COMPUTER NETWORKS

A Systems Approach

Computer Networks: A Systems Approach,

by Larry L. Peterson and Bruce S. Davie,

is the premier title

in the Morgan Kaufmann Series in Networking.

Our series editor is David Clark

of the Massachusetts Institute of Technology.

Larry L. Peterson & Bruce S. Davie

COMPUTER NETWORKS

A Systems Approach

Morgan Kaufmann Publishers, Inc.
San Francisco, California

Sponsoring Editor Jennifer Mann
Production Manager Yonie Overton
Production Editor Julie Pabst
Editorial Assistant Jane Elliott
Cover and Text Design Ross Carron Design
Illustration ST Associates, Inc.
Copyeditor Jeff Van Bueren
Proofreader Ken DellaPenta
Composition Ed Sznyter, Babel Press
Indexer Steve Rath
Printer Courier Corporation

Morgan Kaufmann Publishers, Inc.
Editorial and Sales Office
340 Pine Street, Sixth Floor
San Francisco, CA 94104-3205 USA
Telephone 415/392-2665
Facsimile 415/982-2665
Internet mkp@mkp.com
Order toll free 800/745-7323

Library of Congress Cataloging-in-Publication Data
Peterson, Larry L.
        Computer networks : a systems approach / Larry L. Peterson and Bruce S. Davie.
                p.   cm.
        Includes bibliographical references and index.
        ISBN 1-55860-368-9
        1. Computer networks.   I. Davie, Bruce S.   II. Title.
TK5105.5.P479   1996
004.6'5—dc20   96-1590

To Lynn and Jody

David Clark
Massachusetts Institute of Technology

The term *spaghetti code* is universally understood as an insult. All good computer scientists worship the god of modularity, since modularity brings many benefits, including the all-powerful benefit of not having to understand all parts of a problem at the same time in order to solve it. Modularity thus plays a role in presenting ideas in a book, as well as in writing code. If a book's material is organized effectively—modularly—the reader can start at the beginning and actually make it to the end.

The field of network protocols is perhaps unique in that the "proper" modularity has been handed down to us in the form of an international standard: the seven-layer reference model of network protocols from the ISO. This model, which reflects a layered approach to modularity, is almost universally used as a starting point for discussions of protocol organization, whether the design in question conforms to the model or deviates from it.

It seems obvious to organize a networking book around this layered model. However, there is a peril to doing so, because the OSI model is not really successful at organizing the core concepts of networking. Such basic requirements as reliability, flow control, or security can be addressed at most, if not all, of the OSI layers. This fact has led to great confusion in trying to understand the reference model. At times it even requires a suspension of disbelief. Indeed, a book organized strictly according to a layered model has some of the attributes of spaghetti code.

Which brings us to this book. Peterson and Davie follow the traditional layered model, but they do not pretend that this model actually helps in the understanding of the big issues in networking. Instead, the authors organize discussion of fundamental concepts in a way that is independent of layering. Thus, after reading the book, readers will understand flow control, congestion control, reliability enhancement, data representation, and synchronization, and will separately understand the implications of addressing these issues in one or another of the traditional layers.

This is a timely book. It looks at the important protocols in use today—especially the Internet protocols. Peterson and Davie have a long involvement in and much experience with the Internet. Thus their book reflects not just the theoretical issues in protocol design, but the real factors that matter in practice. The book looks at some of the protocols that are just emerging now, so the reader can be assured of an up-to-date perspective. But most importantly, the discussion of basic issues is presented in a way that derives from the fundamental nature of the problem, not the constraints of the layered reference model or the details of to-day's protocols. In this regard, what this book presents is both timely and timeless. The combination of real-world relevance, current examples, and careful explanation of fundamentals makes this book unique.

C O N T E N T S

Without question, computer networking is one of the most exciting computer science topics to emerge in recent years. The media have done a more than adequate job of popularizing networking, and examples of its rapid spread are plentiful: *USA Today* regularly publishes the addresses of interesting World Wide Web sites; we are encouraged to send comments to *NBC Nightly News* via Internet mail; both the White House and Congress are online (as is Her Majesty's Treasury); and, perhaps most impressively, it is possible to order pizza over the Internet. Surely any technology that receives this much attention must be worth understanding.

The concern, of course, is that there might be little or no intellectual substance once we get beyond the buzzwords. Fortunately, this is not the case. When we peel away all the hype, the field of computer networking contains a wealth of interesting problems and clever solutions founded on solid underlying principles. The challenge is to identify and understand these principles. That is why we decided to write this book. Our intent is that the book should serve as the text for an introductory networking class, at either the graduate or upper-division undergraduate level. We also believe that the book's focus on core concepts should be appealing to industry professionals who are retraining for network-related assignments, as well as current network practitioners who want to understand the "whys" behind the protocols they work with every day.

Approach

It is our experience that people learning about networks for the first time often have the impression that network protocols are some sort of edict handed down from on high, and that their job is to learn as many TLAs (Three Letter Acronyms) as possible. In fact, protocols are the building blocks of a complex system developed through the application of engineering design principles. Moreover, they are constantly being refined, extended, and replaced based on real-world experience. With this in mind, our goal with this book is to do more than survey the protocols in use today. Instead, we explain the underlying principles of sound network design.

This goal implies several things about our approach. Perhaps most importantly, the book takes a systems-oriented view of computer networking. What we mean by this is that the book identifies the underlying building blocks, shows how they can be glued together to construct a complete network, measures the resulting system experimentally, and uses this data to quantitatively analyze various design options. This is in contrast to looking at networking through the eyes of a standardization body, a telephone company executive, or a queuing theorist.

In keeping with our systems perspective, this book explains *why* networks are designed the way they are. It does this by starting from first principles, rather than by simply marching through the set of protocols that happen to be in use today. Moreover, we do not adhere to a rigidly layerist point of view, but instead allow ourselves to address issues that cannot be neatly packaged in any single layer. It is our experience that once you understand the underlying concepts, any new protocol that you are confronted with—especially one that cannot be pigeonholed in an existing layer—will be relatively easy to digest. Given the volatility and explosive growth of networking in the 1990s, this focus on principles rather than artifacts is well justified.

The book does two things to help make these underlying concepts more tangible. First, it draws heavily from the lessons of the Internet. As a functioning, global network, the Internet is rich with examples that illustrate how networks are designed in practice. This book exploits the Internet experience in several ways: as a road map that guides the organization of this book, as a source of examples that illustrate the fundamental ideas underlying computer networks, and as a set of design principles that color our way of looking at computer networks. Second, the book includes code segments from a working network subsystem—the x-kernel. The book is not an exhaustive inspection of the code. Rather, snippets of x-kernel code are given throughout the book to help make the discussion more concrete. The basic strategy is to provide you with not only an understanding of the components of a network, but also a feel for how all the pieces are put together.

How to Use This Book

The chapters of this book can be organized into three groups:

- Introductory material: Chapters 1–2.

- Core topics: Chapters 3–6.

- Advanced topics: Chapters 7–9.

For an undergraduate course, extra class time will most likely be needed to help students digest the introductory material in the first two chapters, probably at the expense of the more advanced topics covered in Chapters 7 through 9. In contrast, the instructor for a graduate course should be able to cover the first two chapters in only a few lectures—with students studying the material more carefully on their own—thereby freeing up additional class time to cover the last three chapters in depth. Both graduate and undergraduate classes will want to cover the core material contained in the middle four chapters, although an undergraduate class might choose to skim the more advanced sections (e.g., 3.2, 3.8, 4.4, and 5.5).

For those of you using the book in self-study, we believe that the topics we have selected cover the core of computer networking, and so we recommend that the book be read sequentially, from front to back. In addition, we have included a liberal supply of references to help you locate supplementary material that is relevant to your specific areas of interest.

There are several other things to note about the topic selection and organization. First, the book takes a unique approach to the topic of congestion control by pulling all topics related to congestion control and resource allocation together in a single place—Chapter 8. We do this because the problem of congestion control cannot be solved at any one level, and we want you to consider the various design options at the same time. (This is consistent with our view that strict layering often obscures important design tradeoffs.) A more traditional treatment of congestion control is possible, however, by studying Section 8.2 in the context of Chapter 4 and Section 8.3 in the context of Chapter 6.

Second, even though Chapter 9 is the only chapter explicitly labeled *High-Speed Networking*, the topic is covered in substantial depth throughout the book. For example, Section 3.8 discusses the role played by network adaptors in delivering high throughput, 4.3 describes ATM networks, 4.4 describes hardware switches used in high-speed networks, 7.2 discusses MPEG video compression, and 8.5 discusses resource reservation. In addition, video applications are used throughout the book to motivate various design decisions. In short, high-speed networking is becoming commonplace, and we believe that it no longer deserves to be treated purely as an advanced topic.

Third, example code from the x-kernel is used throughout the book to illustrate important concepts, with an overview of the x-kernel given in Chapter 2. How much time you spend studying Chapter 2 depends, of course, on how you plan to use the x-kernel throughout the rest of the book. We envision the code being used at one of three levels.

- The code can be *ignored*. Each of the chapters contains a complete discussion of the topic at hand; the code simply punctuates this discussion with tangible evidence that the ideas being presented can be put to practice.

- The code can be *read*. While this certainly involves some effort, the investment is relatively low (the x-kernel was explicitly designed to support network software and so has a high "signal-to-noise" ratio) and the payoff is real (you can see firsthand how the underlying ideas are realized in practice).

- The code can be *written*. Because the complete code is available online, it can be used to provide hands-on experience. Some of the exercises at the end of each chapter suggest programming assignments that you can do using the x-kernel.

Additional information on how (and why) to use the x-kernel is given on page xx.

Finally, the book has several features that we encourage you to take advantage of.

- Each chapter begins with a *Problem* that identifies the next set of issues that must be addressed in the design of a network. Each problem statement introduces the issues to be explored in the chapter that follows and outlines individual topics covered in that chapter.

■ *Shaded sidebars* throughout the text elaborate on the topic being discussed or introduce a related advanced topic. In many cases, these sidebars relate real-world anecdotes about networking.

■ Key paragraphs are *highlighted* and marked in the margin with an icon. These paragraphs often summarize an important nugget of information that we want you to take away from the discussion. In many cases, this nugget is a system design principle that you will see applied in many different situations.

■ Even though the book's focus is on core concepts rather than existing protocol specifications, real protocols are used to illustrate most of the important ideas. As a result, the book can be used as a source of reference for these example protocols. To help you find the descriptions of the protocols, each applicable section heading parenthetically identifies the protocols defined in that section. For example, Section 6.2, which describes the principles of reliable end-to-end protocols, provides a detailed description of TCP, the canonical example of such a protocol.

■ We conclude the main body of each chapter with an *Open Issue*. The idea of this section is to expose you to various unresolved issues that are currently being debated in the research community, the commercial world, and/or society as a whole. We have found that discussing these issues helps to make the subject of networking more relevant and exciting.

■ As part of the Further Reading section at the end of each chapter, a specific *recommended reading list* is given. This list generally contains the seminal papers on the topics discussed in the chapter. We strongly recommend that advanced readers (e.g., graduate students) study the papers in this reading list to supplement the material covered in the chapter.

Software

As mentioned above, this book uses the x-kernel to illustrate how network software is implemented. The x-kernel was designed to support the rapid implementation of efficient network protocols. A protocol implementation can be done rapidly because the x-kernel provides a set of high-level abstractions that are tailored specifically to support protocol implementations. x-kernel protocols are efficient because these abstractions are themselves implemented using highly optimized data structures and algorithms. In fact, the world speed record for delivering network data from an ATM network into a desktop workstation—516 Mbps—is held by the x-kernel at the time of this printing.

Because the x-kernel has the dual goals of running fast and making it easy to implement protocols, it has also proved to be an invaluable pedagogical tool, one that is used extensively in the *Principles of Computer Networking* class at the University of Arizona. There are two aspects to the pedagogical value of the x-kernel. First, because the x-kernel defines a concise framework for implementing protocols, it can be viewed as simply codifying the essential elements of network protocols. An intimate understanding of the interfaces provided by the x-kernel necessarily means appreciating the mechanisms found in all protocols. Second, it provides a convenient means for students to get hands-on experience with network protocols—students are able both to implement protocols and to evaluate their performance.

On the subject of "hands-on experience," many of the exercises at the end of each chapter suggest programming assignments that can be done, some (but not all) of which use the x-kernel. Typically, these assignments take on one of the following four forms:

- Write a small program that tests or measures some narrow aspect of a network system. These assignments are independent of the x-kernel.

- Run and measure existing protocols currently distributed with the x-kernel. Sometimes these assignments involve making simple modifications to existing x-kernel code.

- Implement and evaluate standard protocols based on existing protocol specifications. These assignments use the x-kernel as a protocol implementation framework.

- Design, implement, and evaluate new protocols from scratch. These assignments use the x-kernel as a protocol implementation framework.

For these assignments, students typically run the x-kernel as a user process on Unix workstations connected by an Ethernet. Several flavors of Unix are currently supported, including SunOS, Solaris, OSF/1, IRIX, and Linux. In this case, the x-kernel generates packets that are delivered between machines over the Ethernet. An alternative is to run the x-kernel in *simulation mode*, again on top of Unix. In this case, networks with arbitrary topology, bandwidth, and delay characteristics can be simulated as a single Unix process.

The x-kernel source code is available via anonymous ftp to cs.arizona.edu, cd'ing to directory xkernel, and accessing file xkernel.tar.Z. You can also find the x-kernel home page on the Web at URL

http://www.cs.arizona.edu/xkernel

This page includes a link to online documentation, as well as instructions on how to obtain help with the x-kernel. Additional information about the x-kernel and how it can be used in conjunction with this book can be found at URL

http://www.mkp.com

Acknowledgments

This book would not have been possible without the help of so many people. We would like to thank them for their efforts in improving the end result. Before we do so, however, we should mention that we have done our best to correct the mistakes that the reviewers have pointed out and to accurately describe the protocols and mechanisms that our collegues have explained to us. We alone are responsible for any remaining errors. If you should find any of these, please send email to our publisher, Morgan Kaufmann, at netbugs@mkp.com, and we will endeavor to correct them in future printings of this book.

First and foremost, we would like to thank our series editor, Dave Clark. His involvement in the series played no small part in our decision to write this book with Morgan Kaufmann, and the suggestions, expertise, perspective, and encouragement he offered us throughout the writing process proved invaluable.

Several members of the Network Systems Research Group at the University of Arizona contributed ideas, examples, corrections, data, and code to this book. Andy Bavier fleshed out many of the exercises and examples, and he offered helpful suggestions on the clarity of the early drafts. Lawrence Brakmo answered countless questions about TCP and provided the data used in the figures on TCP congestion control. David Mosberger served as the resident expert on MPEG and JPEG, and he ran many of the performance experiments reported in the book. Andy, Lawrence, and David also wrote most of the x-kernel code fragments that ended up in the book. Richard Schroeppel, Hilarie Orman, and Sean O'Malley were valuable resources on network security and supplied the security-related performance numbers. Sean also helped us organize our thoughts on presentation formatting. Finally, countless people have contributed to the x-kernel over the years. We would especially like to thank (in addition to those mentioned above) Ed Menze, Sandy Miller, Hasnain Karampurwala, Mats Bjorkman, Peter Druschel, Erich Nahum, and Norm Hutchinson.

Several other people were kind enough to answer our questions and correct our misunderstandings. Rich Salz and Franco Travostino from OSF taught us about NDR. Jeffrey Mogul from Digital's Western Research Lab and John Wroclawski from MIT helped us understand how fast workstations can switch packets. Gregg Townsend from the University of Arizona explained how GIF works. Gail Lalk and Tom Robe of Bellcore answered questions about SONET.

We would also like to thank the many people who reviewed drafts of various chapters. The list is long, and includes Chris Edmondson-Yurkanan of the University of Texas at Austin, Willis Marti of Texas A&M University, Frank Young of Rose-Hullman Institute of Technology, Tom Robertazzi of SUNY Stony Brook, Jon Crowcroft of University College London, Eric Crawley of Bay Networks, Jim Metzler of Strategic Networks Consulting, Dan McDonald of the Navy Research Lab, Mark Abbott of IBM, Tony Bogovic of Bellcore, David Hayes of San Jose State University, S. Ron Oliver of California State Polytechnic University-Pomona, Donald Carpenter of the University of Nebraska at Kearney, and Ski Ilnicki of Hewlett-Packard. Their comments and suggestions were invaluable. Also, a special thanks to Professors Peter Druschel of Rice University, Izidor Gertner of CCNY, and Mansoor Alam of the University of Toledo for their feedback based on class-testing the first draft of the book.

We also want to thank the Advanced Research Projects Agency and the National Science Foundation for supporting our research over the past several years. That research helped to shape our perspective on networking, as well as to produce tangible results like the x-kernel. Thanks also to Bell Communications Research, which supported some of our research and writing.

We would like to thank all the people at Morgan Kaufmann who helped shepherd us through the book-writing process, especially our sponsoring editor, Jennifer Mann, our production editor, Julie Pabst, and our production manager, Yonie Overton. We cannot imagine a more enthusiastic or harder-working group of people.

Finally, we wish to thank our long-suffering wives, Lynn Peterson and Jody Davie, who put up with our complete obsession with the book (and consequent neglect of our families), especially in the final months of writing.

RELATED TITLES FROM MORGAN KAUFMANN

Computer Architecture: A Quantitative Approach, Second Edition

John L. Hennessy, Stanford University, and David A. Patterson, University of California, Berkeley
1995; 1004 pages; cloth; ISBN 1-55860-329-8

This landmark revision focuses on the new generation of architectures and design techniques with a view toward the future. It includes increased coverage of pipelining and storage, a comprehensive presentation of caches, and new chapters on shared memory multiprocessing and networking technology. Anyone involved in building computers will profit from the unmatched experience and quantitative approach that Hennessy and Patterson apply to their presentation.

Introduction to Data Compression

Khalid Sayood, University of Nebraska, Lincoln
1995; 475 pages; cloth; ISBN 1-55860-346-8

The fundamental theories and techniques of data compression, with the most complete coverage available of both lossy and lossless methods. Sayood explains the theoretical underpinnings of the algorithms so that readers learn how to model structures in data and design compression packages of their own. Practitioners, researchers, and students will benefit from the balanced presentation of theoretical material and implementations.

Web Server Technology:
The Advanced Guide for World Wide Web Information Providers

Nancy Yeager and Robert E. McGrath, both of the National Center for Supercomputing Applications
April 1996; approximately 400 pages; paper; ISBN 1-55860-376-X

The success of the Web depends not only on the creation of stimulating and valuable information, but also on the speed, efficiency, and convenient delivery of this information to the Web consumer. This authoritative presentation of Web server technology takes you beyond the basics to provide the underlying principles and technical details of how WWW servers really work. It explains current technology and suggests enhanced and expanded methods for disseminating information via the Web.

High-Performance Communications Networks

Jean Walrand and Pravin Varaiya, both of University of California, Berkeley
September 1996; approximately 600 pages; cloth; ISBN 1-55860-341-7

A comprehensive presentation of the technologies used to build high-performance communication networks capable of providing telephone, interactive video, data, and multimedia services. Intended for network hardware and software designers, application developers, network and information system managers, and senior/graduate engineering and computer science students, this book explains how converging networking technologies are combined into high-performance networks and how to plan, manage, and control these networks.

S uppose you want to build a computer network, one that has the potential to grow to global proportions and to support applications as diverse as teleconferencing, video-on-demand, distributed computing, and digital libraries. What available technologies would serve as the underlying building blocks, and what kind of software architecture would you design to integrate these building blocks into an effective communication service? Answering this question is the overriding goal of this book—to describe the available building materials and then to show how they can be used to construct a network from the ground up.

Before we can understand how to design a computer network, we should first agree on exactly what a computer network is. At one time, the term *network* meant the set of serial lines used to attach dumb terminals to mainframe computers. To some, the term implies the voice telephone network. To others, the only interesting network is the cable network used to disseminate video signals. The main thing these networks have in common is that they are specialized to handle one particular kind of data (key strokes, voice, or video) and they typically connect to special-purpose devices (terminals, hand receivers, and television sets).

What distinguishes a computer network from these other types of networks? Probably the most important characteristic of a computer network is its generality. Computer networks are built primarily from general-purpose programmable hardware, and they are not optimized for a particular application like making phone calls or delivering television signals. Instead, they are able to carry many different types of data and they support a wide, and ever growing, range of applications. This chapter looks at some typical applications of computer networks and then discusses the requirements of which a network designer who wishes to support such applications must be aware.

Once we understand the requirements, how do we proceed? Fortunately, we will not be building the first network. Others, most notably the community of researchers respon-

I must Create a System,
or be enslav'd by
another Man's; I will
not Reason and
Compare: my business
is to Create.

—Blake

sible for the Internet, have gone before us. We will use the wealth of experience generated from the Internet to guide our design. This experience is embodied in a *network architecture* that identifies the available hardware and software components and shows how they can be arranged to form a complete network system.

To start us on the road toward understanding how to build a network, this chapter does three things. First, it explores the motivation for building networks, which is primarily to support network applications. Second, it looks at the requirements that different applications and different communities of people (such as network users and network operators) place on the network. Finally, it introduces the idea of a network architecture, which lays the foundation for the rest of the book.

1

Foundation

1.1 Motivation

It has become increasingly difficult to find people who have not made some use of computer networks, whether to send electronic mail (email), to transfer files, or to "surf the net" using a World Wide Web browser like Mosaic.[1] However, just as the vast majority of today's computer users have never written a computer program, the majority of network users know very little about the technology that underlies computer networks. This book explains computer networking technology from a systems perspective, which is to say it explains networking in a way that will teach you how networks are implemented—what sort of hardware is used, how it works, and how to implement the software that turns the hardware components into a useful network. To begin, we consider some of the factors that make computer networking an exciting and worthwhile field of study.

1.1.1 Explosive Growth

While catchy phrases like "information superhighway" help to sell the general public on the idea of networking, computer networks like the Internet are a reality today and have been for over 20 years. In 1989, it was estimated that the Internet connected approximately 100,000 computers. By the end of 1992, the number had reached 1 million. Today, there are over 6 million computers on the Internet, giving an estimated 30 to 50 million users access to its services. If traced back to its origins, the Internet has been doubling in size every year since 1981. Figure 1.1 plots the number of computers connected to the Internet since 1988.

One of the things that has made the Internet such a runaway success is the fact that so much of its functionality is provided by software running in general-purpose computers. The significance of this is that new functionality can be added readily with "just a small matter of programming." As a result, we could not even begin to list all the new applications that have appeared on the Internet in recent years. A few of these applications have been overwhelmingly popular, with the World Wide Web being a particularly notable example.

Adding new functionality to the network is not limited to the creation of new applications but may also include new functions "inside" the network. A good example of the latter is multicast routing, which enables multiparty teleconferencing to take place over the Internet. Our goal in this book is to teach enough about the implementation of networks for you to be able not only to understand the functionality of computer networks but also to expand it.

Another factor that has made computer networking so exciting in recent years is the massive increase in computing power available in commodity machines. While computer networks have always been capable in principle of transporting any kind of information such as digital voice samples, digitized images, and so on, this potential was not particularly interesting if the computers sending and receiving that data were too slow to do anything useful with the information. Virtually all of today's computers are capable of playing back digitized voice

---

[1]Those rare individuals who have not used a computer network will find some help in getting started in that direction later in this section.

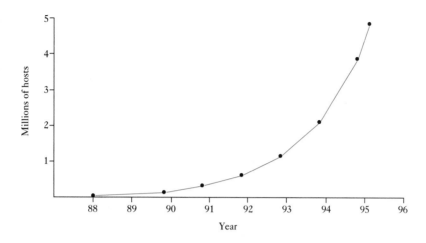

Figure 1.1   Growth in the number of computers connected to the Internet since 1988.

at full speed and can display video at a speed and resolution that is useful for some (but by no means all) applications. Thus, today's networks have begun to support multimedia, and their support for it will only improve as computing hardware becomes inexorably faster. Dealing with multimedia applications and with the demand for ever-faster networks presents some special challenges for network designers; this book will present some of those challenges and provide some tools for dealing with them.

1.1.2   Network Applications

Since the reason for having computer networks in the first place is so that users can run applications over them, it will be helpful to our subsequent discussion to have some understanding of common applications. Any function that is provided in a network can ultimately be traced back to some application need. Application builders take advantage of functions provided by the network, and network designers try to add new functionality to improve the performance of current applications and to enable new ones. The following subsections describe some of the most common applications that motivate our discussion of networking functionality.

FTP: File Transfer Protocol

The acronym FTP is a little confusing because it can interpreted to stand for either File Transfer *Program*, which is an application, or for File Transfer *Protocol*, which is a protocol. The latter definition is actually the correct one but for now we want to focus on applications. The FTP application is one of the oldest on the Internet and continues to be useful. As the name suggests, its function is to enable the transfer of files between computers over a network. The operation of one version of the application is illustrated in the following example:

```
% ftp
ftp> open ds.internic.net
Connected to ds.internic.net.
 [...]
220 ds.internic.net FTP server ready.
Name (ds.internic.net:bsd):anonymous
331 Guest login ok, send ident as password.
Password:
230 Guest login ok, access restrictions apply.
ftp> cd rfc
250 CWD command successful.
ftp> get rfc-index.txt
200 PORT command successful.
150 Opening ASCII mode data connection for rfc-index.txt (245544 bytes).
226 Transfer complete.
local: rfc-index.txt remote: rfc-index.txt
251257 bytes received in 1.2e+02 seconds (2 Kbytes/s)
ftp> close
221 Goodbye.
```

The above example shows an *anonymous* FTP to a machine called ds.internic.net. Anonymous FTP means that a user who does not have an account on the remote machine can still connect to it, by providing the user name **anonymous**. By convention, the user's email address is given as a password. We began the FTP application by typing **ftp**. (All text typed by the user is shown in color in the example.) Then we opened a connection to the remote machine and responded to its request for a user name and password. At that point, the user could perform a range of operations related to retrieving files. For a full listing of commands, the user would type **help**. What we did above was to change to a directory called **rfc** using the **cd** command and then retrieved the file **rfc-index.txt** with the **get** command. Finally, we closed the connection.

You can try out the above example for yourself, provided you have access to an Internet-connected machine that runs FTP. The **rfc** directory actually contains all the Internet *Request for Comments* documents (RFCs), which provide a wealth of information about the Internet from the highly technical to the humorous.

This example allows us to define an important pair of terms: *client* and *server*. In the example, we started an FTP client program on our own machine; our computer connected to the FTP server on ds.internic.net. The client then issued a series of requests to the server, which responded. You may find it helpful to think of the client as the entity that issues requests for a service, just as the client of a business is the person who asks the business for some service. In the current example, the service provided is the storage and retrieval of files.

World Wide Web

The World Wide Web has been so successful and has made the Internet accessible to so many people that sometimes it seems to be synonymous with the Internet. One helpful way to think

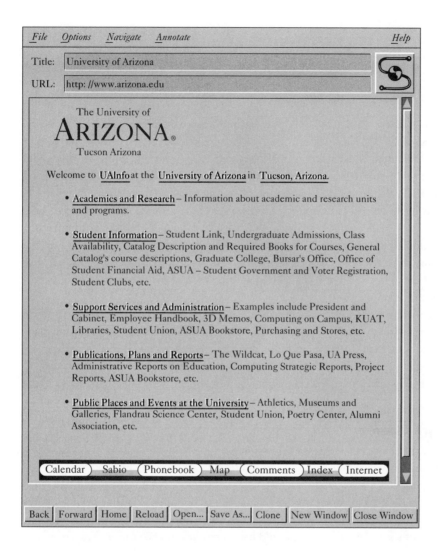

Figure 1.2 The Mosaic Web browser.

of the Web is as a set of cooperating clients and servers, all of whom speak the same language: the HyperText Transfer Protocol (HTTP). Most people are exposed to the Web through a graphical client program, or Web browser, like Mosaic, so we will talk about it from that perspective here. Figure 1.2 shows the Mosaic browser in use, displaying a page of information from the University of Arizona.

Any Web browser has a function that allows the user to "open a URL." URLs (Uniform Resource Locators) provide information about the location of objects on the Web; they look like the following:

http://www.arizona.edu/index.html

If you opened that particular URL, your Web browser would open a connection to the Web server at a machine called www.arizona.edu and would immediately retrieve and display the file called index.html. Most files on the Web contain images and text, and some have audio and video clips; this multimedia flavor is one of the things that has made the Web so appealing to users. Most files also include URLs that point to other files, and your Web browser will have some way in which you can recognize URLs and ask the browser to open them. These embedded URLs are called hypertext links. When you ask your Web browser to open one of these embedded URLs (e.g., by pointing and clicking on it with a mouse), it will open a new connection and retrieve and display a new file. This is called "following a link." It thus becomes very easy to hop from one machine to another around the network, following links to all sorts of information.

It is interesting to note that much of what goes on when browsing the World Wide Web is the same as what goes on when retrieving files with FTP. Remote machines are identified, connections are made to those machines, and files are transferred. We will see that many seemingly disparate applications depend on similar underlying functionality and that one of the network builder's jobs is to provide the right common functionality that many applications can use.

NV: Network Video

A third, rather different application is NV, an acronym for Network Video. NV is used primarily for multiparty videoconferencing on the Internet. To be a sender of video, you need special hardware, called a *frame grabber*, which takes the sequence of images output by a video camera and digitizes them so that they can be fed into a computer. The size of each image, which is called a *frame*, depends on the resolution of the picture. For example, an image one quarter the size of a standard TV image would have a resolution of 352 by 240 pixels; a pixel corresponds to one dot on a display. If each pixel is represented by 24 bits of information, as would be the case for 24-bit color, then the size of each frame would be $(352 \times 240 \times 24)/8 = 247.5$ kilobytes (KB).

The rate at which images are taken is called the frame rate and needs to be about 25–30 frames per second to provide video quality that is as good as television. Frame rates of 15 frames per second are still tolerable, while update rates of greater than 30 frames per second cannot be perceived by a human and are therefore not very useful. NV usually runs at a slower speed, on the order of two or three frames a second, to reduce the rate at which data is sent, because both the computers involved in the conference and the network in between are typically unable to handle data at such high rates with today's commodity technology. In any case, digital images, once provided to the sending host by the frame grabber, are sent over the

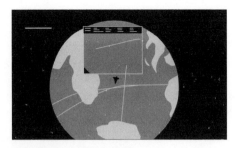

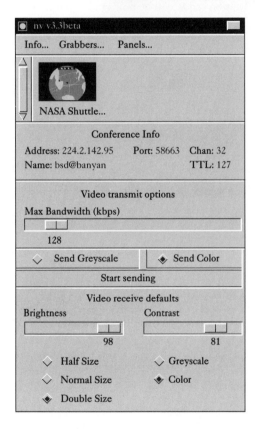

Figure 1.3   The NV video application.

---

network as a stream of messages (frames) to a receiving host. The receiving host then displays the received frames on its monitor at the same rate as they were captured. Figure 1.3 shows the control panel for an NV session along with a frame of the video feed from NASA during a space shuttle mission.

1.2   Requirements

Before trying to understand how a network that supports applications like FTP, WWW, and
NV is designed and implemented, it is important to identify what we expect from a network.
The short answer is that there is no single expectation; computer networks are designed and
built under a large number of constraints and requirements. In fact, the requirements differ
widely depending on your perspective:

- a *network user* would list the services that his or her application needs, for example,
  a guarantee that each message the application sends will be delivered without error
  within a certain amount of time;

- a *network designer* would list the properties of a cost-effective design, for example,
  that network resources are efficiently utilized and fairly allocated to different users;
  and

- a *network provider* would list the characteristics of a system that is easy to administer
  and manage, for example, in which faults can be easily isolated and where it is easy
  to account for usage.

This section attempts to distill these different perspectives into a high-level introduction to
the major considerations that drive network design, and in doing so, identifies the challenges
addressed throughout the rest of this book.

1.2.1   Connectivity

Starting with the obvious, a network must provide connectivity among a set of computers.
Sometimes it is enough to build a limited network that connects only a few select machines.
In fact, for reasons of privacy and security, many private (corporate) networks have the explicit
goal of limiting the set of machines that are connected. In contrast, other networks (of which
the Internet is the prime example), are designed to grow in a way that allows them the potential to connect all the computers in the world. A system that is designed to support growth
to an arbitrarily large size is said to *scale*. Using the Internet as a model, this book addresses
the challenge of scalability.

Links, Nodes, and Clouds

Network connectivity occurs at many different levels. At the lowest level, a network can consist of two or more computers directly connected by some physical medium, such as a coaxial
cable or an optical fiber. We call such a physical medium a *link*, and we often refer to the
computers it connects as *nodes*. (Sometimes a node is a more specialized piece of hardware
rather than a computer, but we overlook that distinction for the purposes of this discussion.)
As illustrated in Figure 1.4, physical links are sometimes limited to a pair of nodes (such a
link is said to be *point-to-point*), while in other cases, more than two nodes may share a single
physical link (such a link is said to be *multiple-access*). Whether a given link supports point-
to-point or multiple-access connectivity depends on how the node is attached to the link. It

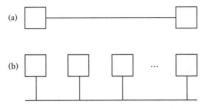

Figure 1.4 Direct links: (a) point-to-point; (b) multiple-access.

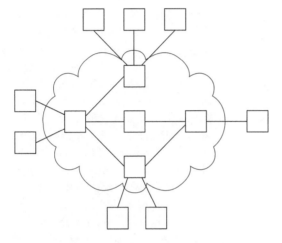

Figure 1.5 Switched network.

is also the case that multiple-access links are often limited in size, in terms of both the geographical distance they can cover and the number of nodes they can connect. The exception is a satellite link, which can cover a wide geographic area.

If computer networks were limited to situations in which all nodes are directly connected to each other over a common physical medium, then networks would either be very limited in the number of computers they could connect or the number of wires coming out of the back of each node would quickly become both unmanageable and very expensive. Fortunately, connectivity between two nodes does not necessarily imply a direct physical connection between them—indirect connectivity may be achieved among a set of cooperating nodes. Consider the following two examples of how a collection of computers can be indirectly connected.

Figure 1.5 shows a set of nodes, each of which is attached to one or more point-to-point links. Those nodes that are attached to at least two links run software that forwards data received on one link out on another. If organized in a systematic way, these forwarding nodes form a *switched network*. There are numerous types of switched networks, of which the two most common are *circuit-switched* and *packet-switched*. The former is most notably employed by the telephone system, while the latter is used for the overwhelming majority of computer networks and will be the focus of this book. The important feature of packet-switched net-

works is that the nodes in such a network send discrete blocks of data to each other. Think of these blocks of data as corresponding to some piece of application data such as a file, a piece of email, or an image. We call each block of data either a *packet* or a *message*, and for now we use these terms interchangeably; we discuss the reason they are not always the same in Section 1.2.2.

Packet-switched networks typically use a strategy called *store-and-forward*. As the name suggests, each node in a store-and-forward network first receives a complete packet over some link, stores the packet in its internal memory, and then forwards the complete packet to the next node. In contrast, a circuit-switched network first establishes a dedicated circuit across a sequence of links and then allows the source node to send a stream of bits across this circuit to a destination node. The major reason for using packet switching rather than circuit switching in a computer network is discussed in the next subsection.

The cloud in Figure 1.5 distinguishes between the nodes on the inside that *implement* the network (they are commonly called *switches* and their sole function is to store and forward packets) and the nodes on the outside of the cloud that *use* the network (they are commonly called *hosts* and they support users and run application programs). Also note that the cloud in Figure 1.5 is one of the most important icons

DANs, LANs, MANs, and WANs

One way to characterize networks is according to their size. Two well-known examples are LANs (local area networks) and WANs (wide area networks)—the former typically extend less than 1 kilometer, while the latter can be worldwide. Other networks are classified as MANs (metropolitan area networks), which, as the name implies, usually span tens of kilometers. The reason such classifications are interesting is that the size of a network often has implications for the underlying technology that can be used, with a key factor being the amount of time it takes for data to propagate from one end of the network to the other; we discuss this issue more in later chapters.

An interesting historical note is that the term wide area network was not applied to the first WANs because there was no other sort of network to differentiate them from. When computers were incredibly rare and expensive, there was no point in

of computer networking. In general, we use a cloud to denote any type of network, whether it is a single point-to-point link, a multiple-access link, or a switched network. Thus, whenever you see a cloud used in a figure, you can think of it as a placeholder for any of the networking technologies covered in this book.

A second way in which a set of computers can be indirectly connected is shown in Figure 1.6. In this situation, a set of independent networks (clouds) are interconnected to form an *internetwork*, or internet for short. We adopt the Internet's convention of referring to a generic internetwork of networks as a lowercase i internet, and the currently operational TCP/IP Internet as the capital I Internet. A node that is connected to two or more networks is commonly called a *router* or *gateway*, and it plays much the same role as a switch—it forwards messages from one network to another. Note that an internet can itself be viewed as another kind of network, which means that an internet can be built from an interconnection of internets. Thus, we can recursively build arbitrarily large networks by interconnecting clouds to form larger clouds.

thinking about how to connect all the computers in the local area—there was only one computer in that area. Only as computers began to proliferate did LANs become necessary, and the term WAN was then introduced to describe the larger networks that interconnected geographically distant computers.

One of the most intriguing kinds of networks that is gaining attention today is the DAN (desk area network). The idea of a DAN is to open up the computer setting on your desk and to treat each component of that computer—e.g., its display, disk, CPU, as well as peripherals like cameras and printers—as a network-accessible device. In essence, the I/O bus is replaced by a network (a DAN) that can, in turn, be interconnected to other LANs, MANs, and WANs. Establishing this interconnection provides uniform access to all the resources that might be required by a network application.

Just because a set of hosts are directly or indirectly connected to each other does not mean that we have succeeded in providing host-to-host connectivity. The final requirement is that each node must be able to say which of the other nodes on the network it wants to communicate with. This is done by assigning an *address* to each node. An address is a byte string that identifies a node; i.e., the network can use a node's address to distinguish it from the other nodes connected to the network. When a source node wants the network to deliver a message to a certain destination node, it specifies the address of the destination node. If the sending and receiving nodes are not directly connected, then the switches and routers of the network use this address to decide how to forward the message toward the destination. The process of determining systematically how to forward messages toward the destination node based on its address is called *routing*.

This brief introduction to addressing and routing has presumed that the source node wants to send a message to a single destination node (*unicast*). While this is the most common scenario, it is also possible that the source node might want to *broadcast* a message to all the nodes on the network. Or a source node might want to send a message to some subset of

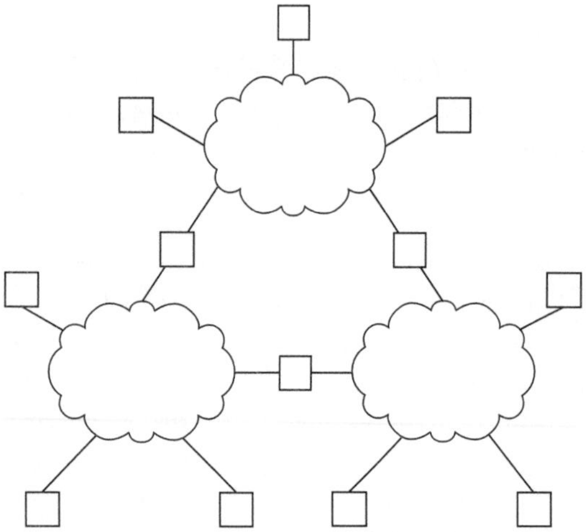

Figure 1.6 Interconnection of networks.

the other nodes, but not all of them, a situation called *multicast*. Thus, in addition to node-specific addresses, another requirement of a network is that it support multicast and broadcast addresses.

The main thing to take away from this discussion is that we can define a *network* recursively as consisting of two or more nodes connected by a physical link, or as two or more networks connected by one or more nodes. In other words, a network can be constructed from a nesting of networks, where at the bottom level, the network is implemented by some physical medium. One of the key challenges in providing network connectivity is to define an address for each node that is reachable on the network (including support for broadcast and multicast connectivity), and to be able to use this address to route messages toward the appropriate destination node(s).

1.2.2 Cost-Effective Resource Sharing

As stated above, this book focuses on packet-switched networks. This section explains the key requirement of computer networks—in short, efficiency—that leads us to packet switching as the strategy of choice.

Given a collection of nodes indirectly connected by a nesting of networks, it is possible for any pair of hosts to send messages to each other across a sequence of links and nodes. Of course, we want to do more than support just one pair of communicating hosts—we want to provide all pairs of hosts with the ability to exchange messages. The question, then, is how do all the hosts that want to communicate share the network, especially if they want to use it at the same time? And, as if that problem isn't hard enough, how do several hosts share the same *link* when they all want to use it at the same time?

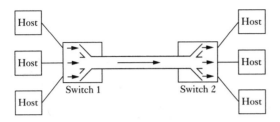

Figure 1.7 Multiplexing multiple logical flows over a single physical link.

To understand how hosts share a network, we need to introduce a fundamental concept, *multiplexing*, which means that a system resource is shared among multiple users. At an intuitive level, multiplexing can be explained by analogy to a timesharing computer system, where a single physical CPU is shared (multiplexed) among multiple jobs, each of which believes it has its own private processor. Similarly, data being sent by multiple users can be multiplexed over the physical links that make up a network.

To see how this might work, consider the simple network illustrated in Figure 1.7, where the three hosts on the left side of the network are sending data to the three hosts on the right by sharing a switched network that contains only one physical link. (For simplicity, assume that the top host on the left is communicating with the top host on the right, and so on.) In this situation, three flows of data—corresponding to the three pairs of hosts—are multiplexed onto a single physical link by Switch 1 and then *demultiplexed* back into separate flows by Switch 2. Note that we are being intentionally vague about exactly what a "flow of data" corresponds to. For the purposes of this discussion, assume that each host on the left has a large supply of data that it wants to send to its counterpart on the right.

There are several different methods for multiplexing multiple flows onto one physical link. One method, which is commonly used in the telephone network, is *synchronous time-division multiplexing* (STDM). The idea of STDM is to divide time into equal-sized quanta, and in a round-robin fashion, give each flow a chance to send its data over the physical link. In other words, during time quantum 1, data from the first flow is transmitted; during time quantum 2, data from the second flow is transmitted; and so on. This process continues until all the flows have had a turn, at which time the first flow gets to go again, and the process repeats. Another common method is *frequency-division multiplexing* (FDM). The idea of FDM is to transmit each flow over the physical link at a different frequency, much the same way that the signals for different TV stations are transmitted at a different frequency on a physical cable TV link.

Although simple to understand, both STDM and FDM are limited in two ways. First, if one of the flows (host pairs) does not have any data to send, its share of the physical link— i.e., its time quantum or its frequency—remains idle, even if one of the other flows has data to transmit. For computer communication, the amount of time that a link is idle can be very large—for example, consider the amount of time you spend reading a Web page (leaving the link idle) compared to the time you spend fetching the page. Second, both STDM and FDM are limited to situations in which the maximum number of flows is fixed and known ahead of time. It is not practical to resize the quantum or to add additional quanta in the case of STDM or to add new frequencies in the case of FDM.

The form of multiplexing that we make most use of in this book is called *statistical multiplexing*. Although the name is not all that helpful for understanding the concept, statistical multiplexing is really quite simple; it involves two key ideas. First, it is like STDM in that the physical link is shared over time—first data from one flow is transmitted over the physical link, then data from another flow is transmitted, and so on. Unlike STDM, however, data is transmitted from each flow on demand rather than during a predetermined time slot. Thus, if only one flow has data to send, it gets to transmit that data without waiting for its quantum to come around and thus without having to watch the quanta assigned to the other flows go by unused. It is this avoidance of idle time that gives packet switching its efficiency.

As defined so far, however, statistical multiplexing has no mechanism to ensure that all the flows eventually get their turn to transmit over the physical link. That is, once a flow begins sending data, we need some way to limit the transmission, so that the other flows can have a turn. To account for this need, statistical multiplexing defines an upper bound on the size of the block of data that each flow is permitted to transmit at a given time. This limited-size block of data is typically referred to as a *packet*, to distinguish it from the arbitrarily large *message* that an application program might want to transmit. The fact that a packet-switched network limits the maximum size of packets means that a host may not be able to send a complete message in one packet—the source may need to fragment the message into several packets, with the receiver reassembling the packets back into the original message.

In other words, each flow sends a sequence of packets over the physical link, with a decision made on a packet-by-packet basis as to which flow's packet to send next. Notice that if only one flow has data to send, then it can send a sequence of packets back to back. However, should more than one of the flows have data to send, then their packets are interleaved on the link. Figure 1.8 depicts a switch multiplexing packets from multiple sources onto a single shared link.

The decision as to which packet to send next on a shared link can be made in a number of different ways. For example, in a network consisting of switches interconnected by links such as the one in Figure 1.7, the decision would be made by the switch that transmits packets onto the shared link. (As we will see later, not all packet-switched networks actually involve switches, and they may use other mechanisms to determine whose packet goes onto the link next.) Each switch in a packet-switched network makes this decision independently, on a packet-by-packet basis. One of the issues that faces a network designer is how to make this decision in a fair manner. For example, a switch could be designed to service the different flows in a round-robin manner, just as in STDM. However, statistical multiplexing does not

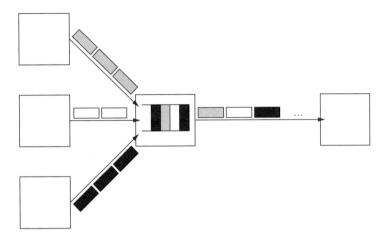

Figure 1.8 A switch multiplexing packets from multiple sources onto one shared link.

require a round-robin approach. In fact, another equally valid choice would be to service each flow's packets on a first-in-first-out (FIFO) basis.

Also, notice in Figure 1.8 that since the switch has to multiplex three incoming packet streams onto one outgoing link, it is possible that the switch will receive packets faster than the shared link can accommodate. In this case, the switch is forced to buffer these packets in its memory. Should a switch receive packets faster than it can send them for an extended period of time, then the switch will eventually run out of buffer space, and some packets will have to be dropped. When a switch is operating in this state, it is said to be *congested*.

The bottom line is that statistical multiplexing defines a cost-effective way for multiple users (e.g., host-to-host flows of data) to share network resources (links and nodes) in a fine-grained manner. It defines the packet as the granularity with which the links of the network are allocated to different flows, with each switch able to schedule the use of the physical links it is connected to on a per-packet basis. Fairly allocating link capacity to different flows and dealing with congestion when it occurs are the key challenges of statistical multiplexing.

1.2.3 Functionality

While the previous section outlined the challenges involved in providing cost-effective connectivity among a group of hosts, it is overly simplistic to view a computer network as simply delivering packets among a collection of computers. It is more accurate to think of a network as providing the means for a set of application processes that are distributed over those computers to communicate. In other words, the next requirement of a computer network is that the application programs running on the hosts connected to the network must be able to communicate in a meaningful way.

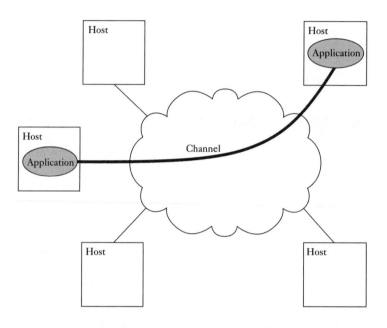

Figure 1.9 Processes communicating over an abstract channel.

When two application programs need to communicate with each other, there are a lot of complicated things that need to happen beyond simply sending a message from one host to another. One option would be for application designers to build all that complicated functionality into each application program. However, since many applications need common services, it is much more logical to implement those common services once and then to let the application designer build the application on top of those services. The challenge for a network designer is to identify the right set of common services. The goal is to hide the complexity of the network from the application without overly constraining the application designer.

Intuitively, we view the network as providing logical *channels* over which application-level processes can communicate with each other; each channel provides the set of services required by that application. In other words, just as we use a cloud to abstractly represent connectivity among a set of computers, we now think of a channel as connecting one process to another. Figure 1.9 shows a pair of application-level processes communicating over a logical channel that is, in turn, implemented on top of a cloud that connects a set of hosts. We can think of the channel as being like a pipe connecting two applications, so that a sending application can put data in one end and expect that data to be delivered by the network to the application at the other end of the pipe.

The challenge is to recognize what functionality the channels should provide to application programs. For example, does the application require a guarantee that messages sent over the channel are delivered, or is it acceptable if some messages fail to arrive? Is it necessary that messages arrive at the recipient process in the same order in which they are sent, or does the recipient not care about the order in which messages arrive? Does the network need to ensure that no third parties are able to eavesdrop on the channel, or is privacy not a concern? In general, a network provides a variety of different types of channels, with each application selecting the type that best meets its needs. The rest of this section illustrates the thinking involved in defining useful channels.

Identifying Common Communication Patterns

Designing abstract channels involves first understanding the communication needs of a representative collection of applications, then extracting their common communication requirements, and finally incorporating the functionality that meets these requirements in the network.

To illustrate how one might define an abstract channel, consider the example applications introduced in Section 1.1.2. One of the earliest applications supported on any network is a file access program like FTP. Although many details vary—for example, whether whole files are transferred across the network or only single blocks of the file are read/written at a given time—the communication component of remote file access is characterized by a pair of processes, one that requests that a file be read or written and a second process that honors this request. Recall that the process that requests access to the file is called the client, and the process that supports access to the file is called the server.

Reading a file involves the client sending a small request message to a server and the server responding with a large message that contains the data in the file. Writing works in the opposite way—the client sends a large message containing the data to be written to the server, and the server responds with a small message confirming that the write to disk has taken place.

A more recent application class that is gaining in popularity, but which in many respects behaves like remote file access, is the digital library program. As exemplified by the World Wide Web, the kind of data being retrieved from a digital library may vary—e.g., it may be a small text file, a very large digital image, or some sort of multimedia object—but the communication pattern looks very similar to the file transfer described above: a client process makes a request and a server process responds by returning the requested data.

A third class of applications that differs substantially from these first two involves the playing of video over the network. While an entire video file could first be fetched from a remote machine using a file access application and then played at the local machine, this would entail waiting for the last second of the video file to be delivered before starting to look at it. Consider instead the case in which the sender and the receiver are, respectively, the source and the sink for the video stream. That is, the source generates a sequence of video frames, each of which is sent across the network as a message and then displayed at the destination as it is received.

Video, in and of itself, is not an application. It is a type of data. Video data might be used as part of a video-on-demand application or in a teleconferencing application like NV.

Although similar, these two applications have a major difference. In the case of video-on-demand, there are no serious timing constraints; if it takes 10 seconds from the time the user starts the video until the first frame is displayed, then the service is still deemed satisfactory. In contrast, a teleconferencing system has very tight timing constraints. Just as when using the telephone, the interactions among the participants must be timely. When a person at one end gestures, then the corresponding video frame must be displayed at the other end as quickly as possible. Added delay makes the system unusable. It is also the case that interactive video implies that frames are flowing in both directions while a video-on-demand application is most likely sending frames in only one direction.

Using these four applications as a representative sample, one might decide to provide the following two types of channels: *request/reply* channels and *message stream* channels. The request/reply channel would be used by the file transfer and digital library applications. It would guarantee that every message sent by one side is received by the other side and that only one copy of each message is delivered. The request/reply channel might also protect the privacy and integrity of the data that flows over it, so that unauthorized parties cannot read or modify the data being exchanged between the client and server processes.

The message stream channel could be used by both the video-on-demand and teleconferencing applications, provided it is parameterized to support both one-way and two-way traffic and to support different delay properties. The message stream channel might not need to guarantee that all messages are delivered, since a video application can operate adequately even if some frames are not received. It would, however, need to ensure that those messages that are delivered arrive in the same order in which they were sent, to avoid displaying frames out of sequence. Like the request/reply channel, the message stream channel might want to ensure the privacy and integrity of the video data. Finally, the message stream channel might need to support multicast, so that multiple parties can participate in the teleconference or view the video.

While it is common for a network designer to strive for the smallest number of abstract channel types that can serve the largest number of applications, there is a danger in trying to get away with too few channel abstractions. Simply stated, if you have a hammer, then everything looks like a nail. For example, if all you have are message stream and request/reply channels, then it is tempting to use them for the next application that comes along, even if neither type provides exactly the semantics needed by the application. Thus, network designers will probably be inventing new types of channels—and adding options to existing channels—for as long as application programmers are inventing new applications.

Reliability

As suggested by the examples just considered, reliable message delivery is one of the most important functions that a network can provide. It is difficult to determine how to provide this reliability, however, without first understanding how networks can fail. The first thing to recognize is that computer networks do not exist in a perfect world. Machines crash and later are rebooted, fibers are cut, electrical interference corrupts bits in the data being transmitted, and if these sorts of physical problems aren't enough to worry about, the software that manages the hardware sometimes forwards packets into oblivion. Thus, a major requirement of a network is to mask (hide) certain kinds of failures, so as to make the network appear more reliable than it really is to the application programs using it.

There are three general classes of failure that network designers have to worry about. First, as a packet is transmitted over a physical link, *bit errors* may be introduced into the data; i.e., a 1 is turned into a 0 or vice versa. Sometimes single bits are corrupted, but more often than not, a *burst error* occurs—several consecutive bits are corrupted. Bit errors typically occur because outside forces, such as lightning strikes and power surges, interfere with the transmission of data. The good news is that such bit errors are fairly rare, affecting on average only one out of every 10^6 to 10^7 bits on a typical copper-based cable and one out of every 10^{12} to 10^{14} bits on a typical optical fiber. As we will see, there are techniques that detect these bit errors with high probability. Once detected, it is sometimes possible to correct for such errors—if we know which bit or bits are corrupted, we can simply flip them—while in other cases the damage is so bad that it is necessary to discard the entire packet. In such a case, the sender may be expected to retransmit the packet.

The second class of failure is at the packet, rather than the bit, level; that is, a complete packet is lost by the network. One reason this can happen is that the packet contains an uncorrectable bit error and therefore has to be discarded. A more likely reason, however, is that the software running on one of the nodes that handles the packet—e.g., a switch that is forwarding it from one link to another—makes a mistake. For example, it might incorrectly forward a packet out on the wrong link, so that the packet never finds its way to the ultimate destination. Even more commonly, the forwarding node is so overloaded that it has no place to store the packet, and therefore is forced to drop it. This is the problem of congestion mentioned in Section 1.2.2. As we will see, one of the main difficulties in dealing with lost packets is distinguishing between a packet that is indeed lost and one that is merely late in arriving at the destination.

The third class of failure is at the node and link level, that is, a physical link is cut or the computer it is connected to crashes. This can be caused by software that crashes, a power failure, or a reckless backhoe operator. While such failures can eventually be corrected, they can have a dramatic effect on the network for an extended period of time. However, they need not totally disable the network. In a packet-switched network, for example, it is sometimes possible to route around a failed node or link. One of the difficulties in dealing with this third class of failure is distinguishing between a failed computer and one that is merely slow, or in the case of a link, between one that has been cut and one that is very flaky and therefore introducing a high number of bit errors.

The thing to take away from this discussion is that defining useful channels involves both understanding the applications' requirements and recognizing the limitations of the underlying technology. The challenge is to fill in the gap between what the application expects and what the underlying technology can provide.

1.2.4   Performance

Like any computer system, computer networks are expected to exhibit high performance, and often more importantly, high performance per unit cost. Computations distributed over multiple machines use networks to exchange data. The effectiveness of these computations often depends directly on the efficiency with which the network delivers that data. While the old programming adage "first get it right and then make it fast" is valid in many settings, in networking it is usually necessary to "design for performance." It is therefore important to understand the various factors that impact network performance.

Bandwidth and Latency

Network performance is measured in two fundamental ways: *bandwidth* (also called *throughput*) and *latency* (also called *delay*). The bandwidth of a network is given by the number of bits that can be transmitted over the network in a certain period of time. For example, a network might have a bandwidth of 10 million bits/second (Mbps), meaning that it is able to deliver 10 million bits every second. It is sometimes useful to think of bandwidth in terms of how long it takes to transmit each bit of data. On a 10-Mbps network, for example, it takes 0.1 microsecond (μs) to transmit each bit.

While you can talk about the bandwidth of the network as a whole, sometimes you want to be more precise, focusing for example on the bandwidth of a single physical link or of a logical process-to-process channel. At the physical level, bandwidth is constantly improving, with no end in sight. Intuitively, if you think of a second of time as a distance you could measure with a ruler and bandwidth as how many bits

Bandwidth and Throughput

Bandwidth and *throughput* are two of the most confusing terms used in networking. While we could try to give you a precise definition of each term, it is important that you know how other people might use them and for you to be aware that they are often used interchangeably.

First of all, bandwidth can be applied to an analog channel, such as a voice-grade telephone line. Such a line supports signals in the range of 300 and 3300 Hz and is said to have a bandwidth of 3300 Hz − 300 Hz = 3000 Hz. If you see the word bandwidth used in a situation in which it is being measured in hertz (Hz), then it probably refers to the range of analog signals that can be accommodated.

When we talk about the bandwidth of a digital link, we normally refer to the number of bits per second that can be transmitted on the link. We might say that the bandwidth of an Ethernet is 10 Mbps. A useful distinction might be made, however, be-

fit in that distance, then you can think of each bit as a pulse of some width. For example, each bit on a 1-Mbps link is 1 μs wide, while each bit in a 2-Mbps link is 0.5 μs wide, as illustrated in Figure 1.10. The more sophisticated the transmitting and receiving technology, the narrower each bit can become, and thus, the higher the bandwidth. For logical process-to-process channels, bandwidth is also influenced by other factors, including how many times the software that implements the channel has to handle, and possibly transform, each bit of data.

The second performance metric, latency, corresponds to how long it takes a single bit to propagate from one end of a network to the other. (As with bandwidth, we could be focused on the latency of a single link or channel.) Latency is measured strictly in terms of time. For example, a transcontinental network might have a latency of 24 milliseconds (ms), that is, it takes a single bit 24 ms to travel from one end of the country to the other. There are many situations in which it is more important to know how long it takes to send a bit from one end of a network to the other and back, rather than the one-way latency. We call this the *round-trip time* (RTT) of the network.

tween the bandwidth that is available on the link and the number of bits per second that we can actually transmit over the link in practice. We tend to use the word *throughput* to refer to the *measured performance* of a system. Thus, because of various inefficiencies of implementation, a pair of nodes connected by a link with a bandwidth of 10 Mbps might achieve a throughput of only 2 Mbps. This would mean that an application on one host could send data to the other host at 2 Mbps.

Finally, we often talk about the bandwidth *requirements* of an application. This is the number of bits per second that it needs to transmit over the network to perform acceptably. For some applications, this might be "whatever I can get," for others it might be some fixed number (preferably no more than the available link bandwidth), and for others it might be a number that varies with time. We will provide more on this topic later in this section.

We often think of latency as having three components. First, there is the speed-of-light propagation delay. This delay occurs because nothing, including a bit on a wire, can travel faster than the speed of light. If you know the distance between two points, you can calculate the speed-of-light latency, although you have to be careful because light travels across different mediums at different speeds: it travels at 3.0×10^8 meters/second in a vacuum, 2.3×10^8 meters/second in a cable, and 2.0×10^8 meters/second in a fiber. Second, there is the amount of time it takes to transmit a unit of data. This is a function of the network bandwidth and the size of the packet in which the data is carried. Third, there may be queuing delays inside the network, since packet switches generally need to store packets for some time before forwarding them on an outbound link, as discussed in Section 1.2.2. So, we could define the total latency as

Latency = Propagation + Transmit + Queue
Propagation = Distance / SpeedOfLight
Transmit = Size / Bandwidth

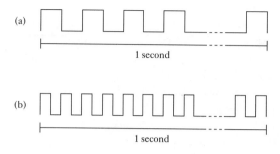

1 second

(b)

1 second

Figure 1.10 Bits transmitted at a particular bandwidth can be regarded as having some width. (a) Bits transmitted at 1 Mbps (each bit 1 μs wide); (b) bits transmitted at 2 Mbps (each bit 0.5 μs wide).

where Distance is the length of the wire over which the data will travel, SpeedOfLight is the effective speed of light over that wire, Size is the size of the packet, and Bandwidth is the bandwidth at which the packet is transmitted.

While there is eternal optimism that network bandwidth will continue to improve, observe that latency is fundamentally limited by the speed of light. We can make Transmit + Queue small by using high-bandwidth links, but, in the words of Scotty from Star Trek, "You cannae change the laws of physics." Thus, the 24-ms latency mentioned above corresponds to the time it takes light to travel through a fiber across the approximately 3000-mile width of the U.S.

Bandwidth and latency combine to define the performance characteristics of a given link or channel. Their relative importance, however, depends on the application. For some applications, latency dominates bandwidth. For example, a client that sends a 1-byte message to a server and receives a 1-byte message in return is latency bound. Assuming that no serious computation is involved in preparing the response, the application will perform much differently on a crosscountry channel with a 100-ms RTT than it will on an across-the-room channel with a 1-ms RTT. Whether the channel is 1 Mbps or 100 Mbps is relatively insignificant, however, since the former implies that the time to transmit a byte (Transmit) is 8 μs and the latter implies Transmit = 0.08 μs.

In contrast, consider a digital library program that is being asked to fetch a 25-megabyte (MB) image—the more bandwidth that is available, the faster it will be able to return the image to the user. Here, the bandwidth of the channel dominates performance. To see this, suppose that the channel has a bandwidth of 10 Mbps. It will take 20 seconds to transmit the image, making it relatively unimportant if the image is on the other side of a 1-ms channel or a 100-ms channel; the difference between a 20.001-second response time and a 20.1-second response time is negligible.

Figure 1.11 gives you a sense of how latency or bandwidth can dominate performance in different circumstances. The graph shows how long it takes to move objects of various sizes

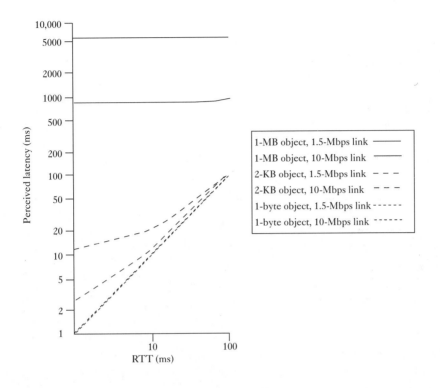

Figure 1.11 Perceived latency (response time) versus round-trip time for various object sizes and link speeds.

(1 byte, 2 KB, 1 MB) across networks with RTTs ranging from 1 to 100 ms and link speeds of either 1.5 or 10 Mbps. We use logarithmic scales to show relative performance. For a 1-byte object (say a keystroke), latency remains almost exactly equal to the RTT, so that you cannot distinguish between a 1.5-Mbps network and a 10-Mbps network. For a 2-KB object (say an email message), the link speed makes quite a difference on a 1-ms-RTT network but a negligible difference on a 100-ms-RTT network. And for a 1-MB object (say a digital image), the RTT makes no difference—it is the link speed that dominates performance across the full range of RTT.

Note that throughout this book we use the terms *latency* and *delay* in a generic way, that is, to denote how long it takes to perform a particular function such as delivering a message or moving an object. When we are referring to the specific amount of time it takes a signal to propagate from one end of a link to another, we use the term *propagation delay*. Also, we make it clear in the context of the discussion whether we are referring to the one-way latency or the round-trip time.

As an aside, computers are becoming so fast that when we connect them to networks, it is sometimes useful to think, at least figuratively, in terms of *instructions per mile*. Con-

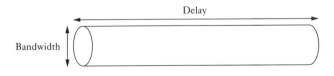

Figure 1.12 Network as a pipe.

sider what happens when a computer that is able to execute 200 million instructions per second sends a message out on a channel with a 100-ms RTT. (To make the math easier, assume that the message covers a distance of 5000 miles.) If that computer sits idle the full 100 ms waiting for a reply message, then it has forfeited the ability to execute 20 million instructions, or 4000 instructions per mile. It had better have been worth going over the network to justify this waste.

Delay × Bandwidth Product

It is also useful to talk about the product of these two metrics, often called the *delay × bandwidth product*. Intuitively, if we think of a channel between a pair of processes as a hollow pipe (see Figure 1.12), where the latency corresponds to the length of the pipe and the bandwidth gives the diameter of the pipe, then the delay × bandwidth product gives the volume of the pipe—the number of bits it holds. Said another way, if latency (measured in time) corresponds to the length of the pipe, then given the width of each bit (also measured in time), you can calculate how many bits fit in the pipe. For example, a transcontinental channel with a one-way latency of 50 ms and a bandwidth of 45 Mbps is able to hold 50×10^{-3} sec × 45 × 10^6 bits/sec = 2.25×10^6 bits, or approximately 280 KB of data. In other words, this example channel (pipe) holds as many bytes as the memory of a personal computer from the early 1980s could hold.

The delay × bandwidth product is important to know when constructing high-performance networks because it corresponds to how many bits the sender must transmit be-

How Big Is a Mega?

There are several pitfalls you need to be aware of when working with the common units of networking—MB, Mbps, KB, and Kbps. The first is to distinguish carefully between bits and bytes. Throughout this book, we always use a lowercase b for bits and a capital B for bytes. The second is to be sure you are using the appropriate definition of mega (M) and kilo (K). Mega, for example, can mean either 2^{20} or 10^6. Similarly, kilo can be either 2^{10} or 10^3. What is worse, in networking we typically use both definitions. Here's why.

Network bandwidth, which is often specified in terms of Mbps, is typically governed by the speed of the clock that paces the transmission of the bits. A clock that is running at 10 megahertz (MHz) is used to transmit bits at 10 Mbps. Because the mega in MHz means 10^6 hertz, Mbps is us-

fore the first bit arrives at the receiver. If the sender is expecting the receiver to somehow signal that bits are starting to arrive, and it takes another channel latency for this signal to propagate back to the sender (i.e., we are interested in the channel's RTT rather than just its one-way latency), then the sender can send up to two delay × bandwidths worth of data before hearing from the receiver that all is well. Also, if the receiver indicates to stop sending, it might receive that much data before the sender manages to respond. In our example above, that amount corresponds to 5.5×10^6 bits (560 KB) of data.

Note that most of the time we are interested in the RTT scenario, which we simply refer to as the delay × bandwidth product, without explicitly saying that this product is multiplied by two. Again, whether the "delay" in "delay × bandwidth" means one-way latency or RTT is made clear by the context.

ually also defined as 10^6 bits per second. (Similarly, Kbps is 10^3 bits per second.) On the other hand, when we talk about a message that we want to transmit, we often give its size in kilobytes. Because messages are stored in the computer's memory, and memory is typically measured in powers of two, the K in KB is usually taken to mean 2^{10}. (Similarly, MB usually means 2^{20}.) When you put the two together, it is not uncommon to talk about sending a 32-KB message over a 10-Mbps channel, which should be interpreted to mean $32 \times 2^{10} \times 8$ bits are being transmitted at a rate of 10×10^6 bits per second. This is the interpretation we use throughout the book, unless explicitly stated otherwise.

The good news is that many times we are satisfied with a back-of-the-envelope calculation, in which case it is perfectly reasonable to

Application Performance Needs

The discussion in this section has taken a network-centric view of performance, that is, we have talked in terms of what a given link or channel will support. The unstated assumption has been that application programs have simple needs—they want as much bandwidth as the network can provide. This is certainly true of the aforementioned digital library program that is retrieving a 25-MB image—the more bandwidth that is available, the faster the program will be able to return the image to the user. However, some applications are able to state an upper limit on how much bandwidth they need. For example, a video application that needs to transmit a 128-KB video frame 30 times a second might request a throughput rate of 32 Mbps. The ability of the network to provide more bandwidth is of no interest to such an application because it has only so much data to transmit in a given period of time.

Unfortunately, the situation is not as simple as this example suggests. Because the difference between any two adjacent frames in a video stream is often small, it is possible to compress the video by transmitting only the differences between adjacent frames. This compressed video does not flow at a constant rate, but varies with time according to factors such the amount of action and detail in the picture and the compression algorithm being used. Therefore, it is possible to say what the average bandwidth requirement will be, but the instantaneous rate may be more or less.

The key issue is the time interval over which the average is computed. Suppose that this example video application can be compressed down to the point that it needs only 2 Mbps, on average. If it transmits 1 megabit in a 1-second interval and 3 megabits in the following 1-second interval, then over the 2-second interval it is transmitting at an average rate of 2 Mbps; however, this will be of little consolation to a channel that was engineered to support no more than 2 megabits in any one second. Clearly, just knowing the average bandwidth needs of an application will not always suffice.

Generally, however, it is possible to put an upper bound on how big of a burst an application like this is likely to transmit. A burst might be described by some peak rate that is maintained for some period of time. Alternatively, it could be described as the number of bytes that can be sent at the peak rate before reverting to the average rate or some lower rate. If this peak rate is higher than the available channel capacity, then the excess data will have to be buffered somewhere, to be transmitted later. Knowing how big of a burst might be sent allows the network designer to allocate sufficient buffer capacity to hold the burst. We will return to the subject of describing bursty traffic accurately in Chapter 9.

Analogous to the way an application's bandwidth needs can be something other than "all it can get," an application's delay requirements may be more complex than simply "as little delay as possible." In the case of delay, it sometimes doesn't matter so much whether the one-way latency of the network is 100 ms or 500 ms as how much the latency varies from packet to packet. The variation in latency is called *jitter*.

Consider the situation in which the source sends a packet once every 33 ms, as

pretend that a byte has 10 bits in it (making it easy to convert between bits and bytes) and that 10^6 is really equal to 2^{20} (making it easy to convert between the two definitions of mega). Notice that the first approximation introduces a 20% error, while the latter introduces only a 5% error.

To help you in your quick-and-dirty calculations, 100 ms is a reasonable number to use for a crosscountry round-trip time (RTT) and 1 ms is a good approximation of an RTT across a local area network. In the case of the former, we increase the 48-ms round-trip time implied by the speed of light over a fiber to 100 ms because there are, as we have said, other sources of delay, such as the processing time in the switches inside the network. You can also be sure that the path taken by the fiber between two points will not be a straight line.

would be the case for a video application transmitting frames 30 times a second. If the packets arrive at the destination spaced out exactly 33 ms apart, then we can deduce that the delay experienced by each packet in the network was exactly the same. If the spacing between when packets arrive at the destination—sometimes called the *interpacket gap*—is variable, however, then the delay experienced by the sequence of packets must have also been variable, and the network is said to have introduced jitter into the packet stream. Such variation is generally not introduced in a single physical link, but it can happen when packets experience different queuing delays in a multihop packet-switched network. This queuing delay corresponds to the Queue component of latency defined earlier in this section, which varies with time.

To understand the relevance of jitter, suppose that the packets being transmitted over the network contain video frames, and in order to display these frames on the screen the receiver needs to receive a new one every 33 ms. If a frame arrives early, then it can simply be saved by the receiver until it is time to display it. Unfortunately, if a frame arrives late, then the receiver will not have the frame it needs in time to update the screen, and the video quality will suffer; it will not be smooth. Note that it is not necessary to eliminate jitter, only to know how bad it is. The reason for this is that if the receiver knows the upper and lower bounds on the latency that a packet can experience, it can delay the time at which it starts playing back the video (i.e., displays the first frame) long enough to ensure that in the future it will always have a frame to display when it needs it. We return to the topic of jitter in Chapter 9.

1.3 Network Architecture

In case you hadn't noticed, the previous section established a pretty substantial set of requirements for network design—a computer network must provide general, cost-effective, fair, robust, and high-performance connectivity among a large number of computers. As if this weren't enough, networks do not remain fixed at any single point in time, but must evolve to accommodate changes in both the underlying technologies upon which they are based as well as changes in the demands placed on them by application programs. Designing a network to meet these requirements is no small task.

To help deal with this complexity, network designers have developed general blueprints—usually called a *network architecture*—that guide the design and implementation of networks. This section defines more carefully what we mean by a network architecture by introducing the central ideas that are common to all network architectures. It also introduces two of the most widely referenced architectures—the OSI architecture and the Internet architecture.

1.3.1 Layering and Protocols

When the system gets complex, the system designer introduces another level of abstraction. The idea of an abstraction is to define a unifying model that can capture some important aspect of the system, encapsulate this model in an object that provides an interface that can be manipulated by other components of the system, and hide the details of how the object is implemented from the users of the object. The challenge is to identify abstractions that simultaneously provide a service that proves useful in a large number of situations and that can be efficiently implemented in the underlying system. This is exactly what we were doing when

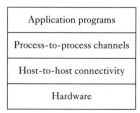

| Application programs |
| Process-to-process channels |
| Host-to-host connectivity |
| Hardware |

Figure 1.13 Example of a layered network system.

we introduced the idea of a channel in the previous section: we were providing an abstraction for applications that hides the complexity of the network from application writers.

Abstractions naturally lead to layering, especially in network systems. The general idea is that you start with the services offered by the underlying hardware, and then add a sequence of layers, each providing a higher (more abstract) level of service. The services provided at the high layers are implemented in terms of the services provided by the low layers. Drawing on the discussion of requirements given in the previous section, for example, one might imagine a network as having two layers of abstraction sandwiched between the application program and the underlying hardware, as illustrated in Figure 1.13. The layer immediately above the hardware in this case might provide host-to-host connectivity, abstracting away the fact that there may be an arbitrarily complex network topology between any two hosts. The next layer up builds on the available host-to-host communication service and provides support for process-to-process channels, abstracting away the fact that the network occasionally loses messages, for example.

Layering provides two nice features. First, it decomposes the problem of building a network into more manageable components. Rather than implementing a monolithic piece of software that does everything you will ever want, you can implement several layers, each of which solves one part of the problem. Second, it provides a more modular design. If you decide that you want to add some new service, you may only need to modify the functionality at one layer, reusing the functions provided at all the other layers.

Thinking of a system as a linear sequence of layers is an oversimplification, however. Many times there are multiple abstractions provided at any given level of the system, each providing a different service to the higher layers but building on the same low-level abstractions. To see this, consider the two types of channels discussed in Section 1.2.3: one provides a request/reply service and one supports a message stream service. These two channels might be alternative offerings at some level of a multilevel networking system, as illustrated in Figure 1.14.

Using this discussion of layering as a foundation, we are now ready to discuss the architecture of a network more precisely. For starters, the abstract objects that make up the layers of a network system are called *protocols*. That is, a protocol provides a communication service that higher-level objects (such as application processes, or perhaps higher-level pro-

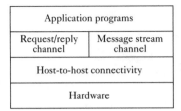

Application programs	
Request/reply channel	Message stream channel
Host-to-host connectivity	
Hardware	

Figure 1.14 Layered system with alternative abstractions available at a given layer.

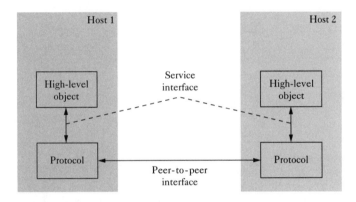

Figure 1.15 Service and peer interfaces.

tocols) use to exchange messages. For example, one could imagine a network that supports a request/reply protocol and a message stream protocol, corresponding to the request/reply and message stream channels discussed above.

Each protocol defines two different interfaces. First, it defines a *service interface* to the other objects on the same computer that want to use its communication services. This service interface defines the operations that local objects can perform on the protocol. For example, a request/reply protocol would support operations by which an application can send and receive messages. Second, a protocol defines a *peer interface* to its counterpart (peer) on another machine. This second interface defines the form and meaning of messages exchanged between protocol peers to implement the communication service. This would determine the way in which a request/reply protocol on one machine communicates with its peer on another machine. In other words, a protocol defines a communication service that it exports locally, along with a set of rules governing the messages that the protocol exchanges with its peer(s) to implement this service. This situation is illustrated in Figure 1.15.

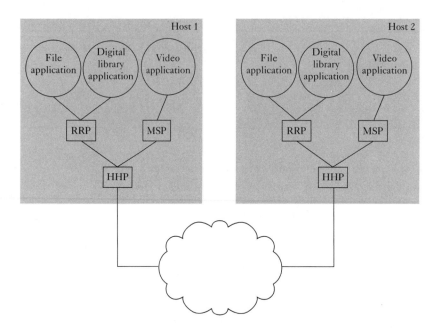

Figure 1.16 Example of a protocol graph.

Except at the hardware level where peers directly communicate with each other over a link, peer-to-peer communication is indirect—each protocol communicates with its peer by passing messages to some lower-level protocol, which in turn delivers the message to *its* peer. In addition, there are potentially multiple protocols at any given level, each providing a different communication service. We therefore represent the suite of protocols that make up a network system with a *protocol graph*. The nodes of the graph correspond to protocols and the edges represent a *depends on* relation. For example, Figure 1.16 illustrates a protocol graph for the hypothetical layered system we have been discussing—protocols RRP (Request/Reply Protocol) and MSP (Message Stream Protocol) implement two different types of process-to-process channels, and both depend on HHP (host-to-host protocol), which provides a host-to-host connectivity service.

In this example, suppose that the file access program on Host 1 wants to send a message to its peer on Host 2 using the communication service offered by protocol RRP. In this case, the file application asks RRP to send the message on its behalf. To communicate with its peer, RRP then invokes the services of HHP, which in turn transmits the message to its peer on the other machine. Once the message has arrived at protocol HHP on Host 2, HHP passes the message up to RRP, which in turn delivers the message to the file application. In this particular case, the application is said to employ the services of the *protocol stack* RRP/HHP.

Note that the term *protocol* is used in two different ways. Sometimes it refers to the abstract interfaces—that is, the operations defined by the service interface and the form and meaning of messages exchanged between peers—and sometimes it refers to the module that actually implements these two interfaces. To distinguish between the interfaces and the module that implements these interfaces, we generally refer to the former as a *protocol specification*. Specifications are generally expressed using a combination of prose, pseudocode, state transition diagrams, pictures of packet formats, and other abstract notations. It should be the case that a given protocol can be implemented in different ways by different programmers, as long as each adheres to the specification. The challenge is ensuring that two different implementations of the same specification can successfully exchange messages. Two or more protocol modules that do accurately implement a protocol specification are said to *interoperate* with each other.

One can imagine many different protocols and protocol graphs that satisfy the communication requirements of a collection of applications. Fortunately, there exist standardization bodies, such as the International Standards Organization (ISO) and the Internet Engineering Task Force (IETF), that establish policies for a particular protocol graph. We call the set of rules governing the form and content of a protocol graph a *network architecture*. Although beyond the scope of this book, standardization bodies such as the ISO and the IETF have established well-defined procedures for introducing, validating, and finally approving protocols in their respective architectures. We briefly describe the architectures defined by the ISO and the IETF shortly, but first there are two additional things we need to explain about the mechanics of a protocol graph.

Encapsulation

Consider what happens in Figure 1.16 when one of the application program sends a message to its peer by passing the message to protocol RRP. From RRP's perspective, the message it is given by the application is an uninterpreted string of bytes. RRP does not care that these bytes represent an array of integers, an email message, a digital image, or whatever; it is simply charged with sending them to its peer. However, RRP must communicate control information to its peer, instructing it how to handle the message when it is received. RRP does this by attaching a *header* to the message. Generally speaking, a header is a small data structure—from a few bytes to a few dozen bytes—that is used among peers to communicate with each other. As the name suggests, headers are usually attached to the front of a message. In some cases, however, this peer-to-peer control information is sent at the end of the message, in which case it is called a *trailer*. The exact format for the header attached by RRP is defined by its protocol specification. The rest of the message—i.e., the data being transmitted on behalf of the application—is called the message's *body*. We say that the application's data is *encapsulated* in the new message created by protocol RRP.

This process of encapsulation is then repeated at each level of the protocol graph; for example, HHP encapsulates RRP's message by attaching a header of its own. If we now assume that HHP sends the message to its peer over some network, then when the message arrives at

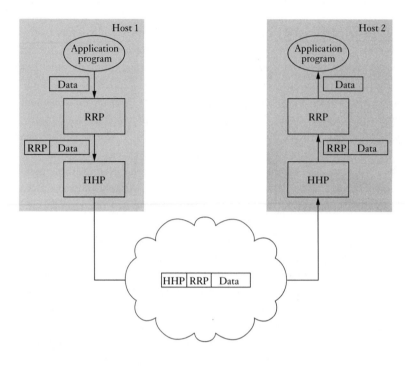

Figure 1.17   High-level messages are encapsulated inside of low-level messages.

the destination host, it is processed in the opposite order: HHP first strips its header off the front of the message, interprets it (i.e., takes whatever action is appropriate given the contents of the header), and passes the body of the message up to RRP, which removes the header that its peer attached, takes whatever action is indicated by that header, and passes the body of the message up to the application program. The message passed up from RRP to the application on Host 2 is exactly the same message as the application passed down to RRP on Host 1; the application does not see any of the headers that have been attached to it to implement the lower-level communication services. This whole process is illustrated in Figure 1.17. Note that in this example, nodes in the network (e.g., switches and routers) may inspect the HHP header at the front of the message.

   Note that when we say a low-level protocol does not interpret the message it is given by some high-level protocol, we mean that it does not know how to extract any meaning from the data contained in the message. It is sometimes the case, however, that the low-level protocol applies some simple transformation to the data it is given, such as to compress or encrypt it. In this case, the protocol is transforming the entire body of the message, including both the original application's data and all the headers attached to that data by higher-level protocols.

Multiplexing and Demultiplexing

Recall from Section 1.2.2 that a fundamental idea of packet switching is to multiplex multiple flows of data over a single physical link. This same idea applies up and down the protocol graph, not just to switching nodes. In Figure 1.16, for example, one can think of RRP as implementing a logical communication channel, with messages from two different applications multiplexed over this channel at the source host and then demultiplexed back to the appropriate application at the destination host.

Practically speaking, all this means is that the header that RRP attaches to its messages contains an identifier that records the application to which the message belongs. We call this identifier RRP's *demultiplexing key*, or *demux key* for short. At the source host, RRP includes the appropriate demux key in its header. When the message is delivered to RRP on the destination host, it strips its header, examines the demux key, and demultiplexes the message to the correct application.

RRP is not unique in its support for multiplexing; nearly every protocol implements this mechanism. For example, HHP has its own demux key to determine which messages to pass up to RRP and which to pass up to MSP. However, there is no uniform agreement among protocols—even those within a single network architecture—on exactly what constitutes a demux key. Some protocols use an 8-bit field (meaning they can support only 256 high-level protocols), and others use 16- or 32-bit fields. Also, some protocols have a single demultiplexing field in their header, while others have a pair of demultiplexing fields. In the former case, the same demux key is used on both sides of the communication, while in the latter case, each side uses a different key to identify the high-level protocol (or application program) to which the message is to be delivered.

1.3.2 OSI Architecture

The ISO was one of the first organizations to formally define a common way to connect computers. Their architecture, called the *Open Systems Interconnection* (OSI) architecture and illustrated in Figure 1.18, defines a partitioning of network functionality into seven layers, where one or more protocols implement the functionality assigned to a given layer. In this sense, the schematic given in Figure 1.18 is not a protocol graph, per se, but rather a *reference model* for a protocol graph. The ISO, usually in conjunction with a second standards organization known as the *International Telecommunications Union* (ITU),[2] publishes a series of protocol specifications based on the OSI architecture. This series is sometimes called the "X dot" series since the protocols are given names like X.25, X.400, X.500, and so on. There have been several networks based on these standards, including the public X.25 network and private networks like Tymnet.

---

[2]A subcommittee of the ITU on telecommunications (ITU-T) replaces an earlier subcommittee of the ITU, which was known by its French name Comité Consultatif International de Télégraphique et Téléphonique (CCITT).

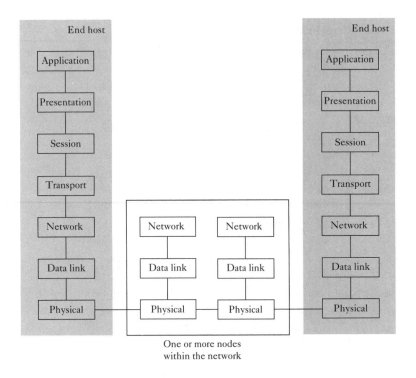

Figure 1.18 OSI network architecture.

Starting at the bottom and working up, the *physical* layer handles the transmission of raw bits over a communications link. The *data link* layer then collects a stream of bits into a larger aggregate called a *frame*. Network adaptors typically implement the data link level, meaning that frames, not raw bits, are actually delivered to hosts. The *network* layer handles routing among nodes within a packet-switched network. At this layer, the unit of data exchanged among nodes is typically called a *packet* rather than a frame, although they are fundamentally the same thing. The lower three layers are implemented on all network nodes, including switches within the network and hosts connected along the exterior of the network. The *transport* layer then implements what we have up to this point been calling a process-to-process channel. Here, the unit of data exchanged is commonly called a *message* rather than a packet or a frame. The transport layer and higher layers typically run only on the end hosts and not on the intermediate switches or routers.

There is less agreement about the definition of the top three layers. Working from the top down, the topmost layer is the *application*. Application layer protocols include things like the file transfer protocol, FTP, which defines a protocol by which file transfer applications can interoperate. Next, the *presentation* layer is concerned with the format of data exchanged between peers, for example, whether an integer is 16, 32, or 64 bits long and whether the

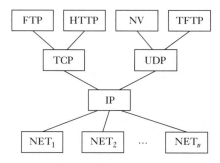

Figure 1.19 Internet protocol graph.

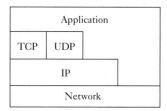

Figure 1.20 Alternative view of the Internet architecture.

most significant bit is transmitted first or last. Finally, the *session* layer provides a name space that is used to tie together the potentially different transport streams that are part of a single application. For example, it might manage an audio stream and a video stream that are being combined in a teleconferencing application.

1.3.3 Internet Architecture

The Internet architecture, which is also sometimes called the TCP/IP architecture after its two main protocols, is depicted in Figure 1.19. An alternative representation is given in Figure 1.20. The Internet architecture evolved out of experiences with an earlier packet-switched network called the ARPANET. Both the Internet and the ARPANET were funded by the Advanced Research Projects Agency (ARPA), one of the R&D funding agencies of the U.S. Department of Defense. The Internet and ARPANET were around before the OSI architecture, and the experience gained from building them was a major influence on the OSI reference model.

While the seven-layer OSI model can, with some imagination, be applied to the Internet, a four-layer model is often used instead. At the lowest level are a wide variety of network protocols, denoted NET_1, NET_2, and so on. In practice, these protocols are implemented by a combination of hardware (e.g., a network adaptor) and software (e.g., a network device driver). For example, one might find Ethernet or Fiber Distributed Data Interface (FDDI) protocols at this layer. (These protocols in turn may actually involve several sublayers, but the Internet architecture does not presume anything about them.) The second layer consists of a single protocol—IP, which stands for the *Internet Protocol*. This is the

protocol that supports the interconnection of multiple networking technologies into a single, logical internetwork. The third layer contains two main protocols—the *Transmission Control Protocol* (TCP) and the *User Datagram Protocol* (UDP). TCP and UDP provide alternative logical channels to application programs—TCP provides a reliable byte stream channel and UDP provides an unreliable datagram delivery channel (*datagram* may be thought of as a synonym for message). In the language of the Internet, TCP and UDP are sometimes called *end-to-end* protocols, although it is equally correct to refer to them as transport protocols.

Running above the transport layer are a range of application protocols, such as FTP, TFTP (Trivial File Transport Protocol), Telnet (remote login), and SMTP (Simple Mail Transfer Protocol, or electronic mail), that enable the interoperation of popular applications. To understand the difference between an application layer protocol and an application, think of all the different World Wide Web browsers that are available (e.g., Mosaic, Netscape, Lynx, etc.). The reason that you can use any one of these application programs to access a particular site on the Web is because they all conform to the same application layer protocol: HTTP (HyperText Transport Protocol). Confusingly, the same word sometimes applies to both an application and the application layer protocol that it uses (e.g., FTP).

The Internet architecture has three features that are worth highlighting. First, as best illustrated by Figure 1.20, the Internet architecture does not imply strict layering. The application is free to bypass the defined transport layers and to directly use IP or one of the underlying networks. In fact, programmers are free

OSI versus Internet Architecture

While there have been countless spirited discussions over the past 15–20 years about the technical advantages of the ISO protocols versus the Internet protocols, such debates are no longer relevant. This is because the ISO protocols, with a handful of exceptions, are largely ignored, while the Internet thrives. (This statement does not imply that the OSI reference architecture is worthless—on the contrary, it continues to be somewhat influential by providing a model for understanding networks, even though the ISO protocols themselves have been a commercial failure.)

One explanation for the success of one and the failure of the other is that some of the technical arguments made against the OSI architecture during these debates were on the mark. There is a more likely explanation, however, one that is surprisingly pragmatic in nature. It is that an implementation of the TCP/IP protocol suite was bundled with the popular

to define new channel abstractions or applications that run on top of any of the existing protocols.

Second, if you look closely at the protocol graph in Figure 1.19, you will notice an hourglass shape—wide at the top, narrow in the middle, and wide at the bottom. This shape actually reflects the central philosophy of the architecture. That is, IP serves as the focal point for the architecture—it defines a common method for exchanging packets among a wide collection of networks. Above IP can be arbitrarily many transport protocols, each offering a different channel abstraction to application programs. Thus, the issue of delivering messages from host to host is completely separated from the issue of providing a useful process-to-process communication service. Below IP, the architecture allows for arbitrarily many different network technologies, ranging from Ethernet to FDDI to ATM to single point-to-point links.

A final attribute of the Internet architecture (or more accurately, of the IETF culture) is that in order for someone to propose a new protocol to be included in the architecture, they must produce both a protocol specification and at least one (and preferably two) representative implementations of the specification. The existence of working implementations is required for standards to be adopted by the IETF. This cultural assumption of the design community helps to ensure that the architecture's protocols can be efficiently implemented. Even with this requirement, the implementations of the protocols in the Internet architecture have evolved quite significantly over time as researchers and practitioners have gained experience using them.

Unix operating system distributed by the University of California at Berkeley in the early 1980s. People are more likely to use software that is readily available than software that requires effort to acquire, and the widespread availability of Berkeley Unix allowed the TCP/IP architecture to achieve a critical mass.

To expand on this point a bit further, the ISO/ITU culture has always been to "specify first and implement later." As the specification process is a long and tedious one, especially when you do not have any working code with which to experiment, the implementation of ISO protocols were always a long time in arriving. In contrast, the Internet culture has been to "implement as you go." In fact, to quote a T-shirt commonly worn at IETF meetings:

We reject kings, presidents, and voting. We believe in rough consensus and running code. (Dave Clark)

1.4 Plan for the Book

Just as a network architecture provides a blueprint for building a computer network, this section gives the blueprint for reading this book. This blueprint has two dimensions. In one dimension, the chapters give a layer-by-layer account of how to design a computer network. While it is accurate to characterize the sequence of chapters as describing a network from the bottom up—i.e., starting at the low levels of the network architecture and moving to the higher layers—we prefer to think of the book as first describing the simplest possible network and then adding functionality and capabilities in later chapters. A summary of the chapters is given below. In the second dimension, there are a set of common themes that run through all the chapters. We think of these themes as collectively representing a *systems approach* to computer networks. Section 1.4.2 identifies the themes that make up the systems approach to networking.

1.4.1 Chapter Organization

Each chapter begins with a statement of the next problem that must be solved—the individual problems have their genesis in Chapter 1—and then develops and evaluates solutions that can be applied to the problem. In this way, each chapter builds on the foundation developed in the previous chapters, with the end result being a recipe for building a computer network from the ground up.

Before studying the lowest layers of the network, Chapter 2 first takes a brief detour by introducing the x-kernel, a framework for implementing network protocols. While it is not essential that you understand the x-kernel in detail, this chapter plays a valuable role in this book. One reason is that we give fragments of x-kernel code in later chapters; reading Chapter 2 helps to make this code more accessible. Another reason is that Chapter 2 describes the underlying data structures used to implement various components of a protocol; seeing these

To understand just how important running code is, we observe that it is even more powerful than the U.S. government. In 1988, the National Institute for Standards and Technology (NIST), an agency within the U.S. government's Department of Commerce, approved a mandate that required government agencies to procure equipment that could run the ISO protocols. (The agencies did not have to use the ISO protocols, but the vendors had to support it or at least demonstrate how their systems could support it.) Since the U.S. government is such a big consumer of computers, this mandate was expected to push the commercial sector toward adopting the ISO protocol suite. In reality, however, computers were shipped with ISO-compliant code, but people kept using TCP/IP. To make a long story short, the mandate was officially rescinded in September 1994.

data structures helps to ground your understanding of networks at the most basic level. The third and perhaps most important reason is that this chapter describes the mechanics of a protocol, and as such, provides a scaffolding for the concepts you learn throughout the rest of the book. Without Chapter 2, this book contains a comprehensive collection of algorithms and protocols that make up computer networks. With Chapter 2, however, you should be able to develop a concrete understanding of how all these algorithms and protocols fit together to provide a functioning computer network.

Chapters 3 and 4 then explore a variety of networking technologies. Chapter 3 begins by considering simple networks in which all the computers are directly connected to each other, either in a point-to-point configuration or with a shared-access medium such as Ethernet or FDDI. It also discusses the point at which the network link connects to the computer—the network adaptor. Chapter 4 then considers switch-based networks in which intermediate nodes forward packets between machines that are not directly connected to each other. Here, routing and contention are the key topics.

Chapter 5 then covers the topic of internetworking. Starting with the problem of connecting a handful of Ethernets, then moving on to the simple interconnection of networks as exemplified by the early days of the Internet, and concluding with the problems associated with a global internet like the one that exists today, Chapter 5 addresses two main issues—scale and heterogeneity.

Assuming a collection of computers connected by some kind of network—either a particular networking technology or the global Internet—Chapters 6 and 7 then look at the end-to-end issues. Chapter 6 considers three forms of end-to-end (transport) protocols: unreliable datagram protocols (UDP), byte-stream protocols (TCP), and request/reply protocols (RPC). Chapter 7 then focuses on application-specific transformations that are applied to the data being communicated. These transformations include encryption, compression, and presentation formatting.

Chapters 8 and 9 discuss advanced topics. Chapter 8 focuses on the issue of congestion control, which is cast as the problem of fair resource allocation. This chapter looks at both "inside the network" and "at the edge of the network" solutions. Chapter 9 then introduces the problems that must be addressed as networks become faster—moving into the gigabit-per-second range—and outlines how some of these problems are being solved.

Finally, so as not to leave you with the false impression that the networking community knows everything there is to know about networking, each chapter concludes with a discussion of some unresolved issue—an Open Issue. Typically, this is a controversial subject that is currently being debated in the networking community. This section is included to show that much more work remains to be done and that networking is an exciting and vibrant subject with plenty of challenges yet to be addressed by the next generation of network designers.

1.4.2 Systems Approach

The approach we take throughout all the chapters is to consider networking from a systems perspective. While the term *systems approach* is terribly overused, we use it to mean that the book first develops a collection of building blocks and then shows how these components can be put together to construct a complete network that satisfies the numerous and sometimes conflicting goals of some user community. This systems-oriented perspective has several implications that are reflected in the content, organization, and emphasis of this book.

First, the systems approach implies doing experimental performance studies, and then using the data you gather both to quantitatively analyze various design options and to guide you in optimizing the implementation. This emphasis on empirical analysis pervades the book, as exemplified by the definition of networking's central performance metrics given earlier in this chapter. Later chapters discuss the performance of the specific component being studied.

Second, system builders do not accept existing artifacts as gospel, but instead strive to understand the concepts that are fundamental to the system. In the context of this book, this means that starting from first principles, we answer the question of *why* networks are designed the way they are rather than simply marching through the set of protocols that happen to be in use today. It is our experience that once you understand the underlying concepts, any new protocol that you are confronted with will be relatively easy to digest.

Third, to help understand the concepts underlying the system in question, system builders often draw on a collection of design principles that have evolved from experience with computer systems in general. For example, a well-known system design rule that we have already seen is to manage complexity by introducing multiple layers of abstraction. As we will see throughout this book, layering is a trick of the trade applied quite frequently in the networking domain. Other rules of thumb guide the decomposition of a system into its component layers. We highlight these design principles as they are introduced throughout the book.

Fourth, the systems approach implies studying successful, working examples; systems cannot be studied in the abstract. For example, this book draws heavily—although not exclusively—from the Internet. As a functioning, global network, the Internet is rich with examples that illustrate how networks are designed. It is also the case that the Internet, because it encompasses every known wide area network (WAN) and local area network (LAN) technology, lends itself to the broadest possible coverage of networking topics. Note that while we plan to use the Internet as a framework for talking about networks, the book is not simply a tutorial on the Internet. The Internet is an evolving network, and in fact is at a juncture where change is rapid. Five years from now, it is very unlikely that the Internet will look anything like it does today. Therefore, our goal is to focus on unifying principles, not just to recount the specifics of the current Internet.

Fifth, a systems approach implies looking at the big picture. That is, you need to evaluate design decisions in terms of how they affect the entire system, not just with the goal of optimizing some small part of the system. In a networking context, this means understanding the entire network architecture before trying to optimize the design of one protocol.

Finally, system design often implies software, and computer networks are no exception. Although the primitive building blocks of a network are the commodity hardware that can be bought from computer vendors and communication services that can be leased from the phone company, it is software that turns this raw hardware into a richly functional, robust, and high-performance network. As mentioned above, one goal of this book is to provide you not only with an understanding of the components of a network but also with a feel for how all the pieces are put together. Code from the x-kernel—a working network subsystem—helps to make this all tangible.

1.5 Summary

Computer networks like the Internet have experienced explosive growth over the past decade and are now positioned to provide a wide range of services—remote file access, digital libraries, video conferencing—to tens of millions of users. Much of this growth can be attributed to the general-purpose nature of computer networks, and in particular to the ability to add new functionality to the network by writing software that runs on affordable, high-performance computers. With this in mind, the overriding goal of this book is to describe computer networks in such a way that when you finish reading it, you should feel that if you had an army of programmers at your disposal, you could actually build a fully functional computer network from the ground up. This chapter lays the foundation for realizing this goal.

The first step we have taken toward this goal is to carefully identify exactly what we expect from a network. For example, a network must first provide cost-effective connectivity among a set of computers. This is accomplished through a nested interconnection of nodes and links, and by sharing this hardware base through the use of statistical multiplexing. This results in a packet-switched network, on top of which we then define a collection of process-to-process communication services. Finally, the network as a whole must offer high performance, where the two performance metrics we are most interested in are latency and throughput.

The second step is to define a layered architecture that will serve as a blueprint for our design. The central objects of this architecture are network protocols. Protocols both provide a communication service to higher-level protocols and define the form and meaning of messages exchanged with their peers running on other machines. We have briefly surveyed two of the most widely used architectures: the OSI architecture and the Internet architecture. This book most closely follows the Internet architecture, both in its organization and as a source of examples.

There is little doubt that computer networks are on the brink of becoming an integral part of the everyday lives of vast numbers of people. What began over 20 years ago as experimental systems like the ARPANET—connecting mainframe computers over long-distance telephone lines—has turned into big business. And where there is big business, there are lots

OPEN   ISSUE

Ubiquitous Networking

of players. In this case, there is the computing industry, which has become increasingly in-volved in supporting packet-switched networking products; the telephone carriers, which rec-ognize the market for carrying all sorts of data, not just voice; and the cable TV industry, which currently owns the entertainment portion of the market.

Assuming that the goal is ubiquitous networking—to bring the network into every household—the first problem that must be addressed is how to establish the necessary physical links. Many would argue that the ultimate answer is to bring an optical fiber into ev-ery home, but at an estimated $1000 per house and 100 million homes in the U.S. alone, this is a $100 billion proposition. The most widely discussed alternative is to use the existing cable TV facilities. The problem is that today's cable facilities are asymmetric—you can deliver 150 channels into every home, but the outgoing bandwidth is severely limited. Such asymmetry implies that there are a small number of information providers, but that most of us are simply information consumers. Many people would argue that in a democracy we should all have an equal opportunity to provide information.

How the struggle between the computer companies, the telephone companies, and the cable industry will play out in the marketplace is anyone's guess. (If we knew the answer, we'd be charging a lot more for this book.) All we know is that there are many technical obsta-cles that stand between the current state of the art and the sort of global, ubiquitous, het-erogeneous network that we believe is possible and desirable—issues of connectivity, levels of service, performance, reliability, and fairness. It is these challenges that are the focus of this book.

FURTHER READING

Computer networks are not the first communication-oriented technology to have found their way into the everyday fabric of our society. For example, the early part of this century saw the introduction of the telephone, and then during the 1950s television became widespread. When considering the future of networking—how widely it will spread and how we will use it—it is instructive to study this history. Our first reference is a good starting point for doing this (the entire issue is devoted to the first 100 years of telecommunications).

The second and third papers are the seminal papers on the OSI and Internet architec-tures, respectively. The Zimmerman paper introduces the OSI architecture and the Clark pa-per is a retrospective. The final two papers are not specific to networking, but ones that every systems person should read. The Saltzer et al. paper motivates and describes one of the most widely applied rules of system design—the *end-to-end argument*. The paper by Mashey de-scribes the thinking behind RISC architectures; as we will soon discover, making good judg-ments about where to place functionality in a complex system is what system design is all about.

- Pierce, J. Telephony—A personal view. *IEEE Communications* 22(5):116–120, May 1984.

- Zimmerman, H. OSI reference model—The ISO model of architecture for open systems interconnection. *IEEE Transactions on Communications* COM-28(4):425–432, April 1980.

- Clark, D. The design philosophy of the DARPA internet protocols. *Proceedings of the SIGCOMM '88 Symposium*, pages 106–114, August 1988.

- Saltzer, J., et al. End-to-end arguments in system design. *ACM Transactions on Computer Systems* 2(4):277–288, November 1984.

- Mashey, J. RISC, MIPS, and the motion of complexity. *UniForum 1986 Conference Proceedings*, pages 116–124, 1986.

Several texts offer an introduction to computer networking. Stallings gives an encyclopedic treatment of the subject, with an emphasis on the lower levels of the OSI hierarchy [Sta91]; Tanenbaum uses the OSI architecture as an organizational model [Tan88]; Comer gives an overview of the Internet architecture [Com95]; and Bertsekas and Gallager discuss networking from a performance modeling perspective [BG92].

For more on the social ramifications of computer networking, articles can be found in almost any newspaper or periodical. Two specific examples that we recommend are Barlow's commentary on the risks of asymmetric networks [Bar95] and an overview of the information revolution published in the National Geographic [Swe95]. (The latter has nice pictures.) Also, we recommend the "Net Surf" column in *Wired* for interesting WWW links.

To put computer networking into a larger context, two books—one dealing with the past and the other looking toward the future—are must reading. The first is Holzmann and Pehrson's *The Early History of Data Networks* [HP95]. Surprisingly, many of the ideas covered in the book you are now reading were invented during the 1700s. The second is *Realizing the Information Future: The Internet and Beyond*, a book prepared by the Computer Science and Telecommunications Board of the National Research Council [Nat94].

A good introduction to the Internet—its growth and some of the new applications that are making it more popular—can be found in the August 1994 issue of the *Communications of the ACM* [Lei94]. To follow the history of the Internet from its beginning, the reader is encouraged to peruse the Internet's *Request for Comments* (RFC) series of documents. These documents, which include everything from the TCP specification to April Fools jokes, are retrievable on the Internet by doing anonymous ftp to hosts ds.internic.net, nic.ddn.mil, or ftp.isi.edu, and changing directory to rfc. For example, the protocol specifications for TCP, UDP, and IP are available in RFC 793, 768, and 791, respectively.

To gain a better appreciation for the Internet philosophy and culture, two references are must reading; both are also quite entertaining. Padlipsky gives a good description of the early days, including a pointed comparison of the Internet and OSI architectures [Pad85]. For a more up-to-date account of what really happens behind the scenes at the Internet Engineering Task Force, we recommend Boorsook's article [Boo95].

Finally, we conclude the Further Reading section of each chapter with a set of live references, that is, URLs for locations on the World Wide Web where you can learn more about the topics discussed in that chapter. Since these references are live, it is possible that they will not remain active for an indefinite period of time. For this reason, we limit the set of live references at the end of each chapter to sites that either export software, provide a service, or report on the activities of an ongoing working group or standardization body. In other words, we only give URLs for the kinds of material that cannot easily be referenced using standard citations. For this chapter, we include four live references:

- http://www.mkp.com: information about this book, including supplements, addendums, and so on;

- http://www.acm.org/sigcomm/sos.html: status of various networking standards, including those of the IETF, ISO, and IEEE;

- http://www.ietf.cnri.reston.va.us/home.html: information about the IETF and its working groups;

- http://www.research.att.com/#netbib: searchable bibliography of network-related research papers.

EXERCISES

1 Use anonymous FTP to connect to ds.internic.net, and retrieve the RFC index. Also retrieve the protocol specifications for TCP, IP, and UDP.

2 Become familiar with a WWW browser such as Mosaic or Netscape. Use the browser to connect to

http://www.cs.arizona.edu/xkernel

Here you can read about current network research under way at the University of Arizona and see a picture of author Larry Peterson. See if you can follow links to find a picture of author Bruce Davie.

3 Learn about a WWW search tool, and then use this tool to locate information about the following topics: MBone, ATM, MPEG, and IPv6.

4 The Unix utility whois can be used to find the domain name corresponding to an organization, or vice versa. Read the man page for whois and experiment with it. Try whois arizona.edu and whois tucson, for starters.

5 Discover what you can about the network technologies that are used within your department or at your campus:

(a) Identify the kinds of hardware that are being used, e.g., link types, switches, routers.

(b) Identify the high-level protocols that are supported.

(c) Sketch the network topology.

(d) Estimate the number of hosts that are connected.

6 Compare and contrast a packet-switched network and a circuit-switched network. What are the relative advantages and disadvantages of each?

7 One useful property of an address is that it is *unique*; without uniqueness, it would be impossible to distinguish between nodes. List other useful properties that addresses might have.

8 Give an example of a situation in which multicast addresses might be beneficial.

9 Explain why STDM is a cost-effective form of multiplexing for a voice telephone network and FDM is a cost-effective form of multiplexing for television and radio networks, yet we reject both as not being cost effective for a general-purpose computer network.

10 How "wide" is a bit on a 1-Gbps link?

11 How long does it take to transmit x KB over a y-Mbps link? Give your answer as a ratio of x and y.

12 Suppose a 100 Mbps point-to-point link is being set up between the earth and a new lunar colony. The distance from the moon to the earth is approximately 240,000 miles, and data travels over the link at the speed of light—186,000 miles per second.

(a) Calculate the minimum RTT for the link.

(b) Using the RTT as the delay, calculate the delay $\times$ bandwidth product for the link.

(c) What is the significance of the delay $\times$ bandwidth product computed in (b)?

(d) A camera on the lunar base takes pictures of the earth and saves them in digital format to disk. Suppose Mission Control on earth wishes to download the most current image, which is 25 MB. What is the minimum amount of time that will elapse between when the request for the data goes out and the transfer is finished?

13 The Unix utility ping can be used to find the RTT to various Internet hosts. Read the man page for ping, and use it to find the RTT to cs.arizona.edu in Tucson and thumper.bellcore.com in New Jersey.

14 For each of the following operations on a remote file server, explain whether they are more likely to be delay sensitive or bandwidth sensitive.

(a) Open a file.

(b) Read the contents of a file.

(c) List the contents of a directory.

(d) Display the attributes of a file.

15 Use the idea of jitter to support the argument that the telephone network should be circuit switched. Can a voice application be implemented on a packet-switched network? Explain your answer.

16 Suppose an application program running on a host connected to an Ethernet sends a message over the TCP/IP Internet. Sketch the message at the time it leaves the source host, including any headers that have been attached to it.

17 Identify at least three different organizations that define network-related standards, and list some of the standards that they are responsible for.

18 Learn about the history of the ARPANET and its successor, NSFNET. Identify the original ARPANET and NSFNET nodes.

19 Discuss the limitations of building a packet-switched network on top of the existing cable TV network. What technical challenges must be addressed to make such a network a reality?

20 Suppose that networks do achieve ubiquity in the next few years. Discuss the potential impact on our daily lives and on society as a whole.

Network architectures and protocol specifications are useful things, but the fact remains that a large part of building a computer network has to do with implementing protocols in software. There are two questions we have to ask about this software. One is what language/compiler are we using to implement the network software? The answer to this question is quite often C. It is the dominant language for implementing systems software in general, and network software is most certainly systems software. This is no accident. C gives the programmer the ability to manipulate data at the bit level (this is often called bit twiddling), which is necessary when implementing network software.

There are three things to be looked to in a building: that it stand on the right spot; that it be securely founded; that it be successfully executed.

—*Goethe*

The second question is what operating system (OS) does the network software use? The answer to this question is, "whatever OS runs on the node in question." Perhaps more importantly, it is necessary to understand the role played by the OS. Simply stated, network software depends on many of the services provided by the OS, and in fact network software almost always runs as part of the OS. For example, network protocols have to call the network device driver to send and receive messages, the system's timer facility to schedule events, and the system's memory subsystem to allocate buffers for messages. In addition, network software is generally a complex concurrent program that depends on the operating system for process support and synchronization. Thus, a network programmer needs to be not only an expert at network protocols, but also an operating system guru.

While each operating system provides its own set of routines to read the clock, allocate memory, synchronize processes, and so on, we use a specific operating system—the x-kernel—to make this book as tangible as possible. We have chosen to use the x-kernel because it was explicitly designed to help out network programmers who are *not* operating system experts. The hope is that by using the network-centric abstractions and interfaces provided by the x-kernel, protocol implementers can concentrate on the algorithms that make up network software. The good news is that because the x-kernel is efficient, protocols implemented in the x-kernel are also efficient.

By the end of this chapter, you probably won't be an OS expert (unless you were one already at the start), but you should know enough about the x-kernel to be able to understand the code segments that appear in the remainder of the book. This will establish the groundwork needed in later chapters to make the discussion of various algorithms and mechanisms more concrete.

Aside from providing background material, and equally importantly, this chapter serves to crystallize the abstract concepts introduced in Chapter 1. This is because the x-kernel is simply a codification of the fundamental components that are common to all protocols. Thus, this chapter introduces a set of objects and operations available in the x-kernel that correspond to the fundamental concepts of networking introduced in the previous chapter. These concepts include protocols, channels, and messages, as well as operations like demultiplexing and encapsulation. It is this codification of fundamental protocol components that makes the x-kernel ideal for learning about network programming.

2

Protocol Implementation

2.1   Object-Based Protocol Implementation

The x-kernel provides an object-based framework for implementing protocols. By using the term *object-based*, we are not just being fashionable; this is actually an important attribute of the x-kernel. While we could probably devote several chapters to developing a precise definition of the concept object-based, it is sufficient to say here that the key abstractions of the x-kernel are represented by objects, most of which we will describe in the following sections. An object may be conveniently thought of as a data structure with a collection of operations that are *exported*, that is, made available for invocation by other objects. Objects that have similar features are grouped into classes, with two obvious object classes for a protocol implementation environment being the *protocol* and the *message*.

To better understand the role played by the x-kernel, recall from Chapter 1 that a protocol is itself an abstract object, one that exports both a service interface and a peer-to-peer interface. The former defines the operations by which other protocols on the same machine invoke the services of this protocol, while the latter defines the form and meaning of messages exchanged between peers (instances of the same protocol running on different machines) to implement this service. In a nutshell, the x-kernel provides a concrete representation for a protocol's service interface. While the protocol's specification defines what it means to send or receive a message using the protocol's service interface, the x-kernel defines the precise way in which these operations are invoked in a given

Languages for Network Software

We claimed in the problem statement at the beginning of this chapter that network protocols are often implemented in C. While this statement is generally true, there is more to say on the subject.

For example, one of the holy grails of networking is the ability to express network functionality in a very high-level language and from this to be able to generate the correct low-level code. The ITU and ISO have developed three different languages for this purpose: SDL, Lotos, and Estelle. These languages are often referred to as *Formal Description Techniques* (FDTs).

The motivation for using an FDT is that it simplifies the process of verifying that a protocol implementation is correct, that is, it adheres to the specification. The idea

system. For example, the x-kernel's operations for sending and receiving a message are xPush and xPop, respectively. An x-kernel protocol object would consist of an implementation of xPush and xPop that adheres to what the protocol specification says it means to send and receive messages using this protocol. In other words, the protocol specification defines the *semantics* of the service interface, while the x-kernel defines one possible *syntax* for that interface.

The fashionableness of object-based programming has been accompanied by a proliferation of object-oriented languages, of which C++ is probably the most well-known example. The x-kernel, however, is written in C, which is not considered to be an object-oriented language. To deal with this, the x-kernel provides its own object infrastructure—the glue that makes it possible for one object to invoke an operation on another object. For example, when an object invokes the operation xOpen on some protocol p (xOpen is the x-kernel operation for opening a communication channel), it includes p as one of the arguments to this operation. The x-kernel's object infrastructure takes care of invoking the actual procedure that implements this operation on protocol p. In other words, the x-kernel uses xOpen(p, ...) in place of the more conventional notation for invoking an operation on an object: p.xOpen(...).

is to express both the specification and the implementation in the same language, thereby avoiding the error-prone translation of the specification into some low-level language like C. The preciseness of the specification/implementation language also helps to avoid ambiguities that occur in less formal, ad hoc specification languages like English.

Unfortunately, the effort to achieve this goal has met with limited success—network software is often too complex to express in a concise high-level language, and even when it can be, the code that is automatically generated from such a language is usually not efficient enough to be of practical use. How to do a better job of compiling protocols implemented in high-level specification languages is a subject of much research.

Before getting into the details of the x-kernel, we have one word of caution—this chapter is not a substitute for an x-kernel programmer's manual. We have taken certain liberties—swept a few uninteresting details under the rug and left out certain features—for the sake of improving the exposition. If you are trying to debug an x-kernel protocol you have written, then you should study the unabridged programmer's manual. Conversely, it is not necessary to understand every detail in this chapter to benefit from the rest of the book; you may want to skim it and return to it later if you find a code segment that seems impenetrable in a subsequent chapter.

2.2 Protocols and Sessions

Recall from Chapter 1 that a network architecture defines a protocol graph, with each protocol in the graph implementing an abstract channel (pipe) through which data can be sent. The x-kernel provides a framework for implementing this graph, including the functionality of each protocol in the graph. To help make the description of this framework more concrete, the following discussion focuses on the protocol graph illustrated in Figure 2.1; it is a portion of a protocol graph defined by the Internet architecture.

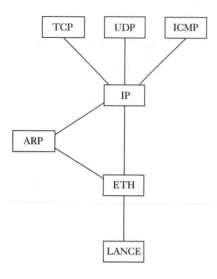

Figure 2.1 Example of a protocol graph.

The two main classes of objects supported by the x-kernel are *protocols* and *sessions*. Protocol objects represent just what you would expect—protocols such as IP or TCP. Session objects represent the local endpoint of a channel, and as such, typically implement the code that interprets messages and that maintains any state associated with the channel. The protocol objects available in a particular network subsystem, along with the relationships among these protocols, is defined by a protocol graph at the time a kernel is configured. Session objects are dynamically created as channels are opened and closed. Loosely speaking, protocol objects export operations for opening channels—resulting in the creation of a session object—and session objects export operations for sending and receiving messages.

The set of operations exported by protocol and session objects is called the *uniform protocol interface*—it defines how protocols and sessions invoke operations on each other. At this stage, the important thing to know about the uniform protocol interface is that it specifies how high-level objects invoke operations on low-level objects to send outgoing messages, as well as how low-level objects invoke operations on high-level objects to handle incoming messages. For example, consider the specific pair of protocols TCP and IP in the Internet architecture, depicted in Figure 2.1. TCP sits directly above IP in this architecture, so the x-kernel's uniform protocol interface defines the operations that TCP invokes on IP, as well as the operations IP invokes on TCP, as illustrated in Figure 2.2.

Keep in mind that the following discussion defines a common interface between protocols, that is, the operations that one protocol is allowed to invoke on the other. This is only half the story, however. The other half is that each protocol has to provide a routine that implements this interface. Thus, for an operation like xOpen, protocols like TCP and IP must

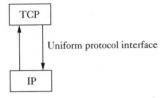

Figure 2.2 Uniform protocol interface.

include a routine that implements xOpen; by convention, we name this routine tcpOpen and ipOpen, respectively. Therefore, the following discussion not only defines the interface to each operation, but it also gives a rough outline of what every protocol's implementation of that operation is expected to do.

2.2.1 Configuring a Protocol Graph

Before presenting the operations that protocol and session objects export, we first explain how a protocol programmer configures a protocol graph. As discussed in Chapter 1, standardization bodies like the ISO and the IETF define a particular network architecture that includes a specific set of protocols. In the Internet architecture, for example, TCP depends on IP by definition. This suggests that it is possible to "hard-code" TCP's dependence on IP into the TCP implementation. While this could be done in the case of TCP, the x-kernel supports a more flexible mechanism for configuring a protocol graph, which makes it easy to plug protocols together in different ways. While this is a powerful thing to be able to do, you must be careful that it makes sense to have any two protocols adjacent to each other in the protocol graph.

Quite simply, a user who wants to configure a protocol graph specifies the graph with a text file of the following form:

```
name=lance;
name=eth protocols=lance;
name=arp protocols=eth;
name=ip protocols=eth,arp;
name=icmp protocols=ip;
name=udp protocols=ip;
name=tcp protocols=ip;
```

This specification results in the protocol graph depicted in Figure 2.1. In this example graph, lance and eth combine to implement an Ethernet device driver: lance is the device-specific half and eth is the device-independent half. Also, arp is the Address Resolution Protocol (it is used to translate IP addresses into Ethernet addresses) and icmp is the Internet Control Message Protocol (it sends error messages on behalf of TCP and IP). The name field in each line specifies a protocol (by name) and the protocols field says which other protocols this protocol depends on. Not shown in this example is a dir field that identifies the directory where the named protocol implementation can be found; by default, it is the same as the name of the protocol. The x-kernel build program, called compose, parses this specification and generates some C code that initializes the protocol graph when the system is booted.

2.2.2 Operations on Protocol Objects

The primary operation exported by a protocol object allows a higher-level entity to *open* a channel to its peer. The return value from an open operation is a session object. Details about the session object are discussed in the following subsection. For now, think of a session as a convenient object for gaining access to the channel; the module that opened the protocol object can send and receive messages using the session object. An object that lets us gain access to something abstract is sometimes called a *handle*—think of it as the thing that makes it easy to grab something that is otherwise quite slippery. Thus, a session object provides a handle on a channel.

In the following discussion, we need a generic way to refer to the entity that opens a channel, since sometimes it is an application program and sometimes it is another protocol. We use the term *participant* for this purpose. That is, we think in terms of a pair of participants at level i that are communicating over a channel implemented by a protocol at level $i-1$ (where the level number decreases as you move down the stack).

Opening a channel is an asymmetric activity. Generally, one participant initiates the channel (we call this party the client). This local participant is therefore able to identify the remote participant and is said to do an *active* open. In contrast, the other participant accepts the channel (we call this party the server). This participant does not know what clients might try to talk to it until one of them actually makes contact. The server, therefore, does a *passive* open—it says to the lower-level protocol that it is willing to accept a channel but does not say with whom the channel will be.

Thus, the exact form of the open operation depends on whether the higher-level entity is doing an active open or a passive open. In the case of an active open, the operation is

    Sessn xOpen(Protl hlp, Protl llp, Part *participants)

This operation says that high-level protocol hlp is opening low-level protocol llp so as to establish a channel with the specified participants. For a typical channel between a pair of participants, this last argument would contain both the local participant's address and the remote participant's address. The low-level protocol does whatever is necessary to establish the channel, which quite often implies opening a channel on a still lower-level protocol. Notice that Protl and Sessn are the C type definitions for protocol and session objects, respectively.

A high-level protocol passively opens a low-level protocol with a pair of operations:

    XkReturn xOpenEnable(Protl hlp, Protl llp, Part *participant)

    XkReturn xOpenDone(Protl hlp, Protl llp, Sessn session, Part *participants)

xOpenEnable is used by high-level protocol hlp to inform low-level protocol llp that it is will-ing to accept a connection. In this case, the high-level protocol usually specifies only a sin-gle participant—itself. The xOpenEnable operation returns immediately; it does not block while waiting for a remote site to try to connect to it. The low-level protocol remembers this enabling; when some remote participant subsequently connects to the low-level protocol, llp calls the high-level protocol's xOpenDone operation to inform it of this event. The low-level protocol llp passes the newly created session as an argument to high-level protocol hlp, along with the complete set of participants, thereby informing the high-level protocol of the ad-dress of the remote entity that just connected to it. XkReturn is the return value of all the uniform protocol interface operations except for xOpen; it indicates whether the operation was successful (XK_SUCCESS) or not (XK_FAILURE).

In addition to these operations for opening a connection, x-kernel protocol objects also support an operation for demultiplexing incoming messages to the appropriate channel (ses-sion). In this case, a low-level session invokes this operation on the high-level protocol that at some earlier time had opened it. The operation is

    XkReturn xDemux(Protl hlp, Sessn lls, Msg *message)

It will be easier to understand how this operation is used after we look at session objects in more detail.

2.2.3   Operations on Session Objects

As already explained, a session can be thought of as a handle on a channel that is implemented by some protocol. You can also view it as an object that exports a pair of operations, one for sending messages and one for receiving messages:

    XkReturn xPush(Sessn lls, Msg *message)

    XkReturn xPop(Sessn hls, Sessn lls, Msg *message, void *hdr)

The implementation of xPush and xPop is where the real work of a protocol is carried out—it's where headers are added to and stripped from messages and then interpreted. In short, these two routines implement the algorithm that defines the protocol.

The operation of xPush is fairly straightforward. It is invoked by a high-level session to pass a message down to some low-level session (lls) that it had opened at some earlier time. lls then goes off and does what is needed with the message—perhaps using xPush to pass it down to a still lower-level session. This is illustrated in Figure 2.3. In this figure we see three sessions, each of which implements one protocol in a stack, passing a message down the stack using xPush.

Passing messages back up the stack using xPop is more complicated. The main problem is that a session does not know what session is above it—all it knows is the protocol that is above it. So, a low-level session lls invokes the xDemux routine of the protocol above it. That protocol, since it did the work of opening the high-level session hls to which this message needs to go, is able to pass the message to hls using its xPop routine. How does a protocol's

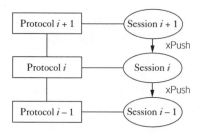

Figure 2.3   Using xPush to pass a message down a stack.

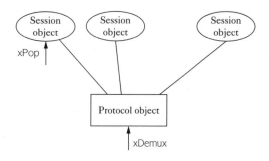

Figure 2.4   Using xDemux and xPop to pass a message up a stack.

xDemux routine know which of its potentially many sessions to pass the message up to? It uses the *demultiplexing key* found in its header.

In addition to the hls that is being called and the message that is being passed to it, xPop takes two other arguments. First, lls identifies the low-level session that handed up this message by means of xDemux. Second, since xDemux has to inspect the message header to select the session on which to call xPop—i.e., it has already gone to the effort of extracting the protocol's header—it passes the header (hdr) on as the final argument to xPop. This chain of events is illustrated in Figure 2.4.

To see how this works in practice, imagine that we want to send a message using the TCP and IP protocols. An application program opens a channel by performing xOpen on TCP; TCP returns a session object to the application. TCP opens an IP channel by performing xOpen on IP; IP returns a session object to TCP. When the application wants to send a message, it invokes the xPush operation of the TCP session; this session in turn invokes the xPush operation of the IP session, which ultimately causes the message to be sent.

Now suppose that an incoming message is delivered to the IP session. This session has no idea about the TCP session above it, so it does the only thing it knows how to do—it passes the message up to the TCP protocol using xDemux. The TCP protocol knows about all the

TCP sessions and thus passes the message up to the appropriate TCP session using xPop. TCP's xDemux uses the demux key it found in the TCP header to select among all the TCP sessions.

The final operation that we need to be able to perform is one to close a session, which in effect closes the channel to the other machine.

    XkReturn xClose(Sessn session)

In addition to sessions and protocols, this discussion has introduced two other x-kernel object classes: messages and participants. Both classes represent exactly what you think they do—the messages that protocols send to each other (corresponding to type definition Msg) and the addresses of participants that are communicating over some channel (corresponding to type definition Part). Message objects are discussed in more detail in Section 2.3. Participants are simple enough that we do not describe them further. (See Section 2.6 for an example of how participants are used.)

2.2.4 Process Models for Protocols

As we have said, protocol implementers typically have to be concerned about a lot of operating system issues. This subsection introduces one of the most important of these issues—the process model.

Most operating systems provide an abstraction called a *process*, or alternatively, a *thread*. Each process runs largely independently of other processes, and the OS is responsible for making sure that resources, such as address space and CPU cycles, are allocated to all the current processes. The process abstraction makes it fairly straightforward to have a lot of things executing concurrently on one machine; for example, each user application might execute in its own process, and various things inside the OS might execute as other processes. When the OS stops one process from executing on the CPU and starts up another one, we call the change a *context switch*.

When designing a protocol implementation framework, one of the first questions to answer is, "Where are the processes?" There are essentially two choices, as illustrated in Figure 2.5. In the first, which we call the *process-per-protocol* model, each protocol is implemented by a separate process. This means that as a message moves up or down the protocol stack, it is passed from one process/protocol to another—the process that implements protocol i processes the message, then passes it to protocol $i - 1$, and so on. How one process/protocol passes a message to the next process/protocol depends on the support the host OS provides for interprocess communication. Typically, there is a simple mechanism for enqueuing a message with a process. The important point, however, is that a context switch is required at each level of the protocol graph—typically a time-consuming operation.

The alternative, which we call the *process-per-message* model, treats each protocol as a static piece of code and associates the processes with the messages. That is, when a message arrives from the network, the OS dispatches a process which it makes responsible for the message as it moves up the protocol graph. At each level, the procedure that implements that pro-

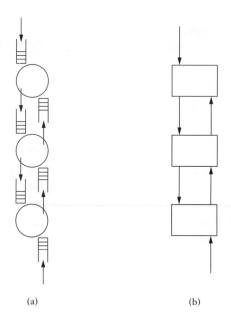

(a)   (b)

Figure 2.5   Alternative process models: (a) process-per-protocol; (b) process-per-message.

tocol is invoked, which eventually results in the procedure for the next protocol being invoked, and so on. For outbound messages, the application's process invokes the necessary procedure calls until the message is delivered. In both directions, the protocol graph is traversed in a sequence of procedure calls.

Although the process-per-protocol model is sometimes easier to think about—I implement my protocol in my process and you implement your protocol in your process—the process-per-message model is generally more efficient for a simple reason: a procedure call is an order of magnitude more efficient than a context switch on most computers. The former model requires the expense of a context switch at each level, while the latter model costs only a procedure call per level.

The x-kernel uses the process-per-message model. Tying this model to the operations outlined above, this means that once a session (channel) is open at each level, a message can be sent down the protocol stack by a sequence of calls to xPush and up the protocol stack by alternating calls to xDemux and xPop. This asymmetry—xPush going down and xDemux/xPop going up—is unappealing, but necessary. This is because when sending a message out, each layer knows which low-level session to invoke xPush on because there is only one choice, while in the incoming case, the xDemux routine at each level has to first demultiplex the message to decide which session's xPop to call.

Notice that the high-level protocol does not reach down and receive a message from the low-level protocol. Instead, the low-level protocol does an *upcall*—a procedure call up the stack—to deliver the message to the high-level protocol. This is because a receive operation would imply that the high-level protocol is executing in a process that is waiting for new messages to arrive, which would then result in a costly context switch between the low-level and high-level protocols. By having the low-level protocol deliver the message to the high-level protocol, incoming messages can be processed by a sequence of procedure calls just as outgoing messages are.

We conclude this discussion of processes by introducing three operations that the x-kernel provides for process synchronization:

```
void semInit(Semaphore *s, int count)

void semSignal(Semaphore *s)

void semWait(Semaphore *s)
```

These operations implement conventional counting semaphores. Specifically, every invocation of semSignal increments semaphore s by 1, and every invocation of semWait decrements s by 1, with the calling process blocked (suspended) should decrementing s cause its value to become less than 0. A process that is blocked during its call to semWait will be allowed to resume as soon as enough semSignal operations have been performed to raise the value of s above 0. Operation semInit initializes the value of s to count.

For those not familiar with how semaphores are used to synchronize processes, the OS-related references given at the end of this chapter give a good introduction. Also, examples of protocols that use semaphores are given in Chapter 3 and 6.

2.3   Messages

We now turn our attention from how protocols invoke operations on each other and consider what goes on inside a particular protocol. One of the most common things that a protocol does is manipulate messages. We have already seen in Chapter 1 how protocols add headers to, and strip headers from, messages. Another common way in which protocols manipulate messages is to break a single message into multiple fragments and later to join these multiple fragments back into a single message. This is necessary because, as we mentioned in Section 1.2.2, most network links allow messages of only a certain size to be transmitted. Thus, a protocol that uses such a link to transmit a large message must first *fragment* the message on the source node and then *reassemble* the fragments back into the original message on the destination node. We will see several examples of protocols that fragment and reassemble messages in later chapters.

Because manipulating messages is a basic part of all protocols, the x-kernel defines an abstract data type—called the *message* and given by the C type definition Msg—that includes an interface for performing these common operations. This section begins by presenting the x-kernel's message abstraction. It then outlines the underlying data structures and algorithms that implement the various operations defined by the interface.

m

abcdefg

Figure 2.6   Message object containing a byte string.

2.3.1   Manipulating Messages

The message abstraction can best be viewed as a byte string of some length. For the purposes of this discussion, we use the term *message* to refer to the abstract object and the term *data* to refer to the actual byte string contained in a message. For example, message *m* schematically depicted in Figure 2.6 contains the data "abcdefg."

In effect, the operations on the message object can be viewed as string manipulations. For example, while processing an outgoing message, each of several protocols may add a header to the message (i.e., two strings are concatenated) and fragment the message into two or more packets (i.e., a string is divided into two substrings). Similarly, while processing an incoming message, each of several protocols may strip headers from the message (i.e., a string is removed from the front of another string) and reassemble message fragments (i.e., two strings are concatenated). In addition, each of several protocols may save references to portions of a message for future use, e.g., to retransmit in the event of an error in the network. Thus, any given byte may be attached to several different strings, removed from several different strings, and referenced by several different protocols.

Adding and Stripping Headers

As outgoing messages move down the protocol graph, each protocol attaches (pushes) its header onto the front of the message. Similarly, as an incoming message moves up the protocol graph, each protocol strips (pops) its header from the front of the message. The message object supports the following two operations for pushing and popping headers:

        char *msgPush(Msg *message, int length)

        char *msgPop(Msg *message, int length)

Both operations return a pointer to a buffer that contains the header. In the case of msgPush, room for length bytes is attached to the front of the message, and a pointer to this memory location is returned. The protocol can then write the header to this location to effectively add the header to the message. In the case of msgPop, length bytes are removed from the front of the message. The protocol can then read the header available at the returned memory location. Figures 2.7 and 2.8 illustrate the semantics of the two operations.

Fragmenting and Reassembling Messages

Fragmenting and reassembling messages is a common activity in network protocols. The *x*-kernel supports the following two operations for manipulating message fragments:

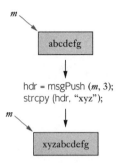

hdr = msgPush (*m*, 3);
strcpy (hdr, "xyz");

Figure 2.7 Effects of msgPush operation.

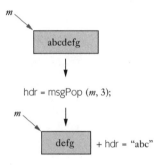

hdr = msgPop (*m*, 3);

+ hdr = "abc"

Figure 2.8 Effects of msgPop operation.

     void msgBreak(Msg *original_message, Msg *fragment_message, int length)

     void msgJoin(Msg *new_message, Msg *fragment1, Msg *fragment2)

The first operation creates a pair of messages by breaking length bytes off the front of the original_message and placing them in (fragment_message). After the operation returns, original_message contains the sequence of bytes that remain after length bytes are removed. The second operation attaches fragment1 to the front of fragment2, producing new_message. The arguments to msgJoin need not refer to distinct messages. One common use of msgJoin is to attach a fragment to the end of a larger message, in which case the first two arguments are the same (the larger message) and the third argument is the fragment. These two operations are illustrated in Figures 2.9 and 2.10.

Other Operations On Messages

There are additional operations that can be applied to message objects, as summarized below:

     void msgConstructEmpty(Msg *message)

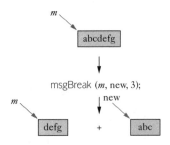

Figure 2.9   Effects of msgBreak operation.

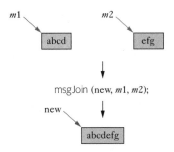

Figure 2.10   Effects of msgJoin operation.

void msgConstructBuffer(Msg *message, char *buffer, int length)

char *msgConstructAllocate(Msg *message, int length)

void msgAssign(Msg *message_1, Msg *message_2)

int msgLength(Msg *message)

The first three operations are used to create messages. Each is used under a different set of circumstances. msgConstructEmpty creates an empty message. It is used in conjunction with msgAssign to save a reference to a message. For example, if a given protocol wants to send a particular message m out over the network, but at the same time save a copy of m in case it needs to retransmit it in the future, it might use msgConstructEmpty to create an empty message n and then do msgAssign(m, n). At this point both m and n represent the same message (the same byte string).

The other two message constructors create messages with an associated data component. msgConstructBuffer builds a message from the existing byte string, referenced by buffer. This operation is used, for example, by an application program that already possesses a buffer of data it wants to transmit; it uses msgConstructBuffer to encapsulate this buffer in a message object. In contrast, msgConstructAllocate is used when a protocol knows it is going to need a message to hold length bytes of data but it does not yet have the data to place in the message. This operation is used, for example, in a device driver that knows it will eventually receive a packet from the network of some given size. It invokes msgConstructAllocate to create the message and in return gets a pointer to a memory buffer that is free to hold the data. The device driver would then program the network adaptor to receive the next packet into this buffer.

Finally, msgLength returns the number of bytes in a given message.

2.3.2 Implementation

The first rule in implementing network protocols is to avoid copying data from one buffer into another. In fact, if this is the only rule your protocol implementation adheres to, your implementation will probably be quite efficient. The reason is that every time you copy data—where copying data implies a loop that loads every word of one buffer into a CPU register and then stores it back into another memory location—you dramatically affect the end-to-end throughput of the network.

To see this, suppose that a phenomenally fast network can deliver messages into your computer's memory at a rate of 622 Mbps. Now suppose that your computer can copy data from one buffer to another at a rate of only 300 Mbps. Copying the data only one time means that the fastest rate seen by the application program is 300 Mbps. Copying the data a second time effectively cuts that rate in half, resulting in an effective bandwidth of 150 Mbps. Copying the data four times—yes, there are systems that copy the data that often—means that the application ends up seeing a little over 35 Mbps, or one twentieth of the network rate. In a sense, you should think of your computer's bus as the last physical link of the network, but if you are not careful, one that gets traversed multiple times.

What does this discussion have to do with the message object? Everything! It is critical that the message operations not touch the data in a message, but rather, only manipulate pointers. For example, when joining two fragments into a new message, rather than allocating a new memory buffer and copying the bytes from the first message into that buffer and then the bytes from the second message into the buffer, the two fragments must be logically joined into a new message: you must create a logical message object that points to the two original message objects.

This implementation of the message object avoids copying by representing messages with a directed acyclic graph (DAG). As illustrated in Figure 2.11, the leaves of the graph correspond to actual memory buffers that hold the bytes of data that make up the message, such that a preorder traversal of the DAG yields the byte string represented by the message. In this data structure, the leftmost leaf is treated as a special case—the root of the message contains a direct pointer to this data buffer. This is because the leftmost leaf of the DAG holds the message header that is manipulated by the msgPush and msgPop operations; this buffer is called the *header stack*. A pointer into the middle of the header stack—the *top of stack* pointer—indicates how much of that buffer is currently filled.

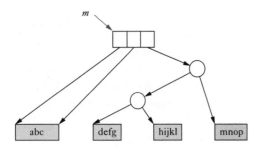

Figure 2.11 Directed acyclic graph for a data structure to implement a message object.

Conceptually, the implementation of the various message operations is straightforward: msgPush and msgPop simply move the top of stack pointer left and right, respectively; msgJoin creates a new interior node that points to the DAG for two original messages; and msgBreak creates a new root node that points into an existing DAG. In practice, however, the devil is in the details.

Because the data contained in a message object is scattered over multiple, noncontiguous memory buffers, the x-kernel provides a final set of operations for "walking" the DAG and extracting the actual data.

```
void msgWalkInit(Context *cxt, Msg *message)

char *msgWalk(Context *cxt, int *len)

void msgWalkDone(Context *cxt)
```

Operation msgWalk traverses the message DAG and returns a pointer to the next chunk of data in the message; it also sets len to the number of bytes in that chunk. Argument cxt maintains the context for the message traversal, so that msgWalk knows how far through the DAG it got on the last invocation. The other two operations—msgWalkInit and msgWalkDone— initialize and destroy this context, respectively.

As a simple example of how one might use msgWalk, device drivers often create an array of pointers to the various pieces of the message (along with each piece's length). Arrays of buffer/length pairs are commonly accepted by network devices, so this might be something that is done by a network device driver to prepare an x-kernel message for transmission over a physical link.

2.4 Events

Another common activity for protocols is to schedule an event to happen some time in the future. To understand how a protocol might use such events, consider the situation in which a network sometimes fails to deliver a message to the destination. A protocol that wants to offer a reliable channel across such a network might, after sending a message, schedule an event that is to occur after a certain period of time. If the protocol has not received confirmation that the message was delivered by the time this event happens, then the protocol retransmits the message. In this case, the event implements a *timeout*; we will see several examples of protocols that use timeouts in later chapters. Note that another use for events is to perform periodic maintenance functions, such as garbage collection.

This section introduces the interface to the x-kernel's event manager, which allows a protocol to schedule a procedure that is to be called after a certain period of time. It also describes two common data structures used to implement events.

2.4.1 Scheduling Timeouts

The event manager defines a single object—the Event—and the following operation:

> Event evSchedule(EvFunc function, void *argument, int time)

This operation schedules an event that executes the specified function with the given argument after a delay of time microseconds. (EvFunc is a pointer to function that returns a void.) A handle to the event is returned, which can be used to cancel the event at some later time. When an event is executed, a new process is created to run the specified function; that is, the event runs asynchronously with respect to the rest of the system. Since each event occurs at most one time, if the protocol wants an event to repeat, then the next incarnation of the event should be rescheduled using evSchedule as the last action taken in the event handling function.

A second operation

> EvCancelReturn evCancel(Event event)

is used to cancel the given Event. evCancel is called, for example, because a source has received confirmation that a message it sent was successfully delivered, and so there is no reason for it to retransmit the message. The operation's return value, as defined by the enumeration type EvCancelReturn, is set to EVENT_FINISHED if the event has already happened, EVENT_RUNNING if the event is currently running, and EVENT_CANCELLED if the event has not run and can be guaranteed to not run.

Finally, the following operation releases a handle to an event.

> void evDetach(Event event)

As soon as function completes, the internal resources associated with the event are freed.

2.4.2 Implementation

How one implements event objects depends on the underlying timer facility available in the system. Sometimes the host OS supports a timer facility that looks very much like the x-kernel's abstraction. If you are implementing an event manager directly on the machine architecture, however, it is more likely that the machine supports a clock that interrupts every so often, e.g., once every 10 ms. The rest of this section describes how to implement an efficient

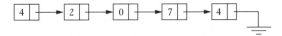

Figure 2.12   Delta list implementation of an event manager.

event facility using clock interrupts of this form. It actually describes two different implementations: the first is simpler, and therefore easier to understand; the second extends this basic idea to provide a more efficient facility.

Delta Lists

A straightforward implementation of an event manager uses a data structure called a *delta list*. The idea is to maintain a linked list of event records, sorted in increasing order of when the event is to occur. Each event record contains the information needed to execute the event—in the x-kernel, for example, this means a function pointer and an integer argument—as well as the number of clock ticks in the future that the event should fire. The time (number of clock ticks) stored in each event record is relative to the preceding event. For example, suppose there are five events scheduled for 4, 6, 6, 13, and 17 clock ticks in the future. This would result in the delta list depicted in Figure 2.12. Notice that the third event record contains a 0 because it occurs 0 time units after the second event.

The event manager depends on an underlying clock that delivers an interrupt once every clock tick, meaning that the underlying clock mechanism calls an "interrupt routine" within the event manager. Each time the clock ticks (and this interrupt routine is called), the event manager subtracts 1 from the time contained in the first record of the link list. Should decrementing this value result in a time of 0, the event manager executes the event. (The event manager also executes all subsequent events with a time of 0.) If the result is nonzero, the event manager simply returns from this routine.

To schedule a new event, the event manager walks down the list and inserts a record for the new event in the appropriate location, being careful to adjust the relative time of both the new event and the event immediately following the new event. Deleting an event from the list is implemented in an analogous way. For example, given the delta list in Figure 2.12, inserting a new event that is to happen 14 clock ticks in the future results in the delta list in Figure 2.13. Notice that the event record following the new one has been adjusted to reflect the fact that the event that was scheduled for 4 clock ticks after the fourth event is now scheduled for 3 clock ticks after the new event.

The final question is exactly what constitutes a clock tick. One answer is that each clock tick corresponds to an interrupt from the machine's hardware clock. For example, on a machine that delivers a hardware clock interrupt once every 10 ms, we might turn every hardware clock interrupt into an event manager clock tick (i.e., every hardware interrupt corresponds to the event manager's interrupt routine being called), meaning that the events given in the preceding example will occur 40 ms, 60 ms, 60 ms, 130 ms, and 170 ms in the future.

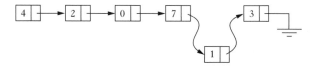

Figure 2.13   Inserting a new event into a delta list.

On the other hand, we could turn every tenth hardware clock interrupt into a call to the event manager's interrupt routine by having the clock interrupt handler do nothing 9 times out of 10. This would give us an effective clock tick (from the event manager's perspective) with a granularity of 100 ms, meaning that the events in the example would happen 400 ms, 600 ms, 600 ms, 1300 ms, and 1700 ms in the future. (Obviously, you would want to know the effective clock granularity before you start scheduling events.) Note that while it is possible to have a clock tick with a granularity greater than or equal to the granularity of the hardware clock, the situation cannot be reversed—the granularity of the clock as seen by the event manager cannot be any finer than the granularity of the hardware clock.

Timing Wheels

The delta list implementation of the event manager is very efficient in terms of the work it does on every clock tick—it simply decrements the time contained in the first element of the list. This can be done in a few instructions and does not depend on the number of events in the list. Inserting and deleting events, however, can become quite expensive, because it is necessary to traverse the list to find the right place to add or remove an event record. In fact, it is quite likely that a new event will be inserted near the end of the list, meaning that the entire list must be traversed.

To overcome this problem without sacrificing the per-tick efficiency of the delta list, this simple linear list can be reorganized into an array of lists, with an overflow list for events that are scheduled for a time beyond the range of the array. For example, all events that are scheduled to happen in the next second might be in the list starting at the first element in the array, all events happening between 1 and 2 seconds in the future could be contained in the list stored at the second element of the array, and so on. Observe that the process of scheduling a new event now involves an insertion into a list of events that will occur during a 1-second interval, rather than insertion into the list of all scheduled events. As time passes (the clock ticks), the event manager cycles through elements of the array. At each clock tick, however, only the first record in the list corresponding to the current element needs to be decremented. This data structure is sometimes called a *timing wheel*.

2.5   Id Map

The final x-kernel tool we describe is the id mapper. This tool provides a facility for maintaining a set of bindings between identifiers. The id mapper supports operations for adding new bindings to the set, removing bindings from the set, and mapping one identifier into another, relative to a set of bindings. Protocol implementations use these operations to translate identifiers extracted from message headers (e.g., addresses, demultiplexing keys) into capabilities for (pointers to) x-kernel objects such as sessions.

2.5.1 Demultiplexing Packets

The id mapper supports two main objects: *maps* and *bindings*, denoted by the types Map and Binding, respectively. A map is simply a table of bindings, where each binding is given by the pair ⟨ external key, internal id ⟩. An external key is a variable-length byte string, and an internal id is a fixed-sized identifier (e.g., a 32- or 64-bit memory address). Typically, an external key is constructed from various fields in a message header, and an internal id is a pointer to a session or protocol object. A map is created with the following operation:

    Map mapCreate(int number, int size)

This operation creates a map that is able to hold number bindings in it, where the external keys bound in this map are size bytes long.

Once a map is created, protocols can perform two basic operations on it. The first puts bindings into the map and the latter resolves external keys according to the map and returns the corresponding internal id:

    Binding mapBind(Map map, void *key, void *id)

    XkReturn mapResolve(Map map, void *key, void **id)

The first operation inserts a binding of key to id into the specified map and returns a pointer to the resulting binding. If key is already bound to some id in the map, then a pointer to that existing binding is returned. The second operation returns the internal id bound to the specified key in the given map. If the key is not found in the map, then mapResolve reports a failure by returning XK_FAILURE.

The id mapper also provides a pair of operations for removing bindings from a map:

    XkReturn mapUnbindBinding(Binding binding, Map map)

    XkReturn mapUnbindKey(void *key, Map map)

The first removes the specified binding—the value returned by an earlier mapBind—and the second removes the binding for the specified key. Both operations return a failure code if the binding does not exist in the map.

Protocols generally maintain two maps: an active map and a passive map. Active maps are used to map keys found in incoming messages into the session that will process the message. Thus, the active map holds information about the set of currently active connections. Passive maps are used to bind keys found in incoming messages into protocol objects, thereby allowing a protocol to create a session when a message that is part of a new connection arrives.

Typically, a protocol binds an active key to a session in its implementation of xOpen and a passive key to a protocol object in its xOpenEnable routine. These bindings are then used in the protocol's xDemux operation. This general pattern is illustrated in the example given Section 2.6.

2.5.2 Implementation

The x-kernel implements each map with a hash table, meaning that each invocation of mapResolve can be completed in a constant time in the average case. The choice of a hash table should come as no surprise. What might be surprising, however, is that this constant can be significant unless the following two optimizations are included.

First, the id mapper maintains a one-element cache for each map. This means that it saves the last binding that mapResolve returns in a special data structure. Then, when mapResolve is invoked the next time, it checks to see if this binding matches the external key before doing the normal lookup in the hash table. This optimization pays off in a big way because maps are typically used by a protocol's demultiplexing routine to look up a demux key that it found in a message header, and it is commonly the case that a given protocol will process consecutively several messages that are destined for the same session (i.e., that contain the same demux key).

This is an example of an important system design rule: *optimize the common case*. In this particular situation, the common case is that packets belonging to the same channel arrive back to back. In general, the idea is to identify the scenarios that are most likely to occur and to optimize them, even if this means that some other scenarios become less efficient. For example, if the common use of a protocol involves opening a channel and then sending and receiving several messages on that channel, then it makes sense to do extra work at the time a channel is opened if that means that you can get by with doing less work each time a message is sent or received.

The second optimization is less obvious. At the heart of the hash table is a subroutine that compares the external key given as an argument to mapResolve with the external key contained in the individual bindings that hash to the same bucket of the hash table. Since the id mapper accepts variable-sized external keys, the naive implementation of this comparison routine would contain a loop that compares each byte in the key, one at a time. This loop involves too much overhead, so the x-kernel's id mapper instead asks the protocol to specify how big the external keys will be when the map is created (see the size argument to mapCreate) and then specializes the comparison subroutine to deal with keys of exactly this size. For example, a 4-byte key comparison is implemented with a single word equality check, an 8-byte key with a pair of word equality tests, and so on. In essence, by knowing the key size in advance, the implementation is able to unroll the comparison loop.

2.6 Example Protocol

This section presents an example protocol—A Simple Protocol (ASP)—that illustrates how the interfaces and support routines described in previous sections are used. ASP is a complete, working protocol that is typically configured on top of IP in an x-kernel protocol graph. Because of its simplicity, ASP does not implement any of the interesting algorithms found in the protocols described throughout this book; it only serves to illustrate the boilerplate code that is common to all protocols.

2.6.1 Protocol Semantics

ASP supports an unreliable message delivery service, where the two endpoints of an ASP channel are identified by a pair of *ports*. In the x-kernel, a session object implements each endpoint of an ASP channel, with each session uniquely identified by the following 4-tuple:

⟨ local IP host, remote IP host, local ASP port, remote ASP port⟩

In other words, ASP demultiplexes each incoming message to the appropriate session by using this 4-tuple as a demux key. This is ASP's only significant function—to add a multiplexing/demultiplexing function to the protocols below it.

ASP does very little processing on each message—it only checks the length of the received messages and truncates the message to the specified length, if necessary. ASP is an unreliable protocol, in the sense that it adds no reliability to the protocols below it; i.e., it does not retransmit lost messages.

2.6.2 Header Files

By convention, the header information required by ASP is organized into two files: asp.h and asp_internal.h. File asp.h contains only definitions required by other protocols; protocols that depend on ASP must have access to asp.h in order to use these definitions. In the case of ASP, asp.h defines the ASP port to be an unsigned short (16-bit value).

```
/*
 * asp.h
 */

typedef u_short AspPort;
```

File asp_internal.h contains ASP-specific definitions that other protocols do not need to know about. For example, it defines the format of the ASP header (AspHdr), protocol-specific state information (ProtlState), and session-specific state information (SessnState).

```
/*
 * asp_internal.h
 */

#include "xkernel.h"
#include "ip.h"
#include "asp.h"

/* ASP header definition */

typedef struct header {
```

```
    AspPort     sport;  /* source port       */
    AspPort     dport;  /* destination port */
    u_short     ulen;   /* ASP length        */
} AspHdr;

#define HLEN    (sizeof(AspHdr))

/* Protocol and session state */

typedef struct pstate {
    Map         activemap;
    Map         passivemap;
} ProtlState;

typedef struct sstate {
    AspHdr      hdr;
} SessnState;

/* Active and passive maps */

typedef struct {
    AspPort     localport;
    AspPort     remoteport;
    Sessn       lls;
} ActiveId;

typedef AspPort PassiveId;

#define ACTIVE_MAP_SIZE 101
#define PASSIVE_MAP_SIZE 23

/* UPI Function Declarations */

void                asp_init( Protl );
static Sessn        aspOpen( Protl, Protl, Part * );
static XkReturn     aspOpenEnable( Protl, Protl, Part * );
static XkReturn     aspDemux( Protl, Sessn, Msg * );
static XkReturn     aspPop( Sessn, Sessn, Msg *, void * );
static XkReturn     aspPush( Sessn, Msg * );
static XkReturn     aspClose( Sessn );

/* Internal Function Declarations */

static Sessn        asp_init_sessn( Protl, Protl, Protl, ActiveId * );
static long         aspHdrLoad( void *, char *, long, Msg * );
static void         aspHdrStore( void *, char *, long, Msg * );
static void         getproc_sessn( Sessn );
static void         getproc_protl( Protl );
```

One of the main definitions contained in **asp_internal.h** concerns the demultiplexing function. In particular, the state associated with the ASP protocol object includes two maps: **activemap** and **passivemap**. The former map is used by ASP's demux routine to map incoming messages to an existing session. It uses **ActiveId** as the demultiplexing key. Although conceptually the active map key is given by the 4-tuple described above, in practice we take advantage of the fact that the underlying IP session already corresponds to a local/remote host pair, and we use this session object in lieu of these two IP addresses.

The second map—**passivemap**—is used to record high-level protocols that have done a passive open on ASP. In this case, the corresponding key that is used to search this map, called the **PassiveId**, is given by the ASP port that the local protocol has done an **xOpenEnable** on.

2.6.3 Initialization

The C functions that implement a given protocol can be distributed across multiple .c files. In the case of ASP, they are all contained in a single file named **asp.c**. The rest of this section examines these functions one at a time.

We begin with function **asp_init**, which is called at system startup time. This function initializes the ASP protocol object, including protocol state and maps. It then does an **xOpenEnable** call on the protocol configured below it (usually IP) to inform it that ASP is willing to accept messages from any host. **xGetDown** is used to obtain a handle for the protocol that was configured below ASP. (In theory, ASP may have many low-level sessions opened; the second argument to **xGetDown** asks for the first of these.)

```
void
asp_init(Protl self)
{
    Part        part;
    ProtlState  *pstate;
    Protl       llp;

    getproc_protl(self);

    /* create and initialize protocol state */
    pstate = (ProtlState *) xMalloc(sizeof(ProtlState));
    bzero((char *)pstate, sizeof(ProtlState));
    self->state = (void *)pstate;
    pstate->activemap = mapCreate(ACTIVE_MAP_SIZE, sizeof(ActiveId));
    pstate->passivemap = mapCreate(PASSIVE_MAP_SIZE, sizeof(PassiveId));

    /* find lower level protocol and do a passive open on it */
    llp = xGetDown(self, 0);
    partInit(&part, 1);
    partPush(part, ANY_HOST, 0);
    xOpenEnable(self, llp, &part);
}
```

Because in this example we are dealing not just with the interfaces between objects but with their implementation, we need to consider some of the internal structure of the Protl and Sessn objects, which we have glossed over until now. For example, in the preceding code we initialized the state data structure in the ASP Protl object. One important part of initialization of the Protl object is to fill in the table that will cause operations on the object (e.g., xOpen) to invoke the appropriate function to implement that operation (e.g., aspOpen). In the case of ASP, the subroutine getproc_protl fills out this operation table:

```
static void
getproc_protl(Protl p)
{
    /* Fill in the function pointers to implement protocol operations */
    p->open = aspOpen;
    p->openenable = aspOpenEnable;
    p->demux = aspDemux;
}
```

2.6.4 Opening Connections

When a high-level protocol wishes to establish an ASP channel to a remote host, it will call xOpen, which causes aspOpen to be called. This function extracts the local and remote ASP ports from the participant list that is passed down by the high-level protocol and passes the resulting participant list, by means of another xOpen call, down to IP. A new ASP session (asp_s) is then created to handle messages sent and received on this channel. If a high-level protocol attempts to reopen a channel—i.e., one that is found in the active map—the open operation fails; otherwise, the newly created session is returned to the calling protocol.

Notice that aspOpen uses the x-kernel operation partPop to extract address information from the participant list; there is also a partPush operation that is used to attach addressing information to the participant list. Briefly, the participant list is an array of addresses, where, by convention, the first element of this array identifies the local participant and the second element identifies the remote participant. Each element in the array, in turn, is represented by a stack of addresses; hence the "push" and "pop" in the operation names. It is a stack rather than a flat structure because a given participant might be identified with a multicomponent address, for example, a host address and a port number. In this example, aspOpen extracts the port number from each stack but leaves the host number on the stack for some lower-level protocol (e.g., IP) to process.

```
static Sessn
aspOpen(Protl self, Protl hlp, Part *p)
{
    Sessn       asp_s;
    Sessn       lls;
    ActiveId    key;
    ProtlState  *pstate = (ProtlState *)self->state;
```

```
    bzero((char *)&key, sizeof(key));

    /* High level protocol must specify both local and remote ASP port */
    key.localport = *((AspPort *) partPop(p[0]));
    key.remoteport = *((AspPort *) partPop(p[1]));

    /* Assume failure until proven otherwise */
    asp_s = XK_FAILURE;

    /* Attempt to open session on protocol below this one */
    lls = xOpen(self, xGetDown(self, 0), p);
    if ( lls != XK_FAILURE )
    {
        key.lls = lls;
        /* Check for this session in the active map */
        if (mapResolve(pstate->activemap, &key, (void **)&asp_s) == XK_FAILURE)
        {
        /* Session wasn't already in map, so initialize it */
            asp_s = asp_init_sessn(self, hlp, &key);
            if ( asp_s != XK_FAILURE )
            {
                /* A successful open */
                return asp_s;
            }
        }

        /* If control makes it this far, an error has occurred */
        xClose(lls);
    }
    return asp_s;
}
```

Note that the real work of initializing the session is performed by asp_init_sessn, presented below. Before we get into the details of that routine, however, we'll take a look at aspOpenEnable. This is the routine that is called indirectly through xOpenEnable by a high-level protocol that wants to do a passive open on ASP. The high-level protocol specifies its willingness to receive messages on a specific ASP port, and aspOpenEnable records this fact in its passive map. Note that the *x*-kernel defines an Enable object that is used by aspOpenEnable to record the necessary information about the passive open, including a reference count (rcnt) of how many times that particular port has been enabled. Also, keep in mind that a session object is not created at this time; it will be created in aspDemux when a message arrives addressed to that port.

```
static XkReturn
aspOpenEnable(Protl self, Protl hlp, Part *p)
{
    ProtlState   *pstate = (ProtlState *)self->state;
```

```
    Enable        *e;
    PassiveId     key;

    key = *((AspPort *) partPop (*p));

    /* Check if this port has already been OpenEnabled */
    if (mapResolve(pstate->passivemap, &key, (void **)&e) != XK_FAILURE)
    {
        if ( e->hlp == hlp )
        {
            /* This port was OpenEnabled previously by the same hlp */
            e->rcnt++;
            return XK_SUCCESS;
        }
        /* This port was OpenEnabled previously by a different hlp - error */
        return XK_FAILURE;
    }

    /* This will be a new enabling, so create and initialize Enable object */
    e = (Enable *)xMalloc(sizeof(Enable));
    e->hlp = hlp;
    e->rcnt = 1;
    /* Enter the binding of port/enable object in the passive map */
    e->binding = mapBind(pstate->passivemap, &key, e);

    return XK_SUCCESS;
}
```

Finally, the actual work of initializing an ASP session is performed in the subroutine asp_init_sessn given below. This subroutine calls an *x*-kernel operation—xCreateSessn—to allocate a new session object and to connect it to other protocol and session objects in the appropriate way; e.g., the new session points to the high-level protocol that created it (hlp) and to the low-level session that it will use to send and receive messages (lls). In addition, the new session object will need to know where to find the routines that implement the various operations it supports, such as xPush and xPop. getproc_sessn (presented below) is the routine that fills in the ASP-specific function pointers for these operations; it is called by xCreateSessn.

Note that asp_init_sessn is not only called from aspOpen but also from aspDemux (shown in next subsection) when it needs to create a new session as a result of an earlier passive open. Also notice that in the case of asp_init_sessn, the only protocol-specific initialization that is required is to set up a header template asph that can later be prepended to the front of outgoing messages.

```
static Sessn
asp_init_sessn(Protl self, Protl hlp, ActiveId *key)
{
    Sessn       s;
```

```
    SessnState *sstate;
    ProtlState *pstate;
    AspHdr     *asph;

    pstate = (ProtlState *)self->state;

    /* create the session object and initialize it */
    s = xCreateSessn(getproc_sessn, hlp, self, 1, &key->lls);
    s->binding = mapBind(pstate->activemap, key, s);
    sstate = (SessnState *)xMalloc(sizeof(SessnState));
    s->state = (char *)sstate;

    /* Create an ASP header */
    asph = &(sstate->hdr);
    asph->sport = key->localport;
    asph->dport = key->remoteport;
    asph->ulen = 0;

    return s;
}

static void
getproc_sessn(Sessn s)
{
    /* Fill in the function pointers to implement session operations */
    s->push = aspPush;
    s->pop = aspPop;
    s->close = aspClose;
}
```

2.6.5 Demultiplexing Incoming Messages

Function **aspDemux** is called indirectly through **xDemux** by an IP session to pass an incoming message up to ASP. (More generally, it could be called by any low-level protocol configured below it, but this protocol will usually be IP.) This function extracts the header information from the message and then demultiplexes the message to the appropriate session as follows. First, **aspDemux** consults the protocol's active map to see if a session already exists for the ASP channel to which the message belongs. If such a session exists, the message is passed to that session by means of the **xPop** operation. If it does not exist, **aspDemux** then checks the passive map to see if the message is addressed to a port on which a high-level session has performed an **xOpenEnable**. If the port is found in the passive map, a new session is created— by invoking **asp_init_sessn**—and the message is dispatched to that session. If an appropriate entry is not found in either the active or the passive map, the message is discarded.

```
static XkReturn
aspDemux(Protl self, Sessn lls, Msg *msg)
{
```

```
        AspHdr          h;
        Sessn           s;
        ActiveId        activeid;
        PassiveId       passiveid;
        ProtlState      *pstate;
        Enable          *e;
        void            *buf;

        pstate = (ProtlState *)self->state;

        /* extract the header from the message */
        buf = msgPop(msg, HLEN);
        aspHdrLoad(&h, buf, HLEN, msg);

        /* construct a demux key from the header */
        bzero((char *)&activeid, sizeof(activeid));
        activeid.localport = h.dport;
        activeid.remoteport = h.sport;
        activeid.lls = lls;

        /* see if demux key is in the active map */
        if (mapResolve(pstate->activemap, &activeid, (void **)&s) == XK_FAILURE)
        {
            /* didn't find an active session, so check passive map */
            passiveid = h.dport;
            if (mapResolve(pstate->passivemap, &passiveid, (void **)&e) == XK_FAILURE)
            {
                /* drop the message */
                return XK_SUCCESS;
            }

            /* port was enabled, so create a new session and inform hlp */
            s = asp_init_sessn(self, e->hlp, &activeid);
            xOpenDone(e->hlp, s, self);
        }
        /* found (or created) an appropriate session, so pop to it */
        return xPop(s, lls, msg, &h);
}
```

Subroutine **aspHdrLoad** is responsible for converting the fields in the ASP header from network byte order into the local host's byte order. (See Section 7.1 for a discussion of byte order.) It uses the library routine **ntohs**, which stand for network-to-host-short. A counterpart routine—**aspHdrStore**—performs the opposite conversion; it translates host byte order to network byte order. This latter routine is used when preparing a message for transmission, as discussed in the next subsection. Notice that both routines simultaneously swap bytes and copy the header between the message and the template.

```
static long
aspHdrLoad(void *hdr, char *src, int len, Msg *m)
{
    /* copy from src to hdr, then convert network byte order to host order */
    bcopy(src, (char *)hdr, HLEN);
    ((AspHdr *)hdr)->ulen = ntohs(((AspHdr *)hdr)->ulen);
    ((AspHdr *)hdr)->sport = ntohs(((AspHdr *)hdr)->sport);
    ((AspHdr *)hdr)->dport = ntohs(((AspHdr *)hdr)->dport);
    return HLEN;
}
static void
aspHdrStore(void *hdr, char *dst, int len, Msg *m)
{
    /* copy from hdr to dst, then convert host byte order to network order */
    ((AspHdr *)hdr)->ulen = htons(((AspHdr *)hdr)->ulen);
    ((AspHdr *)hdr)->sport = htons(((AspHdr *)hdr)->sport);
    ((AspHdr *)hdr)->dport = htons(((AspHdr *)hdr)->dport);
    bcopy((char *)hdr, dst, HLEN);
}
```

2.6.6   Sending and Receiving Messages

We now turn our attention to the ASP-specific implementation of xPush and xPop—aspPush and aspPop—the two routines that embody the semantics of ASP. Because of its simple nature, aspPush simply prepends a copy of the header stored in the session state onto the outgoing message and passes the resulting message to the IP session beneath it. The header template found in the session state already contains the appropriate local and remote ASP ports, since these will not change during the lifetime of a session. However, the message length must be calculated and inserted into the appropriate header field. Subroutine aspHdrStore, as defined in the previous subsection, converts this header template from host byte order to network byte order.

```
static XkReturn
aspPush(Sessn s, Msg *msg)
{
    SessnState  *sstate;
    AspHdr      hdr;
    void        *buf;

    /* create a header by inserting length into header template */
    sstate = (SessnState *) s->state;
    hdr = sstate->hdr;
    hdr.ulen = msgLen(msg) + HLEN;

    /* attach header to message and pass it on down the stack */
    buf = msgPush(msg, HLEN);
    aspHdrStore(&hdr, buf, HLEN, msg);
    return xPush(xGetDown(s, 0), msg);
}
```

Again because of its simplicity, the only work that **aspPop** performs is to check the length field in the message header and truncate the message, if necessary. Notice that the last thing **aspPop** does is to invoke **xDemux** on the high-level protocol that had earlier opened the session. **xGetUp** is a simple routine that returns the high-level protocol that originally opened session **s**.

```
static XkReturn
aspPop(Sessn s, Sessn ds, Msg *msg, void *inHdr)
{
    AspHdr      *h = (AspHdr *) inHdr;

    /* truncate message to length shown in header */
    if ((h->ulen - HLEN) < msgLen(msg))
        msgTruncate(msg, (int) h->ulen);

    /* pass the message to the next protocol up the stack */
    return xDemux(xGetUp(s), s, msg);
}
```

2.6.7 Closing the Connection

Finally, **aspClose** is called indirectly through **xClose** when a high-level protocol wants to close a session it had opened earlier. This routine removes the entry in the active map corresponding to this session, closes the lower-level session, and destroys the session object. As you can see, the session object includes a field in which the binding in the active map for this session was recorded (**binding**). Also, the routine **xGetMyProtl** returns the protocol object that corresponds to this session (e.g., the protocol object that represents ASP).

```
static XkReturn
aspClose(Sessn s)
{
    ProtlState *pstate;
    SessnState *sstate;

    pstate = (ProtlState *)xGetMyProtl(s)->state;
    sstate = (SessnState *)s->state;

    /* remove this session from the active map */
    mapUnbindBinding(pstate->activemap, s->binding);

    /* close the lower level session on which it depends */
    xClose(xGetDown(s, 0));

    /* de-allocate the session object itself */
    xDestroy(s);

    return XK_SUCCESS;
}
```

2.7 Summary

This chapter introduced the x-kernel protocol implementation framework. The x-kernel provides two essential things. First, it defines an interface that protocols can use to invoke each other's services. This interface specifies how to open and close connections and how to send and receive messages. The advantage of having such a protocol-to-protocol interface is that it makes it possible to plug-and-play with different protocol objects. Thus, by configuring a graph of protocol objects that adhere to this interface, you can build the desired network subsystem.

Second, the x-kernel provides a set of support routines that protocol implementations can call to perform the tasks that they must perform, for example, manipulate messages, schedule events, and map identifiers. The key observation is that protocols look alike in many respects. The x-kernel simply codifies these common features and makes them available to protocol implementers in the form of a set of support routines. One advantage of such a framework is that it keeps you from having to reinvent the wheel: a single event manager can be used by all protocols. A second advantage is that a rising tide raises all ships: An improvement made to the algorithm or data structure used by any support routine benefits all protocols that use that routine.

O P E N   I S S U E

Cost of Network Software

In the larger picture, implementing and maintaining network software is a very expensive business. It is estimated that large computer vendors like HP, Sun, SGI, IBM, and Digital each spend approximately \$80 to \$100 million per year to maintain their networking code. This is not an investment that necessarily makes these companies any money—it is something they have to do just to stay competitive. The cost is high because each company typically has to maintain several different protocol stacks across several different architecture/OS bases. There is reason to believe that a protocol implementation framework might help to improve this situation, since vendors would be able to maintain just one instance of each protocol—the one that runs in this framework—and then would be able to port this framework to all of their platforms. In fact, there is a move in the industry to do just this. For example, the System V Streams mechanism is now used in Sun Microsystems' Solaris OS and the x-kernel is included in a recent release of OSF/1.

A related issue is how innovations in protocol design and implementation find their way into commercial offerings. At one time, nearly every vendor had a version of Unix that was derived from the Berkeley version (BSD): HP had HPUX, Digital had Ultrix, and Sun had SunOS. This made technology transfer from the research community fairly easy, since most of the networking researchers were doing their research in BSD Unix. As a result, two years after someone demonstrated a good idea in the BSD implementation of TCP, that idea would show up in Ultrix or SunOS. Today, however, most of the Unix operating systems are quite far removed from BSD Unix—e.g., Solaris is essentially based on System V Unix—not to mention the arrival of new operating systems like NT that have virtually no tie to Unix. This means that the technology transfer path is now broken; it will be much harder to move future innovations from the research world into the commercial world.

A second consequence of this shift away from BSD-based operating systems is that the days when all our implementations of TCP were derived from the same code base are over, meaning that maintaining interoperability is going to become more and more challenging. Again, a common protocol implementation platform might help to address this issue.

FURTHER READING

There are two mature environments for implementing network protocols: the Streams mechanism from System V Unix and the x-kernel. The following two papers give an overview of these two systems and are strongly recommended:

- Ritchie, D. A Stream input-output system. *Bell System Technical Journal* 63(8):311–324, October 1984.

- Hutchinson, N., and L. Peterson. The x-kernel: An architecture for implementing network protocols. *IEEE Transactions on Software Engineering* 17(1):64–76, January 1991.

Probably the most widely used implementation of the TCP/IP protocol stack is that found in BSD Unix. This implementation is well documented in Leffler et al. [LMKQ89] and Stevens and Wright [SW95].

More generally, there is a large body of work that addresses the issue of structuring and optimizing protocol implementations. Clark was one of the first to discuss the relationship between modular design and protocol performance [Cla82]. Later papers then introduce the use of upcalls in structuring protocol code [Cla85] and study the processing overheads in TCP [CJRS89]. Finally, Watson and Mamrak [WM87] describe how to gain efficiency in transport services through appropriate design and implementation choices.

Several papers have introduced specific techniques and mechanisms that can be used to improve protocol performance. For example, Hutchinson et al. [HMPT89] describe some of the mechanisms used in the x-kernel, McKenney and Dove [MD93] discuss various implementations of demultiplexing tables, Varghese and Lanck [VL87] introduce the timing wheel mechanism to manage protocol events, and Druschel and Peterson [DP93] describe an efficient buffer-management strategy. Also, the performance of protocols running on parallel processors—locking is a key issue in such environments—is discussed in Bjorkman and Gunningberg [BG93] and by Nahum et al. [NYKT94].

On a more general note, since many aspects of protocol implementation depend on an understanding of the basics of operating systems, we recommend Finkel [Fin88], Bic and Shaw [BS88], and Tanenbaum [Tan92] for an introduction to OS concepts.

A good introduction to formal specification languages and their use in designing and validating protocols can be found in Holzmann [Hol91]. This book also has a nice discussion of exactly what a protocol is. Also, Giagioni [Gia94] describes an effort to implement a protocol stack in the functional language ML. In contrast to traditional formal specification work that focuses on a single protocol, this effort is concerned with the communication service that results when two or more protocols are composed together.

Finally, we recommend the following live reference:

■ http://www.cs.arizona.edu/xkernel: information on the x-kernel, including programmer's manual and source code.

E X E R C I S E S

1 Use a WWW browser to familiarize yourself with the x-kernel programmer's manual at URL http://www.cs.arizona.edu/xkernel/manual/manual.html.

2 Configure a version of the x-kernel that includes ASP, along with a test protocol called TEST_ASP configured on top of ASP. Run the resulting kernel as a Unix process on a pair of workstations connected by some LAN (e.g., Ethernet or FDDI). Write different versions of TEST_ASP to test different aspects of ASP's performance.

(a) Program TEST_ASP to send a 1-byte message to its peer on the other machine, and have the peer echo the 1-byte message back. Repeat this process 1000 times. Divide the running time of the entire test run by 1000 to determine the round-trip latency for a single 1-byte message.

(b) Program TEST_ASP to repeat the above experiment, but for different message sizes, for example, 1 KB, 2 KB, ..., 32 KB. Use the results to compute the effective throughput rate for each message size. Plot the measured throughput as a function of message size.

3 Repeat the above experiments, but this time use a configuration of the x-kernel that includes TCP and UDP.

4 Configure a version of the x-kernel that includes TCP, along with a test protocol called TEST_TCP configured on top of TCP. Program TEST_TCP to send 1 MB of data from one host to another. Do this in a loop that sends a message of some size, e.g., 1024 iterations of a loop that sends 1-KB messages. Repeat the experiment with different message sizes and plot the results.

5 Study the code that implements the x-kernel's event manager. Implement your own event manager using delta lists. Compare the performance of this new implementation with that of the x-kernel.

6 Study the code that implements the x-kernel's id mapper. Implement your own id mapper, but in a way that is not specialized according to the key size, that is, this new version should be able to bind and resolve variable-length keys. Compare the performance of this new implementation with that of the x-kernel for various key sizes.

7 Study the code that implements the x-kernel's message tool. Implement your own message tool using a linear (linked list) representation for messages. Compare the performance of this new implementation with that of the x-kernel.

8 Experiment with the x-kernel's message operations. Apply different sequences of operations to a collection of buffers and display the contents of the message after these operations have been applied.

9 Write a test program that copies data from one buffer to another. Use this program to measure the copy bandwidth of the computer you use. How does the size of the buffer influence the results? (Hint: think about the cache.)

10 Compare the performance of your buffer-to-buffer copy program (see previous exercise) to library programs for copying that are available on your system (e.g., bcopy, memcpy). Look at the source code to explain the difference between the performance of your program and the standard utilities.

11 Write a test program that reads data from (writes data to) a buffer. For example, this program might consist of a loop that iterates 1000 times, writing an integer (or floating-point number) into successive elements of an array. Compare the read (write) bandwidth of your computer to its copy bandwidth. Explain the relationship between a computer's read, write, and copy bandwidths.

12 For the example protocol ASP, explain why the local and remote IP addresses are included in the demultiplexing key. Why is the low-level session a sufficient replacement for these two IP addresses?

13 Inspect the x-kernel implementations of UDP and TCP.

    (a) Identify the demultiplexing key for each; how many bytes long is each key?

    (b) Print out the data structure that defines the header for each.

    (c) Print out the data structure that defines the session-specific state for each.

14 Discover how many different protocols are implemented in your favorite computer or OS vendor's system.

15 On some operating system for which you have access to the source code, determine what percentage of the system code is network related.

16 Investigate the STREAMS protocol implementation framework from System V Unix. Compare STREAMS to the x-kernel.

17 Suppose that you work for a computer vendor that maintains N different protocols across M different operating systems. Describe an argument that you could present to your boss as to why a common protocol implementation platform like the x-kernel or System V STREAMS is a good idea for your company. How does the argument change if the N protocols are constantly changing rather than fixed?

18 Extend the argument in the previous problem to include what happens if the protocol implementation framework is an industry-wide standard rather than one used by just your company.

The simplest network possible is one in which all the hosts are directly connected by some physical medium. This may be a wire or a fiber, and it may cover a small area (e.g., an office building) or a wide area (e.g., transcontinental). Connecting two or more nodes with a suitable medium is only the first step, however. There are five additional problems that must be addressed before the nodes can successfully exchange packets.

The first is *encoding* bits onto the wire or fiber so that they can be understood by a receiving host. Second is the matter of delineating the sequence of bits transmitted over the link into complete messages that can be delivered to the end node. This is called the *framing* problem, and the messages delivered to the end hosts are often called *frames*. Third, because frames are sometimes corrupted during transmission, it is necessary to detect these errors and take the appropriate action; this is the *error detection* problem. The fourth issue is making a link appear reliable in spite of the fact that it corrupts frames from time to time. Finally, in those cases where the link is shared by multiple hosts—as opposed to a simple point-to-point link—it is necessary to mediate access to this link. This is the *media access control* problem.

Although these five issues—encoding, framing, error detection, reliable delivery, and access mediation—can be discussed in the abstract, they are very real problems that are addressed in different ways by different networking technologies. This chapter considers these issues in the context of three specific network technologies: point-to-point links, Carrier Sense Multiple Access (CSMA) networks (of which Ethernet is the most famous example), and token rings (of which FDDI is the most famous example). The goal of this chapter is simultaneously to survey the available network technology and to explore these five fundamental issues.

Before tackling the specific issues of connecting hosts, this chapter begins by examining the building blocks that will be used: nodes and links. We then explore the first three issues—encoding, framing, and error detection—in the context of a simple point-to-point link. The techniques intro-

It is a mistake to look too far ahead. Only one link in the chain of destiny can be handled at a time.

—*Churchill*

duced in these three sections are general, and therefore apply equally well to multiple access networks. The problem of reliable delivery is considered next. Since link-level reliability is usually not implemented in shared-access networks, this discussion focuses on point-to-point links only. Finally, we address the media access problem by examining the two main approaches to managing access to a shared link: CSMA and the token ring.

Note that these five functions are, in general, implemented in a network adaptor—a board that plugs into a host's I/O bus on one end and into the physical medium on the other end. In other words, bits are exchanged between adaptors, but correct frames are exchanged between nodes. This adaptor is controlled by software running on the node—the device driver—which, in turn, is typically represented as the bottom protocol in a protocol graph. This chapter concludes with a concrete example of a network adaptor and sketches the device driver for such an adaptor.

3

Direct Link Networks

3.1   Hardware Building Blocks

As we saw in Chapter 1, networks are constructed from two classes of hardware building blocks: *nodes* and *links*. This statement is just as true for the simplest possible network—one in which a single point-to-point link connects a pair of nodes—as it is for a worldwide internet. This section gives a brief overview of what we mean by nodes and links, and in so doing, defines the underlying technology that we will assume throughout the rest of this book.

3.1.1   Nodes

Nodes are often general-purpose computers, like a desktop workstation, a multiprocessor, or a PC. For our purposes, let's assume it's a workstation-class machine. This workstation can serve as a host that users run application programs on, it might be used inside the network as a switch that forwards messages from one link to another, or it might be configured as a router that forwards internet packets from one network to another. In some cases, a network node—most commonly a switch or router inside the network, rather than a host—is implemented by special-purpose hardware. This is usually done for performance reasons: it is generally possible to build custom hardware that performs a particular function faster than a general-purpose processor can perform it. When this happens, we will first describe the basic function being performed by the node as though this function is being implemented in software on a general-purpose workstation, and then explain why and how this functionality might instead be implemented by special hardware.

While we could leave it at that, it is useful to know a little bit about what a workstation looks like on the inside. This information becomes particularly important when we become concerned about how well the network performs. Figure 3.1 gives a simple block diagram of the workstation-class machine we assume throughout this book. There are three key features of this figure that are worth noting.

First, the memory on any given machine is finite. It may be 4 megabytes (MB) or it may be 128 MB, but it is not infinite. As pointed out in Section 1.2.2, this is important because memory turns out to be one of the two scarce resources in the network (the other is link bandwidth) that must be carefully managed if we are to provide a fair amount of network capacity to each user. Memory is a scarce resource because on a node that serves as a switch or router, packets must be buffered in memory while waiting their turn to be transmitted over an outgoing link.

Second, each node connects to the network via a *network adaptor*. This adaptor generally sits on the system's I/O bus and delivers data between the workstation's memory and the network link. A software module running on the workstation—the *device driver*—manages this adaptor. It issues commands to the adaptor, telling it, for example, from what memory location outgoing data should be transmitted and into what memory location incoming data should be stored. Adaptors are discussed in more detail in Section 3.8.

Finally, while CPUs are becoming faster at an unbelievable pace, the same is not true of memory. Recent performance trends show processor speeds doubling every 18 months but

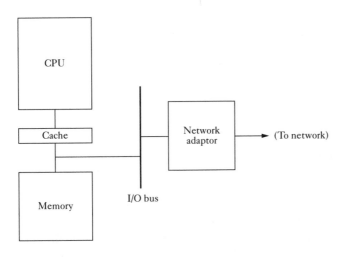

Figure 3.1 Example workstation architecture.

memory speeds improving at a rate of only 7% each year. The relevance of this difference is that as a network node, a workstation runs at memory speeds, not processor speeds, to a first approximation. This means that the network software needs to be careful about how it uses memory and, in particular, about how many times it accesses memory as it processes each message. We do not have the luxury of being sloppy just because processors are becoming infinitely fast.

3.1.2 Links

Network links are implemented on a variety of different physical media, including twisted pair (the wire that your phone connects to), coaxial cable (the wire that your TV connects to), optical fiber (the stuff we all want to connect to), and space (the stuff that radio waves, microwaves, and laser beams propagate through). Whatever the physical medium, it is used to propagate *signals*. Some signals take on discrete values, such as positive and negative voltage pulses. Links over which discrete signals are sent are said to be *digital*. Other links carry continuous electromagnetic signals ranging between, say, 300 Hz and 3300 Hz (the range of voice-grade telephone). Links over which continuous signals are sent are called *analog* links.

Digital and analog links provide the foundation for transmitting all sorts of information, including the kind of data we are interested in transmitting—binary data (1s and 0s). We say that the binary data is *encoded* in the signal. For example, a *modem* (short for *mod*ulator/ *dem*odulator) is a device that encodes binary data onto an analog signal at the transmit side and the analog signal back into binary data on the receive side. A *digital transmitter* is a device that transmits binary (digital) data over a digital link. We return to the problem of encoding binary data on a digital link in Section 3.2.

Cable	Typical Bandwidths and Distances
Category 5 twisted pair	10–100 Mbps, 100 m
50-ohm coax (ThinNet)	10–100 Mbps, 200 m
75-ohm coax (ThickNet)	10–100 Mbps, 500 m
Multimode fiber	100 Mbps, 2 km
Single-mode fiber	100–2400 Mbps, 40 km

Table 3.1 Common types of cables and fibers available for local links.

Another attribute of a link is how many bit streams can be encoded on it at a given time. If the answer is only one, then the nodes connected to the link must share access to the link. This is the case for the multiple-access links described in Sections 3.6 and 3.7. For point-to-point links, however, it is often the case that two bit streams can be simultaneously transmitted over the link at the same time, one going in each direction. Such a link is said to be *full-duplex*. A point-to-point link that supports data flowing in only one direction at a time—such a link is called *half-duplex*—requires that the two nodes connected to the link alternate using it. For the purposes of this book, we assume that all point-to-point links are full-duplex.

The only other property of a link that we are interested in at this stage is a very pragmatic one—how far it reaches. On the one hand, if the nodes you want to connect are in the same room, in the same building, or even on the same site (e.g., a campus), then you can buy a piece of cable and physically string it between the nodes. (Well, you may need the assistance of a backhoe operator, but putting in such a link is within the realm of possibility.) Exactly what type of cable you choose to install depends on the technology you plan to use to transmit data over the link; we'll see several examples later in this chapter. For now, a list of the common cable (fiber) types is given in Table 3.1.

On the other hand, if the two nodes you want to connect are on opposite sides of the country, or even across town, then it is not practical to install the link yourself. Your only option is to lease a link from the telephone company, in which case all you'll need to be able to do is conduct an intelligent conversation with the phone company customer service representative. Table 3.2 gives the common services that can be leased from the phone company. Again, more details are given throughout this chapter.

While these bandwidths appear somewhat arbitrary, there is actually some method to the madness. First, the 64-Kbps capacity of the ISDN (Integrated Services Digital Network) link was chosen because it is the bandwidth commonly used to transmit digitized voice, and one of the goals of ISDN is to handle both voice and data. (A device that encodes analog voice into a digital ISDN link is called a CODEC, for *coder/decoder*.) Second, T1 and T3 are relatively old technologies that are defined for copper-based transmission media. T1 is equal to the aggregation of 24 digital voice circuits, and T3 is equal to 30 T1 links. Finally, all the STS-*N* links are for optical fiber (STS stands for *Synchronous Transport Signal*). STS-1 is the

Service	Bandwidth
ISDN	64 Kbps
T1	1.544 Mbps
T3	44.736 Mbps
STS-1	51.840 Mbps
STS-3	155.250 Mbps
STS-12	622.080 Mbps
STS-24	1.244160 Gbps
STS-48	2.488320 Gbps

Table 3.2   Common bandwidths available from the carriers.

base link speed, and each STS-N has N times the bandwidth of STS-1. An STS-N link is also sometimes called an OC-N link (OC stands for *optical carrier*). The difference between STS and OC is subtle: the former refers to the *electrical* transmission on the devices connected to the link, and the latter refers to the actual *optical* signal that is propagated over the fiber.

All of the above links are digital, as opposed to analog. Also, with the exception of the ISDN link they are also leased as dedicated lines, meaning that the line is always available; it is not necessary to "dial up" a connection before using it. (It is actually possible to have a dial-up T1 link, but T1 is usually leased as a dedicated line.) The alternative, of course, is to use a modem to transmit binary data over a conventional analog, dial-up, voice-grade phone line. Although analog modem technology has improved a great deal recently—a 28.8-Kbps modem costs only a few hundred dollars—this technology has limited potential and is not expected to go much higher.

Keep in mind that the phone company does not implement the "link" we just ordered as a single, unbroken piece of cable or fiber. Instead, it implements the link on its own network. Although the telephone network has historically looked much different from the kind of network described in this book—it was built primarily to provide a voice service, used circuit-switching technology, and was based on analog links—the current trend is toward the style of networking described in this book, particularly the Asynchronous Transfer Mode (ATM) network described in Chapter 4. This is not surprising—the potential market for carrying data, voice, and video is huge.

In any case, whether the link is physical or a logical connection through the telephone network, the problem of building a computer network on top of a collection of such links remains the same. So, we will proceed as though each link is implemented by a single cable/fiber, and only when we are done will we worry about whether we have just built a computer network on top of the underlying telephone network, or whether the computer network we have just built could itself serve as the backbone for the telephone network.

3.2   Encoding (NRZ, NRZI, Manchester, 4B/5B)

The first step in turning nodes and links into usable building blocks is to understand how to connect them in such a way that bits can be transmitted from one node to the other. As mentioned in the preceding section, signals propagate over physical links. The task, therefore, is to encode the binary data that the source node wants to send into the signals that the links are able to carry, and then to decode the signal back into the corresponding binary data at the receiving node. We consider this problem in the context of a digital link, in which case we are most likely working with two discrete signals. We refer to these generically as the high signal and the low signal, although in practice these signals would be two different voltages on a copper-based link and two different power levels on an optical link.

As we have said, most of the functions discussed in this chapter are performed by a network adaptor—a piece of hardware that connects a node to a link. The network adaptor contains a signalling component that actually encodes bits into signals at the sending node and decodes signals into bits at the receiving node. Thus, as illustrated in Figure 3.2, signals travel over a link between two signalling components, and bits flow between network adaptors.

Let's return to the problem of encoding bits onto signals. The obvious thing to do is to map the data value 1 onto the high signal and data value 0 onto the low signal. This is exactly the mapping used by an encoding scheme called, cryptically enough, *non-return to zero* (NRZ). For example, Figure 3.3 schematically depicts the NRZ-encoded signal (bottom) that corresponds to the transmission of a particular sequence of bits (top).

Shannon's Law Meets Your Modem

There has been an enormous body of work done in the related areas of signal processing and information theory, studying everything from how signals degrade over distance to how much data a given signal can effectively carry. The most notable piece of work in this area is a formula known as *Shannon's theorem*. Simply stated, Shannon's theorem gives an upper bound to the capacity of a link, in terms of bits per second (bps), as a function of the signal-to-noise ratio of the link, measured in decibels (dB).

Shannon's law can be used to determine the data rate at which a modem—a device that transmits digital data over analog links—can be expected to transmit binary data over a voice-grade phone line without suffering from too high an error rate. We assume that a voice-grade phone connection supports a frequency range of 300 Hz to 3300 Hz.

Shannon's law is typically given

The problem with NRZ is that a sequence of several consecutive 1s means that the signal stays high on the link for an extended period of time, and similarly, several consecutive 0s means that the signal stays low for a long time. There are several problems caused by long strings of 1s or 0s. First, a prolonged low signal may really correspond to the absence of a signal. Thus, the receiver cannot distinguish between a long string of 0s and a dead link. Second, a sustained high signal potentially confuses the receiver because the receiver uses the average signal level, called the *baseline*, to distinguish between the high and the low signal. Too many consecutive 1s causes this average to change, a situation known as *baseline wander*. Third, frequent transitions from high to low and vice versa are necessary to enable *clock recovery*, as described below.

Intuitively, the clock recovery problem is that both the encoding and the decoding processes are driven by a clock—every clock cycle the sender transmits a bit and the receiver recovers a bit. The sender's and the receiver's clocks have to be precisely synchronized in order for the receiver to recover the same bits the sender transmits. If the receiver's clock is even the slightest bit faster or slower than the sender's clock, then it does not correctly decode the signal. You could imagine sending the clock to the receiver over a separate wire, but this is typically avoided because it makes the cost of cabling twice as high. So instead, the receiver derives the clock from the received signal—the clock recovery process. Whenever the signal changes, such as on a transition from 1 to 0 or from 0 to 1, then the receiver knows it is at a clock cycle boundary, and it can resynchronize itself. However, a long period of time without such a transition leads to clock drift. Thus, clock recovery depends on having lots of transitions in the signal, no matter what data is being sent.

by the following formula:
$$C = B \log_2(1 + S/N)$$

where C is the achievable channel capacity, B is the bandwidth of the line $(3300\,\mathrm{Hz} - 300\,\mathrm{Hz} = 3000\,\mathrm{Hz})$, S is the average signal power, and N is the average noise power. The signal-to-noise ratio (S/N) is usually expressed in decibels (dB), related as follows:

$$dB = 10 \times \log_{10}(S/N)$$

Assuming a typical decibel ratio of 30 dB, this means that $S/N = 1000$. Thus, we have

$$C = 3000 \times \log_2(1001)$$

which equals approximately 30 Kbps, roughly the limit of today's 28.8-Kbps modems. Modems will only be able to achieve higher rates if the quality (signal-to-noise) ratio of the phone network improves, or by using compression.

One approach that addresses this problem, called *non-return to zero inverted* (NRZI), has the sender make a transition from the current signal to encode a 1 and stay at the current signal to encode a 0. This solves the problem of consecutive 1s, but obviously does nothing for consecutive 0s. NRZI is illustrated in Figure 3.4. An alternative, called *Manchester [t] [t] encoding*, does a more explicit job of merging the clock with the signal by transmitting the exclusive-OR of the NRZ-encoded data and the clock. (Think of the local clock as an internal signal that alternates from low to high; a low/high pair is considered one clock cycle.) The

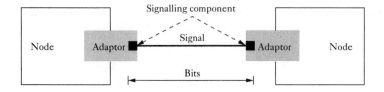

Figure 3.2   Signals travel between signalling components, bits flow between adaptors.

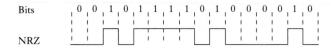

Figure 3.3   NRZ encoding of a bit stream.

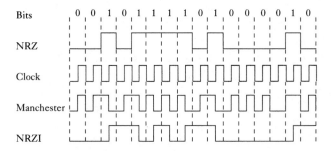

Figure 3.4   Different encoding strategies.

Manchester encoding is also illustrated in Figure 3.4. Observe that the Manchester encoding results in 0 being encoded as a low-to-high transition and 1 being encoded as a high-to-low transition. Because both 0s and 1s result in a transition to the signal, the clock can be effectively recovered at the receiver.

The problem with the Manchester encoding scheme is that it doubles the rate at which signal transitions are made on the link, which means that the receiver has half the time to detect each pulse of the signal. The rate at which the signal changes is called the link's *baud rate*. In the case of the Manchester encoding, the bit rate is half the baud rate, so the encoding is considered only 50% efficient. Keep in mind that if the receiver had been able to keep up with the faster baud rate required by the Manchester encoding in Figure 3.4, then both NRZ and NRZI could have been able to transmit twice as many bits in the same time period.

4-Bit Data Symbol	5-Bit Code
0000	11110
0001	01001
0010	10100
0011	10101
0100	01010
0101	01011
0110	01110
0111	01111
1000	10010
1001	10011
1010	10110
1011	10111
1100	11010
1101	11011
1110	11100
1111	11101

Table 3.3   4B/5B encoding.

A final encoding that we consider, called *4B/5B*, attempts to address the inefficiency of the Manchester encoding without suffering from the problem of having extended durations of high or low signals. The idea of 4B/5B is to insert extra bits into the bit stream so as to break up long sequences of 0s or 1s. Specifically, every 4 bits of actual data are encoded in a 5-bit code that is then transmitted to the receiver; hence the name 4B/5B. The 5-bit codes are selected in such a way that each one has no more than one leading 0 and no more than two trailing 0s. Thus, when sent back to back, no pair of 5-bit codes results in more than three consecutive 0s being transmitted. The resulting 5-bit codes are then transmitted using the NRZI encoding, which explains why the code is only concerned about consecutive 0s— NRZI already solves the problem of consecutive 1s. Note that the 4B/5B encoding results in 80% efficiency.

Table 3.3 gives the 5-bit codes that corresponds to each of the 16 possible 4-bit data symbols. Notice that since 5 bits are enough to encode 32 different codes, and we are using only 16 of these for data, there are 16 codes left over that we can use for other purposes. Of

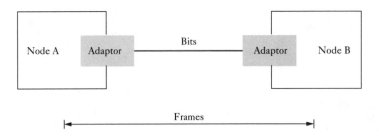

Figure 3.5   Bits flow between adaptors, frames between hosts.

these, code 11111 is used when the line is idle, code 00000 corresponds to when the line is dead, and 00100 is interpreted to mean halt. Of the remaining 13 codes, seven of them are not valid because they violate the one-leading-zero/two-trailing-zero rule, and the other six represent various control symbols. As we will see later in this chapter, some framing protocols (e.g., FDDI) make use of these control symbols.

3.3   Framing

Now that we have seen how to transmit a sequence of bits over a point-to-point link—from adaptor to adaptor—let's consider the scenario illustrated in Figure 3.5. Recall from Chapter 1 that we are focusing on packet-switched networks, which means that blocks of data (called frames at this level), not bit streams, are exchanged between nodes. It is the network adaptor that enables the nodes to exchange frames. When node A wishes to transmit a frame to node B, it tells its adaptor to transmit a frame from its memory. This results in a sequence of bits being sent over the link. The adaptor on node B then collects together the sequence of bits arriving on the link and deposits the corresponding frame in B's memory. Recognizing exactly what set of bits constitute a frame—that is, determining where the frame begins and ends—is the central challenge faced by the adaptor.

There are several ways to address the framing problem. This section uses several different protocols to illustrate the various points in the design space. Note that while we discuss framing in the context of point-to-point links, the problem is a fundamental one that must also be addressed in multiple access networks like CSMA and token ring.

3.3.1   Byte-Oriented Protocols (BISYNC, IMP-IMP, DDCMP)

One of the oldest approaches to framing—it has its roots in connecting terminals to mainframes—is to view each frame as a collection of bytes (characters) rather than a collection of bits. Such a *byte-oriented* approach is exemplified by the BISYNC (Binary Synchronous Communication) protocol developed by IBM in the late 1960s, the DDCMP (Digital Data Communication Message Protocol) used in Digital Equipment Corporation's DECNET, and the IMP-IMP protocol used in the original ARPANET. (IMP stands for Interface Message Processor, which is what the packet-switching nodes in the ARPANET were originally

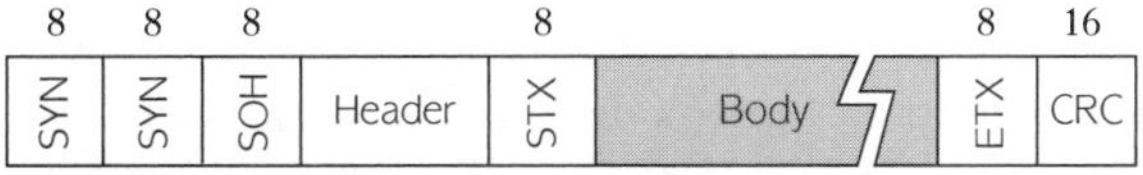

Figure 3.6 BISYNC frame format.

Figure 3.7 IMP-IMP frame format.

called.) Sometimes these protocols assume a particular character set—e.g., BISYNC can support ASCII, EBCDIC, and IBM's 6-bit Transcode—but this is not necessarily the case.

Although similar in many respects, these three protocols can be classified as using two different framing techniques, the sentinel approach and the byte-counting approach.

Sentinel Approach

The BISYNC and IMP-IMP protocols illustrate the sentinel approach to framing; their frame formats are depicted in Figures 3.6 and 3.7, respectively. These figures are the first of many that you will see in this book that are used to illustrate frame or packet formats, so a few words of explanation are in order. We show a packet as a sequence of labeled fields. Above each field is a number indicating the length of that field in bits. Note that the packets are transmitted beginning with the leftmost field.

In both the BISYNC and the IMP-IMP protocol, the beginning of a frame is denoted by sending a special SYN (synchronization) character. The data portion of the frame is then contained between special *sentinel characters*. In BISYNC, STX (start-of-text) and ETX (end-of-text) enclose the data, while in IMP-IMP, DLE/STX and DLE/ETX enclose the data (DLE stands for data-link-escape). The SOH (start of header) field in the BISYNC frame serves much the same purpose as the STX field.

The problem with the sentinel approach, of course, is that the ETX character might appear in the data portion of the frame. BISYNC overcomes this problem by "escaping" the ETX character by preceding it with a DLE character whenever it appears in the body of a frame; the DLE character is also escaped (by preceding it with an extra DLE) in the frame body. (C programmers may notice that this is analogous to the way a quotation mark is escaped by the backslash when it occurs inside a string.) Because the IMP-IMP protocol already puts DLE before the STX and ETX characters at the ends of the frame, it only needs to escape the DLE character in the frame body.

Both frame formats include a field (labeled CRC, or cyclic redundancy check) that is used to detect transmission errors; various algorithms for error detection are presented in Section 3.4. Also, both formats include room for additional header information. This additional header information is used for, among other things, the link-level reliable delivery algorithm. Examples of these algorithms are given in Section 3.5.

Byte-Counting Approach

As every Computer Sciences 101 student knows, the alternative to detecting the end of a file with a sentinel value is to include the number of items in the file at the beginning of the file. The same is true in framing—the number of bytes contained in a frame can be included as a field in the frame header. The DECNET's DDCMP protocol uses this approach, as illustrated in Figure 3.8. In this example, the COUNT field specifies how many bytes are contained in the frame's body.

One danger with this approach is that a transmission error could corrupt the count field, in which case the end of the frame would not be correctly detected. (A similar problem exists with the sentinel-based approach if the ETX field becomes corrupted.) Should this happen, the receiver will accumulate as many bytes as the bad COUNT field indicates and then use the error-detection field to determine that the frame is bad. This is sometimes called a *framing error*. The receiver will then wait until it sees the next SYN character to start collecting the bytes that make up the next frame. It is therefore possible that a framing error will cause back-to-back frames to be incorrectly received.

3.3.2 Bit-Oriented Protocols (HDLC)

Unlike these byte-oriented protocols, a bit-oriented protocol is not concerned with byte boundaries—it simply views the frame as a collection of bits. These bits might come from

What's in a Layer?

One of the important contributions of the OSI reference model presented in Chapter 1 was to provide some vocabulary for talking about protocols, and in particular, protocol layers. This vocabulary has provided fuel for plenty of arguments along the lines of "your protocol does function X at layer Y, and the OSI reference model says it should be done at layer Z—that's a layer violation." In fact, figuring out the right layer at which to perform a given function can be very difficult, and the reasoning is usually a lot more subtle than "what does the OSI model say?" It is partly for this reason that this book avoids a rigidly layerist approach. Instead, it shows you a lot of functions that need to be performed by protocols and looks at some ways that they have been successfully implemented.

In spite of our nonlayerist approach, sometimes we need convenient ways to talk about classes of protocols, and the name of the layer at which they operate is often the best choice. Thus, for example, this chapter focuses primarily on link-layer protocols. (Bit encoding,

some character set, such as ASCII, or they might be pixel values in an image or instructions and operands from an executable file. The Synchronous Data Link Control (SDLC) protocol developed by IBM is an example of a bit-oriented protocol; SDLC was later standardized by the OSI as the High-Level Data Link Control (HDLC) protocol. The more recent Point-to-Point Protocol (PPP) is similar to HDLC. In the following discussion, we use HDLC as an example; its frame format is given in Figure 3.9.

described in Section 3.2, is the exception, being considered a physical layer function.) Link-layer protocols can be identified by the fact that they run over single links—the type of network discussed in this chapter. Network-layer protocols, by contrast, run over switched networks that contain lots of links interconnected by switches or routers. Topics related to network-layer protocols are discussed in Chapter 4.

The important thing to note about protocol layers is that they are supposed to be helpful—they provide helpful ways to talk about classes of protocols, and they help us divide the problem of building networks into manageable subtasks. However, they are not meant to be overly restrictive—the mere fact that something is a layer violation does not end the argument about whether it is a worthwhile thing to do. In other words, layering makes a good slave, but a poor master. A particularly interesting argument about the best layer to place a certain function comes up when we look at congestion control in Chapter 8.

HDLC denotes both the beginning and the end of a frame with the distinguished bit sequence 01111110. This sequence is also transmitted during any times that the link is idle so that the sender and receiver can keep their clocks synchronized. In this way, both protocols essentially use the sentinel approach. Because this sequence might appear anywhere in the body of the frame—in fact, the bits 01111110 might cross byte boundaries—bit-oriented protocols use the analogue of the DLE character, a technique known as *bit stuffing*.

Bit stuffing in the HDLC protocol works as follows. On the sending side, any time five consecutive 1s have been transmitted from the body of the message (i.e., excluding when the sender is trying to transmit the distinguished 01111110 sequence), the sender inserts a 0 before transmitting the next bit. On the receiving side, should five consecutive 1s arrive, the receiver makes its decision based on the next bit it sees (i.e., the bit following the five 1s). If the next bit is a 0, it must have been stuffed, and so the receiver removes it. If the next bit is a 1, then one of two things is true: either this is the end-of-frame marker or an error has been introduced into the bit stream. By looking at the *next* bit, the receiver can distinguish between these two cases: if it sees a 0 (i.e., the last eight bits it has looked at are 01111110), then it is the end-of-frame marker; if it sees a 1 (i.e., the last eight bits it has looked at are 01111111), then there must have been an error and the

Figure 3.8 DDCMP frame format.

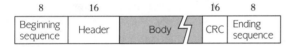

Figure 3.9 HDLC frame format.

whole frame is discarded. In the latter case, the receiver has to wait for the next 01111110 before it can start receiving again, and as a consequence, there is the potential that the receiver will fail to receive two consecutive frames. Obviously, there are still ways that framing errors can go undetected, such as when an entire spurious end-of-frame pattern is generated by errors, but these failures are relatively unlikely. Robust ways of detecting errors are discussed in Section 3.4.

An interesting characteristic of bit stuffing, as well as of the escaping of sentinel values, is that the size of a frame is dependent on the data that is being sent in the payload of the frame. It is in fact not possible to make all frames exactly the same size, given that the data that might be carried in any frame is arbitrary. (To convince yourself of this, consider what happens if the last byte of a frame's body is the ETX character.) A form of framing that ensures that all frames are the same size is described in the next subsection.

3.3.3 Clock-Based Framing (SONET)

A third approach to framing is exemplified by the Synchronous Optical Network (SONET) standard. For lack of a widely accepted generic term, we refer to this approach simply as *clock-based framing*. SONET was first proposed by Bell Communications Research (Bellcore), and then developed under the American National Standards Institute (ANSI) for digital transmission over optical fiber; it has since been adopted by the ITU-T. Who standardized what and when is not the interesting issue though. The thing to remember about SONET is that it defines how telephone companies transmit data over optical networks.

An important thing to know about SONET before we go any further is that the full specification is substantially larger than this book. Thus, the following discussion will necessarily cover only the high points of the standard. Also, SONET addresses both the framing problem and the encoding problem. It also addresses a problem that is very important for phone companies—the multiplexing of several low-speed links onto one high-speed link. We begin with framing, and discuss the other issues following.

As with the previously discussed framing schemes, a SONET frame has some special information that tells the receiver where the frame starts and ends. However, that is about as far as the similarities go. Notably, no bit stuffing is used, so that a frame's length does not depend on the data being sent. So the question to ask is, How does the receiver know where each frame starts and ends? We consider this question for the lowest-speed SONET link, which is known as STS-1 and runs at 51.84 Mbps. An STS-1 frame is shown in Figure 3.10. It is arranged as 9 rows of 90 bytes each, and the first 3 bytes of each row are overhead, with the rest being available for data that is being transmitted over the link. The first 2 bytes of the frame contain a special bit pattern, and it is these bytes that enable the receiver to determine where the frame starts. However, since bit stuffing is not used, there is no reason why this pattern will not occasionally turn up in the payload portion of the frame. To guard against this, the receiver looks for the special bit pattern consistently, hoping to see it appearing once every 810 bytes, since each frame is $9 \times 90 = 810$ bytes long. When the special pattern turns up in the right place enough times, the receiver concludes that it is in sync and can then interpret the frame correctly.

One of the things we are not describing due to the complexity of SONET is the detailed use of all the other overhead bytes. Part of this complexity can be attributed to the fact that SONET runs across the carrier's optical network, not just over a single link. (Recall that we are glossing over the fact that the carriers implement a network, and we are instead focusing on the fact that we can lease a SONET link from them and then use this link to build our own packet-switched network.) Additional complexity comes from the fact that SONET provides a considerably richer set of services than just data transfer. For example, 64 Kbps of a SONET link's capacity is set aside for a voice channel that is used for maintenance.

Bit Rates and Baud Rates

Many people use the terms bit rate and baud rate interchangeably, even though as we see with the Manchester encoding, they are not the same thing. While the Manchester encoding is an example of a case in which a link's baud rate is greater than its bit rate, it is also possible to have a bit rate that is greater than the baud rate. This would imply that more than one bit is encoded on each pulse sent over the link.

To see how this might happen, suppose you could transmit four distinguished signals over a link rather than just two. On an analog link, for example, these four signals might correspond to four different frequencies. Given four different signals, it is possible to encode two bits of information on each signal. That is, the first signal means 00, the second signal means 01, and so on. Now, a sender (receiver) that is able to transmit (detect) 1000 pulses per second would be able to send (receive) 2000 bits of information per second. That is, it would be a 1000-baud/2000-bps link.

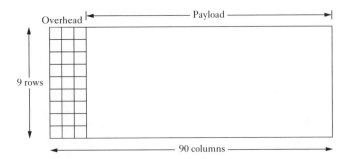

Figure 3.10   A SONET STS-1 frame.

The overhead bytes of a SONET frame are encoded using NRZ, the simple encoding described in the previous section where 1s are high and 0s are low. However, to ensure that there are plenty of transitions to allow the receiver to recover the sender's clock, the payload bytes are *scrambled*. This is done by calculating the exclusive-OR (XOR) of the data to be transmitted and by the use of a well-known bit pattern. The bit pattern, which is 127 bits long, has plenty of transitions from 1 to 0, so that XORing it with the transmitted data is likely to yield a signal with enough transitions to enable clock recovery.

SONET supports the multiplexing of multiple low-speed links in the following way. A given SONET link runs at one of a finite set of possible rates, ranging from 51.84 Mbps (STS-1) to 2488.32 Mbps (STS-48), and beyond. (See Table 3.2 in Section 3.1 for the full set of SONET data rates.) Note that all of these rates are integer multiples of STS-1. The significance for framing is that a single SONET frame can contain subframes for multiple lower rate channels. A second related feature is that each frame is 125 μs long. This means that at STS-1 rates, a SONET frame is 810 bytes long, while at STS-3 rates, each SONET frame is 2430 bytes long. Notice the synergy between these two features: $3 \times 810 = 2430$, meaning that three STS-1 frames fit exactly in a single STS-3 frame.

Intuitively, the STS-N frame can be thought of as consisting of N STS-1 frames, where the bytes from these frames are interleaved; i.e., a byte from the first frame is transmitted, then a byte from the second frame is transmitted, and so on. The reason for interleaving the bytes from each STS-N frame is to ensure that the bytes in each STS-1 frame are evenly paced, that is, bytes show up at the receiver at a smooth 51 Mbps, rather than all bunched up during one particular $1/N$th of the 125-μs interval.

Although it is accurate to view an STS-N signal as being used to multiplex N STS-1 frames, the payload from these STS-1 frames can be linked together to form a larger STS-N payload; such a link is denoted STS-Nc (for *concatenated*). One of the fields in the overhead is used for this purpose. Figure 3.11 schematically depicts concatenation in the case of three STS-1 frames being concatenated into a single STS-3c frame. The significance of a SONET link being designated as STS-3c rather than STS-3 is that, in the former case, the user of the

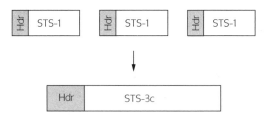

Figure 3.11   Three STS-1 frames multiplexed onto one STS-3c frame.

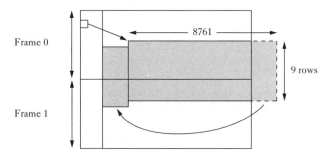

Figure 3.12   SONET frames out of phase.

link can view it as a single 155.25-Mbps pipe, whereas an STS-3 should really be viewed as three 51.84-Mbps links that happen to share a fiber.

Finally, the preceding description of SONET is overly simplistic in that it assumes that the payload for each frame is completely contained within the frame. (Why wouldn't it be?) In fact, one should view the STS-1 frame just described as simply a placeholder for the frame, where the actual payload may *float* across frame boundaries. This situation is illustrated in Figure 3.12. Here we see both the STS-1 payload floating across two STS-1 frames, and the payload shifted some number of bytes to the right and, therefore, wrapped around. One of the fields in the frame overhead points to the beginning of the payload. The value of this capability is that it simplifies the task of synchronizing the clocks used throughout the carriers' networks, which is something that carriers spend a lot of their time worrying about.

3.4   Error Detection

As discussed in Chapter 1, bit errors are sometimes introduced into frames. This happens, for example, because of electrical interference or thermal noise. Although errors are rare, especially on optical links, some mechanism is needed to detect these errors so that corrective action can be taken. Otherwise, the end user is left wondering why the C program that successfully compiled just a moment ago now suddenly has a syntax error in it, when all that happened in the interim is that it was copied across a network file system.

There is a long history of techniques for dealing with bit errors in computer systems, dating back to Hamming and Reed/Solomon codes that were developed for use when storing data on magnetic disks and in early core memories. In networking, the dominant method for detecting transmission errors is a technique known as the *cyclic redundancy check* (CRC). It is used in nearly all the link-level protocols discussed in the previous section—e.g., IMP-IMP, HDLC, DDCMP—as well as in the CSMA and token ring protocols described later in this chapter. This section outlines the basic CRC algorithm. It also introduces two other approaches to error detection—*two-dimensional parity* and *checksums*. The former is used by the BISYNC protocol when it is transmitting ASCII characters (CRC is used as the error code when BISYNC is used to transmit EBCDIC), and the latter is used by several Internet protocols.

3.4.1 Cyclic Redundancy Check

The basic idea behind any error detection scheme is to add redundant information to a frame that can be used to determine if errors have been introduced. In the extreme, one could imagine transmitting two complete copies of the data. If the two copies are identical at the receiver, then it is probably the case that both are correct. If they differ, then an error was most likely introduced into one (or both) of them, and they must be discarded. Fortunately, we can do a lot better than sending n redundancy bits for an n-bit message. In general, we need to send only k redundancy bits for an n-bit message, where $k << n$. On an Ethernet, for example, a frame carrying up to 12,000 bits (1500 bytes) of data requires only a 32-bit CRC code, or as it is commonly expressed, uses CRC-32. Such a code will catch the overwhelming majority of errors, as we will see below.

You don't reliably detect errors in a 12,000 bit message with only 32 redundant bits unless you have some fairly powerful mathematics behind you. In this case, the theoretical foundation of the cyclic redundancy check is rooted in finite fields. We will discuss the errors detected by CRC below; for now, we are only interested in the mechanics of the CRC algorithm. To start, think of an n-bit message as being represented by an $n - 1$ degree polynomial, where the value of each bit (0 or 1) is the coefficient for each term in the polynomial. For example, a message containing the bits 10011010 corresponds to the polynomial $M(x) = x^7 + x^4 + x^3 + x^1$. We also let k be the degree of some divisor polynomial $C(x)$. For our example, suppose $C(x) = x^3 + x^2 + 1$. In this case, $k = 3$. The answer to the question "Where did $C(x)$ come from?" is "You look it up in a book." Again, we will discuss this more below.

What we are going to do is transmit a polynomial that is exactly divisible by $C(x)$; the transmitted polynomial will be $P(x)$. (We'll explain how to generate $P(x)$ below.) Then, if some error occurs, it will be as if an error term $E(x)$ has been added to $P(x)$. When the recipient of the message divides $(P(x) + E(x))$ by $C(x)$, the result will be 0 in only two cases: $E(x)$ is 0 (i.e., there is no error), or $E(x)$ is exactly divisible by $C(x)$. A clever choice of $C(x)$

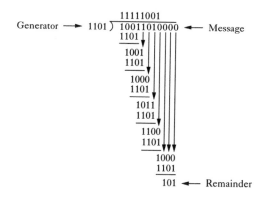

Figure 3.13   CRC calculation using polynomial long division.

can make the second case extremely rare, so that we can safely conclude that a 0 result means that the message is error free, and a nonzero result means that an error occurred.

It will help to understand the following if you know a little about polynomial arithmetic; it is just slightly different from normal integer arithmetic. We first take $M(x)$ and multiply it by x^k, to obtain $x^{10} + x^7 + x^6 + x^4$, or 10011010000 in our example. Then we divide this by $C(x)$, which corresponds to 1101 in this case. Figure 3.13 shows the polynomial long division operation. This calculation is just like integer long division with two differences: $C(x)$ divides any polynomial $B(x)$ that is of the same degree as $C(x)$, and the remainder is the exclusive-OR (XOR) of $B(x)$ and $C(x)$. Thus in the first step of our example, we see that $C(x)$, which is 1101 in this case, divides into the polynomial 1001 since they are of the same degree, and leaves a remainder of 100 (1101 XOR 1001). The next step is to bring down digits from the message polynomial until we get another polynomial with the same degree as $C(x)$, calculate the remainder again, and continue until the calculation is complete.

You can see from Figure 3.13 that the remainder of the example calculation is 101. So we know that 10011010000 minus 101 would be exactly divisible by $C(x)$, and this is what we send. The minus operation in polynomial arithmetic is the logical XOR operation, so we actually send 10011010101. Note that this turns out to be just the original message with the remainder for the CRC calculation appended to it. The recipient divides the received polynomial $P(x) + E(x)$ by $C(x)$ and, if the result is 0, concludes that there were no errors. If the result is nonzero, it may be necessary to discard the errored message; with some codes, it may be possible to *correct* a small error (e.g., if the error affected only one bit). A code that enables error correction is called an *error-correcting code* or ECC.

Now we will consider the question of where the polynomial $C(x)$ comes from. Intuitively, the idea is to select this polynomial so that it does not divide evenly into a message that has errors introduced into it, or, said another way, we want to ensure that $C(x)$ does not divide evenly into polynomial $E(x)$ that represents the error. For example, an error in the single bit

CRC	$C(x)$
CRC-8	$x^8 + x^2 + x^1 + 1$
CRC-10	$x^{10} + x^9 + x^5 + x^4 + x^1 + 1$
CRC-12	$x^{12} + x^{11} + x^3 + x^2 + 1$
CRC-16	$x^{16} + x^{15} + x^2 + 1$
CRC-CCITT	$x^{16} + x^{12} + x^5 + 1$
CRC-32	$x^{32} + x^{26} + x^{23} + x^{22} + x^{16} + x^{12} + x^{11} +$ $x^{10} + x^8 + x^7 + x^5 + x^4 + x^2 + x + 1$

Table 3.4 Common CRC polynomials.

i can be expressed as $E(x) = x^i$. If we select $C(x)$ such that the first and the last term are nonzero, then we already have two terms that cannot divide evenly into the one term $E(x)$. Such a $C(x)$ can, therefore, detect all single-bit errors. In general, it is possible to prove the following statements about the errors that can be detected by a $C(x)$ with the stated properties:

- All single-bit errors, as long as the x^k and x^0 terms have nonzero coefficients.

- All double-bit errors, as long as $C(x)$ has a factor with at least three terms.

- Any odd number of errors, as long as $C(x)$ contains the factor $(x + 1)$.

- Any "burst" error (i.e., sequence of consecutive errored bits) for which the length of the burst is less than k bits. (Most burst errors of larger than k bits can also be detected.)

Six versions of $C(x)$ are widely used in link-level protocols. They are shown in Table 3.4. For example, the Ethernet and FDDI networks described later in this chapter use CRC-32, while HDLC uses CRC-CCITT. ATM, as described in Chapter 4, uses CRC-8 and CRC-10.

Finally, we note that the CRC algorithm, while seemingly complex, is easily implemented in hardware using a k-bit shift register and XOR gates.

3.4.2 Two-Dimensional Parity

Two-dimensional parity is exactly what the name suggests. Whereas simple parity involves adding an extra bit to a 7-bit code to balance the number of 1s in the byte—e.g., odd parity sets the eighth bit to 1 if needed to give an odd number of 1s in the byte, and even parity sets the eighth bit to 1 if needed to give an even number of 1s in the byte—two-dimensional parity does a similar calculation for each bit position across each of the bytes contained in the frame. This results in an extra parity byte for the entire frame, in addition to a parity bit for each

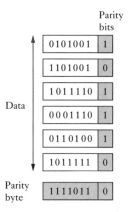

Figure 3.14 Two-dimensional parity.

byte. Figure 3.14 illustrates how two-dimensional, even parity works for an example frame containing 6 bytes of data. Notice that the third bit of the parity byte is 1 since there is an odd number of 1s in the third bit across the 6 bytes in the frame. Two-dimensional parity catches all 1-, 2-, and 3-bit errors, and most 4-bit errors.

3.4.3 Internet Checksum Algorithm

A third approach to error detection is exemplified by the Internet checksum. Although it is not used at the link level, it nevertheless provides the same sort of functionality as CRCs and parity, so we discuss it here. We will see examples of its use in Sections 5.2, 6.1, and 6.2.

The idea behind the Internet checksum is very simple—you add up all the words that are transmitted and then transmit the result of that sum. The result is called the *checksum*. The receiver performs the same calculation on the received data and compares the result with the received checksum. If any transmitted data, including the checksum itself, is corrupted, then the results will not match, so the receiver knows that an error occurred. Unlike CRCs, however, this checksum does not have very strong error detection properties. For example, the checksum will not detect any errors resulting from words being misordered.

You can imagine many different variations on the basic idea of a checksum. The exact scheme used by the Internet protocols works as follows. Consider the data being checksummed as a sequence of 16-bit integers. Add them together using 16-bit ones complement arithmetic (explained below) and then take the ones complement of the result. That 16-bit number is the checksum. The following routine gives a straightforward implementation of the Internet's checksum algorithm. The count argument gives the length of buf measured in 16-bit units. The routine assumes that buf has already been padded with 0s to a 16-bit boundary.

```
u_short
cksum(u_short *buf, int count)
{
    register u_long sum = 0;

    while (count--)
    {
        sum += *buf++;
        if (sum & 0xFFFF0000)
        {
            /* carry occurred, so wrap around */
            sum &= 0xFFFF;
            sum++;
        }
    }
    return ~(sum & 0xFFFF);
}
```

This code ensures that the calculation uses ones complement arithmetic, rather than the twos complement that is used in most machines. In ones complement arithmetic, a negative integer $-x$ is represented as the complement of x, i.e., each bit of x is inverted. When adding numbers in ones complement arithmetic, a carryout from the most significant bit needs to be added to the result. This is the reason for the if statement inside the while loop.

The reason for using an algorithm like this in spite of its weaker protection against errors than a CRC is simple: this algorithm is much easier to implement in software. Experience in the ARPANET suggested that a checksum of this form was adequate. One reason it is adequate is that this checksum is the last line of defense in an end-to-end protocol; the majority of errors are picked up by stronger error detection algorithms at the link level.

One final note on the word *checksum*. You can see that the Internet checksum is appropriately named: it is an error check that uses a summing algorithm. The word *checksum* is often used imprecisely to mean any form of error-detecting code, including CRCs. This can be confusing, so we urge you to use the word *checksum* only to apply to codes that actually do use addition and to use *error-detecting code* to refer to the general class of codes we have described in this section.

3.5 Reliable Transmission

As we saw in the previous section, frames are sometimes corrupted while in transit, with an error code like CRC used to detect such errors. While some error codes are strong enough also to correct errors, in practice the state of the art in error-correcting codes is not advanced enough to handle the range of bit and burst errors that can be introduced on a network link, and as a consequence, corrupt frames must be discarded. A link-level protocol that wants to deliver frames reliably must somehow recover from these discarded (lost) frames.

This is usually accomplished using a combination of two fundamental mechanisms—*acknowledgments* and *timeouts*. An acknowledgment (ACK for short) is a small control frame that a protocol sends back to its peer saying that it has received an earlier frame. By control frame we mean a header without any data, although a protocol can *piggyback* an ACK on a data frame it just happens to be sending in the opposite direction. The receipt of an acknowledgment indicates to the sender of the original frame that its frame was successfully delivered. If the sender does not receive an acknowledgment after a reasonable amount of time, then it *retransmits* the original frame. This action of waiting a reasonable amount of time is called a *timeout*.

The general strategy of using acknowledges and timeouts to implement reliable delivery is sometimes called *automatic repeat request*, normally abbreviated ARQ. This section describes three different ARQ algorithms using generic language; i.e., we do not give detailed information about a particular protocol's header fields.

3.5.1 Stop-and-Wait

The simplest ARQ scheme is the *stop-and-wait* algorithm. The idea of stop-and-wait is straightforward: after transmitting one frame, the sender waits for an acknowledgment before transmitting the next frame. If the acknowledgment does not arrive after a certain period of time, the sender times out and retransmits the original frame.

Figure 3.15 illustrates four different scenarios that result from this basic algorithm. This figure is a timeline, a common way to depict a protocol's behavior. The sending side is represented on the left, the receiving side is depicted on the right, and time flows from top to bottom. Figure 3.15(a) shows the situation in which the ACK is received before the timer expires, (b) and (c) show the situation in which the original frame and the ACK, respectively, are lost, and (d) shows the situation in which the timeout fires too soon. Recall that by "lost" we mean that the frame was corrupted while in transit, that this corruption was detected by an error code on the receiver, and that the frame was subsequently discarded.

There is one important subtlety in the stop-and-wait algorithm. Suppose the sender sends a frame and the receiver acknowledges it, but the acknowledgment is either lost or delayed in arriving. This situation is illustrated in timelines (c) and (d) of Figure 3.15. In both cases, the sender times out and retransmits the original frame, but the receiver will think that it is the next frame, since it correctly received and acknowledged the first frame. This has the potential to cause duplicate copies of a frame to be delivered. To address this problem, the header for a stop-and-wait protocol usually includes a 1-bit sequence number—i.e., the sequence number can take on the values 0 and 1—and the sequence numbers used for each frame alternate, as illustrated in Figure 3.16. Thus, when the sender retransmits frame 0, the receiver can determine that it is seeing a second copy of frame 0 rather than the first copy of frame 1 and therefore can ignore it (the receiver still acknowledges it).

The main shortcoming of the stop-and-wait algorithm is that it allows the sender to have only one outstanding frame on the link at a time, and this may be far below the link's capacity. Consider, for example, a 1.5-Mbps link with a 45-ms round-trip time (RTT). This

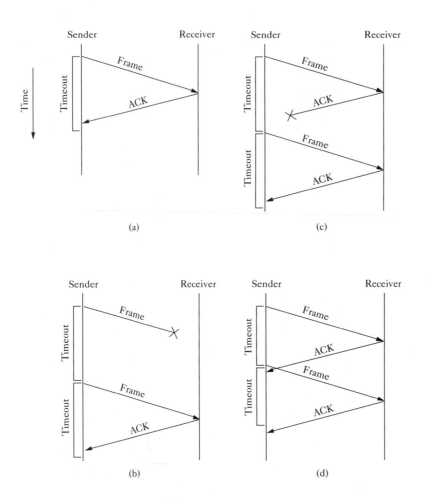

Figure 3.15 Timeline showing four different scenarios for the stop-and-wait algorithm. (a) The ACK is received before the timer expires; (b) the original frame is lost; (c) the ACK is lost; (d) the timeout fires too soon.

link has a delay $\times$ bandwidth product of 67.5 Kb, or approximately 8 KB. Since the sender can send only one frame per RTT, and assuming a frame size of 1 KB, this implies a maximum sending rate of $1024 \times 8/0.045 = 182$ Kbps, or about one-eighth of the link's capacity. To use the link fully, then, we'd like the sender to be able to transmit up to eight frames before having to wait for an acknowledgment.

The significance of the bandwidth $\times$ delay product is that it represents the amount of data that could be in transit. We would like to be able to send this much data without waiting for the first acknowledgment. The principle at work here is often referred to as *keeping the pipe full*. The algorithms presented in the following two subsections do exactly this.

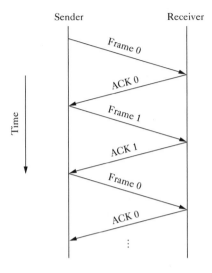

Figure 3.16 Timeline for stop-and-wait with 1-bit sequence number.

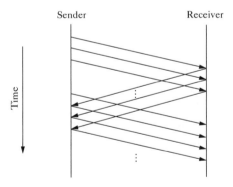

Figure 3.17 Timeline for the sliding window algorithm.

3.5.2 Sliding Window

Consider again the scenario in which the link has a delay × bandwidth product of 8 KB and frames are of 1 KB size. We would like the sender to be ready to transmit the ninth frame at pretty much the same moment that the ACK for the first frame arrives. The algorithm that allows us to do this is called *sliding window*, and an illustrative timeline is given in Figure 3.17.

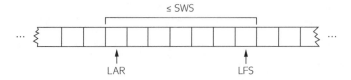

Figure 3.18   Sliding window on sender.

The Sliding Window Algorithm

The sliding window algorithm works as follows. First, the sender assigns a *sequence number*, denoted SeqNum, to each frame. For now, let's ignore the fact that SeqNum is implemented by a finite-size header field and instead assume that it can grow infinitely large. The sender maintains three variables: the *send window size*, denoted SWS, gives the upper bound on the number of outstanding (unacknowledged) frames that the sender can transmit; LAR denotes the sequence number of the *last acknowledgment received*; and LFS denotes the sequence number of the *last frame sent*. The sender also maintains the following invariant:

$$\text{LFS} - \text{LAR} + 1 \leq \text{SWS}.$$

This situation is illustrated in Figure 3.18.

When an acknowledgment arrives, the sender moves LAR to the right, thereby allowing the sender to transmit another frame. Also, the sender associates a timer with each frame it transmits, and it retransmits the frame should the timer expire before an ACK is received. Notice that the sender has to be willing to buffer up to SWS frames since it must be prepared to retransmit them until they are acknowledged.

The receiver maintains the following three variables: the *receive window size*, denoted RWS, gives the upper bound on the number of out-of-order frames that the receiver is willing to accept; LFA denotes the sequence number of the *last frame acceptable*; and NFE denotes the sequence number of the *next frame expected*. The receiver also maintains the following invariant:

$$\text{LFA} - \text{NFE} + 1 \leq \text{RWS}.$$

This situation is illustrated in Figure 3.19.

When a frame with sequence number SeqNum arrives, the receiver takes the following action. If SeqNum < NFE or SeqNum > LFA, then the frame is outside the receiver's window and it is discarded. If NFE $\leq$ SeqNum $\leq$ LFA, then the frame is within the receiver's window and it is accepted. Now the receiver needs to decide whether or not to send an ACK. Let SeqNumToAck denote the largest sequence number not yet acknowledged, such that all frames with sequence numbers less than SeqNumToAck have been received. The receiver acknowledges the receipt of SeqNumToAck, even if higher numbered packets have been received. This acknowledgment is said to be cumulative. It then sets NFE = SeqNumToAck + 1 and adjusts LFA = SeqNumToAck + RWS.

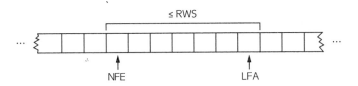

Figure 3.19 Sliding window on receiver.

For example, suppose NFE = 5 (i.e., the last ACK the receiver sent was for sequence number 4), and RWS = 4. This implies that LFA = 9. Should frames 6 and 7 arrive, they will be buffered because they are within the receiver's window. However, no ACK needs to be sent since frame 5 is yet to arrive. Frames 6 and 7 are said to have arrived out of order. (Technically, the receiver could resend an ACK for frame 4 when frames 6 and 7 arrive.) Should frame 5 then arrive—perhaps it is late because it was lost the first time and had to be retransmitted, or perhaps it was simply delayed—the receiver acknowledges frame 7, bumps NFE to 8, and sets LFA to 12. If frame 5 is in fact lost, then a timeout will occur at the sender and frame 5 will be resent. Because the sender has to backtrack by some number of frames (potentially as many as the window size), this scheme is known as *go-back-n*.

We observe that when a timeout occurs, the amount of data in transit decreases, since the sender is unable to advance its window until frame 5 is acknowledged. This means that when packet losses occur, this scheme is no longer keeping the pipe full. The longer it takes to notice that a packet loss has occurred, the more severe this problem becomes.

Notice that in this example, the receiver could have sent a *negative acknowledgment* (NAK) for frame 5 as soon as frame 6 arrived. However, this is unnecessary since the sender's timeout mechanism is sufficient to catch this situation, and sending NAKs adds additional complexity to the receiver. Also, as we mentioned, it would have been legitimate to send additional acknowledgments of frame 4 when frames 6 and 7 arrived; in some cases, a sender can use duplicate ACKs as a clue that a frame was lost. Both approaches help to improve performance by allowing early detection of packet losses.

Yet another variation on this scheme would be to use *selective acknowledgments*. That is, the receiver could acknowledge exactly those frames it has received, rather than just the highest-numbered frame received in order. So, in the above example, the receiver could acknowledge the receipt of frames 6 and 7. Giving more information to the sender makes it potentially easier for the sender to keep the pipe full, but adds complexity to the implementation.

The sending window size is selected according to how many frames we want to have outstanding on the link at a given time; SWS is easy to compute for a given delay × bandwidth product.[1] On the other hand, the receiver can set RWS to whatever it wants. Two common

---

[1]Easy, that is, if we know the delay and the bandwidth. Sometimes we do not, and estimating them well is a challenge to protocol designers. We discuss this further in Chapter 6.

settings are RWS = 1, which implies that the receiver will not buffer any frames that arrive out of order, and RWS = SWS, which implies that the receiver can buffer any of the frames the sender transmits.

Finite Sequence Numbers and Sliding Window

We now have to return to the one simplification we introduced into the algorithm—our assumption that sequence numbers can grow infinitely large. In practice, of course, a frame's sequence number is specified in a header field of some finite size. For example, a 3-bit field means that there are eight possible sequence numbers, $0 \ldots 7$. This makes it necessary to reuse sequence numbers, or, stated another way, sequence numbers wrap around. This introduces the problem of being able to distinguish between different incarnations of the same sequence numbers, which implies that the number of possible sequence numbers must be larger than the number of outstanding frames allowed. For example, stop-and-wait allowed one outstanding frame at a time and had two distinct sequence numbers.

Suppose we have one more number in our space of sequence numbers than we have potentially outstanding frames; i.e., SWS $\leq$ MaxSeqNum - 1, where MaxSeqNum is the number of available sequence numbers. Is this sufficient? The answer is no. To see this, consider the situation in which we have the eight sequence numbers 0 through 7, and SWS = RWS = 7. Suppose the sender transmits frames 0..6, they are successfully received, but the ACKs are lost. The receiver is now expecting frames 7,0..5, but the sender times out and sends frames 0..6. Unfortunately, the receiver is expecting the second incarnation of frames 0..5, but gets the first incarnation of these frames. This is exactly the situation we wanted to avoid.

It turns out that the sending window size can be no more than half as big as the number of available sequence numbers, or stated more precisely,

$$\text{SWS} < (\text{MaxSeqNum} + 1)/2.$$

Intuitively, what this is saying is that the sliding window protocol alternates between the two halves of the sequence number space, just as stop-and-wait alternates between sequence numbers 0 and 1. The only difference is that it continually slides between the two halves rather than discretely alternating between them.

Implementation of Sliding Window

The following code sequences show the x-kernel routines that implement the sending and receiving sides of the sliding window algorithm. The routines are taken from a working x-kernel protocol named, appropriately enough, Sliding Window Protocol (SWP).

We start by defining a pair of data structures. First, the frame header is very simple: it contains a sequence number (SeqNum) and an acknowledgment number (AckNum). It also contains a Flags field that indicates whether the frame is an ACK or carries data.

```
typedef u_char  SwpSeqno;

typedef struct {
    SwpSeqno    SeqNum;         /* sequence number of this frame */
    SwpSeqno    AckNum;         /* ack of received frame */
    u_char      Flags;          /* up to 8 bits worth of flags */
} SwpHdr;
```

Next, the state of the sliding window algorithm has the following structure. For the sending side of the protocol, this state includes variables **LAR** and **LFS**, as described earlier in this section, as well as a queue that holds frames that have been transmitted but not yet acknowledged (**txq**). The sending state also includes a *semaphore* called **sendWindowNotFull**. We will see how this is used below.

For the receiving side of the protocol, the state includes the variable **NFE**, as described earlier in this section, plus a queue that holds frames that have been received out of order (**rxq**). Finally, although not shown, the sender and receiver sliding window sizes are defined by constants **SWS** and **RWS**, respectively.

```
typedef struct {
    /* sender side state: */
    SwpSeqno    LAR;                /* seqno of last ACK received */
    SwpSeqno    LFS;                /* last frame sent */
    Semaphore   sendWindowNotFull;
    SwpHdr      hdr;                /* pre-initialized header */
    struct txq_slot {
        Event   timeout;           /* event associated with send-timeout */
        Sessn   lls;               /* session to resend message on */
        Msg     msg;
    } txq[SWS];

    /* receiver side state: */
    SwpSeqno    NFE;                /* seqno of next frame expected */
    struct rxq_slot {
        int     received;          /* is msg valid? */
        Msg     msg;
    } rxq[RWS];
} SState;
```

The sending side of SWP is implemented by procedure **swpPush**. This routine is rather simple. First, **semWait** causes this process to block until it is OK to send another frame. Once allowed to proceed, **swpPush** sets the sequence number in the frame's header, saves a copy of the frame in the transmit queue, sends the frame to the next-lower-level protocol, and schedules a timeout event to handle the case in which the frame is not acknowledged.

The one piece of complexity in this routine is the use of **semWait** and the **sendWindowNotFull** semaphore. **sendWindowNotFull** is a *counting semaphore* that is initialized to the size of the sender's sliding window (**SWS**). Each time the sender transmits a frame, the semWait operation decrements this count and blocks the sender should the count go to 0. Each time an ACK is received, the semSignal operation invoked in swpPop (see below) increments this count, thus unblocking any waiting sender.

```
static XkReturn
swpPush(Sessn s, Msg *msg)
{
    SwpState *state = (SwpState *)s->state;
    struct txq_slot *slot;

    /* wait for send window to open before sending anything */
    semWait(&state->sendWindowNotFull);
    state->hdr.SeqNum = ++state->LFS;
    slot = &state->txq[state->hdr.SeqNum % SWS];
    bcopy(&state->hdr, msgPush(msg, sizeof(SwpHdr)), sizeof(SwpHdr));
    msgConstructCopy(&slot->msg, msg);
    slot->lls = xGetDown(s, 0);
    slot->timeout = evSchedule(swpTimeout, slot, SWP_SEND_TIMEOUT);
    return xPush(slot->lls, msg);
}
```

The receiving side of SWP is implemented in the x-kernel routine swpPop. This routine actually handles two different kinds of incoming messages: ACKs for frames sent earlier from this node and data frames arriving at this node. In a sense, the ACK half of this routine is the counterpart to the sender side of the algorithm given in swpPush. A decision as to whether the incoming message is an ACK or a data frame is made by checking the Flags field in the header. Note that this particular implementation does not support piggybacking ACKs on data frames.

When the incoming frame is an ACK, swpPop simply finds the slot in the transmit queue (txq) that corresponds to the ACK, and both frees the frame saved there and cancels the timeout event. This work is actually done in a loop since the ACK may be cumulative. The only other thing to notice about this case is the call to subroutine swpInWindow. This subroutine, which is given below, ensures that the sequence number for the frame being acknowledged is within the range of ACKs that the sender currently expects to receive.

When the incoming frame contains data, swpPop first calls swpInWindow to make sure the sequence number of the frame is within the range of sequence numbers that it expects. If it is, the routine loops over the set of consecutive frames it has received and passes them up to the higher-level protocol by invoking the xDemux routine. It also sends a cumulative ACK back to the sender, but does so by looping over the receive queue (it does not use the SeqNumToAck variable used in the prose description given earlier in this section).

```
static XkReturn
swpPop(Sessn s, Sessn ds, Msg *dg, void *inHdr)
{
    SwpState *state = (SwpState *)s->state;
```

```
SwpHdr   *hdr = (SwpHdr *)inHdr;

if (hdr->Flags & FLAG_ACK_VALID)
{
    /* received an acknowledgment---do SENDER-side */
    if (swpInWindow(hdr->AckNum, state->LAR + 1, state->LFS))
    {
        do
        {
            struct txq_slot *slot;

            slot = &state->txq[++state->LAR % SWS];
            evCancel(slot->timeout);
            msgDestroy(&slot->msg);
            semSignal(&state->sendWindowNotFull);
        } while (state->LAR != hdr->AckNum);
    }
}
if (hdr->Flags & FLAG_HAS_DATA)
{
    struct rxq_slot *slot;

    /* received data packet---do RECEIVER side */
    slot = &state->rxq[hdr->SeqNum % RWS];
    if (!swpInWindow(hdr->SeqNum, state->NFE, state->NFE + RWS - 1))
    {
        /* drop the message */
        return XK_SUCCESS;
    }
    msgConstructCopy(&slot->msg, dg);
    slot->received = TRUE;
    if (hdr->SeqNum == state->NFE)
    {
        SwpHdr ackhdr;
        Msg m;

        while (slot->received)
        {
            xDemux(xGetUp(s), s, &slot->msg);
            msgDestroy(&slot->msg);
            slot->received = FALSE;
            slot = &state->rxq[++state->NFE % RWS];
        }
        /* send ACK: */
        ackhdr.AckNum = state->NFE - 1;
        ackhdr.Flags = FLAG_ACK_VALID;
        msgConstructBuffer(&m, (char *)&ackhdr, sizeof(ackhdr));
        xPush(ds, &m);
```

```
        msgDestroy(&m);
      }
   }
   return XK_SUCCESS;
}
```

Finally, **swpInWindow** is a simple subroutine that checks to see if a given sequence number falls between some minimum and maximum sequence number.

```
static bool
swpInWindow(SwpSeqno seqno, SwpSeqno min, SwpSeqno max)
{
    SwpSeqno pos, maxpos;

    pos   = seqno - min;       /* pos *should* be in range [0..MAX) */
    maxpos = max - min + 1;    /* maxpos is in range [0..MAX] */
    return pos < maxpos;
}
```

Frame Order and Flow Control

The sliding window protocol is perhaps the best-known algorithm in computer networking.
What is easily confusing about the algorithm, however, is that it can used to serve three different roles. The first role is the one we have been concentrating on in this section—to reliably
deliver frames across an unreliable link. (In general, the algorithm can be used to reliably deliver messages across an unreliable network.) This is the core function of the algorithm.

The second role that the sliding window algorithm can serve is to preserve the order
in which frames are transmitted. This is easy to do at the receiver—since each frame has a
sequence number, the receiver just makes sure that it does not pass a frame up to the next-
higher-level protocol until it has already passed up all frames with a smaller sequence number.
That is, the receiver buffers (i.e., does not pass along) out-of-order frames. The version of the
sliding window algorithm described in this section does preserve frame order, although one
could imagine a variation in which the receiver passes frames to the next protocol without
waiting for all earlier frames to be delivered. A question we should ask ourselves is whether we
really need the sliding window protocol to keep the frames in order, or whether, instead, this
is unnecessary functionality at the link level. Unfortunately, we have not yet seen enough of
the network architecture to answer this question—we first need to understand how a sequence
of point-to-point links is connected by switches to form an end-to-end path.

The third role that the sliding window algorithm sometimes plays is to support *flow
control*—a feedback mechanism by which the receiver is able to throttle the sender. Such a
mechanism is used to keep the sender from overrunning the receiver, that is, from transmitting
more data than the receiver is able to process. This is usually accomplished by augmenting the
sliding window protocol so that the receiver not only acknowledges frames it has received, but
also informs the sender of how many frames it has room to receive. The number of frames
that the receiver is capable of receiving corresponds to how much free buffer space it has. As

in the case of ordered delivery, we need to make sure that flow control is necessary at the link level before incorporating it into the sliding window protocol.

One important thing to take away from this discussion is the system design principle we call *separation of concerns*. That is, you must be careful to distinguish between different functions that are sometimes rolled together in one mechanism, and you must make sure that each function is necessary and being supported in the most effective way. In this particular case, reliable delivery, ordered delivery, and flow control are sometimes combined in a single sliding window protocol, and we should ask ourselves if this is the right thing to do at the link level. With this question in mind, we revisit the sliding window algorithm in Chapter 4 (we show how X.25 networks use it to implement hop-by-hop flow control) and in Chapter 6 (we describe how TCP uses it to implement a reliable byte-stream channel).

3.5.3 Concurrent Logical Channels

The IMP-IMP protocol used in the ARPANET provides an interesting alternative to the sliding window protocol, in that it is able to keep the pipe full while still using the simple stop-and-wait algorithm. One important consequence of this approach is that the frames sent over a given link are not kept in any particular order. The IMP-IMP protocol also implies nothing about flow control.

The idea underlying the IMP-IMP protocol, which we refer to as *concurrent logical channels*, is to multiplex several logical channels onto a single point-to-point link and to run the stop-and-wait algorithm on each of these logical channels. There is no relationship maintained among the frames sent on any of the logical channels, yet because a different frame can be outstanding on each of the several logical channels, the sender can keep the link full.

More precisely, the sender keeps three bits of state for each channel: a boolean, saying whether the channel is currently busy; the 1-bit sequence number to use the next time a frame is sent on this logical channel; and the next sequence number to expect on a frame that arrives on this channel. When the node has a frame to send, it uses the lowest idle channel, and otherwise it behaves just like stop-and-wait.

In practice, the ARPANET supported eight logical channels over each ground link and 16 over each satellite link. In the ground-link case, the header for each frame included a 3-bit channel number and a 1-bit sequence number, for a total of 4 bits. This is exactly the number of bits the sliding window protocol requires to support up to eight outstanding frames on the link.

3.6 CSMA/CD (Ethernet)

Easily the most successful local area networking technology of the last 20 years is the Ethernet. Developed in the mid-1970s by researchers at the Xerox Palo Alto Research Center (PARC), the Ethernet is a working example of the more general Carrier Sense, Multiple Access with Collision Detect (CSMA/CD) local area network technology. The Ethernet supports a transmission rate of 10 Mbps. This section focuses on the most common or "classic" form of Ethernet. While the basic algorithms have not changed, Ethernet has adapted over the years to run at a variety of speeds and over a range of physical media.

As indicated by the CSMA name, the Ethernet is a multiple access network (a set of nodes send and receive frames over a shared link). You can, therefore, think of an Ethernet as being like a bus that has multiple stations plugged into it. The "carrier sense" in CSMA/CD means that all the nodes can distinguish between an idle and a busy link, and "collision detect" means that a node listens as it transmits and can therefore detect when a frame it is transmitting has interfered (collided) with a frame transmitted by another node.

The Ethernet has its roots in an early packet-radio network, called Aloha, developed at the University of Hawaii to support computer communication across the Hawaiian islands. Like the Aloha network, the fundamental problem faced by the Ethernet is how to mediate access to a shared medium fairly and efficiently (in Aloha the medium was the atmosphere, while in Ethernet the medium is a coax cable). That is, the core idea in both Aloha and the Ethernet is an algorithm that controls when each node can transmit.

3.6.1 Physical Properties

A segment of Ethernet is implemented on a coaxial cable of up to 500 meters (m). This cable is similar to the type used for cable TV, except that it typically has an impedance of 50 ohms instead of cable TV's 75 ohms. Hosts connect to an Ethernet segment by tapping into it; taps must be at least 2.5 m apart. A *transceiver*—a small device directly attached to the tap—detects when the line is idle and drives the signal when the host is transmitting. The transceiver is, in turn, connected to an Ethernet adaptor, which is plugged into the host. All the logic that makes up the Ethernet protocol, as described in this section, is implemented in the adaptor (not the transceiver).

Multiple Ethernet segments can be joined together by *repeaters*. A repeater is a device that forwards digital signals, much like an amplifier forwards analog signals. However, no more than two repeaters may be positioned between any pair of hosts, meaning that an Ethernet has a total reach of only 1500 m. Having two repeaters between any pair of hosts does support a configuration similar to the one illustrated in Figure 3.20, i.e., a segment running down the spine of a building with a segment on each floor. All told, an Ethernet is limited to supporting a maximum of 1024 hosts.

Any signal placed on the Ethernet by a host is broadcast over the entire network; i.e., the signal is propagated in both directions and repeaters forward the signal on all outgoing segments. Terminators attached to the end of each segment absorb the signal and keep it from bouncing back and interfering with trailing signals. The Ethernet uses the Manchester encoding scheme described in Section 3.2.

We refer to the Ethernet just described as "classic" because alternative technologies have been introduced over the years. For example, rather than using a 50-ohm coax cable, an Ethernet can be constructed from a thinner cable known as 10Base2; the original cable is called 10Base5 (the two cables are commonly called *thin-net* and *thick-net*, respectively). The "10" in 10Base2 means that the network operates at 10 Mbps, "Base" refers to the fact that the cable

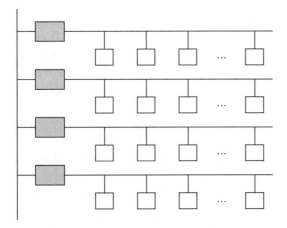

Figure 3.20 Ethernet repeater.

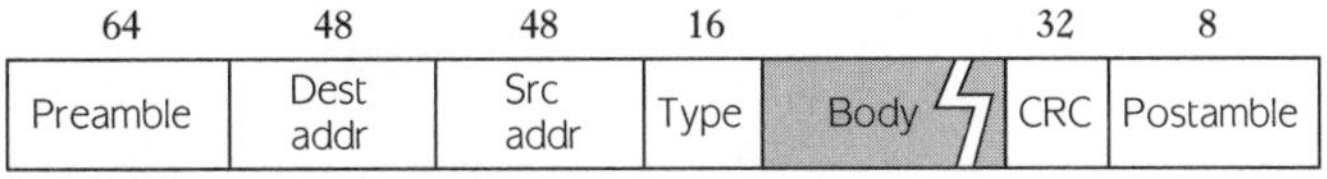

64	48	48	16		32	8
Preamble	Dest addr	Src addr	Type	Body	CRC	Postamble

Figure 3.21 Ethernet frame format.

is used in a *baseband* system, and the "2" means that a given segment can be no longer than 200 m (a segment of the original 10Base5 cable can be up to 500 m long). An even newer technology is called 10BaseT, where the "T" stands for twisted pair. 10BaseT is similar to the line coming into a standard telephone, although a bit thicker. A 10BaseT segment is usually limited to under 100 m in length.

Because the cable is so thin, you do not tap into a 10Base2 or 10BaseT cable in the same way as you would with 10Base5 cable. With 10Base2, a T-joint is spliced into the cable. In effect, 10Base2 is used to daisy-chain a set of hosts together. With 10BaseT, the common configuration is to have several point-to-point segments coming out of a multiway repeater.

3.6.2 Access Protocol

We now turn our attention to the Ethernet protocol implemented in hardware on the network adaptor. We will not describe the hardware per se, but instead focus on the algorithm it implements.

Frame Format

Each Ethernet frame is defined by the format given in Figure 3.21. The 64-bit preamble allows the receiver to synchronize with the signal; it is a sequence of alternating 0s and 1s. Both the source and destination hosts are identified with a 48-bit address. The packet type field serves as the demultiplexing key, that is, it identifies to which of possibly many higher-level protocols this frame should be delivered. Each frame contains up to 1500 bytes of data. Minimally, a frame must contain at least 46 bytes of data, even if this means the host has

to pad the frame before transmitting it. The reason for this minimum frame size is that the frame must be long enough to detect a collision; we discuss this more below. Finally, each frame includes a 32-bit CRC and an 8-bit postamble that denotes the end of the frame. Like the HDLC protocol described in Section 3.3.2, the Ethernet is a bit-oriented framing protocol. Note that from the host's perspective, an Ethernet frame has a 14-byte header: two 6-byte addresses and a 2-byte type field. The sending adaptor attaches the preamble, CRC, and postamble before transmitting, and the receiving adaptor removes them.

The frame format just described is taken from the Ethernet standard defined collectively by Xerox, Digital Equipment Corporation, and Intel Corporation in 1978. A similar standard, known as IEEE 802.3, was later defined. The two standards are essentially equivalent, except 802.3 substitutes a 16-bit length field for the Ethernet's 16-bit type field. This length field is used to determine how long the frame is, rather than depending on the end-of-frame marker;

Future of the Ethernet

An interesting question today is whether or not the Ethernet has a future as the network of choice for local area environments. The problem, of course, is that 10 Mbps is no longer considered particularly high speed. While no one knows for sure, we can point to two ways in which the Ethernet has evolved in an effort to survive.

The first thing to have happened is that Ethernets have been configured with a single host per segment, with a switch being used to connect several segments together. As long as the switch has enough aggregate capacity to support all the hosts/segments connected to it, each host effectively gets

802.3 uses information in the data portion of the message to demultiplex the frame. In practice, the Ethernet standard, not 802.3, is the dominant format in use. Interestingly, since the Ethernet standard has avoided using any type values less than 1500 (the maximum length found in an 802.3 header), it is possible to distinguish between the two formats.

Addresses

Each host on an Ethernet—in fact, every Ethernet host in the world—has a unique Ethernet address. Technically, the address belongs to the adaptor, not the host—it is burned into ROM. Ethernet addresses are typically printed in a form humans can read as a sequence of six numbers separated by colons. Each number corresponds to 1 byte of the 6-byte address, and is given by a pair of hexadecimal digits, one for each of the 4-bit nibbles in the byte; leading 0s are dropped. For example, 8:0:2b:e4:b1:2 is the human-readable representation of Ethernet address:

$$00001000 \quad 00000000 \quad 00101011$$
$$11100100 \quad 10110001 \quad 00000010.$$

To ensure that each adaptor gets a unique address, each of the manufacturers of Ethernet devices is allocated a different prefix that must be prepended to the address on every adaptor they build. For example, Advanced Micro Devices (AMD) has been assigned the 20-bit prefix x08002 (or 8:0:2). A given manufacturer then makes sure the address suffixes it produces are unique.

access to a private 10-Mbps link. It does not have to share this bandwidth with other hosts. While 10 Mbps is not considered particularly fast in a world of 622-Mbps STS-12 links, it does provide each host with enough network capacity to drive half a dozen compressed video streams.

The second thing is that the Ethernet has adapted over the years to run at a variety of speeds, up to and including 100 Mbps. This is done without changing the basic protocol. One hundred Mbps certainly makes the Ethernet competitive with FDDI networks (see the next section), and when coupled with switching, puts it in the same ballpark as a 155-Mbps ATM network (see the next chapter).

Each frame transmitted on an Ethernet is received by every adaptor connected to that Ethernet. Each adaptor recognizes those frames addressed to its address and passes only those frames on to the host. (An adaptor can be programmed to run in *promiscuous* mode, in which case it delivers all received frames to the host.) In addition to these *unicast* addresses, an Ethernet address consisting of all 1s is treated as a *broadcast* address; all adaptors pass frames addressed to the broadcast address up to the host. Similarly, an address that has the first bit set to 1 but is not the broadcast address is called a *multicast* address. A given host can program its adaptor to accept some set of multicast addresses. Multicast addresses are used to send messages to some subset of the hosts on an Ethernet; e.g., all file servers. To summarize, an Ethernet adaptor receives all frames, and accepts

■ frames addressed to its own address;

■ frames addressed to the broadcast address;

■ frames addressed to a multicast address, if it has been instructed to listen to that address;

■ all frames, if it has been placed in promiscuous mode.

It passes to the host only the frames that it accepts.

Transmitter Algorithm

As we have just seen, the receiver side of the Ethernet protocol is simple; the real smarts are implemented at the sender's side. The transmitter algorithm is defined as follows.

When the adaptor has a frame to send and the line is idle, it transmits the frame immediately; there is no negotiation with the other adaptors. The upper bound of 1500 bytes in the message means that the adaptor can occupy the line for only a fixed length of time Moreover, an adaptor must wait at least 51 μs before it can transmit another frame. This gives other adaptors a chance to send their frames and therefore keeps any one adaptor from sending back-to-back frames so close together that it is able to maintain continuous control of the network.

When an adaptor has a frame to send and the line is busy, it waits for the line to go idle and then transmits immediately. The Ethernet is said to be a *1-persistent* protocol because an adaptor with a frame to send transmits with probability 1 whenever a busy line goes idle. In general, a *p-persistent* algorithm transmits with probability $0 \leq p \leq 1$ after a line becomes idle. The reasoning behind choosing a $p < 1$ is that there might be multiple adaptors waiting for the busy line to become idle, and we don't want all of them to begin transmitting at the same time. If each adaptor transmits immediately with a probability of, say, 33%, then up to three adaptors can be waiting to transmit and the odds are that only one will begin transmitting when the line becomes idle. Despite this reasoning, an Ethernet adaptor always transmits immediately after noticing that the network has become idle and has been very effective in doing so.

Because there is no centralized control, it is possible for two (or more) adaptors to begin transmitting at the same time, either because both found the line to be idle or because both had been waiting for a busy line to become idle. When this happens, the two (or more) frames are said to collide on the network. Each sender, because the Ethernet supports collision detection, is able to determine that a collision is in progress. At the moment an adaptor detects that its frame is colliding with another, it first makes sure to transmit at least 512 bits of the frame and then stops the transmission.

This 512-bit minimum jam time comes from the fact that on a maximally sized Ethernet of 1500 m, the delay from one end to the other can be as high as 51.2 μs. This is enough time on a 10-Mbps network to transmit 512 bits; i.e., the delay × bandwidth of Ethernet is 512 bits. Because we want to make sure that two transmitting adaptors on opposite ends of the Ethernet both detect that a collision has occurred, they both need to transmit enough bits to fill the Ethernet pipe—512 bits. This need to transmit a minimum of 512 bits explains why every Ethernet frame must contain at least 46 bytes of data: 14 bytes of header plus 46 bytes of data plus 4 bytes of CRC equals 64 bytes, or 512 bits.

Notice that the fact that a maximally sized Ethernet's delay × bandwidth product is 512 bits also explains why an adaptor must wait 51.2 μs between sending back-to-back frames—it must wait long enough for the pipe to empty so that other nodes have a chance to transmit.

Once an adaptor has detected a collision and stopped its transmission, it waits a certain amount of time and tries again. Each time it tries to transmit but fails, the adaptor doubles the amount of time it waits before trying again. This strategy of doubling the delay interval between each retransmission attempt is a general technique known as *exponential backoff*. More precisely, the adaptor first delays an amount of time uniformly distributed between 0 and 51.2 μs. If this effort fails, it then waits an amount of time uniformly distributed between 0 and 102.4 μs before trying again; then between 0 and 204.8 μs; and so on. The adaptor gives up after a given number of tries (usually 16), and reports a transmit error to the host.

3.6.3 Experience with Ethernet

Because Ethernets have been around for so many years and are so popular, we have a great deal of experience in using them. One of the most important observations people have made about Ethernets is that they work best under lightly loaded conditions. This is because under heavy loads—typically, a utilization of over 30% is considered heavy on an Ethernet—too much of the network's capacity is wasted by collisions.

Fortunately, most Ethernets are used in a far more conservative way than the standard allows. For example, most Ethernets have fewer than 200 hosts connected to them, which is far fewer than the maximum of 1024. (See if you can discover a reason for this upper limit of around 200 hosts in Chapter 5.) Similarly, most Ethernets are far shorter than 1500 m, with a propagation delay of closer to 5 μs than 51.2 μs. Another factor that makes Ethernets practical is that, even though Ethernet adaptors do not implement link-level flow control, the hosts typically provide an end-to-end flow control mechanism. As a result, it is rare to find situations in which any one host is continuously pumping frames onto the network.

Finally, it is worth saying a few words about why Ethernets have been so successful, so that we can understand the properties we should emulate with any LAN technology that tries to replace it. First, an Ethernet is extremely easy to administer and maintain: there are no switches that can fail, no routing or configuration tables that have to be kept up to date, and it is easy to add a new host to the network. It is going to be a major challenge to make any of the switch-based networks described in the next chapter this simple to operate. Second, it is inexpensive: cable is cheap and the only other cost is the network adaptor on each host. Again, any switch-based approach will involve an investment in an expensive infrastructure (the switches), in addition to the incremental cost of each adaptor.

3.7 Token Rings (FDDI)

Alongside the Ethernet, token rings are the other significant class of shared media network. There are more different types of token rings than there are types of Ethernet; this section will discuss only one type in detail—FDDI (Fiber Distributed Data Interface). Earlier token ring networks include the 10-Mbps and 80-Mbps PRONET ring, IBM's 4-Mbps token ring, and the 16-Mbps IEEE 802.5 token ring. In many respects, the ideas embodied in FDDI are a superset of the ideas found in any other token ring network. This makes FDDI a good example for studying token rings in general.

As the name suggests, a token ring network like FDDI consists of a set of nodes connected in a ring. (See Figure 3.22.) Data always flows in a particular direction around the ring, with each node receiving frames from its upstream neighbor and then forwarding them to its

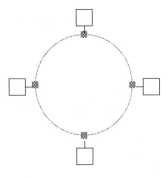

Figure 3.22   Token ring network.

downstream neighbor. This ring-based topology is in contrast to the Ethernet's bus topology. Like the Ethernet, however, the ring is viewed as a single shared medium; it does not behave as a collection of independent point-to-point links that just happen to be configured in a loop. Thus, a token ring shares two key features with an Ethernet: first, it involves a distributed algorithm that controls when each node is allowed to transmit, and second, all nodes see all frames, with the node identified in the frame header as the destination saving a copy of the frame as it flows past.

The term *token* in token ring comes from the way access to the shared ring is managed. The idea is that a token, which is really just a special sequence of bits (e.g., 01111110) circulates around the ring; each node receives and then forwards the token. When a node that has a frame to transmit sees the token, it takes the token off the ring (i.e., it does not forward the special bit pattern) and instead inserts its frame into the ring. Each node along the way simply forwards the frame, with the destination node saving a copy and forwarding the message onto the next node on the ring. When the frame makes its way back around to the sender, this node strips its frame off the ring (rather than continuing to forward it) and reinserts the token. In this way, some node downstream will have the opportunity to transmit a frame. The media access algorithm is fair in the sense that as the token circulates around the ring, each node gets a chance to transmit. Nodes are serviced in a round robin fashion.

3.7.1   Physical Properties

Unlike the simple illustration given in Figure 3.22, an FDDI ring can have a more complex configuration than one might imagine. First, an FDDI network really consists of a dual ring—two independent rings that transmit data in opposite directions, as illustrated in Figure 3.23(a). The second ring is not used during normal operation but instead comes into play only if the primary ring fails, as depicted in Figure 3.23(b). That is, the ring loops back on the secondary fiber to form a complete ring, and as a consequence, an FDDI network is able to tolerate a single break in the cable.

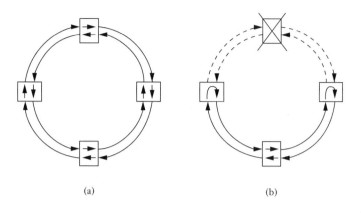

(a)   (b)

Figure 3.23   Dual-fiber ring.

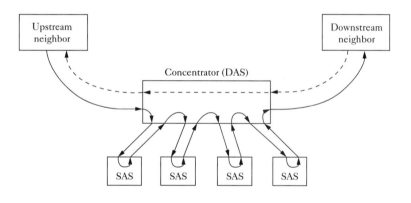

Figure 3.24   SASs connected to a concentrator.

Each node is connected to the ring by four fibers—one coming in and one going out for the primary ring, and one coming in and one going out for the secondary ring. These four fibers are actually bundled into two cables, one running to each of the node's two neighbors. Also, these cables attach to an FDDI network adaptor (rather than to the host itself). The FDDI protocol described in Section 3.7.2 is implemented on this adaptor.

The second complexity in the configuration of an FDDI ring is that because of the expense of the dual-ring configuration, FDDI allows nodes to attach to the network by means of a single cable. Such nodes are called *single attachment stations* (SAS); their dual-connected counterparts are called, not surprisingly, *dual attachment stations* (DAS). A concentrator is used to attach several SASs to the dual ring, as illustrated in Figure 3.24. Notice how the single-cable (two-fiber) connection into an SAS forms a connected piece of the ring. Should this SAS fail, the concentrator detects this situation and uses an *optical bypass* to isolate the failed SAS, thereby keeping the ring connected. Also note that in this illustration, the second (backup) ring is denoted with a dotted line.

The third complexity is that each station implements a small *elasticity buffer* that temporarily holds the bits of a frame as they pass through the station. This allows frames to be sent over the ring without all the stations having to be synchronized: the buffer separates the receipt of bits from the upstream neighbor from the transmission of bits to the downstream neighbor. The buffer needs to be able to hold at least 9 bits but is sometimes as large as 80 bits. Note that this elasticity buffer means that each station introduces delay into the time it takes data to circulate around the ring. For example, because FDDI is a 100-Mbps network, it has a 10-nanosecond (ns) bit time (each bit is 10 ns wide). If each station implements a 10-bit buffer, and waits for the buffer to be half full before starting to transmit, then each station introduces a $5 \times 10\,\text{ns} = 50\,\text{ns}$ delay into the total ring rotation time.

FDDI has other physical characteristics. For example, the standard limits a single network to at most 500 stations (hosts), with a maximum distance of 2 km between any pair of stations. Overall, the network is limited to a total of 200 km of fiber, which means that, because of the dual nature of the ring, the total amount of cable connecting all stations is limited to 100 km. Also, although the "F" in FDDI implies that optical fiber serves as the underlying physical medium, the standard has been defined to run over a number of different physical media, including coax and twisted pair. Of course, you still have to be careful about the total distance covered by the ring. As we will see in Section 3.7.2, the amount of time it takes the token to traverse the network plays an important role in the access-control algorithm.

FDDI uses 4B/5B encoding, as discussed in Section 3.2 of this chapter. Since FDDI was the first popular networking technology to use fiber, and 4B/5B chipsets operating at FDDI rates became widely available, 4B/5B has enjoyed considerable popularity as an encoding scheme for fiber.

3.7.2 Timed-Token Algorithm

The actual access-control algorithm used by FDDI is more complicated than the brief description given in the introduction to this section. We now develop this algorithm more thoroughly.

The first issue we must address is how much data a given node is allowed to transmit each time it possesses the token, or said another way, how long a given node is allowed to hold the token. We call this the *token holding time* (THT). If we assume that most nodes on the network do not have data to send at any given time—a reasonable assumption, and certainly one that the Ethernet takes advantage of—then we could make a case for letting a node that possesses the token transmit as much data as it has before passing the token on to the next node. This would mean setting the THT to infinity. It would be silly in this case to limit a node to sending a single message, and to force it to wait until the token circulates all the way around the ring before getting a chance to send another message. Of course, "as much data as it has" would be dangerous because a single station could keep the token for an arbitrarily long time, but we could certainly set the THT to some very large value.

It is easy to see that the more bytes a node can send each time it has the token, the better the utilization of the ring you can achieve in the situation in which only a single node has data to send. The downside, of course, is that this strategy does not work well when multiple nodes have data to send—it favors nodes that have a lot of data to send over nodes that have only a small message to send, even when it is important to get this small message delivered as soon as possible. The situation is analogous to finding yourself in line at the bank behind a customer who is taking out a car loan, even though you simply want to cash a check.

Overall, it is possible to define the *token rotation time* (TRT) to be the amount of time it takes a token to traverse the ring as viewed by a given node. It is easy to see that

$$\text{TRT} \leq \text{ActiveNodes} \times \text{THT} + \text{RingLatency}$$

where RingLatency denotes how long it takes the token to circulate around the ring when no one has data to send and ActiveNodes denotes the number of nodes that have data to transmit.

To ensure that a given node has the opportunity to transmit within a certain amount of time—that is, to put an upper bound on the TRT observed by any node—we define a *target token rotation time*, denoted TTRT, and all nodes agree to live within the limits of the TTRT. (How the nodes agree to a particular TTRT is described in the next subsection.) Specifically, each node measures the time between successive arrivals of the token. We call this the node's *measured* TRT. If this measured TRT is greater than the agreed upon TTRT, then the token is late, and the node does not transmit any data. If this measured TRT is less than the TTRT, then the token is early, and the node is allowed to hold the token for the difference between TTRT and the measured TRT.

Although it may seem that we are now done, the algorithm we have just developed does not ensure that a node concerned with sending a frame with a bounded delay will actually be able to do so. The problem is that a node with lots of data to send has the opportunity, upon seeing an early token, to hold the token for so long that by the time a downstream node gets the token, its measured TRT is equal to or exceeds the TTRT, meaning that it still cannot transmit its frame. To account for this possibility, FDDI defines two classes of traffic: *synchronous* and *asynchronous*.[2] When a node receives a token, it is always allowed to send synchronous data, without regard for whether the token is early or late. In contrast, a node can send asynchronous traffic only when the token is early.

Note that the terms *synchronous* and *asynchronous* are somewhat misleading. By synchronous, FDDI means that the traffic is delay sensitive. For example, one would send voice or video as synchronous traffic on an FDDI network. In contrast, asynchronous means that the application is more interested in throughput than delay. A file transfer application would be asynchronous FDDI traffic.

Are we done yet? Not quite. Because synchronous traffic can transmit without regard to whether the token is early or late, it would seem that if each node had a sizable amount of synchronous data to send, then the target rotation time would again be meaningless. To

---

[2]Originally, FDDI defined two subclasses of asynchronous traffic: *restricted* and *unrestricted*. In practice, however, the restricted asynchronous case is not supported, and so we describe only the unrestricted case and refer to it simply as "asynchronous."

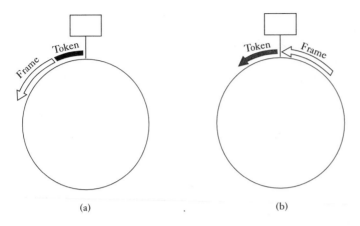

(a)   (b)

Figure 3.25   Immediate (a) versus delayed (b) token release.

account for this, the total amount of synchronous data that can be sent during one token rotation is also bounded by TTRT. This means that in the worst case, the nodes with asynchronous traffic first use up one TTRT's worth of time, and then the nodes with synchronous data consume another TTRT's worth of time, meaning that it is possible for the measured TRT at any given node to be as much as $2 \times$ TTRT. Note that if the synchronous traffic has already consumed one TTRT's worth of time, then the nodes with asynchronous traffic will not send any data because the token will be late. Thus, it is not possible to have back-to-back rotations of the token that take $2 \times$ TTRT amount of time.

This completes the discussion, except for cleaning up two loose ends. First, there is a question of exactly when the sending node releases the token. As illustrated in Figure 3.25, the sender can insert the token back onto the ring immediately following its frame (this is called *immediate release*) or after the frame it transmits has gone all the way around the ring and been removed (this is called *delayed release*). If the delay around the ring is larger than the time it takes to transmit a frame, then delayed release wastes ring bandwidth. FDDI uses immediate token release. IEEE 802.5 originally used delayed token release, but support for immediate token release has now been added.

The second loose end concerns precisely how a node determines if it can send asynchronous traffic. As stated above, a node sends if the measured TRT is less than the TTRT. The question then arises: What if the measured TRT is less than the TTRT, but by such a small amount that it's not possible to send the full message without exceeding the TTRT? The answer is that the node is allowed to send in this case. As a consequence, the measured TRT is actually bounded by TTRT plus the time it takes to send a full FDDI frame.

3.7.3 Token Maintenance

The algorithm just described obviously relies on the existence of a valid token. Since a token is just a special bit pattern, and bit errors happen, it is possible to lose the token. A token can also be lost when a node that is holding it fails. Token ring networks, therefore, need a method for monitoring the validity of the token and generating a new token should the old one be lost. A new token also needs to be generated when a ring is initialized. We first consider the problem of generating a token and then discuss how FDDI monitors the validity of the token.

Generating a Token

A new token is potentially generated whenever a new node joins the ring or a node suspects that some kind of error has occurred. It is during the process of generating a token that the nodes on the ring agree upon the current TTRT.

The algorithm, also called the *token claim process*, is straightforward. Each node sends a special *claim frame*, which includes the node's *bid* for the TTRT, i.e., the token rotation time that the node needs to make its applications happy. A node can send a claim frame without holding the token and typically does so whenever it suspects a failure or when it first joins the network. If this claim frame makes it all the way around the ring, then the sender removes it, knowing that its TTRT bid was the lowest. That node now holds the token—i.e., it is responsible for inserting a valid token on the ring—and may proceed with the normal token algorithm.

When a node receives a claim frame, it checks to see if the TTRT bid in the frame is less than its own. If it is, then the node resets its local definition of the TTRT to that contained in the claim frame and forwards the frame to the next node. If the bid TTRT is greater than that node's minimum required TTRT, then the claim frame is removed from the ring and the node enters the bidding process by putting its own claim frame on the ring. Should the bid TTRT be equal to the node's required TTRT, the node compares the address of the claim frame's sender with its own and the higher address wins. Thus, if a claim frame makes it all the way back around to the original sender, that node knows that it is the only active bidder and that it can safely claim the token.

Monitoring for a Valid Token

In a correctly functioning ring, each node should see a valid transmission—either a data frame or the token—every so often. The greatest idle time between valid transmissions that a given node should experience is equal to the ring latency plus the time it takes to transmit a full frame, which on a maximally sized ring is a little less than 2.5 ms. Therefore, each node sets a timer event that fires after 2.5 ms. If this timer expires, the node suspects that something has gone wrong and transmits a claim frame. Every time a valid transmission is received, however, the node resets the timer back to 2.5 ms.

3.7.4 Frame Format

We are now ready to define the FDDI frame format, which is depicted in Figure 3.26. FDDI uses 4B/5B encoding, as described in Section 3.2. This means that many of the fields in its header—e.g., the start and end of frame markers—are actually given by 4B/5B control symbols.

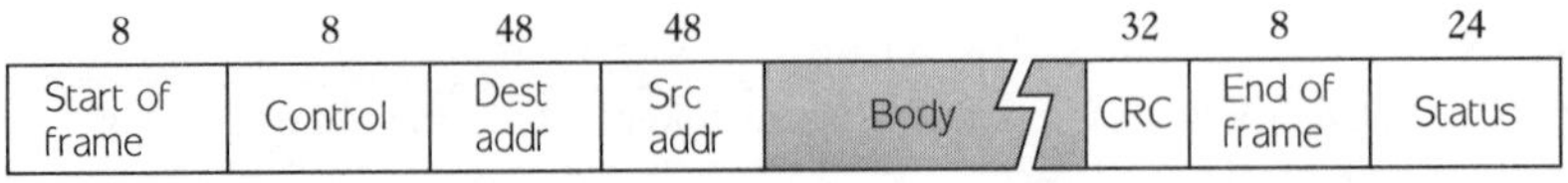

8	8	48	48		32	8	24
Start of frame	Control	Dest addr	Src addr	Body	CRC	End of frame	Status

Figure 3.26 FDDI frame format.

Similar to the Ethernet, FDDI addresses are 48 bits long. The FDDI standard actually allows for smaller, 16-bit addresses, but 48-bit addresses are typically used. When 48-bit addresses are used, they are interpreted in exactly the same way as on an Ethernet. Also like the Ethernet, FDDI uses bit-oriented framing, with a unique bit sequence denoting the beginning and ending of a frame. The FDDI frame also includes a 32-bit CRC. FDDI frames may be up to 4500 bytes long, including the FDDI header, meaning that up to 4478 bytes of data can be transmitted in a frame that uses 48-bit addresses.

The 8-bit control field in the FDDI header contains several pieces of information about the frame: the first bit indicates whether the frame carries asynchronous (0) or synchronous (1) traffic, the second bit says whether 16-bit (0) or 48-bit (1) addresses are being used, and the final 6 bits give a demultiplexing key for the frame (i.e., these 6 bits serve the same role as the 8-bit type field in the Ethernet header). Certain frame types are reserved for use internally by the FDDI protocol; they do not identify higher-level protocols. For example, the token itself, as well as a claim frame, are denoted by special bit patterns in this field.

Finally, the FDDI header includes a 24-bit frame status field. This field is typically set by the recipient of the frame to report status information back to the sender. (Recall that the frame travels all the way around the ring and is removed by the sender, which can then read this status field.) Specifically, the receiver can say whether there was an error in the frame it received, whether or not it recognized the address, and whether or not it copied the frame as it went by. These last two pieces of information seem redundant, since a node that recognizes its address in the header normally also saves a copy of the frame. It is possible, however, for a node to recognize its address in the destination field, but because it does not have enough buffer space available, for it to refuse to copy the frame into its local memory. In this way, FDDI allows the receiver to send flow control information back to the sender.

3.8 Network Adaptors

Nearly all the networking functionality described in this chapter is implemented in the network adaptor: framing, error detection, and the media access protocol. The only exceptions are the point-to-point automatic repeat request (ARQ) schemes described in Section 3.5, which are typically implemented in the lowest-level protocol running on the host. We conclude this chapter by describing the design of a generic network adaptor, and the device driver software that controls it.

When reading this section, keep in mind that no two network adaptors are exactly alike; they vary in countless small details. Our focus, therefore, is on their general characteristics, although we do include some examples from an actual adaptor to make the discussion more tangible.

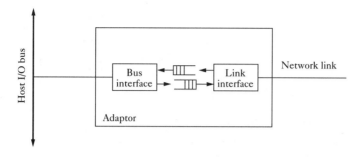

Figure 3.27 Block diagram of a typical network adaptor.

3.8.1 Components

A network adaptor serves as an interface between the host and the network, and as a result, can be thought of as having two main components: a bus interface that understands how to communicate with the host and a link interface that speaks the correct protocol on the network. There must also be a communication path between these two components, over which incoming and outgoing data is passed. A simple block diagram of a network adaptor is depicted in Figure 3.27.

Network adaptors are always designed for a specific I/O bus, which is why it's generally not possible to move an adaptor from one vendor's machine to another. Each bus, in effect, defines a protocol that is used by the host's CPU to program the adaptor, by the adaptor to interrupt the host's CPU, and by the adaptor to read and write memory on the host. One of the main features of an I/O bus is the data transfer rate that it supports. For example, a typical bus might have a 32-bit-wide data path (i.e., it can transfer 32 bits of data in parallel) running at 25 MHz (i.e., the bus's cycle time is 40 ns), giving it a peak transfer rate of 800 Mbps, which would be enough to support a (unidirectional) 622-Mbps STS-12 link. Of course, the peak rate tells us almost nothing about the average rate, which may be much lower.

The link-half of the adaptor implements the link-level protocol. For fairly mature technologies like Ethernet and FDDI, the link-half of the adaptor is implemented by a chip set that can be purchased on the commodity market. For newer link technologies, however, the link-level protocol may be implemented in software on a general-purpose microprocessor or perhaps with some form of programmable hardware, such as a field-programmable gate array (FPGA). These approaches generally add to the cost of the adaptor but make it more flexible—it is easier to modify software than hardware and easier to reprogram FPGAs than to redesign boards.

Because the host's bus and the network link are, in all probability, running at different speeds, there is a need to put a small amount of buffering between the two halves of the adaptor. Typically, a small FIFO (byte queue) is enough to hide the asynchrony between the bus and the link.

3.8.2 View from the Host

Since we have spent most of this chapter discussing various protocols that are implemented by the link-half of the adaptor, we now turn our attention to the host's view of the network adaptor.

Control Status Register

A network adaptor, like any other device, is ultimately programmed by software running on the CPU. From the CPU's perspective, the adaptor exports a *control status register* (CSR) that is readable and writable from the CPU. The CSR is typically located at some address in the memory, thereby making it possible for the CPU to read and write just like any other memory location. The CPU writes to the CSR to instruct it to transmit and/or receive a frame and reads from the CSR to learn the current state of the adaptor.

The following is an example CSR from the Lance Ethernet device, which is manufactured by Advanced Microsystem Devices (AMD). The Lance device actually has four different control status registers; the following shows the bit masks used to interpret the 16-bit CSR0. To set a bit on the adaptor, the CPU does an inclusive-OR of the mask corresponding to the bit it wants to set, and CSR0. To determine if a particular bit is set, the CPU compares the AND of the contents of CSR0 and the mask against 0.

```
/*
 * Control and status bits for CSR0.
 *
 * Legend:
 *   RO  - Read Only
 *   RC  - Read/Clear (writing 1 clears, writing 0 has no effect)
 *   RW  - Read/Write
 *   W1  - Write-1-only (writing 1 sets, writing 0 has no effect)
 *   RW1 - Read/Write-1-only (writing 1 sets, writing 0 has no effect)
 */

#define LE_ERR      0x8000      /* RO BABL | CERR | MISS | MERR */
#define LE_BABL     0x4000      /* RC transmitted too many bits */
#define LE_CERR     0x2000      /* RC No Heartbeat */
#define LE_MISS     0x1000      /* RC Missed an incoming packet */
#define LE_MERR     0x0800      /* RC Memory Error; no acknowledge */
#define LE_RINT     0x0400      /* RC Received packet Interrupt */
#define LE_TINT     0x0200      /* RC Transmitted packet Interrupt */
#define LE_IDON     0x0100      /* RC Initialization Done */
#define LE_INTR     0x0080      /* RO BABL|MISS|MERR|RINT|TINT|IDON */
#define LE_INEA     0x0040      /* RW Interrupt Enable */
#define LE_RXON     0x0020      /* RO Receiver On */
#define LE_TXON     0x0010      /* RO Transmitter On */
#define LE_TDMD     0x0008      /* W1 Transmit Demand (send it now) */
#define LE_STOP     0x0004      /* RW1 Stop */
#define LE_STRT     0x0002      /* RW1 Start */
#define LE_INIT     0x0001      /* RW1 Initialize */
```

This definition says, for example, that the host writes a 1 to the least significant bit of CSR0 (0x0001) to initialize the Lance chip. Similarly, if the host sees a 1 in the sixth significant bit (0x0020) and in the fifth significant bit (0x0010), then it knows that the Lance chip is enabled to receive and transmit frames, respectively.

Interrupts

The host CPU could sit in a tight loop reading the adaptor's control status register until something interesting happens and then take the appropriate action. On the Lance chip, for example, it could continually watch for a 1 in the eleventh significant bit (0x0400), which would indicate that a frame has just arrived. This is called *polling*, and although it is not an unreasonable design in certain situations—e.g., a network router that has nothing better to do than wait for the next frame—it is not typically done on end hosts that could better spend their time running application programs.

Instead of polling, most hosts only pay attention to the network device when the adaptor interrupts the host. The device raises an interrupt when an event that requires host intervention occurs—for example, a frame has been successfully transmitted or received, or an error occurred when the device was attempting to transmit or receive a frame. The host's architecture includes a mechanism that causes a particular procedure inside the operating system to be invoked when such an interrupt occurs. This procedure is known as an *interrupt handler*, and it inspects the CSR to determine the cause of the interrupt and then takes the appropriate action.

While servicing an interrupt, the host typically *disables* additional interrupts. This keeps the device driver from having to service multiple interrupts at one time. Because interrupts are disabled, the device driver must finish its job quickly (it does not have the time to execute the entire protocol stack), and under no circumstances can it afford to block (that is, suspend execution while awaiting some event). In the x-kernel, for example, this is accomplished by having the interrupt handler dispatch a process to take care of the message and then return. Thus, the handler makes sure that the message will get processed without having to spend valuable time actually processing the message itself.

Direct Memory Access versus Programmed I/O

One of the most important issues in network adaptor design is how the bytes of a frame are transferred between the adaptor and the host memory. There are two basic mechanisms: *direct memory access* (DMA) and *programmed I/O* (PIO). With DMA, the adaptor directly reads and writes the host's memory without any CPU involvement; the host simply gives the adaptor a memory address and the adaptor reads to (writes from) it. With PIO, the CPU is directly responsible for moving data between the adaptor and the host memory: to send a frame, the CPU sits in a tight loop that first reads a word from host memory and then writes it to the adaptor; to receive a frame, the CPU reads words from the adaptor and writes them to memory. We now consider DMA and PIO in more detail.

When using DMA, there is no need to buffer frames on the adaptor; the adaptor reads and writes host memory. (A few bytes of buffering are needed to stage data be-

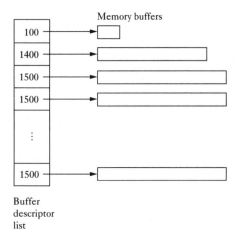

Figure 3.28   Buffer descriptor list.

tween the bus and the link, as described above, but complete frames are not buffered on the adaptor.) The CPU is therefore responsible for giving the adaptor a pair of *buffer descriptor lists*; one to transmit out of and one to receive into. A buffer descriptor list is an array of address/length pairs, as illustrated in Figure 3.28.

When receiving frames, the adaptor uses as many buffers as it needs to hold the incoming frame. For example, the descriptor illustrated in Figure 3.28 would cause an Ethernet adaptor that was attempting to receive a 1450-byte frame to put the first 100 bytes in the first buffer and the next 1350 bytes in the second buffer. If a second 1500-byte frame arrived immediately after the first, it would be placed entirely in the third buffer. That is, separate frames are placed in separate buffers, although a single frame may be scattered across multiple buffers. This latter feature is usually called *scatter-read*. In practice, scatter-read is used when the network's maximum frame size is so large that it is wasteful to allocate all buffers big enough to contain the largest possible arriving frame. A mechanism like the *x*-kernel message data structure would then be used to link to-

Frames, Buffers, and Messages

As this section has suggested, the network adaptor is the place where the network comes in physical contact with the host. It also happens to be the place where three different worlds intersect: the network, the host architecture, and the host operation system. It turns out that each of these has a different terminology for talking about the same thing. It is important to recognize when this is happening.

From the network's perspective, the adaptor transmits *frames* from the host and receives *frames* into the host. Most of this chapter has been presented from the network

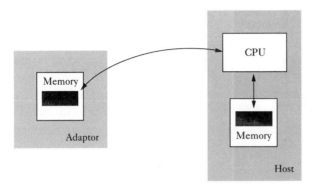

Figure 3.29 Programmed I/O (PIO).

gether all the buffers that make up a single frame. Scatter-read is typically not used on an Ethernet because preallocating 1500-byte buffers does not excessively waste memory.

Output works in a similar way. When the host has a frame to transmit, it puts a pointer to the buffer that contains the frame in the transmit descriptor list. Devices that support *gather-write* allow the frame to be fragmented across multiple physical buffers. In practice, gather-write is more widely used than scatter-read because outgoing frames are often constructed in a piecemeal fashion, with more than one protocol contributing a buffer. For example, by the time a message makes it down the protocol stack and is ready to be transmitted, it consists of a buffer that contains the aggregate header (the collection of headers attached by various protocols that processed the message) and a separate buffer that contains the application's data.

perspective, so you should have a good understanding of what the term *frame* means. From the perspective of the host architecture, each frame is received into or transmitted from a *buffer*, which is simply a region of main memory of some length and starting at some address. Finally, from the operating system's perspective (in this particular case we are talking about the *x*-kernel), a *message* is an abstract object that holds network frames. Messages are implemented by a data structure that includes pointers to different memory locations (buffers).

In the case of PIO, the network adaptor must contain some amount of buffering—the CPU copies frames between host memory and this adaptor memory, as illustrated in Figure 3.29. The basic fact that necessitates buffering is that, with most operating systems, you can never be sure when the CPU will get around to doing something, so you need to be prepared to wait for it. One important question that must be addressed is how much memory is needed on the adaptor. There certainly needs to be at least one frame's worth of memory in both the transmit and the receive direction. In addition, adaptors that use PIO usually have additional memory that can be used to hold a small number of incoming frames until the CPU can get around to copying them into host memory. Although the computer system axiom that "memory is cheap" would seem to suggest putting a huge amount of memory on the adaptor, this memory must be of the more expensive dual-ported type because both the CPU and the adaptor read/write it. PIO-based adaptors typically have something on the order of 64 to 256 KB of adaptor memory, although there are adaptors with as much as 1 MB of memory.

3.8.3 Example Device Driver

This section describes an x-kernel device driver for the Lance Ethernet adaptor. One of our objectives in giving this example is to demonstrate how an x-kernel protocol graph is anchored in a device driver. In the following example, variable csr is a pointer to the Lance's CSR0; we have hidden the details of manipulating the Lance's transmit and receive buffer descriptor lists in functions next_xmit_buffer, next_rcv_desc, and install_rcv_desc; and routine copy_data_to_lance copies the data found in a message object into a contiguous buffer of memory that is readable by the Lance device. Also, we assume the availability of the following low-level kernel routines that implement the obvious functions: process_create, disable_interrupts, and enable_interrupts.

The code shown is for the device-dependent half of the Ethernet protocol; there is also a device-independent half that exports the standard x-kernel operations—such as xPush—to higher-level protocols. This device-dependent half of the Ethernet protocol supports three procedures: one that is called by the device-independent ethPush routine to transmit a frame (lance_transmit), one that is called by the host operating system to service an interrupt from the Lance adaptor (lance_interrupt_handler), and one that is called at system boot time to initialize the Lance device (not shown).

```
lance_transmit(Msg *msg)
{
    char *src, *dst;
    Context c;
    int len;

    semWait(xmit_queue);
    semWait(mutex);
    disable_interrupts();
    dst = next_xmit_buf();
    msgWalkInit(&c, msg);
    while ((src = msgWalk(&c, &len)) != 0)
        copy_data_to_lance(src, dst, len);
    msgWalkDone(&c);
    enable_interrupts();
    semSignal(mutex);
    return;
}
```

The lance_transmit routine takes a message **msg** that is to be transmitted on the Lance device. It first waits on a counting semaphore that ensures that there is a free transmit buffer on the device to handle this message. This semaphore (**xmit_queue**) is initialized to the number of transmit buffers supported by this device, typically 64. This means that up to 64 messages can be queued at any one time on the transmit list (and the calling process allowed to return), and it's not until a process tries to enqueue the 65th message that it is blocked. Any number of processes can block on this semaphore while trying to enqueue their message on the transmit list.

Once there is an available transmit buffer, the invoking process protects itself from other transmitting processes by waiting on a mutual exclusion (mutex) semaphore and from the device by disabling interrupts. The transmit routine then uses the **msgWalk** operation to traverse the message data structure and to extract all the individual buffers that contain portions of the message. In this example, the transmit routine copies the data from the message buffers into the single transmit buffer; an alternative would be simply to give the device the addresses and lengths of the individual buffers in the message. The routine then signals the mutex semaphore, enables interrupts, and returns.

```
lance_interrupt_handler()
{
    Msg *msg,  *replacement_msg;
    char *buf;

    disable_interrupts();

    /* some error occurred */
    if (csr & LE_ERR)
    {
        print_error(csr);
        /* clear error bits */
        csr = LE_BABL | LE_CERR | LE_MISS | LE_MERR | LE_INEA;
        enable_interrupts();
        return();
    }

    /* transmit interrupt */
    if (csr & LE_TINT)
    {
        /* clear interrupt */
        csr = LE_TINT | LE_INEA;

        /* signal blocked senders */
        semSignal(xmit_queue);

        enable_interrupts();
        return(0);
    }
```

```
/* receive interrupt */
if (csr & LE_RINT)
{
    /* clear interrupt */
    csr = LE_RINT | LE_INEA;

    /* loop over all received messages */
    while (rdl = next_rcv_desc())
    {
        /* create process to handle this message */
        msg = rdl->msg;
        process_create(ethDemux, msg);

        /* msg eventually freed in ethDemux; now allocate a replacement */
        buf = msgConstructAllocate(replacement_msg, LANCE_MTU);
        rdl->msg = replacement_msg;
        rdl->buf = buf;
        install_rcv_desc(rdl);
    }
    enable_interrupts();
    return();
}
}
```

The lance_interrupt_handler routine is called to service an interrupt from the Lance adaptor. When this routine is invoked, one of three things has just happened: an error has occurred, a transmit request has completed, or a frame has been received. In the first case, the handler prints a message and clears the error bits; routine print_error inspects the CSR and reports which bits were set. In the second case, we know that a transmit request that was queued earlier by lance_transmit has completed, meaning that there is now a free transmit buffer that can be reused. Thus, we signal semaphore xmit_queue, which permits another process blocked in lance_transmit to proceed.

The third case in lance_interrupt_handler—receive interrupt—is the interesting one. First, notice the while loop. This allows us to process as many frames as have arrived with just one interrupt; next_rcv_buf keeps returning entries in the receive buffer descriptor list as long as it contains frames that have not yet been processed. (Each entry in a receive descriptor list contains a flag saying whether the host or the adaptor owns it; next_rcv_buf uses that flag to identify unprocessed frames.) Second, each entry in the receive descriptor list—represented by variable rdl—contains a pointer to both an x-kernel message (a data structure) and to the actual buffer that implements the message (a piece of memory). The adaptor only understands the buffer, but we need to remember which message that buffer belongs to so we can process that message when the buffer has been filled with new network data.

Once we have located the message (msg), we dispatch a process that will cause the message to travel up through the protocol graph; this new process begins by executing the bottom entry point into the device-independent half of the Ethernet protocol—ethDemux. The ethDemux routine does exactly what any protocol's demultiplexing routine does: it demultiplexes the frame to a session based on the type field in the header. Also, the message is freed as the very last action in ethDemux.

At this point, the interrupt handler is done processing the message that just arrived; the new process does the rest of the work. However, the interrupt handler now has to prepare a replacement message and install it in the receive descriptor list. It uses the msgConstructAllocate operation for this purpose and resets the buffer descriptor entry (rdl) to know about both the new message and the corresponding buffer.

There is one final point to make. Notice that the lance_interrupt_handler routine does not wait on the mutex semaphore. This is because only one process can be running in the interrupt handler at a time; there is no other source of interference in an interrupt handler on a uniprocessor.

3.9 Summary

This chapter introduced the hardware building blocks of a computer network—nodes and links—and discussed the five key problems that must be solved so that two or more nodes that are directly connected by a physical link can exchange messages with each other.

First, physical links carry signals. It is therefore necessary to encode the bits that make up a binary message into the signal at the source node and then to recover the bits from the signal at the receiving node. This is the encoding problem, and it is made challenging by the need to keep the sender's and receiver's clocks synchronized. We discussed four different encoding techniques—NRZ, NRZI, Manchester, and 4B/5B—which differ largely in how they encode clock information along with the data being transmitted. One of the key attributes of an encoding scheme is its efficiency, that is, the ratio of signal pulses to encoded bits.

Once it is possible to transmit bits between nodes, the next step is to figure out how to package these bits into frames. This is the framing problem, and it boils down to being able to recognize the beginning and end of each frame. Again, we looked at several different techniques, including byte-oriented protocols, bit-oriented protocols, and clock-based protocols.

Assuming that each node is able to recognize the collection of bits that make up a frame, the third problem is to determine if those bits are in fact correct, or if they have possibly been corrupted in transit. This is the error detection problem, and we looked at three different approaches: cyclic redundancy codes, two-dimensional parity, and checksums. Of these, the CRC approach gives the strongest guarantees and is the most widely used at the link level.

Given that some frames will arrive at the destination node containing errors and thus will have to be discarded, the next problem is how to recover from such losses. The goal is to make the link appear reliable. The general approach to this problem is called ARQ and involves using a combination of acknowledgments and timeouts. We looked at three specific ARQ algorithms: stop-and-wait, sliding window, and concurrent channels. What makes these algorithms interesting is how effectively they use the link, with the goal being to keep the pipe full.

The final problem is not relevant to point-to-point links, but it is the central issue in multiple-access links. The problem is how to mediate access to a shared link so that all nodes eventually have a chance to transmit their data. In this case, we looked at two different media access protocols—CSMA/CD and token ring—which have been put to practical use in the Ethernet and FDDI local area networks, respectively. What both of these technologies have in common is that control over the network is distributed over all the nodes connected to the network; there is no dependence on a central arbitrator.

We concluded the chapter by observing that in practice, most of the algorithms that address these five problems are implemented on the adaptor that connects the host to the link. It turns out that the design of this adaptor is of critical importance in how well the network, as a whole, performs.

OPEN ISSUE

Does It Belong in Hardware?

One of the most important questions in the design of any computer system is, What belongs in hardware and what belongs in software? In the case of networking, the network adaptor finds itself at the heart of this question. For example, why is the Ethernet algorithm, presented in Section 3.6 of this chapter, typically implemented on the network adaptor, while the higher-level protocols discussed later in this book are not?

It is certainly possible to put a general-purpose microprocessor on the network adaptor, which gives you the opportunity to move high-level protocols there, such as TCP/IP. The reason that this is typically not done is complicated, but it comes down to the economics of computer design: the host processor is usually the fastest processor on a computer, and it would be a shame if this fast host processor had to wait for a slower adaptor processor to run TCP/IP when it could have done the job faster itself. On the flip side, some protocol processing does belong on the network adaptor. The general rule of thumb is that any processing for which a fixed processor can keep pace with the link speed—i.e., a faster processor would not improve the situation—is a good candidate for being moved to the adaptor. In other words, any function that is already limited by the link speed, as opposed to the processor at the end of the link, might be effectively implemented on the adaptor.

In general, making the call as to what functionality belongs on the network adaptor and what belongs on the host computer is a difficult one, and it is a problem that is reexamined each time someone designs a new network adaptor.

Independent of exactly what protocols are implemented on the network adaptor, it is generally the case that the data will eventually find its way onto the main computer, and when it does, the efficiency with which the data is moved between the adaptor and the computer's memory is very important. Recall from Section 3.1.1 that memory bandwidth—the rate at which data can be moved from one memory location to another—is typically the limiting factor in how a workstation-class machine performs. An inefficient host/adaptor data transfer mechanism can, therefore, limit the throughput rate seen by application programs running on the host. First, there is the issue of whether DMA or programmed I/O is used; each has advantages in different situations. Second, there is the issue of how well the network adaptor is integrated with the operating system's buffer mechanism; a carefully integrated system is usually able to avoid copying data at a higher level of the protocol graph, thereby improving application-to-application throughput.

FURTHER READING

One of the most important contributions in computer networking over the last 20 years is the original paper by Metcalf and Boggs (1976) introducing the Ethernet. Many years later, Boggs, Mogul, and Kent reported (1988) their practical experiences with Ethernet, debunking many of the myths that had found their way into the literature over the years. Both papers are must reading. The third paper on our reading list describes FDDI, with a particular emphasis on the standardization process.

- Metcalf, R., and D. Boggs. Ethernet: Distributed packet switching for local computer networks. *Communications of the ACM* 19(7):395–403, July 1976.

- Boggs, D., J. Mogul, and C. Kent. Measured capacity of an Ethernet. *Proceedings of the SIGCOMM '88 Symposium*, pages 222–234, August 1988.

- Ross, F., and J. Hamstra. Forging FDDI. *IEEE Journal of Selected Areas in Communication (JSAC)* 11:181–190, February 1993.

There are countless textbooks with a heavy emphasis on the lower levels of the network hierarchy, with a particular focus on *telecommunications*—networking from the phone company's perspective. Books by Spragins et al. [SHP91] and Minoli [Min93] are two good examples. Several other books concentrate on various local area network technologies. Of these, Stallings's book is the most comprehensive [Sta90], while Jain gives a thorough description of FDDI [Jai94]. Jain's book also gives a good introduction to the low-level details of optical communication. Also, a comprehensive overview of FDDI can be found in Ross [Ros86].

For an introduction to information theory, Blahut's book is a good place to start [Bla87], along with Shannon's seminal paper on link capacity [Sha48].

For a general introduction to the mathematics behind error codes, Rao and Fujiwara [RF89] is recommended. For a detailed discussion of the mathematics and a description of how the hardware works that is generally used for CRC calculation in particular, see Peterson and Brown [PB61].

On the topic of network adaptor design, much work has been done recently as researchers try to connect hosts to networks running at higher and higher rates. For example, see

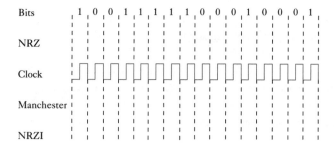

Figure 3.30   Diagram for exercise 2.

Druschel et al. [DPD94], Davie [Dav91], Traw and Smith [TS93], Ramakrishnan [Ram93], Edwards et al. [EWL⁺94], Metcalf [Met93], Kanakia and Cheriton [KC88], Cohen et al. [CFFD93], and Steenkiste [Ste94a].

For general information on computer architecture, Hennessy and Patterson's book [HP96] is an excellent reference, while Sites [Sit92] explains the DEC Alpha architecture in detail. (Many of the performance experiments discussed in this book were run on the DEC Alpha.)

Finally, we recommend the following live reference:

■ http://stdsbbs.ieee.org/: status of various IEEE network-related standards.

E X E R C I S E S

1 Many different media can be used to transmit information between network nodes, in addition to those mentioned in this chapter. For example, communication may be done by means of laser beam, microwave beam, radio waves, sound waves, and infrared. Select two or three of these media and investigate the advantages, capabilities, and drawbacks of each. Summarize your studies by indicating the situations and environments where each of the media you have studied would be most appropriately used.

2 Show the NRZ, Manchester, and NRZI encodings for the bit pattern shown in Figure 3.30. Assume that the NRZI signal starts out low.

3 Show the 4B/5B encoding, and the resulting NRZI signal, for the bit sequence 1110 0101 0000 0011.

4 Assuming a framing protocol that uses bit stuffing, show the bit sequence transmitted over the link when the frame contains the following bit sequence:

1101011110101111101011111110

Mark the stuffed bits.

5 Suppose the following sequence of bits arrive over a link:

110101111010111100101111110110

Show the resulting frame after any stuffed bits have been removed. Indicate any errors that might have been introduced into the frame.

6 Suppose you want to send some data using the BISYNC framing protocol, and the last two bytes of your data are DLE and ETX. What sequence of bytes would be transmitted immediately prior to the CRC? What would your answer be if the IMP-IMP protocol were used?

7 Suppose we want to transmit the message 11001001 and protect it from errors using the CRC polynomial $x^3 + 1$.

   (a) Use polynomial long division to determine the message that should be transmitted.

   (b) Suppose the leftmost bit of the message is inverted due to noise on the transmission link. What is the result of the receiver's CRC calculation? How does the receiver know that an error has occurred?

8 What are the advantages of a CRC over the IP checksum algorithm? What are the disadvantages?

9 Give an example of a 4-bit error that would not be detected by two-dimensional parity, using the data in Figure 3.14. What is the general set of circumstances under which 4-bit errors will be undetected?

10 Typically the checksum field is included in the data being checksummed, with this field zeroed out by the sender when computing the checksum. On the receiver, when the result of computing the checksum (again including the checksum field) results in an answer of 0, the receiver accepts the message as correct. Explain why it does. Give a small example that illustrates your answer.

11 Consider an ARQ protocol that uses only negative acknowledges (NAKs), but no positive acknowledgments (ACKs). Describe what timeouts would need to be scheduled. Explain why an ACK-based protocol is usually preferred to a NAK-based protocol.

12 Consider an ARQ algorithm running over a 20-km point-to-point fiber link.

(a) Compute the propagation delay for this link, assuming that the speed of light is 2×10^8 meters per second in the fiber.

(b) Suggest a suitable timeout value for the ARQ algorithm to use.

(c) Why might it still be possible for the ARQ algorithm to timeout and retransmit a frame, given this timeout value?

13 In the sliding window protocol, why doesn't having RWS greater than SWS make any sense?

14 Suppose you are designing a sliding window protocol for a 1-Mbps point-to-point link to the moon, which has a one-way latency of 1.25 second. Assuming that each frame carries 1 KB of data, how many bits do you need for the sequence number?

15 This chapter suggests that the sliding window protocol can be used to implement flow control. We can imagine doing this by having the receiver delay ACKs, that is, not send the ACK until there is free buffer space to hold the next frame. In doing so, each ACK would simultaneously acknowledge the receipt of the last frame and tell the source that there is now free buffer space available to hold the next frame. Explain why implementing flow control in this way is not a good idea.

16 Implement the concurrent logical channel protocol in the x-kernel.

17 Extend the x-kernel implementation of SWP to piggyback ACKs on data frames.

18 Extend the x-kernel implementation of SWP to support selective ACKs.

19 Experiment with the send window size (**SWS**) in the x-kernel implementation of SWP. Plot the effective throughput for **SWS** = 1,...,32 on whatever network you have available. Running SWP over an Ethernet is fine; you can also vary the link latency by configuring x-kernel protocol VDELAY into your protocol graph. (See the Appendix of the *x-kernel Programmer's Manual* for a description of VDELAY.)

20 What company manufactures the Ethernet adaptor for the machine you most commonly use? Determine what address prefix has been assigned to this manufacturer.

21 Why is it important for protocols configured on top of the Ethernet to have a length field in their header, indicating how long the message is?

22 Considering that the maximum length of an Ethernet is 1500 m, compute the worst-case propagation delay of an Ethernet. Explain why the Ethernet algorithm uses 51.2 μs instead of the number you just computed.

23 Some network applications are a better match for an Ethernet, and some are a better match for an FDDI network. Which network would be the better match for a remote terminal application (e.g., Telnet) and which would be a better match for a file transfer application (e.g., FTP)? Would your answer be the same if you assumed a 100-Mbps Ethernet, rather than 10 Mbps? Give a general explanation for what it is about each of these applications that suggests that one type of network is a better match than the other.

24 For a 100-Mbps token ring network that uses delayed release, has a token rotation time of 200 μs, and allows each station to transmit one 1-KB packet each time it possesses the token, determine the network's maximum effective throughput rate.

25 Consider a token ring network like FDDI in which a station is allowed to hold the token for some period of time (the *token holding time* or THT). Let RingLatency denote the time it takes the token to make one complete rotation around the network when none of the stations have any data to send.

(a) In terms of THT and RingLatency, express the efficiency of this network when only a single station is active.

(b) What setting of THT would be optimal for a network that had only one station active (with data to send) at a time?

(c) In the case where N stations are active, give an upper bound on the token rotation time, or TRT, for the network.

26 Consider a token ring with a ring latency of 200μs. Assuming that the delayed token release stategy is used, what is the effective throughput rate that can be achieved if the ring has a bandwidth of 4 Mbps? What is the effective throughput rate that can be achieved if the ring has a bandwidth of 100 Mbps?

27 Repeat the previous problem for a ring that uses immediate token release.

28 Give the code fragment that determines whether the Lance Ethernet adaptor has just issued a receive interrupt.

29 Sketch the implementation of the device-independent half of an x-kernel Ethernet driver. Compare your implementation to protocol ETH distributed with the x-kernel.

The directly connected networks described in the previous chapter suffer from two limitations. First, there is a limit to how many hosts can be attached. For example, only two hosts can be attached to a point-to-point link, and an Ethernet can connect up to only 1024 hosts. Second, there is a limit to how large of a geographic area a single network can serve. For example, an Ethernet can span only 1500 meters, and even though point-to-point links can be quite long, they do not really serve the area between the two ends. Since our goal is to build networks that can be global in scale, the next problem is therefore to enable communication between hosts that are not directly connected.

Nature seems . . . to reach many of her ends by long circuitous routes.

—Lotze

This problem is not unlike the one addressed in the telephone network: your phone is not directly connected to every person you might want to call, but instead is connected to an exchange that contains a *switch*. It is the switches that create the impression that you have a connection to the person at the other end of the call. Similarly, computer networks use *packet switches* (as distinct from the *circuit switches* used for telephony) to enable packets to travel from one host to another, even when no direct connection exists between those hosts. This chapter introduces the major concepts of packet switching, which lies at the heart of computer networking.

A packet switch is a device with several inputs and outputs leading to and from the hosts that the switch interconnects. There are three main problems that a packet switch must address. First, the core job of a switch is to take packets that arrive on an input and *forward* (or *switch*) them to the right output so that they will reach their appropriate destination. Knowing which output is the right one requires the switch to know something about the possible routes to the destination. The process of accumulating and sharing this knowledge, the second problem for a packet switch, is called *routing*. Third, a switch must deal with the fact that its outputs have a certain bandwidth. If the number of packets arriving at a switch that need to be sent out on a certain output exceeds the capacity of that output, then we have a problem of *contention*. The switch queues (buffers) packets until the contention subsides, but if it lasts too long, the switch will run out of buffer space and be forced to discard packets. When packets are discarded too frequently, the switch is said to be *congested*. The ability of a switch to handle contention is a key aspect of its performance, and many high-performance switches use exotic hardware to reduce the effects of contention.

This chapter introduces these three issues of packet switching: forwarding, routing, and contention. For the most part, these discussions apply to a wide range of packet-switched technologies. There is one particular technology, however, that has attracted so much attention recently that it warrants more specific attention. That technology is *asynchronous transfer mode* (ATM). The third section of this chapter introduces ATM, providing a handy backdrop for a discussion of the hardware that can be used to implement a packet switch, which is the subject of the final section. This discussion of switches focuses on contention; we postpone the related problem of congestion until Chapter 8.

4

Packet
Switching

4.1 Switching and Forwarding

In the simplest terms, a switch is a mechanism that allows us to interconnect links to form a larger network. The switch does this by adding a star topology (see Figure 4.1) to the point-to-point link, bus (Ethernet), and ring (FDDI) topologies established in the last chapter. There are several nice features of a star topology:

- We can connect hosts to the switch using point-to-point links, which typically means that we can build networks of large geographic scope.

- Even though a switch has a fixed number of inputs and outputs, which limits the number of hosts that can be connected to a single switch, large networks can be built by interconnecting a number of switches.

- Adding a new host to the network by connecting it to the switch does not necessarily mean that the hosts already connected will get worse performance from the network.

This last claim cannot be made for the shared-media networks discussed in the last chapter. For example, it is impossible for two hosts on the same Ethernet to transmit continuously at 10 Mbps because they share the same transmission medium. Every host on a switched network has its own link to the switch, so it may be entirely possible for many hosts to transmit at the full link speed (bandwidth), provided that the switch is designed with enough aggregate capacity. Providing high aggregate throughput is one of the design goals for a switch; we return to this topic in Section 4.4. In general, switched networks are considered more *scalable* (i.e., more capable of growing to large numbers of nodes) than shared-media networks because of this ability to support many hosts at full speed.

A switch is connected to a set of links and, for each of these links, runs the appropriate data link protocol to communicate with the node at the other end of the link. A switch's primary job is to receive incoming packets on one of its links and to transmit them on some other link. This function is sometimes referred to as either *switching* or *forwarding* and, in terms of the OSI architecture, it is the main function of the network layer. Figure 4.2 shows the protocol graph that would run on a switch that is connected to two T3 links and one STS-1 SONET link. A representation of this same switch is given in Figure 4.3. In this figure, we have split the input and output halves of each link, and we refer to each input or output as a *port*. (In general, we assume that each link is bidirectional, and hence supports both input and output.) In other words, this example switch has three input ports and three output ports.

The question, then, is how does the switch decide which output port to place each packet on? The general answer is that it looks at the header of the packet for an identifier that it uses to make the decision. The details of how it uses this identifier vary, but there are two common approaches. The first is the *datagram* or *connectionless* approach. The second is the *virtual circuit* or *connection-oriented* approach. A third approach, *source routing*, is less common than these other two, but it is the simplest to explain and does have some useful applications. We will describe it first.

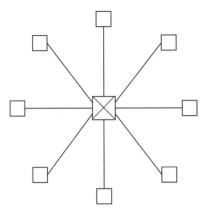

Figure 4.1   A switch provides a star topology.

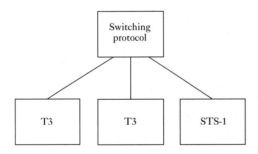

Figure 4.2   Example protocol graph running on a switch.

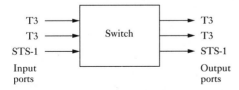

Figure 4.3   Example switch with three input and output ports.

One thing that is common to all networks is that we need to have a way to identify the end nodes. Such identifiers are usually called addresses. We have already seen examples of addresses in the previous chapter, for example, the 48-bit address used for Ethernet. The only requirement for Ethernet addresses is that no two nodes on a network have the same address. This is accomplished by making sure that all Ethernet cards are assigned a *globally unique* identifier. For the following discussions, we assume that each host has a globally unique address. Later on, we consider other useful properties that an address might have, but global uniqueness is all we need to get started.

Another assumption that we need to make is that there is some way to identify the input and output ports of each switch. There are at least two sensible ways to identify ports: one is to number each port, and the other is to identify the port by the name of the node (switch or host) to which it leads. For now, we use numbering of the ports.

4.1.1 Source Routing

One way to tell a switch which output to place each packet on would be to assign a number to each output of the switch and to place that number in the header of the packet. The switching function is then very simple: for each packet that arrives on an input, the switch would read the port number in the header and transmit the packet on that output. However, we should assume that in a switched network there will in general be more than one switch in the path between the sending and the receiving host. What this means is that the header for the packet needs to contain enough information to allow every switch in the path to determine which output the packet needs to be placed on. One way to do this would be to put an ordered list of switch ports in the header and to rotate the list so that the next switch in the path is always at the front of the list. Figure 4.4 illustrates this idea.

In this example, the packet needs to traverse three switches to get from host A to host B. At switch 1, it needs to exit on port 1, at the next switch it needs to exit at port 0, and at the third switch it needs to exit at port 3. Thus, the original header when the packet leaves host A contains the list of ports (3,0,1), where we assume that each switch reads the right-most element of the list. To make sure that the next switch gets the appropriate information, each switch rotates the list after it has read its own entry. Thus, the packet header as it leaves switch 1 en route to switch 2 is now (1,3,0); switch 2 performs another rotation and sends out a packet with (0,1,3) in the header. Although not shown, switch 3 performs yet another rotation, restoring the header to what it was when host A sent it.

There are several things to note about this approach. First, it assumes that host A knows enough about the topology of the network to form a header that has all the right directions in it for every switch in the path. For a large network, obtaining this topological information is problematic. Second, observe that we cannot predict how big the header needs to be, since it must be able to hold one word of information for every switch on the path. This implies that headers are probably of variable length with no upper bound, unless we can predict with absolute certainty the maximum number of switches through which a packet will ever need to pass. Third, there are some variations on this approach. For example, rather than rotate the

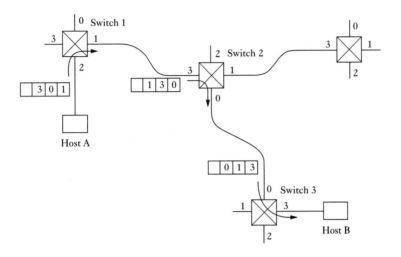

Figure 4.4   Source routing in a switched network (where the switch reads the rightmost number).

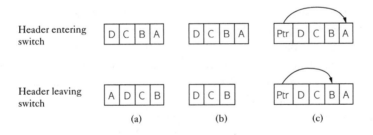

Figure 4.5   Three ways to handle headers for source routing: (a) rotation; (b) stripping; (c) pointer.

header, each switch could just strip the first element as it uses it. Rotation has an advantage over stripping, however: host B gets a copy of the complete header, which may help it figure out how to get back to host A. Yet another alternative is to have the header carry a pointer to the current "next port" entry, so that each switch just updates the pointer rather than rotating the header; this may be more efficient to implement. We show these three approaches in Figure 4.5. In each case, the entry that this switch needs to read is A and the entry that the next switch needs to read is B.

The main reason source routing is not used extensively is that it suffers from a scaling problem. In any reasonably large network, it is very hard for a host to get the complete path information it needs to construct correct headers.

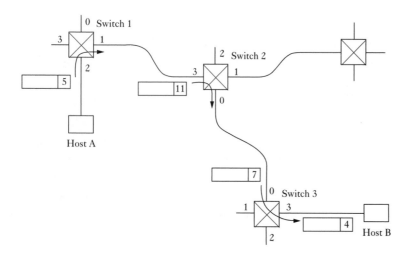

Figure 4.6 An example of a virtual circuit network.

4.1.2 Virtual Circuit Switching

A widely used technique for packet switching uses the concept of a *virtual circuit*. This approach, which is also called a connection-oriented model, requires that we first set up a virtual connection from the source host to the destination host. To understand how this works, consider Figure 4.6, where host A again wants to send packets to host B. It begins by sending a connection request message toward host B, which arrives at switch 1. This request message contains an address for host B and a *virtual circuit identifier* or VCI, which the switch will use to identify subsequent packets that A wants to send to B. The only requirement for this identifier is that it must not currently be in use on the link between host A and switch 1. In this example, let's assume host A picks the identifier 5.

When switch 1 receives the connection request, it tries to determine how to get to host B. For the moment, we assume that switch 1 knows enough about the network topology to figure out that it can get to host B using port 1. It creates an entry in its virtual circuit table that says, "when packets arrive on port 2 with identifier 5, send them out on port 1." Also, since the identifier 5 was only unique on the link from host A to switch 1, the switch chooses a new identifier that it knows to be unused on the link to switch 2. Let's assume it chooses 11. Thus, switch 1 really adds the following information to the table: "when packets arrive on port 2 with identifier 5, replace the identifier with 11 and send the packet out on port 1." A piece of the virtual circuit table for switch 1 is shown in Table 4.1. The third line of the table shows how to handle packets from host A with identifier 5; the other lines correspond to other connections that have already been established.

When switches 2 and 3 receive the connection request message, they behave similarly to switch 1, and eventually the tables are set up in all three switches and the connection request

Input Port	Incoming Identifier	Output Port	Outgoing Identifier
2	1	2	4
2	4	0	3
2	5	1	11
2	6	0	4

Table 4.1   Segment of virtual circuit table for switch 1.

message can be delivered to host B. Host B accepts (or rejects) the connection and sends an acceptance notice back toward A. Once host A receives the acceptance, it knows that all the switches are set up, and all it has to do is send packets with the identifier 5 in the header and it can rely on the switches to get them to the destination. The identifier 5 gets remapped to 11 at the first switch, to 7 at the second switch, and to 4 at the last switch. Host B knows when it sees a packet with identifier 4 that it belongs to this connection, and thus that it came from host A, even though the packet contains neither the address of host A nor even the identifier that A chose for the connection.

When host A no longer wants to send data to host B, it tears down the connection by sending a teardown message to switch 1. The switch removes the relevant entry from its table and forwards the message on to the other switches in the path, which similarly delete the appropriate table entries. At this point, if host A were to send a packet with a VCI of 5 to switch 1, it would be dropped as if the connection had never existed.

There are several things to note about virtual circuit switching:

- Since host A has to wait for the connection request to reach the far side of the network and return before it can send its first data packet, there is at least one RTT of delay before data is sent.[1]

- While the connection request contains the full address for host B (which might be quite large, being a global identifier on the network), each data packet contains only a small identifier, which is only unique on one link. Thus, the per-packet overhead caused by the header is reduced.

- If a switch or a link in a connection fails, the connection is broken and a new one will need to be established. Also, the old one needs to be torn down to free up table storage space in the switches.

- The issue of how a switch decides which link to forward the connection request on has been glossed over. We discuss this issue in Section 4.2.

---

[1] This is not strictly true. Some people have proposed sending a data packet immediately after sending the connection request.

One of the nice aspects of virtual circuits is that by the time the host gets the go-ahead to send data, it knows quite a lot about the network—for example, that there really is a route to the receiver and that the receiver is willing and able to receive data. It is also possible to allocate resources to the virtual circuit at the time it is established. For example, an X.25 network—a packet-switched network that uses the connection-oriented model—employs the following three-part strategy: (1) buffers are allocated to each virtual circuit when the circuit is initialized; (2) the sliding window protocol is run between each pair of nodes along the virtual circuit, and this protocol is augmented with flow control to keep the sending node from overrunning the buffers allocated at the receiving node; and (3) the circuit is rejected by a given node if not enough buffers are available at that node when the connection request message is processed. In doing these three things, each node is ensured of having the buffers it needs to queue the packets that arrive on that circuit. This basic strategy is usually called *hop-by-hop flow control*.

By generalizing this idea, one could imagine providing each circuit with a different *quality of service* (QoS). In this setting, the term *quality of service* is usually taken to mean that the network gives the user some kind of performance-related guarantee, which in turn implies that switches set aside the resources they need to meet this guarantee. For example, the switches along a given virtual circuit might allocate a percentage of each outgoing link's bandwidth to that circuit. As another example, a sequence of switches might ensure that packets belonging to a particular circuit not be delayed (queued) for more than a certain amount of time. We return to the topic of resource allocation and quality of service in Chapters 8 and 9.

4.1.3 Datagrams

The alternative to connection-oriented communication is a connectionless approach. In switched networks, this is also called a *datagram* model. The idea behind datagrams is incredibly simple: you do not set up a connection, you just make sure that every packet contains enough information to get it to its destination. That is, every packet contains the complete destination address. Consider the example network illustrated in Figure 4.7, in which the hosts have addresses A, B, C, and so on. To decide how to forward a packet, a switch consults a *forwarding table* (often called a *routing table*), an example of which is depicted in Table 4.2. This particular table shows the forwarding information that switch 2 needs to forward datagrams in the example network. It is pretty easy to figure out such a table when you have a complete map of a simple network like that depicted here; it is a lot harder for large, complex networks with potentially changing topology and multiple paths between destinations. That harder problem is the topic of Section 4.2. Note that the problem of forwarding datagrams is essentially the same problem as getting the virtual circuit connection request to follow the right path in a connection-oriented network.

Connectionless (datagram) networks have the following characteristics:

■ There is no round-trip-time delay in waiting for a connection setup; a host can send data as soon as it is ready.

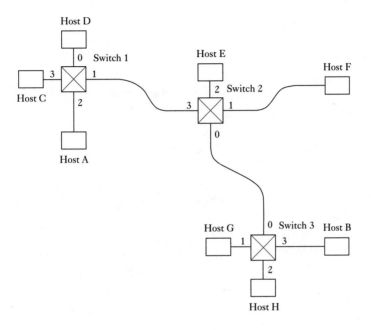

Figure 4.7 Datagram routing: an example network.

Destination	Switch Port
A	3
B	0
C	3
D	3
E	2
F	1
G	0
H	0

Table 4.2 Forwarding table for switch 2.

■ When a host sends a packet, it has no way of knowing if the network is capable of delivering it or if the destination host is even up and running.

■ Each packet is forwarded independently of previous packets that might have been sent to the same destination. Thus, a switch or link failure might not have any serious effect on communication, if it is possible to find an alternate route around the failure and to update the forwarding table accordingly. In contrast, a connection-oriented network would lose the connection in the event of a link failure and a new connection would need to be established.

■ Since every packet must carry the full address of the destination, the overhead per packet is higher than for the connection-oriented model (all other things being equal).

Introduction to Congestion

Recall the distinction between contention and congestion: contention occurs when multiple packets have to be queued at a switch because they are competing for the same output link, while congestion means that the switch has so many packets queued that it runs out of buffer space and has to start dropping packets. We return to the topic of congestion in Chapter 8, after we have seen the transport protocol component of the network architecture. At this point, however, we observe that the decision as to whether your network uses virtual circuits or datagrams has an impact on how you deal with congestion.

On the one hand, suppose that each switch allocates enough buffers to handle the packets belonging to each virtual circuit it supports, as is done in an X.25 network. In this case, the network has defined away the problem of congestion—a switch never encounters a situation in which it has more packets to queue than it has buffer space, since it does not allow the connection to be established in the first place unless it can dedicate

Notice that since there is no connection-establishment phase and each switch processes each packet independently, it is not obvious how a datagram network would allocate resources in a meaningful way. Instead, each arriving packet competes with all other packets for buffer space. If there are no free buffers, the incoming packet must be discarded. We observe, however, that even in a datagram-based network, a source host often sends a sequence of packets to the same destination host. It is possible for each switch to distinguish among the set of packets it currently has queued, based on the source/destination pair, and thus for the switch to ensure that the packets belonging to each source/destination pair are receiving a fair share of the switch's buffers. We discuss this idea in much greater depth in Chapter 8.

4.1.4 Implementation and Performance

So far, we have talked about what a switch must do without discussing how to do it. There is a very simple way to build a switch: buy a general-purpose workstation and equip it with a number of network interfaces. Such a device can receive packets, perform any of the switching functions described above, and send packets out over its interfaces. This is in fact a popular way to build experimental switches when you want to be able to do things like develop new routing protocols, because it offers extreme flexibility and a familiar programming environment.

enough resources to it to avoid this situation. The problem with this approach, however, is that it is extremely conservative—it is unlikely that all the circuits will need to use all of their buffers at the same time, and as a consequence, the switch is potentially underutilized.

On the other hand, the datagram model seemingly invites congestion—you do not know that there is enough contention at a switch to cause congestion until you run out of buffers. At that point, it is too late to prevent the congestion and your only choice is to try to recover from it. The good news, of course, is that you are likely to get much better utilization out of your switches since you are not holding buffers in reserve for a worst-case scenario that is unlikely to happen.

As is quite often the case, nothing is strictly black and white—there are design advantages for defining congestion away (as the X.25 model does) and for doing nothing about congestion until after it happens (as the simple datagram model does). We describe some of these design points in Chapter 8.

Figure 4.8 shows a workstation with three network interfaces used as a switch. The figure shows a path that a packet might take from the time it arrives on interface 1 until it is output on interface 2. We have assumed here that the workstation has a mechanism to move data directly from an interface to its main memory without having to be directly copied by the CPU; i.e., direct memory access (DMA) as described in Section 3.8. Once the packet is in memory, the CPU examines its header to determine which interface the packet should be sent out on. It then uses DMA to move the packet out to the appropriate interface. Note that Figure 4.8 does not show the packet going to the CPU because the CPU inspects only the header of the packet; it does not have to read every byte of data in the packet.

The main problem with using a workstation as a switch is that its performance is limited by the fact that all packets must pass through a single point of contention: in the example shown, each packet crosses the I/O bus twice and is written to and read from main memory once. The upper bound on aggregate throughput of such a device (the total sustainable data rate summed over all inputs) is, thus, either half the main memory bandwidth or half the I/O bus bandwidth, whichever is

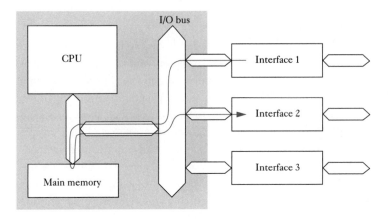

Figure 4.8 A workstation used as a packet switch.

less.   (Usually, it's the I/O bus bandwidth.)   For many applications, this limit will
make performance too low.   This upper bound also assumes that moving data is the
only problem—a fair approximation for long packets but a bad one when packets are
short.   In the latter case, the cost of processing each packet—parsing its header, and
deciding which output link to transmit it on—is likely to dominate. Suppose, for example,
that a workstation could switch 15,000 packets each second. (This is an achievable number
on today's systems.) If the average packet is short, say 64 bytes, this would imply a throughput
of 7.68 Mbps—substantially below the range that users are demanding from their networks
today. Bear in mind that this 7.68 Mbps would be shared by all users connected to the switch,
just as the 10 Mbps of an Ethernet (or the 100 Mbps of an FDDI ring) is shared among all
users connected to the shared medium.

   To address this problem, hardware designers have come up with a large array of switch
designs that reduce the amount of contention and provide high aggregate throughput. Note
that some contention is unavoidable: if every input has data to send to a single output, then
they cannot all send it at once. However, if data destined for different outputs is arriving at
different inputs, a well-designed switch will be able to move data from inputs to outputs in
parallel, thus increasing the aggregate throughput. We discuss some approaches to handling
contention in Section 4.4.

4.2 Routing

The preceding discussion assumes that either the hosts (in the case of source routing) or the
switches have enough knowledge of the network topology so they can choose the right port
onto which each packet should be output. In the case of virtual circuits, routing is an issue
only for the connection request packet; all subsequent packets follow the same path as the
request. In datagram networks, routing is an issue for every packet. In either case, a switch

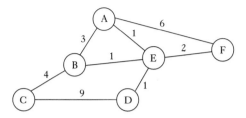

Figure 4.9   Network represented as a graph.

needs to be able to look at the packet's destination address and then to determine which of the output ports is the best choice to get the packet to that address. As we saw in Section 4.1.3, the switch makes this decision by consulting a forwarding table. The fundamental problem of routing is, How do switches acquire the information in their forwarding tables?

We need to make an important distinction, which is often neglected, between *forwarding* and *routing*. Forwarding consists of taking a packet, looking at its destination address, consulting a table, and sending the packet in a direction determined by that table. Routing is the process by which forwarding tables are built and is a topic to which people devote entire careers.

4.2.1   Network as a Graph

Routing is, in essence, a problem of graph theory. Figure 4.9 shows a graph representing a network. The nodes of the graph, labeled A through F, may be either hosts or switches, although for our purposes, we limit the graph to just the switches in the network. We can do this because hosts are typically connected to just one switch, making their forwarding decision trivial; they need not be concerned with routing. The edges of the graph correspond to the network links. Each edge has an associated *cost*, which gives some indication of the desirability of sending traffic over that link. A discussion of how edge costs are assigned is given in Section 4.2.4.[2]

The basic problem of routing is to find the lowest-cost path between any two nodes, where the cost of a path equals the sum of the costs of all the edges that make up the path. For a simple network like the one in Figure 4.9, you could imagine just calculating all the shortest paths and loading them into some non-volatile storage on each node. Such a static approach has several shortcomings:

  ■ It does not deal with node or link failures.

  ■ It does not consider the addition of new nodes or links.

---

[2]In the example networks (graphs) used throughout this chapter, we use undirected edges and assign each edge a single cost. This is actually a slight simplification. It is more accurate to make the edges directed, which typically means that there would be a pair of edges between each node—one flowing in each direction and each with its own edge cost.

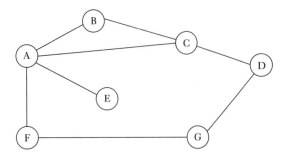

Figure 4.10 Distance-vector routing: an example network.

- It implies that edge costs cannot change, even though we might reasonably wish to temporarily assign a high cost to a link that is heavily loaded.

For these reasons, routing is achieved in most practical networks by running routing protocols among the switches. These protocols provide a distributed, dynamic way to solve the problem of finding the lowest-cost path in the presence of link and node failures and changing edge costs. Note the word "distributed" in the last sentence: centralization is the enemy of scalability, so all good routing protocols are distributed. To begin our analysis, we assume that we know the edge costs and we look at the two main classes of routing protocols: *distance vector* and *link state*. In Section 4.2.4 we return to the problem of calculating edge costs in a meaningful way.

Note that this section discusses the principles of routing. These principles are being applied at the time of this writing to define routing protocols for the main packet-switched network discussed in this chapter (see the coverage of ATM in Section 4.3), but these protocols are not yet at a stage of maturity to describe in this book. It turns out that the most widely used and mature routing protocols in use today were developed for the Internet, which is the topic of the next chapter. Therefore, we postpone giving concrete examples of routing protocols until then and concentrate instead on the important ideas.

4.2.2 Distance Vector

The idea behind the distance-vector algorithm is suggested by its name: "distance" is really some metric (measurement) that we want to minimize and "vector" is simply the first step (direction) in the route that we want packets to follow. The starting assumption for distance-vector routing is that each node knows the cost of the link to each of its directly connected neighbors. A link that is down is assigned an infinite cost.

Global Perspective

To see how a distance-vector routing algorithm works, it is easiest to consider an example like the one depicted in Figure 4.10. In this example, the cost of each link is set to 1, so that a least-cost path is simply the one with the fewest hops. (Since all edges have the same cost,

Information	Distance to Reach Node						
Stored at Node	A	B	C	D	E	F	G
A	0	1	1	∞	1	1	∞
B	1	0	1	∞	∞	∞	∞
C	1	1	0	1	∞	∞	∞
D	∞	∞	1	0	∞	∞	1
E	1	∞	∞	∞	0	∞	∞
F	1	∞	∞	∞	∞	0	1
G	∞	∞	∞	1	∞	1	0

Table 4.3 Initial distances stored at each node (global view).

we do not show the costs in the graph.) We can represent each node's knowledge about the distances to all other nodes as a table like the one given in Table 4.3. Note that each node only knows the information in one row of the table (the one that bears its name in the left column). The global view that is presented here is not available at any single point in the network.

We may consider each row in Table 4.3 as a list of distances from one node to all other nodes, representing the current beliefs of that node. Initially, each node sets a cost of 1 to its directly connected neighbors and ∞ to all other nodes. Thus, A initially believes that it can reach B in one hop and that D is unreachable. The next step in distance-vector routing is that every node sends a message to its directly connected neighbors containing its personal list of distances. Thus, for example, the top line of the table above describes A's beliefs about the distances to the other nodes, so it sends that information to its neighbors B, C, E, and F. If any of the recipients of the information from A find that A is advertising a path shorter than the one they currently know about, they update their list to give the new path length and note that they should send packets for that destination through A.

For example, node B learns from A that node E can be reached at a cost of 1; B also knows it can reach A at a cost of 1, so it adds these to get the cost of reaching E by means of A. This total cost of 2 is less than the current cost of infinity, so B records that it can reach E at a cost of 2 by going through A. In the next cycle, B passes on to C the information that E can be reached through B at a cost of 2. However, C will by then have learned that it can reach E at a cost of 2 by means of A. To reach E through B would mean a total cost of 3, so C does not update its distance list. Thus, after every node has exchanged a few updates with its directly connected neighbors (and in the absence of any topology changes), all nodes will know the least-cost path to all the other nodes. The final set of distances stored at each node is given in Table 4.4.

Information	Distance to Reach Node						
Stored at Node	A	B	C	D	E	F	G
A	0	1	1	2	1	1	2
B	1	0	1	2	2	2	3
C	1	1	0	1	2	2	2
D	2	2	1	0	3	2	1
E	1	2	2	3	0	2	3
F	1	2	2	2	2	0	1
G	2	3	2	1	3	1	0

Table 4.4 Final distances stored at each node (global view).

In addition to updating their list of distances when they receive updates, the nodes need to keep track of which node told them about the path that they used to calculate the cost, so that they can create their forwarding table. For example, B knows that it was A who said "I can reach E in one hop" and so B puts an entry in its table that says "To reach E, use the link to A." This is the vector part of distance-vector routing—the vector is the direction in which to send packets to reach a given destination.

Per-Node Perspective

The preceding discussion takes a somewhat global view of how the distance-vector algorithm works. In practice, each node's forwarding table consists of a set of triples of the form:

(Destination, Cost, NextHop).

For example, Table 4.5 shows the complete routing table maintained at node B for the network in Figure 4.10. Also, each node then sends updates to (and receives updates from) its neighbors. Each of these updates is a list of pairs of the form:

(Destination, Cost).

Whenever a node receives an update from a neighbor that includes a route that is better than one of its current routes, it changes the route in its forwarding table. Note that Table 4.5 shows that the best route to node G is through node A, even though B could also use node C to reach G at the same cost (3). The route that gets used depends on which of its neighbors B happened to hear from first.

There are two circumstances under which a given node decides to send an update to its neighbors. First, each node automatically sends an update message every so often, even if nothing has changed. This serves to let the other nodes know that this node is still running. It also makes sure that they keep getting information that they may need if their current routes

Destination	Cost	NextHop
A	1	A
C	1	C
D	2	C
E	2	A
F	2	A
G	3	A

Table 4.5   Routing table maintained at node B.

become unviable. The frequency of these periodic updates varies from protocol to protocol, but it is typically on the order of several seconds to several minutes. The second mechanism, sometimes called a *triggered* update, happens whenever a node receives an update from one of its neighbors that causes it to change one of the routes in its forwarding table. That is, whenever a node's forwarding table changes, it sends an update to its neighbors, which may lead to a change in their tables, causing them to send an update to their neighbors.

Now consider what happens when a link or node fails. The nodes that notice first send new lists of distances to their neighbors and, normally, the system settles down fairly quickly to a new state. As to the question of how a node detects a failure, there are a couple of different answers. In one approach, a node continually tests the link to another node by sending a control packet and seeing if it receives an acknowledgment. In another approach, a node determines that the link (or the node at the other end of the link) is down if it does not receive the expected periodic routing update for the last few update cycles.

To understand what happens when a node detects a link failure, consider what happens when F detects that its link to G has failed. First, F sets its new distance to G to infinity and passes that information along to A. Since A knows that its 2-hop path to G is through F, A would also set its distance to G to infinity. However, with the next update from C, A would learn that C has a 2-hop path to G. Thus A would know that it could reach G in 3 hops through C, which is less than infinity, and so A would update its table accordingly. When it advertises this to F, node F would learn that it can reach G at a cost of 4 through A, which is less than infinity, and the system would again become stable.

Unfortunately, slightly different circumstances can prevent the network from stabilizing. Suppose, for example, that the link from A to E goes down. In the next round of updates, A advertises a distance of infinity to E, but B and C advertise a distance of 2 to E. Depending on the exact timing of events, the following might happen: node B, upon hearing that E can be reached in 2 hops from C, concludes that it can reach E in 3 hops and advertises this to A; node A concludes that it can reach E in 4 hops and advertises this to C; node C concludes that it can reach E in 5 hops; and so on. This cycle stops only when the distances reach some number that is large enough to be considered infinite. In the meantime, none of the nodes actually knows that E is unreachable, and the routing tables for the network do not stabilize.

There are several partial solutions to this problem. One technique to break routing loops is called *split horizon*. The idea is that when a node sends a routing update to its neighbors, it does not send those routes it learned from each neighbor back to that neighbor. For example, if B has the route (E, 2, A) in its table, then it knows it must have learned this route from A, and so whenever B sends a routing update to A, it does not include the route (E, 2) in that update. In a stronger variation of split horizon, called *split horizon with poison reverse*, B actually sends that route back to A, but it puts negative information in the route to ensure that A will not eventually use B to get to E. For example, B sends the route (E, ∞) to A. The problem with both of these techniques is that they only work for routing loops that involve two nodes. For larger routing loops, more drastic measures are called for. Continuing the above example, if B and C had waited for a while after hearing of the link failure from A before advertising routes to E, they would have found that neither of them really had a route to E. Unfortunately, this approach delays the convergence of the protocol; speed of convergence is one of the key advantages of its competitor, link-state routing.

Implementation

The code that implements this algorithm is very straightforward; we give only some of the basics here. Structure Route defines each entry in the forwarding table, and constant MAX_TTL specifies how long an entry is kept in the table before it is discarded.

```
#define MAX_ROUTES      128     /* maximum size of routing table */
#define MAX_TTL         120     /* time (in seconds) until route expires */

typedef struct {
    NodeAddr    Destination;    /* address of destination */
    NodeAddr    NextHop;        /* address of next hop */
    int         Cost;           /* distance metric */
    u_short     TTL;            /* time to live */
} Route;

int     numRoutes = 0;
Route   routingTable[MAX_ROUTES];
```

The routine that updates the local node's forwarding table based on a new route is given by mergeRoute. Although not shown, a timer function periodically scans the list of routes in the node's routing table, decrements the TTL (time to live) field of each route, and discards any routes that have a time to live of 0. Notice, however, that the TTL field is reset to MAX_TTL any time the route is reconfirmed by an update message from a neighboring node.

```
void
mergeRoute (Route *new)
{
    int i;
```

```
for (i = 0; i < numRoutes; ++i)
{
    if (new->Destination == routingTable[i].Destination)
    {
        if (new->Cost + 1 < routingTable[i].Cost)
        {
            /* found a better route: */
            break;
        } else if (new->NextHop == routingTable[i].NextHop) {
            /* metric for current next-hop may have changed: */
            break;
        } else {
            /* route is uninteresting---just ignore it */
            return;
        }
    }
}
routingTable[i] = *new;
/* reset TTL */
routingTable[i].TTL = MAX_TTL;
/* account for hop to get to next node */
++routingTable[i].Cost;
if (i == numRoutes)
{
    /* this is a completely new route */
    ++numRoutes;
}
}
```

Finally, the procedure updateRoutingTable is the main routine that calls mergeRoute to incorporate all the routes contained in a routing update that is received from a neighboring node.

```
void
updateRoutingTable (Route *newRoute[], int numNewRoutes)
{
    int i;

    for (i=0; i < numNewRoutes; ++i)
    {
        mergeRoute(&newRoute[i]);
    }
}
```

4.2.3 Link State

The starting assumptions for link-state routing are rather similar to those for distance-vector routing. Each node is assumed to be capable of finding out the state of the link to its neighbors (up or down) and the cost of each link. Again, we want to provide each switch with enough information to enable it to find the least-cost path to any destination. The basic idea behind link-state protocols is very simple: every node knows how to reach its directly connected neighbors, and if we make sure that the totality of this knowledge is disseminated to every node, then every node will have enough knowledge of the network to determine correct routes to any destination. In fact, each node will have enough information to let it build a complete map of the network. Thus, link-state routing protocols rely on two mechanisms: reliable dissemination of link-state information and the calculation of routes from the sum of all the accumulated link-state knowledge.

Reliable Flooding

Reliable flooding is the process of making sure that all the nodes participating in the routing protocol get a copy of the link-state information from all the other nodes. As the term "flooding" suggests, the basic idea is for a node to send its link-state information out on all of its directly connected links, with each node that receives this information forwarding it out on all of *its* links. This process continues until the information has reached all the nodes in the network.

More precisely, each node creates an update packet, also called a link-state packet (LSP), that contains the following information:

■ the ID of the node that created the LSP;

■ a list of directly connected neighbors of that node, with the cost of the link to each one;

■ a sequence number;

■ a time to live (TTL) for this packet.

The first two items are needed to enable route calculation; the last two are used to make the process of flooding the packet to all nodes reliable. Reliability includes making sure that you have the most recent copy of the information, since there may be multiple, contradictory LSPs from one node traversing the network. Making the flooding reliable has proven to be quite difficult. (For example, an early version of link-state routing used in the ARPANET caused that network to fail in 1981.)

Flooding works in the following way. When a node X receives a copy of an LSP that originated at some other node Y, it checks to see if it has already stored a copy of an LSP from Y. If not, it stores the LSP. If it already has a copy, it compares the sequence numbers; if the new LSP has a larger sequence number, it is assumed to be the more recent, and that LSP is stored, replacing the old one (otherwise it is discarded). The new LSP is then forwarded on to all neighbors of X except the neighbor from which the LSP was just received. Thus, the most recent copy of the LSP reaches all nodes.

Each node generates a new LSP periodically. Each time it generates a new LSP, it increments the sequence number by 1. Unlike most sequence numbers used in protocols, these sequence numbers are not expected to wrap, so the field needs to be quite large (say 64 bits). If a node goes down and then comes back up, it starts with a sequence number of 0. If the node was down for a long time, all the old LSPs for that node will have timed out (as described below); otherwise, this node will eventually receive a copy of its own LSP with a higher sequence number, which it can then use to set its own sequence number.

The aging process aims to delete old LSPs. This is done by decrementing the TTL of stored LSPs at a suitable rate. Some subtle aspects of this process that have improved the reliability of flooding include always decrementing the TTL of an LSP before forwarding a copy of it, and reflooding a stored LSP when its TTL reaches 0, so that all the nodes delete it at the same time.

Route Calculation

Once a given node has a copy of the LSP from every other node, it is able to compute a complete map for the topology of the network, and from this map to decide the best route to each destination. The question, then, is exactly how it calculates routes from this information. The solution is based on a well-known algorithm from graph theory—Dijkstra's shortest-path algorithm.

We first define Dijkstra's algorithm in graph-theoretic terms. Imagine that a node takes all the LSPs it has received and constructs a graphical representation of the network, in which N denotes the set of nodes in the graph, $l(i, j)$ denotes the non-negative cost (weight) associated with the edge between nodes $i, j \in N$, and $l(i, j) = \infty$ if no edge connects i and j. In the following description, we let $s \in N$ denote this node, that is, the node executing the algorithm to find the shortest path to all the other nodes in N. Also, the algorithm maintains the following two variables: M denotes the set of nodes incorporated so far by the algorithm, and $C(n)$ denotes the cost of the path from s to each node n. Given these definitions, the algorithm is defined as follows:

$M = \{s\}$
for each n in $N - \{s\}$
    $C(n) = l(s, n)$
while ($N \neq M$)
    $M = M \cup \{w\}$ such that $C(w)$ is the minimum for all w in $(N - M)$
    for each n in $(N - M)$
        $C(n) = \text{MIN}(C(n), C(w) + l(w, n))$

Basically, the algorithm works as follows. We start with M containing this node s and then initialize the table of costs (the $C(n)$s) to other nodes using the known costs to directly connected nodes. We then look for the node that is reachable at the lowest cost (w) and add it to M. Finally, we update the table of costs by considering the cost of reaching nodes through w. In the last line of the algorithm, we choose a new route to node n that goes through node w if the total cost of going from the source to w and then following the link from w to n is less

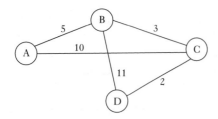

Figure 4.11 Link-state routing: an example network.

than the old route we had to n. This procedure is repeated until all nodes are incorporated in M.

In practice, each switch computes its routing table directly from the LSPs it has collected using a realization of Dijkstra's algorithm called the *forward search* algorithm. Specifically, each switch maintains two lists, known as Tentative and Confirmed. Each of these lists contains a set of entries of the form (Destination, Cost, NextHop). The algorithm works as follows:

1 Initialize the Confirmed list with an entry for myself; this entry has a cost of 0.

2 For the node just added to the Confirmed list in the previous step, call it node Next, select its LSP.

3 For each neighbor (Neighbor) of Next, calculate the cost (Cost) to reach this Neighbor as the sum of the cost from myself to Next and from Next to Neighbor.

    (a) If Neighbor is currently on neither the Confirmed nor the Tentative list, then add (Neighbor, Cost, NextHop) to the Tentative list, where NextHop is the direction I go to reach Next.

    (b) If Neighbor is currently on the Tentative list, and the Cost is less that the currently listed cost for Neighbor, then replace the current entry with (Neighbor, Cost, NextHop), where NextHop is the direction I go to reach Next.

4 If the Tentative list is empty, stop. Otherwise, pick the entry from the Tentative list with the lowest cost, move it to the Confirmed list, and return to step 2.

This will become a lot easier to understand when we look at an example. Consider the network depicted in Figure 4.11. Note that, unlike our previous example, this network has a range of different edge costs. Table 4.6 traces the steps for building the routing database for node D. We denote the two outputs of D by using the names of the nodes to which they connect, B and C. Note the way the algorithm seems to head off on false leads (like the 11-unit cost path to B that was the first addition to the Tentative list) but ends up with the least-cost paths to all nodes.

Step	Confirmed	Tentative	Comments
1	(D,0,-)		Since D is the only new member of the confirmed list, look at its LSP.
2	(D,0,-)	(B,11,B) (C,2,C)	D's LSP says we can reach B through B at cost 11, which is better than anything else on either list, so put it on Tentative list; same for C.
3	(D,0,-) (C,2,C)	(B,11,B)	Put lowest-cost member of Tentative (C) onto Confirmed list. Next, examine LSP of newly confirmed member (C).
4	(D,0,-) (C,2,C)	(B,5,C) (A,12,C)	Cost to reach B through C is 5, so replace (B,11,B). C's LSP tells us that we can reach A at cost 12.
5	(D,0,-) (C,2,C) (B,5,C)	(A,12,C)	Move lowest-cost member of Tentative (B) to Confirmed, then look at its LSP.
6	(D,0,-) (C,2,C) (B,5,C)	(A,10,C)	Since we can reach A at cost 5 through B, replace the Tentative entry.
7	(D,0,-) (C,2,C) (B,5,C) (A,10,C)		Move lowest-cost member of Tentative (A) to Confirmed, and we are all done.

Table 4.6   Steps for building routing database for node D (Figure 4.11).

The link-state routing algorithm has many nice properties: it has been proven to be self-stabilizing quickly; it does not generate much traffic; and it responds rapidly to topology changes or node failures. On the downside, the amount of information stored at each node (one LSP for every other node in the network) can be quite large. This is one of the fundamental problems of routing and is an instance of a more general problem known as *scalability*. Some solutions to both the specific problem, the amount of storage potentially required at each node, and the general problem, scalability, will be discussed in the next chapter.

Thus, the difference between the distance-vector and link-state algorithms can be summarized as follows. In distance vector, each nodes talks only to its directly connected neighbors, but it tells them everything it has learned (i.e., its entire forwarding table). In link state, each node talks to all other nodes, but it tells them only what it knows for sure (i.e., only the state of its directly connected links).

4.2.4 Metrics

The preceding discussion assumes that link costs, or metrics, are known when we execute the routing algorithm. In this section, we look at some ways to calculate link costs that have proven effective in practice. One example that we have seen already, which is quite reasonable and very simple, is to assign a cost of 1 to all links—the least-cost route will then be the one with the fewest hops. Such an approach has several drawbacks, however. First, it does not distinguish between links on a latency basis. Thus, a satellite link with 250-ms latency looks just as attractive to the routing protocol as a terrestrial link with 1 ms latency. Second, it does not distinguish between routes on a capacity basis, making a 9.6-Kbps link look just as good as a 45-Mbps link. Finally, it does not distinguish between links based on their current load, making it impossible to route around overloaded links. It turns out that this last problem is the hardest because you are trying to capture the complex and dynamic characteristics of a link in a single scalar cost.

The ARPANET was the testing ground for a number of different approaches to link-cost calculation. (It was also the place where the superior stability of link-state over distance-vector routing was demonstrated; the original mechanism used distance vector while the later version used link state.) The following discussion traces the evolution of the ARPANET routing metric, and in so doing, explores the subtle aspects of the problem.

The original ARPANET routing metric measured the number of packets that were queued waiting to be transmitted on each link, meaning that a link with 10 packets queued waiting to be transmitted was assigned a larger cost weight than a link with 5 packets queued for transmission. Using queue length as a routing metric did not work well, however, since queue length is an artificial measure of load—it moves packets toward the shortest queue rather than toward the destination, a situation all too familiar to those of us who hop from line to line at the grocery store. Stated more precisely, the original ARPANET routing mechanism suffered from the fact that it did not take either the bandwidth or the latency of the link into consideration.

A second version of the ARPANET routing algorithm, sometimes called the "new routing mechanism," took both link bandwidth and latency into consideration and used delay, rather than queue length, as a measure of load. This was done as follows. First, each incoming packet was timestamped with its arrival time (ArrivalTime); its departure time (DepartTime) was also recorded. Second, when the link-level ACK was received from the other side, the node computed the delay for that packet as

$$\text{Delay} = (\text{DepartTime} - \text{ArrivalTime}) + \text{TransmissionTime} + \text{Latency}$$

where TransmissionTime and Latency were statically defined for the link and captured the link's bandwidth and latency, respectively. Notice that in this case, DepartTime − ArrivalTime represents the amount of time the packet was delayed (queued) in the node due to load. If the

ACK did not arrive, but instead the packet timed out, then DepartTime was reset to the time
the packet was *retransmitted*. In this case, DepartTime − ArrivalTime captures the reliability
of the link—the more frequent the retransmission of packets, the less reliable the link, and
the more we want to avoid it. Finally, the weight assigned to each link was derived from the
average delay experienced by the packets recently sent over that link.

Although an improvement over the original mechanism, this approach also had a lot of
problems. Under light load, it worked reasonably well, since the two static factors of delay
dominated the cost. Under heavy load, however, a congested link would start to advertise
a very high cost. This caused all the traffic to move off that link, leaving it idle, so then it
would advertise a low cost, thereby attracting back all the traffic, and so on. The effect of
this instability was that, under heavy load, many links would in fact spend a great deal of time
being idle, which is the last thing you want under heavy load.

Another problem was that the range of link values was much too large. For example, a
heavily loaded 9.6-Kbps link could look 127 times more costly than a lightly loaded 56-Kbps
link. This means that the routing algorithm would choose a path with 126 hops of lightly
loaded 56-Kbps links in preference to a 1-hop 9.6-Kbps path. While shedding some traffic
from an overloaded line is a good idea, making it look so unattractive that it loses all its traffic
is excessive. Using 126 hops when 1 hop will do is in general a bad use of network resources.
Also, satellite links were unduly penalized, so that an idle 56-Kbps satellite link looked considerably more costly than an idle 9.6-Kbps terrestrial link, even though the former would
give better performance for high-bandwidth applications.

A third approach, called the "revised ARPANET routing metric" addressed these problems. The major changes were to compress the dynamic range of the metric considerably, to
account for the link type, and to smooth the variation of the metric with time.

The smoothing was achieved by several mechanisms. First, the delay measurement was
transformed to a link utilization and this number was averaged with the last reported utilization to suppress sudden changes. Second, there was a hard limit on how much the metric
could change from one measurement cycle to the next. By smoothing the changes in the cost,
the likelihood that all nodes would abandon a route at once is greatly reduced.

The compression of the dynamic range was achieved by feeding the measured utilization, the link type, and the link speed into a function that is shown graphically in Figure 4.12.
Observe the following:

- a highly loaded link never shows a cost of more than three times its cost when idle;

- the most expensive link is only seven times the cost of the least expensive;

- a high-speed satellite link is more attractive than a low-speed terrestrial link;

- cost is a function of link utilization only at moderate to high loads.

All these factors mean that a link is much less likely to be universally abandoned, since a three-
fold increase in cost is likely to make the link unattractive for some paths while letting it remain the best choice for some others. The slopes, offsets, and breakpoints for the curves in

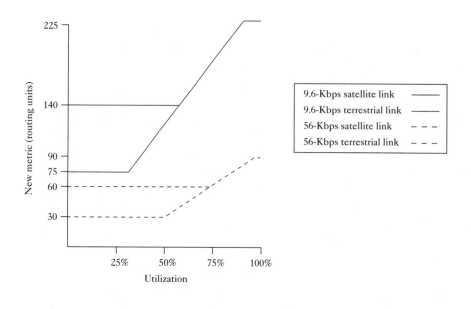

Figure 4.12 Revised ARPANET routing metric versus link utilization.

Figure 4.12 were arrived at by a great deal of trial and error, and they were carefully tuned to provide good performance.

There is one final issue related to calculating edge weights—the frequency with which each node calculates the weights on its links. There are two things to keep in mind. First, none of the metrics are instantaneous. That is, whether a node is measuring queue length, delay, or utilization, it is actually computing an average over a period of time. Second, just because a metric changes does not mean that the node sends out an update message. In practice, updates are sent only when the change to an edge weight is larger than some threshold.

4.2.5 Routing, Addressing, and Hierarchy

When we mentioned addresses at the start of this chapter, all we asked was that they provide a globally unique identifier for each node. Such an address, which provides no semantics other than its uniqueness, is normally called a *flat* address. Ethernet addresses are flat. The problem with flat addresses is that our forwarding tables need to have one entry for every host. This is a serious scaling problem: a forwarding table that grows linearly with the number of hosts clearly will not work for a global network. Also, recall that the link-state routing protocol requires each node to store an entire LSP for every other node in the network.

The most common technique to handle these problems is *route aggregation*, which is achieved using *hierarchical* addresses. For example, telephone numbers are a form of hierarchical address: in North America, they consist of a three-digit area code, followed by a seven-digit local phone number (which has some additional hierarchy that we ignore for now).

Route aggregation enables a switch to begin the process of routing a call by looking only at the area code. When a switch in the 201 area code of northern New Jersey sees a phone number that has an area code of 520 (southern Arizona), it does not need to look any further. It looks in its routing table for area code 520 and decides to send the call out on a westbound link. If the switch had seen an area code of 201, it would have looked further into the address, perhaps using the next three digits to decide which part of New Jersey to send the call to.

Hierarchical addressing and route aggregation, which are two sides of the same coin, have been widely used in the Internet. This is one of the reasons that the Internet has scaled up so successfully. We look at the specifics of Internet addressing and routing in the next chapter.

4.3 Cell Switching (ATM)

Now that we have discussed some of the general issues associated with switched networks, it is time to focus on one particular switching technology: *asynchronous transfer mode* (ATM). ATM has become a tremendously important technology in recent years for a variety of reasons, not the least of which is that it has been embraced by the telephone industry, which has historically been less than active in data communications except as a supplier of links on top of which other people have built networks. ATM also happened to be in the right place at the right time, as a high-speed switching technology that appeared on the scene just when shared media like Ethernet and FDDI were starting to look a bit too slow for many users of computer networks.

ATM is a connection-oriented, packet-switched network, which is to say, it uses virtual circuits very much in the manner described in Section 4.1.2. In ATM terminology, the connection setup phase is called *signalling*. At the time of this writing, the ATM Forum (the standards body that governs ATM) is still hammering out the details of an ATM signalling protocol known as Q.2931. In addition to discovering a suitable route across an ATM network, Q.2931 is also responsible for allocating resources at the switches along the circuit. This is done in an effort to ensure the circuit a particular quality of service. We return to this topic in Chapter 9, where we discuss it in the context of similar efforts to implement QoS.

The thing that makes ATM really unusual is that the packets that are switched in an ATM network are of fixed length. That length happens to be 53 bytes—5 bytes of header followed by 48 bytes of payload—a rather interesting choice that is discussed in more detail below. To distinguish these fixed-length packets from the more common variable-length packets normally used in computer networks, they are given a special name: *cells*. ATM may be thought of as the canonical example of cell switching.

4.3.1 Cells

All the packet-switching technologies we have looked at so far have used variable-length packets. Variable-length packets are normally constrained to fall within some bounds. The lower bound is set by the minimum amount of information that needs to be contained in the packet, which is typically a header with no optional extensions. The upper bound may be set by a variety of factors; the maximum FDDI packet size, for example, determines how long each station is allowed to transmit without passing on the token, and thus determines how long a station might have to wait for the token to reach it. Cells, in contrast, are both fixed in length and small in size. While this seems like a simple enough design choice, there are actually a lot of factors involved, as explained in the following paragraphs.

Cell Size

Variable-length packets have some nice characteristics. If you only have 1 byte to send (e.g., to acknowledge the receipt of a packet), you put it in a minimum-sized packet. If you have a large file to send, however, you break it up into as many maximum-sized packets as you need. You do not need to send any extraneous padding in the first case, and in the second, you drive down the ratio of header to data bytes, thus increasing bandwidth efficiency. You also minimize the total number of packets sent, thereby minimizing the total processing incurred by per-packet operations. This can be particularly important in obtaining high throughput, since many network devices are limited not by how many *bits* per second they can process but rather by the number of *packets* per second.

So, why use fixed-length cells? One of the main reasons was to facilitate the implementation of hardware switches. When ATM was being created in the mid and late 1980s, 10-Mbps Ethernet was the cutting-edge technology in terms of speed. To go much faster, most people thought in terms of hardware. Also, in the telephone world, people think big when they think of switches—telephone switches often serve tens of thousands of customers. Fixed-length packets turn out to be a very helpful thing if you want to build fast, highly scalable switches. There are two main reasons for this:

1 It is easier to build hardware to do simple jobs, and the job of processing packets is simpler when you already know how long each one will be.

2 If all packets are the same length, then you can have lots of switching elements all doing much the same thing in parallel, each of them taking the same time to do its job.

This second reason, the enabling of parallelism, greatly improves the scalability of switch designs. We will examine a highly scalable, parallel switch in Section 4.4.4. It would be overstating the case to say that fast, parallel hardware switches can only be built using fixed-length cells. However, it is certainly true that cells ease the task of building such hardware and that there was a lot of knowledge available about how to build cell switches in hardware at the time the ATM standards were being defined.

Another nice property of cells relates to the behavior of queues. Queues build up in a switch when traffic from several inputs may be heading for a single output. In general, once you extract a packet from a queue and start transmitting it, you need to continue until the whole packet is transmitted; it is not practical to preempt the transmission of a packet. (Recall that this idea is at the heart of statistical multiplexing.) The longest time that a queue output can be tied up is equal to the time it takes to transmit a maximum-sized packet. Fixed-length cells mean that a queue output is never tied up for more than the time it takes to transmit one cell, which is almost certainly shorter than the maximum-sized packet on a variable-length packet network. Thus, if tight control over the latency that is being experienced by cells when they pass through a queue is important, cells provide some advantage. Of course, long queues can still build up and there is no getting around the fact that some cells will have to wait their turn. What you get from cells is not much-shorter queues but potentially finer control over the behavior of queues.

An example will help to clarify this idea. Imagine a network with variable-length packets, where the maximum packet length is 4 KB and the link speed is 100 Mbps. The time to transmit a maximum-sized packet is $4096 \times 8/100 = 327.68\,\mu s$. Thus, a high-priority packet that arrives just after the switch starts to transmit a 4-KB packet will have to sit in the queue $327.68\,\mu s$ waiting for access to the link. In contrast, if the switch were forwarding 53-byte cells, the longest wait would be $53 \times 8/100 = 4.24\,\mu s$. This may not seem like a big deal, but the ability to control delay and especially to control its variation with time (jitter) can be important for some applications.

Queues of cells also tend to be a little shorter than queues of packets, for the following reason. When a packet begins to arrive in an empty queue, it is typical for the switch to have to wait for the whole packet to arrive before it can start transmitting the packet on an outgoing link. This means that the link sits idle while the packet arrives. However, if you imagine a large packet being replaced by a "train" of small cells, then as soon as the first cell in the train has entered the queue, the switch can transmit it. Imagine in the example above what would happen if two 4-KB packets arrived in a queue at about the same time. The link would sit idle for $327.68\,\mu s$ while these two packets arrive, and at the end of that period we would have 8 KB in the queue. Only then could the queue start to empty. If those same two packets were sent as trains of cells, then transmission of the cells could start $4.24\,\mu s$ after the first train started to arrive. At the end of $327.68\,\mu s$, the link would have been active for a little over $323\,\mu s$ and there would be just over 4 KB of data left in the queue, not 8 KB as before. Shorter queues mean less delay for all the traffic.

Having decided to use small, fixed-length packets, the next question is, What is the right length to fix them at? If you make them too short, then the amount of header information that needs to be carried around relative to the amount of data that fits in one cell gets larger, so the percentage of link bandwidth that is actually used to carry data goes down. Even more seriously, if you build a device that processes cells at some maximum number of cells per second, then as cells get shorter, the total data rate drops in direct proportion to cell size. An example of such a device might be a network adaptor that reassembles cells into larger units before handing them up to the host. The performance of such a device depends directly on cell size. On the other hand, if you make the cells too big, then there is a problem of wasted bandwidth caused by the need to pad transmitted data to fill a complete cell. If the cell payload size is 48 bytes and you want to send 1 byte, you'll need to send 47 bytes of padding. If this happens a lot, then the utilization of the link will be very low.

Efficient link utilization is not the only factor that influences cell size. For example, cell size has a particular effect on voice traffic, and since ATM grew out of the telephony community, one of the major concerns was that it be able to carry voice effectively. The standard digital encoding of voice is done at 64 Kbps (8-bit samples taken at 8 KHz). To maximize efficiency, you want to collect a full cell's worth of voice samples before transmitting a cell. A sampling rate of 8 KHz means that 1 byte is sampled every 125 μs, so the time it takes to fill an n-byte cell with samples is $n \times 125 \mu$s. If cells are, say, 1000 bytes long, it would take 125 ms just to collect a full cell of samples before you even start to transmit it to the receiver. That amount of latency starts to be quite noticeable to a human listener. Even considerably smaller latencies create problems for voice, particularly in the form of echoes. Echoes can be eliminated by a piece of technology called an echo canceler, but this adds cost to a telephone network that many network operators would rather avoid.

All of the above factors caused a great deal of debate in the international standards bodies when ATM was being standardized, and the fact that no length was perfect in all cases was used by those opposed to ATM to argue that fixed-length cells were a bad idea in the first place. As is so often the case with standards, the end result was a compromise that pleased almost no one: 48 bytes was chosen as the length for the ATM cell payload. Probably the greatest tragedy of this choice is that it is not a power of two, which means that it is quite a mismatch to most things that computers handle, like pages and cache lines. Rather

A Compromise of 48 Bytes

The explanation for why the payload of an ATM cell is 48 bytes is an interesting one and makes an excellent case for studying the process of standardization. As the ATM standard was evolving, the U.S. telephone companies were pushing for a 64-byte cell size, while the European companies were advocating 32-byte cells. The reason that the Europeans wanted the smaller size was that since the countries they served were of a small enough size, they would not have to install echo cancelers if they were able to keep the latency induced by generating a complete cell small enough. Thirty-two-byte cells were adequate for this purpose. In contrast, the U.S. is a large enough country that the phone companies had to install echo cancelers anyway, and so the larger cell size reflected a desire to improve the header-to-payload ratio.

Averaging is a classic form of compromise—48 bytes is simply the average of 64 bytes and 32 bytes. So as not to leave the false impression that this use of compromise-by-averaging is an isolated incident, we note that the seven-layer OSI model was actually a comprise between six and eight layers.

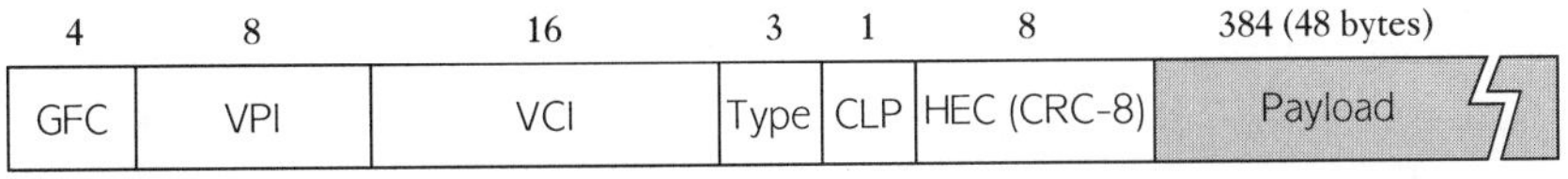

4	8	16	3	1	8	384 (48 bytes)
GFC	VPI	VCI	Type	CLP	HEC (CRC-8)	Payload

Figure 4.13   ATM cell format at the UNI.

less controversially, the header was fixed at 5 bytes. The format of an ATM cell is shown in Figure 4.13.

Cell Format

The ATM cell actually comes in two different formats, depending on where you look in the network. The one shown in Figure 4.13 is called the UNI (user-network interface) format; the alternative is the NNI (network-network interface). The UNI format is used when transmitting cells between a host and a switch, while the NNI format is used when transmitting cells between switches. The only difference is that the NNI format replaces the GFC field with 4 extra bits of VPI. Clearly, understanding all the three-letter acronyms (TLAs) is a key part of understanding ATM.

Starting from the leftmost byte of the cell (which is the first one transmitted), the UNI cell has 4 bits for Generic Flow Control (GFC). The use of these bits is not well defined at the time of this writing, but they are intended to have local significance at a site and may be overwritten in the network. The basic idea behind the GFC bits is to provide a means to arbitrate access to the link if the local site uses some shared medium to connect to ATM.

The next 24 bits contain an 8-bit Virtual Path Identifier (VPI) and a 16-bit Virtual Circuit Identifier (VCI). The difference between the two is explained below, but for now it is adequate to think of them as a single 24-bit identifier that is used to identify a virtual connection, just as in Section 4.1.2. Following the VPI/VCI is 3-bit Type field that has eight possible values. Four of them, when the first bit in the field is set, relate to management functions. When that bit is clear, it means that the cell contains user data. In this case, the second bit is the "explicit forward congestion indication" (EFCI) bit and the third is the "user signalling" bit. The former can be set by a congested switch to tell an end node that it is congested; it has its roots in the DECbit described in Section 8.4.1 and, although the standards are not yet firm on this point, it is intended to be used similarly. The latter is used primarily in conjunction with ATM Adaptation Layer 5 to delineate frames, as discussed below.

Next is a bit to indicate Cell Loss Priority (CLP); a user or network element may set this bit to indicate cells that should be dropped preferentially in the event of overload. For example, a video coding application could set this bit for cells that, if dropped, would not dramatically degrade the quality of the video. A network element might set this bit for cells that have been transmitted by a user in excess of the amount that was negotiated.

The last byte of the header is an 8-bit CRC, known as the Header Error Check (HEC). It uses the CRC-8 polynomial given in Section 3.4.1 and provides error detection and single-

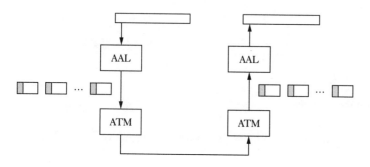

Figure 4.14 Segmentation and reassembly in ATM.

bit error-correction capability on the cell header only. Protecting the cell header is particularly important because an error in the VCI will cause the cell to be misdelivered.

4.3.2 Segmentation and Reassembly

Up to this point, we have assumed that a low-level protocol could just accept the packet handed down to it by a high-level protocol, attach its own header, and pass the packet on down. This is not possible with ATM, however, since the packets handed down from above are often larger than 48 bytes, and thus, will not fit in the payload of an ATM cell. The solution to this problem is to *fragment* the high-level message into low-level packets at the source, transmit the individual low-level packets over the network, and then reassemble the fragments back together at the destination. This general technique is usually called *fragmentation and re-assembly*. In the case of ATM, however, it is often called *segmentation and reassembly*.

Segmentation is not unique to ATM, but it is much more of a problem than in a network with a maximum packet size of, say, 1500 bytes. To address the issue, a protocol layer was added that sits between ATM and the variable-length packet protocols that might use ATM, such as IP. This layer is called the ATM Adaptation Layer (AAL), and to a first approximation, the AAL header simply contains the information needed by the destination to reassemble the individual cells back into the original message. The relationship between the AAL and ATM is illustrated in Figure 4.14.

Because ATM was designed to support all sorts of services, including voice, video, and data, it was felt that different services would have different AAL needs. Thus, four adaptation layers were originally defined: 1 and 2 were designed to support applications, like voice, that require guaranteed bit rates, while 3 and 4 were intended to provide support for packet data running over ATM. The idea was that AAL3 would be used by connection-oriented packet services (such as X.25) and AAL4 would be used by connectionless services (such as IP). Eventually, the reasons for having different AALs for these two types of service were found to be insufficient, and the AALs merged into one that is inconveniently known as AAL3/4. Meanwhile, some perceived shortcomings in AAL3/4 caused a fifth AAL to be proposed,

8	8	16	< 64 KB	8	0–24	8	16
CPI	Btag	BASize	User data	Pad	0	Etag	Len

Figure 4.15 ATM Adaptation Layer 3/4 packet format.

called AAL5. Thus, there are now four AALs: 1, 2, 3/4, and 5. The two that support computer communications are described below.

ATM Adaptation Layer 3/4

The main function of AAL3/4 is to provide enough information to allow variable-length packets to be transported across the ATM network as a series of fixed-length cells. That is, the AAL supports the segmentation and reassembly process. Since we are now working at a new layer of the network hierarchy, convention requires us to introduce a new name for a packet—in this case, we call it a *protocol data unit* (PDU). The task of segmentation/reassembly involves two different packet formats. The first of these is the *convergence sublayer protocol data unit* (CS-PDU), as depicted in Figure 4.15. The CS-PDU defines a way of encapsulating variable-length PDUs prior to segmenting them into cells. The PDU passed down to the AAL layer is encapsulated by adding a header and a trailer, and the resultant CS-PDU is segmented into ATM cells.

The CS-PDU format begins with an 8-bit common part indicator (CPI), which is like a version field, indicating which version of the CS-PDU format is in use. Only the value 0 is currently defined. The next 8 bits contain the beginning tag (Btag), which is supposed to match the end tag (Etag) for a given PDU. This protects against the situation in which the loss of the last cell of one PDU and the first cell of another causes two PDUs to be inadvertently joined into a single PDU and passed up to the next layer in the protocol stack. The buffer allocation size (BASize) field is not necessarily the length of the PDU (which appears in the trailer); it is supposed to be a hint to the reassembly process as to how much buffer space to allocate for the reassembly. The reason for not including the actual length here is that the sending host might not have known how long the CS-PDU was when it transmitted the header.

The CS-PDU trailer contains the Etag, the real length of the PDU (Len), and a padding byte of 0s.

The second part of AAL3/4 is the header and trailer that is carried in each cell, as depicted in Figure 4.16. Thus, the CS-PDU is actually segmented into 44-byte chunks; an AAL3/4 header and trailer is attached to each one, bringing it up to 48 bytes, which is then carried as the payload of an ATM cell.

The first two bits of the AAL3/4 header contain the Type field, which indicates if this is the first cell of a CS-PDU, the last cell of a CS-PDU, a cell in the middle of a CS-PDU,

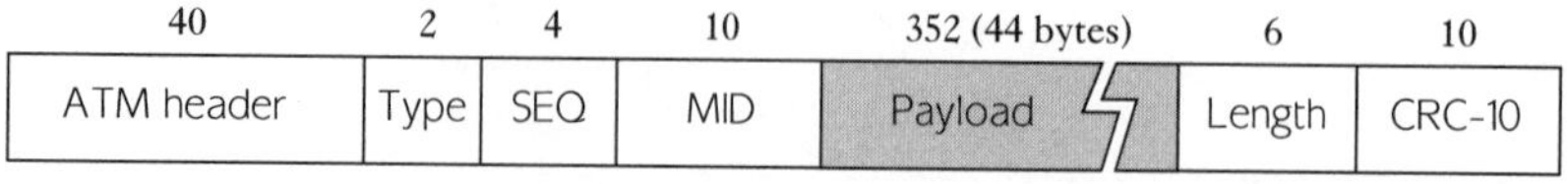

40	2	4	10	352 (44 bytes)	6	10
ATM header	Type	SEQ	MID	Payload	Length	CRC-10

Figure 4.16   ATM cell format for AAL3/4.

Value	Name	Meaning
10	BOM	Beginning of message
00	COM	Continuation of message
01	EOM	End of message
11	SSM	Single-segment message

Table 4.7   AAL3/4 type field.

or a single-cell PDU (in which case it is both first and last). The official names for these four conditions are shown in Table 4.7, along with the bit encodings.

Next is a 4-bit sequence number (**SEQ**), which is intended simply to detect cell loss or misordering so that reassembly can be aborted. Clearly, a sequence number this small can miss cell losses if the number of lost cells is large enough. This is followed by a multiplexing identifier (**MID**), which can be used to multiplex several PDUs onto a single connection. The 6-bit **Length** field shows the number of bytes of PDU that are contained in the cell; it must equal 44 for BOM and COM cells. Finally, a 10-bit CRC is used to detect errors anywhere in the 48-byte cell payload.

One thing to note about AAL3/4 is that it exacerbates the fixed per-cell overhead that we discussed above. With 44 bytes of data to 9 bytes of header, the best possible bandwidth utilization would be 83%.

ATM Adaptation Layer 5

One thing you may have noticed in the discussion of AAL3/4 is that it seems to take a lot of fields and thus a lot of overhead to perform the conceptually simple function of segmentation and reassembly. This observation was, in fact, made by several people in the early days of ATM, and numerous competing proposals arose for an AAL to support computer communications over ATM. There was a movement known informally as "Back the Bit" which argued that if we could just have 1 bit in the ATM header (as opposed to the AAL header) to delineate the end of a frame, then segmentation and reassembly could be accomplished without using any of the 48-byte ATM payload for segmentation/reassembly information. This movement eventually led to the definition of the user signalling bit described above and to the standardization of AAL5.

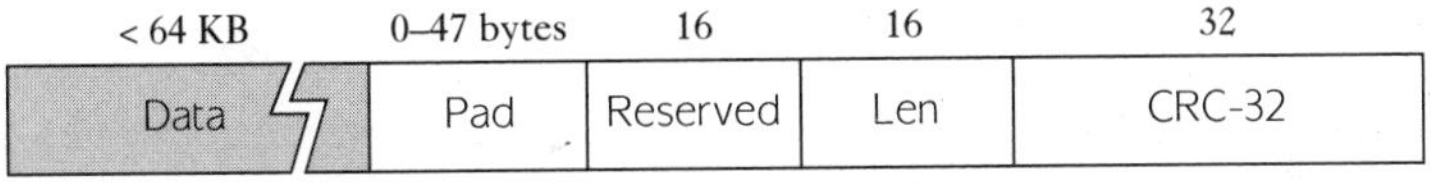

< 64 KB	0–47 bytes	16	16	32
Data	Pad	Reserved	Len	CRC-32

Figure 4.17   ATM Adaptation Layer 5 packet format.

What AAL5 does is replace the 2-bit **Type** field of AAL3/4 with 1 bit of framing information in the ATM cell header. By setting that 1 bit, we can identify the last cell of a PDU; the next cell is assumed to be the first cell of the next PDU, and subsequent cells are assumed to be COM cells until another cell is received with the user signalling bit set. All the pieces of AAL3/4 that provide protection against lost, corrupt, or misordered cells, including the loss of an EOM cell, are provided by the AAL5 CS-PDU packet format depicted in Figure 4.17.

The AAL5 CS-PDU consists simply of the data portion (the PDU handed down by the higher-layer protocol) and an 8-byte trailer. To make sure that the trailer always falls at the tail end of an ATM cell, there may be up to 47 bytes of padding between the data and the trailer. The first 2 bytes of the trailer are currently reserved and must be 0. The length field (**Len**) is the number of bytes carried in the PDU, not including the trailer or any padding before the trailer. Finally, there is a 32-bit CRC.

Somewhat surprisingly, AAL5 provides almost the same functionality as AAL3/4 without using 4 bytes out of every cell. For example, the CRC-32 detects lost or misordered cells as well as bit errors in the data. In fact, having a checksum over the entire PDU rather than doing it on a per-cell basis as in AAL3/4 provides stronger protection. For example, it protects against the loss of 16 consecutive cells, an event that would not be picked up by the sequence number checking of AAL3/4. Also, a 32-bit CRC protects against longer burst errors than a 10-bit CRC.

The main feature missing from AAL5 is the ability to provide an additional layer of multiplexing onto one virtual circuit using the **MID**. It is not clear whether this is a significant loss. For example, if you are being charged for every virtual circuit you set up across a network, then multiplexing traffic from lots of different applications onto one connection might be a plus. However, this approach has the drawback that all applications will have to live with whatever quality of service (e.g., delay and bandwidth guarantees) has been chosen for that one connection, which may mean that some applications are not receiving appropriate service. Certainly the large (24-bit) space available for **VCI/VPI** combinations suggests that it should be possible for a host to open many virtual connections and to avoid multiplexing at this level, in which case the **MID** is of little value.

In general, AAL5 has been wholeheartedly embraced by the computer communications community (at least by that part of the community that has embraced ATM at all). For example, it is the preferred AAL in the IETF for transmitting IP datagrams over ATM. Its more efficient use of bandwidth and simple design are the main features that make it more appealing than AAL3/4.

4.3.3 Virtual Paths

As mentioned above, ATM uses a 24-bit identifier for virtual circuits, and these circuits operate almost exactly like the ones described in Section 4.1.2. The one twist is that the 24-bit identifier is split into two parts: an 8-bit Virtual Path Identifier (VPI) and a 16-bit Virtual Circuit Identifier (VCI). This provides some hierarchy in the identifier, just as there may be a hierarchy in addresses as we discussed in Section 4.2.5. To understand how a hierarchical virtual circuit identifier might be used, consider the following example. (We ignore the fact that in some places there might be a network-network interface (NNI) with a different-sized VPI; just assume that 8-bit VPIs are used everywhere.)

Suppose that a corporation has two sites that connect to a public ATM network, and that at each site the corporation has a network of ATM switches. We could imagine establishing a virtual path between two sites using only the VPI field. Thus, the switches in the public network would use the VPI as the only field on which to make forwarding decisions. From their point of view, this is a virtual circuit network with 8-bit circuit identifiers. The 16-bit VCI is of no interest to these public switches, and they neither use the field for switching nor remap it. Within the corporate sites, however, the full 24-bit space is used for switching. Any traffic that needs to flow between the two sites is routed to a switch that has a connection to the public network, and its top 8 bits (the VPI) are mapped onto the appropriate value to get the data to the other site. This idea is illustrated in Figure 4.18. Note that the virtual path acts like a fat pipe that contains a bundle of virtual circuits, all of which have the same 8 bits in their most significant byte.

> ### ATM in the LAN
>
> As we mentioned above, ATM grew out of the telephony community, who envisioned it as a way to build large public networks that could transport voice, video, and data traffic. However, it was subsequently embraced by the computer and data communications industries as a technology to be used in LANs—a replacement for Ethernet and FDDI. Its popularity in this realm can be attributed to many factors, most notably the fact that it offered significantly higher bandwidth than Ethernet and, unlike FDDI, its bandwidth is switched rather than shared, meaning that in theory every host can send or receive at the full link speed.
>
> The problem with running ATM in a LAN, however, is that it doesn"t look like a "traditional" LAN. Because most LANs (i.e., Ethernets and token rings) are shared-media networks (i.e., every node on the LAN is connected to the same link) it is easy to implement things like broadcast (sending to everybody) and multicast (sending to a group). Thus, many of the protocols that people depend on in their LANs—e.g., the Address Resolution Protocol (ARP) described in

The advantage of this approach is clear: although there may be thousands or millions of virtual connections across the public network, the switches in the public network behave as if there is only one connection. This means that there needs to be much less connection-state information stored in the switches, avoiding the need for big, expensive tables of per-VCI information.

Section 5.2.5—depend in turn on the ability of the LAN to support multicast and broadcast. However, because of its connection-oriented and switched nature, ATM behaves rather differently than a shared-media LAN. For example, how can you broadcast to all nodes on an ATM LAN if you don't know all their addresses?

There are two possible solutions to this problem, and both of them have been explored. One is to redesign the protocols that assume things about LANs that are not in fact true of ATM. Thus, for example, there is a new protocol called AT-MARP that, unlike traditional ARP, does not depend on broadcast. The alternative is to make ATM behave more like a shared-media LAN—in the sense of supporting multicast and broadcast—without losing the performance advantages of a switched network. This approach has been explored by the ATM Forum as "LAN emulation" (which might be more correctly called "shared-media emulation"). This approach aims to add functionality to ATM LANs so that anything that runs over a shared-media LAN can operate over an ATM LAN.

4.3.4 Physical Layers for ATM

While the layered approach to protocol design might lead you to think that we do not need to worry about what type of point-to-point link ATM runs on top of, this turns out not to be the case. From a simple pragmatic point of view, when you buy an ATM adaptor for a workstation or an ATM switch, it comes with some physical medium over which ATM cells will be sent. Of course, this is also true for other networking protocols such as FDDI and Ethernet. Like these protocols, ATM can also run over several different physical media and physical layer protocols.

From early in the process of standardizing ATM, it has been assumed that ATM will run on top of a SONET physical layer (see Section 3.3.3). Some people even get ATM and SONET confused because they have been so tightly coupled for so long. While it is true that standard ways of carrying ATM cells inside a SONET frame have been defined, and that you can now buy ATM-over-SONET products, the two are entirely separable. For example, you can lease a SONET link from a phone company and send whatever you want over it, including variable-length packets. Also, you can send ATM cells over many other physical layers instead of SONET, and standards have been (or are being) defined for these encapsulations.

When you send ATM cells over some physical medium, the main issue is how to find the boundaries of the ATM cells; this is exactly the framing problem described in Chapter 3. With SONET, there are two easy ways to find the boundaries. One of the overhead bytes in the SONET frame can be used as a pointer into the SONET payload to the start of an ATM cell. Having found the start of one cell, it is known that the next cell starts 53 bytes further on in the SONET payload, and so on. In

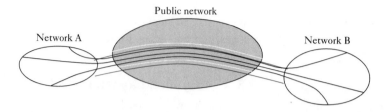

Figure 4.18   Example of a virtual path.

theory, you only need to read this pointer once, but in practice, it makes sense to read it every time the SONET overhead goes by so that you can detect errors or resynchronize if needed.

The other way to find the boundaries of ATM cells takes advantage of the fact that every cell has a CRC in the fifth byte of the cell. Thus, if you run a CRC calculation over the last 5 bytes received and the answer comes out to indicate no errors, then it is probably true that you have just read an ATM header. If this happens several times in a row at 53-byte intervals, you can be pretty sure you have found the cell boundary.

4.4   Switching Hardware

Whether a switch has to handle virtual circuits or datagrams, variable-length packets or fixed-length cells, the basic issues that have to be addressed remain the same. A switch is a multi-input, multi-output device, and its job is to get as many packets as possible from the inputs to the appropriate outputs. Most of what we have talked about in the previous sections of this chapter has revolved around deciding which output to send a particular packet to. In this section, we look at how to make the process of getting packets from the inputs to the outputs as fast as possible.

Recall from Section 4.1.4 that the performance of a switch implemented in software on a general-purpose processor is limited by the bandwidth of the machine's I/O bus (among other factors). When you consider that each packet must traverse the bus twice—once from the adaptor to memory and once from memory to the adaptor—it is easy to see that a processor with a 1-Gbps I/O bus would be able to handle at most ten T3 (45-Mbps) links, up to three STS-3 (155-Mbps) links, and not even one STS-12 (622-Mbps) link. Considering that the whole purpose of a switch is to connect reasonably large numbers of links, this is not an ideal situation. Fortunately, switches can be implemented by special-purpose hardware, as we now discuss.

4.4.1   Design Goals

There are two major challenges in the design of switching hardware. The first is throughput—the number of packets the switch can forward each second. The second is size or scalability—how many inputs/outputs it can connect. Before we discuss these challenges, we need one item of terminology. We normally describe a switch in terms of the number of inputs and outputs it has; an $n \times m$ (read "n by m") switch is one with n inputs and m outputs. It is often (but not always) the case that $n = m$; this configuration obviously makes sense if the links to the switch are bidirectional. Another interesting special case is the one in which all link speeds are the same, but it is sometimes the case that a switch will have links of various speeds.

Throughput

It turns out to be very difficult to define the throughput of a switch. Intuitively, we might think that if a switch has n inputs that each support a link speed of s_n, then the throughput would just be the sum of all the s_n. This is actually the best possible throughput that such a switch could provide, but virtually no real switch can guarantee that level of performance. The reason for this is simple to understand. Suppose that, for some period of time, all the traffic arriving at the switch needed to be sent to the same output. As long as the bandwidth of that output is less than the sum of the input bandwidths, then some of the traffic will need to be either buffered or dropped. With this particular traffic pattern, the switch could not provide a sustained throughput higher than the link speed of that one output.

The first thing to notice about the above example is that the throughput of the switch is a function of the traffic to which it is subjected. One of the things that switch designers spend a lot of their time doing is trying to come up with traffic models that realistically imitate real traffic. This turns out to be extremely difficult, because real traffic is annoyingly awkward to model. There are several elements to a traffic model. The main ones are: (1) when do packets arrive, (2) what outputs are they destined for, and (3) how big are they. (This last factor is obviously the easy one for ATM switches.)

Traffic modeling is a well-established science that has been extremely successful in the world of telephony, enabling telephone companies to engineer their networks to carry expected loads quite efficiently. This is partly because the way people use the phone network does not change that much over time: the frequency with which calls are placed, the amount of time taken for a call, and the tendency of everyone to make calls on Mother's Day have stayed fairly constant for many years. By contrast, the rapid evolution of computer communications, where a new application like the World Wide Web can change the traffic patterns almost overnight, has made effective modeling of computer networks much more difficult. Nevertheless, there are some excellent books and articles on the subject that we list at the end of the chapter.

Aside from the difficulty of obtaining good traffic models, the main problem that we run up against in switch design is *contention*. The above example (sending all traffic to the same output) illustrates the problem of output contention. This sort of contention is pretty much unavoidable: you cannot fit more traffic into an output link than that link will carry. However, most switch designs are also subject to some degree of internal contention, and the amount of contention under different traffic loads determines the performance of the switch.

Scalability

The other issue that switch designers tend to be concerned about is scalability. Typically, the amount of hardware needed to build a switch is a function of the number of inputs and outputs. The question is, How fast does hardware cost rise with increasing n? For example, a switch design for which the hardware cost increases in proportion to n^2 would be considered more scalable than one that increases in proportion to n^3. Furthermore, most switch designs run into problems at some maximum number of inputs and outputs, for example because some piece of wire gets too long to run at full speed or the fanout of a device is exceeded. Thus, scalability can be measured in terms of both the rate of increase in cost and the maximum possible switch size.

One of the reasons that scalability has been a big issue for ATM switches is that ATM was originally conceived as the technology that would replace current telephone switching technology. Telephone switches, since they are bought by companies with millions of subscribers, tend to have very large numbers of ports—tens of thousands are common. Thus, many designers were thinking in terms of similarly huge ATM switches. Interestingly, the thing that has caused ATM to take off is the availability of small switches, on the order of 16 to 32 ports. These switches can use less-scalable designs, which may lead to simpler implementation for a small switch. It remains to be seen whether very large switches will be commercially successful or whether large networks will be built from many small switches.

The next few sections look at a number of switch designs. Each has advantages and disadvantages in terms of its ability to handle contention, its complexity, and its scalability. Before examining them, however, we need to look in a little more detail at the component parts of a switch.

4.4.2 Ports and Fabrics

Most switches look conceptually similar to the one shown in Figure 4.19. They consist of a number of *input ports* and *output ports* and a *fabric*. The ports have to communicate with the outside world. They may contain fiberoptic receivers and lasers, buffers to hold packets (cells) that are waiting to be switched or transmitted, and often a significant amount of other circuitry that enables the switch to function. The fabric has a very simple and well-defined job: when presented with a packet, deliver it to the right output.

One of the jobs of the ports, then, is to deal with the complexity of the real world in such a way that the fabric can do its relatively simple job. For example, suppose that this switch is supporting a virtual circuit model of communication. In general, the process of setting up and managing virtual circuits is handled in the ports. The ports maintain tables of virtual circuit identifiers that are currently in use, with information about what output a packet should be sent out on for each VCI and how the VCI needs to be remapped to ensure uniqueness on the outgoing link. Similarly, the ports of a datagram switch may store tables that map between datagram addresses and output ports. In general, when a packet is handed from an input port to the fabric, the port has figured out where the packet needs to go, and either the port sets

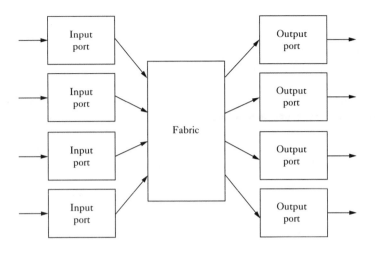

Figure 4.19 A 4 × 4 switch.

up the fabric accordingly or it attaches enough information to the packet (e.g., an output port number) to allow the fabric to do its job.

A key function of ports is buffering. While some fabrics have internal buffering, some do not, and in almost all cases it is necessary to provide some if not most of the buffering on the ports. The design of these buffers, in terms of both their capacity and the way data is managed in them, can have a profound impact on the performance of the switch. We talk more about these issues in Chapter 8. It is worth noting that although there have been many more papers published on fabrics than on ports, a switch's functionality, size, and cost often depend more on the ports than on the fabric. However, it is probably fair to say that the opportunities for innovative research have been greater in the area of fabrics.

Observe that buffering can happen in either the input or the output port; it can also happen within the fabric. In the latter case, it is called *internal buffering.* In the switch examples that follow, internal and output buffering are discussed; none of the designs use input buffering. One reason for this is that input buffering has some serious limitations. The simplest way to build an input buffer is to use a FIFO. As packets arrive at the switch, they are placed in the input buffer. The switch then tries to forward the packets at the front of each FIFO to their appropriate output port. However, if the packets at the front of several different input ports are destined for the same output port at the same time, then only one of them can be forwarded;[3] the rest must stay in their input buffers.

---

[3] For a simple input-buffered switch, one packet at a time can be sent to a given output port. It is possible to design switches that can forward more than one packet to the same output at once, at a cost of higher switch complexity, but there is always some upper limit on the number.

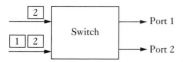

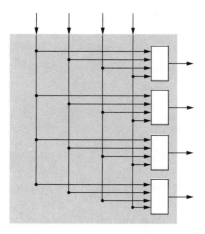

Figure 4.20 Simple illustration of head-of-line blocking.

Figure 4.21 A 4 × 4 crossbar switch.

The drawback of this feature is that those packets left at the front of the input buffer prevent other packets further back in the buffer from getting a chance to go to their chosen outputs, even though there may be no contention for those outputs. This phenomenon is called *head-of-line blocking*. A simple example of head-of-line blocking is given in Figure 4.20, where we see a packet destined for port 1 blocked behind a packet contending for port 2. It can be shown that when traffic is uniformly distributed among outputs, head-of-line blocking limits the throughput of an input-buffered switch to 59% of the theoretical maximum (which is the sum of the link bandwidths for the switch).

4.4.3 Crossbar Switches

Crossbar switches are a good place to start in our discussion of switch designs because they are conceptually very simple. The only contention problem they exhibit is the output port contention we mentioned above. Figure 4.21 shows a 4 × 4 crossbar switch.

Note that every input is connected to every output. The complexity of the switch lies primarily in the deceptively small box sitting in front of each output. (We consider this box part of the output port, not the fabric.) This box has to do two things:

1 recognize the packets that are destined for this output (this is necessary since the fabric delivers all inputs to each output);

2 deal with the contention that arises when multiple packets are sent to the same output simultaneously.

In general, the complexity of the output port grows in proportion to or faster than the number of inputs n, and since there are also n outputs, that means that the complexity of the switch as a whole grows at least as fast as n^2. However, it takes some clever design work to come up with an output port that only grows linearly with n. One example of such a design is the Knockout switch developed by Yeh, Hluchyj, and Acampora, which we now examine in more detail.

The Knockout Switch

The Knockout switch is in fact not quite a "perfect" crossbar—some assumptions about traffic are made to reduce the complexity of the output ports. A true crossbar would be able to deal with the situation in which every switch input had a packet to send to a given output at exactly the same time. For a small switch like the one in Figure 4.21, this might be easy enough to implement; for a large switch, it would not only be quite difficult, it would be overkill. For most reasonable traffic scenarios, the likelihood that many inputs would all need to send to the same output simultaneously is very small. So, the idea is to design an output port that can accept l packets simultaneously, with $l < n$. We would clearly like to pick l to be small enough to keep our cost down, yet large enough that the likelihood of more than l packets arriving all at once is acceptably small. Here again we are in the realm of traffic models; it is relatively easy to figure out a good value of l if you assume that the traffic arriving at each input port is independent of the traffic arriving at all other ports. Sadly, that may be a bad assumption if someone has just connected a popular Web site to one output of the switch. The phenomenon of traffic collecting to "beat up" on one port of a switch is referred to as a *hot spot*, and it is likely to be quite common in an environment where many clients communicate with a server. We do not delve deeper into this problem, except to note that ignoring it when you calculate l might be a bad idea.

The output port of the Knockout switch, then, is made up of three parts:

- ■ a set of packet filters that recognize packets destined for this port;

- ■ the "knockout" part, called a *concentrator*, that selects up to l packets from those destined for this port and discards any excess packets on the (hopefully) rare occasions when they occur;

- ■ a queue that accepts up to l packets at a time and buffers them while they await transmission.

The filters use simple matching hardware to identify the packets that contain the right output port number. The concentrator's job turns out to be the hard part, primarily because

Inputs

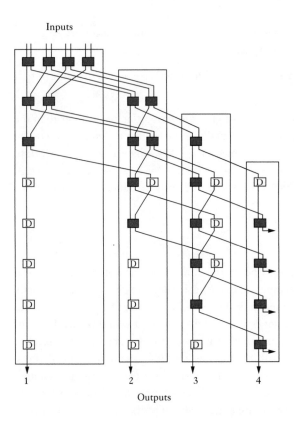

1   2   3   4

Outputs

Figure 4.22   An 8 to 4 knockout concentrator.

of the need to ensure fairness: we need to be sure that no one input port is singled out for bad treatment every time the output is overloaded. Fairness is achieved by "playing" the packets against each other in a form of knockout "tournament" to select l winners from n contestants. One game in the tournament involves two packets. These two packets compete by entering a 2×2 switching element, which randomly selects a winner. Picking the overall winner is easy—it is exactly the way the winner is picked in a knockout tennis tournament, that is, you play $\log_2 n$ rounds and the losers of each round are knocked out until only one winner remains. To pick l winners is a bit more complicated—the process is illustrated in Figure 4.22 in the case in which $n = 8$ and $l = 4$. For the following discussion, we assume that packets are all of the same length, as they would be in an ATM switch.

We can think of the tournament as having l sections designed to pick a winner, a runner up, a third-place finisher, and so on, up to the lth place finisher. The first section is the traditional knockout tournament, which selects one winner. All the losers from that section go to compete to be runner up. Any packet that loses in the second section goes on to the third, and so on. If a packet loses in l sections, it is dropped. Since each section selects just one packet as the winner of that section, we end up selecting l packets and dropping all the rest, if there were in fact more than l packets submitted.

This process is much easier to understand when you look at an example like the one in Figure 4.22. The leftmost section looks like the quarterfinal round at Wimbledon, and selects one winner. The first-round losers from this section go straight to the second section and play off against each other, to be joined at later stages by second- and third-round losers from the first section. With each loss, a packet moves right to another section of competition, while each win advances it further within its current section. With enough losses, a packet is eliminated; if it goes undefeated in a given section, it reaches the output of that box. Sometimes at a particular stage a section has an odd number of players, so one packet needs to wait in a delay element, marked D, before moving on to the next round. Delay elements are also used to ensure that all winning packets exit at the same time in spite of the different tournament lengths.

The other interesting part of the Knockout design is the output buffer, which must accept up to l packets in a single cycle and then transmit one packet each cycle. Rather than implementing this as a FIFO with an input that runs l times faster than the output, which would be awkward, the Knockout designers used an array of l buffers preceded by a shifter, as shown in Figure 4.23. The shifter moves arriving packets into different buffers to ensure that they are filled in round-robin order, and thus that they never differ by more than one packet in their level of occupancy. At the same time, packets are read out one at a time, also in round-robin order, so that packet order is preserved. Clearly, if the number of packets arriving in each cycle is more than one for a significant period of time, the buffer will overflow. In Figure 4.23(a), three packets arrive and are placed in the first three buffers. In the next cycle, Figure 4.23(b), three more arrive and are shifted right by three positions, while the first packet is sent out from the second buffer. Finally, in Figure 4.23(c), one packet arrives, is shifted right by 2 positions (6 mod 4, since 6 packets arrived previously) and stored, while a packet is transmitted from the third buffer.

To estimate the complexity of this switch for large values of n, and thus to evaluate its scalability, we note first that l can remain fixed at some reasonably small value, such as 8, and still provide quite good performance. Since the shared buffer scales with l, its cost is constant. The complexity of the concentrator for a large n value approaches $n \times l$, so it scales with n. The number of packet filters needed per port is clearly n. Thus, the complexity of the output port, most of which is in the concentrator, is proportional to n. Since there are n output ports, the total switch complexity is roughly proportional to n^2—not great, but not awful either.

Probably the greatest flaw of the Knockout switch is that it rests on the assumption that traffic arriving at different ports is uncorrelated and equally likely to go to any output. However, its n^2 cost is also a drawback. Self-routing fabrics are the type of switch design that have generally achieved greatest scalability, as we discuss in the next section.

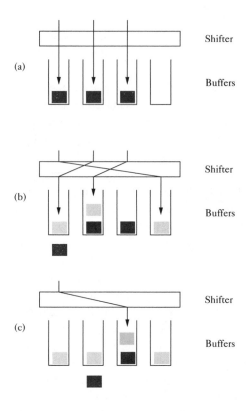

(a)

(b)

(c)

Figure 4.23 The shared buffer of a knockout switch. (a) Three packets arrive; (b) three packets arrive, one leaves; (c) one packet arrives, one leaves.

4.4.4 Self-Routing Fabrics

Self-routing fabrics are a class of switches made up of many small, interconnected switching elements in which packets find their own way through the fabric based on a sequence of local switching decisions made at each small switching element. Figure 4.24 shows a self-routing fabric of the type known as a *banyan network*, so-called because of its similarity to the banyan tree. It may seem strange to call this a banyan "network," but in a sense the fabric is a miniature network inside the switch.

The general principle behind self-routing fabrics is that each packet carries enough information in its header to allow the small switching elements to make a local decision, without consulting any other elements or any central controller. This is normally done by having the input port add an extra (internal) header to the packet before it arrives at the fabric, and then having the output port remove this header before the packet is transmitted to the next switch. This header is called a *self-routing header*. In a virtual circuit switch, for example, the virtual circuit number in an arriving packet is used to look up the appropriate switch output port, and

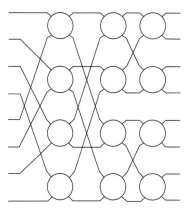

Figure 4.24   An eight-input banyan network.

this port number is then placed in the self-routing header. (Notice the similarity between a self-routing header and source routing, as described in Section 4.1.1.)

Banyan Networks

Self-routing fabrics are often made from simple 2×2 switching elements that switch based on just one bit in the self-routing header. For example, the 2×2 switches in the banyan network just look at one bit in each packet header, and route toward the upper output if it is set or toward the lower output if it is clear. Obviously, if two packets arrive at a banyan element at the same time and both have this bit set to the same value, then they want to be routed to the same output and a collision will occur. Either preventing or dealing with these collisions is a main challenge for self-routing switch design. The banyan network is a clever arrangement of 2×2 switching elements that routes all packets to the correct output without collisions if the packets are presented in ascending order. We can see how this works in an example, as shown in Figure 4.25.

In this example, the first column of switch elements look at the most significant bit of the output port number contained in the self-routing header and route packets to the top or bottom output based on whether it is a 0 (top) or a 1 (bottom). Switch elements in the second column look at the second bit, and those in the last column look at the least significant bit. You can see from this example that the packets are routed to the correct destination port without collisions. Notice how the top outputs from the first column of switches all lead to the top half of the network, thus getting packets with port numbers 0–3 into the right half of the network. The next column gets packets to the right quarter of the network, and the final column gets them to the right output port. The clever part is the way switches are arranged to avoid collisions. Part of the arrangement includes the "perfect shuffle" wiring pattern at the start of the network.

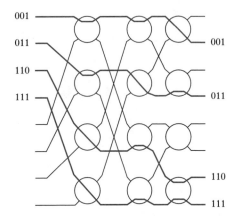

001

011

110

111

001

011

110

111

Figure 4.25   Routing packets through a banyan network.

From this discussion it should be apparent that a banyan network with n inputs needs to have $\log_2 n$ stages, each of which has $n/2$ switching elements, so that the complexity is on the order of $n \log_2 n$.

Batcher Networks

Since a banyan network can route a set of packets without collisions when those packets are presented in ascending order, one thing you might think of doing—and which has been done successfully in several switches—is to precede a banyan network with a different sort of self-routing network that sorts packets into order. The *Batcher network*, named after its inventor, is just such a network. An example Batcher network is illustrated in Figure 4.26. When you put a Batcher network in front of a banyan network, you get a Batcher-banyan fabric, which has the property that it is *nonblocking*, i.e., there will be no collisions as long as the packets presented to it are all destined for unique output ports.

The 2×2 switching element of a Batcher network differs substantially from that of a banyan network. It does a complete comparison of the self-routing headers, routing the packet with the numerically greater tag to one output and the one with the lesser tag to the other output. If the tags are equal, it makes a random choice. There are actually two types of switch element in a Batcher network: those that sort "up" (i.e., send the higher number to the top output) and those that sort "down" (i.e., send the higher number to the bottom output). In the figure, the "up" elements are shaded.

In essence, the Batcher network implements a recursive merge-sort algorithm in hardware. You can see how this works by looking first at the six switching elements in the top left corner of Figure 4.26. The basic 2×2 element can sort two packets, so if we take a "down" element and an "up" element, we get a pair of two-member ordered lists—one in ascending order and one in descending order. Using two more columns of "down" elements, we can

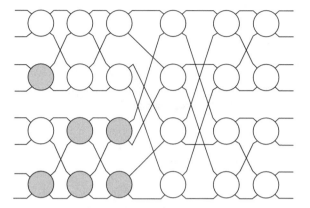

Figure 4.26   An 8 × 8 Batcher network. The elements that send the higher number to the top output are shaded.

merge these two lists into a four-member list in ascending order. (By ascending, we mean that the numbers get bigger as you go down the picture.) Meanwhile, the six switching elements in the bottom left corner are just like the ones in the top left except all the "up" sorters have been replaced by "down" sorters and vice versa. Thus, they provide a list of packets sorted in *descending* order. With three more columns of "down" sorters, we can merge our two four-member lists into one eight-member list. By now, it should be fairly clear how you could build arbitrarily large Batcher networks. For example, a 16-input version would be made from two eight-input versions followed by four rows of sorters to do the merge function. While it may not be totally obvious, this means that the number of stages in an n-input Batcher network is $\log_2 n \times (1 + \log_2 n)/2$. Since there are $n/2$ switching elements per stage, the total complexity is on the order of $n \log_2^2 n$, which is actually better (i.e., grows less quickly) than n^2.

The important idea behind how merging works is that the merger depends on the fact that it is presented with a pair of ordered lists, one in ascending order and one in descending order. Without going into the details, you should note that the first column of the merger (the fourth column from the left in the figure) sends packets to the correct half of the network (top or bottom), the next column sends them to the correct quarter, and the final column sends them to the correct output.

Sunshine Switch

With a combination of Batcher and banyan networks, we can construct a fabric that delivers all packets to the right output port, as long as there are no duplicate packets heading for the same port. Unfortunately, that is a rather severe restriction. A switch this simple would need to drop packets every time two or more were destined for the same output. There have been many switch architectures designed around Batcher-banyan networks that aim to deal with

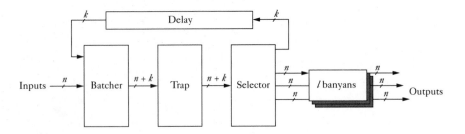

Figure 4.27   The Sunshine switch.

this limitation. An interesting one that uses a combination of techniques to avoid collisions is the Sunshine switch, depicted in Figure 4.27.

The Sunshine switch complements the Batcher and banyan networks with three additional elements: a trap, a selector, and a set of delay boxes. It also uses multiple parallel banyans. The multiple banyans enable multiple packets to go to one output at the same time. Like the Knockout switch, this means that the output port (not shown) must be able to accept l packets at once if there are l parallel banyans. When more than l packets are destined for a single output in the same cycle, they are recirculated through the delay box and resubmitted to the switch in the next cycle. This means that the Batcher network needs to be able to sort $n + k$ packets—n from the input ports and up to k that have been recirculated. The trap network identifies those packets that will be able to exit the switch through the banyans (up to l of them per output port) and marks the rest for recirculation. The selector makes sure that, if l packets are going to the same output, they get sent to separate banyans to avoid collisions, and any extras get sent to the recirculator. The packets include a priority field that is incremented each time they get recirculated, which ensures that "older" packets have a better chance of getting out through the banyans than newly arrived packets; this feature ensures that packet order is preserved through the switch, a requirement for ATM networks.

The Sunshine switch turns out to be a very good compromise design. It has lower complexity than the Knockout switch, and rather than discarding the extra packets when more than l are destined for one output, it recirculates the extras. The only way packets get dropped before reaching the output is when the number of packets getting recirculated is greater than k. The Sunshine designers simulated and analyzed the design for a very wide range of traffic scenarios and found that with well-chosen values for l and k they could make these losses very rare.

4.4.5 Shared-Media Switches

There are lots of other ways to build switches. One popular method is to collapse a shared-media network (such as FDDI) down into a box and then to use it as a switching fabric. Shared-media switches tend not to scale terribly well, however, since the shared resource either gets more overloaded or needs to get faster as the switch size grows. We consider one

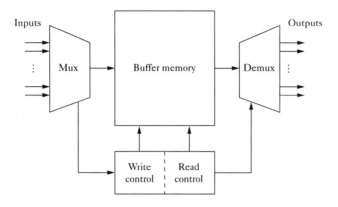

Figure 4.28   A shared-memory switch.

example of a shared-media switch in some detail—a shared-memory switch, as illustrated in Figure 4.28.

The nice thing about a shared-memory switch is that it is basically one big buffer, which can be built out of off-the-shelf memory chips. It can be made to work like a perfect crossbar, only better: since the buffering is shared among all the output ports, you can get better utilization out of the buffering. To understand why utilization is better, recall that an output-buffered crossbar only loses packets when the rate at which packets are arriving at one output exceeds the rate at which they can be transmitted, for a long enough period to overflow the buffer at that output. As a consequence, you need to provide enough buffering at each output to make this overflow a rare occurrence. But the likelihood that all your outputs will be simultaneously overloaded is very low, so it would be nice if you could borrow unused buffer space from another output and give it to the overloaded output. This is exactly what a shared-buffer memory does for you.

The memory switch in Figure 4.28 is only capable of writing one packet into the shared memory at a time. This means that the bus connecting the multiplexer to the memory must run n times faster than the line speed of a single link, something that would typically be achieved by making it a very wide bus. Each arriving packet has its header passed to the write-control logic. Upon examining the output port number, the write control gets an address of a free location from a free list, writes the packet to this address, and links the packet to a linked list associated with the appropriate output port. Similarly, the read control takes packets from the linked list for each output, sends them to the appropriate port through the demultiplexer, and returns the memory addresses to the free list.

Note that the main limitation on size for this sort of switch is the rate at which the control logic can operate, since unlike the buffer memory, the control logic can not be made faster by widening it.

4.5 Summary

This chapter has started to look at some of the issues involved in building large, scalable networks by using switches, rather than just links, to interconnect hosts. There are several different ways to decide how to switch packets, the two main ones being the datagram (connectionless) model and the virtual circuit (connection-oriented) model.

One of the hardest parts of building large switched networks is figuring out what direction to send a packet from any given node in the network so that it will reach its intended destination. This is the routing problem, and what makes it hard is that no one node has global knowledge of the network. The solution is that every node must be involved in a routing protocol to exchange information with its neighbors in an effort to build up a reasonable global picture. Such protocols have to be robust in the face of node and link failures, and they must be able to adapt to the addition of new nodes and links. Ideally, they should also be sensitive to the different characteristics of the links, such as latency, throughput, and the current load. In this context, we studied two general routing algorithms: distance vector and link state.

Independent of the switching model and of how routing is done, switches need to forward packets from inputs to outputs at a high rate, and in some circumstances, switches need to grow to a large size to accommodate hundreds or thousands of ports. Building switches that both scale and offer high performance is complicated by the problem of contention, and as a consequence, switches often employ special-purpose hardware rather than being built from general-purpose workstations. Some switch designers have targeted the "central office switch" for design improvement, which would allow the telephone companies to provide ATM instead of a simple voice telephone line to everyone's home. Building such large, fast switches is a tough problem that has yielded a wealth of clever switch architectures.

In addition to the issues for forwarding, routing, and contention, we observe that the related problem of congestion has come up throughout this chapter. We will postpone our discussion of congestion control until Chapter 8, after we have seen more of the network architecture. We do this because it is impossible to fully appreciate congestion (both the problem and how it to address it) without understanding both what happens inside the network (the topic of this and the next chapter) and what happens at the edges of the network (the topic of Chapter 6).

OPEN ISSUE

What Makes a Route Good?

It is tempting to think that all the hard problems of routing have been solved by the algorithms described in this chapter. This is certainly not the case, as the large number of people who continue to work on routing problems will attest. One challenge for routing is the support of mobile hosts. If you have a wireless link to your laptop and roam around the country, or even if you unplug your computer from the wall in New Jersey and take it to Arizona and plug it back in, how can packets be efficiently delivered? Moreover, will these mechanisms be scalable enough to support an environment in which much of the world's population has a mobile computing device? This is one of the hard problems currently being tackled.

Also, routing promises to become even more difficult as application requirements become more demanding and networks try to provide a range of qualities of service that meet different application needs. For example, a high-resolution video broadcast application would probably prefer to be routed over a high-speed satellite link than over a lower-speed, lower-latency terrestrial link, whereas an interactive video application with a smaller bandwidth requirement might prefer the lower-speed, lower-latency link. In other words, link cost becomes a function of application needs, not something that can be calculated in isolation.

Coupled with all these problems is the unavoidable fact that networks continue to grow beyond the expectations of the original designers. Thus, the scaling problem for routing continues to get harder, something we will look at more closely in the next chapter.

FURTHER READING

Among the more accessible and interesting papers on routing are the two papers that describe the "new" (1980) and the "revised" (1988) ARPANET routing mechanisms. The third paper in our reading list gives a broader perspective on routing. The current level of interest in ATM has yielded plenty of survey papers. We recommend the article by Lyles and Swinehart as a good early example, partly because it discusses ATM from the perspective of the desktop rather than from the perspective of the telephone company. Finally, the last paper describes the Sunshine switch and is especially interesting because it provides insights into the important role of traffic analysis in switch design. In particular, the Sunshine designers were among the first to realize that cells were unlikely to arrive at a switch in a totally uncorrelated way and thus were able to factor these correlations into their design.

- McQuillan, J., et al. The new routing algorithm for the ARPANET. *IEEE Transactions on Communications* COM-28(5):711–719, May 1980.

- Khanna, A., and J. Zinky. The revised ARPANET routing metric. *Proceedings of the SIGCOMM '88 Symposium*, pages 45–56, August 1988.

- Schwartz, M., and T. Stern. Routing techniques used in computer communication networks. *IEEE Transactions on Communications* COM-28(4):539–552, April 1980.

- Lyles, J., and D. Swinehart. The emerging gigabit environment and the role of the local ATM. *IEEE Communications* 30(4):52–58, April 1992.

- Giacopelli, J. N., et al. Sunshine: A high-performance self-routing broadband packet-switched architecture. *IEEE Journal of Selected Areas in Communications (JSAC)* 9(8):1289–1298, October 1991.

A good general overview of routing protocols and issues can be found in works by Perlman [Per92, Per93]. *Interconnections: Bridges and Routers* includes a description of the circumstances that led to the ARPANET crash in 1981.

For more information on ATM, one of the early overview books is by De Prycker [Pry91]. Also, as one of the key ATM standards-setting bodies, the ATM Forum produces new specifications for ATM; the User Network Interface (UNI) specification, version 3.1, is the most recent at the time of this writing. (See live reference below.)

There have been literally thousands of papers published on switch architectures. One early paper that explains Batcher networks well is, not surprisingly, one by Batcher himself [Bat68]. Sorting networks are explained by Drysdale and Young [DY75], and the Knockout switch is described by Yeh et al. [YHA87]. A reasonable survey of ATM switch architectures appears in Partridge [Par94], and a good overview of the performance of different switching fabrics can be found in Robertazzi [Rob93]. An example of a modern non-ATM switch can be found in Gopal and Guerin[GG94].

An excellent text to read if you want to learn about the mathematical analysis of network performance is by Kleinrock [Kle75], one of the pioneers of the ARPANET. Many papers have been published on the applications of queuing theory to packet switching. We recommend the article by Paxson and Floyd [PF94] as a recent contribution focused on the Internet, and one by Leland et al. [LTWW94], a significant paper that introduces the important concept of "long-range dependence" and shows the inadequacy of many traditional approaches to traffic modeling.

Finally, we recommend the following live reference:

■ http://www.atmforum.com: current activities of the ATM Forum.

E X E R C I S E S

1 Give a list of network applications that would be better suited for a datagram-based network than a connection-oriented network, and vice versa. Justify why each application belongs on one list or the other.

2 Using the example network given in Figure 4.29, give the virtual circuit tables for all the switches after each of the following connections is established. Assume that the sequence of connections is cumulative, that is, the first connection is still up when the second connection is established, and so on. Also assume that the VCI assignment always picks the lowest unused VCI on an outbound link.

(a) Host A connects to host B.

(b) Host C connects to host G.

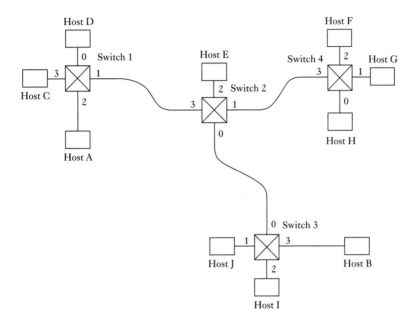

Figure 4.29 Example network for exercise 2.

(c) Host E connects to host I.

(d) Host D connects to host B.

(e) Host F connects to host J.

(f) Host H connects to host A.

3 For the network given in Figure 4.30, give the datagram forwarding table for each node. Assume that a short-path-first algorithm is used to select the route to each destination.

4 For the network given in the previous problem, show how the link-state algorithm builds the routing table for node D.

5 For the same network used in problem 3, show the sequence of global routing tables—one for each update cycle—that would be created by the distance-vector algorithm.

6 Even though the Ethernet supports multiple access, it can be used as a point-to-point link; you just limit it to one node at each end. Suppose you built a network similar to the one used in problem 3. How would the fact that you used an Ethernet for each link

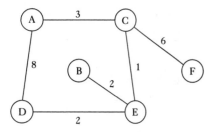

Figure 4.30   Network for exercise 3.

complicate the routing algorithm? (Hint: Think about how you assign weights to each link.)

7 Read the article by McQuillan et al., "New routing algorithm for the ARPANET," given in the recommended reading list for this chapter. List all the reasons why the algorithm described in this paper was an improvement over the original algorithm.

8 What percentage of an ATM link's total bandwidth is consumed by the ATM cell headers?

9 Explain why AAL3/4 will not detect the loss of 16 cells within a PDU.

10 The IP datagram for a TCP ACK message is 40 bytes long: it contains 20 bytes of TCP header and 20 bytes of IP header. Assume that this ACK is traversing an ATM network that uses AAL5 to encapsulate IP packets. How many ATM packets will it take to carry the ACK? What if AAL3/4 is used instead?

11 The CS-PDU for AAL5 contains up to 47 bytes of padding, while the AAL3/4 CS-PDU only contains up to 3 bytes of padding. Explain why the effective bandwidth of AAL5 is always the same as, or higher than, that of AAL3/4, given a PDU of a particular size.

12 Assuming DMA in and out of main memory, how many interfaces to 45-Mbps T3 links could a workstation-based switch handle if its I/O bus speed is 800 Mbps and the memory bandwidth is 2 Gbps?

13 Suppose a switch can forward packets at a rate of 15,000 per second. Plot the aggregate throughput of the switch as a function of packet size. At what packet size does the bus bandwidth become the limiting factor, assuming the workstation parameters described in the previous problem?

14 Implement a simple switching protocol for a datagram-based network in the x-kernel. Measure the packets per second that this protocol can process.

15 Read the paper by Giacopelli et al., "Sunshine: A high performance self-routing broadband packet-switched architecture," given in the recommended reading list for this chapter. Explain how the Sunshine switch is able to keep cells in order, even when they have to be recirculated. Be precise.

16 Give a schematic for a 16 to 6 Knockout concentrator, similar to the one given in Figure 4.22.

17 A stage of an $n \times n$ banyan network consists of $(n/2)$ 2×2 switching elements. The first stage directs packets to the correct half of the network, the next stage to the correct quarter, and so on, until the packet is routed to the correct output. Derive an expression for the number of 2×2 switching elements needed to make an $n \times n$ banyan network. Verify your answer for $n = 8$.

18 An $n \times n$ Batcher network can be made from two Batcher networks of size $n/2 \times n/2$ plus a merge network of size $n/2 \log_2 n$. Assuming that a 2×2 Batcher network has a complexity of 1 (i.e., it has one switching element), derive the expression for the complexity (number of switching elements) of an $n \times n$ Batcher network. Check your result for $n = 8$ against Figure 4.26.

We have now seen how to build a single network
using point-to-point links, shared media, and
switches. The problem is that lots of people
have built networks with these various technologies and they
all want to be able to communicate with each other, not just
with the other users of a single network. This chapter is about
the problem of interconnecting different networks.

*There is a certain scale
of duties, there is a
certain Hierarchy of
upper and lower
commands.*

—Milton

There are two important problems that must be addressed when
connecting networks: *heterogeneity*
and *scale*. Simply stated, the problem
of heterogeneity is that users on one
type of network want to be able to
communicate with users on other
types of networks. To further com-
plicate matters, establishing connectivity between hosts on
two different networks may require traversing several other
networks in between, each of which may be of yet another
type. These different networks may be Ethernets, token
rings, point-to-point links, or switched networks of various
kinds, and each of them is likely to have its own addressing
scheme, media-access protocols, service model, and so on.
The challenge of heterogeneity is to provide a useful and
fairly predictable host-to-host service over this hodgepodge
of different networks. To understand the problem of scaling,
it is worth considering the growth of the Internet, which has
roughly doubled in size each year for 20 years. This sort of
growth forces us to think about how to do routing efficiently
in a network that might have billions of nodes, and this issue
is closely related to how we do addressing.

This chapter looks at a series of approaches to interconnecting networks, starting with a simple approach that supports only very limited amounts of heterogeneity and scalability, and ending with the introduction of a new standard
for building a global internetwork. In between these two extremes, we trace the evolution of the TCP/IP Internet in an
effort to understand the problems of heterogeneity and scale
in detail, along with the general techniques that can be applied
to them.

The chapter begins with a description of bridging as a way of interconnecting networks. Bridges basically allow us to take a number of LANs and to interconnect them to form an extended LAN—something that behaves like a LAN but does not suffer from the same limitations of physical size or number of attached hosts. As a way of interconnecting networks, however, bridging accommodates very little heterogeneity, and it does not scale to large sizes.

The next section introduces the Internet Protocol (IP) and shows how it can be used to build a scalable, heterogeneous internetwork. This section includes a discussion of the Internet's service model, which is the key to its ability to handle heterogeneity. It also describes how the Internet's hierarchical addressing and routing scheme has allowed the Internet to scale to a modestly large size.

The following section then discusses several of the problems (growing pains) that the Internet has experienced over the past several years and introduces the techniques that have been employed to address these problems. In particular, this section discusses the Internet's routing protocols, which are based on the principles outlined in Chapter 4.

The experience gained from using these techniques has led to the design of a new version of IP, which is known as Next Generation IP, or IP version 6 (IPv6). This new version of IP has been developed to allow further scaling of the Internet, and it is described in the next section. Throughout all these discussions, we see the importance of hierarchy in building scalable networks.

The chapter concludes by considering two issues related to internetworking. First, we show how multicast delivery—the ability to deliver packets efficiently to a set of receivers—can be incorporated into an internet. Second, we describe a naming scheme that can be used to identify objects, such as hosts, in a large internet.

5

Internetworking

5.1   Bridges and Extended LANs

Suppose you have a pair of Ethernets that you want to interconnect. One thing you might do is put a repeater between them, as described in Chapter 3. This would not be a workable solution, however, if doing so exceeded the physical limitations of the Ethernet. (Recall that no more than two repeaters between any pair of hosts and no more than a total of 1500 m in length is allowed.) An alternative would be to put a node between the two Ethernets and have the node forward frames from one Ethernet to the other. This node would be in promiscuous mode, accepting all frames transmitted on either of the Ethernets, so it could forward them to the other.

The node we have just described is typically called a *bridge*, and a collection of LANs connected by one or more bridges is usually said to form an *extended LAN*. While bridges look a lot like the switches described in the previous chapter, they are different in that they connect two or more multi-access networks rather than a set of point-to-point links. Bridges simply accept and forward LAN frames, without the need for a higher-level packet header that is used to make a routing decision. It is for this reason that we say that a bridge is a link-level node that forwards frames rather than a network-level node that switches packets.

While the simple "accept and forward all frames" algorithm just described works, and it corresponds to the functionality provided by early bridges, this strategy has been refined to make bridges an even more effective mechanism for interconnecting a set of LANs. The rest of this section fills in the more interesting details.

5.1.1   Learning Bridges

The first optimization we can make to a bridge is to observe that it need not forward all frames that it receives. Consider the bridge in Figure 5.1. Whenever a frame from host A that is addressed to host B arrives on port 1, there is no need for the bridge to forward the frame out over port 2. The question, then, is how does a bridge come to learn on which port the various hosts reside?

One option would be to have a human download a table into the bridge similar to the one given in Table 5.1. Then, whenever the bridge receives a frame on port 1 that is addressed to host A, it would not forward the frame out on port 2; there would be no need because host A would have already directly received the frame on the LAN connected to port 1. Any time a frame addressed to host A was received on port 2, the bridge would forward the frame out on port 1.

Having a human maintain this table is quite a burden, especially considering that there is a simple trick by which a bridge can learn this information for itself. The idea is for each bridge to inspect the *source* address in all the frames it receives. Thus, when host A sends a frame to a host on either side of the bridge, the bridge receives this frame and records the fact that a frame from host A was just received on port 1. In this way, the bridge can build a table just like Table 5.1.

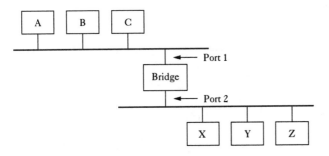

Figure 5.1 Illustration of a learning bridge.

Host	Port
A	1
B	1
C	1
X	2
Y	2
Z	2

Table 5.1 Forwarding table maintained by a bridge.

When a bridge first boots, this table is empty; entries are added over time. Also, a timeout is associated with each entry, and the bridge discards the entry after a specified period of time. This is to protect against the situation in which a host—and as a consequence, its LAN address—is moved from one network to another. Thus, this table is not necessarily complete. Should the bridge receive a frame that is addressed to a host not currently in the table, it goes ahead and forwards the frame out on all the other ports. In other words, this table is simply an optimization that filters out some frames; it is not required for correctness.

5.1.2 Spanning Tree Algorithm

The preceding strategy works just fine until the extended LAN has a loop in it, in which case it fails in a horrible way—frames potentially loop through the extended LAN forever. This is easy to see in the example depicted in Figure 5.2, where, for example, bridges B1, B4, and B6 form a loop. How does an extended LAN come to have a loop in it? One possibility is that the network is managed by more than one administrator, for example, because it spans multiple departments in an organization. In such a setting, it is possible that no single person

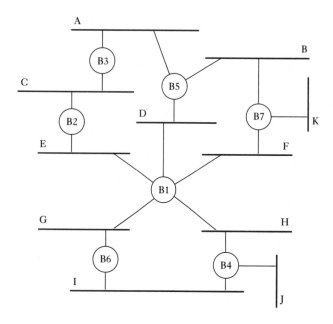

Figure 5.2   Extended LAN with loops.

knows the entire configuration of the network, meaning that a bridge that closes a loop might be added without anyone knowing. A second, more likely scenario is that loops are built into the network on purpose—to provide redundancy in case of failure.

Whatever the cause, bridges must be able to correctly handle loops. While one could imagine addressing this problem by having the bridges run one of the routing algorithms described in Chapter 4, the problem is instead addressed by having the bridges run a distributed *spanning tree* algorithm. If you think of the extended LAN as being represented by a graph that possibly has loops (cycles), then a spanning tree is a subgraph of this graph that covers (spans) all the vertices, but contains no cycles. That is, a spanning tree keeps all of the vertices of the original graph, but throws out some of the edges. For example, Figure 5.3 shows a cyclic graph on the left and one of possibly many spanning trees on the right.

The spanning tree algorithm, which was developed by Radia Perlman at Digital, is a protocol used by a set of bridges to agree upon a spanning tree for a particular extended LAN. (The IEEE 802.1 specification for LAN bridges is based on this algorithm.) In practice, this means that each bridge decides the ports over which it is and is not willing to forward frames. In a sense, it is by removing ports from the topology that the extended LAN is reduced to an acyclic tree.[1] It is even possible that an entire bridge will not participate in forwarding frames,

---

[1]Representing an extended LAN as an abstract graph is a bit awkward. Basically, you let both the bridges and the LANs correspond to the vertices of the graph, and the ports correspond to the graph's edges. However, the spanning tree we are

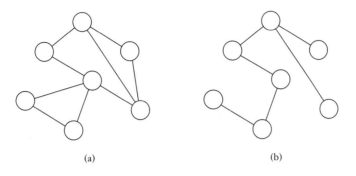

Figure 5.3 Example of (a) a cyclic graph; (b) a corresponding spanning tree.

which seems kind of strange when you consider that the one reason we intentionally have loops in the network in the first place is to provide redundancy. The algorithm is dynamic, however, meaning that the bridges are always prepared to reconfigure themselves into a new spanning tree should some bridge fail.

The main idea of the spanning tree is for the bridges to select the ports over which they will forward frames. The algorithm selects ports as follows. Each bridge has a unique identifier; for our purposes, we use the labels B1, B2, B3, and so on. The algorithm first elects the bridge with the smallest id as the root of the spanning tree; exactly how this election takes place is described below. The root bridge always forwards frames out over all of its ports. Next, each bridge computes the shortest path to the root and notes which of its ports is on this path. This port is also selected as the bridge's preferred path to the root. Finally, all the bridges connected to a given LAN elect a single *designated* bridge that will be responsible for forwarding frames toward the root bridge. Each LAN's designated bridge is the one that is closest to the root, and if two or more bridges are equally close to the root, then the bridges" identifiers are used to break ties; the smallest id wins. Of course, each bridge is connected to more than one LAN, so it participates in the election of a designated bridge for each LAN it is connected to. In effect, this means that each bridge decides if it is the designated bridge relative to each of its ports. The bridge forwards frames over those ports for which it is the designated bridge.

Figure 5.4 shows the spanning tree that corresponds to the extended LAN shown in Figure 5.2. In this example, B1 is the root bridge, since it has the smallest id. Notice that both B3 and B5 are connected to LAN A, but B5 is the designated bridge since it is closer to the root. Similarly, both B5 and B7 are connected to LAN B, but in this case, B5 is the designated bridge since it has the smaller id; both are an equal distance from B1.

going to compute for this graph needs to span only those nodes that correspond to networks. It is possible that nodes corresponding to bridges will be disconnected from the rest of the graph. This corresponds to a situation in which all the ports connecting a bridge to various networks get removed by the algorithm.

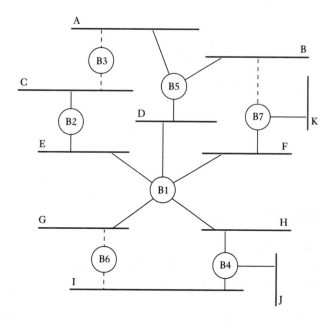

Figure 5.4 Spanning tree with some ports not selected.

While it is possible for a human to look at the extended LAN given in Figure 5.2 and to compute the spanning tree given in Figure 5.4 according to the rules given above, the bridges in an extended LAN do not have the luxury of being able to see the topology of the entire network, let alone peek inside other bridges to see their ids. Instead, the bridges have to exchange configuration messages with each other and then decide whether or not they are the root or a designated bridge based on these messages.

Specifically, the configuration messages contain three pieces of information:

1 the id for the bridge that is sending the message;

2 the id for what the sending bridge believes to be the root bridge;

3 the distance, measured in hops, from the sending bridge to the root bridge.

Each bridge records the current best configuration message it has seen on each of its ports, including both messages it has received from other bridges and messages that it has itself transmitted.

Initially, each bridge thinks it is the root, and so it sends a configuration message out on each of its ports identifying itself as the root and giving a distance to the root of 0. Upon receiving a configuration message over a particular port, the bridge checks to see if that new message is better than the current best configuration message recorded for that port. The new configuration message is considered "better" than the currently recorded information if it identifies a root with a smaller id; it identifies a root with an equal id but with a shorter distance; or if the root id and distance are equal, but the sending bridge has a smaller id. If the new message is better than the currently recorded information, the bridge discards the old information and saves the new information. However, it first adds 1 to the distance-to-root field since the bridge is one hop farther away from the root than the bridge that sent the message.

When a bridge receives a configuration message indicating that it is not the root bridge—that is, a message from a bridge with a smaller id—the bridge stops generating configuration messages on its own and instead only forwards configuration messages from other bridges. Likewise, when a bridge receives a configuration message that indicates it is not the designated bridge for that port—that is, a message from a bridge that is closer to the root or equally far from the root but with a smaller id—the bridge stops sending configuration messages over that port. Thus, when the system stabilizes, only the root bridge is still generating configuration messages, and the other bridges are forwarding these messages—after first adding 1 to the distance field—only over ports for which they are the designated bridge.

Even after the system has stabilized, the root bridge continues to send configuration messages periodically and the other bridges continue to forward these messages as described in the previous paragraph. Should a particular bridge fail, the downstream bridges will not receive these configuration messages, and after waiting a specified period of time, they will once again claim to be the root, and the algorithm just described will kick in again to elect a new root and new designated bridges.

One important thing to notice is that although the algorithm is able to reconfigure the spanning tree whenever a bridge fails, it is not able to forward frames over alternative paths for the sake of routing around a congested bridge.

5.1.3 Broadcast and Multicast

The preceding discussion has focused on how bridges forward unicast frames from one LAN to another. Since the goal of a bridge is to transparently extend a LAN across multiple networks, and since most LANs support both broadcast and multicast, then bridges must also support these two features. Broadcast is simple—each bridge forwards a frame with a destination broadcast address out on each active (selected) port other than the one on which the frame was received.

Multicast can be implemented in exactly the same way, with each host deciding for itself whether or not to accept the message. This is exactly what is done in practice. Notice, however, that since not all the LANs in an extended LAN necessarily have a host that is a member of a particular multicast group, it is possible to do better. Specifically, the spanning tree algorithm can be extended to prune networks over which multicast frames need not be forwarded. Consider a frame sent to group M by a host on LAN A in Figure 5.4. If there is no host on LAN J that belongs to group M, then there is no need for bridge B4 to forward the frames over that network. On the other hand, not having a host on LAN H that belongs to group M does not necessarily mean that bridge B1 can avoid forwarding multicast frames onto LAN H. It all depends on whether or not there are members of group M on LANs I and J.

How does a given bridge learn whether it should forward a multicast frame over a given port? It learns exactly the same way that a bridge learns whether it should forward a unicast frame over a particular port—by observing the *source* addresses that it receives over that port. Of course, groups are not typically the source of frames, so we have to cheat a little. In particular, each host that is a member of group M must periodically send a frame with the address for group M in the source field of the frame header. This frame would have as its destination address the multicast address for the bridges.

Note that while the multicast extension just described has been proposed, it is not widely adopted. Instead, multicast is implemented in exactly the same way as broadcast on today's extended LANs.

5.1.4 Limitations of Bridges

The bridge-based solution just described is meant to be used in only a fairly limited setting— to connect a handful of similar LANs. It does not really address either the issue of scale or the issue of heterogeneity outlined in the problem statement for this chapter.

On the issue of scale, it is not realistic to connect more than a few LANs by means of bridges, where in practice "few" typically means "tens of." One reason for this is that the spanning tree algorithm scales linearly, that is, there is no provision for imposing a hierarchy on the extended LAN. A second reason is that bridges forward all broadcast frames. While it is reasonable for all hosts within a limited setting (say, a department) to see each other's broadcast messages, it is unlikely that all the hosts in a larger environment (say, a large company or university) would want to have to be bothered by each other's broadcast messages. Said another way, broadcast does not scale, and as a consequence, extended LANs do not scale.

On the issue of heterogeneity, bridges are fairly limited in the kinds of networks they can interconnect. In particular, bridges make use of the network's frame header and so can support only networks that have exactly the same format for addresses. Thus, bridges can be used to connect Ethernets to Ethernets, FDDI to FDDI, and Ethernets to FDDI, since both networks support the same 48-bit address format. Bridges do not generalize to other kinds of networks, such as ATM.

Despite these limitations, bridges are a very important part of the complete networking picture. Their main advantage is that they allow multiple LANs to be transparently connected, that is, the networks can be connected without the end hosts having to run any additional protocols (or even be aware, for that matter). The one potential exception is when the hosts are expected to announce their membership in a multicast group, as described in Section 5.1.3.

Notice, however, that this transparency can be dangerous. If a host, or more precisely, the application and transport protocol running on that host, is programmed under the assumption that it is running on a single LAN, then inserting bridges between the source and designation hosts can have unexpected consequences. For example, if a bridge becomes congested, it may have to drop frames; in contrast, it is rare that a single Ethernet ever drops a frame. As another example, the latency between any pair of hosts on an extended LAN becomes both larger and more highly variable; in contrast, the physical limitations of a single Ethernet make the latency both small and predictable. As a final example, it is possible (although unlikely) that frames will be reordered in an extended LAN; in contrast, frame order is never shuffled on a single Ethernet. The bottom line is that it is never safe to design network software under the assumption that it will run over a single Ethernet segment. Bridges happen.

5.2   Simple Internetworking (IP)

The remainder of this chapter explores some ways to go beyond the limitations of bridged networks, enabling us to build large, highly heterogeneous networks with reasonably efficient routing. We refer to such networks as internetworks. In the next three sections, we make a steady progression toward larger and larger internetworks. We start with the basic functionality of the currently deployed version of the Internet Protocol (IP), and then we examine various techniques that have been developed to extend the scalability of the Internet in Section 5.3. This discussion culminates in Section 5.4, in which we describe the "next generation" IP, also known as IP version 6 (IPv6). Before delving into the details of an internetworking protocol, however, let's consider more carefully what the word *internetwork* means.

5.2.1   What Is an Internetwork?

We use the term *internetwork*, or sometimes just internet with a lowercase i, to refer to an arbitrary collection of networks interconnected to provide some sort of host-to-host packet delivery service. For example, a corporation with many sites might construct a private internetwork by interconnecting the LANs at their different sites with point-to-point links leased from the phone company. When we are talking about the widely used, global internetwork to which a large percentage of networks are now connected, we call it the *Internet* with a capital I. In keeping with the first-principles approach of this book, we mainly want you to learn about the principles of "lowercase i" internetworking, but we illustrate these ideas with real-world examples from the "big I" Internet.

Another piece of terminology that can be confusing is the difference between networks, subnetworks, and internetworks. We are going to avoid subnetworks (or subnets) altogether until Section 5.3. For now, we use *network* to mean either a directly connected or a switched network of the kind that was discussed in the last two chapters. Such a network uses one technology, such as FDDI, Ethernet, or ATM. An *internetwork* is an interconnected collection of such networks. Sometimes, to avoid ambiguity, we refer to the underlying networks that we are interconnecting as *physical* networks. An internet is a *logical* network built out of a collection of physical networks.

Figure 5.5 shows an example internetwork. An internetwork is often referred to as a "network of networks" because it is made up of lots of smaller networks. In this figure, we see

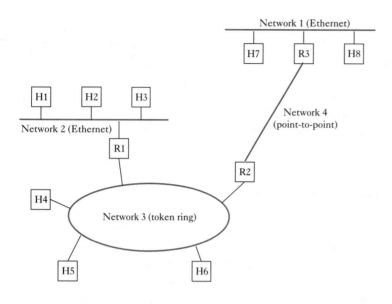

Figure 5.5   A simple internetwork. Hn = host; **R**n = router.

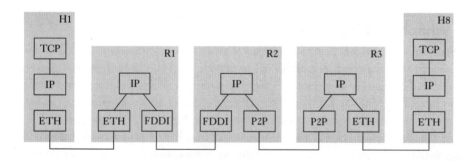

Figure 5.6   A simple internetwork, showing the protocol layers used to connect H1 to H8 in Figure 5.5.

Ethernets, a token ring, and a point-to-point link. Each of these is a single-technology network. The nodes that interconnect the networks are called *routers*. They are also sometimes called *gateways*, but since this term has several other connotations, we restrict our usage to router.

The Internet Protocol (IP) is the key tool used today to build scalable, heterogeneous internetworks. It was originally known as the Kahn-Cerf protocol after its inventors. One way to think of IP is that it runs on all the nodes (both hosts and routers) in a collection of networks and defines the infrastructure that allows these nodes and networks to function as a single logical internetwork. For example, Figure 5.6 shows how hosts H1 and H8 are logically connected by the internet in Figure 5.5, including the protocol graph running on each node. Note that higher-level protocols, such as TCP and UDP, typically run on top of IP on the hosts.

Most of the rest of this chapter is about various aspects of IP. While it is certainly possible to build an internetwork that does not use IP—for example, Novell supports an internetworking protocol called IPX, which is in turn based on the XNS internet designed by Xerox— IP is the most interesting case to study simply because of the size of the Internet. Said another way, it is only the IP Internet that has really faced the issue of scale.

5.2.2 Service Model

A good place to start when you build an internetwork is to define its *service model*, that is, the host-to-host services you want to provide. The main concern in defining a service model for an internetwork is that we can provide only a host-to-host service if this service can somehow be provided over each of the underlying physical networks. For example, it would be no good deciding that our internetwork service model was going to provide guaranteed delivery of every packet in 1 ms or less if there were underlying network technologies that could arbitrarily delay packets. The philosophy used in defining the IP service model, therefore, was to make it undemanding enough that just about any network technology that might turn up in an internetwork would be able to provide the necessary service.

The IP service model can be thought of as having two parts: an addressing scheme, which provides a way to identify all hosts in the internetwork, and a datagram (connectionless) model of data delivery. This service model is sometimes called *best effort* because while IP makes every effort to deliver datagrams, it makes no guarantees. We postpone a discussion of the addressing scheme for now and look first at the data delivery model.

Datagram Delivery

The IP datagram is fundamental to the IP. Every datagram carries enough information to let the network forward the packet to its correct destination; there is no need for any advance setup mechanism to tell the network what to do when the packet arrives. You just send it, and the network does its best to get it to the desired destination. The best effort part means that if something goes wrong and the packet gets lost, corrupted, misdelivered, or in any way fails to reach its intended destination, the network does nothing—it made its best effort, and that is all it has to do. It does not make any attempt to recover from the failure. This is sometimes called an *unreliable* service.

Best effort, connectionless service is about the simplest service you could ask for from an internetwork, and this is a great strength. For example, if you provide best effort service over a network that provides a reliable service, then that's fine—you end up with a best effort service that just happens to always deliver the packets. If, on the other hand, you had a reliable service model over an unreliable network, you would have to put lots of extra functionality into the routers to make up for the deficiencies of the underlying network. Keeping the routers as simple as possible was one of the original design goals of IP.

The ability of IP to "run over anything" is frequently cited as one of its most important characteristics. It is noteworthy that many of the technologies over which IP runs today did not exist when IP was invented. So far, no networking technology has been invented that has proven too bizarre for IP; it has even been claimed that IP can run over a network that consists of two tin cans and a piece of string.

Best effort delivery does not just mean that packets can get lost. Sometimes they can get delivered out of order, and sometimes the same packet can get delivered more than once. The higher-level protocols or applications that run above IP need to be aware of all these possible failure modes.

Packet Format

Clearly, a key part of the IP service model is the type of packets that can be carried. The IP datagram, like most packets, consists of a header followed by a number of bytes of data. The format of the header is shown in Figure 5.7. Note that we have adopted a different style of representing packets than the one we used in previous chapters. This is because packet formats at the internetworking layer and above, where we will be focusing our attention for the next few chapters, are almost invariably designed to align on 32-bit boundaries to simplify the task of processing them in software. Thus, the common way of representing them (used in Internet Requests for Comments [RFCs], for example) is to draw them as a succession of 32-bit words. The top word is the one transmitted first, and the leftmost byte of each word is the one transmitted first. In this representation, you can easily recognize fields that are a multiple of 8 bits long. On the odd occasion when fields are not an even multiple of 8 bits, you can determine the field lengths by looking at the bit positions marked at the top of the packet.

Looking at each field in the IP header, we see that the "simple" model of best effort datagram delivery still has some subtle features. The **Version** field specifies the version of IP. The current version of IP is 4, and it is sometimes called IPv4.[2] Observe that putting this field right at the start of the datagram makes it easy for everything else in the packet format to be redefined in subsequent versions; the header processing software starts off by looking at the version and then branches off to process the rest of the packet according to the appropriate format. The next field, **HLen**, specifies the length of the header in 32-bit words. When there are no options, which is most of the time, the header is 5 words (20 bytes) long. The 8-bit **TOS** (type of service) field has never been used widely enough to be really useful, but in principle it allows packets to be treated differently based on application needs. It contains 3 priority bits to describe how important the packet is and 3 bits that may be set to request low delay, high throughput, or high reliability.

---

[2]Next Generation IP, which is discussed later in this chapter, has a new version number 6 and is known as IPv6. The version number 5 was used for an experimental protocol called ST-II.

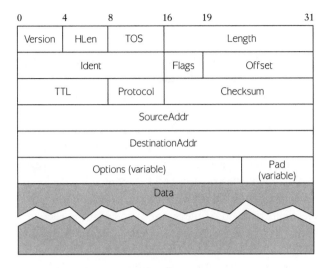

Figure 5.7   IPv4 packet header.

The next 16 bits of the header contain the **Length** of the datagram, including the header. Unlike the **HLen** field, the **Length** field counts bytes rather than words. Thus, the maximum size of an IP datagram is 65,535 bytes. The physical network over which IP is running, however, may not support such long packets. For this reason, IP supports a fragmentation and reassembly process, which is described below. The second word of the header contains information about fragmentation.

Moving on to the third word of the header, the next byte is the **TTL** (time to live) field. Its name reflects its historical meaning rather than the way it is commonly used today. The intent of the field is to catch packets that have been going around in routing loops and discard them, rather than let them consume resources indefinitely. Originally, **TTL** was set to a specific number of seconds that the packet would be allowed to live, and routers along the path would decrement this field until it reached 0. However, since it was rare for a packet to sit for as long as 1 second in a router, and routers did not all have access to a common clock, most routers just decremented the **TTL** by 1 as they forwarded the packet. Thus, it became more of a hop count than a timer, which is still a perfectly good way to catch packets that are stuck in routing loops. One subtlety is in the initial setting of this field by the sending host: set it too high and packets could circulate rather a lot before getting dropped; set it too low and they may not reach their destination. The value 64 is the current default.

The **Protocol** field is simply a demultiplexing key that identifies the higher-level protocol to which this IP packet should be passed. There are values defined for TCP (6), UDP (17), and many other protocols that may sit above IP in the protocol graph.

The Checksum is calculated by considering the entire IP header as a sequence of 16-bit words, adding them up using ones complement arithmetic and taking the ones complement of the result. This is the IP checksum algorithm described in Section 3.4. Thus, if any bit in the header is corrupted in transit, the checksum will not contain the correct value upon receipt of the packet. Since a corrupted header may contain an error in the destination address— and, as a result, may have been misdelivered—it makes sense to discard any packet that fails the checksum. It should be noted that this type of checksum does not have the same strong error-detection properties as a CRC, but it is much easier to calculate in software.

The last two required fields in the header are the SourceAddr and the DestinationAddr for the packet. The latter is the key to datagram delivery: every packet contains a full address for its intended destination so that forwarding decisions can be made at each router. The source address is required to allow recipients to decide if they want to accept the packet and to enable them to reply. IP addresses are discussed in Section 5.2.3—for now, the important thing to know is that IP defines its own global address space, independent of whatever physical networks it runs over. As we will see, this is one of the keys to supporting heterogeneity.

Finally, there may be a number of options at the end of the header. The presence or absence of options may be determined by examining the header length (HLen) field. While options are used fairly rarely, a complete IP implementation must handle them all.

Fragmentation and Reassembly

One of the problems of providing a uniform host-to-host service model over a heterogeneous collection of networks is that each network technology tends to have its own idea of how large a packet can be. For example, an Ethernet can accept packets up to 1500 bytes long, while FDDI packets may be 4500 bytes long. This leaves two choices for the IP service model: make sure that all IP datagrams are small enough to fit inside one packet on any network technology or provide a means by which packets can be fragmented and reassembled when they are too big to go over a given network technology. The latter turns out to be a good choice, especially when you consider the fact that new network technologies are always turning up, and IP needs to run over all of them; this would make it hard to pick a suitably small bound on datagram size. This also means that a host will not send needlessly small packets, which wastes bandwidth and consumes processing resources by requiring more headers per byte of data sent. For example, two hosts connected to FDDI networks that are interconnected by a point-to-point link would not need to send packets small enough to fit on an Ethernet.

The central idea here is that every network type has a *maximum transmission unit* (MTU), which is the largest IP datagram that it can carry in a frame. Note that this value is smaller than the largest packet size on that network because the IP datagram needs to fit in the *payload* of the link-layer frame. Also, note that in ATM networks, the "frame" is the CS-PDU, not the ATM cell; the fact that CS-PDUs get segmented into cells is not visible to IP.

When a host sends an IP datagram, therefore, it can choose any size that it wants. A reasonable choice is the MTU of the network to which the host is directly attached. Then, fragmentation will only be necessary if the path to the destination includes a network with a

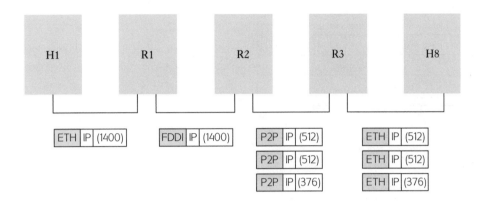

Figure 5.8 IP datagrams traversing the sequence of physical networks graphed in Figure 5.5.

smaller MTU. Should the transport protocol that sits on top of IP give IP a packet larger than the local MTU, however, then the source host must fragment it.

Fragmentation typically occurs in a router when it receives a datagram that it wants to forward over a network that has an MTU that is smaller than the received datagram. To enable these fragments to be reassembled at the receiving host, they all carry the same identifier in the Ident field. This identifier is chosen by the sending host and is intended to be unique among all the datagrams that might arrive at the destination from this source over some reasonable time period. Since all fragments of the original datagram contain this identifier, the reassembling host will be able to recognize those fragments that go together. Should all the fragments not arrive at the receiving host, the host gives up on the reassembly process and discards the fragments that did arrive. IP does not attempt to recover from missing fragments.

To see what this all means, consider what happens when host H1 sends a datagram to host H8 in the example internet shown in Figure 5.5. Assuming that the MTU is 1500 bytes for the two Ethernets, 4500 bytes for the FDDI network, and 532 bytes for the point-to-point network, then a 1420-byte datagram (20-byte IP header plus 1400 bytes of data) sent from H1 makes it across the first Ethernet and the FDDI network without fragmentation but must be fragmented into three datagrams at router R2. These three fragments are then forwarded by router R3 across the second Ethernet to the destination host. This situation is illustrated in Figure 5.8. This figure also serves to reinforce two important points: (1) each fragment is itself a self-contained IP datagram that is transmitted over a sequence of physical networks, independent of the other fragments; and (2) each IP datagram is re-encapsulated for each physical network over which it travels.

The fragmentation process can be understood in detail by looking at the header fields of each datagram, as is done in Figure 5.9. The unfragmented packet, shown at the top, has 1400 bytes of data and a 20-byte IP header. When the packet arrives at router R2, which has an MTU of 532 bytes, it has to be fragmented. A 532-byte MTU leaves 512 bytes for data

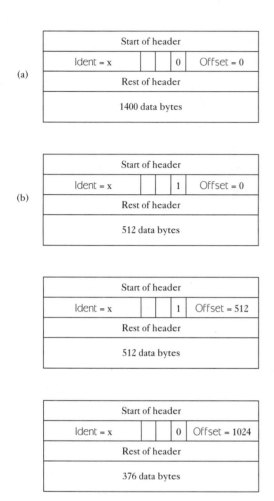

Figure 5.9   Header fields used in IP fragmentation. (a) Unfragmented packets; (b) fragmented packets.

after the 20-byte IP header, so the first fragment contains 512 bytes of data. The router sets the M bit in the Flags field (see Figure 5.7), meaning that there are more fragments to follow, and it sets the Offset to 0, since this fragment contains the first part of the original datagram. The data carried in the second fragment starts with the 513th byte of the original data, so the Offset field in this header is set to 512, and again the M bit is set. In the third fragment go the last 376 bytes of data, and the offset is now $2 \times 512 = 1024$. Since this is the last fragment, the M bit is not set. A minor detail that we have not mentioned up to this point is that the Offset field counts 8-byte units of data, not individual bytes. This means that a datagram must be fragmented on 8-byte boundaries, which happens to be the case in this example. We leave it as an exercise for you to figure out why the Offset field specifies 8-byte chunks of data rather than individual bytes.

Observe that the fragmentation process is done in such a way that it could be repeated if a fragment arrived at another network with an even smaller MTU. Fragmentation produces smaller, valid IP datagrams that can be readily reassembled into the original datagram upon receipt, independent of the order of their arrival. Reassembly is done at the receiving host and not at each router.

Implementation

We conclude this discussion of IP fragmentation and reassembly by giving the x-kernel routine that performs reassembly. One reason we give this particular piece of code is that it is representative of a large proportion of networking code—it does little more than tedious and unglamorous bookkeeping.

First, we define the key data structure (FragList) that is used to hold the individual fragments that arrive at the destination. Incoming fragments are saved in this data structure until all the fragments in the original datagram have arrived, at which time they are reassembled into a complete datagram and passed up to some higher-level protocol. Note that each element in FragList contains either a fragment or a hole.

```
#define FRAGOFFMASK        0x1fff
#define FRAGOFFSET(flag)   ((fragflag) & FRAGOFFMASK)
#define INFINITE_OFFSET    0xffff

typedef struct fid {
    IpHost   source;
    IpHost   dest;
    u_char   prot;
    u_char   pad;
    u_short  ident;
} FragId;

typedef struct hole {
    u_int    first;
    u_int    last;
} Hole;

#define HOLE   1
#define FRAG   2

typedef struct fragif {
    u_char type;
    union {
        Hole     hole;
        Msg      frag;
    } u;
```

```
    struct fragif *next, *prev;
} FragInfo;

typedef struct FragList {
    u_short     nholes;
    FragInfo    head;    /* dummy header node */
    Bind        binding;
    bool        gcMark;
} FragList;
```

The reassembly routine, **ipReassemble**, takes the session to which the datagram belongs
(**s**), an incoming datagram (**msg**), and the IP header for that datagram (**hdr**) as arguments.
The final argument (**fragMap**) is used to map the incoming datagram into the appropriate
FragList. (Recall that the group of fragments that are being reassembled together are uniquely
identified by several fields in the IP header, as defined by structure **FragId** given above.)

The actual work done in **ipReassemble** is straightforward; as stated above, it is mostly
bookkeeping. First, the routine extracts the fields from the IP header that uniquely identify
the datagram to be reassembled, constructs a key from these fields, and looks this key up in
fragMap to find the appropriate **FragList**. Next, it inserts the new fragment into this **FragList**.
This involves comparing the sum of the offset and length of this fragment with the offset of
the next fragment in the list. Some of this work is done in subroutine **hole_create**, which is
given below. Finally, **ipReassemble** checks to see if all the holes are filled. If all the fragments
are present, it calls the x-kernel routine **msgJoin** to actually reassemble the fragments into a
whole datagram and then calls **xDemux** to pass this datagram up the protocol graph.

```
static XkReturn
ipReassemble(Sessn s, Msg *dg, IpHdr *hdr, Map fragMap)
{
    FragId      fragid;
    FragList    *list;
    FragInfo    *fi, *prev;
    Hole        *hole;
    u_short     offset, len;

    /* extract fragmentation info from header and create id for this frag */
    offset = FRAGOFFSET(hdr->frag)*8;
    len = hdr->dlen - GET_HLEN(hdr) * 4;
    bzero((char *)&fragid, sizeof(FragId));
    fragid.source = hdr->source;
    fragid.dest = hdr->dest;
    fragid.prot = hdr->prot;
    fragid.ident = hdr->ident;

    /* find reassembly list for this frag; create one if none exists */
    if (mapResolve( fragMap, &fragid, (void **)&list) == XK_FAILURE )
    {
```

```
        list = X_NEW(FragList);
        list->binding = mapBind( fragMap, &fragid, list );

        /* initialize list with a single hole spanning the whole datagram */
        list->nholes = 1;
        list->head.next = fi = X_NEW(FragInfo);
        fi->next = 0;
        fi->type = HOLE;
        fi->u.hole.first = 0;
        fi->u.hole.last = INFINITE_OFFSET;
    }
    list->gcMark = FALSE;

    prev = &list->head;
    for ( fi = prev->next; fi != 0; prev = fi, fi = fi->next )
    {
        if ( fi->type == FRAG )
        {
            continue;
        }
        hole = &fi->u.hole;
        if ( (offset < hole->last) && ((offset + len) > hole->first) )
        {
            /* check to see if frag overlaps previously received frags */
            if ( offset < hole->first )
            {
                /* truncate message from left */
                msgPop(dg, hole->first - offset);
                offset = hole->first;
            }
            if ( (offset + len) > hole->last )
            {
                /* truncate message from right */
                msgTruncate(dg, hole->last - offset);
                len = hole->last - offset;
            }

            /* now check to see if new hole(s) need to be made */
            if (((offset + len) < hole->last) && (hdr->frag & MOREFRAGMENTS))
            {
                /* creating new hole above */
                hole_create(prev, fi, (offset+len), hole->last);
                list->nholes++;
            }
            if ( offset > hole->first )
            {
                /* creating new hole below */
                hole_create(fi, fi->next, hole->first, (offset));
```

```
                        list->nholes++;
             }

             /* change this FragInfo structure to be FRAG */
             list->nholes--;
             fi->type = FRAG;
             msgConstructCopy(&fi->u.frag, dg);
             break;
         } /* if found a hole */
    } /* for loop */

    /* check to see if we're done, and if so, pass datagram up */
    if ( list->nholes == 0 )
    {
        Msg fullMsg;

        /* now have a full datagram */
        msgConstructEmpty(&fullMsg);
        for( fi = list->head.next; fi != 0; fi = fi->next )
        {
            msgJoin(&fullMsg, &fi->u.frag, &fullMsg);
        }
        mapRemoveBinding(fragMap, list->binding);
        ipFreeFragList(list);
        xDemux(xGetUp(s), s, &fullMsg);
        msgDestroy(&fullMsg);
    }
    return XK_SUCCESS;
}
```

Subroutine hole_create creates a new hole in the fragment list that begins at offset first and continues to offset last. It makes use of the x-kernel utility X_NEW, which creates an instance of the given structure.

```
static int
hole_create(FragInfo *prev, FragInfo *next, u_int first, u_int last)
{
    FragInfo    *fi;

    /* creating new hole from first to last */
    fi = X_NEW(FragInfo);
    fi->type = HOLE;
    fi->u.hole.first = first;
    fi->u.hole.last = last;
    fi->next = next;
    prev->next = fi;
}
```

Finally, note that these routines do not capture the entire picture of reassembly. What is not shown is a background process (an x-kernel event) that periodically checks to see if there has been any recent activity on this datagram (it looks at field gcMark), and if not, deletes the corresponding FragList. IP does not attempt to recover from the situation in which one or more of the fragments does not arrive; it simply gives up and reclaims the memory that was being used for reassembly.

5.2.3 Global Addresses

In the above discussion of the IP service model, we mentioned that one of the things that it provides is an addressing scheme. After all, if you want to be able to send data to any host on any network, there needs to be a way of identifying all the hosts. Thus, we need a global addressing scheme—one in which no two hosts have the same address. Global uniqueness is the first property that should be provided in an addressing scheme.

Ethernet addresses are globally unique, but that alone does not suffice for an addressing scheme in a large internetwork. Ethernet addresses are also *flat*, which means that they have no structure and provide very few clues to routing protocols. In contrast, IP addresses are *hierarchical*, by which we mean that they are made up of several parts that correspond to some sort of hierarchy in the internetwork. Specifically, IP addresses consist of two parts, a network part and a host part. This is a fairly logical structure for an internetwork, which is made up of many interconnected networks. The network part of an IP address identifies the network to which the host is attached; all hosts attached to the same network have the same network part in their IP address. The host part then identifies each host uniquely on that particular network. Thus, in the simple internetwork of Figure 5.5, the addresses of the hosts on network 1, for example, would all have the same network part and different host parts.

Note that the routers in Figure 5.5 are attached to two networks. They need to have an address on each network, one for each interface. For example, router R1, which sits between network 2 and network 3, has an IP address on the interface to network 2 that has the same network part as the hosts on network 2, and it has an IP address on the interface to network 3 that has the same network part as the hosts on network 3. Thus, bearing in mind that a router might be implemented as a host with two network interfaces, it is more precise to think of IP addresses as belonging to interfaces than to hosts.

Now, what do these hierarchical addresses look like? Unlike some other forms of hierarchical address, the sizes of the two parts are not the same for all addresses. Instead, IP addresses are divided into three different classes, as shown in Figure 5.10, each of which defines different-sized network and host parts. (There are also class D addresses that specify a multicast group, discussed in Section 5.5, and class E addresses that are currently unused.) In all cases, the address is 32 bits long.

The class of an IP address is identified in the most significant few bits. If the first bit is 0, it is a class A address. If the first bit is 1 and the second is 0, it is a class B address. If the first two bits are 1 and the third is 0, it is a class C address. Thus, of the approximately 4 billion possible IP addresses, half are class A, one-quarter are class B, and one-eighth are class

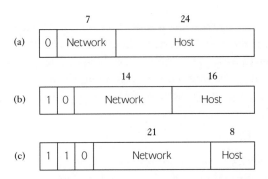

Figure 5.10 IP addresses: (a) class A; (b) class B; (c) class C.

C. Each class allocates a certain number of bits for the network part of the address and the rest for the host part. Class A networks have 7 bits for the network part and 24 bits for the host part, meaning that there can be only 128 class A networks but each of them can accommodate up to 2^{24} (about 16 million) hosts. Class B addresses allocate 14 bits for the network and 16 bits for the host, meaning that each class B network has room for 65535 hosts. Finally, class C addresses have only 8 bits for the host and 21 for the network part. Therefore, a class C network can have only 256 unique host identifiers, which means only 255 attached hosts (one host identifier, 255, is reserved for broadcast). However, the addressing scheme supports 2^{21} (about 2 million) class C networks.

On the face of it, this addressing scheme has a lot of flexibility, allowing networks of vastly different sizes to be accommodated fairly efficiently. The original idea was that the Internet would consist of a small number of wide area networks (these would be class A networks), a modest number of site- (campus-) sized networks (these would be class B networks), and a large number of LANs (these would be class C networks). However, as we shall see in Section 5.3, additional flexibility has been needed, and some innovative ways to provide it are now in use. Because one of these techniques actually removes the distinction between address classes, the addressing scheme just described is now known as "classful" addressing to distinguish it from the newer "classless" approach.

Before we look at how IP addresses get used, it is helpful to look at some practical matters, such as how you write them down. By convention, IP addresses are written as four *decimal* integers separated by dots. Each integer represents the decimal value contained in 1 byte of the address, starting at the most significant. For example, the address of the computer on which this sentence was typed is 128.96.33.81.

It is important not to confuse IP addresses with Internet domain names, which are also hierarchical. Domain names tend to be ASCII strings separated by dots, such as cicada.cs.arizona.edu. We will be talking about those in Section 5.6. The important thing about IP addresses is that they are what is carried in the headers of IP packets, and it is those addresses that are used to make routing decisions.

5.2.4 Datagram Forwarding in IP

We are now ready to look at the basic mechanism by which IP routers forward datagrams in an internetwork. (Things get a lot more complicated when we start to worry about scale and the distribution of authority in the Internet, but we postpone those concerns until Section 5.3.) Recall from Chapter 4 that *forwarding* is the process of taking a packet from an input and sending it out on the appropriate output, while *routing* is the process of building up the tables that allow the correct output for a packet to be determined. The discussion here focuses on forwarding—we take up routing in Section 5.3.2.

The main points to bear in mind as we discuss the forwarding of IP datagrams are the following:

- Every IP datagram contains the IP address of the destination host.

- The "network part" of an IP address uniquely identifies a single physical network that is part of the larger Internet.

- All hosts and routers that share the same network part of their address are connected to the same physical network and can thus communicate with each other by sending frames over that network.

- Every physical network that is part of the Internet has at least one router that, by definition, is also connected to at least one other physical network; this router can exchange packets with hosts or routers on either network.

Forwarding IP datagrams can therefore be handled in the following way. A datagram is sent from a source host to a destination host, possibly passing though several routers along the way. Any node, whether it is a host or a router, first tries to establish whether it is connected to the same physical network as the destination. To do this, it compares the network part of the destination address with the network part of the address of each of its network interfaces. (Hosts normally have only one interface, while routers normally have two or more, since they are typically connected to two or more networks.) If a match occurs, then that means that the destination lies on the same physical network as the interface, and the packet can be directly delivered over that network. Section 5.2.5 explains some of the details of this process.

If the node is not connected to the same physical network as the destination node, then it needs to send the datagram to a router. In general, each node will have a choice of several routers, and so it needs to pick the best one or at least one that has a reasonable chance of getting the datagram closer to its destination. It does this by consulting its forwarding table. The forwarding table is just a list of ⟨NetworkNum, NextHop⟩ pairs. Normally, there is also a default router that is used if none of the entries in the table match the destination's network number. For a host, it may be quite acceptable to have a default router and nothing else—this

NetworkNum	NextHop
1	R3
2	R1

Table 5.2   Example forwarding table for router R2 in Figure5.5.

means that all datagrams destined for hosts not on the physical network to which the sending host is attached will be sent out through the default router.

We can describe the datagram forwarding algorithm in the following way:

```
if (NetworkNum of destination = NetworkNum of one of my interfaces) then
        deliver packet to destination over that interface
else
        if (NetworkNum of destination is in my forwarding table) then
                deliver packet to NextHop router
        else
                deliver packet to default router
```

For a host with only one interface and only a default router in its forwarding table, this simplifies to

```
if (NetworkNum of destination = my NetworkNum) then
        deliver packet to destination directly
else
        deliver packet to default router
```

Let's see how this works in the example internetwork of Figure 5.5. First, suppose that H1 wants to send a datagram to H2. Since they are on the same physical network, H1 and H2 have the same network number in their IP address. Thus, H1 deduces that it can deliver the datagram directly to H2 over the Ethernet. The one issue that needs to be resolved is how H1 finds out the correct Ethernet address for H2—this is the address resolution mechanism described in Section 5.2.5.

Now suppose H1 wants to send a datagram to H8. Since these hosts are on different physical networks, they have different network numbers, so H1 deduces that it needs to send the datagram to a router. R1 is the only choice, so H1 sends the datagram over the Ethernet to R1. Similarly, R1 knows that it cannot deliver a datagram directly to H8 because neither of R1s interfaces is on the same network as H8. Suppose R1s default router is R2; R1 then sends the datagram to R2 over the token ring network. Now suppose R2 has the forwarding table shown in Table 5.2. R2 looks at the network number of H8, sees that it is on network 1, and forwards the datagram to R3. Finally, R3, since it is on the same network as H8, forwards the datagram directly to H8.

Note that it is possible to include the information about directly connected networks in the forwarding table. For example, we could label the network interfaces of router R2 as

NetworkNum	NextHop
1	R3
2	R1
3	Interface 1
4	Interface 0

Table 5.3 Complete forwarding table for router R2 in Figure 5.5.

interface 0 for the point-to-point link (network 4) and interface 1 for the token ring (network 3). Then R2 would have the forwarding table shown in Table 5.3.

The forwarding table used by R2 is simple enough that it could be manually configured. Usually, however, these tables are more complex and would be built up by running a routing protocol such as one of those described in Section 5.3.2. Also note that, in practice, the network numbers are usually longer, e.g., 128.96.

We can now see how hierarchical addressing—splitting the address into network and host parts—has improved the scalability of a large network. Routers now contain forwarding tables that list only a set of network numbers, rather than all the nodes in the network. In our simple example, that meant that R2 could store the information needed to reach all the hosts in the network (of which there were eight) in a four-entry table. Even if there were 100 hosts on each physical network, R2 would still only need those same four entries. This is a good first step (although by no means the last) in achieving scalability.

▶   This illustrates one of the most important principles of building scalable networks: to achieve scalability, you need to reduce the amount of information that is stored in each node and that is exchanged between nodes. The most common way to do that is *hierarchical aggregation*. IP introduces a two-level hierarchy, with networks at the top level and nodes at the bottom level. We have aggregated information by letting routers deal only with reaching the right network; the information that a router needs to deliver a datagram to any node on a given network is represented by a single, aggregated piece of information.

5.2.5 Address Translation (ARP)

The last section talked about how to get IP datagrams to the right physical network, but it glossed over the issue of how to get a datagram to a particular host or router on that network. The main issue is that IP datagrams contain IP addresses, but the physical interface hardware on the host or router to which you want to send the datagram only understands the addressing scheme of that particular network. Thus, we need to translate the IP address to a link-level address that makes sense on this network; e.g., a 48-bit Ethernet address. We can then encapsulate the IP datagram inside a frame that contains that link-level address and send it either to the ultimate destination or to a router that promises to forward the datagram toward the ultimate destination.

One simple way to map an IP address into a physical network address is to encode a host's physical address in the host part of its IP address. For example, a host with physical address 00010001 00101001 (which has the decimal value 33 in the upper byte and 81 in the lower byte) might be given the IP address 128.96.33.81. While this solution has been used on some networks, it is limited in that the network's physical addresses can be no more than 16 bits long in this example; they can be only 8 bits long on a class C network. This clearly will not work for 48-bit Ethernet addresses.

A more general solution would be for each host to maintain a table of address pairs, that is, the table would map IP addresses into physical addresses. While this table could be centrally managed by a system administrator and then copied to each host on the network, a better approach would be for each host to dynamically learn the contents of the table using the network. This can be accomplished using the Address Resolution Protocol (ARP). The goal of ARP is to enable each host on a network to build up a table of mappings between IP addresses and link-level addresses. Since these mappings may change over time (e.g., because an Ethernet card in a host breaks and is replaced by a new one with a new address), the entries are timed out periodically and removed. This happens on the order of every 15 minutes. The set of mappings currently stored in a host is known as the ARP cache or ARP table.

ARP takes advantage of the fact that many link-level network technologies, such as Ethernet and FDDI, support broadcast. If a host wants to send an IP datagram to a host (or router) on the same network, it first checks for a mapping in the cache. If no mapping is found, it needs to invoke the address resolution proto-

Bridges, Switches, and Routers

It is easy to become confused about the distinction between bridges, switches, and routers. There is good reason for such confusion, since at some level, they all forward messages from one link to another. One distinction people make is based on layering: bridges are link-level nodes (they forward frames from one link to another to implement an extended LAN), switches are network-level nodes (they forward packets from one link to another to implement a packet-switched network), and routers are internet-level nodes (they forward datagrams from one network to another to implement an internet). In some sense, however, this is an artificial distinction. It is certainly the case that networking companies do not ask the layering police for permission to sell new products that do not fit neatly into one layer or another.

For example, there are now products on the market called Ethernet

col over the network. It does this by broadcasting an ARP query onto the network. This query contains the IP address in question (the "target IP address"). Each host receives the query and checks to see if it matches its IP address. If it does match, the host sends a response message that contains its link-layer address back to the originator of the query. The originator adds the information contained in this response to its ARP table.

The query message also includes the IP address and link-layer address of the sending host. Thus, when a host broadcasts a query message, each host on the network can learn the sender's link-level and IP addresses and place that information in its ARP table. However, not every host adds this information to its ARP table. If the host already has an entry for that host in its table, it "refreshes" this entry, that is, it resets the length of time until it discards the entry. If that host is the target of the query, then it adds the information about the sender to its table, even if it did not already have an entry for that host. This is because there is a good chance that the source host is about to send it an application-level message, and it may eventually have to send a response or ACK back to the source; it will need the source's physical address to do this. If a host is not the target and does not already have an entry for the source in its ARP table, then it does not add an entry for the source. This is because there is no reason to believe that this host will ever need the source's link-level address; there is no need to clutter its ARP table with this information.

switches. The idea is that if you put one host on each Ethernet segment and connect a set of segments into a star configuration using an Ethernet switch, then each host gets a full 10 Mbps of bandwidth; it does not have to share that bandwidth with the other hosts. Although a set of Ethernet switches can be interconnected into an arbitrary configuration (i.e., you are not limited to a single star-shaped network), these switches behave fundamentally like the bridges we discuss in Section 5.1. This is because the switches do not run a routing protocol, but instead they use the spanning tree algorithm to logically restrict the topology to a loop-free tree. The only real difference between a bridge and an Ethernet switch is that the latter typically has more ports and a higher aggregate switching capacity. In other words, an Ethernet switch is just a bridge on steroids.

So, we have one important distinction: bridges depend on the span-

Figure 5.11 shows the ARP packet format for IP-to-Ethernet address mappings. In fact, ARP can be used for lots of other kinds of mappings—the major differences are in the address sizes. In addition to the IP and link-layer addresses of both sender and target, the packet contains

- a HardwareType field, which specifies the type of physical network (e.g., Ethernet);

- a ProtocolType field, which specifies the higher-layer protocol (e.g., IP);

- HLEN and PLEN fields, which specify the length of the link-layer address and higher-layer protocol address, respectively;

- an Operation field, which specifies whether this is a request or a response;

■ the source and target hardware (Ethernet) and protocol (IP) addresses.

▶ We have now seen the basic mechanisms that IP provides for dealing with both heterogeneity and scale. On the issue of heterogeneity, IP begins by defining a best effort service model that makes minimal assumptions about the underlying networks; most notably, this service model is based on unreliable datagrams. IP then adds two important things to this starting point: (1) a common packet format (fragmentation/reassembly is the mechanism that makes this format work over networks with different MTUs); and (2) a global address space for identifying all hosts (ARP is the mechanism that makes this global address space work over networks with different physical addresses). On the issue of scale, IP uses hierarchical aggregation to reduce the amount of information needed to forward packets. Specifically, IP addresses are partitioned into network and host components, with packets first routed toward the destination network and then delivered to the correct host on that network.

5.2.6   Error Reporting (ICMP)

We conclude this section by noting that while IP is perfectly willing to drop datagrams when the going gets tough—for example, when a router does not know how to forward the datagram or when one fragment of a datagram fails to arrive at the destination—it does not fail silently. IP is always configured with a companion protocol, known as the Internet Control Message Protocol (ICMP), that defines a collection of error messages that are sent back to the source host whenever a router or host is unable to process an IP datagram successfully.

ning tree algorithm, while switches and routers run routing protocols that allow each switch/router to learn the topology of the whole network. This is an important distinction because knowing the whole network topology allows the switches to discriminate among different routes, while in contrast, the spanning tree algorithm locks in a single tree over which messages are forwarded. It is also the case that the spanning tree approach does not scale as well.

What about switches and routers: are they fundamentally the same thing or are they different in some important way? Here, the distinction is much less clear. For starters, since a single point-to-point link is itself a legitimate network, a router can be used to connect a set of such links. In such a situation, a router looks just like a switch. In fact, because there are a lot of Internet router products available on the market today, and they use mature Internet routing protocols

For example, ICMP defines error messages indicating that the destination host is unreachable (perhaps due to a link failure), that the reassembly process failed, that the TTL had reached 0, that the IP header checksum failed, and so on.

ICMP also defines a handful of control messages that a router can send back to a source host. One of the most useful control messages, called an ICMP-Redirect, tells the source host that there is a better route to the destination. ICMP-Redirects are used in the following situation. Suppose a host is connected to a network that has two routers attached to it, called R1 and R2, where the host uses R1 as its default router. Should R1 ever receive a datagram from the host, where based on its forwarding table it knows that R2 would have been a better choice for a particular destination address, it sends an ICMP-Redirect back to the host, instructing it to use R2 for all future datagrams addressed to that destination. The host then adds this new route to its forwarding table.

like the Routing Information Protocol (RIP) and Open Shortest Path First (OSPF), it is easier to extend the Internet one link at a time rather than to build an entire self-contained network (like the ARPANET or an X.25 network) and then to connect that network to the Internet.

Having said this, there is one packet-switching technology that does continue to thrive as a self-contained network—the ATM networks described in Section 4.3. The big difference between an ATM network built from switches and the Internet built from routers is that the Internet is able to accommodate heterogeneity, whereas ATM consists of homogeneous links. Whether this fact will remain an important distinction between switches and routers is yet to be seen, since networking companies are now starting to build switch/router boxes that allow you to interconnect ATM and other link technologies.

5.3 Global Internet

At this point, we have seen how to connect a heterogeneous collection of networks to create an internetwork and how to use the simple hierarchy of the IP address to make routing in an internet somewhat scalable. We say "somewhat" scalable because even though each router does not need to know about all the hosts connected to the internet, it does need to know about all the networks connected to the internet. Today's Internet has tens of thousands of networks connected to it. Route propagation protocols, such as those discussed in Chapter 4, do not scale to those kinds of numbers. This section looks at three techniques that greatly improve scalability and that have enabled the Internet to grow as far as it has.

Before getting to these techniques, we need to have a general picture in our heads of what the global Internet looks like. It is not just a random interconnection of Ethernets, but instead it takes on a shape that reflects the fact that it interconnects many different organizations. Figure 5.12 gives a simple depiction of the state of the Internet in 1990. Since that time, the Internet's topology has grown much more complex than this figure suggests—we present a more accurate picture of the current Internet in Section 5.3.2 and Figure 5.18—but this picture will do for now.

The salient features of this topology are that it consists of multiple sites (e.g., University

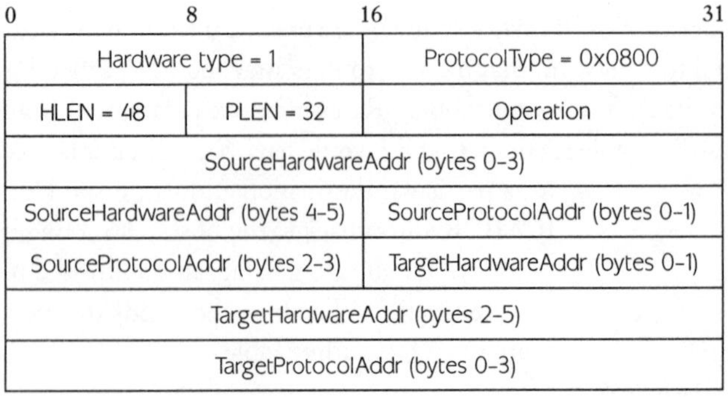

0
8
16
31
Hardware type = 1
ProtocolType = 0x0800
HLEN = 48
PLEN = 32
Operation
SourceHardwareAddr (bytes 0–3)
SourceHardwareAddr (bytes 4–5)
SourceProtocolAddr (bytes 0–1)
SourceProtocolAddr (bytes 2–3)
TargetHardwareAddr (bytes 0–1)
TargetHardwareAddr (bytes 2–5)
TargetProtocolAddr (bytes 0–3)

Figure 5.11 ARP packet format for mapping IP addresses into Ethernet addresses.

NSFNET backbone
Stanford
BARRNET
regional
Berkeley
PARC
Westnet
regional
NCAR
UA
UNM
...
MidNet
regional
ISU
UNL
KU

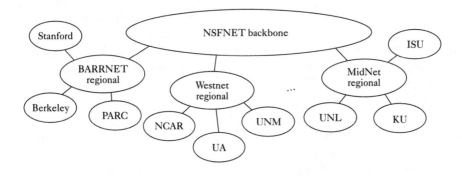

Figure 5.12 The tree structure of the Internet in 1990.

of Arizona), with nearby sites interconnected by a regional network (e.g., Westnet connects sites in Arizona, New Mexico, Utah, and Colorado). The regional networks are, in turn, connected by a nationwide backbone. In 1990, this backbone was funded by the National Science Foundation (NSF) and was therefore called the NSFNET backbone. Although the detail is not shown in this figure, the backbone and each of the regional networks is a packet-switched network typically built from T1 and T3 links, and each site is typically not a single network, but instead consists of multiple physical networks connected by routers and bridges.

The fact that the Internet has a discernible structure can be used to our advantage as we tackle the problem of scalability. This is especially true in the case of routing protocols, which we discuss in Section 5.3.2. The other scaling problem we have to deal with is address utilization—that is, making sure that the IP address space does not get consumed too quickly. We examine why this is a problem, and a way to mitigate it, in Section 5.3.1. Finally, a technique that deals with the efficiency of both routing protocols and address assignment is discussed in Section 5.3.3.

5.3.1 Subnetting

The original intent of IP addresses was that the network part would uniquely identify exactly one physical network. It turns out that this approach has a couple of drawbacks. Imagine a large campus that has lots of internal networks and that decides to connect to the Internet. For every network, no matter how small, the site needs at least a class C network address. Even worse, for any network with more than 255 hosts, they need a class B address. This may not seem like a big deal, and indeed it wasn't when the Internet was first envisioned, but there are only a finite number of network numbers, and there are far fewer class B addresses than class Cs. Class B addresses tend to be in particularly high demand because you never know if your network might expand beyond 255 nodes, so it is easier to use a class B address from the start than to have to renumber every host when you run out of room on a class C network. The problem we observe here is address assignment inefficiency: a network with two nodes uses an entire class C network address, thereby wasting 253 perfectly useful addresses; a class B network with slightly more than 255 hosts wastes over 64,000 addresses.

Assigning one network number per physical network, therefore, uses up the IP address space potentially much faster than we would like. While we would need to connect over 4 billion hosts to use up all the valid addresses, we only need to connect 2^{14} (about 16,000) class B networks before that part of the address space runs out. Therefore, we would like to find some way to use the network numbers more efficiently.

Assigning many network numbers has another drawback that becomes apparent when you think about routing. Recall that the amount of state that is stored in a node participating in a routing protocol is proportional to the number of other nodes, and that routing in an internet consists of building up forwarding tables that tell a router how to reach different networks. Thus, the more network numbers there are in use, the bigger the forwarding tables get. Big forwarding tables add cost to routers, and they are slower to search than smaller tables for a given technology, so they degrade router performance. This provides another motivation for assigning network numbers carefully.

Subnetting provides an elegantly simple way to reduce the total number of network numbers that are assigned. The idea is to take a single IP network number and allocate the IP addresses with that network number to several physical networks, which are now referred to as *subnets*. Several things need to be done to make this work. First, the subnets should be close to each other. This is because at a distant point in the Internet, they will all look like a single network, having only one network number between them. This means that a router will only be able to select one route to reach any of the subnets, so they had better all be in the same general direction. A perfect situation in which to use subnetting is a large campus or corporation that has many physical networks. From outside the campus, all you need to know to reach any subnet inside the campus is where the campus connects to the rest of the Internet.

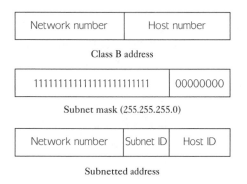

Figure 5.13 **Subnet addressing.**

This is often at a single point, so one entry in your forwarding table will suffice. Even if there are multiple points at which the campus is connected to the rest of the Internet, knowing how to get to one point in the campus network is still a good start.

The mechanism by which a single network number can be shared among multiple networks involves configuring all the nodes on each subnet with a *subnet mask*. With simple IP addresses, all hosts on the same network must have the same network number. The subnet mask enables us to introduce a *subnet number*; all hosts on the same physical network will have the same subnet number, which means that hosts may be on different physical networks but share a single network number.

What the subnet mask effectively does is introduce another level of hierarchy into the IP address. For example, suppose that we want to share a single class B address among several physical networks. We could use a subnet mask of 255.255.255.0. (Subnet masks are written down just like IP addresses; this mask is therefore all 1s in the upper 24 bits and 0s in the lower 8 bits.) In effect, this means that the top 24 bits (where the mask has 1s) are now defined to be the network number, and the lower 8 bits (where the mask has 0s) are the host number. Since the top 16 bits identify the network in a class B address, we may now think of the address as having not two parts but three: a network part, a subnet part, and a host part. This is shown in Figure 5.13.

What subnetting means to a host is that it is now configured with both an IP address and a subnet mask for the subnet to which it is attached. For example, host H1 in Figure 5.14 is configured with an address of 128.96.34.15 and a subnet mask of 255.255.255.128. (All hosts on a given subnet are configured with the same mask, i.e., there is exactly one subnet mask per subnet.) The bitwise AND of these two numbers defines the subnet number of the host and of all other hosts on the same subnet. In this case, 128.96.34.15 AND 255.255.255.128 equals 128.96.34.0, so this is the subnet number for the topmost subnet in the figure.

When the host wants to send a packet to a certain IP address, the first thing it does is to perform a bitwise AND between its own subnet mask and the destination IP address. If the

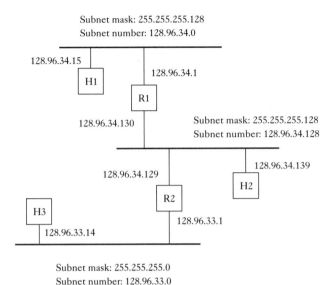

Subnet mask: 255.255.255.128
Subnet number: 128.96.34.0

128.96.34.15

H1

128.96.34.1

R1

128.96.34.130

Subnet mask: 255.255.255.128
Subnet number: 128.96.34.128

128.96.34.129

128.96.34.139

H2

R2

H3

128.96.33.1

128.96.33.14

Subnet mask: 255.255.255.0
Subnet number: 128.96.33.0

Figure 5.14   An example of subnetting.

result equals the subnet number of the sending host, then it knows that the destination host is on the same subnet and the packet can be delivered directly over the subnet. If the results are not equal, the packet needs to be sent to a router to be forwarded to another subnet. For example, if H1 is sending to H2, then H1 ANDs its subnet mask (255.255.255.128) with the address for H2 (128.96.34.139) to obtain 128.96.34.128. This does not match the subnet number for H1 (128.96.34.0) so H1 knows that H2 is on a different subnet. Since H1 cannot deliver the packet to H2 directly over the subnet, it sends the packet to its default router R1.

The job of a router also changes when we introduce subnetting. Recall that, for simple IP, a router has a forwarding table that consists of entries of the form ⟨NetworkNum, NextHop⟩. To support subnetting, the table must now hold entries of the form ⟨SubnetNumber, SubnetMask, NextHop⟩. To find the right entry in the table, the router ANDs the packet's destination address with the SubnetMask for each entry in turn; if the result matches the SubnetNumber of the entry, then this is the right entry to use, and it forwards the packet to the next hop router indicated. In the example network of Figure 5.14, router R1 would have the entries shown in Table 5.4.

Continuing with the example of a datagram from H1 being sent to H2, R1 would AND H2's address (128.96.34.139) with the subnet mask of the first entry (255.255.255.128) and compare the result (128.96.34.128) with the network number for that entry (128.96.34.0). Since this is not a match, it proceeds to the next entry. This time a match does occur, so R1 delivers the datagram to H2 using interface 1, which is the interface connected to the same network as H2.

SubnetNumber	SubnetMask	NextHop
128.96.34.0	255.255.255.128	Interface 0
128.96.34.128	255.255.255.128	Interface 1
128.96.33.0	255.255.255.0	R2

Table 5.4   Example forwarding table with subnetting for Figure 5.14.

We can now describe the datagram forwarding algorithm in the following way:

```
D = destination IP address
for each forwarding table entry ⟨SubnetNumber, SubnetMask, NextHop⟩
      D1 = SubnetMask & D
      if D1 = SubnetNumber
            if NextHop is an interface
                  deliver datagram directly to destination
            else
                  deliver datagram to NextHop (a router)
```

Although not shown in this example, a default router would usually be included in the table and would be used if no explicit matches were found. We note in passing that a naive implementation of this algorithm—one involving repeated ANDing of the destination address with a subnet mask that may not be different every time, and a linear table search—would be very inefficient.

A few fine points about subnetting need to be mentioned. First, it is not necessary for all the 1s in a subnet mask to be contiguous. For example, it would be quite possible to use a subnet mask of 255.255.1.0. All of the mechanisms described above should continue to work, but now you can't look at a contiguous part of the IP address and say "that is the subnet number." This makes administration more difficult. It may also fail to work with implementations that assume that no one would use noncontiguous masks, and so it is not recommended in practice.

Second, we can actually put multiple subnets on a single physical network. The effect of this would be to force hosts on the same network to talk to each other through a router, which might be useful for administrative purposes; for example, to provide isolation between different departments sharing a LAN.

A third point to which we have alluded is that different parts of the internet see the world differently. From outside our hypothetical campus, routers see a single network. In the example above, routers outside the campus see the collection of networks in Figure 5.14 as just the network 128.96, and they keep one entry in their forwarding tables to tell them how to reach it. Routers within the campus, however, need to be able to route packets to the right subnet. Thus, not all parts of the internet see exactly the same routing information. The next section takes a closer look at how the propagation of routing information is done in the Internet.

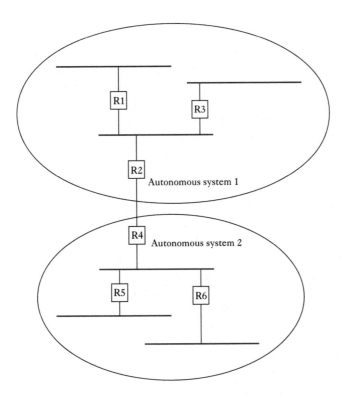

Figure 5.15   A network with two autonomous systems.

▶ The bottom line is that subnetting helps solve our scalability problems in two ways. First, it improves our address assignment efficiency by letting us not use up an entire class C or class B address every time we add a new physical network. Second, it helps us aggregate information. From a reasonable distance, a complex collection of physical networks can be made to look like a single network, so that the amount of information that routers need to store to deliver datagrams to those networks can be reduced.

5.3.2   Route Propagation (RIP, OSPF, BGP)

The preceding section talked about a hypothetical corporation with a complex internal network and introduced the idea that it might not need to reveal all that complexity to the rest of the Internet. This situation can be generalized by introducing the concept of an *autonomous system* (AS). An autonomous system is a region of the Internet that is under the administrative control of a single entity. That entity might be our aforementioned corporation, or it might be a regional Internet service provider or an Internet backbone provider. Figure 5.15 shows a simple network with two autonomous systems. In the Internet, each AS has a unique 16-bit identifier.

The basic idea behind autonomous systems is to provide an additional way to hierarchically aggregate routing information in a large internet, thus improving scalability. We now divide the routing problem up into two parts: routing within a single autonomous system and routing between autonomous systems. Since another name for autonomous systems in the Internet is routing *domains*, we refer to the two parts of the routing problem as interdomain routing and intradomain routing. In addition to improving scalability, the AS model decouples the intradomain routing that takes place in one AS from that taking place in another. Thus, each AS can run whatever intradomain routing protocols it chooses. It can even use static routes or multiple protocols if desired. The interdomain routing problem is then one of having different ASs share reachability information with each other.

One feature of the autonomous system idea is that it enables some ASs to dramatically reduce the amount of routing information they need to care about by using *default routes*. For example, if a corporate network is connected to the rest of the Internet by a single router—this router is typically called a *border router* since it sits at the boundary between the AS and the rest of the Internet—then it is pretty easy for a host or router *inside* the autonomous system to figure out where it should send packets that are headed for a destination *outside* of this AS—they first go to the AS's border router. This is the default route. Similarly, a regional Internet service provider can keep track of how to reach the networks of all its directly connected customers and can have a default route to some other provider (typically a backbone provider) for everyone else. Of course, this passing of the buck has to stop at some point; eventually the packet should reach a router connected to a backbone network that knows how to reach everything. Managing the amount of routing information in the backbones is an important issue that we discuss under the heading of interdomain routing, and we return to this subject in Section 5.4. Before doing that, however, we examine intradomain routing.

Intradomain Routing Protocols

One of the most widely used intradomain routing protocols is the Routing Information Protocol (RIP). Its widespread use is due in no small part to the fact that it was distributed along with the popular Berkeley Software Distribution (BSD) version of Unix, from which many commercial versions of Unix were derived. RIP uses the distance-vector algorithm described in Section 4.2.2.

Recall that in distance vector routing, each node transmits messages to its neighbors stating the cost of reaching all other nodes through this node. For an intradomain protocol, the nodes sending messages are the routers, and the costs they advertise are distances to other networks. Routers running RIP send their advertisements every 30 seconds; a router also sends an update message whenever an update from another router causes it to change its forwarding table. The packet format for these routing information exchanges is shown in Figure 5.16.

RIP is in fact a fairly straightforward implementation of distance-vector routing. The main point of interest, apart from the fact that the distances advertised are to networks rather than to single nodes, is that it supports multiple address families, not just IP. The majority

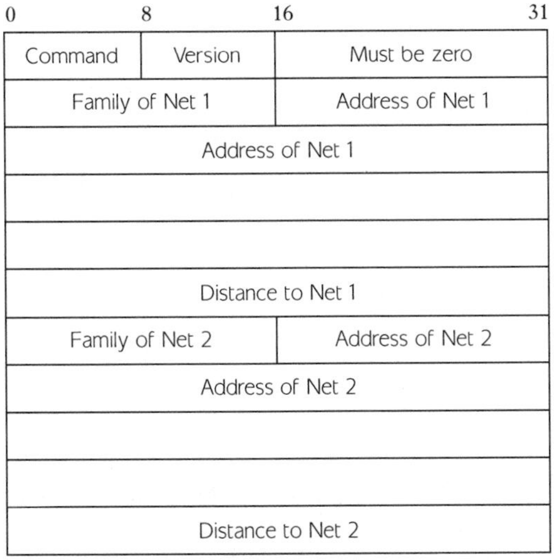

```
0           8           16                    31
```

Command	Version	Must be zero
Family of Net 1		Address of Net 1
Address of Net 1		
Distance to Net 1		
Family of Net 2		Address of Net 2
Address of Net 2		
Distance to Net 2		

Figure 5.16   RIP packet format.

of the packet is taken up with ⟨network-address, distance⟩ pairs, but the network-address is itself represented as a ⟨family, address⟩ pair. Fourteen bytes are allocated for the network address, which means that 10 bytes are unused when the address family is IP. (More precisely, they are unused in RIP version 1. Version 2 allows these spare bytes to be used for various things, notably subnet masks, which enables RIPv2 to support subnetting.)

Recall that many different metrics can be used for the link costs in a routing protocol. RIP is implemented with link costs of 1, so that it always tries to find the minimum hop route and does not worry about link speed or traffic level. Valid distances are 1 through 15, with 16 representing infinity. This also limits RIP to running on fairly small networks—those with no paths longer than 15 hops.

A second example of an intradomain protocol is OSPF, which stands for Open Shortest Path First. The first word refers to the fact that it is an open, nonproprietary standard, created under the auspices of the IETF. The "SPF" part comes from an alternate name for link-state routing, of which OSPF is a popular example. OSPF adds quite a number of features to the basic link-state algorithm described in Section 4.2.3. These features include

■ authentication of routing messages: This is a nice feature, since it is all too common for some misconfigured host to decide that it can reach every host in the universe at a cost of 0. When the host advertises this fact, every router in the surrounding neighborhood updates its forwarding tables to point to that host, and said host receives a vast amount of data which, in reality, it has no idea what to do with. It typically drops it all, bringing the network to a halt. Such disasters can be averted in many cases by requiring routing updates to be authenticated. The only form of authen-

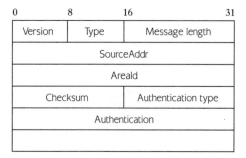

Figure 5.17   OSPF header format.

tication currently supported by OSPF is an 8-byte password. This is not a strong enough form of authentication to prevent dedicated malicious users, but it alleviates many problems caused by mis-configuration. (A similar form of authentication was added to RIP in version 2.)

■ additional hierarchy: Hopefully you have noticed by now that hierarchy helps to make systems more scalable. OSPF introduces another layer of hierarchy by allowing a domain to be partitioned into *areas*. This means that a router within a domain does not necessarily need to know how to reach every network within that domain— it may be able to get by with knowing how to get to the right area. Once again, we observe a reduction in the amount of information that must be transmitted to and stored in each node.

■ load balancing: OSPF allows multiple routes to the same place to be assigned the same cost and will cause traffic to be distributed evenly over those routes.

There are several different types of OSPF messages, but all begin with the same header, as shown in Figure 5.17. The Version field is currently set to 2, and the Type field may take the values 1 through 5. The SourceAddr identifies the sender of the message, and the AreaId is a 32-bit identifier of the *area* in which the node is located. The Authentication type can be either 0 (none) or 1, in which case the next 8 bytes contain a password.

Of the five OSPF message types, type 1 is the "hello" message, which is used by a node to convince its neighbors that it is alive and reachable. If a router fails to receive these messages from one of its neighbors for some period of time, it assumes that that node is no longer directly reachable and updates its link-state information accordingly. The remaining types are used to request, send, and acknowledge the receipt of link-state messages.

Interdomain Routing Protocols

There have been two major interdomain routing protocols in the recent history of the Internet. The first was the Exterior Gateway Protocol (EGP). EGP had a number of limitations,

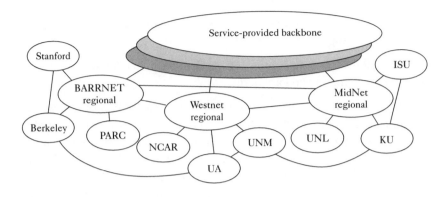

Figure 5.18   Today's multibackbone Internet.

perhaps the most severe of which was that it constrained the topology of the Internet rather significantly. EGP basically forced a tree-like topology onto the Internet, or to be more precise, it was designed when the Internet had a tree-like topology, such as that illustrated in Figure 5.12. EGP did not allow for the topology to become more general. Note that in this simple tree-like structure, there is a single backbone, and autonomous systems are connected only as parents and children and not as peers.

The replacement for EGP is the Border Gateway Protocol (BGP), which is in its fourth version at the time of this writing (BGP-4). BGP is also known for being rather complex, although perhaps not as bad as OSPF, if the length of the RFC is anything to judge by. This section presents the highlights of BGP-4.

As a starting position, BGP assumes that the Internet is an arbitrarily interconnected set of ASs. This model is clearly general enough to accommodate non-tree-structured internetworks, like the present-day multibackbone Internet shown in Figure 5.18.[3] Unlike the simple tree-structured internet shown in Figure 5.12, today's Internet consists of an interconnection of multiple-backbone networks (they are usually called *service provider networks* and they are operated by private companies rather than the government), and sites are connected to each in arbitrary ways.

Given this rough sketch of the Internet, if we define *local traffic* as traffic that originates at or terminates on nodes within an AS, and *transit traffic* as traffic that passes through an AS, we can classify ASs into three types:

■ *stub AS:* an AS that has only a single connection to one other AS; such an AS will only carry local traffic.

---

[3]In an interesting stretch of metaphor, the Internet has recently acquired multiple backbones, having had only one for most of its life. The authors know of no other animal that has this characteristic.

- *multihomed AS:* an AS that has connections to more than one other AS but that refuses to carry transit traffic.

- *transit AS:* an AS that has connections to more than one other AS and that is designed to carry both transit and local traffic.

The administrator of each AS picks at least one node to be a "BGP speaker," which is essentially a spokesperson for the entire AS. In addition, the AS has one or more border gateways, which need not be the same as the speakers. The border gateways are the routers through which packets reach the AS. In our simple example in Figure 5.15, routers R2 and R4 would be border gateways. Note that we have avoided using the word "gateway" until this point, because it tends to be confusing. We can't avoid it here, given the name of the protocol we are describing. The important thing to understand here is that, in the context of interdomain routing, a border gateway is simply an IP router that is charged with the task of forwarding packets between ASs.

Whereas the discussion of routing in Section 4.2 focused on finding optimal paths based on minimizing some sort of link metric, the problem of interdomain routing turns out to be so difficult—due to the problem of scale—that the goals are rather more modest. First and foremost, the goal is to find *any* path to the intended destination that is loop free. That is, we are more concerned with reachability than optimality. Finding a path that is anywhere close to optimal is considered a great achievement. We will see why this is so as we look at the details of BGP.

The BGP speaker advertises *reachability* information for all the networks within that AS, and in the case of a transit AS, the speaker also advertises networks that can be reached through this AS. The concept of reachability is basically a statement that "you can reach this network through this AS." The need to introduce this concept arises because each AS may run its own interior routing protocols. This means that they may all have different routing metrics and thus that it is impossible to calculate meaningful path costs for a path that crosses multiple ASs. As a result, reachability is all that can be advertised. This means that for BGP to pick an optimal path is essentially impossible. However, BGP does have the capability to make choices between multiple paths based on a wide range of policies, such as "use the path that crosses the fewest number of ASs" or "use AS x in preference to AS y." The goal is to specify policies that lead to "good" paths, if not to optimal ones.

Note that BGP does not belong to either of the two main classes of routing protocols (distance-vector and link-state protocols) described in the previous chapter. Unlike these protocols, BGP advertises *complete paths* as an enumerated list of ASs to reach a particular network. This is necessary to enable the sorts of policy decisions described above to be made in accordance with the wishes of a particular AS. It also enables routing loops to be readily detected.

To see how this works, consider the example network in Figure 5.19. Assume that the backbone and regional providers are transit networks, while the customer networks are stubs. A BGP speaker for the AS of regional provider A (AS 2) would be able to advertise reacha-

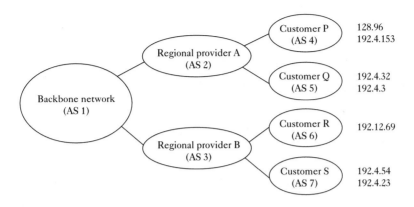

Figure 5.19 Example of a network running BGP.

bility information for each of the network numbers assigned to customers P and Q. Thus, it would say, in effect, "The networks 128.96, 192.4.153, 192.4.32, and 192.4.3 can be reached directly from AS 2." The backbone network, on receiving this advertisement, can advertise "The networks 128.96, 192.4.153, 192.4.32, and 192.4.3 can be reached along the path ⟨AS 1,AS 2⟩." Similarly, it could advertise "The networks 192.12.69, 192.4.54, and 192.4.23 can be reached along the path ⟨AS 1,AS 3⟩."

As well as advertising paths, BGP speakers need to be able to cancel previously advertised paths if a critical link or node on a path goes down. This is done with a form of negative advertisement known as a *withdrawn route*. Both positive and negative reachability information are carried in a BGP update message, the format of which is shown in Figure 5.20. (Note that the fields in this figure are multiples of 16 bits, unlike other packet formats in this chapter.)

We will not delve further into the details of BGP-4, except to point out that all the protocol does is specify how reachability information should be exchanged among autonomous systems. BGP speakers obtain enough information by this exchange to calculate loop-free routes to all reachable networks, but how they choose the "best" routes is largely left to the policies of the AS.

Let's return to the real question: how does all this help us to build scalable networks? First, the number of nodes participating in BGP is on the order of the number of ASs, which is much smaller than the number of networks. Second, finding a good interdomain route is only a matter of finding a path to the right border router, of which there are only a few per AS. Thus, we have neatly subdivided the routing problem into manageable parts, once again using a new level of hierarchy to increase scalability. The complexity of interdomain routing is now on the order of the number of ASs, and the complexity of intradomain routing is on the order of the number of networks in a single AS. The one flaw, however, is that the BGP speakers are still passing around information about every single network, so the amount of

0   15

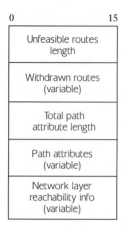

| Unfeasible routes length |
| Withdrawn routes (variable) |
| Total path attribute length |
| Path attributes (variable) |
| Network layer reachability info (variable) |

Figure 5.20 BGP-4 update packet format.

state information that is stored in a border router still grows in proportion to the number of assigned networks. Subnetting is a partial solution to this problem, but there are also other solutions, as the following section illustrates.

5.3.3 Classless Routing (CIDR)

Classless interdomain routing (CIDR, pronounced "cider") is a technique that addresses two scaling concerns in the Internet: the growth of forwarding tables that we alluded to in the previous subsection and the potential for the 32-bit IP address space to be exhausted well before the 4 billionth host is attached to the Internet. We have already mentioned the problem that would cause this address space exhaustion: address assignment inefficiency. The inefficiency arises because the IP address structure, with class A, B, and C addresses, forces us to hand out network address space in fixed-sized chunks of three very different sizes. A network with two hosts needs a class C address, giving an address assignment efficiency of $2/255 = 0.78\%$, while a network with 256 hosts needs a class B address for an efficiency of only $256/65535 = 0.39\%$. Even though subnetting can help us to assign addresses carefully, it does not get around the fact that any autonomous system with more than 255 hosts, or an expectation of eventually having that many, wants a class B address.

As it turns out, exhaustion of the IP address space centers on exhaustion of the class B network numbers. One way to deal with that would seem to be saying no to any AS that requests a class B address unless they can show a need for something close to 64K addresses, and instead giving them an appropriate number of class C addresses to cover the expected number of hosts. Since we would now be handing out address space in chunks of 256 addresses at a time, we could more accurately match the amount of address space consumed to the size of the AS. For any AS with at least 256 hosts (which means the majority of ASs), we can guarantee an address utilization of at least 50%.

This solution, however, raises exactly the problem we were trying to avoid at the end of the last section: excessive storage requirements at the routers. If a single AS has, say, 16 class C network numbers aligned to it, that means every BGP router that is not using a default route—that is, those routers in the backbone networks—needs 16 entries in its forwarding tables for that AS. This is true even if the path to every one of those networks is the same. If we had assigned a class B address to the AS, the same routing information could be stored in one table entry. However, our address assignment efficiency would then be only $16 \times 255/65536 = 6.2\%$.

CIDR, therefore, tries to balance the desire to minimize the number of routes that a router needs to know against the need to hand out addresses efficiently. To do this, CIDR helps us to *aggregate* routes. That is, it lets us use a single entry in a forwarding table to tell us how to reach a lot of different networks. As you may have guessed from the name, it does this by breaking the rigid boundaries between address classes. To understand how this works, consider our hypothetical AS with 16 class C network numbers. Instead of handing out 16 addresses at random, we can hand out a block of *contiguous* class C addresses. Suppose we assign the class C network numbers from 192.4.16 through 192.4.31. Observe that the top 20 bits of all the addresses in this range are the same (11000000 00000100 0001). Thus, what we have effectively created is a 20-bit network number—something that is between a class B network number and a class C number in terms of the number of hosts that it can support. In other words, we get both the high address efficiency of handing out addresses 256 nodes at a time and a single network prefix that can be used in forwarding tables. Observe that for this scheme to work, we need to hand out blocks of class C addresses that share a common prefix, which means that each block must contain a number of class C networks that is a power of two.

All we need now to make CIDR solve our problems is a routing protocol that can deal with these "classless" addresses, which means that it must understand that a network number may be of any length. BGP-4 does exactly that. The network numbers that are carried in a BGP-4 update message are represented simply by ⟨length, value⟩ pairs, where the length gives the number of bits in the network prefix—20 in the above example. Note that representing a network address in this way is similar to the ⟨mask, value⟩ approach used in subnetting, as long as masks consist of contiguous bits starting from the most significant bit. Also note that we used subnetting to share one address among multiple physical networks, while CIDR aims to collapse the multiple addresses that would be assigned to a single AS onto one address. The similarity between the two approaches is reflected in the original name for CIDR—supernetting.

In fact, the ability to aggregate routes in the way that we have just shown is only the first step. Imagine a regional network, whose primary job is to provide Internet connectivity to a large number of corporations and campuses. If we assign network numbers to the corporations in such a way that all the different corporations connected to the regional network share a common address prefix, then we can get even greater aggregation of routes. Consider the

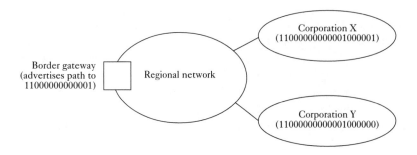

Figure 5.21   Route aggregation with CIDR.

example in Figure 5.21. The two corporations served by the regional network have been assigned adjacent 20-bit network prefixes. Since both of the corporations are reachable through the regional network, it can advertise a single route to both of them by just advertising the common 19-bit prefix they share. In general, it is possible to aggregate routes repeatedly if addresses are assigned carefully. This means that we need to pay attention to which regional network a corporation is attached to before assigning it an address if this scheme is to work. One way to accomplish that is to assign a portion of address space to the regional network and then to let the regional network provider assign addresses from that space to its customers.

The important thing to take away from our discussion of scaling in the Internet is that there are two main problems: the amount of routing information transmitted between and stored in each node as the network grows, and the efficient use of address space. We have focused rather more heavily on the former problem and have seen that most of the techniques for dealing with it involve the addition of levels of hierarchy. One challenge in adding hierarchy is to allow enough flexibility to accommodate the complex structure of the Internet. In the next section, we will see what lies around the corner when the present methods for dealing with scaling reach their limits.

5.4   Next Generation IP (IPv6)

In many respects, the motivation for Next Generation IP (IPng) is the same as the motivation for the techniques described in the last section: to deal with scaling problems caused by the Internet's massive growth. Subnetting and CIDR (and BGP-4, which helps CIDR to be deployed) have helped to contain the rate at which the Internet address space is being consumed (the address depletion problem) and have also helped to control the growth of routing table information needed in the Internet's routers (the routing information problem). However, there will come a point at which these techniques are no longer adequate. In particular, it is virtually impossible to achieve 100% address utilization efficiency, so the address space will probably be exhausted well before the 4 billionth host is connected to the Internet. Even if we were able to use all 4 billion addresses, it's not too hard to imagine ways that that number could be exhausted, such as the assignment of IP addresses to set-top boxes for cable TV or to electricity meters. All of these possibilities argue that a bigger address space than that provided by 32 bits will eventually be needed.

5.4.1 Historical Perspective

The IETF began looking at the problem of evolving the IP address space in 1991, and several alternatives were proposed. Since the IP address is carried in the header of every IP packet, increasing the size of the address dictates a change in the packet header. This means a new version of the Internet Protocol, and as a consequence, a need for new software for every host and router in the Internet. This is clearly not a trivial matter—it is a major change that needs to be thought about very carefully.

The significance of the change to a new version of IP caused a snowball effect. The general feeling among network designers was that if you are going to make a change of this magnitude, you might as well fix as many other things in IP as possible at the same time. Consequently, the IETF solicited white papers from anyone who cared to write one, asking for input on the features that might be desired in a new version of IP. In addition to the need to accommodate scalable routing and addressing, some of the things that arose as wish list items for IPng were

- support for real-time services;

- security support;

- autoconfiguration (i.e., the ability of hosts to automatically configure themselves with such information as their own IP address and domain name);

- enhanced routing functionality, including support for mobile hosts.

In addition to the wish list, one absolutely nonnegotiable feature for IPng was that there must be a transition plan to move from the current version of IP (version 4) to the new version. With the Internet being so large and having no centralized control, it would be completely impossible to have a "flag day" on which everyone shut down their hosts and routers and installed a new version of IP. Thus, there will probably be a long transition period in which some hosts and routers will run IPv4 only, some will run IPv4 and IPng, and some will run IPng only.

The IETF appointed a committee called the IPng Directorate to collect all the inputs on IPng requirements and to evaluate proposals for a protocol to become IPng. Over the life of this committee there were a number of proposals, some of which merged with other proposals, and eventually one was chosen by the Directorate to be the basis for IPng. That proposal was called SIPP (Simple Internet Protocol Plus). SIPP originally called for a doubling of the IP address size to 64 bits. When the Directorate selected SIPP, they stipulated several changes, one of which was another doubling of the address to 128 bits (16 bytes). Once it was decided to assign IP version number 6 to the new protocol, it became known as IPv6. The rest of this section describes the features of IPv6. At the time of this writing, most of the specifications for IPv6 are moving to Proposed Standard status in the IETF.

5.4.2   Addresses and Routing

First and foremost, IPv6 provides a 128-bit address space, as opposed to the 32 bits of version 4. Thus, while version 4 can potentially address 4 billion nodes if address assignment efficiency reaches 100%, IPv6 can address 3.4×10^{38} nodes, again assuming 100% efficiency. As we have seen, though, 100% efficiency in address assignment is not likely. Some analysis of other addressing schemes, such as those of the French and U.S. telephone networks, as well as that of IPv4, have turned up some empirical numbers for address assignment efficiency. Based on the most pessimistic estimates of efficiency drawn from this study, the IPv6 address space is predicted to provide over 1500 addresses per square foot of the earth's surface, which certainly seems like it should serve us well even when toasters on Venus have IP addresses.

Address Space Allocation

IPv6 addresses do not have classes, but the address space is subdivided based on prefixes just as in IPv4. Rather than specifying different address classes, the prefixes specify different uses of the IPv6 address. The current assignment of prefixes is listed in Table 5.5.

This allocation of the address space turns out to be easier to explain than it looks. First, the entire functionality of IPv4's three main address classes (A, B, and C) is contained inside the 010 prefix. Provider-based unicast addresses, as we will see shortly, are a lot like classless IPv4 addresses, only much longer. These are the main ones of interest at this point, with one-eighth of the address space allocated to this important form of address. Obviously, large chunks of address space have been left unassigned to allow for future growth and new features. Two portions of the address space (0000 001 and 0000 010) have been reserved for encoding of other (non-IP) address schemes. NSAP addresses are used by the ISO protocols, and IPX addresses are used by Novell's network-layer protocol. Exactly how these encodings will work is not yet defined.

Geographic unicast addresses are not yet defined, but the idea is that you should be able to have an address that relates to where you are physically rather than one that depends on who your network provider is. This is the flip side of the coin to provider-based addressing. The challenge is to design a geographic scheme that scales well.

The idea behind "link local use" addresses is to enable a host to construct an address that will work on the network to which it is connected without being concerned about global uniqueness of the address. This may be useful for autoconfiguration, as we will see in Section 5.4.3. Similarly, the "site local use" addresses are intended to allow valid addresses to be constructed on a site that is not connected to the larger Internet; again, global uniqueness need not be an issue.

Finally, the multicast address space is for multicast, thereby serving the same role as class D addresses in IPv4. Note that multicast addresses are easy to distinguish—they start with a byte of all 1s.

Prefix	Use
0000 0000	Reserved
0000 0001	Unassigned
0000 001	Reserved for NSAP allocation
0000 010	Reserved for IPX allocation
0000 011	Unassigned
0000 1	Unassigned
0001	Unassigned
001	Unassigned
010	Provider-based unicast addresses
011	Unassigned
100	Reserved for geographic-based unicast addresses
101	Unassigned
110	Unassigned
1110	Unassigned
1111 0	Unassigned
1111 10	Unassigned
1111 110	Unassigned
1111 1110 0	Unassigned
1111 1110 10	Link local use addresses
1111 1110 11	Site local use addresses
1111 1111	Multicast addresses

Table 5.5 Address prefix assignments for IPv6.

Within the reserved address space (addresses beginning with 1 byte of 0s) are some important special types of addresses. A node may be assigned an "IPv4-compatible IPv6 address" by zero-extending a 32-bit IPv4 address to 128 bits. A node that is only capable of understanding IPv4 can be assigned an "IPv4-mapped IPv6 address" by prefixing the 32-bit IPv4 address with 2 bytes of all 1s and then zero-extending the result to 128 bits. These two special address types have uses in the IPv4-to-IPv6 transition.

Address Notation

Just as with IPv4, there is some special notation for writing down IPv6 addresses. The standard representation is x:x:x:x:x:x:x:x where each "x" is a hexadecimal representation of a 16-bit piece of the address. An example would be

47CD:1234:4422:ACO2:0022:1234:A456:0124

Any IPv6 address can be written using this notation. Since there are a few special types of IPv6 addresses, there are some special notations that may be helpful in certain circumstances. For example, an address with a large number of contiguous 0s can be written more compactly by omitting all the 0 fields. For example,

47CD:0000:0000:0000:0000:0000:A456:0124

could be written

47CD::A456:0124

Clearly, this form of shorthand can only be used for one set of contiguous 0s in an address to avoid ambiguity.

Since there are two types of IPv6 addresses that contain an embedded IPv4 address, these have their own special notation which make extraction of the IPv4 address easier. For example, the "IPv4-mapped IPv6 address" of a host whose IPv4 address was 128.96.33.81 could be written as

::00FF:128.96.33.81

That is, the last 32 bits are written in IPv4 notation, rather than as a pair of hexadecimal numbers separated by a colon. Note that the double colon at the front indicates the leading 0s.

Provider-Based Unicast Addresses

By far the most important thing that IPv6 must provide when it is deployed is plain old unicast addressing. It must do this in a way that supports the rapid rate of addition of new hosts to the Internet and that allows routing to be done in a scalable way as the number of physical networks in the Internet grows. Thus, at the heart of IPv6 is the unicast address allocation plan that determines how provider-based addresses—those with the 010 prefix—will be assigned to service providers, autonomous systems, networks, hosts, and routers.

In fact, the address allocation plan that is proposed for IPv6 unicast addresses is extremely similar to that being deployed with CIDR in IPv4. To understand how it works and how it provides scalability, it is helpful to define some new terms. We may think of a non-transit AS (i.e., a stub or multihomed AS) as a *subscriber* and we may think of a transit AS as a *provider*. Furthermore, we may subdivide providers into *direct* and *indirect*. The former are directly connected to subscribers and are often referred to as *regional networks*. The latter primarily connect other providers, are not connected directly to subscribers, and are often known as *backbone networks*.

3	m	n	o	p	125–m–n–o–p
010	RegistryID	ProviderID	SubscriberID	SubnetID	InterfaceID

Figure 5.22   An IPv6 provider-based unicast address.

With this set of definitions, we can see that the Internet is not just an arbitrarily inter-connected set of ASs; it has some intrinsic hierarchy. The difficulty is in making use of this hierarchy without inventing mechanisms that fail when the hierarchy is not strictly observed, as happened with EGP. For example, the distinction between direct and indirect providers becomes blurred when a subscriber connects to a backbone or when a direct provider starts connecting to many other providers.

As with CIDR, the goal of the IPv6 address allocation plan is to provide aggregation of routing information to reduce the burden on intradomain routers. Again, the key idea is to use an address prefix—a set of contiguous bits at the most significant end of the address—to aggregate reachability information to a large number of networks and even to a large number of ASs. The main way to achieve this is to assign an address prefix to a direct provider and then for that direct provider to assign longer prefixes that begin with that prefix to its subscribers. This is exactly what we observed in Figure 5.21. Thus, a provider can advertise a single prefix for all of its subscribers. It should now be clear why this scheme is referred to as "provider-based addressing." The IPv6 addresses assigned to a site under this scheme will all contain a prefix that identifies the provider for that site.

Of course, the drawback is that if a site decides to change providers, it will need to obtain a new address prefix and renumber all the nodes in the site. This could be a colossal undertaking, enough to dissuade most people from ever changing providers. It is for this reason that geographic addressing schemes are being investigated. For now, however, provider-based addressing is necessary to make routing work efficiently.

One question is whether it makes sense for hierarchical aggregation to take place at other levels in the hierarchy. For example, should all providers obtain their address prefixes from within a prefix allocated to the backbone to which they connect? Given that most providers connect to multiple backbones, this probably doesn't make sense. Also, since the number of providers is much smaller than the number of sites, the benefits of aggregating at this level are much less.

One place where aggregation may make sense is at the national or continental level. Continental boundaries form natural divisions in the Internet topology, and if all addresses in Europe, for example, had a common prefix, then a great deal of aggregation could be done, so that most routers in other continents would only need one routing table entry for all networks with the Europe prefix. Providers in Europe would all select their prefixes such that they began with the European prefix. Using this scheme, an IPv6 address might look like Figure 5.22. The **RegistryID** might be an identifier assigned to a European address registry, with different

IDs assigned to other continents or countries. Note that prefixes would be of different lengths under this scenario. For example, a provider with few customers could have a longer prefix (and thus less total address space available) than one with many customers.

One tricky situation could occur when a subscriber is connected to more than one provider. Which prefix should the subscriber use for his (or her) site? There is no perfect solution to the problem. For example, suppose a subscriber is connected to two providers X and Y. If the subscriber takes his prefix from X, then Y has to advertise a prefix that has no relationship to its other subscribers and that as a consequence cannot be aggregated. If the subscriber numbers part of his AS with the prefix of X and part with the prefix of Y, he runs the risk of having half his site become unreachable if the connection to one provider goes down. One solution that works fairly well if X and Y have a lot of subscribers in common is for them to have three prefixes between them: one for subscribers of X only, one for subscribers of Y only, and one for the sites that are subscribers of both X and Y.

5.4.3   IPv6 Features

As mentioned at the beginning of this section, the primary motivation behind the development of IPv6 was to support the continued growth of the Internet. Once the IP header had to be changed for the sake of the addresses, however, the door was open for more far-reaching changes, including changes to the Internet's underlying best-effort service model.

Although many of these extensions are not yet well defined, enough hooks have been put into the IPv6 packet format to support them once they are more mature. We therefore limit our discussion to an overview of the IPv6 header and an introduction to two features that are easy to explain given the material covered so far in this book—autoconfiguration and source-directed routing. Many of the other features that may one day end up in IPv6 are covered elsewhere in this book—multicast is discussed in Section 5.5, network security is the topic of Section 7.3, and a new service model proposed for the Internet is described in Section 9.3.

Packet Format

Despite the fact that IPv6 extends IPv4 in several ways, its header format is actually simpler. This simplicity is due to a concerted effort to remove unnecessary functionality from the protocol. Figure 5.23 shows the result. (For comparison with IPv4, see the header format shown in Figure 5.7.)

As with many headers, this one starts with a Version field, which is set to 6 for IPv6. The Version field is in the same place relative to the start of the header as IPv4's Version field so that header-processing software can immediately decide which header format to look for. The Priority and FlowLabel fields both relate to quality of service issues, as discussed in Section 9.3.

The PayloadLen field gives the length of the packet, excluding the IPv6 header, measured in bytes. The NextHeader field cleverly replaces both the IP options and the Protocol field of IPv4. If options are required, then they are carried in one or more special headers following the IP header, and this is indicated by the value of the NextHeader field. If there are no special headers, the NextHeader field is the header for the higher-level protocol running over

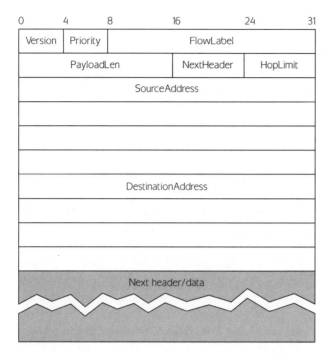

| 0 | 4 | 8 | 16 | 24 | 31 |

Figure 5.23   IPv6 packet header.

IP (e.g., TCP or UDP), that is, it serves the same purpose as the IPv4 **Protocol** field. Also, fragmentation is now handled as an optional header, which means that the fragmentation-related fields of IPv4 are not included in the IPv6 header. The **HopLimit** field is simply the **TTL** of IPv4, renamed to reflect the way it is actually used.

Finally, the bulk of the header is taken up with the source and destination addresses, each of which is 16 bytes (128 bits) long. Thus, the IPv6 header is always 40 bytes long. Considering that IPv6 addresses are four times longer than those of IPv4, this compares quite well with the IPv4 header, which is 20 bytes long in the absence of options.

The way that IPv6 handles options is quite an improvement over IPv4. In IPv4, if any options were present, every router had to parse the entire options field to see if any of the options were relevant. This is because the options were all buried at the end of the IP header, as an unordered collection of ⟨type, length, value⟩ tuples. In contrast, IPv6 treats options as *extension headers* that must, if present, appear in a specific order. This means that each router can quickly determine if any of the options are relevant to it; in most cases, they will not be. Usually this can be determined by just looking at the **NextHeader** field. The end result is that option processing is much more efficient in IPv6, which is an important factor in router performance. In addition, the new formatting of options as extension headers means that they

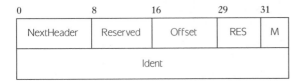

0	8	16	29	31
NextHeader	Reserved	Offset	RES	M
Ident				

Figure 5.24 IPv6 fragmentation extension header.

can be of arbitrary length, whereas in IPv4 they were limited to 44 bytes at most. We will see
how some of the options are used below.

To see how extension headers work, consider the fragmentation header shown in Figure 5.24. This header provides functionality similar to the fragmentation fields in the IPv4 header described in Section 5.2.2, but it is only present if fragmentation is necessary. If it were the first or only extension header, then the NextHeader field of the IPv6 header would contain the value 44, which indicates that the next header is a fragmentation header. In this case, the NextHeader field of the fragmentation header contains a value describing the header that follows it. For example, if there are no more extension headers, then the next header might be the TCP header, which results in NextHeader containing the value 6. (Note that when the next header is a higher-layer protocol, not an extension header, the value of the NextHeader field is the same as the value of the Protocol field in an IPv4 header.) If the fragmentation header were followed by, say, an authentication header, then the fragmentation header's NextHeader field would contain the value 51.

Autoconfiguration

While the Internet's growth has been impressive, one factor that has inhibited faster acceptance of the technology is the fact that getting connected to the Internet has typically required a fair amount of system administration expertise. In particular, every host that is connected to the Internet needs to be configured with a certain minimum amount of information, such as a valid IP address, a subnet mask for the link to which it attaches, and the address of a name server. Thus, it has not been possible to unpack a new computer and connect it to the Internet without some preconfiguration. One goal of IPv6, therefore, is to provide support for autoconfiguration, sometimes referred to as "plug-and-play" operation.

There are various aspects to autoconfiguration, but the most crucial step is *address autoconfiguration*, since a host cannot communicate with anything else until it gets an IP address. There are two proposed approaches to address autoconfiguration: a *stateful* approach, in which hosts talk to a configuration server, and a *stateless* approach, in which hosts construct their IP address essentially on their own. The latter is the one that is being standardized at the time of this writing.

Recall that IPv6 unicast addresses are hierarchical, and that the least significant portion is the interface ID. Thus, we can subdivide the autoconfiguration problem into two parts:

1 obtain an interface ID that is unique on the link to which the host is attached;

2 obtain the correct address prefix for this subnet.

The first part turns out to be rather easy, since every host on a link must have a unique link-level address.For example, all hosts on an Ethernet have a unique 48-bit Ethernet address. This can be turned into a valid link local use address by adding the appropriate prefix from Table 5.5 (1111 1110 10) followed by enough 0s to make up 128 bits. For some devices—for example, printers or hosts on a small routerless network that do not connect to any other networks—this address may be perfectly adequate. Those devices that need a globally valid address depend on a router on the same link to periodically advertise the appropriate prefix for the link. Clearly, this requires that the router be configured with the correct address prefix, and that this prefix be chosen in such a way that there is enough space at the end (e.g., 48 bits) to attach an appropriate link-level address.

The ability to embed link-level addresses as long as 48 bits into IPv6 addresses was one of the reasons for choosing such a large address size. Not only does 128 bits allow the embedding, but it leaves plenty of space for the multilevel hierarchy of addressing that we discussed above.

Advanced Routing Capabilities

Another of IPv6's extension headers is the routing header. In the absence of this header, routing for IPv6 differs very little from that of IPv4 under CIDR. The routing header contains a list of IPv6 addresses that represent nodes or topological areas that the packet should visit en route to its destination. A topological area may be, for example, a backbone provider's network. Specifying that packets must visit this network would be a way of implementing provider selection on a packet-by-packet basis. Thus, a host could say that it wants some packets to go through a provider that is cheap, others through a provider that provides high reliability, and still others through a provider that the host trusts to provide security.

Transition from IPv4 to IPv6

The most important idea behind the transition from IPv4 to IPv6 is that the Internet is far too big and decentralized to have a "flag day"—one specified day on which every host and router is upgraded from IPv4 to IPv6. Thus, IPv6 needs to be deployed incrementally in such a way that hosts and routers that only understand IPv4 can continue to function for as long as possible. Ideally, IPv4 nodes should be able to talk to other IPv4 nodes and some set of other IPv6-capable nodes indefinitely. Also, IPv6 hosts should be capable of talking to other IPv6 nodes even when some of the infrastructure between them may only support IPv4. Two major mechanisms have been defined to help this transition: *dual-stack operation* and *tunneling*.

The idea of dual stacks is fairly straightforward: IPv6 nodes run both IPv6 and IPv4 and use the Version

To provide the ability to specify topological entities rather than individual nodes, IPv6 defines an *anycast* address. An anycast address is assigned to a set of interfaces, and packets sent to that address will go to the "nearest" of those interfaces, with nearest being determined by the routing protocols. For example, all the routers of a backbone provider could be assigned a single anycast address, which would be used in the routing header.

The anycast address and the routing header are also expected to be used to provide enhanced routing support to mobile hosts. The detailed mechanisms for providing this support are still being defined.

5.5 Multicast

As we saw in Chapter 3, multi-access networks like Ethernet and FDDI implement multicast in hardware. This section describes how to extend multicast, in software, across an internetwork of such networks. The approach described in this section is based on an implementation of multicast used in the current Internet (IPv4). Multicast will also be supported in the next generation of IP (IPv6), but first the scalability of the solution must be improved. Several proposals for how to do this are currently being considered; see the references at the end of this chapter for more information.

The motivation for developing multicast is that there are applications that want to send a packet to more than one destination host. Instead of forcing the source host to send a separate packet to each of the destination hosts, we want the source to be able to send a single packet to a *multicast address*, and for the network—or internet, in this case—to deliver a copy of that packet to each of a group of hosts. Hosts can then choose to join or leave this group at will, without synchronizing or negotiating with other members of the group. Also, a host may belong to more than one group at a time.

field to decide which stack should process an arriving packet. In this case, the IPv6 address could be unrelated to the IPv4 address, or it could be the "IPv4-mapped IPv6 address" described earlier in this section.

Tunneling is a technique used in a variety of situations in which an IP packet is sent as the *payload* of an IP packet; that is, a new IP header is attached in front of the header of an IP packet. For IPv6 transition, tunneling is used to send an IPv6 packet over a piece of the network that only understands IPv4. This means that the IPv6 packet is encapsulated within an IPv4 header that has the address of the tunnel endpoint in its header, is transmitted across the IPv4-only piece of network, and then is decapsulated at the endpoint. The endpoint could be either a router or a host; in either case, it must be IPv6-capable to be able to process the IPv6 packet

Internet multicast can be implemented on top of a collection of networks that support hardware multicast (or broadcast) by extending the forwarding function implemented by the routers that connect these networks. This section describes two such extensions: one that extends the distance-vector protocol used by some routers (e.g., RIP), and one that extends the link-state protocol used by other routers (e.g., OSPF). Notice that both extensions involve adding a specially designated multicast address type to the internet address. For example, multicast addresses have been added to IPv4 by defining a new address class; IPv6 was defined from the start to support multicast addresses.

5.5.1 Link-State Multicast

Adding multicast to a link-state routing algorithm is fairly straightforward, so we describe it first. Recall that in link-state routing, each router monitors the state of its directly connected links and sends an update message to all of the other routers whenever the state changes. Since each router receives enough information to reconstruct the entire topology of the network, it is able to use Dijkstra's algorithm to compute the shortest-path spanning tree rooted at itself and reaching all possible destinations. The router uses this tree to determine the best next hop for each packet it forwards.

after decapsulation. If the endpoint is a host with an IPv4-mapped IPv6 address, then tunneling can be done automatically, by extracting the IPv4 address from the IPv6 address and using it to form the IPv4 header. Otherwise, the tunnel must be configured manually. In this case, the encapsulating node needs to know the IPv4 address of the other end of the tunnel, since it cannot be extracted from the IPv6 header. From the perspective of IPv6, the other end of the tunnel looks like a regular IPv6 node that is just one hop away, even though there may be many hops of IPv4 infrastructure between the tunnel endpoints.

Tunneling is a very powerful technique with applications beyond addressing. One of the main challenges in implementing tunneling is dealing with all the special cases, such as fragmentation within the tunnel and error handling.

All we have to do to extend this algorithm to support multicast is to add the set of groups that have members on a particular link (LAN) to the "state" for that link. The only question is how each router determines which groups have members on which links. As suggested in Section 5.1.3, the solution is to have each host periodically announce to the LAN the groups to which it belongs. The router simply monitors the LAN for such announcements. Should such announcements stop arriving after a period of time, the router then assumes that the host has left the group.

Given full knowledge of which groups have members on which links, each router is able to compute the *shortest-path multicast tree* from any source to any group, again using Dijkstra's algorithm. For example, given the internet illustrated in Figure 5.25, where the shaded hosts belong to group G, the routers would compute the shortest-path multicast trees given in Figure 5.26 for sources A, B, and C. The routers would use these trees to decide how to forward packets addressed to multicast group G. For example, router R3 would forward a packet going from host A to group G to R6.

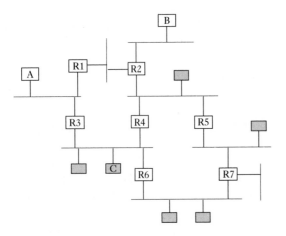

Figure 5.25   Example internet with members of group G shaded.

Keep in mind that each router must potentially keep a separate shortest-path multicast tree from every source to every group. This is obviously very expensive, so instead, the router just computes and stores a cache of these trees—one for each source/group pair that is currently active.

5.5.2   Distance-Vector Multicast

Adding multicast to the distance-vector algorithm is a bit trickier because the routers do not know the entire topology of the internet. Instead, recall that each router maintains a table of ⟨Destination, Cost, NextHop⟩ tuples, and exchanges a list of ⟨ Destination, Cost ⟩ pairs with its directly connected neighbors. Extending this algorithm to support multicast is a two-stage process. First, we need to design a broadcast mechanism that allows a packet to be forwarded to all the networks on the internet. Second, we need to refine this mechanism so that it prunes back networks that do not have hosts that belong to the multicast group.

Reverse-Path Broadcast (RPB)

Since each router knows that the current shortest path to a given destination goes through NextHop whenever it receives a multicast packet from source S, the router forwards the packet on all outgoing links (except the one on which the packet arrived) if and only if the packet arrived over the link that is on the shortest path to S (i.e., the packet came *from* the NextHop associated with S in the routing table). This strategy effectively floods packets outward from S, but does not loop packets back toward S.

There are two major shortcomings to this approach. The first is that it truly floods the network; it has no provision for avoiding LANs that have no members in the multicast group. We address this problem in the next subsection. The second limitation is that a given packet will be forwarded over a LAN by each of the routers connected to that LAN. This is due to the forwarding strategy of flooding packets on all links other than the one on which the packet

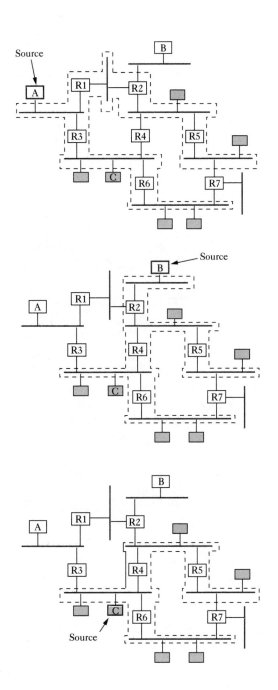

Figure 5.26 Example shortest-path multicast trees.

arrived, without regard to whether or not those links are part of the shortest-path tree rooted at the source.

The solution to this second limitation is to eliminate the duplicate broadcast packets that are generated when more than one router is connected to a given LAN. One way to do this is to designate one router as the "parent" router for each link, relative to the source, where only the parent router is allowed to forward multicast packets from that source over the LAN. The router that has the shortest path to source S is selected as the parent; a tie between two routers would be broken according to which router has the smallest address. A given router can learn if it is the parent for the LAN (again relative to each possible source) based upon the distance-vector messages it exchanges with its neighbors.

Notice that this refinement requires that each router keep, for each source, a bit for each of its incident links indicating whether or not it is the parent for that source/link pair. Keep in mind that in an internet setting, a "source" is a network, not a host, since an internet router is only interested in forwarding packets between networks. The resulting mechanism is sometimes called reverse-path broadcast (RPB).

Reverse-Path Multicast (RPM)

RPB implements shortest-path broadcast. We now want to prune the set of networks that receive each packet addressed to group G to exclude those that have no hosts that are members of G. This can be accomplished in two stages. First, we need to recognize when a *leaf* network has no group members. Determining that a network is a leaf is easy—if the parent router as described in RPB is the only router on the network, then the network is a leaf. Determining if any group members reside on the net-

MBone

Multicast is one of the core features supported by IPv6, but it is also available under IPv4 in the form of the MBone—multicast backbone. The MBone is a logical internet layered over the top of the current Internet. It uses class D addresses and tunneling. That is, multicast-enhanced routers tunnel to each other through the existing Internet. Any regular routers between two multicast-enhanced routers see only their own headers, and hence they never have to worry about multicast addresses.

At last report, the MBone connects approximately 1500 networks; it has been growing exponentially for the past three years. It is used as a testbed for various applications that want to exploit its multicast capabilities. One of the most popular applications is NV (network video), which supports multiparty videoconferencing. NV is used to broadcast both seminars and meetings across the Internet. In fact, IETF meetings—which are a week long and attract hundreds of participants—are generally broadcast over the MBone.

work is accomplished by having each host that is a member of group G periodically announce this fact over the network, as described in our earlier description of link-state multicast. The router then uses this information to decide whether or not to forward a multicast packet addressed to G over this LAN.

The second stage is to propagate this "no members of G here" information up the shortest-path tree. This is done by having the router augment the ⟨ Destination, Cost ⟩ pairs it sends to its neighbors with the set of groups for which the leaf network is interested in receiving multicast packets. This information can then be propagated from router to router, so that for each of its links, a given router knows for what groups it should forward multicast packets.

Note that including all of this information in the routing update is a fairly expensive thing to do. In practice, therefore, this information is exchanged only when some source starts sending packets to that group. In other words, the strategy is to use RPB, which adds a small amount of overhead to the basic distance-vector algorithm, until a particular multicast address becomes active. At that time, routers that are not interested in receiving packets addressed to that group speak up, and that information is propagated to the other routers.

5.6 Host Names (DNS)

The addresses we have been using to identify hosts, while perfectly suited for processing by routers, are not exactly user friendly. It is for this reason that a unique *name* is also typically assigned to each host in a network. Host names differ from host addresses in two important ways. First, they are usually of variable length and mnemonic, thereby making them easier for humans to remember. (In contrast, fixed-length numeric addresses are easier for routers to process.) Second, names typically contain no information that helps the network locate (route packets toward) the host. Addresses, in contrast, sometimes have routing information embedded in them; *flat* addresses (those not divisible into component parts) are the exception.

Before getting into the details of how hosts are named in a network, we first introduce some basic terminology. First, a *name space* defines the set of possible names. A name space can be either *flat* (names are not divisible into components), or it can be *hierarchical* (Unix file names are the obvious example). Second, the naming system maintains a collection of *bindings* of names to values. The value can be anything we want the naming system to return when presented with a name; in many cases it is an address. Finally, a *resolution mechanism* is a procedure that, when invoked with a name, returns the corresponding value. A *name server* is a specific implementation of a resolution mechanism that is available on a network and that can be queried by sending it a message.

Because of its large size, the Internet has a particularly well-developed naming system in place—the *domain name system* (DNS). We therefore use DNS as a framework for discussing the problem of naming hosts. Note that the Internet did not always use DNS. Early in its history, when there were only a few hundred hosts on the Internet, a central authority called the Network Information Center (NIC) maintained a flat table of name-to-address bindings; this table was called hosts.txt. Whenever a site wanted to add a new host to the Internet, the site administrator sent email to the NIC giving the new host's name/address pair. This

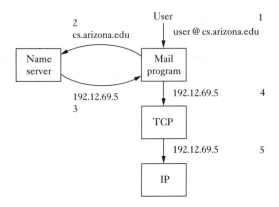

Figure 5.27   Names translated into addresses, where the numbers 1–5 show the sequence of steps in the process.

information was manually entered into the table, the modified table was mailed out to the various sites every few days, and the system administrator at each site installed the table on every host at the site. Name resolution was then simply implemented by a procedure that looked up a host's name in the local copy of the table and returned the corresponding address.

It should come as no surprise that the hosts.txt approach to naming did not work well as the number of hosts in the Internet started to grow. Therefore, in the mid-1980s, the domain naming system was put into place. DNS employs a hierarchical name space rather than a flat name space, and the "table" of bindings that implements this name space is partitioned into disjoint pieces and distributed throughout the Internet. These subtables are made available in name servers that can be queried over the network.

Note that we are jumping the gun a little bit by introducing host names at this point. What happens in the Internet is that a user presents a host name to an application program (possibly embedded in a compound name such as an email address or URL), and this program engages the naming system to translate this name into a host address. The application then opens a connection to this host by presenting some transport protocol (e.g., TCP) with the host's IP address. This situation is illustrated (in the case of sending email) in Figure 5.27. We discuss name resolution in this chapter, rather than in some later chapter, because the main problem that the naming system must address is exactly the same problem that an internetwork itself must solve—the problem of scale.

5.6.1   Domain Hierarchy

DNS implements a hierarchical name space for Internet objects. Unlike Unix file names, which are processed from left to right with the naming components separated with slashes, DNS names are processed from right to left and use periods as the separator. (Although they are "processed" from right to left, humans still "read" domain names from left to right.) An

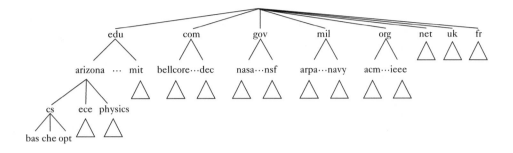

Figure 5.28 Example of a domain hierarchy.

example domain name for a host is cheltenham.cs.arizona.edu. Notice that we said domain names are used to name Internet "objects." What we mean by this is that DNS is not strictly used to map host names into host addresses. It is more accurate to say that DNS maps domain names into values. For the time being, we assume that these values are IP addresses; we will come back to this issue later in this section.

Like the Unix file hierarchy, the DNS hierarchy can be visualized as a tree, where each node in the tree corresponds to a domain and the leaves in the tree correspond to the hosts being named. Figure 5.28 gives an example of a domain hierarchy. Note that one should not assign any semantics to the term "domain" other than that it is simply a context in which additional names can be defined.

There was actually a substantial amount of discussion that took place when the domain name hierarchy was first being developed as to what conventions would govern the names that were to be handed out near the top of the hierarchy. Without going into that discussion in any detail, notice that the hierarchy is not very wide at the first level. There are domains for each country, plus the "big six" domains: edu, com, gov, mil, org, and net. These six domains are all based in the U.S.; the only domain names that don't explicitly specify a country are those in the U.S. Aside from this U.S. bias, you might notice a military bias in the hierarchy. This is easy to explain, since the development of DNS was originally funded by ARPA, the major research arm of the U.S. Department of Defense.

5.6.2 Name Servers

The complete domain name hierarchy exists only in the abstract. We now turn our attention to the question of how this hierarchy is actually implemented. The first step is to partition the hierarchy into subtrees called *zones*. For example, Figure 5.29 shows how the hierarchy given in Figure 5.28 might be divided into zones. Each zone can be thought of as corresponding to some administrative authority that is responsible for that portion of the hierarchy. For example, the top level of the hierarchy forms a zone that is managed by the NIC. Below this is a zone that corresponds to the University of Arizona. Within this zone, some departments do not want the responsibility of managing the hierarchy (and so they remain in

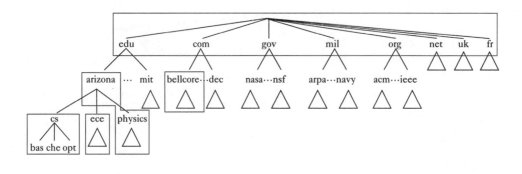

Figure 5.29 Domain hierarchy partitioned into zones.

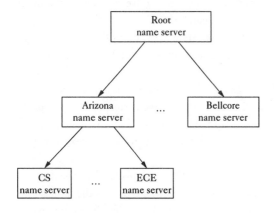

Figure 5.30 Hierarchy of name servers.

the university-level zone), while others, like the Department of Computer Science, manage their own department-level zone.

The relevance of a zone is that it corresponds to the fundamental unit of implementation in DNS—the name server. Specifically, the information contained in each zone is implemented in two or more name servers. Each name server, in turn, is a program that can be accessed over the Internet. Clients send queries to name servers, and name servers respond with the requested information. Sometimes the response contains the final answer that the client wants, and sometimes the response contains a pointer to another server that the client should query next. Thus, from an implementation perspective, it is more accurate to think of DNS as being represented by a hierarchy of name servers rather than by a hierarchy of domains, as illustrated in Figure 5.30.

Note that each zone is implemented in two or more name servers for the sake of redundancy; that is, the information is still available even if one name server fails. On the flip side, a given name server is free to implement more than one zone.

Each name server implements the zone information as a collection of *resource records*. In essence, a resource record is a name-to-value binding, or more specifically, a 5-tuple that contains the following fields:

⟨ Name, Value, Type, Class, TTL ⟩

The Name and Value fields are exactly what you would expect, while the Type field specifies how the Value should be interpreted. For example, Type=A indicates that the Value is an IP address. Thus, A records implement the name-to-address mapping we have been assuming. Other record types include

- NS: the Value field gives the domain name for a host that is running a name server that knows how to resolve names within the specified domain.

- CNAME: the Value field gives the canonical name for a particular host; it is used to define aliases.

- MX: the Value field gives the domain name for a host that is running a mail server that accepts messages for the specified domain.

The Class field was included to allow entities other than the NIC to define useful record types. To date, the only widely used Class is the one used by the Internet; it is denoted IN. Finally, the TTL field show how long this resource record is valid. It is used by servers that cache resource records from other servers; when the TTL expires, the server must evict the record from its cache.

To better understand how resource records represent the information in the domain hierarchy, consider the following examples drawn from the domain hierarchy given in Figure 5.28. To simplify the examples, we ignore the TTL field and we give the relevant information for only one of the name servers that implement each zone.

First, the root name server contains an NS record for each second-level server. It also has an A record that translates this name into the corresponding IP address. Taken together, these two records effectively implement a pointer from the root name server to each of the second-level servers.

⟨ arizona.edu, telcom.arizona.edu, NS, IN ⟩
⟨ telcom.arizona.edu, 128.196.128.233, A, IN ⟩

⟨ bellcore.com, thumper.bellcore.com, NS, IN ⟩
⟨ thumper.bellcore.com, 128.96.32.20, A, IN ⟩

...

Next, the domain arizona.edu has a name server available on host telcom.arizona.edu that contains the following records. Note that some of these records give the final answer (e.g., the address for host saturn.physics.arizona.edu), while others point to third-level name servers.

⟨ cs.arizona.edu, optima.cs.arizona.edu, NS, IN ⟩
⟨ optima.cs.arizona.edu, 192.12.69.5, A, IN ⟩

⟨ ece.arizona.edu, helios.ece.arizona.edu, NS, IN ⟩
⟨ helios.ece.arizona.edu, 128.196.28.166, A, IN ⟩

⟨ jupiter.physics.arizona.edu, 128.196.4.1, A, IN ⟩
⟨ saturn.physics.arizona.edu, 128.196.4.2, A, IN ⟩
⟨ mars.physics.arizona.edu, 128.196.4.3, A, IN ⟩
⟨ venus.physics.arizona.edu, 128.196.4.4, A, IN ⟩

...

Finally, a third-level name server, such as the one managed by domain cs.arizona.edu, contains A records for all of its hosts. It might also define a set of aliases (CNAME records) for each of those hosts, in addition to a maildrop (MX record) for the whole domain. This latter record is useful because it allows an administrator to change which host receives mail on behalf of the domain without having to change everyone's email address.

⟨ cs.arizona.edu, optima.cs.arizona.edu, MX, IN ⟩

⟨ cheltenham.cs.arizona.edu, 192.12.69.60, A, IN ⟩
⟨ che.cs.arizona.edu, cheltenham.cs.arizona.edu, CNAME, IN ⟩

⟨ optima.cs.arizona.edu, 192.12.69.5, A, IN ⟩
⟨ opt.cs.arizona.edu, optima.cs.arizona.edu, CNAME, IN ⟩

⟨ baskerville.cs.arizona.edu, 192.12.69.35, A, IN ⟩
⟨ bas.cs.arizona.edu, baskerville.cs.arizona.edu, CNAME, IN ⟩

...

5.6.3 Name Resolution

Given a hierarchy of name servers, we now consider the issue of how a client engages these servers to resolve a domain name. To illustrate the basic idea, suppose the client wants to resolve the name cheltenham.cs.arizona.edu relative to the set of servers given in the previous subsection. The client first sends a query containing this name to the root server. The root server, unable to match the entire name, returns the best match it has—the NS record for arizona.edu. The server also returns all records that are related to this record, in this case, the A record for telcom.arizona.edu. The client, having not received the answer it was after, next sends the same query to the name server at IP host 128.196.128.233. This server also cannot match the whole name, and so returns the NS and corresponding A records for the

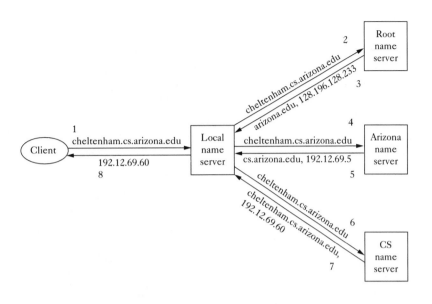

Figure 5.31 Name resolution in practice, where the numbers 1–8 show the sequence of steps in the process.

cs.arizona.edu domain. Finally, the client sends the same query as before to the server at IP host 192.12.69.5, and this time gets back the A record for cheltenham.cs.arizona.edu.

This example still leaves a couple of questions about the resolution process unanswered. The first question is, how did the client locate the root server in the first place, or said another way, how do you resolve the name of the server that knows how to resolve names? This is a fundamental problem in any naming system, and the answer is that the system has to be bootstrapped in some way. In this case, the name-to-address mapping for one or more root servers is well known, that is, published through some means outside the naming system itself.

In practice, however, not all clients know about the root servers. Instead, the client program running on each Internet host is initialized with the address of a *local* name server. For example, all the hosts in the Department of Computer Science at the University of Arizona know about the server on optima.cs.arizona.edu. This local name server, in turn, has resource records for one or more of the root servers, for example:

⟨ 'root', venera.isi.edu, NS, IN ⟩
⟨ venera.isi.edu, 128.9.0.32, A, IN ⟩

Thus, resolving a name actually involves a client querying the local server, which in turn acts as a client that queries the remote servers on the original client's behalf. This results in the client/server interactions illustrated in Figure 5.31. One advantage of this model is that all the hosts in the Internet do not have to be kept up to date on where the current root servers are located; only the servers have to know about the root. A second advantage is that the local server gets to see the answers that come back from queries that are posted by all the local clients. The local server caches these responses and is sometimes able to resolve future queries without having to go out over the network. The TTL field in the resource records returned by remote servers indicates how long each record can be safely cached.

The second question is how the system works when a user submits a partial name (e.g., cheltenham) rather than a complete domain name (e.g., cheltenham.cs.arizona.edu). The answer is that the client program is configured with the local domain in which the host resides (e.g., cs.arizona.edu) and it appends this string to any simple names before sending out a query.

▶ Just to make sure we are clear, we have now seen three different levels of identifiers—domain names, IP addresses, and physical network addresses—and the mapping of identifiers at one level into identifiers at another level happens at different points in the network architecture. First, users specify domain names when interacting with the application. Second, the application engages DNS to translate this name into an IP address; it is the IP address that is placed in each datagram, not the domain name. (As an aside, this translation process involves IP datagrams being sent over the Internet, but these datagrams are addressed to a host that runs a name server, not to the ultimate destination.) Third, IP does forwarding at each router, which often means that it maps one IP address into another; i.e., it maps the ultimate destination's address into the address for the next-hop router. Finally, IP engages ARP to translate the next hop IP address into the physical address for that machine; the next hop might be the ultimate destination or it might be an intermediate router. Frames sent over the physical network have these physical addresses in their headers.

Naming Conventions

Our description of DNS focuses on the underlying *mechanisms*, that is, how the hierarchy is partitioned over multiple servers and how the resolution process works. There is an equally interesting, but much less technical, issue of the *conventions* that are used to decide the names to use in the mechanism. For example, it is by convention that all U.S. universities are under the edu domain, while English universities are under the ac (academic) subdomain of the uk (United Kingdom) domain. In fact, the very existence of the uk domain, rather than a gb (Great Britain) domain, was a source of great controversy in the early days of DNS, since the latter does not include Northern Ireland.

The thing to understand about conventions is that they are sometimes defined without anyone making an explicit decision. For example, by convention a site hides the exact host that serves as its mail

5.7 Summary

The main theme of this chapter was how to build big networks by interconnecting smaller networks. We looked first at bridging, a technique that is mostly used to interconnect asmall to moderate number of similar networks. What bridging does not do well is tackle the two closely related problems of building very large networks: heterogeneity and scale. The Internet Protocol (IP) is the key tool for dealing with these problems, and it provided most of the examples for this chapter.

exchange behind the MX record. An alternative would have been to adopt the convention of sending mail to user@mail.cs.arizona.edu, much as we expect to find a site's public FTP directory at ftp.cs.arizona.edu and its WWW server at www.cs.arizona.edu.

Conventions also exist at the local level, where an organization names its machines according to some consistent set of rules. Given that the host names venus, saturn, and mars are among the most popular in the Internet, it's not too hard to figure out one common naming convention. Some host naming conventions are more imaginative, however. For example, one site named its machines up, down, crashed, rebooting, and so on, resulting in confusing statements like "rebooting has crashed" and "up is down." Of course, there are also less imaginative namers, such as those who name their machines after the integers.

IP tackles heterogeneity by defining a simple, common service model for an internetwork, which is based on the best-effort delivery of IP datagrams. An important part of the service model is the global addressing scheme, which enables any two nodes in an internetwork to uniquely identify each other for the purposes of exchanging data. The IP service model is simple enough to be supported by any known networking technology, and the ARP mechanism is used to translate global IP addresses into local link-layer addresses.

We then saw a succession of scaling problems and the ways that IP deals with them. The major scaling issues are the efficient use of address space and the growth of routing tables as the Internet grows. The hierarchical IP address format, with its network and host parts, gives us one level of hierarchy to manage scale. Subnetting lets us make more efficient use of network numbers and helps consolidate routing information; in effect, it adds one more level of hierarchy to the address. Autonomous systems allow us to partition the routing problem into two parts, interdomain and intradomain routing, each of which is much smaller than the total routing problem would be. Classless routing, provided by CIDR and BGP-4, lets us introduce more levels of hierarchy and achieve further

routing aggregation. These mechanisms have enabled today's Internet to sustain remarkable growth.

Eventually, all of these mechanisms will be unable to keep up with the Internet's growth and a new address format will be needed. This will require a new IP datagram format and a new version of the protocol. Originally known as Next Generation IP (IPng), this new protocol is now known as IPv6 and it will provide a 128-bit address with CIDR-like addressing and routing. At the same time, it will add considerable functionality to IP, including auto-configuration, support for multicast, and advanced routing capabilities.

O P E N   I S S U E
IP versus ATM

While we have presented IP as the only protocol for global internetworking, there are other contenders, most notably ATM. One of the design goals of ATM, from day one, has been that it could provide all sorts of services, including voice, video, and data applications. Many proponents of ATM are so enamored of this planned capability that they argue that ATM is the only rational choice for future networks. They tend to refer to any network that uses variable-length packets as a "legacy network" and assume that the future of global networking lies in ATM LANs connected to ATM WANs, with all serious users having direct ATM connections into their workstations. Of course, many researchers, users, and network designers in the IP community have a slightly different view. They see ATM as just another technology over which you can run IP. After all, IP has run over every other technology that has come along, so why should ATM be any different? They tend to refer to ATM as "just another subnet technology." (One IP proponent responded to the use of the term "legacy network" by asserting that ATM will never be successful enough even to become a legacy.) As you might expect, this does not go over well with the more strident proponents of ATM.

There are challenges for both IP and ATM if either is to succeed on a global scale. For ATM, the main obstacle is likely to be the huge installed base of non-ATM technology. It is hard to believe that all those users will want to discard their existing network adaptors, hubs, routers, wiring, and so on. For IP, one of the biggest challenges will be to provide quality of service guarantees that are suitable for high-quality voice and video, something that is likely to be available in ATM networks from the outset. In a sense, ATM does not deal well with heterogeneous technologies: it works best when everyone uses ATM. IP, at present, does not deal well with a wide range of applications: it is best suited to those without real-time constraints. As we will see in Chapter 9, the IP community is working to address that shortcoming of IP.

In the end, the real challenge is likely to be the integration of IP and ATM. The IETF is already working on some IP-over-ATM issues, having generated proposed standards for both the encapsulation of IP datagrams inside ATM CS-PDUs and for an address resolution mechanism that maps between the ATM and IP address spaces. At the time of this writing, the efficient support of IP multicast over ATM networks is high on the IETF agenda. A likely challenge for the future integration of ATM and IP is the provision of end-to-end quality of service guarantees in an internetwork that includes both ATM and non-ATM technologies.

F U R T H E R   R E A D I N G

Not surprisingly, there have been countless papers written on various aspects of the Internet. Of these, we recommend two as must reading: the paper by Cerf and Kahn is the one that originally introduced the TCP/IP architecture and is worth reading just for its historical perspective; the paper by Bradner and Mankin gives an informative overview on how the rapidly growing Internet has stressed the scalability of the original architecture, ultimately resulting in the next generation IP. The paper by Perlman describes the spanning tree algorithm and is the seminal paper on this topic. The next three papers discuss multicast: the article by Deering and Cheriton is a seminal paper on the topic and describes the approach to multicast currently used on the MBone, while the papers by Ballardie et al. and by Thyagarajan and Deering present more scalable solutions. Finally, the paper by Mockapetris and Dunlap describes many of the design goals behind the domain name system.

- Cerf, V., and R. Kahn. A protocol for packet network intercommunication. *IEEE Transactions on Communications* COM-22(5):637–648, May 1974.

- Bradner, S., and A. Mankin. The recommendation for the next generation IP protocol. *Request for Comments* 1752, January 1995.

- Perlman, R. An algorithm for distributed computation of spanning trees in an extended LAN. *Proceedings of the Ninth Data Communications Symposium*, pages 44–53, September 1985.

- Deering, S., and D. Cheriton. Multicast routing in datagram internetworks and extended LANs. *ACM Transactions on Computer Systems* 8(2):85–110, May 1990.

- Ballardie, T., P. Francis, and J. Crowcroft. Core Based Trees (CBT): An architecture for scalable inter-domain multicast routing. *Proceedings of the SIGCOMM '93 Symposium*, pages 85–95, September 1993.

- Thyagarajan, A., and S. Deering. Hierarchical distance vector multicast routing for the MBone. *Proceedings of the SIGCOMM '95 Symposium*, pages 60–67, August 1995.

- Mockapetris, P., and K. Dunlap. Development of the Domain Name System. *Proceedings of the SIGCOMM '88 Symposium*, pages 123–133, August 1988.

Beyond these papers, Perlman gives an excellent explanation of routing in an internet, including coverage of both bridges and routers [Per92]. The description of the spanning tree algorithm presented in Chapter 3 of Perlman's book is actually easier to understand than the paper cited in the above reading list. Also, the book by Lynch and Rose gives general information on the scalability of the Internet [Cha93].

Many of the techniques and protocols developed to help the Internet scale are described in RFCs: subnetting is described in Mogul and Postel [MP85], CIDR is described in Fuller et al. [FLYV93], RIP is defined in Hedrick [Hed88] and Malkin [Mal93], OSPF is defined

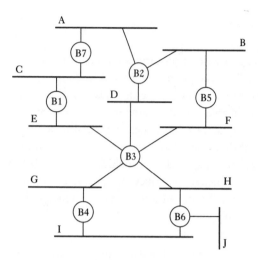

Figure 5.32   Extended LAN for exercise 1.

in Moy [Moy94], and BGP-4 is defined in Rekhter and Li [RL95]. The OSPF specification, at 212 pages, is one of the longer RFCs around. Also, explanations of how IP and ATM can coexist are given in Heinanen [Hei93], Laubach [Lau94], and Borden et al. [BCDB95]. A collection of RFCs related to IPv6 can be found in Bradner and Mankin [BM95].

There are a wealth of papers on naming, as well as on the related issue of resource discovery (finding out what resources exist in the first place). General studies of naming can be found in Terry [Ter86], Comer and Peterson [CP89], Birrell et al. [BLNS82], Saltzer [Sal78], Shoch [Sho78], and Watson [Wat81]; attribute-based (descriptive) naming systems are described in Peterson [Pet88] and Bowman et al. [BPY90]; and resource discovery is the subject of Bowman et al. [BDMS94].

Finally, we recommend the following live references:

■ http://www.ietf.cnri.reston.va.us: the IETF home page, from which you can get RFCs, internet drafts, and working group charters;

■ http://playground.sun.com/pub/ipng/html/ipng-main.html: current state of IPv6;

■ http://boom.cs.ucl.ac.uk/ietf/idmr/: current state of the MBone.

E X E R C I S E S

1 Given the extended LAN shown in Figure 5.32, indicate which ports are not selected by the spanning tree algorithm.

2 Identify the class of each of the following IP addresses:

(a) 128.36.199.3

(b) 21.12.240.17

(c) 183.194.76.253

(d) 192.12.69.248

(e) 89.3.0.1

(f) 200.3.6.2

3 Why does the Offset field in the IP header measure the offset in 8-byte units? (Hint: Recall that the Offset field is 13 bits long.)

4 Suppose that a TCP message that contains 2048 bytes of data and 20 bytes of TCP header is passed to IP for delivery across two networks of the Internet (i.e., from the source host to a router to the destination host). The first network uses 14-byte headers and has an MTU of 1024 bytes; the second uses 8-byte headers with an MTU of 512 bytes. (Each network's MTU gives the total packet size that may be sent, including the network header.) Also, recall that the IP header size is 20 bytes. Schematically depict the packets that are delivered to the network layer at the destination host.

5 Give an explanation for why IP does reassembly at the destination host rather than at the routers.

6 Identify the differences in IP fragmentation/reassembly and ATM segmentation/reassembly. (Consider both AAL3/4 and AAL5.) Explain why these differences lead to different header formats.

7 In IP, why is it necessary to have one address per interface, rather than just one address per host?

8 Read the man page for the Unix utility netstat. Use netstat to display the current IP routing table on your host.

9 Use the Unix utility ping to determine the round-trip time to various hosts in the Internet. Read the man page for ping to determine how it is implemented.

10 Explain why having each entry in the ARP table timeout after 10–15 minutes is reasonable. Describe the problems that occur if the timeout value is too small or too large.

SubnetNumber	SubnetMask	NextHop
128.96.39.0	255.255.255.128	Interface 0
128.96.39.128	255.255.255.128	Interface 1
128.96.40.0	255.255.255.128	R2
192.4.153.0	255.255.255.192	R3
⟨default⟩		R4

Table 5.6   A router's forwarding table.

11 Sketch the ARP procedure that determines if a request message that was just received should be used to update the ARP table. Implement the complete ARP protocol in the x-kernel.

12 Use the Unix utility traceroute to determine how many hops it is from your host to other hosts in the Internet (e.g., cs.arizona.edu or thumper.bellcore.com). How many routers do you traverse just to get out of your local site? Explain how traceroute is implemented. (Hint: read the man page.)

13 Suppose a router has built up the routing table shown as Table 5.6. The router can deliver packets directly over interfaces 0 and 1, or it can forward packets to routers R2, R3, or R4. Describe what the router does with a packet addressed to each of the following destinations:

(a) 128.96.39.10

(b) 128.96.40.12

(c) 128.96.40.151

(d) 192.4.153.17

(e) 192.4.153.90

14 Sketch the data structures and procedures for an IP forwarding table that supports subnetting. Implement IP in the x-kernel.

15 This chapter claimed that IP is designed to run on top of any network technology. Explain the main complication that arises when IP is implemented on top of a connection-oriented network, such as X.25. How might the IP routers connected to such a network work around this complication?

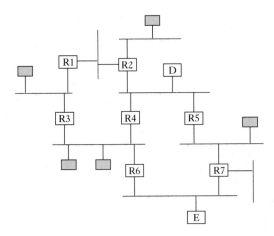

Figure 5.33 Example internet for exercise 19.

16 What would be the disadvantage to placing the IP version number in a place other than in the first byte of the header?

17 Why was the time to live (TTL) field of IPv4 renamed HopLimit in IPv6?

18 Why is it unnecessary to use ARP in conjunction with IPv6?

19 Consider the example internet shown in Figure 5.33, in which sources D and E send packets to multicast group G, whose members are shaded in gray. Show the shortest-path multicast trees for each source.

20 Determine if your site is connected to the MBone. If so, investigate and experiment with any MBone tools, such as sd and nv.

21 The original Internet mechanism for looking up names used a central hosts.txt table, which was distributed to all hosts every few days. Describe the reasons why this mechanism is no longer used.

22 When hosts maintained hosts.txt files, IP addresses could easily be mapped back into host names. Describe how this might be done using DNS.

23 Read the man page for nslookup, a Unix utility for communicating interactively with DNS servers. Determine the sequence of name servers to contact to resolve the name cheltenham.cs.arizona.edu.

The previous three chapters have described various technologies that can be used to connect together a collection of computers: direct links (including LAN technologies like Ethernet and FDDI), packet-switched networks (including cell-based networks like ATM), and internetworks. The next problem is to turn this host-to-host packet delivery service into a process-to-process communication channel. This is the role played by the *transport* level of the network architecture, which, because it supports communication between the end application programs, is sometimes called the *end-to-end* protocol.

PROBLEM

Getting Processes to Communicate

Two forces shape the end-to-end protocol. From above, the application-level processes that use its services have certain requirements. The following list itemizes some of the common properties that a transport protocol can be expected to provide:

■ guarantees message delivery;

■ delivers messages in the same order they are sent;

■ delivers at most one copy of each message;

■ supports arbitrarily large messages;

■ supports synchronization between the sender and the receiver;

■ allows the receiver to apply flow control to the sender;

■ supports multiple application processes on each host.

Victory is the beautiful, bright coloured flower. Transport is the stem without which it could never have blossomed.

—Churchill

Note that this list does not include all the functionality that application processes might want from the network. For example, it does not include security, which is typically provided by protocols that sit above the transport level.

From below, the underlying network upon which the transport protocol operates has certain limitations in the level of service it can provide. Some of the more typical limitations of the network are that it may

■ drop messages;

- reorder messages;

- deliver duplicate copies of a given message;

- limit messages to some finite size;

- deliver messages after an arbitrarily long delay.

Such a network is said to provide a *best-effort* level of service, as exemplified by the Internet.

The challenge, therefore, is to develop algorithms that turn the less-than-desirable properties of the underlying network into the high level of service required by application programs. Different transport protocols employ different combinations of these algorithms. This chapter looks at these algorithms in the context of three representative services—a simple asynchronous demultiplexing service, a reliable byte-stream service, and a request/reply service.

In the case of the demultiplexing and byte-stream services, we use the Internet's UDP and TCP protocols, respectively, to illustrate how these services are provided in practice. In the third case, we first give a collection of algorithms that implement the request/reply (plus other related) services and then show how these algorithms can be combined to implement a Remote Procedure Call (RPC) protocol. This discussion is capped off with a description of a widely used RPC protocol, SunRPC, in terms of these component algorithms. Finally, the chapter concludes with a section that introduces a popular application programming interface (API) that application programs use to access the services of the transport protocol, and with a section that discusses the performance of the different transport protocols.

6

End-to-End Protocols

6.1 Simple Demultiplexer (UDP)

The simplest possible transport protocol is one that extends the host-to-host delivery service of the underlying network into a process-to-process communication service. There are likely to be many processes running on any given host, so the protocol needs to add a level of demultiplexing, thereby allowing multiple application processes on each host to share the network. Aside from this requirement, the transport protocol adds no other functionality to the best-effort service provided by the underlying network. The Internet's User Datagram Protocol (UDP) is an example of such a transport protocol. So is A Simple Protocol (ASP) described in Chapter 2.

The only interesting issue in such a protocol is the form of the address used to identify the target process. Although it is possible for processes to *directly* identify each other with an OS-assigned process id (pid), such an approach is only practical in a "closed" distributed system in which a single OS runs on all hosts and assigns each process a unique id. A more common approach, and the one used by both ASP and UDP, is for processes to *indirectly* identify each other using an abstract locater, often called a *port* or *mailbox*. The basic idea is for a source process to send a message to a port and for the destination process to receive the message from a port.

The header for an end-to-end protocol that implements this demultiplexing function typically contains an identifier (port) for both the sender (source) and the receiver (destination) of the message. For example, the UDP header is given in Figure 6.1. Notice that the UDP port field is only 16 bits long. This means that there are up to 64-K possible ports, clearly not enough to identify all the processes on all the hosts in the Internet. Fortunately, ports are not interpreted across the entire Internet, but only on a single host. That is, a process is really identified by a port on some particular host—a ⟨port, host⟩ pair. In fact, this pair constitutes the demultiplexing key for the UDP protocol.

The next issue is how a process learns the port for the process to which it wants to send a message. Typically, a client process initiates a message exchange with a server process. Once a client has contacted a server, the server knows the client's port (it was contained in the message header) and can reply to it. The real problem, therefore, is how the client learns the server's port in the first place. A common approach is for the server to accept messages at a *well-known port*. That is, each server receives its messages at some fixed port that is widely published, much like the emergency telephone service is available at the well-known phone number 911. In the Internet, for example, the Domain Name Server (DNS) receives messages at well-known port 53 on each host, the Unix talk program accepts messages at well-known port 517, and so on. This mapping is published periodically in an RFC and is available on most Unix systems in file /etc/services. Sometimes a well-known port is just the starting point for communication: the client and server use the well-known port to agree on some other port that they will use for subsequent communication, leaving the well-known port free for other clients.

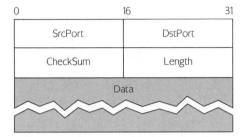

Figure 6.1   Format for UDP header.

As just mentioned, a port is purely an abstraction. Exactly how it is implemented differs from system to system, or more precisely, from OS to OS. Typically, a port is implemented by a message queue. When a message arrives, the protocol (e.g., UDP) appends the message to the end of the queue. Should the queue be full, the message is discarded. There is no flow-control mechanism that tells the sender to slow down. When an application process wants to receive a message, one is removed from the front of the queue. If the queue is empty, the process blocks until a message becomes available.

Finally, although UDP does not implement flow control or reliable/ordered delivery, it does a little more work than to simply demultiplex messages to some application process—it also ensures the correctness of the message by the use of a checksum. (The UDP checksum is optional in the current Internet, but will become mandatory with IPv6.) UDP computes its checksum over the UDP header, the contents of the message body, and something called the *pseudoheader*. The pseudoheader consists of three fields from the IP header: length, source IP address, and destination IP address. UDP uses the same checksum algorithm as IP, as defined in Section 3.4.3. The motivation behind having the pseudoheader is to verify that this message has been delivered between the correct two endpoints. For example, if the destination IP address was modified while the packet was in transit, causing the packet to be misdelivered, this fact would be detected by the UDP checksum.

6.2   Reliable Byte Stream (TCP)

In contrast to a simple demultiplexing protocol like UDP, a more sophisticated transport protocol is one that offers a connection-oriented, reliable byte-stream service. Such a service has proven useful to a wide assortment of applications because it frees the application from having to worry about missing or reordered data. The Internet's Transmission Control Protocol (TCP) is probably the most widely used protocol of this type. It is also the most carefully optimized, which makes it an interesting protocol to study.

In terms of the properties of transport protocols given in the problem statement at the start of this chapter, TCP guarantees the reliable, in-order delivery of a stream of bytes. It is a full-duplex protocol, meaning that each TCP connection supports a pair of byte streams, one flowing in each direction. It also includes a flow-control mechanism for each of these byte streams that allows the receiver to limit how much data the sender can transmit. Finally, like UDP, TCP supports a demultiplexing mechanism that allows multiple application programs on any given host to simultaneously carry on a conversation with their peers.

In addition to the above features, TCP also implements a highly tuned congestion-control mechanism. The idea of this mechanism is to throttle how fast TCP sends data, not for the sake of keeping the sender from overrunning the receiver, but so as to keep the sender from overloading the network. A description of TCP's congestion-control mechanism is postponed until Chapter 8, where we discuss it in the larger context of how network resources are fairly allocated.

Since many people confuse congestion control and flow control, we restate the difference. *Flow control* involves preventing senders from overrunning the capacity of receivers. *Congestion control* involves preventing too much data from being injected into the network, thereby causing switches or links to become overloaded. Thus, flow control is an end-to-end issue, while congestion control is more of an issue of how hosts and networks interact.

6.2.1 End-to-End Issues

At the heart of TCP is the sliding window algorithm. Even though this is the same basic algorithm we saw in Section 3.5.2, because TCP runs over the Internet rather than a point-to-point link there are many important differences. This subsection identifies these differences and explains how they complicate TCP. The following five subsections then describe how TCP addresses these complications.

First, whereas the sliding window algo-

TCP Extensions

We have mentioned at three different points in this section that proposed extensions to TCP may help to mitigate some problem that TCP is facing. These proposed extensions are designed to have as small an impact on TCP as possible. In particular, they are realized as options that can be added to the TCP header. (We glossed over this point earlier, but the reason that the TCP header has a HdrLen field is that the header can be of variable length; the variable part of the TCP header contains the options that have been added.) The significance of adding these extensions as options rather than changing the core of the TCP header is that hosts can still communicate using TCP even if they do not implement the options. Hosts that do implement the optional extensions, however, can take advantage of them. The two sides agree that they will use the options during TCP's connection-establishment phase.

The first extension helps to improve TCP's timeout mechanism. Instead of measuring the RTT using a coarse-grained event, TCP can read the actual system clock when it is about to send a segment, and put

rithm presented in Section 3.5.2 runs over a single physical link that always connects the same two computers, TCP supports logical connections between processes that are running on any two computers in the Internet. This means that TCP needs an explicit connection-establishment phase during which the two sides of the connection agree to exchange data with each other. This difference is analogous to having to dial up the other party, rather than having a dedicated phone line. TCP also has an explicit connection-teardown phase. One of the things that happens during connection establishment is that the two parties establish some shared state to enable the sliding window algorithm to begin.

this time—think of it as a 32-bit *timestamp*—in the segment's header. The receiver then echoes this time-stamp back to the sender in its acknowledgment, and the sender subtracts this timestamp from the current time to measure the RTT. In essence, the timestamp option provides a convenient place for TCP to "store" the record of when a segment was transmitted; it stores the time in the segment itself. Note that the endpoints in the connection do not need synchronized clocks, since the timestamp is written and read at the same end of the connection.

The second extension addresses the problem of TCP's 32-bit SequenceNum field wrapping around too soon on a high-speed network. Rather than define a new 64-bit sequence number field, TCP uses the 32-bit timestamp just described to effectively extend the sequence number space. In other words, TCP decides whether to accept or reject a segment based on a 64-bit identifier that has the SequenceNum field in the low-order 32 bits and the timestamp in the high-order 32 bits. Since the timestamp is always

Second, whereas a single physical link that always connects the same two computers has a fixed RTT, TCP connections have highly variable round-trip times. For example, a TCP connection between a host in Tucson and a host in New York, which are separated by several thousand kilometers, might have an RTT of 100 ms, while a TCP connection between a host in Tucson and a host in Phoenix, only a few hundred kilometers away, might have an RTT of only 10 ms. The same TCP protocol must be able to support both of these connections. To make matters worse, the TCP connection between hosts in Tucson and New York might have an RTT of 100 ms at 3 a.m., but an RTT of 500 ms at 3 p.m. Variations in the RTT are even possible during a single TCP connection that lasts only a few minutes. What this means to the sliding window algorithm is that the timeout mechanism that triggers retransmissions must be adaptive. (Certainly, the timeout for a point-to-point link must be a settable parameter, but it is not necessary to adapt this timer frequently.)

The third difference is also related to the variable RTT of a logical connection across the Internet, but it is concerned with the pathological situation in which a packet is delayed in the network for an extended period of time. Recall from Section 5.2 that the time to live (TTL) field of the IP header limits the number of hops that a packet can traverse. (In IPv6, the TTL field is renamed the HopLimit field.) TCP makes use of the fact that limiting the number of hops indirectly limits how long a packet can circulate in the Internet. Specifically, TCP assumes that each packet has a maximum lifetime of no more than 60 seconds. Keep in mind that IP does not directly enforce this 60-second value; it is simply a conservative estimate that TCP makes

of how long a packet might live in the Internet. This sort of delay is simply not possible in a point-to-point link—a packet put into one end of the link must appear at the other end in an amount of time closely related to the speed of light. The implication of this difference is significant—TCP has to be prepared for very old packets to suddenly show up at the receiver, potentially confusing the sliding window algorithm.

Fourth, the computers connected to a point-to-point link are generally engineered to support the link. For example, if a link's delay $\times$ bandwidth product is computed to be 8 KB—meaning that a window size is selected to allow up to 8 KB of data to be unacknowledged at a given time—then it is likely that the computers at either end of the link have the ability to buffer up to 8 KB of data. Designing the system otherwise would be silly. On the other hand, almost any kind of computer can be connected to the Internet, making the amount of resources dedicated to any one TCP connection highly variable, especially considering that any one host can potentially support hundreds of TCP connections at the same time. This means that TCP must include a mechanism that each side uses to "learn" what resources (e.g., how much buffer space) the other side is able to apply to the connection.

Fifth, because the transmitting side of a directly connected link cannot send any faster than the bandwidth of the link allows, and only one host is pumping data into the link, it is not possible to unknowingly congest the link. Said another way, the load on the link is visible in the

increasing, it serves to distinguish between two different incarnations of the same sequence number. Note that the timestamp is being used in this setting only to protect against wraparound; it is not treated as part of the sequence number for the purpose of ordering or acknowledging data.

The third extension allows TCP to advertise a larger window, thereby allowing it to fill larger delay $\times$ bandwidth pipes that are made possible by high-speed networks. This extension involves an option that defines a *scaling factor* for the advertised window. That is, rather than interpreting the number that appears in the AdvertisedWindow field as indicating how many bytes the sender is allowed to have unacknowledged, this option allows the two sides of TCP to agree that the AdvertisedWindow field counts larger chunks (e.g., how many 16-byte units of data the sender can have unacknowledged). In other words, the window scaling option specifies how many bits each side should left-shift the AdvertisedWindow field before using its contents to compute an effective window.

form of a queue of packets at the sender. In contrast, the sending side of a TCP connection has no idea what links will be traversed to reach the destination. For example, the sending

machine might be directly connected to a relatively fast Ethernet—and so, capable of sending
data at a rate of 10 Mbps—but somewhere out in the middle of the network, a 1.5-Mbps T1
link must be traversed. And to make matters worse, data being generated by many different
sources might be trying to traverse this same slow link. This leads to the problem of network
congestion. Discussion of this topic is delayed until Chapter 8.

We conclude this discussion of end-to-end issues by comparing TCP's approach to providing a reliable/ordered delivery service with the approach used by X.25 networks. In TCP,
the underlying IP network is assumed to be unreliable and to deliver messages out of order;
TCP uses the sliding window algorithm on an end-to-end basis to provide reliable/ordered
delivery. In contrast, X.25 networks use the sliding window protocol within the network, on
a hop-by-hop basis. The assumption behind this approach is that if messages are delivered
reliably and in order between each pair of nodes along the path between the source host and
the destination host, then the end-to-end service also guarantees reliable/ordered delivery.

The problem with this latter approach is that a sequence of hop-by-hop guarantees does
not necessarily add up to an end-to-end guarantee. First, if a heterogeneous link (say, across
an Ethernet) is added to one end of the path, then there is no guarantee that this hop will
preserve the same service as the other hops. Second, just because the sliding window protocol
guarantees that messages are delivered correctly from node A to node B, and then from node B
to node C, it does not guarantee that node B behaves perfectly. For example, network nodes
have been known to introduce errors into messages while transferring them from an input
buffer to an output buffer. They have also been known to accidentally reorder messages. As a
consequence of these small windows of vulnerability, it is still necessary to provide true end-
to-end checks to guarantee reliable/ordered service, even though the lower levels of the system
also implement that functionality.

This discussion serves to illustrate one of the most important principles in system design—
the *end-to-end argument*. In a nutshell, the end-to-end argument says that a function (in our
example, providing reliable/ordered delivery) should not be provided in the lower levels of the
system unless it can be completely and correctly implemented at that level. Therefore, this rule
argues in favor of the TCP/IP approach. This rule is not absolute, however. It does allow for
functions to be incompletely provided at a low level as a performance optimization. This is
why it is perfectly consistent with the end-to-end argument to perform error detection (e.g.,
CRC) on a hop-by-hop basis; detecting and retransmitting a single corrupt packet across one
hop is preferable to having to retransmit an entire file end-to-end.

6.2.2 Segment Format

TCP is a byte-oriented protocol, which means that the sender writes bytes into a TCP connection and the receiver reads bytes out of the TCP connection. Although "byte stream" describes the service TCP offers to application processes, TCP does not, itself, transmit individual bytes over the Internet. Instead, TCP on the source host buffers enough bytes from the
sending process to fill a reasonably sized packet and then sends this packet to its peer on the
destination host. TCP on the destination host then empties the contents of the packet into

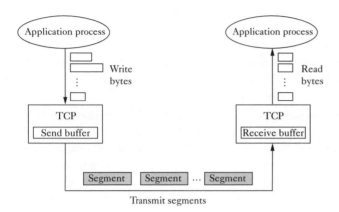

Figure 6.2   How TCP manages a byte stream.

a receive buffer, and the receiving process reads from this buffer at its leisure. This situation is illustrated in Figure 6.2, which, for simplicity, shows data flowing in only one direction. Remember that, in general, a single TCP connection supports byte streams flowing in both directions.

The packets exchanged between TCP peers in Figure 6.2 are called *segments*, since each one carries a segment of the byte stream. One question you might ask is, how does TCP decide that it has enough bytes to send a segment? The answer is that TCP has three mechanisms to trigger the transmission of a segment. First, TCP maintains a threshold variable, typically called the maximum segment size (MSS), and it sends a segment as soon as it has collected MSS bytes from the sending process. MSS is usually set to the size of the largest segment TCP can send without causing the local IP to fragment. That is, MSS is set to the MTU of the directly connected network, minus the size of the TCP and IP headers. The second thing that triggers TCP to transmit a segment is that the sending process has explicitly asked it to do so. Specifically, TCP supports a *push* operation, and the sending process invokes this operation to effectively flush the buffer of unsent bytes. (This push operation is not the same as the the x-kernel's xPush.) This operation is used in terminal emulators like Telnet because each byte has to be sent as soon as it is typed. The final trigger for transmitting a segment is a timer that periodically fires; the resulting segment contains as many bytes as are currently buffered for transmission.

Each TCP segment contains the header schematically depicted in Figure 6.3. The relevance of most of these fields will become apparent throughout this section. For now, we simply introduce them.

The SrcPort and DstPort fields identify the source and destination ports, respectively, just as in UDP. These two fields, plus the source and destination IP addresses, combine to uniquely identify each TCP connection. That is, TCP's demux key is given by the 4-tuple:

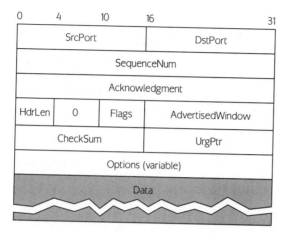

Figure 6.3 TCP header format.

Figure 6.4 Simplified illustration (showing only one direction) of TCP process, with data flow in one direction and ACKs in the other.

⟨ SrcPort, SrcIPAddr, DstPort, DstIPAddr ⟩.

Note that because TCP connections come and go, it is possible for a connection between a particular pair of ports to be established, used to send and receive data, and closed, and then at a later time for the same pair of ports to be involved in a second connection. We sometimes refer to this situation as two different *incarnations* of the same connection.

The Acknowledgment, SequenceNum, and AdvertisedWindow fields are all involved in TCP's sliding window algorithm. Because TCP is a byte-oriented protocol, each byte of data has a sequence number; the SequenceNum field contains the sequence number for the first byte of data carried in that segment. The Acknowledgment and AdvertisedWindow fields carry information about the flow of data going in the other direction. To simplify our discussion, we ignore the fact that data can flow in both directions, and we concentrate on data that has a particular SequenceNum flowing in one direction and Acknowledgment and AdvertisedWindow values flowing in the opposite direction, as illustrated in Figure 6.4. The use of these three fields is described more fully in Section 6.2.4.

The 6-bit Flags field is used to relay control information between TCP peers. The possible flags include SYN, FIN, RESET, PUSH, URG, and ACK. The SYN and FIN flags are used when establishing and terminating a TCP connection, respectively. Their use is described in Section 6.2.3. The ACK flag is set any time the Acknowledgment field is valid, implying that the receiver should pay attention to it. The URG flag signifies that this segment contains urgent data. When this flag is set, the UrgPtr field indicates where the non-urgent data contained in this segment begins. The urgent data is contained at the front of the segment body, up to and including a value of UrgPtr bytes into the segment. The PUSH flag signifies that the sender invoked the push operation, which indicates to the receiving side of TCP that it should notify the receiving process of this fact. We discuss these last two features more in Section 6.2.6. Finally, the RESET flag signifies that the receiver has become confused—for example, because it received a segment it did not expect to receive—and so wants to abort the connection.

Finally, the CheckSum field is used in exactly the same way as in UDP—it is computed over the TCP header, the TCP data, and the pseudoheader, which is made up of the source address, destination address, and length fields from the IP header. The checksum is required for TCP in both IPv4 and IPv6. Also, since the TCP header is of variable length (options can be attached after the mandatory fields), a HdrLen field is included that gives the length of the header in 32-bit words. This field is also known as the Offset field, since it measures the offset from the start of the packet to the start of the data.

6.2.3 Connection Establishment and Termination

A TCP connection begins with a client (caller) doing an active open to a server (callee). Assuming that the server had earlier done a passive open, the two sides engage in an exchange of messages to establish the connection. (Recall from Chapter 2 that a party wanting to initiate a connection performs an active open, while a party willing to accept a connection does a passive open.) Only after this connection-establishment phase is over do the two sides begin sending data. Likewise, as soon as a participant is done sending data, it closes its half of the connection, which causes TCP to initiate a round of connection-termination messages. Notice that while connection setup is an asymmetric activity—one side does a passive open and the other side does an active open—connection teardown is symmetric—each side has to close the connection independently. Therefore, it is possible for one side to have done a close, meaning that it can no longer send data, but for the other side to keep its half of the bidirectional connection open and to continue sending data.

Three-Way Handshake

The algorithm used by TCP to establish and terminate a connection is called a *three-way handshake*. We first describe the basic algorithm and then show how it is used by TCP. The three-way handshake involves the exchange of three messages between the client and the server, as illustrated by the timeline given in Figure 6.5.

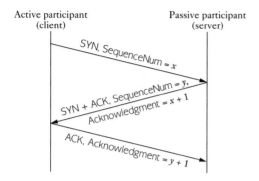

Active participant
(client)

Passive participant
(server)

SYN, SequenceNum = x

SYN + ACK, SequenceNum = y,
Acknowledgment = $x + 1$

ACK, Acknowledgment = $y + 1$

Figure 6.5   Timeline for three-way handshake algorithm.

The idea is that two parties want to agree on a set of parameters, which, in the case of opening a TCP connection, are the starting sequence numbers the two sides plan to use for their respective byte streams. In general, the parameters might be any facts that each side wants the other to know about. First, the client (the active participant) sends a segment to the server (the passive participant) stating the initial sequence number it plans to use (**Flags =** **SYN, SequenceNum** = x). The server then responds with a single segment that both acknowledges the client's sequence number (**Flags = ACK, Ack** = $x + 1$) and states its own beginning sequence number (**Flags = SYN, SequenceNum** = y). That is, both the **SYN** and **ACK** bits are set in the **Flags** field of this second message. Finally, the client responds with a third segment that acknowledges the server's sequence number (**Flags = ACK, Ack** = $y + 1$). The reason that each side acknowledges a sequence number that is one larger than the one sent is that the **Acknowledgment** field actually identifies the "next sequence number expected," thereby implicitly acknowledging all earlier sequence numbers. Although not shown in this timeline, a timer is scheduled for each of the first two segments, and if the expected response is not received, the segment is retransmitted.

You may be asking yourself why the client and server have to exchange starting sequence numbers with each other at connection setup time. It would be simpler if each side simply started at some "well-known" sequence number, such as 0. In fact, the TCP specification requires that each side of a connection select an initial starting sequence number at random. The reason for this is to protect against two incarnations of the same connection reusing the same sequence numbers too soon, that is, while there is still a chance that a segment from an earlier incarnation of a connection might interfere with a later incarnation of the connection.

State-Transition Diagram

TCP is complex enough that its specification includes a state-transition diagram. A copy of this diagram is given in Figure 6.6. This diagram shows only the states involved in opening a connection (everything above ESTABLISHED) and in closing a connection (everything

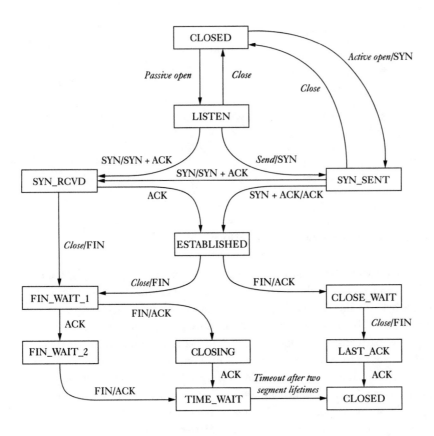

Figure 6.6 TCP state-transition diagram.

below ESTABLISHED). Everything that goes on while a connection is open—i.e., the operation of the sliding window algorithm—is hidden in the ESTABLISHED state.

TCP's state-transition diagram is fairly easy to understand. Each circle denotes a state that any TCP connection can find itself in. All connections start in the CLOSED state. As the connection progresses, the connection moves from state to state according to the arcs. Each arc is labeled with a tag of the form *event/action*. Thus, if a connection is in the LISTEN state and a SYN segment arrives (i.e., a segment with the **SYN** flag set), the connection makes a transition to the SYN_RCVD state and takes the action of replying with an ACK + SYN segment.

Notice that two kinds of events trigger a state transition: (1) a segment arrives from the peer (e.g., the event on the arc from LISTEN to SYN_RCVD), and (2) the local application process invokes an operation on TCP (e.g., the *active open* event on the arc from CLOSE to SYN_SENT). In other words, TCP's state-transition diagram effectively defines the *semantics* of both its peer-to-peer interface and its service interface, as defined in Section 1.3.1. The *syntax* of these two interfaces is given by the segment format (as illustrated in Figure 6.3), and by some application programming interface (an example of which is given in Section 6.4), respectively.

Now let's trace the typical transitions taken through the diagram in Figure 6.6. Keep in mind that at each end of the connection, TCP makes different transitions from state to state. When opening a connection, the server first invokes a passive open operation on TCP, which causes TCP to move to the LISTEN state. At some later time, the client does an active open, which causes its end of the connection to send a SYN segment to the server and to move to the SYN_SENT state. When the SYN segment arrives at the server, it moves to the SYN_RCVD state and responds with a SYN+ACK segment. The arrival of this segment causes the client to move to the ESTABLISHED state and to send an ACK back to the server. When this ACK arrives, the server finally moves to the ESTABLISHED state. In other words, we have just traced the three-way handshake.

There are three things to notice about the connection-establishment half of the state-transition diagram. First, if the client's ACK to the server is lost, corresponding to the third leg of the three-way handshake, then the connection still functions correctly. This is because the client side is already in the ESTABLISHED state, so the local application process can start sending data to the other end. Each of these data segments will have the ACK flag set, and the correct value in the Acknowledgment field, so the server will move to the ESTABLISHED state when the first data segment arrives. This is actually an important point about TCP— every segment reports what sequence number the sender is expecting to see next, even if this repeats the same sequence number contained in one or more previous segments.

The second thing to notice about the state-transition diagram is that there is a funny transition out of the LISTEN state whenever the local process invokes a *send* operation on TCP. That is, it is possible for a passive participant to identify both ends of the connection (i.e., itself and the remote participant that it is willing to have connect to it), and then for it to change its mind about waiting for the other side and instead actively establish the connection. To the best of our knowledge, this is a feature of TCP that no system-specific interface allows the application process to take advantage of.

The final thing to notice about the diagram is the arcs that are not shown. Specifically, most of the states that involve sending a segment to the other side also schedule a timeout that eventually causes the segment to be resent if the expected response does not happen. These retransmissions are not depicted in the state-transition diagram.

Turning our attention now to the process of terminating a connection, the important thing to keep in mind is that the application process on both sides of the connection must independently close its half of the connection. This complicates the state-transition diagram because it must account for the possibility that the two sides invoke the *close* operator at the same time, as well as the possibility that first one side invokes close and then at some later time, the other side invokes close. Thus, on any one side there are three combinations of transitions that get a connection from the ESTABLISHED state to the CLOSED state:

- This side closes first:
  ESTABLISHED → FIN_WAIT_1 → FIN_WAIT_2 → TIME_WAIT → CLOSED.

- The other side closes first:
  ESTABLISHED → CLOSE_WAIT → LAST_ACK → CLOSED.

- Both sides close at the same time:
  ESTABLISHED → FIN_WAIT_1 → CLOSING → TIME_WAIT → CLOSED.

There is actually a fourth, although rare, sequence of transitions that lead to the CLOSED state; it follows the arc from FIN_WAIT_1 to TIME_WAIT. We leave it as an exercise for you to figure out what combination of circumstances leads to this fourth possibility.

The main thing to recognize about connection teardown is that a connection in the TIME_WAIT state cannot move to the CLOSED state until it has waited for two times the maximum amount of time an IP datagram might live in the Internet (i.e., 120 seconds). The reason for this is that while the local side of the connection has sent an ACK in response to the other side's FIN segment, it does not know that the ACK was successfully delivered. As a consequence, the other side might retransmit its FIN segment, and this second FIN segment might be delayed in the network. If the connection were allowed to move directly to the CLOSED state, then another pair of application processes might come along and open the same connection (i.e., use the same pair of port numbers), and the delayed FIN segment from the earlier incarnation of the connection would immediately initiate the termination of the later incarnation of that connection.

6.2.4 Sliding Window Revisited

We are now ready to discuss TCP's variant of the sliding window algorithm. As discussed in Section 3.5.2, the sliding window serves several purposes: (1) it guarantees the reliable delivery of data, (2) it ensures that data is delivered in order, and (3) it enforces flow control between the sender and the receiver. TCP's use of the sliding window algorithm is the same as we saw in Section 3.5.2 in the case of the first two of these three functions. Where TCP differs from the earlier algorithm is that it folds the flow-control function in as well. In particular, rather than having a fixed-sized sliding window, the receiver *advertises* a window size to the sender. This is done using the AdvertisedWindow field in the TCP header. The sender is then limited to having no more than a value of AdvertisedWindow bytes of unacknowledged data at any given time. The receiver selects a suitable value for AdvertisedWindow based on the amount of memory allocated to the connection for the purpose of buffering data. The idea is to keep the sender from overrunning the receiver's buffer. We discuss this at greater length below.

Reliable and Ordered Delivery

To see how the sending and receiving sides of TCP interact with each other to implement reliable and ordered delivery, consider the situation illustrated in Figure 6.7. TCP on the sending

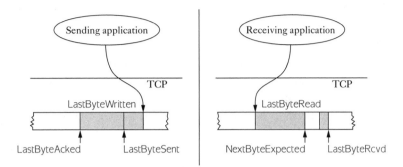

Figure 6.7   Relationship between TCP send buffer (left) and receive buffer (right).

side (pictured on the left) maintains a send buffer. This buffer is used to store data that has been sent but not yet acknowledged, as well as data that has been written by the sending application, but not transmitted. On the receiving side, TCP maintains a receive buffer. This buffer holds data that arrives out of order, as well as data that is in the correct order (i.e., there are no missing bytes earlier in the stream) but that the application process has not yet had the chance to read.

To make the following discussion simpler to follow, we initially ignore the fact that both the buffers and the sequence numbers are of some finite size, and hence will eventually wrap around. Also, we do not distinguish between a pointer into a buffer where a particular byte of data is stored and the sequence number for that byte.

Looking first at the sending side, three pointers are maintained into the send buffer, each with an obvious meaning: LastByteAcked, LastByteSent, and LastByteWritten. Clearly,

$$LastByteAcked \leq LastByteSent$$

since the receiver cannot have acknowledged a byte that has not yet been sent, and

$$LastByteSent \leq LastByteWritten$$

since TCP cannot send a byte that the application process has not yet written. Also note that none of the bytes to the left of LastByteAcked need to be saved in the buffer because they have already been acknowledged, and none of the bytes to the right of LastByteWritten need to be buffered because they have not yet been generated.

A similar set of pointers (sequence numbers) are maintained on the receiving side: LastByteRead, NextByteExpected, and LastByteRcvd. The inequalities are a little less intuitive, however, because of the problem of out-of-order delivery. The first relationship

$$LastByteRead < NextByteExpected$$

is true because a byte cannot be read by the application until it is received *and* all preceding bytes have also been received. NextByteExpected points to the byte immediately after the latest byte to meet this criterion. Second,

$$NextByteExpected \leq LastByteRcvd + 1$$

since, if data has arrived in order, NextByteExpected points to the byte after NextByteExpected, whereas if data has arrived out of order, NextByteExpected points to the start of the first gap in the data, as in Figure 6.7. Note that bytes to the left of LastByteRead need not be buffered because they have already been read by the local application process, and bytes to the right of LastByteRcvd need not be buffered because they have not yet arrived.

Flow Control

Most of the above discussion is similar to that found in Section 3.5.2, the only real difference being that this time we elaborated on the fact that the sending and receiving application processes are filling and emptying their local buffer, respectively. (The earlier discussion glossed over the fact that data arriving from an upstream node was filling the send buffer, and data being transmitted to a downstream node was emptying the receive buffer).

You should make sure you understand this much before proceeding, because now comes the point where the two algorithms differ more significantly. In what follows, we reintroduce the fact that both buffers are of some finite size, denoted MaxSendBuffer and MaxRcvBuffer, although we don't worry about the details of how they are implemented. In other words, we are only interested in the number of bytes being buffered, not in where those bytes are actually stored.

Recall that in a sliding window protocol, the size of the window sets the amount of data that can be sent without waiting for acknowledgment from the receiver. Thus, the receiver throttles the sender by advertising a window that is no larger than the amount of data that it can buffer. Observe that TCP on the receive side must keep

$$LastByteRcvd - NextByteRead \leq MaxRcvBuffer$$

to avoid overflowing its buffer. It therefore advertises a window size of

$$AdvertisedWindow = MaxRcvBuffer - (LastByteRcvd - NextByteRead),$$

which represents the amount of free space remaining in its buffer. As data arrives, the receiver acknowledges it as long as all the preceding bytes have also arrived. In addition, LastByteRcvd moves to the right (is incremented), meaning that the advertised window potentially shrinks. Whether or not it shrinks depends on how fast the local application process is consuming data. If the local process is reading data just as fast as it arrives (causing NextByteRead to be incremented at the same rate as LastByteRcvd), then the advertised window stays open (i.e., AdvertisedWindow = MaxRcvBuffer). If, however, the receiving process falls behind, perhaps because it performs a very expensive operation on each byte of data that it reads, then the advertised window grows smaller with every segment that arrives, until it eventually goes to 0.

TCP on the send side must then adhere to the advertised window it gets from the receiver. This means that at any given time, it must ensure that

$$LastByteSent - LastByteAcked \leq AdvertisedWindow.$$

Said another way, the sender computes an *effective* window that limits how much data it can send:

$$\text{EffectiveWindow} = \text{AdvertisedWindow} - (\text{LastByteSent} - \text{LastByteAcked})$$

Clearly, EffectiveWindow must be greater than 0 before the source can send more data. It is possible, therefore, that a segment arrives acknowledging x bytes, thereby allowing the sender to increment LastByteAcked by x, but because the receiving process was not reading any data, the advertised window is now x bytes smaller than the time before. In such a situation, the sender would be able to free buffer space, but not to send any more data.

All the while this is going on, the send side must also make sure that the local application process does not overflow the send buffer, that is, that

$$\text{LastByteWritten} - \text{LastByteAcked} \leq \text{MaxSendBuffer}.$$

If the sending process tries to write y bytes to TCP, but

$$(\text{LastByteWritten} - \text{LastByteAcked}) + y > \text{MaxSendBuffer},$$

then TCP blocks the sending process and does not allow it to generate more data.

It is now possible to understand how a slow receiving process ultimately stops a fast sending process. First, the receive buffer fills up, which means the advertised window shrinks to 0. An advertised window of 0 means that the sending side cannot transmit any data, even though data it has previously sent has been successfully acknowledged. Finally, not being able to transmit any data means that the send buffer fills up, which ultimately causes TCP to block the sending process. As soon as the receiving process starts to read data again, the receive-side TCP is able to open its window back up, which allows the send-side TCP to transmit data out of its buffer. When this data is eventually acknowledged, LastByteAcked is incremented, the buffer space holding this acknowledged data becomes free, and the sending process is unblocked and allowed to proceed.

There is only one remaining detail that must be resolved—how does the sending side know that the advertised window is no longer 0? As mentioned above, TCP *always* sends a segment in response to a received data segment, and this response contains the latest values for the Acknowledge and AdvertisedWindow fields, even if these values have not changed since the last time they were sent. The problem is this. Once the receive side has advertised a window size of 0, the sender is not permitted to send any more data, which means it has no way to discover that the advertised window is no longer 0 at some time in the future. TCP on the receive side does not spontaneously send nondata segments; it only sends them in response to an arriving data segment.

TCP deals with this situation as follows. Whenever the other side advertises a window size of 0, the sending side persists in sending a segment with 1 byte of data every so often. It knows that this data will probably not be accepted, but it tries anyway, because each of these 1-byte segments triggers a response that contains the current advertised window. Eventually, one of these 1-byte probes triggers a response that reports a nonzero advertised window.

Bandwidth	Time until Wraparound
T1 (1.5 Mbps)	6.4 hours
Ethernet (10 Mbps)	57 minutes
T3 (45 Mbps)	13 minutes
FDDI (100 Mbps)	6 minutes
STS-3 (155 Mbps)	4 minutes
STS-12 (622 Mbps)	55 seconds
STS-24 (1.2 Gbps)	28 seconds

Table 6.1 Time until 32-bit sequence number space wraps around.

▶ Note that the reason the sending side periodically sends this probe segment is that TCP is designed to make the receive side as simple as possible—it simply responds to segments from the sender, and it never initiates any activity on its own. This is an example of a well-recognized (although not universally applied) protocol design rule, which, for lack of a better name, we call the *smart sender/dumb receiver* rule. Recall that we saw another example of this rule when we discussed the use of NAKs in Section 3.5.2.

Keeping the Pipe Full

We now turn our attention to the size of the SequenceNum and AdvertisedWindow fields and the implications of their sizes on TCP's correctness and performance. TCP's SequenceNum field is 32 bits long and its AdvertisedWindow field is 16 bits long, meaning that TCP has easily satisfied the requirement of the sliding window algorithm that the sequence number space be twice as big as the window size: $2^{32} >> 2 \times 2^{16}$. However, this requirement is not the interesting thing about these two fields. Consider each field in turn.

The relevance of the 32-bit sequence number space is that the sequence number used on a given connection might wrap around—a byte with sequence number x could be sent at one time, and then at a later time, a second byte with the same sequence number x might be sent. Once again, we assume that packets cannot survive in the Internet for longer than 60 seconds. Thus, we need to make sure that the sequence number does not wrap around within a 60-second period of time. Whether or not this happens depends on how fast data can be transmitted over the Internet, that is, how fast the 32-bit sequence number space can be consumed. (This discussion assumes that we are trying to consume the sequence number space as fast as possible, but of course we will be if we are doing our job of keeping the pipe full.) Table 6.1 shows how long it takes for the sequence number to wrap around on networks with various bandwidths.

As you can see, the 32-bit sequence number space is adequate for today's networks, but it won't be long (STS-12) until a larger sequence number space is needed. The IETF is already

Bandwidth	Delay × Bandwidth Product
T1 (1.5 Mbps)	18 KB
Ethernet (10 Mbps)	122 KB
T3 (45 Mbps)	549 KB
FDDI (100 Mbps)	1.2 MB
STS-3 (155 Mbps)	1.8 MB
STS-12 (622 Mbps)	7.4 MB
STS-24 (1.2 Gbps)	14.8 MB

Table 6.2   Required window size for 100 ms RTT.

working on an extension to TCP that effectively extends the sequence number space to protect against the sequence number wrapping around.

The relevance of the 16-bit AdvertisedWindow field is that it must be big enough to allow the sender to keep the pipe full. Clearly, the receiver is free to not open the window as large as the AdvertisedWindow field allows; we are interested in the situation in which the receiver has enough buffer space to handle as much data as the largest possible AdvertisedWindow allows.

In this case, it is not just the network bandwidth but the delay × bandwidth product that dictates how big the AdvertisedWindow field needs to be—the window needs to be opened far enough to allow a full delay × bandwidth product's worth of data to be transmitted. Assuming an RTT of 100 ms (a typical number for a crosscountry connection in the U.S.), Table 6.2 gives the delay × bandwidth product for several network technologies.

As you can see, TCP's AdvertisedWindow field is in even worse shape than its SequenceNum field—it is not big enough to handle even a T3 connection across the continental U.S., since a 16-bit field allows us to advertise a window of only 64 KB. The very same TCP extension mentioned above provides a mechanism for effectively increasing the size of the advertised window.

6.2.5   Adaptive Retransmission

Because TCP guarantees the reliable delivery of data, it retransmits each segment if an ACK is not received in a certain period of time. TCP sets this timeout as a function of the RTT it expects between the two ends of the connection. Unfortunately, given the range of possible RTTs between any pair of hosts in the Internet, as well as the variation in RTT between the same two hosts over time, choosing an appropriate timeout value is not that easy. To address this problem, TCP uses an adaptive retransmission mechanism. We now describe this mechanism and how it has evolved over time as the Internet community has gained more experience using TCP.

Original Algorithm

We begin with a simple algorithm for computing a timeout value between a pair of hosts. This is the algorithm that was originally described in the TCP specification—and the following description presents it in those terms—but it could be used by any end-to-end protocol.

The idea is to keep a running average of the RTT and then to compute the timeout as a function of this RTT. Specifically, every time TCP sends a data segment, it records the time. When an ACK for that segment arrives, TCP reads the time again, and then takes the difference between these two times as a SampleRTT. TCP then computes an EstimatedRTT as a weighted average between the previous estimate and this new sample. That is,

$$\text{EstimatedRTT} = \alpha \times \text{EstimatedRTT} + \beta \times \text{SampleRTT}$$

where

$$\alpha + \beta = 1.$$

The parameters α and β are selected to *smooth* the EstimatedRTT. A large β value tracks changes in the RTT but is perhaps too heavily influenced by temporary fluctuations. On the other hand, a large α value is more stable but perhaps not quick enough to adapt to real changes. The original TCP specification recommended a setting of α between 0.8 and 0.9 and β between 0.1 and 0.2. TCP then uses EstmatedRTT to compute the timeout in a rather conservative way:

$$\text{TimeOut} = 2 \times \text{EstimatedRTT}.$$

Karn/Partridge Algorithm

After several years of use on the Internet, a rather obvious flaw was discovered in this simple algorithm. The problem was that an ACK does not really acknowledge a transmission; it actually acknowledges the receipt of data. In other words, whenever a segment is retransmitted and then an ACK arrives at the sender, it is impossible to determine if this ACK should be associated with the first or the second transmission of the segment for the purpose of measuring the sample RTT. It is necessary to know which transmission to associate it with so as to compute an accurate SampleRTT. As illustrated in Figure 6.8, if you assume that the ACK is for the original transmission but it was really for the second, then the SampleRTT is too large (a), while if you assume that the ACK is for the second transmission but it was actually for the first, then the SampleRTT is too small (b).

The solution is surprisingly simple. Whenever TCP retransmits a segment, it stops taking samples of the RTT; it only measures SampleRTT for segments that have been sent only once. This solution is known as the Karn/Partridge algorithm, after its inventors. Their proposed fix also includes a second small change to TCP's timeout mechanism. Each time TCP retransmits, it sets the next timeout to be twice the last timeout, rather than basing it on the last EstimatedRTT. That is, Karn and Partridge proposed that TCP use exponential backoff, just as the Ethernet does.

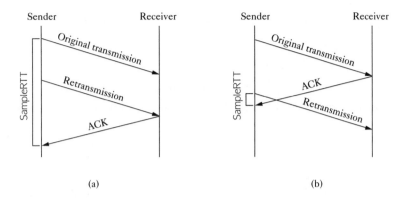

Figure 6.8 Associating the ACK with original transmission (a) versus retransmission (b).

Jacobson/Karels Algorithm

The Karn/Partridge algorithm was introduced at a time when the Internet was suffering from high levels of network congestion. Their approach was designed to fix some of the causes of that congestion, and although it was an improvement, the congestion was not eliminated. A couple of years later, two other researchers—Jacobson and Karels—proposed a more drastic change to TCP to battle congestion. The bulk of that proposed change is described in Chapter 8. Here, we focus on the aspect of that proposal that is related to deciding when to timeout and retransmit a segment.

As an aside, it should be clear how the timeout mechanism is related to congestion—if you timeout too soon, you may unnecessarily retransmit a segment, which only adds to the load on the network. As we will see in Chapter 8, the other reason for needing an accurate timeout value is that a timeout is taken to imply congestion, which triggers a congestion-control mechanism. Finally, note that there is nothing about the Jacobson/Karels timeout computation that is specific to TCP. It could be used by any end-to-end protocol.

The main problem with the original computation is that it does not take the variance of the sample RTTs into account. Intuitively, if the variation among samples is small, then the EstimatedRTT can be better trusted and there is no reason for multiplying this estimate by 2 to compute the timeout. On the other hand, a large variance in the samples suggests that the timeout value should not be too tightly coupled to the EstimatedRTT.

In the new approach, the sender measures a new SampleRTT as before. It then folds this new sample into the timeout calculation as follows:

Difference = SampleRTT − EstimatedRTT
EstimatedRTT = EstimatedRTT + (δ × Difference)
Deviation = Deviation + δ (|Difference| − Deviation)

where δ is a fraction between 0 and 1. That is, we calculate both the mean RTT and the variation in that mean.

TCP then computes the timeout value as a function of both EstimatedRTT and Deviation as follows:

$$\text{TimeOut} = \mu \times \text{EstimatedRTT} + \phi \times \text{Deviation}$$

where based on experience, μ is typically set to 1 and ϕ is set to 4. Thus, when the variance is small, TimeOut is close to EstimatedRTT, while a large variance causes the Deviation term to dominate the calculation.

Implementation

There are two items of note regarding the implementation of timeouts in TCP. The first is that it is possible to implement the calculation for EstimatedRTT and Deviation without using floating-point arithmetic. Instead, the whole calculation is scaled by 2^n, with δ selected to be $1/2^n$. This allows us to do integer arithmetic, implementing multiplication and division using shifts, thereby achieving higher performance. The resulting calculation is given by the following code fragment, where $n = 3$ (i.e., $\delta = 1/8$). Note that EstimatedRTT and Deviation are stored in their scaled up forms, while the value of SampleRTT at the start of the code and of TimeOut at the end are real, unscaled values. If you find the code hard to follow, you might want to try plugging some real numbers into it and verifying that it gives the same results as the equations above.

```
{
    SampleRTT -= (EstimatedRTT >> 3);
    EstimatedRTT += SampleRTT;
    if (SampleRTT < 0)
        SampleRTT = -SampleRTT;
    SampleRTT -= (Deviation >> 3);
    Deviation += SampleRTT;
    TimeOut = (EstimatedRTT >> 3) + (Deviation >> 1);
}
```

The second point of note is that Jacobson and Karels's algorithm is only as good as the clock used to read the current time. On a typical Berkeley Unix implementation, the clock granularity is as large as 500 ms, which is significantly larger than the average crosscountry RTT of somewhere between 100 and 200 ms. To make matters worse, the Berkeley Unix implementation of TCP only checks to see if a timeout should happen every time this 500-ms clock ticks, and it only takes a sample of the round-trip time once per RTT. The combination of these two factors quite often means that a timeout happens 1 second after the segment was transmitted. Once again, the proposed extensions to TCP include a mechanism that makes this RTT calculation a bit more precise.

6.2.6 Record Boundaries

As mentioned earlier in this section, TCP is a byte-stream protocol. This means that the number of bytes written by the sender are not necessarily the same as the number of bytes read by the receiver. For example, the application might write 8 bytes, then 2 bytes, then 20 bytes to a TCP connection, while on the receiving side, the application reads 5 bytes at a time inside a loop that iterates 6 times. TCP does not interject record boundaries between the eighth and ninth bytes, nor between the tenth and eleventh bytes. This is in contrast to a message-oriented protocol, such as UDP, in which the message that is sent is exactly the same length as the message that is received.

Even though TCP is a byte-stream protocol, it has two different features that can be used by the sender to effectively insert record boundaries into this byte stream, thereby informing the receiver how to break the stream of bytes into records. (Being able to mark record boundaries is useful, for example, in many database applications.) Both of these features were originally included in TCP for completely different reasons; they have only come to be used for this purpose over time.

The first mechanism is the *push* operation. Originally, this mechanism was designed to allow the sending process to tell TCP that it should send whatever bytes it had collected to its peer. This was, and still is, used in terminal emulators like Telnet because each byte has to be sent as soon as it is typed. However, push can be used to implement record boundaries because the specification says that TCP should inform the receiving application that a push was performed; this is the reason for the PUSH flag in the TCP header. This act of informing the receiver of a push can be interpreted as marking a record boundary.

The second mechanism for inserting end-of-record markers into a byte stream is the urgent data feature, as implemented by the URG flag and the UrgPtr field in the TCP header. Originally, the urgent data mechanism was designed to allow the sending application to send *out-of-band* data to its peer. By "out of band" we mean data that is separate from the normal flow of data, e.g., a command to interrupt an operation already under way. This out-of-band data was identified in the segment using the UrgPtr field and was to be delivered to the receiving process as soon as it arrived, even if that meant delivering it before data with an earlier sequence number. Over time, however, this feature has not been used, so instead of signifying "urgent" data, it has come to be used to signify "special" data, such as a record marker. This use has developed because, as with the push operation, TCP on the receiving side must inform the application that "urgent data" has arrived. That is, the urgent data in itself is not important. It is the fact that the sending process can effectively send a signal to the receiver that is important.

Of course, the application program is always free to insert record boundaries without any assistance from TCP. For example, it can send a field that indicates the length of a record that is to follow, or it can insert its own record boundary markers into the data stream.

6.3 Remote Procedure Call

As discussed in Chapter 1, a common pattern of communication used by application programs is the request/reply paradigm, also called message transaction: a client sends a request message to a server, the server responds with a reply message, and the client blocks (suspends execution) waiting for this response. Figure 6.9 illustrates the basic interaction between the client and server in such a message transaction. A transport protocol that supports the request/reply paradigm is much more than a UDP message going in one direction, followed by a UDP message going in the other direction.

It also involves overcoming all of the limitations of the underlying network, as outlined in the problem statement at the beginning of this chapter. While TCP overcomes these limitations by providing a reliable byte-stream channel, it provides very different semantics from the request/reply abstraction that many applications need. This section looks at how we provide such an abstraction.

The request/reply communication paradigm is at the heart of a Remote Procedure Call (RPC) mechanism. RPC is a popular mechanism for structuring distributed systems because it is based on the semantics of a local procedure call—the application program makes a call into a procedure without regard for whether it is local or remote and blocks until the call returns. A complete RPC mechanism actually involves two major components:

1 a protocol that manages the messages sent between the client and the server processes and that deals with the potentially undesirable properties of the underlying network;

2 programming language and compiler support to package the arguments into a request message on the client machine and then to translate this message back into the arguments on the server machine, and likewise with the return value (this piece of the RPC mechanism is usually called a *stub compiler*).

What Layer Is RPC?

Once again, the "what layer is this" issue raises its ugly head. To many people, especially those who adhere to the Internet architecture, RPC is implemented on top of a transport protocol (usually UDP) and so cannot itself (by definition) be a transport protocol. It is equally valid, however, to argue that the Internet should have an RPC protocol, since it offers a process-to-process service that is fundamentally different from that offered by TCP and UDP. The usual response to such a suggestion, however, is that the Internet architecture does not prohibit network designers from implementing their own RPC protocol on top of UDP. (In general, UDP is viewed as the Internet architecture's "escape hatch," since effectively it just adds a layer of demultiplexing to IP.) Whichever side of the issue of whether the Internet should have an official RPC protocol you support, the important point is that the way you implement RPC in the Internet architecture says nothing about whether RPC should be considered a transport protocol or not.

Figure 6.10 schematically depicts what happens when a client invokes a remote procedure. First, the client calls a local stub for the procedure, passing it the arguments required by the procedure. This stub hides the fact that the procedure is remote by translating the arguments into a request message and then invoking an RPC protocol to send the request message to the server machine. At the server, the RPC protocol delivers the request message to the server stub, which translates it into the arguments to the procedure and then calls the local procedure. After the server procedure completes, it returns the answer to the server stub, which packages this return value in a reply message that it hands off to the RPC protocol for transmission back to the client. The RPC protocol on the client passes this message up to the client stub, which translates it into a return value that it returns to the client program.

This section considers just the protocol-related aspects of an RPC mechanism. That is, it ignores the stubs and focuses instead on the RPC protocol that transmits messages between client and server; the transformation of arguments into messages and vice versa is covered in Chapter 7. An RPC protocol, as we will see, fulfills a different set of needs than either TCP or UDP, and it performs a rather complicated set of functions. Indeed, even though we call this an RPC "protocol" in the above discussion, the task being performed is complicated enough that instead of treating RPC as a single, monolithic protocol, we develop it as a "stack" of three smaller protocols: BLAST, CHAN, and SELECT. Each of these smaller protocols, which we sometimes call a *microprotocol*, contains a single algorithm that addresses one of the problems outlined at the start of this chapter. As a brief overview:

Interestingly, there are other people who believe that RPC is the most interesting protocol in the world and that TCP/IP is just what you do when you want to go "off site." This is the predominant view of the operating systems community, which has built countless OS kernels for distributed systems that contain exactly one protocol—you guessed it, RPC—running on top of a network device driver.

The water gets even muddier when you implement RPC as a combination of three different microprotocols, as is the case in this section. In such a situation, which of the three is the "transport" protocol? Our answer to this question is that any protocol that offers process-to-process service, as opposed to node-to-node or host-to-host service, qualifies as a transport protocol. Thus, RPC is a transport protocol, and in fact can be implemented from a combination of microprotocols that are themselves valid transport protocols.

- BLAST: fragments and reassembles large messages;

- CHAN: synchronizes request and reply messages;

- SELECT: dispatches request messages to the correct process.

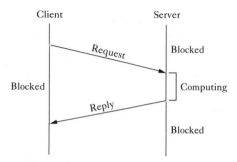

Figure 6.9   Timeline for RPC.

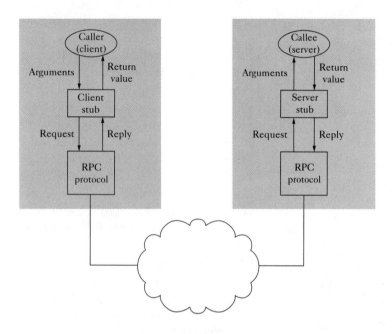

Figure 6.10   Complete RPC mechanism.

These microprotocols are complete, self-contained protocols that can be used in different combinations to provide different end-to-end services. Section 6.3.4 shows how they can be combined to implement RPC.

Note that BLAST, CHAN, and SELECT are not standard protocols in the sense that TCP, UDP, and IP are. They are simply protocols of our own invention, but ones that demonstrate the various algorithms needed to implement RPC. They also serve to illustrate the protocol design process, and in particular, a design philosophy in which each protocol is limited to doing just one thing and then is composed with other one-function protocols to provide more complex communication services. This is in contrast to designing protocols that attempt to provide a wide range of services to many different applications. Because this section is not constrained by the artifacts of what has been designed in the past, it provides a particularly good opportunity to examine the principles of protocol design.

6.3.1 Bulk Transfer (BLAST)

The first problem we are going to tackle is how to turn an underlying network that delivers messages of some small size (say, 1 KB) into a service that delivers messages of a much larger size (say, 32 KB). While 32 KB does not qualify as "arbitrarily large," it is large enough to be of practical use for many applications, including most distributed file systems. Ultimately, a stream-based protocol like TCP (see Section 6.2) will be needed to support an arbitrarily large message, since any message-oriented protocol is likely to have some upper limit to the size of the message it can handle, and you can always imagine needing to transmit a message that is larger than this limit.

We have already examined the basic technique that is used to transmit a large message over a network that can accommodate only smaller messages—fragmentation and reassembly. We now describe the BLAST protocol, which uses this technique. One of the unique properties of BLAST is how hard it tries to deliver all the fragments of a message. Unlike the AAL segmentation/reassembly mechanism used with ATM (see Section 4.3) or the IP fragmentation/reassembly mechanism (see Section 5.2), BLAST attempts to recover from dropped fragments by retransmitting them. However, BLAST does not go so far as to *guarantee* message delivery. The significance of this design choice will become clear later in this section.

BLAST Algorithm

The basic idea of BLAST is for the sender to break a large message passed to it by some high-level protocol into a set of smaller fragments, and then for it to transmit these fragments back to back over the network. Hence the name BLAST—the protocol does not wait for any of the fragments to be acknowledged before sending the next. The receiver then sends a *selective retransmission request* (SRR) back to the sender, indicating which fragments arrived and which did not. (The SRR message is sometimes called a *partial* or *selective* acknowledgment.) Finally, the sender retransmits the missing fragments. In the case in which all the fragments have arrived, the SRR serves to fully acknowledge the message. Figure 6.11 gives a representative timeline for protocol BLAST.

We now consider the send and receive sides of BLAST in more detail. On the sending side, after fragmenting the message and transmitting each of the fragments, the sender sets a timer called DONE. Whenever an SRR arrives, the sender retransmits the requested fragments and resets timer DONE. Should the SRR indicate that all the fragments have arrived, the sender frees its copy of the message and cancels timer DONE. If timer DONE ever expires, the sender frees its copy of the message; i.e., it gives up.

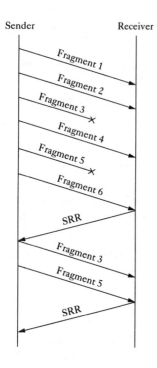

Figure 6.11   Representative timeline for BLAST.

On the receiving side, whenever the first fragment of a message arrives, the receiver initializes a data structure to hold the individual fragments as they arrive and sets a timer LAST_FRAG. Each time a fragment for that message arrives, the receiver adds it to this data structure, and should all the fragments then be present, it reassembles them into a complete message and passes this message up to the higher-level protocol. There are four exceptional conditions, however, that the receiver watches for:

- If the last fragment arrives (the last fragment is specially marked) but the message is not complete, then the receiver determines which fragments are missing and sends an SRR to the sender. It also sets a timer called RETRY.

- If timer LAST_FRAG expires, then the receiver determines which fragments are missing and sends an SRR to the sender. It also sets timer RETRY.

- If timer RETRY expires for the first or second time, then the receiver determines which fragments are still missing and retransmits an SRR message.

- If timer RETRY expires for the third time, then the receiver frees the fragments that have arrived and cancels timer LAST_FRAG; i.e., it gives up.

There are three aspects of BLAST worth noting. First, two different events trigger the initial transmission of an SRR: the arrival of the last fragment and the firing of the LAST_FRAG timer. In the case of the former, because the network may reorder packets, the arrival of the last fragment does not necessarily imply that an earlier fragment is missing (it may just be late in arriving), but since this is the most likely explanation, BLAST aggressively sends an SRR message. In the latter case, we deduce that the last fragment was either lost or seriously delayed.

Second, the performance of BLAST does not critically depend on how carefully the timers are set. Timer DONE is used only to decide that it is time to give up and delete the message that is currently being worked on. This timer can be set to a fairly large value since its only purpose is to reclaim storage. Timer RETRY is only used to retransmit an SRR message. Any time the situation is so bad that a protocol is re-executing a failure-recovery process, performance is the last thing on its mind. Finally, timer LAST_FRAG has the potential to influence performance—it sometimes triggers the sending by the receiver of an SRR message—but this is an unlikely event: it only happens when the last fragment of the message happens to get dropped in the network.

Third, while BLAST is persistent in asking for and retransmitting missing fragments, it does not guarantee that the complete message will be delivered. To understand this, suppose that a message consists of only one or two fragments and that these fragments are lost. The receiver will never send an SRR, and the sender's DONE timer will eventually expire, causing the sender to release the message. To guarantee delivery, BLAST would need for the sender to timeout the interval it waits for an SRR and then retransmit the last set of fragments it had transmitted. While BLAST certainly could have been designed to do this, we chose not to because the purpose of BLAST is to deliver large messages, not to guarantee message delivery. Other protocols can be configured on top of BLAST to guarantee message delivery. You might wonder why we put any retransmission capability at all into BLAST if we need to put a guaranteed delivery mechanism above it anyway. The reason is that we'd prefer to retransmit only those fragments that were lost rather than having to retransmit the entire larger message whenever one fragment is lost. So we get the guarantees from the higher-level protocol but some improved efficiency by retransmitting fragments in BLAST.

BLAST Message Format

The BLAST header has to convey several pieces of information. First, it must contain some sort of message identifier so that all the fragments that belong to the same message can be identified. Second, there must be a way to identify where in the original message the individual fragments fit, and likewise, an SRR must be able to indicate which fragments have arrived and which are missing. Third, there must be a way to distinguish the last fragment, so that the receiver knows when it is time to check to see if all the fragments have arrived. Finally, it must be possible to distinguish a data message from an SRR message. Some of these items are encoded in a header field in an obvious way, but others can be done in a variety of different

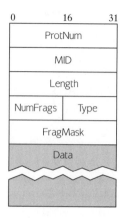

0   16   31

ProtNum	
MID	
Length	
NumFrags	Type
FragMask	
Data	

Figure 6.12 Format for BLAST message header.

ways. Figure 6.12 gives the header format used by BLAST. The following discussion explains the various fields and considers alternative designs.

The **MID** field uniquely identifies this message. All fragments that belong to the same message have the same value in their **MID** field. The only question is how many bits are needed for this field. This is similar to the question of how many bits are needed in the **SequenceNum** field for TCP. The central issue in deciding how many bits to use in the **MID** field has to do with how long it will take before this field wraps around and the protocol starts using message ids over again. If this happens too soon—i.e., the **MID** field is only a few bits long—then it is possible for the protocol to become confused by a message that was delayed in the network, so that an old incarnation of some message id is mistaken for a new incarnation of that same id. So, how many bits are enough to ensure that the amount of time it takes for the **MID** field to wrap around is longer than the amount of time a message can potentially be delayed in the network?

In the worst-case scenario, each BLAST message contains a single fragment that is 1 byte long, which means that BLAST might need to generate a new **MID** for every byte it sends. On a 10-Mbps Ethernet, this would mean generating a new **MID** roughly once every microsecond, while on a 1.2-Gbps STS-24 link, a new **MID** would be required once every 7 nanoseconds. Of course, this is a ridiculously conservative calculation—the overhead involved in preparing a message is going to be more than a microsecond. Thus, suppose a new **MID** is potentially needed once every microsecond, and a message may be delayed in the network for up to 60 seconds (our standard worst-case assumption for the Internet), then we need to ensure that there are more than 60 million **MID** values. While a 26-bit field would be sufficient ($2^{26} = 67,108,864$), it is easier to deal with header fields that are even multiples of a byte, so we will settle on a 32-bit **MID** field.

▶   This conservative (you could say paranoid) analysis of the MID field illustrates an important point. When designing a transport protocol, it is tempting to take shortcuts, since not all networks suffer from all the problems listed in the problem statement at the beginning of this chapter. For example, messages do not get stuck in an Ethernet for 60 seconds, and similarly, it is physically impossible to re-order messages on an Ethernet. The problem with this way of thinking, however, is that if you want the transport protocol to work over any kind of network, then you have to *design for the worst case*. This is because the real danger is that as soon as you assume that an Ethernet does not re-order packets, someone will come along and put a bridge or a router in the middle of it.

Let's move on to the other fields in the BLAST header. The Type field indicates whether this is a DATA message or an SRR message. Notice that while we certainly don't need 16 bits to represent these two types, as a general rule we like to keep the header fields aligned on 32-bit (word) boundaries, so as to improve processing efficiency. The ProtNum field identifies the high-level protocol that is configured on top of BLAST; incoming messages are demultiplexed to this protocol. The Length field indicates how many bytes of data are in *this* fragment; it has nothing to do with the length of the entire message. The NumFrags field indicates how many fragments are in this message. This field is used to determine when the last fragment has been received. An alternative is to include a flag that is only set for the last fragment.

Finally, the FragMask field is used to distinguish among fragments. It is a 32-bit field that is used as a bit mask. For messages of Type=DATA, the ith bit is 1 (all others are 0) to indicate that this message carries the ith fragment. For messages of Type=SRR, the ith bit is 1 to indicate that the ith fragment has arrived, and it is set to 0 to indicate that the ith fragment is missing. Note that there are several ways to identify fragments. For example, the header could have contained a simple "fragment ID" field, with this field set to i to denote the ith fragment. The tricky part with this approach, as opposed to a bit-vector, is how the SRR specifies which fragments have arrived and which have not. If it takes an n-bit number to identify each missing fragment—as opposed to a single bit in a fixed-sized bit-vector—then the SRR message will be of variable length, depending on how many fragments are missing. Variable-length headers are allowed, but they are a little trickier to process. On the other hand, one limitation of the BLAST header given above is that the length of the bit-vector limits each message to only 32 fragments. If the underlying network has an MTU of 1 KB, then this is sufficient to send up to 32-KB messages.

Implementation of BLAST

We conclude our discussion of BLAST by giving the x-kernel implementation of BLAST's xPush routine, which contains the for loop that generates and transmits all the fragments in a message. Notice that it is not necessary to calculate how long the last fragment is because the msgBreak operation automatically makes each fragment the lesser of the specified size (FRAGMENT_SIZE) and however many bytes are left in the message.

```
static XkReturn
blastPush(Sessn s, Msg *msg)
{
    int         num_frags, i;
    Msg         *fragment;
    char        *buf;
    BlastHdr    *hdr;
    BlastState  *state;

    /* get header template and set MID, incrementing last value used*/
    state = s->state;
    hdr = state->hdr_template;
    if (state->mid == MAX_SEQ_NUM)
        state->mid = 0;
    hdr->MID = ++state->mid;

    /* determine number of fragments */
    if (msgLen(msg) <= FRAGMENT_SIZE)
        num_frags = 1;
    else
        num_frags = (msgLen(msg) + FRAGMENT_SIZE - 1)/FRAGMENT_SIZE;
    hdr->NumFrags = num_frags;

    /* create and transmit individual fragments */
    for ( i=1; i <= num_frags; i++ )
    {

        /* carve a fragment off of original msg */
        msgConstructEmpty(fragment);
        msgBreak(msg, fragment, FRAGMENT_SIZE);

        /* fill in dynamic parts of header */
        hdr->len = msgLen(fragment);
        set_fragment_mask(hdr->mask, i);

        /* add header and send fragment */
        buf = msgPush(fragment, HDR_LEN);
        blast_hdr_store(hdr, buf, HDR_LEN, fragment);
        xPush(xGetDown(s, 0), fragment);

        /* save copy of fragment for future retransmit */
        save_for_retransmit(state->frag_list, fragment, i);
    }
    /* schedule DONE timer */
    state->event = evSchedule(giveup, 0, DONE);
    return;
}
```

6.3.2 Request/Reply (CHAN)

The next microprotocol, CHAN, implements the request/reply algorithm that is at the core of RPC. In terms of the common properties of transport protocols given in the problem statement at the beginning of this chapter, CHAN guarantees message delivery, ensures that only one copy of each message is delivered, and allows the communicating processes to synchronize with each other. In the case of this last item, the synchronization we are after mimics the behavior of a procedure call—the caller (client) blocks while waiting for a reply from the callee (server).

At-Most-Once Semantics

The name CHAN comes from the fact that the protocol implements a logical request/reply *channel* between a pair of participants. At any given time, there can be only one message transaction active on a given channel. Like the concurrent logical channel protocol described in Section 3.5.3, the participants have to open multiple channels if they want to have more than one request/reply transaction between them at the same time.

The most important property of each channel is that it preserves a semantics known as *at-most-once*. This means that for every request message that the client sends, at most one copy of that message is delivered to the server. Stated in terms of the RPC mechanism that CHAN is designed to support, for each time the client calls a remote procedure, that procedure is invoked at most one time on the server machine. We say "at most once" rather than "exactly once" because it is always possible that either the network or the server machine has failed, making it impossible to deliver even one copy of the request message.

As obvious as at-most-once sounds, not all RPC protocols support this behavior. Some support a semantics that is facetiously called *zero-or-more* semantics, that is, each invocation on a client results in the remote procedure being invoked zero or more times. It is not hard to understand how this would cause problems for a remote procedure that changed some local state variable (e.g., incremented a counter) or that had some externally visible side effect (e.g., launched a missile) each time it was invoked.

CHAN Algorithm

The request/reply algorithm has several subtle aspects, hence we develop it in stages. The basic algorithm is straightforward, as illustrated by the timeline given in Figure 6.13. The client sends a request message and the server acknowledges it. Then, after executing the procedure, the server sends a reply message and the client acknowledges the reply.

Because the reply message often comes back with very little delay, and it is sometimes the case that the client turns around and makes a second request on the same channel immediately after receiving the first reply, this basic scenario can be optimized by using a technique called *implicit acknowledgments*. As illustrated in Figure 6.14, the reply message serves to acknowledge the request message, and a subsequent request acknowledges the preceding reply.

There are two factors that potentially complicate the rosy picture we have painted so far. The first is that either a message carrying data (a request message or a reply message) or

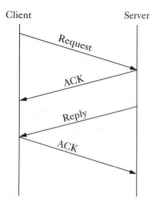

Figure 6.13   Simple time-line for CHAN.

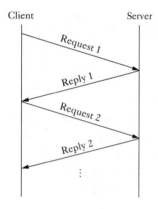

Figure 6.14   Timeline for CHAN when using implicit ACKs.

the ACK sent to acknowledge that message, may be lost in the network. To account for this possibility, both client and server save a copy of each message they send until an ACK for it has arrived. Each side also sets a RETRANSMIT timer and resends the message should this timer expire. Both sides reset this timer and try again some agreed-upon number of times before giving up and freeing the message.

Recall from Section 3.5.1 that this acknowledgment/timeout strategy means that it is possible for duplicate copies of a message to arrive—the original message arrives, the ACK is lost, and then the retransmission arrives. Thus, the receiver must remember what messages it has seen and discard any duplicates. This is done through the use of a **MID** field in the header.

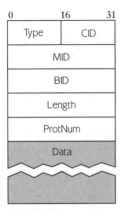

0   16   31

Type	CID
MID	
BID	
Length	
ProtNum	
Data	

Figure 6.15 Format for CHAN message header.

Any message whose **MID** field does not match the next expected **MID** is discarded instead of being passed up to the high-level protocol configured on top of CHAN.

The second complication is that the server may take an arbitrarily long time to produce the result, and worse yet, it may crash (either the process or the entire machine) may crash before generating the reply. Keep in mind that we are talking about the period of time after the server has acknowledged the request but before it has sent the reply. To help the client distinguish between a slow server and a dead server, CHAN's client side periodically sends an "are you alive" message to the server, and CHAN's server side responds with an ACK. Alternatively, the server could send "I am still alive" messages to the client without the client having first solicited them, but we prefer the client-initiated approach because it keeps the server as simple as possible (i.e., it has one less timer to manage).

CHAN Message Format

The CHAN message format is given in Figure 6.15. As with BLAST, the Type field specifies the type of the message; in this case, the possible types are REQ, REP, ACK, and PROBE. (PROBE is the "are you alive" message discussed above.) Similarly, the ProtNum field identifies the high-level protocol that depends on CHAN.

The CID field uniquely identifies the logical channel to which this message belongs. This is a 16-bit field, meaning that CHAN supports up to 64-K concurrent request/reply transactions between any pair of hosts. Of course, a given host can be participating in channels with many other hosts at the same time.

The MID field uniquely identifies each request/reply pair; the reply message has the same MID as the request. Note that because CHAN permits only one message transaction at a time on a given channel, you might think that a 1-bit MID field is sufficient, just as for the stop-and-wait algorithm presented in Section 3.5.1. However, as with BLAST, we have to be concerned about messages that wander around the network for an extended period of time and then suddenly appear at the destination, confusing CHAN. Thus, using much the same reasoning as we used in Section 6.3.1, CHAN uses a 32-bit MID field.

Finally, the BID field gives the *boot id* for the host. A machine's boot id is a number that is incremented each time the machine reboots; this number is read from disk, incremented, and written back to disk during the machine's startup procedure. This number is then put in every message sent by that host. The role played by the BID field is much the same as the role played by the large MID field—it protects against old messages suddenly appearing at the destination—although in this case, the old message is not due to an arbitrary delay in the network but rather to a machine that has crashed and rebooted.

To understand the use of the boot id, consider the following pathological situation. A client machine sends a request message with MID=0, then crashes and reboots, and then sends an unrelated request message, also with MID=0. The server may not have been aware that the client crashed and rebooted, and upon seeing a request message with MID=0, acknowledges it and discards it as a duplicate. To protect against this possibility, each side of CHAN makes sure that the ⟨BID, MID⟩ pair, not just the MID, matches what it is expecting. BID is also a 32-bit field, which means that if we assume that it takes at least 10 minutes to reboot a machine, it will wrap around once every 40 billion minutes (approximately 80,000 years). In effect, the BID and MID combine to form a unique 64-bit id for each transaction; the low-order 32 bits are incremented for each transaction but reset to 0 when the machine reboots, and the high-order 32 bits are incremented each time the machine reboots.

Synchronous versus Asynchronous Protocols

One way to characterize a protocol is by whether it is *synchronous* or *asynchronous*. These two terms have significantly different meanings, depending on where in the protocol hierarchy you use them. At the transport layer, it is most accurate to think of synchrony as a spectrum of possibilities rather than as two alternatives, where the key attribute of any point along the spectrum is how much the sender knows, after the operation to send a message returns. In other words, if we assume that an application program invokes a send operation on a transport protocol, then the question is, exactly what does the application know about the success of the operation when the send operation returns?

At the *asynchronous* end of the spectrum, the application knows absolutely nothing when send returns. It not only doesn't know if the message was received by its peer, but it doesn't even know for sure that the message has successfully left the local

Timeouts

CHAN involves three different timers: there is a RETRANSMIT timer on both the client and server, and the client also manages a PROBE timer. The PROBE timer is not critical to performance and thus can be set to a conservatively large value—on the order of several seconds. The RETRANSMIT timer, however, does influence the performance of CHAN. If it is set too large, then CHAN might wait an unnecessarily long time before retransmitting a message that was lost by the network. This clearly hurts performance. If the RETRANSMIT timer is set too small, however, then CHAN may load the network with unnecessary traffic.

machine. At the *synchronous* end of the spectrum, the send operation typically returns a reply message. That is, the application not only knows that the message it sent was received by its peer, but it knows that the peer has returned an answer. Thus, synchronous protocols implement the request/reply abstraction, while asynchronous protocols are used if the sender wants to be able to transmit many messages without having to wait for a response. Using this definition, CHAN is obviously a synchronous protocol.

Although we have not discussed them in this chapter, there are interesting points between these two extremes. For example, the transport protocol might implement send so that it blocks (does not return) until the message has been successfully received at the remote machine, but returns before the sender's peer on that machine has actually processed and responded to it. This is sometimes called a *reliable datagram protocol*.

If CHAN is designed to run on a local area network only, or even over a campus-size extended LAN, then RETRANSMIT can be set to a fixed value. Something on the order of 20 milliseconds would be reasonable. This is because the RTT of a LAN is not that variable. If CHAN is expected to run over the Internet, however, then selecting a suitable value for RETRANSMIT is similar to the problem faced by TCP. Thus, CHAN would calculate the RETRANSMIT timeout using a mechanism similar to the one described in Section 6.2.5. The only difference is that CHAN has to take into account the fact that the message it is sending ranges in size from 1 B to 32 KB, whereas TCP is always transmitting segments of approximately the same size.

Implementation of CHAN

We conclude our discussion of CHAN by giving fragments of x-kernel code that implement its client side. One of the interesting aspects of CHAN is that it exports a *synchronous* interface to higher-level protocols—the caller blocks until a reply can be returned. This is in contrast to the *asynchronous* interface we have been using, in which there is no reply value for the caller to wait for.

Clearly, the xPush/xDemux/xPop paradigm we have been using is not going to work for synchronous protocols since it makes no provision for a return value. The x-kernel accommodates synchronous protocols by providing a parallel set of operations for sending and receiving messages:

XkReturn xCall(Sessn session, Msg *request, Msg *reply)

XkReturn xCallPop(Sessn session, Msg *request, Msg *reply, void *hdr)

XkReturn xCallDemux(Protl hlp, Sessn session, Msg *request, Msg *reply)

The key difference, of course, is that each operation now returns a reply message (reply); for clarity, we refer to the message given as an argument as the request. The operations are synchronous in the sense that each cannot return until the reply message is available.

So far so good: some protocols are purely asynchronous (they export xPush, xPop, and xDemux operations), and some are purely synchronous (they export xCall, xCallPop, and xCallDemux operations). However, if all protocols were either asynchronous or synchronous, then the entire protocol graph would have to consist of only asynchronous or synchronous protocols—an asynchronous protocol can only call xPush on an adjacent protocol, meaning that it could never be composed with a synchronous protocol.

Fortunately, there can be hybrid protocols that are half synchronous and half asynchronous. This does not mean that they support all six operations, but rather that they look like a synchronous protocol to higher-level protocols and like an asynchronous protocol to lower-level protocols. This is exactly what CHAN does: it supports the xCall operation rather than xPush on top, while from below, it still supports the asynchronous xDemux/xPop interface. That is, CHAN is a protocol that turns an underlying asynchronous communication service into a synchronous communication service. It does this by having the sending process (caller) block on a semaphore while waiting for a reply message.

We now turn to the details of CHAN, beginning with CHAN's two key data structures: ChanHdr and ChanState. Both of these data structures are defined in a private .h file (e.g., chan_internal.h), rather than the chan.h file included by other protocols. The fields in ChanHdr have already been explained. The fields in ChanState will be explained by the code that follows. The one thing to note at this point is that ChanState includes a hdr_template field, which is a copy of the CHAN header. Many of the fields in the CHAN header remain the same for all messages sent out over this channel. These fields are filled in when the channel is created (not shown); only the fields that change are modified before a given message is transmitted.

```
typedef struct {
    u_short    Type;            /* message type: REQ, REP, ACK, PROBE */
    u_short    CID;             /* unique channel id */
    int        MID;             /* unique message id */
    int        BID;             /* unique boot id */
    int        Length;          /* length of message */
    int        ProtNum;         /* high-level protocol number */
} ChanHdr;

typedef struct {
    u_char     type;            /* type of session: CLIENT or SERVER */
```

```
    u_char      status;          /* status of session: BUSY or IDLE */
    Event       event;           /* place to save timeout event */
    int         retries;         /* number of times retransmitted */
    int         timeout;         /* timeout value */
    XkReturn    ret_val;         /* place to save return value */
    Msg         *request;        /* place to save request message */
    Msg         *reply;          /* place to save reply message */
    Semaphore   reply_sem;       /* semaphore the client blocks on */
    int         mid;             /* message id for this channel */
    int         bid;             /* boot id for this channel */
    ChanHdr     hdr_template;    /* header template for this channel */
} ChanState;
```

The CHAN-specific implementation of xCall is given by the following routine, named chanCall. The first thing to notice is that ChanState includes a field named status that indicates whether or not this channel is being used. If the channel is currently in use, then chanCall returns failure.

The next thing to notice about chanCall is that after filling out the message header and transmitting the request message, the calling process is blocked on a semaphore (reply_sem); semWait is the x-kernel semaphore operation introduced in Section 2.2. When the reply message eventually arrives, it is processed by CHAN's xPop routine (see below), which copies the reply message into state variable reply and signals this blocked process. The process then returns. Should the reply message not arrive, then timeout routine retransmit is called (see below). This event is scheduled in the body of chanCall.

```
static XkReturn
chanCall(Sessn self, Msg *msg, Msg *rmsg)
{
    ChanState   *state = (ChanState *)self->state;
    ChanHdr     *hdr;
    char        *buf;

    /* ensure only one transaction per channel */
    if ((state->status != IDLE))
        return XK_FAILURE;
    state->status = BUSY;

    /* save a copy of request msg and pointer to reply msg*/
    msgConstructCopy(&state->request, msg);
    state->reply = rmsg;

    /* fill out header fields */
    hdr = state->hdr_template;
    hdr->Length = msgLen(msg);
    if (state->mid == MAX_MID)
        state->mid = 0;
    hdr->MID = ++state->mid;
```

```
    /* attach header to msg and send it */
    buf = msgPush(msg, HDR_LEN);
    chan_hdr_store(hdr, buf, HDR_LEN);
    xPush(xGetDown(self, 0), msg);

    /* schedule first timeout event */
    state->retries = 1;
    state->event = evSchedule(retransmit, self, state->timeout);

    /* wait for the reply msg */
    semWait(&state->reply_sem);

    /* clean up state and return */
    flush_msg(state->request);
    state->status = IDLE;
    return state->ret_val;
}
```

The next routine (retransmit) is called whenever the retransmit timer fires. It is scheduled for the first time in chanCall, but each time it is called, it reschedules itself. Once the request message has been retransmitted four times, CHAN gives up: it sets the return value to XK_FAILURE and wakes up the blocked client process. Finally, the reason retransmit first checks to see if the event was cancelled is that there is a potential race condition between when evCancel is invoked (evCancel is called in chanClientPop, which is given below) and when the event actually executes. Note that each time retransmit executes and sends another copy of the request message, it needs to re-save the message in state variable request. This is because each time a protocol calls the xPush operation on a message, it loses its reference to the message.

```
static void
retransmit(Event ev, int *arg)
{
    Sessn        s = (Sessn)arg;
    ChanState    *state = (ChanState *)s->state;
    Msg          tmp;

    /* see if event was cancelled */
    if ( evIsCancelled(ev) )
        return;

    /* unblock the client process if we have retried 4 times */
    if (++state->retries > 4)
    {
        state->ret_val = XK_FAILURE;
        semSignal(state->rep_sem);
        return;
```

```
    }

    /* retransmit request message */
    msgConstructCopy(&tmp, &state->request);
    xPush(xGetDown(s, 0), &tmp);

    /* reschedule event with exponential backoff */
    evDetach(state->event);
    state->timeout = 2*state->timeout;
    state->event = evSchedule(retransmit, s, state->timeout);
}
```

CHAN's **chanPop** routine is very simple. This is because CHAN is an asymmetric protocol: the code that implements CHAN on the client machine is completely distinct from the code that implements CHAN on the server machine. In fact, any given CHAN session will always be a purely client session or a purely server session, and this fact is stored in a session state variable (**type**). Thus, all **chanPop** does is check to see whether it is a server session (one that expects **REQ** messages) or a client session (one that expects **REP** messages), and then it calls the appropriate client- or server-specific routine. In this case, we show only the client-specific routine.

```
static XkReturn
chanPop(Sessn self, Sessn lls, Msg *msg, void *inHdr)
{
    /* see if this is a CLIENT or SERVER session */
    if (self->state->type == SERVER)
       return(chanServerPop(self, lls, msg, inHdr));
    else
       return(chanClientPop(self, lls, msg, inHdr));
}
```

The client-specific pop routine (**chanClientPop**) is given below. This routine first checks to see if it has received the expected message, for example, that it has the right **MID**, the right **BID**, and that the message is of type **REP** or **ACK**. This check is made in subroutine clnt_msg_ok (not shown). If it is a valid acknowledgment message, then **chanClientPop** cancels the RE-TRANSMIT timer and schedules the PROBE timer. The PROBE timer is not shown, but would be similar to the RETRANSMIT timer given above. If the message is a valid reply, then **chanClientPop** cancels the RETRANSMIT timer, saves a copy of the reply message in state variable **reply**, and wakes up the blocked client process. It is this client process that actually returns the reply message to the high-level protocol; the process that called **chanClientPop** simply returns back down the protocol stack.

```
static XkReturn
chanClientPop(Sessn self, Sessn lls, Msg *msg, void *inHdr)
{
    ChanState    *state = (ChanState *)self->state;
```

```
    ChanHdr        *hdr = (ChanHdr *)inHdr;

    /* verify correctness of msg header */
    if (!clnt_msg_ok(state, hdr))
        return XK_FAILURE;

    /* cancel retransmit timeout event */
    evCancel(state->event);

    /* if this is an ACK, then schedule PROBE timer and exit*/
    if (hdr->Type == ACK)
    {
        state->event = evSchedule(probe, s, PROBE);
        return XK_SUCCESS;
    }

    /* msg must be a REP, so save it and signal blocked client process */
    msgAssign(state->reply, msg);
    state->ret_val = XK_SUCCESS;
    semSignal(&state->reply_sem);

    return XK_SUCCESS;
}
```

6.3.3 Dispatcher (SELECT)

The final microprotocol, called SELECT, dispatches request messages to the appropriate procedure. It is the RPC protocol stack's version of a demultiplexing protocol like UDP, the main difference being that it is a purely synchronous protocol rather than an asynchronous protocol. What this means is that on the client side, SELECT is given a procedure number that the client wants to invoke, it puts this number in its header, and then it invokes a lower-level request/reply protocol like CHAN. When this invocation returns, SELECT merely lets the return pass on through to the client; it has no real demultiplexing work to do. On the server side, SELECT uses the procedure number it finds in its header to select the right local procedure to invoke. When this procedure returns, SELECT simply returns to the low-level protocol that just invoked it.

This situation, labeled with the corresponding x-kernel calls, is illustrated in Figure 6.16. The corresponding x-kernel code for selectCall and selectCallPop is given below. Notice that SELECT is like CHAN in that it is asymmetric—each session is either a client session or a server session. Unlike CHAN, however, SELECT exports the synchronous interface to both higher-level protocols (xCall) and lower-level protocols (xCallDemux and xCallPop).

```
static XkReturn
selectCall(Sessn self, Msg *msg, Msg *rmsg)
{
    SelectState    *state = (SelectState *)self->state;
```

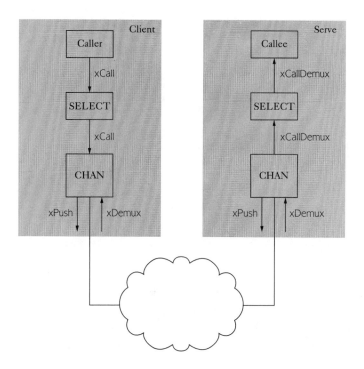

Figure 6.16 **Relationship between SELECT and neighboring modules.**

```
char          *buf;

buf = msgPush(msg, HLEN);
select_hdr_store(state->hdr, buf, HLEN);
return xCall(xGetDown(self, 0), msg, rmsg);
}

static XkReturn
selectCallPop(Sessn s, Sessn lls, Msg *msg, Msg *rmsg, void *inHdr)
{
    return xCallDemux(xGetUp(s), s, msg, rmsg);
}
```

It may seem that SELECT is so simple that it is not worthy of being treated as a separate protocol. After all, CHAN already has its own demultiplexing field that could be used to dispatch incoming request messages to the appropriate procedure. The reason we separate SELECT into a self-contained protocol is that this makes it possible to change the address space with which procedures are identified simply by configuring a different version of SELECT into the protocol graph.

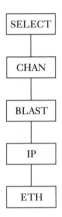

Figure 6.17   A simple RPC stack.

In some settings, it is sufficient to define a *flat* address space for procedures—e.g., a 16-bit selector field allows you to identify 64 K different procedures. In other settings, however, a flat address space is hard to manage—who decides which procedure gets which procedure number? In this case, it might be better to have a hierarchical address space, that is, a two-part procedure number. First, each program could be given a program number, where a program corresponds to something like a "file server" or a "name server." Next, each program could be given the responsibility to assign unique procedure numbers to its own procedures. For example, within the file server program, read might be procedure 1, write might be procedure 2, seek might be procedure 3, and so on, whereas within the name server program, insert might be procedure 1 and lookup might be procedure 2.

6.3.4   Putting It All Together (SunRPC)

We are now ready to construct an RPC stack from the microprotocols described in the three previous subsections. This involves the introduction of a technique for building protocol graphs that is facilitated by the x-kernel's configurability. This section also explains a widely used RPC protocol, SunRPC, in terms of our three microprotocols.

A Simple RPC Stack

Figure 6.17 depicts a simple protocol stack that implements RPC. At the bottom are the protocols that implement the underlying network. Although this stack could contain protocols corresponding to any of the networking technologies discussed in the three previous chapters, we use IP running on top of an Ethernet for illustrative purposes.

On top of IP is BLAST, which turns the small message size of the underlying network into a communication service that supports messages of up to 32 KB in length. Notice that it is not strictly true that the underlying network provides for only small messages; IP can handle messages of up to 64 KB. However, because IP has to fragment such large messages before sending them out over the Ethernet, and BLAST's fragmentation/reassembly algorithm is superior to IP's (because it is able to selectively retransmit missing fragments), we prefer to treat IP as though it supports exactly the same MTU as the underlying physical network. This puts the fragmentation/reassembly burden on BLAST, unless IP has to perform fragmentation out in the middle of the network somewhere.

Next, CHAN implements the request/reply algorithm. Recall that we chose not to implement reliable delivery in BLAST, but instead postponed solving this issue until a higher-level protocol. In this case, CHAN's timeout and acknowledgment mechanism makes sure messages are reliably delivered. Other protocols might use different techniques to guarantee delivery, or, for that matter, might choose not to implement reliable delivery at all. This is an example of the end-to-end argument at work—do not do at low levels of the system (e.g., BLAST) what has to be done at higher levels (e.g., CHAN) anyway.

Finally, SELECT defines an address space for identifying remote procedures. As suggested in Section 6.3.3, different versions of SELECT, each defining a different method for identifying procedures, could be configured on top of CHAN. In fact, it would even be possible to write a version of SELECT that mimics some existing RPC package's address space for procedures (such as SunRPC's), and then to use CHAN and BLAST underneath this new SELECT to implement the rest of the RPC stack. This new stack would not interoperate with the original protocol, but it would allow you to slide a new RPC system underneath an existing collection of remote procedures without having to change the interface.

A More Interesting RPC Stack

While the protocol graph given in Figure 6.17 functions correctly, the x-kernel, because it makes it easy to configure protocols together in different ways, gives us the freedom to specialize the protocol graph to produce an even better RPC mechanism. While the following technique is not available in all operating systems, we think that it is important to illustrate what is possible in network design rather than to limit ourselves to the workings of artifacts that happen to be in use today. Note that the following discussion is necessarily specific to the x-kernel.

In the x-kernel, we sometimes implement modules called *virtual protocols*. Virtual protocols are configured into a protocol graph just like any other protocol, but they are different from regular protocols in that they do not add a header to messages, i.e., they do not directly communicate with their peer on the other machine. Instead, virtual protocols serve to "route messages" through the protocol graph. For example, we have designed a virtual protocol named VSIZE that is configured on top of two low-level protocols. VSIZE takes a message from some high-level protocol, and based on how big the message is (this can be determined using the x-kernel's msgLen operation), decides which of the two low-level protocols to pass the message on to. Figure 6.18 illustrates how VSIZE might be configured into the protocol graph to route large messages (those greater than 1 KB) to BLAST and small messages (those less than or equal to 1 KB) to IP. As before, BLAST still sits on top of IP. The advantage of using a protocol like VSIZE is that it prevents messages that are too small to need fragmenting from incurring the overhead of yet another protocol layer.

Figure 6.19 shows an RPC stack that includes several virtual protocols. It also shows how multiple instantiations of a single protocol can be configured into a protocol graph. VADDR is a virtual protocol that decides which of two low-level protocols to use, based upon the address of the destination host. If the destination is on the same network, then IP is unnecessary and can be bypassed; otherwise, the message must be handed off to IP. Again, this strategy has the advantage of avoiding the overhead of IP in a situation in which IP adds no value to the process-to-process communication.

This introduces a complication, however. Because we do not want to force the application program at the top of the protocol stack to know whether or not IP is going to be used, we want the application to always identify the remote host with an IP address. This means that even when IP is bypassed, this IP address must be translated into a physical network address somewhere in the protocol graph. This translation is done by a virtual protocol called VNET, which sits between IP and the underlying network protocols. IP still decides which machine to route each message to, but now lets VNET map the IP address for this machine into the corresponding physical address. Other protocols can then use VNET without using IP; they simply present VNET with the IP address of the destination machine.

Finally, we put virtual protocol VCHAN above CHAN in the protocol stack to manage concurrency. The idea is that VCHAN opens multiple CHAN sessions, thereby allowing the client to have multiple outstanding calls to the remote procedure. Each time a calling process comes down into VCHAN, it sends the process out on an idle channel (session). If all the channels are currently active, then VCHAN blocks the calling process until a channel becomes idle. The following code gives the implementation of VCHAN's xCall routine. It uses a stack to keep track of idle channels (sessions).

```
static XkReturn
vchanCall(Sessn s, Msg *msg, Msg *rmsg)
{
    Sessn         chan;
    XkReturn      result;
    VchanState    *state = (VchanState *)s->state;

    /* wait for an idle channel */
    semWait(&state->available);
    chan = state->stack[--state->tos];

    /* use the channel */
    result = xCall(chan, msg, rmsg);

    /* free the channel */
    state->stack[state->tos++] = chan;
    semSignal(&state->available);

    return result;
}
```

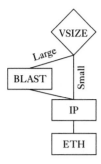

Figure 6.18   An RPC protocol graph that uses VSIZE.

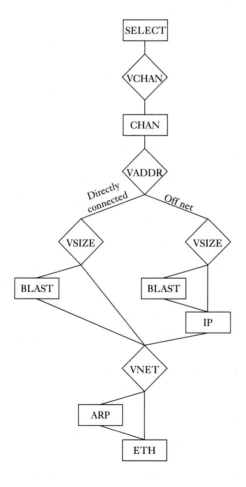

Figure 6.19   An RPC protocol graph that uses virtual protocols.

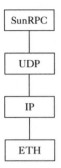

Figure 6.20   Protocol graph for SunRPC.

SunRPC

SELECT, CHAN, and BLAST, although complete and correctly functioning protocols, have not be standardized by any standardization body. We conclude our discussion of RPC by looking at a widely used RPC protocol—SunRPC. Ironically, SunRPC has also not been approved by any standardization body, but it has become a de facto standard, thanks to its wide distribution with Sun workstations and to the central role it plays in Sun's popular Network File System (NFS). Actually, the IETF is now considering officially adopting SunRPC as a standard Internet protocol, but under the name *Open Network Computing* (ONC) rather than SunRPC.

Fundamentally, any RPC protocol must worry about three issues: fragmenting large messages, synchronizing request and reply messages, and dispatching request messages to the appropriate procedure. SunRPC is no exception. Unlike the SELECT/CHAN/BLAST stack, however, SunRPC addresses these three functions in a different order and using slightly different algorithms. The basic SunRPC protocol graph is given in Figure 6.20.

First, SunRPC implements the core request/reply algorithm; it is CHAN's counterpart. SunRPC differs from CHAN, however, in that it does not technically guarantee at-most-once semantics; there are obscure circumstances under which a duplicate copy of a request message is delivered to the server (see below). Second, the role of SELECT is split between UDP and SunRPC—UDP dispatches to the correct program, and SunRPC dispatches to the correct procedure within the program. (We discuss how procedures are identified in more detail below.) Finally, the ability to send request and reply messages that are larger than the network MTU, corresponding to the functionality implemented in BLAST, is handled by IP. Keep in mind, however, that IP is not as persistent as BLAST is in implementing fragmentation; BLAST uses selective retransmission, whereas IP does not.

As just mentioned, SunRPC uses two-tier addresses to identify remote procedures: a 32-bit program number and a 32-bit procedure number. (There is also a 32-bit version number, but we ignore that in the following discussion.) For example, the NFS server has been assigned program number x00100003, and within this program, getattr is procedure 1, setattr

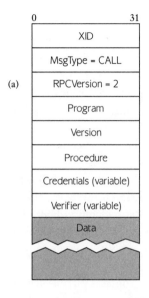
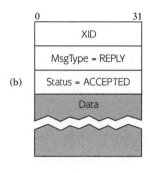

Figure 6.21 SunRPC header formats: (a) request; (b) reply.

is procedure 2, read is procedure 6, write is procedure 8, and so on. Each program is reachable by sending a message to some UDP port. When a request message arrives at this port, SunRPC picks it up and calls the appropriate procedure.

To determine which port corresponds to a particular SunRPC program number, there is a separate SunRPC program, called the Port Mapper, that maps program numbers to port numbers. The Port Mapper itself also has a program number (x00100000) that must be translated into some UDP port. Fortunately, the Port Mapper is always present at a well-known UDP port (111). The Port Mapper program supports several procedures, one of which (procedure number 3) is the one that performs the program-to-port number mapping.

Thus, to send a request message to NFS's read procedure, a client first sends a request message to the Port Mapper at well-known UDP port 111, asking that procedure 3 be invoked to map program number x00100003 to the UDP port where the NFS program currently resides. (In practice, NFS is such an important program that it is given its own well-known UDP port, so the Port Mapper need not be involved in finding it.) The client then sends a SunRPC request message with procedure number 6 to this UDP port, and the SunRPC module listening at that port calls the NFS read procedure. The client also caches the program-to-port number mapping so that it need not go back to the Port Mapper each time it wants to talk to the NFS program.

The actual SunRPC header is defined by a complex nesting of data structures. Figure 6.21 gives the essential details for the case in which the call completes without any problems.

XID is a unique transaction id, much like CHAN's MID field. The reason that SunRPC cannot guarantee at-most-once semantics is that on the server side, SunRPC does not remember that it has already seen a particular XID once it has successfully completed the transaction. This is only a problem if the client retransmits a request message as a result of a timeout and that request message is in transit at exactly the same time as the reply to the original request is on its way from the server back to the client. When the retransmitted request arrives at the server, it looks like a new transaction, since the server thinks it has already completed the transaction with this XID. Clearly, if the reply arrives at the client before the timeout, then the request will not be retransmitted. Likewise, if the retransmitted request arrives at the server before the reply has been generated, then the server will recognize that transaction XID is already in progress, and it will discard the duplicate request message. So it is really quite unlikely that this erroneous behavior will occur. Note that the server's short-term memory about XIDs also means that it cannot protect itself against messages that have been delayed for a long time in the network. This has not been a serious problem with SunRPC, however, because it was originally designed for use on a LAN.

Returning to the SunRPC header format, the request message contains variable-length Credentials and Verifier fields, both of which are used by the client to authenticate itself to the server, that is, to give evidence that the client has the right to invoke the server. How a client authenticates itself to a server is a general issue that must be addressed by any protocol that wants to provide a reasonable level of security. This topic is discussed in more detail in the next chapter.

6.4   Application Programming Interface

We now turn our attention from the *implementation* of various end-to-end protocols to the *interface* these protocols provide to application programs. This has not been a serious issue for the protocols covered in earlier chapters because they only interface with other protocols, and this interaction is typically buried deep in the operating system kernel. Transport protocols, however, are often directly available to application programs, and as a result, special attention is paid to how application programs gain access to the communication services they provide. This interface is generically called the *application programming interface*, or API.

Although each operating system is free to define its own protocol API (and most have), over time certain of these APIs have become widely supported, that is, they have been ported to operating systems other than their native system. The reason this happens is easy to understand: if a common API is supported on a wide range of systems, then it should be easy to port application programs written to this API to all of those systems. A word of warning is called for, however, since "easy" is a relative term. A network application that uses other OS facilities, such as processes, files, and memory objects, is still tightly bound to that OS.

What is not easy to understand is why a particular API becomes more popular than another. In the realm of networking, the most popular API is the *socket interface* originally developed in the Berkeley implementation of Unix. Because of its popularity, the socket in-

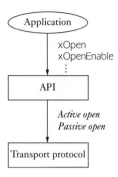

Figure 6.22   Relationship between the API and the protocol.

terface has been ported to nearly all versions of Unix, and a version is now even available on Microsoft Windows. This section gives a brief introduction to the socket interface.

Before describing the socket interface, it is important to keep two concerns separate in your mind. (Since we have not yet described the socket interface, we use the x-kernel interface to illustrate the point.) On the one hand, the protocol defines the *semantics* of the communication. For example, protocols define abstractions like "ports" and "connections," as well as abstract operations like "active open" and "passive open." The state-transition diagram for TCP given in Figure 6.6 identifies some of the abstract operations that TCP supports. On the other hand, the API defines the *syntax* for the communication. For example, it defines its own set of objects (sessions and participants) and it defines its own set of operations (xOpen and xOpenEnable). The implementation is then responsible for mapping the tangible set of operations and objects defined by the API onto the abstract set of operations and objects defined by the protocol, for example, sessions onto ports and xOpen onto "active open." This situation is illustrated in Figure 6.22.

We are now ready to describe the socket interface, which we cover in only enough detail to illustrate the relationship between the API and the transport protocols. In particular, we limit ourselves to showing how the socket interface is used in conjunction with TCP. The main abstraction of the socket interface, not surprisingly, is the *socket*. A good way to think of a socket is as the point where a local application process attaches to the network. The interface defines operations for creating a socket, attaching the socket to the network, sending/receiving messages through the socket, and closing the socket.

The first step is to create a socket, which is done with the following operation:

```
int socket(int domain, int type, int protocol)
```

The reason that this operation takes three arguments is that the socket interface was designed to be general enough to support any underlying protocol suite. Specifically, the **domain** argument specifies the protocol *family* that is going to be used. **PF_INET** is used to denote the Internet family; **PF_UNIX** is an alternative that denotes the Unix pipe facility. The **type** argument indicates the semantics of the communication. SOCK_STREAM is used to denote a byte stream; SOCK_DGRAM is an alternative that denotes a message-oriented service. Finally, the protocol argument identifies the specific protocol that is going to be used. In our case, this argument is UNSPEC because the combination of PF_INET and SOCK_STREAM implies TCP. Finally, the return value from socket is a handle for the newly created socket. It is given as an argument to other socket operations.

The next step depends on whether you are a client or a server. On a server machine, the application process invokes the following three instructions to effect the passive open:

    int bind(int socket, struct sockaddr *address, int addr_len)

    int listen(int socket, int backlog)

    int accept(int socket, struct sockaddr *address, int *addr_len)

The bind operation, as its name suggests, binds the newly created socket to the specified address. This is the address of the *local* participant, i.e., the server. Note that, when used with the Internet protocols, address is a data structure that includes both the IP address of the server and a UDP or TCP port number. The listen operation then defines how many connections can be pending on the specified socket. Finally, the accept operation carries out the passive open. It is a blocking operation that does not return until a remote participant has established a connection, and when it does complete, it returns a *new* socket that corresponds to this just-established connection, and the address argument contains the *remote* participant's address. It is possible to specify a "don't care" value, to enable any client to connect to this server.

Note that when accept returns, the original socket that was created and given as an argument to it still exists and still corresponds to the passive open; it is used in future invocations of accept. Also note that even though the server does not block until it invokes the accept operation, it is by invoking the listen operation that the application process causes TCP to make the transition to the LISTEN state.

On the client machine, the application process invokes a single operation to effect the active open:

    int connect(int socket, struct sockaddr *address, int addr_len)

This operation does not return until the three-way handshake algorithm has successfully completed, meaning that the application can then begin sending data. In this case, address contains both the local and the remote participant's addresses. In practice, the client usually specifies only the remote participant's address and lets the system fill in the local information. Unlike a server that depends on a well-known port, a client typically does not care which port it uses for itself; the OS simply selects an unused one.

Once a connection is established, the application processes invoke the following two operations to send and receive data:

    int write(int socket, char *message, int msg_len, int flags)

```
int read(int socket, char *buffer, int buf_len, int flags)
```

The first operation sends the given **message** over the specified **socket**, while the second operation receives a message from the specified **socket** into the given **buffer**. Both operations take a set of **flags** that control certain details of the operation.

One of the interesting properties of an API is whether or not it allows the application to gain access to all the features of the underlying protocol. In the case of TCP, for example, the interface needs to give a program the ability to indicate that the data it is sending is urgent. This is done in the socket interface by setting the out-of-band flag (**MSG_OOB**) in the call to **write**. Similarly, on the receiving host, the interface needs to provide a mechanism by which TCP informs the application that urgent data has arrived. Delivering such protocol-to-application signals is typically the trickiest part of interface design. In the socket interface, for example, Unix delivers a **SIGURG** signal to the application process. In some cases, the API does not support a feature defined by the protocol. For example, the socket interface does not support a process's ability to send data while in the LISTEN state.

6.5 Performance

Recall that Chapter 1 introduced the two quantitative metrics by which network performance is evaluated: latency and throughput. As mentioned in that discussion, these metrics are influenced not only by the underlying hardware (e.g., propagation delay and link bandwidth), but also by software overheads. Now that we have a complete software-based protocol graph available to us that includes alternative transport protocols, we can discuss how to meaningfully measure its performance; we can hold a sort of protocol track meet. The importance of such measurements is that they represent the performance seen by application programs.

6.5.1 Experimental Method

We begin, as any report of experimental results should, by describing our experimental method. This includes the apparatus used in the experiments.

We ran our experiments on a pair of DEC 3000/600 workstations (with an Alpha 21064 processor running at 175 MHz) connected by an isolated 10-Mbps Ethernet. Each workstation was configured with a stand-alone version of the x-kernel, configured with the protocol graph illustrated in Figure 6.23. Each of the protocols at the top of the protocol graph (TSTTCP, TSTUDP, TSTRPC) ran a series of independent experiments (TST stands for "test"). Each experiment involved running five identical versions of the same test. Each test, in turn, involved sending a message of some specified size back and forth between the two machines 10,000 times. The system's clock was read at the beginning and end of each test, and the difference between these two times was divided by 10,000 to determine the time taken for each round trip. The average of these five times (the five runs of the test) are reported for each experiment below.

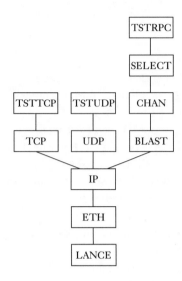

Figure 6.23 Protocol stack configuration used in performance measurements.

Each experiment involved a different-sized message. The latency numbers reported in Section 6.5.2 were for message sizes of 1 byte, 100 bytes, 200 bytes, ..., 1000 bytes. The throughput results presented in Section 6.5.3 were for message sizes of 1 KB, 2 KB, 4 KB, 8 KB, ..., 32 KB. The test protocol is like any other protocol, except that it doesn't have to support the top half of the uniform protocol interface because there are no protocols above it to call xOpen, xPush, and so on. On the client side, the test protocol initiates the tests and reads the system clock, while on the server side, it simply returns (reflects) the exact message it just received.

6.5.2 Latency

Table 6.3 gives the results of the latency test. As you would expect, latency increases with message size. Although there are sometimes special cases where you might be interested in the latency of, say, a 200-byte message, typically the most important latency number is the 1-byte case. This is because the 1-byte case represents the overhead involved in processing each message that does not depend on the amount of data contained in the message. It is typically the lower bound on latency, representing factors like the speed-of-light delay and the time taken to process headers.

We also observe that there is little difference between the latency experienced by the three different protocols (we use RPC as a shorthand for the SELECT/CHAN/BLAST stack). UDP is a bit faster than TCP or RPC, but this is to be expected since it provides less functionality.

Message Size (Bytes)	UDP	TCP	RPC
1	279	365	428
100	413	519	593
200	572	691	753
300	732	853	913
400	898	1016	1079
500	1067	1185	1247
600	1226	1354	1406
700	1386	1514	1566
800	1551	1676	1733
900	1719	1845	1901
1000	1878	2015	2062

Table 6.3   Measured round-trip latencies (μs) for various message sizes and protocols.

Another interesting data point is how much of this round-trip latency is due to the hardware (link + adaptor) and how much can be attributed to the software that implements the protocol stack. Since it is difficult to isolate the cost of the device driver—and in any case, network hardware without a device driver isn't worth very much—we settle for knowing how much all the software above ETH contributes to the RTT. This can be done by reconfiguring the x-kernel to include only a TEST protocol, ETH, and LANCE, and then rerunning the latency experiment. In our particular case, the 1-byte latency was 216 μs, meaning that the UDP/IP stack added 58 μs to the round trip latency. Since each round trip involves traversing the protocol stack four times—twice outgoing and twice incoming—this means that each traversal takes on average about 15 μs. Keep in mind, however, that we do not have enough information to determine the relative times required to send and receive a message. Generally, the receive side takes longer, although the difference is small. (A similar analysis can be done for TCP and RPC.)

6.5.3 Throughput

The results of the throughput test are given in Figure 6.24. Here, we show only the results for UDP; the performance of TCP and RPC are not noticeably different. The key thing to notice in this graph is that throughput improves as the messages get larger. This makes sense—each message involves a certain amount of overhead, so a larger message means that this overhead is amortized over more bytes. The throughput curve flattens off at about 16 KB, at which

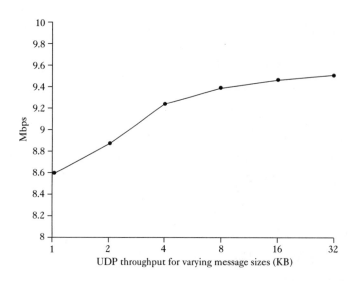

Figure 6.24   Measured throughput using UDP, for various message sizes.

point the per-message overhead becomes insignificant when compared to the large number of bytes that the protocol stack has to process.

A second thing to notice is that the throughput curve tops out at about 9.5 Mbps. This is good news since the experiment was run on an Ethernet, which has a bandwidth of 10 Mbps. Although it can't be deduced from these measurements, it turns out that the factor preventing our system from running at the full Ethernet speed is a limitation of the network adaptor rather than the software. We'll look more closely at this sort of limitation on throughput in Chapter 9.

6.6   Summary

This chapter has described three very different end-to-end protocols, has discussed the API by which application programs engage these protocols, and has reported on their performance.

The first protocol we considered is a simple demultiplexer, as typified by UDP. All such a protocol does is dispatch messages to the appropriate application process based on a port number. It does not enhance the best-effort service model of the underlying network in any way, or said another way, it offers an unreliable, connectionless datagram service to application programs.

The second type is a reliable byte-stream protocol, and the specific example of this type that we looked at is TCP. The challenges faced with such a protocol are to recover from messages that may be lost by the network, to deliver messages in the same order in which they are sent, and to allow the receiver to do flow control on the sender. TCP uses the basic sliding window algorithm, enhanced with an advertised window, to implement this functionality. The other item of note for this protocol is the importance of an accurate timeout/retransmission mechanism.

The third transport protocol we looked at is a request/reply protocol that forms the basis for RPC. In this case, a combination of three different algorithms are employed to implement the request/reply service: a selective retransmission algorithm that is used to fragment and reassemble large messages, a synchronous-channel algorithm that pairs the request message with the reply message, and a dispatch algorithm that causes the correct remote procedure to be invoked.

What should be clear after reading this chapter is that transport protocol design is a tricky business. As we have seen, getting a transport protocol right in the first place is hard enough, but changing circumstances make matters more complicated. The challenge is finding ways to adapt to these changes.

OPEN ISSUE

Application-Specific Protocols

One thing that can change is our experience with using the protocol. As we saw with TCP's timeout mechanism, experience led to a series of refinements in how TCP decides to retransmit a segment. None of these changes affected the format of the TCP header, however, and so they could be incorporated into TCP one implementation at a time. That is, there was no need for everyone to upgrade their version of TCP on the same day.

Another thing that can change is the characteristics of the underlying network. For many years, TCP's 32-bit sequence number and 16-bit advertised window were more than adequate. Recently, however, higher-bandwidth networks have meant that the sequence number is not large enough to protect against wraparound, and the advertised window is too small to allow the sender to fill the network pipe. While an obvious solution would have been to redefine the TCP header to include a 64-bit sequence number field and a 32-bit advertised window field, this would have introduced the very serious problem of how 5 million Internet hosts would make the transition from the current header to this new header. While such transitions have been performed on production networks, including the telephone network, they are no trivial matter. It was decided, therefore, to implement the necessary extensions as options and to allow hosts to negotiate with each other as to whether or not they will use the options for each connection.

This approach will not work indefinitely, however, since the TCP header has room for only 44 bytes of options. (This is because the HdrLen field is 4 bits long, meaning that the total TCP header length cannot exceed 16 × 32 bit words, or 64 bytes.) Of course, a TCP option that extends the space available for options is always a possibility, but you have to wonder how far it is worth going for the sake of backward compatibility.

Perhaps the hardest changes to accommodate are the adaptations to the level of service required by application programs. It is inevitable that some applications will have a good reason for wanting a slight variation from the standard services. For example, some applications want RPC most of the time, but occasionally want to be able to send a stream of request messages without waiting for any of the replies. While this is no longer technically the semantics of RPC, a common scenario is to modify an existing RPC protocol to allow this flexibility. As another example, because video is a stream-oriented application, it is tempting to use TCP as the transport protocol. Unfortunately, TCP guarantees reliability, which is not important to the video application. In fact, a video application would rather drop a frame (segment) than wait for it to be retransmitted. Rather than invent a new transport protocol from scratch, however, some designers have proposed that TCP should support an option that effectively turns off its reliability feature. It seems that such a protocol could hardly be called TCP any more, but we are talking about the pragmatics of getting an application to run.

How to develop transport protocols that can evolve to satisfy diverse applications, many of which have not yet been imagined, is a hard problem. It is possible that the ultimate answer to this problem is the one-function-per-protocol style promoted by the x-kernel or some similar mechanism by which the application programmer is allowed to program, configure, or otherwise stylize the transport protocol.

FURTHER READING

There is no doubt that TCP is a complex protocol and that in fact it has subtleties not illuminated in this chapter. Therefore, the recommended reading list for this chapter includes the original TCP specification. Our motivation for including this specification is not so much to fill in the missing details, as to expose you to what an honest-to-goodness protocol specification looks like. The other two papers in the recommended reading list focus on RPC. The paper by Birrell and Nelson is the seminal paper on the topic, while the article by O'Malley and Peterson describes the x-kernel's one-function-per-protocol design philosophy in more detail.

- USC-ISI. Transmission Control Protocol. *Request for Comments* 793, September 1981.

- Birrell, A., and B. Nelson. Implementing remote procedure calls. *ACM Transactions on Computer Systems* 2(1):39–59, February 1984.

- O'Malley, S., and L. Peterson. A dynamic network architecture. *ACM Transactions on Computer Systems* 10(2):110–143, May 1992.

Beyond the protocol specification, the most complete description of TCP, including its implementation in Berkeley Unix, can be found in Stevens [Ste94b]. Also, the third volume of Comer and Steven's TCP/IP series of books describes how to write client/server applications on top of TCP and UDP, using both the socket interface [CS93] and the System V Unix TLI interface [CS94].

Several papers evaluate the performance of different transport protocols at a very detailed level. For example, the article by Clark et al. [CJRS89] measures the processing overheads of TCP, while Thekkath and Levy [TL93] and Schroeder and Burrows [SB89] examine RPC's performance in great detail.

The original TCP timeout calculation was described in the TCP specification (see above), while the Karn/Partridge algorithm was described in [KP91] and the Jacobson/Karels algorithm was proposed in [Jac88]. The TCP extensions are defined by Jacobson et al. [JBB92], while O'Mallery and Peterson [OP91] argue that extending TCP in this way is not the right approach to solving the problem.

Finally, there are several distributed operating systems that have defined their own RPC protocol. Notable examples include the V system, described by Cheriton and Zwaenepoel [CZ85]; Sprite, described by Ousterhout et al. [OCD$^+$88]; and Amoeba, described by Mullender [Mul90]. The latest version of SunRPC, which is also known as ONC, is defined by Srinivasan [Sri95a].

E X E R C I S E S

1 Inspect your host's /etc/services file. Investigate the services named there. (A good starting place is the man pages.)

2 This chapter explains three sequences of state transitions during TCP connection teardown. There is a fourth possible sequence, which traverses the arc from FIN_WAIT_1 to TIME_WAIT. Explain the circumstances that result in this sequence of state transitions.

3 When closing a TCP connection, why is the two-segment lifetime timeout not necessary on the transition from LAST_ACK to CLOSED?

4 Assume that an operating system can give more memory to, or request memory back from, a TCP connection, based on memory availability and the connection's requirements. What would be the effects of increasing the memory available to a connection? What about decreasing the memory?

5 A sender on a TCP connection that receives a 0 advertised window periodically probes the receiver to discover when the window becomes nonzero. Why would the receiver need

an extra timer if it were responsible for reporting that its advertised window had become nonzero (i.e., if the sender did not probe)?

6 Read the man page for the Unix utility **netstat**. Use **netstat** to see the state of the local TCP connections.

7 The sequence number field in the TCP header is 32 bits long, which is big enough to cover over 4 billion bytes of data. Even if this many bytes were never transferred over a single connection, why might the sequence number still wrap around from $2^{32} - 1$ to 0?

8 You are hired to design a reliable byte-stream protocol that uses a sliding window (like TCP). This protocol will run over a 100-Mbps network. The RTT of the network is 100 ms, and the maximum segment lifetime is 60 seconds. How many bits would you include in the **AdvertisedWindow** and **SequenceNum** fields of your protocol header?

9 What is the justification for assuming that the maximum segment lifetime in the Internet is 60 seconds?

10 What is the justification for the exponential increase in timeout value proposed by Karn and Partridge?

11 Explain why there is room for only 44 bytes of options in the TCP header.

12 Find out the generic format for TCP header options from *Request for Comments* 793 [UI81]. Outline a strategy that would expand the space available for options beyond the current 44 bytes.

13 Sketch the design of a record-oriented protocol that runs on top of TCP. Implement this protocol in the x-kernel. What problems does this protocol encounter as record sizes grow large?

14 The TCP header does not have a **BID** field, like CHAN does. How does TCP protect itself against the crash-and-reboot scenario that motivates CHAN's **BID**? Why doesn't CHAN use this same strategy?

15 Redesign the BLAST header so that both **DATA** and **SRR** messages use 8-bit integers for fragment identifiers, rather than a bit vector. Implement this change in the x-kernel.

16 Discuss various ways in which flow control can be added to BLAST. How does the x-kernel version of BLAST implement flow control? Implement one of the alternative designs that you have identified.

17 What information must be contained in the active keys for BLAST and CHAN? Recall that each BLAST session can handle multiple outstanding messages and that BLAST on a server may receive messages from multiple client hosts. Also, remember that CHAN on a server can receive the same CID from multiple hosts.

18 Design a timeout mechanism for CHAN. Keep in mind that CHAN messages are of variable sizes.

19 Configure a protocol graph with CHAN and VCHAN. Vary the number of concurrent calls that VCHAN supports. Plot the request/reply throughput (i.e., calls per second) that can be supported on whatever network is available to you. At what point does this throughput curve flatten out? Why does it flatten?

20 How does virtual protocol VADDR know if the destination host is on the same network as the sender?

21 Suppose that the Internet had an official RPC protocol. The Simple Network Management Protocol SNMP (see Appendix) could have made use of this protocol; explain how. Identify other network support functions we have seen that could make use of such a protocol. Note that this question is asking about support functions, not end-user applications.

22 Draw a protocol graph that configures the two RPC protocol stacks discussed in this chapter (SELECT/CHAN/BLAST and SunRPC) under a virtual protocol, VSunRPC, which is used to choose between them. How does VSunRPC know which stack an outgoing message should be directed down?

23 Virtual protocols route messages going down the protocol graph on the sender. How do messages find their way back up the protocol graph on the receiver? Look at the definition of xOpen in the *x-kernel Programmer's Manual* and at the source code for VADDR and VSIZE.

24 Sketch an implementation of a circular send/receive buffer that supports socket-like read and write operations.

25 Write a program that implements a client and server that communicate using a TCP socket. The client opens a text file and streams the text to the server (through the socket), and the server prints the text on the display.

26 Write a test program that uses the socket interface to send messages between a pair of Unix workstations connected by some LAN (e.g., Ethernet, ATM, or FDDI). Use this test program to perform the following experiments.

(a) Measure the round-trip latency of TCP and UDP for different message sizes, e.g., 1 byte, 100 byte, 200 byte, ..., 1000 byte.

(b) Measure the throughput of TCP and UDP for 1-KB, 2-KB, 3-KB, ..., 32-KB messages. Plot the measured throughput as a function of message size.

(c) Measure the throughput of TCP by sending 1 MB of data from one host to another. Do this in a loop that sends a message of some size, e.g., 1024 iterations of a loop that sends 1-KB messages. Repeat the experiment with different message sizes and plot the results.

O ur focus up to this point has been on the hierarchy of protocols that deliver messages from one process to another. What we sometimes forget is that these messages carry data—information that is somehow meaningful to the application processes using the network. While this data is by nature application-specific, there are certain common transformations that application programs apply to their data before they send it. This chapter considers three such transformations: presentation formatting, compression, and encryption. These transformations are sometimes called *data manipulations*.

Presentation formatting has to do with translating data from the representation used internally by the application program into a representation that is suitable for transmission over a network. It is concerned with how different data types (e.g., integers, floating-point numbers, character strings) are encoded in messages and with the fact that different machines typically use different encodings. Presentation formatting also deals with the representation of complex data structures (which may include pointers that have only local significance) in a way that they can be transmitted to a remote machine.

Compression is concerned with reducing the number of bits it takes to represent a particular piece of data, with the goal being to transmit the data using as little network bandwidth as possible. Data is typically compressed before it is given to the transport protocol on the sending side and then decompressed on the receiving side before the application begin to process it.

The third transformation, *encryption*, is used to ensure that anyone who might be eavesdropping on the network—that is, snooping packets as they fly by on a shared-access network or as they sit in a router queue—is not able to read the data in the message. Encryption is also used to authenticate participants and to ensure message integrity.

One of the important aspects of the data manipulations studied in this chapter is that they involve processing every byte of data in the message. This is in contrast to most of the protocols we have seen up to this point, which process a mes-

PROBLEM

What Do We Do with the Data?

It is a capital mistake to theorize before one has data.

—Conan Doyle

sage without ever looking at its contents. Because of this need to read, compute on, and write every byte of data in a message, data manipulations strongly affect the end-to-end throughput we can achieve over a network. In fact, these manipulations are often the limiting factor.

Note that there is a fourth common function that processes every byte of data in a message—error checking. We considered error checking in an earlier chapter (Section 3.4) because it is usually implemented at lower levels of the protocol hierarchy; it is typically not implemented above the end-to-end protocol.

7

End-to-End
Data

7.1 Presentation Formatting

From the network's perspective, application programs send messages to each other. From the application's perspective, however, these messages contain various kinds of *data*—arrays of integers, video frames, lines of text, digital images, and so on. For some of this data, well-established formats have been defined. For example, video is typically transmitted in Moving Pictures Experts Group (MPEG) format, still images are usually transmitted in Joint Photographic Experts Group (JPEG) or Graphical Interchange Format (GIF) format, multimedia documents are transmitted in HyperText Markup Language (HTML) or Multipurpose Internet Mail Extensions (MIME) format, and text is typically transmitted in American Standard Code for Information Interchange (ASCII) format.[1] For other types of data, however, there is no universal agreement about the format; each computer defines its own representation. This is certainly true for the kinds of data that regular programs compute on, such as integers, floating-point numbers, character strings, arrays, and structures.

One of the most common transformations of network data is from the representation used by the application program into a form that is suitable for transmission over a network and vice versa. This transformation is typically called *presentation formatting*. As illustrated in Figure 7.1, the sending program translates the data it wants to transmit from the representation it uses internally into a message that can be transmitted over the network; that is, the data is *encoded* in a message. On the receiving side, the application translates this arriving message into a representation that it can then process; that is, the message is *decoded*. Encoding is sometimes called *argument marshalling*, and decoding is sometimes called *unmarshalling*. This terminology comes from the RPC world, where the client thinks it is invoking a procedure with a set of arguments, but these arguments are then "brought together and ordered in an appropriate and effective way"[2] to form a network message.

You might ask what makes this problem challenging enough to warrant a name like marshalling. One reason is that computers represent data in different ways. For example, some computers represent floating-point numbers in IEEE standard 754 format, while other machines still use their own nonstandard format. Even for something as simple as integers, different architectures use different sizes (e.g., 16 bit, 32 bit, 64 bit). To make matters worse, on some machines integers are represented in *big-endian* form (the most significant bit of a word is in the byte with the highest address), while on other machines integers are represented in *little-endian* form (the most significant bit is in the byte with the lowest address). The Motorola 680x0 is an example of a big-endian architecture and the Intel 80x86 is an example of a little-endian architecture. For example, the big-endian and little-endian representation of the integer 34,677,374 is given in Figure 7.2.

Another reason that marshalling is difficult is that application programs are written in different languages, and even when you are using a single language, there may be more than

---

[1] We will study GIF, JPEG, and MPEG in Section 7.2, in the context of data compression. In effect, however, these standards combine elements of presentation formatting and data compression.
[2] This is a definition of *marshalling* taken from Webster's New Collegiate Dictionary.

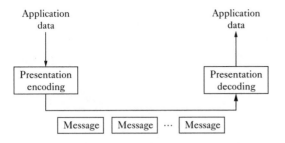

Figure 7.1 Presentation formatting involves encoding and decoding application data.

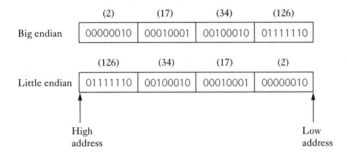

Figure 7.2 Big-endian and little-endian byte order for the integer 34,677,374.

one compiler. For example, compilers have a fair amount of latitude in how they lay out structures (records) in memory, such as how much padding they put between the fields that make up the structure. Thus, you could not simply transmit a structure from one machine to another, even if both machines were of the same architecture and the program was written in the same language, because the compiler on the destination machine might align the fields in the structure differently.

7.1.1 Taxonomy

While anyone who has worked on argument marshalling would tell you that no rocket science is involved—it is a small matter of bit twiddling—there are a surprising number of design choices that you must address. We begin by giving a simple taxonomy for argument marshalling systems. The following is by no means the only viable taxonomy, but it is sufficient to cover most of the interesting alternatives.

Data Types

The first question is what data types the system is going to support. In general, we can classify the types supported by an argument marshalling mechanism at three levels. Each level complicates the task faced by the marshalling system.

At the lowest level, a marshalling system operates on some set of *base types*. Typically, the base types include integers, floating-point numbers, and characters. The system might also support ordinal types and booleans. As described above, the implication of the set of base types is that the encoding process must be able to convert each base type from one representation to another, for example, convert an integer from big-endian to little-endian.

At the next level are *flat types*—structures and arrays. While flat types might at first not appear to complicate argument marshalling, the reality is that they do. The problem is that the compilers used to compile application programs sometimes insert padding between the fields that make up the structure so as to align these fields on word boundaries. The marshalling system typically *packs* structures so that they contain no padding.

At the highest level, the marshalling system might have to deal with *complex types*—those types that are built using pointers. That is, the data structure that one program wants to send to another might not be contained in a single structure, but might instead involve pointers from one structure to another. A tree is a good example of a complex type that involves pointers. Clearly, the data encoder must prepare the data structure for transmission over the network because pointers are implemented by memory addresses, and just because a structure lives at a certain memory address on one machine does not mean it will live at the same address on another machine. In other words, the marshalling system must *linearize* (flatten) complex data structures.

In summary, depending on how complicated the type system is, the task of argument marshalling usually involves converting the base types, packing the structures, and linearizing the complex data structures, all to form a contiguous message that can be transmitted over the network. Figure 7.3 illustrates this task.

Conversion Strategy

Once the type system is established, the next issue is what conversion strategy the argument marshaller will use. There are two general options: *canonical intermediate form* and *receiver-makes-right*. We consider each, in turn.

The idea of canonical intermediate form is to settle on an external representation for each type; the sending host translates from its internal representation to this external representation before sending data, and the receiver translates from this external representation into its local representation when receiving data. To illustrate the idea, consider integer data; other types are treated in a similar manner. You might declare that the big-endian format will be used as the external representation for integers. The sending host must translate each integer it sends into big-endian form and the receiving host must translate big-endian integers into whatever representation it uses. (This is what is done in the Internet for protocol headers.)

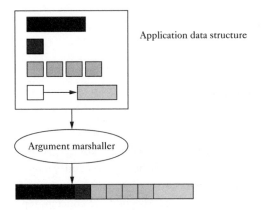

Application data structure

Figure 7.3   Argument marshalling: converting, packing, and linearizing.

Of course, a given host might already use big-endian form, in which case no conversion is necessary.

The alternative, which is sometimes called receiver-makes-right, has the sender transmit data in its own internal format; the sender does not convert the base types, but usually has to pack and flatten more complex data structures. The receiver is then responsible for translating the data from the sender's format into its own local format. The problem with this strategy is that every host must be prepared to convert data from all other machine architectures. In networking, this is known as an *N-by-N solution*: each of N machine architectures must be able to handle all N architectures. In contrast, in a system that uses a canonical intermediate form, each host needs to know only how to convert between its own representation and a single other representation—the external one.

Using a common external format is clearly the correct thing to do, right? This has certainly been the conventional wisdom in the networking community for the past 20 years. The answer is not cut and dried, however. It turns out that there are not that many different representations for the various base classes, or said another way, N is not that large. In addition, the most common case is for two machines of the same type to be communicating with each other. In this situation, it seems silly to translate data from that architecture's representation into some foreign external representation, only to have to translate the data back into the same architecture's representation on the receiver.

A third option, although we know of no existing system that exploits it, is to use receiver-makes-right if the sender knows that the destination has the same architecture; the sender would use some canonical intermediate form if the two machines use different architectures. How would a sender learn the receiver's architecture? It could either learn this information from a name server, or by first using a simple test case to see if the appropriate result occurs.

Figure 7.4 A 32-bit integer encoded in a tagged message.

Tags

The third issue in argument marshalling is how the receiver knows what kind of data is contained in the message it receives. There are two common approaches: *tagged* and *untagged* data. The tagged approach is most intuitive, so we describe it first.

A tag is any additional information included in a message—beyond the concrete representation of the base types—that helps the receiver decode the message. There are several possible tags that might be included in a message. For example, each data item might be augmented with a *type* tag. A type tag indicates that the value that follows is an integer, a floating-point number, or whatever. Another example is a *length* tag. Such a tag is used to indicate the number of elements in an array or the size of an integer. A third example is an *architecture* tag, which might be used in conjunction with the receiver-makes-right strategy to specify the architecture on which the data contained in the message was generated. Figure 7.4 depicts how a simple 32-bit integer might be encoded in a tagged message.

The alternative, of course, is not to use tags. How does the receiver know how to decode the data in this case? It knows because it was programmed to know. In other words, if you call a remote procedure that takes two integers and a floating-point number as arguments, then there is no reason for the remote procedure to inspect tags to know what it has just received. It simply assumes that the message contains two integers and a float, and decodes it accordingly. Note that while this works for most cases, the one place it breaks down is when sending variable-length arrays. In such a case, a length tag is commonly used to indicate how long the array is.

It is also worth noting that the untagged approach means that the presentation formatting is truly end to end. It is not possible for some intermediate agent to interpret the message unless the data is tagged. Why would an intermediate agent need to interpret a message, you might ask? Stranger things have happened, mostly resulting from ad hoc solutions to unexpected problems that the system was not engineered to handle. Poor network design is beyond the scope of this book.

Stubs

A stub is the piece of code that implements argument marshalling. Stubs are typically used to support RPC. On the client side, the stub marshals the procedure arguments into a message that can be transmitted by means of the RPC protocol. On the server side, the stub converts the message back into a set of variables that can be used as arguments to call the remote procedure. Stubs can either be interpreted or compiled.

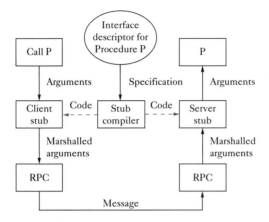

Figure 7.5 Stub compiler takes interface description as input and outputs client and server stubs.

In a compilation-based approach, each procedure has a "customized" client and server stub. This stub is typically generated by a stub compiler, based on a description of the procedure's interface. This situation is illustrated in Figure 7.5. Since the stub is compiled, it is usually very efficient. In an interpretation-based approach, the system provides "generic" client and server stubs that have their parameters set by a description of the procedure's interface. Because it is easy to change this description, interpreted stubs have the advantage of being flexible. Compiled stubs are more common in practice.

7.1.2 Examples (XDR, ASN.1, NDR)

We now briefly describe three popular network data representations in terms of this taxonomy. We use the integer base type to illustrate how each system works.

XDR

External Data Representation (XDR) is the network format used with SunRPC. It supports the C type system but without function pointers, it defines a canonical intermediate form, it does not use tags (except to indicate array lengths), and its stubs are compiled.

An XDR integer is a 32-bit data item that encodes a C integer. It is represented in twos complement notation, with the most significant byte of the C integer in the first byte of the XDR integer, and the least significant byte of the C integer in the fourth byte of the XDR integer. That is, XDR uses big-endian format for integers. XDR supports both signed and unsigned integers, just as C does.

XDR represents variable-length arrays by first specifying an unsigned integer (4 bytes) that gives the number of elements in the array, followed by that many elements of the appropriate type. XDR encodes the components of a structure in the order of their declaration in the structure. For both arrays and structures, the size of each element/component is repre-

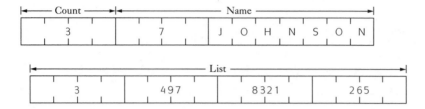

Figure 7.6 Example encoding of a structure in XDR.

sented in a multiple of 4 bytes. Smaller data types are padded out to 4 bytes with 0s. The exception to this "pad to 4 bytes" rule is made for characters, which are encoded one per byte.

The following code fragment gives an example C structure (item) and the XDR routine that encodes/decodes this structure (xdr_item). Figure 7.6 schematically depicts XDR's on-the-wire representation of this structure when the field name is seven characters long and the array list has three values in it.

In this example, xdr_array, xdr_int, and xdr_string are three primitive functions provided by XDR to encode and decode arrays, integers, and character strings, respectively. Argument xdrs is a "context" variable that XDR uses to keep track of where it is in the message being processed; it includes a flag that indicates whether this routine is being used to encode or decode the message. In other words, routines like xdr_item are used on both the client and the server. Note that the application programmer can either write the routine xdr_item by hand or use a stub compiler called rpcgen (not shown) to generate this encoding/decoding routine. In the latter case, rpcgen takes the remote procedure that defines the data structure item as input, and outputs the corresponding stub.

```
#define MAXNAME 256;
#define MAXLIST 100;

struct item {
    int     count;
    char    name[MAXNAME];
    int     list[MAXLIST];
};

bool_t
xdr_item(XDR *xdrs, struct item *ptr)
{
    return(xdr_int(xdrs, &ptr->count) &&
        xdr_string(xdrs, &ptr->name, MAXNAME) &&
        xdr_array(xdrs, &ptr->list, &ptr->count, MAXLIST, sizeof(int), xdr_int));
}
```

Exactly how XDR performs depends, of course, on the complexity of the data. In a simple case of an array of integers, where each integer has to be converted from one byte order to

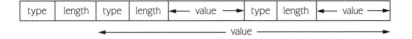

Figure 7.7   Compound types created by means of nesting in ASN.1/BER.

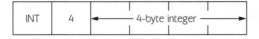

Figure 7.8   ASN.1/BER representation for a 4-byte integer.

another, an average of 2.75 instructions are required for each byte on a DEC Alpha, meaning that converting the whole array is a memory-bound operation. On the 175-MHz Alpha we have been using throughout this book, for example, this means an upper limit on the order of 70 MBps. More complex conversions that require more instructions per byte will run slower.

ASN.1

Abstract Syntax Notation One (ASN.1) is an ISO standard that defines, among other things, a representation for data sent over a network. The representation-specific part of ASN.1 is called the Basic Encoding Rules (BER). ASN.1 supports the C type system without function pointers, defines a canonical intermediate form, uses type tags, and its stubs can be either interpreted or compiled.

ASN.1 represents each data item with a triple of the form

⟨ tag, length, value ⟩.

The tag is typically an 8-bit field, although ASN.1 allows for the definition of multi-byte tags. The length field specifies how many bytes make up the value; we discuss length more below. Compound data types, such as structures, can be constructed by nesting primitive types, as illustrated in Figure 7.7.

If the value is 127 or fewer bytes long, then the length is specified in a single byte. Thus, for example, a 32-bit integer is encoded as a 1-byte type, a 1-byte length, and the 4 bytes that encode the integer, as illustrated in Figure 7.8. The value itself, in the case of an integer, is represented in twos complement notation and big-endian form, just as in XDR. Keep in mind that even though the value of the integer is represented in exactly the same way in both XDR and ASN.1, the XDR representation has neither the type nor the length tags associated with that integer. These two tags both take up space in the message, and more importantly, require processing during marshalling and unmarshalling. This is one reason that ASN.1 is not as efficient as XDR. Another is that the very fact that each data value is preceded by a length field means that the data value is unlikely to fall on a natural byte boundary (e.g., an integer beginning on a word boundary). This complicates the encoding/decoding process.

(a)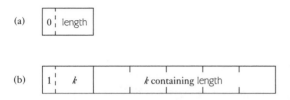

(b)

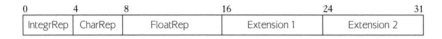

Figure 7.9   ASN.1/BER representation for length: (a) 1 byte; (b) multibyte.

0	4	8	16	24	31
IntegrRep	CharRep	FloatRep	Extension 1	Extension 2	

Figure 7.10   NDR's architecture tag.

If the value is 128 or more bytes long, then multiple bytes are used to specify its length. At this point you may be asking why a byte can specify a length of up to 127 bytes rather than 256. The reason is that 1 bit of the length field is used to denote how long the length field is. A 0 in the eighth bit indicates a 1-byte length field. To specify a longer length, the eighth bit is set to 1, and the other 7 bits indicate how many additional bytes make up the length. Figure 7.9 illustrates a simple 1-byte length and a multibyte length.

NDR

Network Data Representation (NDR) is the data-encoding standard used in the Distributed Computing Environment (DCE).[3] Unlike XDR and ASN.1, NDR uses receiver-makes-right. It does this by inserting an architecture tag at the front of each message; individual data items are untagged. NDR uses a compiler to generate stubs. This compiler takes a description of a program written in the Interface Definition Language (IDL) and generates the necessary stubs. IDL looks pretty much like C, and so essentially supports the C type system.

Figure 7.10 illustrates the 4-byte architecture-definition tag that is included at the front of each NDR-encoded message. The first byte contains two 4-bit fields. The first field, IntegrRep, defines the format for all integers contained in the message. A 0 in this field indicates big-endian integers and a 1 indicates little-endian integers. The CharRep field indicates what character format is used: 0 means ASCII and 1 means EBCDIC. Next, the FloatRep byte defines which floating-point representation is being used: 0 means IEEE 754, 1 means VAX, 2 means Cray, and 3 means IBM. The final 2 bytes are reserved for future use.

---

[3]DCE is defined by the Open Software Foundation (OSF), which is a consortium of companies that includes IBM, Digital, and Hewlett Packard.

Note that in simple cases, such as arrays of integers, NDR does the same amount of work as XDR, and so it is able to achieve the same performance.

7.2 Data Compression

It is sometimes the case that application programs need to send more data in a timely fashion than the bandwidth of the network supports. For example, a video application might have a 10-Mbps video stream that it wants to transmit, but it has only a 1-Mbps network available to it. In cases like this, the data can first be *compressed* at the sender, then transmitted over the network, and finally *decompressed* at the receiver.

The field of data compression has a rich history, dating back to Shannon's pioneer work on information theory in the 1940s. If you think of information theory as the study of techniques for encoding data, then compression is about the efficiency of those encodings—how few bits are needed. In a nutshell, data compression is concerned with removing redundancy from the encoding.

In many ways, compression is inseparable from data encoding. That is, in thinking about how to encode a piece of data in a set of bits, we might just as well think about how to encode the data in the smallest set of bits possible. For example, if you have a block of data that is made up of the symbols A through Z, and if all of these symbols have an equal chance of occurring in the data block you are encoding, then encoding each symbol in 5 bits is the best you can do. If, however, the symbol R occurs 50% of the time, then it would be a good idea to use fewer bits to encode the R than any of the other symbols. In general, if you know the relative probability that each symbol will occur in the data, then you can assign a different number of bits to each possible symbol in a way that minimizes the number of bits it takes to encode a given block of data. This is the essential idea of *Huffman codes*, one of the important early developments in data compression.

For our purposes, there are two classes of compression algorithms. The first, called *lossless compression*, ensures that the data recovered from the compression/decompression process is exactly the same as the original data. A lossless compression algorithm is used to compress file data, such as executable code, text files, and numeric data, because programs that process such file data cannot tolerate mistakes in the data. In contrast, *lossy compression* does not promise that the data received is exactly the same as the data sent. This is because a lossy algorithm removes information that it cannot later restore. Hopefully, however, the lost information will not be missed by the receiver. Lossy algorithms are used to compress digital imagery, including video. This makes sense because such data often contains more information than the human eye can perceive, and for that matter, may already contains errors and imperfections that the human eye is able to compensate for. It is also the case that lossy algorithms typically achieve much better compression ratios than do their lossless counterparts; they can be as much as an order of magnitude better.

It might seem that compressing your data before sending it would always be a good idea, since the network would be able to deliver compressed data in less time than uncompressed data. This is not necessarily the case, however. Compression/decompression algorithms often involve time-consuming computations. The question you have to ask is whether or not the time it takes to compress/decompress the data is worthwhile given such factors as the host's processor speed and the network bandwidth. Specifically, if B_c is the average bandwidth at which data can be pushed through the compressor and decompressor (in series), B_n is the network bandwidth (including network processing costs) for uncompressed data, r is the average compression ratio, and if we assume that all the data is compressed before any of it is transmitted, then the time taken to send x bytes of uncompressed data is x/B_n, whereas the time to compress it and send the compressed data is $x/B_c + x/(rB_n)$. Thus, compression is beneficial if

$$x/B_c + x/(rB_n) < x/B_n$$

which is equivalent to

$$B_c > r/(r-1) \times B_n$$

For example, for a compression ratio of 2, B_c would have to be greater than $2 \times B_n$ for compression to make sense.

7.2.1 Lossless Compression Algorithms

We begin by introducing three lossless compression algorithms. We do not describe these algorithms in much detail—we just give the essential idea—since it is the lossy algorithms used to compress image and video data that are of the greatest interest in today's network environment. We do comment, though, on how well these lossless algorithms work on digital imagery. Some of the ideas exploited by these lossless techniques show up again in later sections when we consider the lossy algorithms that are used to compress images.

Run Length Encoding

Run length encoding (RLE) is a compression technique with a brute-force simplicity. The idea is to replace consecutive occurrences of a given symbol with only one copy of the symbol, plus a count of how many times that symbol occurs; hence the name "run length." For example, the string AAABBCDDDD would be encoded as 3A2B1C4D.

RLE can be used to compress digital imagery by comparing adjacent pixel values and then encoding only the changes. For images that have large homogeneous regions, this technique is quite effective. For example, it is not uncommon that RLE can achieve compression ratios on the order of 8-to-1 for scanned text images. RLE works well on such files because they often contain a large amount of white space that can be removed. In fact, RLE is the key compression algorithm used to transmit faxes. However, for images with even a small degree of local variation, it is not uncommon for compression to actually increase the image byte size, since it takes two bytes to represent a single symbol when that symbol is not repeated.

Differential Pulse Code Modulation

Another simple lossless compression algorithm is Differential Pulse Code Modulation (DPCM). The idea here is to first output a reference symbol, and then for each symbol in the data, to output the difference between that symbol and the reference symbol. For example, using symbol A as the reference symbol, the string AAABBCDDDD would be encoded as A0001123333 since A is the same as the reference symbol, B has a difference of 1 from the reference symbol, and so on. Note that this simple example does not illustrate the real benefit of DPCM, which is that when the differences are small, they can be encoded with fewer bits than the symbol itself. In this example, the range of differences 0–3 can be represented with 2 bits each, rather than the 7 or 8 bits required by the full character. As soon as the difference becomes too large, a new reference symbol is selected.

DPCM works better than RLE for most digital imagery, since it takes advantage of the fact that adjacent pixels are usually similar. Due to this correlation, the dynamic range of the differences between the adjacent pixel values can be significantly less than the dynamic range of the original image, and this range can therefore be represented using fewer bits. Using DPCM, we have measured compression ratios of 1.5-to-1 on digital images.

Dictionary-Based Methods

The final lossless compression method we consider is the dictionary-based approach, of which the Lempel-Ziv (LZ) compression algorithm is the best known. The Unix compress command uses a variation of the LZ algorithm.

The idea of a dictionary-based compression algorithm is to build a dictionary (table) of variable-length strings (think of them as common phrases) that you expect to find in the data, and then to replace each of these strings when it appears in the data with the corresponding index to the dictionary. For example, instead of working with individual characters in text data, you could treat each word as a string and output the index in the dictionary for that word. To further elaborate on this example, the word "compression" has the index 4978 in one particular dictionary; it is the 4978th word in /usr/share/dict/words. To compress a body of text, each time the string "compression" appears, it would be replaced by 4978. Since this particular dictionary has just over 25,000 words in it, it would take 15 bits to encode the index, meaning that the string "compression" could be represented in 15 bits rather than the 77 bits required by 7-bit ASCII. This is a compression ratio of 5-to-1!

Of course, this leaves the question of where the dictionary comes from. One option is to define a static dictionary, preferably one that is tailored for the data being compressed. A more general solution, and the one used by LZ compression, is to adaptively define the dictionary based on the contents of the data being compressed. In this case, however, the dictionary constructed during compression has to be sent along with the data so that the decompression half of the algorithm can do its job. Exactly how you build an adaptive dictionary has been a subject of extensive research; we discuss important papers on the subject at the end of this chapter.

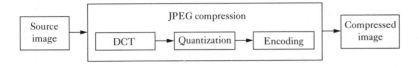

Figure 7.11   Block diagram of JPEG compression.

A variation of the LZ algorithm is used to compress digital images in the Graphical Interchange Format (GIF). Before doing that, GIF first reduces 24-bit color images to 8-bit color images. This is done by identifying the colors used in the picture, of which there will typically be considerably fewer than 2^{24}, and then picking the 256 colors that most closely approximate the colors used in the picture. These colors are stored in a table, which can be indexed with an 8-bit number, and the value for each pixel is replaced by the appropriate index. Note that this is an example of lossy compression for any picture with more than 256 colors. GIF then runs an LZ variant over the result, treating common sequences of pixels as the strings that make up the dictionary. Using this approach, GIF is sometimes able to achieve compression ratios on the order of 10-to-1, but only when the image consists of a relatively small number of discrete colors. Images of natural scenes, which often include a more continuous spectrum of colors, cannot be compressed at this ratio using GIF. As another data point, we were able to get a 2-to-1 compression ratio when we applied the LZ-based Unix compress command to the x-kernel distribution.

7.2.2   Image Compression (JPEG)

Given the increase in the use of digital imagery in the past few years—this use was spawned by the invention of graphical displays, not high-speed networks—the need for compression algorithms designed for digital imagery data has grown more and more critical. In response to this need, the ISO has defined a digital image format known as JPEG, named after the Joint Photographic Experts Group that designed it. (The "Joint" in JPEG stands for a joint ISO/ITU effort.) This section describes the compression algorithm at the heart of JPEG. The next section then describes a related format—MPEG—that is used for video data.

Before describing JPEG compression, one point that needs to be made is that JPEG, as well as GIF and MPEG, is more than just a compression algorithm. They also define the *format* for image or video data, much the same way that XDR, NDL, and ASN.1 define the format for numeric and string data. However, this section concentrates on the compression aspects of these standards.

JPEG compression takes place in three phases, as illustrated in Figure 7.11. On the compression side, the image is fed through these three phases one 8×8 block at a time. The first phase applies the Discrete Cosine Transform (DCT) to the block. If you think of the image as a signal in the spatial domain, then DCT transforms this signal into an equivalent signal in the *spatial frequency* domain. After the DCT, the second phase applies a quantization to the resulting signal, and in so doing, loses the least significant bits of that signal. The third phase encodes the final result, but in so doing, adds an element of lossless compression to the lossy compression achieved by the first two phases. Decompression follows these same three phases, but in reverse order.

The following discussion describes each phase in more detail. It is simplified by considering only grayscale images; color images are discussed at the end of this section. In the case of grayscale images, each pixel in the image is given by an 8-bit value that indicates the grayness (brightness) of the pixel, where 0 equals white and 255 equals black.

DCT Phase

DCT is a transformation closely related to the Fast Fourier Transform (FFT). It takes an 8×8 matrix of pixel values as input and outputs an 8×8 matrix of frequency coefficients. You can think of the input matrix as a 64-point signal that is defined in two spatial dimensions (x and y); DCT breaks this signal into 64 spatial frequencies. To get an intuitive feel for spatial frequency, imagine yourself moving across a picture in, say, the x direction. You would see the value of each pixel varying as some function of x. If this value changes slowly with increasing x, then it has a low spatial frequency, and if it changes rapidly, it has a high spatial frequency. So the low frequencies correspond to the gross features of the picture, while the high frequencies correspond to fine detail. The idea behind the DCT is to separate the gross features, which are essential to viewing the image, from the fine detail, which is less essential and, in some cases, might be barely perceived by the eye.

DCT, along with its inverse which is performed during decompression, is defined by the following formulas:

$$DCT(i,j) = \frac{1}{\sqrt{2N}} C(i)C(j) \sum_{x=0}^{N-1} \sum_{y=0}^{N-1} pixel(x,y) \cos\left[\frac{(2x+1)i\pi}{2N}\right] \cos\left[\frac{(2y+1)i\pi}{2N}\right]$$

$$pixel(x,y) = \frac{1}{\sqrt{2N}} \sum_{i=0}^{N-1} \sum_{j=0}^{N-1} C(i)C(j)DCT(i,j) \cos\left[\frac{(2x+1)i\pi}{2N}\right] \cos\left[\frac{(2y+1)i\pi}{2N}\right]$$

$$C(x) = \frac{1}{\sqrt{2}} \quad \text{if } x = 0, \text{else } 1 \text{ if } x > 0$$

The first frequency coefficient, at location (0,0) in the output matrix, is called the *DC coefficient*. Intuitively, we can see that the DC coefficient is a measure of the average value of the 64 input pixels. The other 63 elements of the output matrix are called the *AC coefficients*. They add the higher-spatial-frequency information to this average value. Thus, as you go from the first frequency coefficient toward the 64th frequency coefficient, you are moving from low-frequency information to high-frequency information; from the broad strokes of the image to finer and finer detail. These higher-frequency coefficients are increasingly unimportant to the perceived quality of the image. It is the second phase of JPEG that decides which portion of which coefficients to throw away.

Quantization Phase

The second phase of JPEG is where the compression becomes lossy; DCT does not itself lose information, it just transforms the image into a form that makes it easier to know what information to remove. (Although not lossy, per se, there is of course some loss of precision during the DCT phase due to the use of fixed-point arithmetic.) Quantization is easy to understand—it's simply a matter of dropping the insignificant bits of the frequency coefficients.

To see how the quantization phase works, imagine that you want to compress some whole numbers less than 100, e.g., 45, 98, 23, 66, and 7. If you decided that knowing these numbers truncated to the nearest multiple of 10 is sufficient for your purposes, then you could divide each number by the quantum 10 using integer arithmetic, yielding 4, 9, 2, 6, and 0. These numbers can each be encoded in 4 bits rather than the 7 bits needed to encode the original numbers.

Rather than using the same quantum for all 64 coefficients, JPEG uses a quantization table that gives the quantum to use for each of the coefficients, as specified in the formula given below. You can think of this table (Quantum) as a parameter that can be set to control how much information is lost, and correspondingly, how much compression is achieved. In practice, the JPEG standard specifies a set of quantization tables that have proven effective in compressing digital images; an example quantization table is given in Table 7.1. In tables like this one, the low coefficients have a quantum close to 1 (meaning that little low-frequency information is lost) and the high coefficients have larger values (meaning that more high-frequency information is lost). Notice that as a result of such quantization tables, many of the high-frequency coefficients end up being set to 0 after quantization, making them ripe for further compression in the third phase.

The basic quantization equation is

$$\mathsf{QuantizedValue}(i, j) = \mathsf{IntegerRound}(DCT(i, j)/\mathsf{Quantum}(i, j))$$

where

$$\mathsf{IntegerRound}(x) = \begin{cases} \lfloor x + 0.5 \rfloor & \text{if } x \geq 0 \\ \lfloor x - 0.5 \rfloor & \text{if } x < 0 \end{cases}$$

Decompression is then simply defined as

$$DCT(i, j) = \mathsf{QuantizedValue}(i, j) \times \mathsf{Quantum}(i, j)$$

For example, if the DC coefficient (i.e., DCT(0,0)) for a particular block was equal to 25, then the quantization of this value using Table 7.1 would result in $\lfloor 25/3 + 0.5 \rfloor = 8$. During decompression, this coefficient would then be restored as $8 \times 3 = 24$.

$$
\text{Quantum} =
\begin{bmatrix}
3 & 5 & 7 & 9 & 11 & 13 & 15 & 17 \\
5 & 7 & 9 & 11 & 13 & 15 & 17 & 19 \\
7 & 9 & 11 & 13 & 15 & 17 & 19 & 21 \\
9 & 11 & 13 & 15 & 17 & 19 & 21 & 23 \\
11 & 13 & 15 & 17 & 19 & 21 & 23 & 25 \\
13 & 15 & 17 & 19 & 21 & 23 & 25 & 27 \\
15 & 17 & 19 & 21 & 23 & 25 & 27 & 29 \\
17 & 19 & 21 & 23 & 25 & 27 & 29 & 31
\end{bmatrix}
$$

Table 7.1 Example JPEG quantization table.

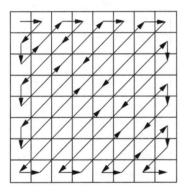

Figure 7.12 Zigzag traversal of quantized frequency coefficients.

Encoding Phase

The final phase of JPEG encodes the quantized frequency coefficients in a compact form. This results in additional compression, but this compression is lossless. Starting with the DC coefficient in position (0,0), the coefficients are processed in the zigzag sequence shown in Figure 7.12. Along this zigzag, a form of run length encoding is used—RLE is applied to only the 0 coefficients, which is significant because many of the later coefficients are 0. The individual coefficient values are then encoded using a Huffman code. (The JPEG standard allows the implementer to use an arithmetic coding instead of the Huffman code.)

In addition, because the DC coefficient contains a large percentage of the information about the 8×8 block from the source image, and images typically change slowly from block to block, each DC coefficient is encoded as the difference from the previous DC coefficient. This is not unlike the strategy used in DPCM, described in Section 7.2.1.

Color Images

The preceding discussion assumed that each pixel was given by a single grayscale value. In the case of a color image, there are many different representations for each pixel to choose from. One representation, called RGB, represents each pixel with three color components: red, green, and blue. RGB is the representation of color typically supported by graphical input and output devices. Another representation, called YUV, also has three components: one luminance (Y) and two chrominance (U and V). Just like RGB, YUV is a three-dimensional coordinate system. However, compared to RGB, its coordinates are rotated to better match the human visual system. This is advantageous because the human visual system is not uniformly sensitive to colors. For example, we can distinguish the luminance (brightness) of a pixel much better than its hue (color).

Exactly why the three components in each of the two representations can be combined to produce acceptable color is an interesting question. The simple answer is that two-coordinate color systems have been defined, but they have proven inadequate for faithfully reproducing colors as perceived by humans. What is important to our discussion is that each pixel in a color image is given by three separate values. To compress such an image, each of these three components is processed independently in exactly the same way as the single grayscale value was processed. In other words, you can think of a color image as three separate images, where these separate images are overlaid on top of each other when displayed. Note that in general, JPEG is not limited to three-component images; it is possible to compress a multispectral image using JPEG.

JPEG includes a number of variations that control how much compression you achieve versus the fidelity of the image. This can be done, for example, by using different quantization tables. These variations, plus the fact that different images have different characteristics, make it impossible to say with any precision the compression ratios that can be achieved with JPEG. The widely accepted generalization, however, is that JPEG is able to compress 24-bit color images by a ratio of roughly 30-to-1: the image can first be compressed by a factor of three by reducing the 24 bits of color to 8 bits of color (as described for GIF) and then by another factor of 10 by using the algorithm described in this section.

7.2.3 Video Compression (MPEG)

We now turn our attention to the MPEG format, which is named after the Moving Pictures Expert Group that defined it. To a first approximation, a moving picture (i.e., video) is simply a succession of still images (frames) displayed at some video rate. Each of these frames can be compressed using the same DCT-based technique used in JPEG. Stopping at this point would be a mistake, however, because it fails to remove the frame-to-frame redundancy present in a video sequence. For example, two successive frames of video will contain almost identical information if there is not much motion in the scene, so it would be unnecessary to send the

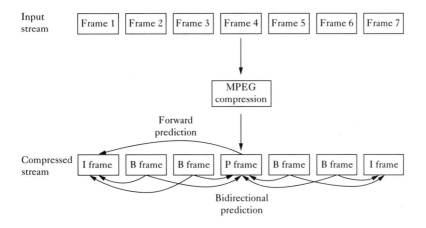

Figure 7.13 Sequence of I, P, and B frames generated by MPEG.

same information twice. Even when there is motion, there may be plenty of redundancy since a moving object may not change from one frame to the next; in some cases, only its position changes. MPEG takes this interframe redundancy into consideration. MPEG also defines a mechanism for encoding an audio signal with the video, but we consider only the video aspect of MPEG in this section.

Frame Types

MPEG takes a sequence of video frames as input and compresses them into three types of frames, called *I frames* (intrapicture), *P frames* (predicted picture), and *B frames* (bidirectional predicted picture). Each frame of input is compressed into one of these three frame types. I frames can be thought of as reference frames; they are self-contained, depending on neither earlier frames nor later frames. To a first approximation, an I frame is simply the JPEG compressed version of the corresponding frame in the video source. P and B frames are not self-contained; they specify relative differences from some reference frame. More specifically, a P frame specifies the differences from the previous I frame, while a B frame gives an interpolation between the previous and subsequent I or P frames.

Figure 7.13 illustrates a sequence of seven video frames that, after being compressed by MPEG, result in a sequence of I, P, and B frames. The two I frames stand alone; each can be decompressed at the receiver independently of any other frames. The P frame depends on the preceding I frame; it can be decompressed at the receiver only if the preceding I frame also arrives. Each of the B frames depend on both the preceding I or P frame and the subsequent I or P frame. Both of these reference frames must arrive at the receiver before MPEG can decompress the B frame to reproduce the original video frame.

Note that because each B frame depends on a later frame in the sequence, the compressed frames are not transmitted in sequential order. Instead, the sequence I B B P B B I

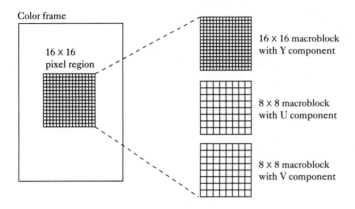

Figure 7.14 Each frame as a collection of macroblocks.

shown in Figure 7.13 is transmitted as I P B B I B B. Also, MPEG does not define the ratio of I frames to P and B frames; this ratio may vary depending on the required compression and picture quality. For example, it is permissible to transmit only I frames. This would be similar to using JPEG to compress the video.

In contrast to the preceding discussion of JPEG, the following focuses on the *decoding* of an MPEG stream. It is a little easier to describe, and it is the operation that is more often implemented in networking systems today, since MPEG coding is so expensive that it is normally done offline, i.e., not in real time. For example, in a video-on-demand system, the video would be encoded and stored on disk ahead of time. When a viewer wanted to watch the video, the MPEG stream would then be transmitted to the viewer's machine which would decode and display the stream in real time.

Let's look more closely at the three frame types. As mentioned above, I frames are approximately equal to the JPEG compressed version of the source frame. The main difference is that MPEG works in units of 16×16 *macroblocks*. For a color video represented in YUV, the U and V components in each macroblock are "down sampled" into an 8×8 block. That is, each 2×2 subblock in the macroblock is given by one U value and one V value—the average of the four pixel values. The subblock still has four Y values. This can be done because the U and V components can be transmitted less accurately without visibly disturbing the image, since humans are less sensitive to color than they are to brightness. The relationship between a frame and the corresponding macroblocks is given in Figure 7.14.

The P and B frames are also processed in units of macroblocks. Intuitively, we can see that the information they carry for each macroblock captures the motion in the video, that is, it shows in what direction and how far the macroblock moved relative to the reference frame(s). The following describes how a B frame is used to reconstruct a frame during decompression; P frames are handled in a similar manner, except that they depend on only one reference frame instead of two.

Before getting to the details of how a B frame is decompressed, we first note that each macroblock in a B frame is not necessarily defined relative to both an earlier and a later frame, as suggested above, but may instead simply be specified relative to just one or the other. In fact, a given macroblock in a B frame can use the same intracoding as is used in an I frame. This flexibility exists because if the motion picture is changing too rapidly, then it sometimes makes sense to give the intrapicture encoding rather than a forward- or backward-predicted encoding. Thus, each macroblock in a B frame includes a type field that indicates which encoding is used for that macroblock. In the following discussion, however, we consider only the general case in which the macroblock uses bidirectional predictive encoding.

In such a case, each macroblock in a B frame is represented with a 4-tuple: (1) a coordinate for the macroblock in the frame, (2) a motion vector relative to the previous reference frame, (3) a motion vector relative to the subsequent reference frame, and (4) a delta (δ) for each pixel in the macroblock (i.e., how much each pixel has changed relative to the two reference pixels). For each pixel in the macroblock, the first task is to find the corresponding reference pixel in the past and future reference frames. This is done using the two motion vectors associated with the macroblock. Then, the delta for the pixel is added to the average of these two reference pixels. Stated more precisely, if we let F_p and F_f denote the past and future reference frames, respectively, and the past/future motion vectors are given by (x_p, y_p) and (x_f, y_f), then the pixel at coordinate (x, y) in the current frame (denoted F_c) is computed as

$$F_c(x, y) = (F_p(x + x_p, y + y_p) + F_f(x + x_f, y + y_f))/2 + \delta(x, y)$$

where δ is the delta for the pixel as specified in the B frame. These deltas are encoded in the same way as pixels in I frames. That is, they are run through DCT and then quantized. Since the deltas are typically small, most of the DCT coefficients are 0 after quantization, hence they can be effectively compressed.

It should be fairly clear from the preceding discussion how encoding would be performed, with one exception. When generating a B or P frame during compression, MPEG must decide where to place the macroblocks. Recall that each macroblock in a P frame, for example, is defined relative to a macroblock in an I frame, but that the macroblock in the P frame need not be in the same part of the frame as the corresponding macroblock in the I frame—the difference in position is given by the motion vector. You would like to pick a motion vector that makes the macroblock in the P frame as similar as possible to the corresponding macroblock in the I frame, so that the deltas for that macroblock can be as small as possible. This means that you need to figure out where objects in the picture moved from one frame to the next. This is the problem of *motion estimation*, and several techniques (heuristics) for solving this problem are known. (We discuss papers that consider this problem at the end of this chapter.) The difficulty of this problem is one of the reasons that MPEG encoding takes longer than decoding on equivalent hardware. MPEG does not specify any particular technique; it only defines the format for encoding this information in B and P frames and the algorithm for reconstructing the pixel during decompression, as given above.

Effectiveness and Performance

MPEG typically achieves a compression ratio of 90-to-1, although ratios as high as 150-to-1 are not unheard of. In terms of the individual frame types, one can expect a compression ratio of approximately 30-to-1 for the I frames (this is consistent with the ratios achieved using JPEG when 24-bit color is first reduced to 8-bit color), while P and B frame compression ratios are typically three to five times smaller than the rates for the I frame. Without first reducing the 24 bits of color to 8 bits, the achievable compression with MPEG is typically between 30-to-1 and 50-to-1.

MPEG involves an expensive computation. On the compression side, it is typically done offline, which is not a problem for preparing movies for a video-on-demand service. Video can be compressed in real time using hardware, but such devices are fairly expensive today. On the decompression side, low-cost MPEG video boards are available, but they do little more than YUV color lookup, which fortunately is the most expensive step. Most of the actual MPEG decoding is done in software. Until recently, processors have not been fast enough to keep pace with 30-frames-per-second video rates when decoding MPEG streams purely in software. With a 175-MHz RISC architecture available in 1994, however, it is possible to decompress MPEG fast enough to keep up with a 320×240 video stream running at 30 frames per second.

7.3 Security

Computer networks are typically a shared resource used by many applications for many different purposes. Sometimes the data transmitted between application processes is confidential, and the applications would prefer that others not be able to read it. For example, when purchasing a product over the World Wide Web, users sometimes transmit their credit card numbers over the network. This is a dangerous thing to do since it is easy for someone to eavesdrop on the network and read all the packets that fly by. Therefore, a third transformation made to data sent over an end-to-end channel is to *encrypt* it, with the goal of keeping anyone who is eavesdropping on the channel from being able to read the contents of the message.

The idea of encryption is simple enough: the sender applies an *encryption* function to the original *plaintext* message, the resulting *ciphertext* message is sent over the network, and the receiver applies a reverse function (called *decryption*) to recover the original plaintext. The encryption/decryption process generally depends on a secret *key* shared between the sender and the receiver. When a suitable combination of a key and an encryption algorithm is used, it is sufficiently difficult for an eavesdropper to break the ciphertext and the sender and receiver can rest assured that their communication is secure.

This familiar use of cryptography is designed to ensure privacy—preventing the unauthorized release of information. Privacy, however, is not the only service that cryptography provides. It can also be used to support other equally important services, including authentication (verifying the identity of the remote participant) and message integrity (making sure that the message has not been altered). This section first introduces the basic idea of

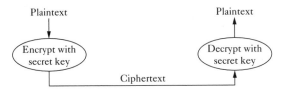

Figure 7.15   Secret key encryption.

cryptography—including a description of the two most common encryption algorithms, the
Data Encryption Standard (DES) and Rivest, Shamir, and Adleman (RSA)—and then shows
how these algorithms can be used to provide authentication and integrity services.

One thing to keep in mind while reading this section is that the various algorithms and
protocols for privacy, authentication, and integrity are being described in isolation. In practice, constructing a secure system requires an intricate combination of just the right set of protocols and algorithms. This is a challenging task because each protocol is vulnerable to a different set of attacks. To make matters worse, determining when a security protocol is "good
enough" is as much art and politics as science. A thorough analysis of these different attacks,
and how you might build a complete system that minimizes the risk of compromise, is beyond
the scope of this book.

7.3.1   Secret Key versus Public Key Cryptography

Broadly speaking, there are two types of cryptographic algorithms: *secret key* algorithms and
public key algorithms. Secret key algorithms are symmetric in the sense that both participants[4]
in the communication share a single key. Figure 7.15 illustrates the use of secret key encryption to transmit data over an otherwise insecure channel. The Data Encryption Standard
(DES) is the best-known example of a secret key encryption function.

In contrast to a pair of participants sharing a single secret key, *public key* cryptography involves each participant having a *private* key that is shared with no one else and a *public* key that
is published so everyone knows it. To send a secure message to this participant, you encrypt
the message using the widely known public key. The participant then decrypts the message
using his or her private key. This scenario is depicted in Figure 7.16. RSA—named after its
inventors, Rivest, Shamir, and Adleman—is the best-known public key encryption algorithm.

There is actually a third type of cryptography algorithm, called a *hash* or *message digest*
function. Unlike the preceding two types of algorithms, cryptographic hash functions involve
the use of no keys. Instead, the idea is to map a potentially large message into a small fixed-
length number, analogous to the way a regular hash function maps values from a large space
into values from a small space.

---

[4]We use the term *participant* for the parties involved in a secure communication since that is the term we have been using
throughout the book to identify the two endpoints of a channel. In the security world, they are typically called *principals*.

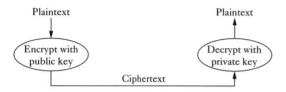

Figure 7.16 Public key encryption.

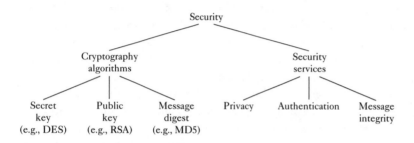

Figure 7.17 Taxonomy of network security.

The best way to think of a cryptographic hash function is that it computes a *cryptographic checksum* over a message. That is, just as a regular checksum protects the receiver from accidental changes to the message, a cryptographic checksum protects the receiver from malicious changes to the message. This is because all cryptographic hash algorithms are carefully selected to be one-way functions—given a cryptographic checksum for a message, it is virtually impossible to figure out what message produced that checksum. Said another way, it is not computationally feasible to find two messages that hash to the same cryptographic checksum. The relevance of this property is that if you are given a checksum for a message (along with the message) and you are able to compute exactly the same checksum for that message, then it is highly likely that this message produced the checksum you were given.

Although we will not describe it in detail, the most widely used cryptographic checksum algorithm is Message Digest version 5 (MD5). An important property of MD5, in addition to those properties outlined in the previous paragraph, is that it is much more efficient to compute than either DES or RSA. We will see the relevance of this fact later in this section.

To re-emphasize, cryptography algorithms like DES, RSA, and MD5 are just building blocks from which a secure system can be constructed. Figure 7.17 gives a simple taxonomy that illustrates this point. In looking at these services and building blocks, we should consider the following question: How did the participants get the various keys in the first place? This is the *key distribution* problem, one of the central problems in security, as we will see in the following subsections.

7.3.2 Encryption Algorithms (DES, RSA)

Before showing how encryption algorithms are used to build secure systems, we first describe how the two best-known algorithms—DES and RSA—work. We will also give some insight into *why* they work, but there is only so much we can do on this front since the design principles that underlie DES are not public knowledge. In the case of RSA, a deep explanation for why it works would require a background in number theory that is beyond the scope of this book, but we can provide some intuition into the underlying principles. Before looking at either algorithm, however, let's step back and ask what we want from an encryption algorithm.

Requirements

The basic requirement for an encryption algorithm is that it be able to turn plaintext into ciphertext in such a way that only the intended recipient—the holder of the decryption key—can recover the plaintext. What this means is that the encryption method should be safe from attacks by people who do not hold the key. As a starting point, we should assume that the encryption algorithm itself is known and that only the key is kept secret. The reason for this assumption is that if you depend on the algorithm being kept secret, then you have to throw it out when you believe it is no longer secret. This means potentially frequent changes of algorithm, which is problematic since it takes a lot of work to develop a new algorithm. Also, one of the best ways to know that an algorithm is effective is to use it for a long time—if no one breaks it, it's probably secure. (Fortunately, there are plenty of people who will try to break algorithms and who will let it be widely known when they have succeeded, so no news is generally good news.) Thus, there is considerable risk in deploying a new algorithm. Therefore, our first requirement is that secrecy of the key, and not of the algorithm itself, is the only thing that is needed to ensure the privacy of the data.

It is important to realize that when someone receives a piece of ciphertext, they may have more information at their disposal than just the ciphertext itself. For example, they may know that the plaintext was written in English, which means that the letter e occurs more often in the plaintext that any other letter; the frequency of many other letters and common letter combinations can also be predicted. This information can greatly simplify the task of finding the key. Similarly, they may know something about the likely contents of the message; e.g., the word "login" is likely to occur at the start of a remote login session. This may enable a "known plaintext" attack, which has a much higher chance of success than a "ciphertext only" attack. Even better is a "chosen plaintext" attack, which may be enabled by feeding some information to the sender that you know the sender is likely to transmit—such things have happened in wartime, for example.

The best cryptographic algorithms, therefore, can prevent the attacker from deducing the key even when the individual knows both the plaintext and the ciphertext. One approach, the one taken in DES, is to make the algorithm so complicated that virtually none of the structure of the plaintext remains in the ciphertext. This leaves the attacker with no choice but to search the space of possible keys exhaustively. This can be made infeasible by choosing a suit-

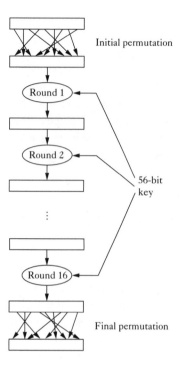

Initial permutation

Round 1

Round 2

56-bit
key

⋮

Round 16

Final permutation

Figure 7.18   High-level outline of DES.

ably large key space and by making the operation of checking a key reasonably costly. As we will see, DES is now becoming only marginally secure on that basis.

DES

DES encrypts a 64-bit block of plaintext using a 64-bit key. The key actually contains only 56 usable bits—the last bit of each of the 8 bytes in the key is a parity bit for that byte. Also, messages larger than 64 bits can be encrypted using DES, as described below.

DES has three distinct phases: (1) the 64 bits in the block are permuted (shuffled), (2) 16 rounds of an identical operation are applied to the resulting data and the key, and (3) the inverse of the original permutation is applied to the result. This high-level outline of DES is depicted in Figure 7.18.

A table representing part of the initial permutation is shown in Table 7.2. The final permutation is the inverse (e.g., bit 40 would be permuted to bit position 1). It is generally agreed that these two permutations add nothing to the security of DES. Some security experts speculate that they were included to make the computation take longer, but it is just as likely that they are an artifact of the initial hardware implementation, involving some restriction of pin layout, for example.

Input Position	1	2	3	4	5	...	60	61	62	63	64
Output Position	40	8	48	16	56	...	9	49	17	57	25

Table 7.2   Initial (and final) DES permutation.

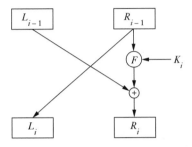

Figure 7.19   Manipulation at each round of DES.

During each round, the 64-bit block is broken into two 32-bit halves, and a different 48 bits are selected from the 56-bit key. If we denote the left and right halves of the block at round i as L_i and R_i, respectively, and the 48-bit key at round i as K_i, then these three pieces are combined during round i according to the following rule:

$$L_i = R_{i-1}$$
$$R_i = L_{i-1} \oplus F(R_{i-1}, K_i)$$

where F is a combiner function described below and $\oplus$ is the exclusive-OR (XOR) operator. Figure 7.19 illustrates the basic operation of each round. Note that L_0 and R_0 correspond to the left and right halves of the 64-bit block that results from the initial permutation, and that L_{16} and R_{16} are combined back together to form the 64-bit block to which the final inverse permutation is applied.

We now need to define function F and show how each K_i is derived from the 56-bit key. We start with the key. Initially, the 56-bit key is permuted according to Table 7.3. Note that every eighth bit is ignored (i.e., bit 64 is missing from the table), reducing the key from 64 bits to 56 bits. Then for each round, the current 56 bits are divided into two 28-bit halves and each half is independently shifted left either one or two digits, depending on the round. The number of bits shifted in each round is given in Table 7.4. The 56 bits that result from this shift are used as both input for the next round (i.e., the preceding shift is repeated) and to select the 48 bits that make up the key for the current round. Table 7.5 shows how 48 of the 56 bits are selected; note that they are simultaneously selected and permuted. For example, the bit in position 9 is not selected because it is not in the table.

Function F combines the resulting 48-bit key for round i (K_i) with the right half of the data block after round $i - 1$ (R_{i-1}), as follows. To simplify our notation, we refer to K_i and

Input Position	1	2	3	4	5	...	59	60	61	62	63
Output Position	8	16	24	56	52	...	17	25	45	37	29

Table 7.3   DES key permutation.

Round	1	2	3	4	5	6	7	8	9	10	11	12	13	14	15	16
Shift	1	1	2	2	2	2	2	2	1	2	2	2	2	2	2	1

Table 7.4   DES key shifts per round.

Input Position	1	2	3	4	5	6	7	8	10	11	12	13	14	15	16	17
Output Position	5	24	7	16	6	10	20	18	12	3	15	23	1	9	19	2

Input Position	19	20	21	23	24	26	27	28	29	30	31	32	33	34	36	37
Output Position	14	22	11	13	4	17	21	8	47	31	27	48	35	41	46	28

Input Position	39	40	41	42	44	45	46	47	48	49	50	51	52	53	55	56
Output Position	39	32	25	44	37	34	43	29	36	38	45	33	26	42	30	40

Table 7.5   DES compression permutation.

R_{i-1} as K and R, respectively. First, function F expands R from 32 bits into 48 bits so that it can be combined with the 48-bit K. It does this by breaking R into eight 4-bit chunks and expanding each chunk into 6 bits by stealing the rightmost and leftmost bit from the left and right adjacent 4-bit chunks, respectively. This expansion is illustrated in Figure 7.20, where R is treated as circular in the sense that the first and last chunks get their extra bit from each other.

Next, the 48-bit K is divided into eight 6-bit chunks, and each chunk is XORed with the corresponding chunk that resulted from the previous expansion of R. Finally, each resulting 6-bit value is fed through something called a *substitution box* (S box), which reduces each 6-bit chunk back into 4 bits. There are actually eight different S boxes, one for each of the 6-bit chunks. You can think of an S box as just performing a many-to-one mapping from 6-bit numbers to 4-bit numbers. Table 7.6 gives part of the S box function for the first chunk. We are now done with round i.

Notice that the preceding description does not distinguish between encryption and decryption. One of the nice features of DES is that both sides of the algorithm work exactly

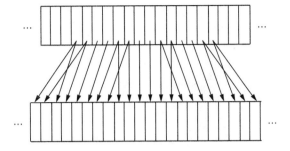

Figure 7.20 Expansion phase of DES.

Input	000000	000001	000010	000011	000100	000101	...
Output	1110	0100	1101	0001	0010	1111	...

Input	...	111010	111011	111100	111101	111110	111111
Output	...	0011	1110	1010	0000	0110	1101

Table 7.6 Example DES S box (bits 1-6).

the same. The only difference is that the keys are applied in the reverse order, i.e., K_{16}, $K_{15}, \ldots, K_1$.

Also keep in mind that the preceding discussion is limited to a single 64-bit data block. To encrypt a longer message using DES, a technique known as *cipher block chaining* (CBC) is typically used. The idea of CBC is simple: the ciphertext for block i is XORed with the plaintext for block $i + 1$ before running it through DES. An *initialization vector* (IV) is used in lieu of the nonexistent ciphertext for block 0. This vector IV, which is a random number generated by the sender, is sent along with the message so that the first block of plaintext can be retrieved. CBC on the encryption side is shown in Figure 7.21 for a 256-bit (four-block) message. Decryption works in the expected way since XOR is its own inverse, with the process starting with the last block and moving toward the front of the message.

We conclude by noting that there is no mathematical proof that DES is secure. What security it achieves it does through the application of two techniques: confusion and diffusion. (Having just plowed through the algorithm, you should now have a deep understanding of these two techniques.) What we can say is that the only known way to break DES is to exhaustively search all possible 2^{56} keys, although on average you would expect to have to search only half of the key space, or $2^{55} = 3.6 \times 10^{16}$ keys. On a 175-MHz DEC Alpha workstation, it is possible to do one encryption in $4\,\mu s$, meaning that it would take $1.4 \times 10^{17}\,\mu s$ to break

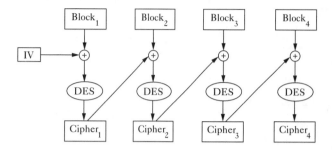

Figure 7.21 Cipher block chaining (CBC) for large messages.

a key (approximately 4500 years). While that may seems like a long time, keep in mind that searching a key space is a *highly* parallel task, meaning that if you could throw 9000 Alphas at the job, it would take only six months to break a key.

This amount of time is considered borderline-secure in many circles, especially considering that processor speeds are doubling every 18 months. For this reason, many applications are starting to use triple-DES, that is, encrypting the data three times. This can be done with three separate keys, or with two keys: the first is used, then the second, and finally the first key is used again.

RSA

RSA is a much different algorithm, not only because it involves different keys for encryption (public key) and decryption (private key), but also because it is grounded in number theory. In fact, the essential aspect of RSA comes down to how these two keys are selected. The act of encrypting or decrypting a message is expressed as a simple function, although this function requires enormous computational power. In particular, RSA commonly uses a key length of 512 bits, making it much more expensive to compute than DES; we discuss this more below.

Breaking RSA

In 1977, a challenge was issued to break a 129-digit (430-bit) message that was encrypted using RSA. It was believed that the code was impregnable, requiring 40 quadrillion years of computation using the currently known algorithms for factoring large numbers. In April of 1994, a mere 17 years later, four scientists reported that they had broken the code. The hidden message was

THE MAGIC WORDS ARE
SQUEAMISH OSSIFRAGE

The task was accomplished using a factoring method that requires approximately 5000 MIP-years. This was done over an eight-month period of time by dividing the

The first task is to generate a public and private key. To do this, choose two large prime numbers p and q, and multiply them together to get n. Both p and q should be roughly 256 bits long. Next, choose the encryption key e, such that e and $(p-1) \times (q-1)$ are relatively prime. (Two numbers are relatively prime if they have no common factor greater than 1.) Finally, compute the decryption key d such that

$$d = e^{-1} \bmod ((p-1) \times (q-1))$$

The public key is constructed from the pair $\langle e, n \rangle$ and the private key is given by the pair $\langle d, n \rangle$. The original prime numbers p and q are no longer needed. They can be discarded, but they must not be disclosed.

Given these two keys, encryption is defined by the following formula:

$$c = m^e \bmod n$$

and decryption is defined by

$$m = c^d \bmod n$$

where m is the plaintext message and c is the resulting ciphertext. Note that m must be less than n, which means that it can be no more than the 512 bits long. A larger message is simply treated as the concatenation of multiple 512-bit blocks.

Notice that when two participants want to encrypt data they are sending to each other using a public key algorithm like RSA, a pair of public/private key pairs is required. It doesn't work to encrypt with your private key and let the other side decrypt with the public key because everyone has access to the public key and so could decrypt the message. In other words, participant A encrypts data it sends to participant B using B's public key and B uses its private key to decrypt this data, while B encrypts data it sends to A using A's public key and A decrypts this message using its private key. Observe that A cannot decrypt a message that it has sent to B; only B has the requisite private key.

RSA security comes from the premise that factoring large numbers is a computationally expensive proposition. In particular, if you could factor n, you could recover p and q, which would compromise d. The speed at which large numbers can be factored is a function

problem into smaller pieces and shipping these pieces, using email, to computers all over the world.

Keep in mind that it doesn't always take 5000 MIP-years to break a key, especially when the key is poorly chosen. For example, a security hole was recently exposed in a WWW browser that used RSA to encrypt credit card numbers that were being sent over the Internet. The problem was that the system used a highly predictable method (a combination of process ID plus time of day) to generate a random number that was, in turn, used to generate a private and public key. Such keys are easily broken.

of both the available processor speed and the factoring algorithm being used. It is estimated that 512-bit numbers will be factorable in the next few years, and in fact, people are already starting to use 768- and 1024-bit keys. Keep in mind that while we are concentrating on the security of data as it moves through the network—i.e., the data is sometimes vulnerable for only a short period of time—in general, security people have to consider the vulnerability of data that needs to be stored in archives for tens of years.

Implementation and Performance

DES is two to three orders of magnitude faster than RSA, depending on whether the implementations are done in hardware or software. When implemented in software, we have measured DES to process data at 36 Mbps and RSA to process data at only 1 Kbps on a 175-MHz DEC Alpha workstation. For comparison, a software implementation of MD5 can process data at a rate of 80 Mbps on the same workstation. When implemented in hardware, that is, by custom VLSI chips, it has been reported that DES can achieve rates approaching 1 Gbps and RSA can achieve a whopping 64 Kbps.

Perhaps surprisingly, DES is the more likely of the two algorithms to be implemented in hardware on a given computer. This is because even when implemented in hardware, RSA is still too slow to be of any practical use in encrypting data messages. Instead, RSA is typically used to encrypt secret keys that are passed between two participants. These participants then use DES, possibly implemented in hardware, to secure their communication using this key. Because the secret key would only be used for as long as these two participants want to communicate, it is called a *session* key. We discuss this more in following subsections.

7.3.3 Authentication Protocols (Kerberos)

Before two participants are likely to establish a secure channel between themselves—i.e., use DES or RSA to encrypt messages they exchange—they must each first establish that the other participant is who he or she claims to be. This is the problem of authentication. If you think about authentication in the context of a client/server relationship, say a remote file system, then it is understandable that the server would want to establish the identity of the client: If the client is going to be allowed to modify or delete John's file, then the server is obligated to make sure that the client is, in fact, John. It is also the case, however, that the client often wants to verify the identity of the server. After all, you would not want to start writing sensitive data to what you thought was a file server, only to later discover that it was an imposter process.

This section describes three common protocols for implementing authentication. The first two use secret key cryptography (e.g., DES), while the third uses public key cryptography (e.g., RSA). Note that it is often during the process of authentication that the two participants establish the session key that is going to be used to ensure privacy during subsequent communication. The following includes a discussion of how this process gets bootstrapped.

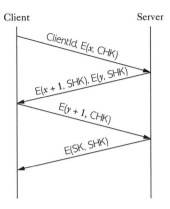

Client   Server

ClientId, E(x, CHK)

E(x + 1, SHK), E(y, SHK)

E(y + 1, CHK)

E(SK, SHK)

Figure 7.22   **Three-way handshake protocol for authentication.**

Simple Three-Way Handshake

A simple authentication protocol is possible when the two participants who want to authenticate each other—think of them as a client and a server—already share a secret key. This situation is analogous to a user (the client) having an account on a computer system (the server), where both client and server know the password for the account.

The client and server authenticate each other using a simple three-way handshake protocol similar to the one described in Section 6.2.3. In the following, we use E(m,k) to denote the encryption of message m with key k and D(m,k) to denote the decryption of message m with key k.

As illustrated in Figure 7.22, the client first selects a random number x and encrypts it using its secret key, which we denote as **CHK** (client handshake key). The client then sends E(x, **CHK**), along with an identifier (ClientId) for itself to the server. The server uses the key it thinks corresponds to client ClientId (call it **SHK** for server handshake key) to decrypt the random number. The server adds 1 to the number it recovers, and sends the result back to the client. It also sends back a random number y that has been encrypted with **SHK**. Next, the client decrypts the first half of this message and if the result is 1 more than the random number x that it sent to the server, it knows that the server possesses its secret key. At this point, the client has authenticated the server. The client also decrypts the random number the server sent it (this should yield y), encrypts this number plus 1, and sends the result to the server. If the server is able to recover $y + 1$ then it knows the client is legitimate.

After the third message, each side has authenticated itself to the other. The fourth message in Figure 7.22 corresponds to the server sending the client a session key (**SK**), encrypted using **SHK** (which is equal to **CHK**). Typically, the client and server then use **SK** to encrypt any future data they send to each other. The advantage of using a session key is that it means that

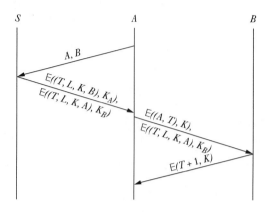

Figure 7.23   Third-party authentication in Kerberos.

the permanent secret key is only used for a small number of messages, making it harder for an attacker to gather data that might be used to determine the key.

This only begs the question of where the client and server handshake keys came from in the first place. One possibility is that they correspond to a password that a user entered; the ClientId could be the login identifier in this situation. Because a user-selected password might not make a suitable secret key, a transformation is often performed to turn it into a legitimate 56-bit DES key, for example.

Trusted Third Party

A more likely scenario is that the two participants know nothing about each other, but both trust a third party. This third party is sometimes called an *authentication server*, and it uses a protocol to help the two participants authenticate each other. There are actually many different variations of this protocol. The one we describe is the one used in Kerberos, a TCP/IP-based security system developed at MIT.

In the following, we denote the two participants who want to authenticate each other as A and B, and we call the trusted authentication server S. The Kerberos protocol assumes that A and B each share a secret key with S; we denote these two keys as K_A and K_B, respectively. As before, E(m,k) denotes message m encrypted with key k.

As illustrated in Figure 7.23, participant A first sends a message to server S that identifies both itself and B. The server then generates a timestamp T, a lifetime L, and a new session key K. Timestamp T is going to serve much the same purpose as the random number in the simple three-way handshake protocol given above, plus it is used in conjunction with L to limit the amount of time that session key K is valid. Participants A and B will have to go back to server S to get a new session key when this time expires. The idea here is to limit the vulnerability of any one session key.

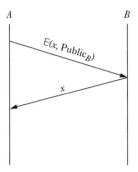

Figure 7.24 Public key authentication.

Server S then replies to A with a two-part message. The first part encrypts the three values T, L, and K, along with the identifier for participant B, using the key that the server shares with A. The second part encrypts the three values T, L, and K, along with participant A's identifier, but this time using the key that the server shares with B. Clearly, when A receives this message, it will be able to decrypt the first part but not the second part. A simply passes this second part on to B, along with the encryption of A and T using the new session key K. (A was able to recover T and K by decrypting the first part of the message it got from S.) Finally, B decrypts the part of the message from A that was originally encrypted by S, and in so doing, recovers T, K, and A. It uses K to decrypt the half of the message encrypted by A, and upon seeing that A and T are consistent in the two halves of the message, replies with a message that encrypts $T + 1$ using the new session key K.

A and B can now communicate with each other using the shared secret session key K to ensure privacy.

Public Key Authentication

Our final authentication protocol uses public key cryptography; e.g., RSA. The public key protocol is a useful one because the two sides need not share a secret key; they only need to know the other side's public key. As shown in Figure 7.24, participant A encrypts a random number x using participant B's public key, and B proves it knows the corresponding private key by decrypting the message and sending x back to A. A could authenticate itself to B in exactly the same way.

As to the question of where a participant learns the other's public key, it is tempting to believe that individual participants should be allowed to post their public keys on a bulletin board. This approach does not work, however, because it would be possible for participant A to post its own public key and claim that it is the key for participant B. This would allow A to masquerade as B. Instead, public keys must be retrieved from a trusted source, typically known as a *certificate authority* (CA). That is, you go to the trusted CA to get some other participant's public key, and you have to prove through some external mechanism that you are who you say you are when you register your public key with the CA. This reduces the problem to one of every participant having to know just one public key—that of the CA. Note that in general, it is possible to build a hierarchy of CAs: you start at the root CA to get the public key for a second-level CA, which gives you the public key for the third-level CA, and so on, until you learn the public key for the participant you want to communicate with. The root CA would be published in some other trusted source, for example, the *New York Times*.

An alternative to a tree-structured hierarchy is to build a nonhierarchical mesh of trust. We defer discussion of this approach until we have discussed digital signatures, on which this approach depends.

7.3.4   Message Integrity Protocols

Sometimes two communicating participants do not care whether an eavesdropper is able to read the messages they are sending to each other, but they are worried about the possibility of an imposter sending messages that claims to be from one of them. That is, the participants want to ensure the integrity of their messages.

One way to ensure the integrity of a message is to encrypt it using DES with cipher block chaining, and then to use the CBC *residue* (the last block output by the CBC process) as a *message integrity code* (MIC). (For the CBC example given in Figure 7.21, $cipher_4$ is the CBC residue.) The plaintext message plus the MIC would be transmitted to the receiver, with the MIC acting as a sort of checksum—if the receiver could not reproduce the attached MIC using the secret key it shares with the sender, then the message was either not sent by the sender, or it was modified since it was transmitted. Note that you would not want to use DES with CBC to both encrypt the message for privacy and to generate the MIC for integrity, because you would simply end up transmitting the CBC-encrypted message with the last block repeated. Thus, anyone who wanted to tamper with the CBC-encrypted message could take the value of the final block they wanted to send, and send it twice.

This section looks at three alternatives for ensuring message integrity. The first uses RSA to produce a digital signature. RSA used on its own tends to be slow, but it can be used in combination with MD5 to yield a much more efficient technique. The second and third approaches use MD5 in conjunction with RSA to guarantee message integrity.

Digital Signature Using RSA

A *digital signature* is a special case of a message integrity code, where the code can only have been generated by one participant. The easiest digital signature algorithm to understand is an RSA signature, which works in the obvious way—since a given participant is the only one that knows its own private key, the participant uses this key to produce the signature. Any other participant can verify this signature using the corresponding public key. In other words, to sign a message, you encrypt it using your private key, and to verify a signature, you decrypt it using the public key of the purported sender. Clearly, this means that producing an RSA signature is as slow as RSA, which we have already seen is two or three orders of magnitude slower than DES. Observe that the use of keys is exactly reversed relative to their use for privacy:

the sender encrypts with the sender's private key rather than with the receiver's public key, and the receiver decrypts with the sender's public key rather than with the receiver's private key.

Note that the National Institute for Standards and Technology (NIST) has proposed a digital signature standard known as DSS that is similar to the approach just described, except that it uses an alternative algorithm, called El Gamel, instead of RSA.

Keyed MD5

Recall that MD5 produces a cryptographic checksum for a message. This checksum does not depend on a secret key, so it does not prevent an imposter from creating a message that claims to be from someone else and computing an MD5 checksum for that message. However, there are two ways to use MD5 in combination with a public key algorithm like RSA to implement message integrity. Both approaches overcome the performance problems inherent in using RSA alone.

The first method, which is commonly referred to as *keyed MD5*, works as follows. The sender generates a random key k and runs MD5 over the concatenation of the message (denoted m) and this key. In practice, the random key k is attached to either the front or back of the message for the purpose of running MD5; k is then removed from the message once MD5 is finished. The random key is then encrypted using RSA and the sender's private key. The original message, the MD5 checksum, and the encrypted version of the random key are then packaged together and sent to the receiver. The following summarizes the complete message transmitted by the sender:

$$m + \text{MD5}(m + k) + \text{E}(k, \textit{private})$$

where MD5(s) represents applying the MD5 algorithm to string s, and $a+b$ denotes the concatenation of strings a and b.

The receiver recovers the random key using the purported sender's public RSA key and then applies MD5 to the concatenation of this random key and the body of the message. If the result matches the checksum sent with the message, then the message must have been sent by the participant who generated the random key.

MD5 with RSA Signature

The second method for using MD5 in combination with RSA works as follows. The sender runs MD5 over the original message it wants to protect, producing an MD5 checksum. It then signs this checksum with its own private RSA key. That is, the sender does not sign the entire message, it just signs the checksum. The original message, the MD5 checksum, and the RSA signature for the checksum are then transmitted. Using the same notation as above, this means that the sender transmits

$$m + \text{MD5}(m) + \text{E}(\text{MD5}(m), \textit{private}).$$

The receiver verifies the message by making sure that the signature is correct, that is, by decrypting the signature with the sender's public key and comparing the result with the MD5 checksum sent with the message. The two should be equal.

Using Digital Signatures for Key Distribution

We mentioned above that digital signatures can be used to build a mesh of trust by which keys can be distributed, as an alternative to a strict hierarchy. Now that we know how digital signatures work, providing us with a way to say "this message was generated by participant X and has not been altered," we can describe the mesh approach.

To begin, suppose participants A and B exchange public keys while they are in the same room; that is, they can verify that the keys really belong to the right people. At some later time, A exchanges public keys with C. A can now use his or her private key to sign the public key of C and send it to B. In other words, A sends a message that says, in effect, "I was in a room with C and I believe that this is C's public key," and signs this message using his or her own private key. Because B has a trustworthy copy of A's public key, B can verify the signature on this message. As long as B trusts that A was not fooled into mistakenly signing C's key, B now has a trustworthy copy of C's public key.

Thus, a reasonable strategy is for C to get his or her key signed by lots of people, and with luck, anyone with whom C wants to communicate will be able to find one person they trust in the set of people who have signed C's public key. Note that there can be arbitrarily many links in the chain of trust, but if one person in the chain signs a key when they are not sure it really belongs to the right person, then the chain of trust is broken. As an aside, note that key-signing parties—a lot of As, Bs, and Cs in a room with their laptops—have become a regular feature of IETF meetings. This approach to key management is used by the Pretty Good Privacy (PGP) suite of software.

Security Support in IPv6

IPv6 includes hooks to support authentication, message integrity, and encryption. First, IPv6 provides an Authentication extension header, which contains only two fields of interest: a Security Parameters Index (SPI) and some amount of Authentication Data. This provides a very general way to support a wide range of authentication algorithms and key management strategies without needing to redefine the header format. It is assumed that any two parties (hosts or routers) that wish to authenticate packets from each other will be able to agree on everything needed to provide authentication, notably an algorithm and a key. Once they have done this, the sending host uses the SPI to identify the appropriate set of agreements to the receiver. The sender then uses the agreed-upon algorithm and key to calculate a checksum over the entire datagram, and the receiver uses the

7.4 Summary

This chapter has described three different data manipulations that applications apply to their data before sending it over a network. Unlike the protocols described earlier in this book, which you can think of as processing *messages*, these three transformations process *data*.

The first data manipulation is presentation formatting, where the problem is encoding the different types of data that application programs compute on—e.g., integers, floating-point numbers, character strings, arrays, structures—into packets that can be transmitted over a network. This involves both translating between machine and network byte order, and linearizing compound data structures. We outlined the design space for presentation formatting and discussed three specific mechanisms that fall on different points in this design space: XDR, ASN.1, and NDR.

The second data manipulation is compression, which is concerned with reducing the bandwidth required to transmit different types of data. Compression algorithms can be either lossless or lossy, with lossy algorithms being most appropriate for image and video data. JPEG and MPEG are examples of lossy compression protocols for still images and video data, respectively.

The third data manipulation is encryption, which is used to protect the privacy of data sent over a network. We looked at two basic encryption algorithms: shared key algorithms (e.g., DES) and public key algorithms (e.g., RSA). As we have seen, encryption algorithms actually play a much bigger role in network security than just supporting privacy; they also form the basis for protocols that are used to ensure authentication and message integrity.

same algorithm and key to verify the checksum. If the packet has been modified in any way, the checksum will fail, which is how we achieve integrity. If someone other than the purported sender tries to send the packet, since they do not know the key to the algorithm, they will be unable to forge the correct checksum.

A similarly general approach is used for encryption. Specifically, another extension header, called the Encapsulating Security Payload (ESP) header, is used. All headers that precede the ESP header, most notably the IPv6 header, are unencrypted, so that routers do not need to decrypt packets before forwarding them. The only mandatory field of the ESP header is the SPI, which again provides an identifier by which the receiver can look up the algorithm and key needed to decrypt the data. Everything that follows the ESP header in the packet is then encrypted.

At one time, data manipulations such as the ones discussed in this chapter were treated as an afterthought by networking people. There were various reasons for this. In the case of presentation formatting, the network was so slow that no one cared how bad the encoding strategy was. In the case of compression, it is the recent advances in CD-ROM and graphical I/O devices (i.e., the growing popularity of multimedia) that have made the compression of images a fruitful area to pursue. In the case of security, it is the recent explosion of the World Wide Web, and the implications of using the Web for commerce, that have made people more security conscious. (Of course, the military has always been highly interested in security.) Today, however, one could argue that the data manipulation level of the network architecture is where the action is. In short, it is the set of data manipulation functions available to application programs that is limiting what we can do with computer networks.

Network security is a good example of services that are just around the corner. Using the basic cryptography algorithms like DES, RSA, and MD5, people are designing security protocols that do much more than ensure privacy, authentication, and message integrity. For example, there are now protocols that support anonymous digital cash, certified mail, secure elections, and simultaneous contract signing.

In the case of data compression, formats like MPEG were not specifically designed for use on a network; they were designed to provide a format for storing video on disk. It is not completely clear that MPEG makes sense for sending video over a network. For example, if a B or P frame is dropped by the network, then it is possible to simply replay the previous frame without seriously compromising the video; 1 frame out of 30 is no big deal. On the other hand, a lost I frame has serious consequences—none of the subsequent B and P frames can be processed without it. Thus, losing an I frame would result in losing multiple frames of the video. While you could retransmit the missing I frame, the resulting delay would probably not be acceptable in a real-time video conference. One interesting avenue of research is to have the application "teach" the network how to treat different types of messages; for example, it is OK to drop messages carrying B and P frames but not messages carrying I frames. Note, however, that this is a significant departure from the current model in which all messages are treated equally by the network.

One final issue to consider is the relationship among these three transformations. In most cases, you would perform presentation encoding before compression or encryption—the application first packs and linearizes a data structure before trying to compress or encrypt it. Between compression and encryption, you would always compress before encrypting. This is for two reasons. First, if the encryption algorithm is a good one, then there is no obvious redundancy for the compression algorithm to remove. The second reason is that by first compressing the data, you are able to make the ciphertext that results from encryption even more obscure, and therefore more difficult to break.

FURTHER READING

Our recommended reading list for this chapter includes two papers on compression and two papers on network security. The two articles on compression give an overview of the JPEG and MPEG standards, respectively. Their main value is in explaining the various factors that shaped the standards. The two security-related papers, taken together, give a good overview of the topic. The article by Lampson et al. contains a formal treatment of security, while the Satyanarayanan paper gives a nice description of how a secure system is designed in practice.

The final paper on the reading list discusses the importance of data manipulations to network performance and gives two architectural principles that should guide the design of future protocols.

- Wallace, G. K. The JPEG still picture compression standard. *Communications of the ACM* 34(1):30–44, April 1991.

- Le Gall, D. MPEG: A video compression standard for multimedia applications. *Communications of the ACM* 34(1):46–58, April 1991.

- Lampson, B., et al. Authentication in distributed systems: Theory and practice. *ACM Transactions on Computer Systems* 10(4):265–310, November 1992.

- Satyanarayanan, M. Integrating security in a large distributed system. *ACM Transactions on Computer Systems* 7(3):247–280, August 1989.

- Clark, D., and D. Tennenhouse. Architectural considerations for a new generation of protocols. *Proceedings of the SIGCOMM '91 Symposium*, pages 200–208, September 1991.

Unfortunately, there is no single paper that gives a comprehensive treatment of presentation formatting. Aside from the XDR, ASN.1/BER, and NDR specifications (see Srinivasan [Sri95b], the CCIT recommendations [dTeT92a, dTeT92b], and the Open Software Foundation [Ope94]), three other papers cover topics related to presentation formatting: those by O'Malley et al. [OPM94], Lin [Lin93], and Chen et al. [CLNZ89]. All three discuss performance-related issues.

On the topic of compression, a good place to start is with Huffman encoding, which was originally defined in [Huf52]. The original LZ algorithm is presented in Ziv and Lempel [ZL77], and an improved version of that algorithm by the same authors can be found in [ZL78]. Both of these papers are of a theoretical nature. The work that brought the LZ approach into widespread practice can be found in Welch [Wel84]. For a more complete overview of the topic of compression, Nelson's article [Nel92] is recommended. You can also learn about compression in any of several recent books on multimedia. We recommend Witten et al. [WMB94], which has an extremely high science-to-hype ratio, and Buford [Buf94], which is a collection of contributed chapters that span the range of multimedia topics.

On the topic of network security, there are several good books to choose from. We recommend Schneier [Sch94] and Kaufman et al. [KPS95]. The former gives a comprehensive treatment of the topic, including sample code, while the latter gives a very readable overview of the subject.

Finally, we recommend the following two live references:

- http://roger-rabbit.cs.berkeley.edu/mpeg/index.html: a collection of MPEG-related programs, some of which are used in the following exercises;

- ftp://cert.org/pub: a collection of security-related notices posted by the Computer Emergency Response Team (CERT).

E X E R C I S E S

1 Consider the following C structure definitions:

```
#define  MAXSTR 100

struct date {
    char   month[MAXSTR];
    int    day;
    int    year;
};

struct employee {
    char    name[MAXSTR];
    int     ssn;
    struct date *hireday;
    int     salary_history[10];
    int     num_raises;
}
```

where num_raises + 1 corresponds to the number of valid entries in array salary_history. Show the on-the-wire representation of structure employee that is generated by XDR.

2 For the data structures given in the previous problem, give the XDR routine that encodes/decodes these structures. If you have XDR available to you, run this routine and measure how long it takes to encode and decode an example instance of structure employee.

3 Using Unix utilities like bcopy and htonl, implement a routine that generates the same on-the-wire representation of the structures given in the problem 1 as XDR does. Compare the performance of your "by hand" encoder/decoder with the corresponding XDR routines.

4 Retrieve the Universal Stub Compiler (USC) byte-swapping program from ftp.cs.arizona.edu, and write the USC specification that encodes/decodes the data structures given in problem 1. (USC does not handle pointers, so you will need to encode/decode that part by hand.) Compare the performance of your USC encoder/decoder with the XDR and by-hand versions from the previous two exercises.

5 Use USC, XDR, and htonl to encode a 1000-element array of integers. Measure and compare the performance of each. How do the three compare to a simple loop that reads and writes a 1000-element array of integers? Perform the experiment on a computer for which the native byte order is the same as the network byte order, as well as on a computer for which the native byte order and the network byte order are different.

6 Give the ASN.1 encoding for the following three integers:

(a) 101

(b) 10,120

(c) 21,645

7 Give the big-endian and little-endian representation for the integers from the previous problem.

8 Determine the byte order for the following architectures: Alpha, MIPS, Sparc, and PA-RISC.

9 XDR is used to encode/decode the header for the SunRPC protocol described in Chapter 6. What difficulties might arise in using XDR in this way?

10 Why might you want to compress your data before doing presentation formatting?

11 Write a routine that implements RLE and DPCM compression. Apply these routines to different types of data, and report the compression ratios that each algorithm achieves.

12 Experiment with the Unix compress utility. What compression ratios is this program able to achieve? See if you can generate data files for which compress can achieve 5:1 or 10:1 compression ratios.

13 Think about what functions might reasonably be expected from a video standard: fast forward, editing capabilities, random access, and so on. (See the paper by LeGall, "MPEG: A video compression standard for multimedia applications," given in this chapter's recommended reading list, for further ideas.) Explain MPEG's design in terms of these features.

14 The frequency of I frames in the MPEG stream defines the granularity of fast forward and reverse. Explain why.

15 Use mpeg_play to play an MPEG-encoded video. Experiment with options, particularly -nob and -nop, which are used to omit the B and P frames, respectively, from the stream. What are the visible effects of omitting these frames?

16 The mpeg_stat program can be used to display statistics for video streams. Use it to determine, for several streams:

(a) number and sequence of I, B, and P frames.

(b) average compression rate for the entire video.

(c) average compression rate for each type of frame.

17 Write a program that implements forward and backward DCT. Run the program on a sample grayscale image. (It would be easiest to use PBM to read and write images.) Since DCT is lossless, the image output by the program should match the input. Now modify your program so that it throws away or changes some of the higher-frequency components and see how the output image is affected.

18 The Unix des command encrypts and decrypts data using the Data Encryption Standard algorithm. If it is available on your system, read the man page and experiment with it. Measure how fast it is able to encrypt or decrypt data.

19 Prove that the RSA decryption algorithm recovers the original message.

20 In the three-way handshake described as an authentication mechanism, why is the server unsure of the client's identity until it receives the third message?

21 Figure 7.21 shows CBC encryption. Give the corresponding diagram for decryption.

22 Show how two-way authentication works using RSA.

23 Learn about the Clipper encryption scheme. What are the pros and cons of Clipper?

24 What sort of attacks are authentication schemes like Kerberos susceptible to?

N ow that we have seen all the layers that make up a network architecture, we return to an issue that spans the entire protocol hierarchy—how to effectively and fairly allocate the available resources among a collection of competing users. The resources being shared include the bandwidth of the links and the buffers on the routers (switches) where packets are queued waiting to be transmitted over these links. Packets *contend* at a router for the use of a link, with each contending packet placed in a queue waiting its turn to be transmitted over the link. When enough packets are contending for the same link, the queue overflows and packets have to be dropped. It is at this stage that the network is said to be *congested*. Most networks provide a *congestion-control* mechanism to deal with just such a situation.

Congestion control and resource allocation are two sides of the same coin. On the one hand, if the network takes an active role in allocating resources—for example, scheduling which virtual circuit gets to use a given physical link during a certain period of time—then congestion can be avoided, thereby making congestion control unnecessary. Allocating network resources with any precision is extremely difficult to do, however, because the resources in question are distributed throughout the network; multiple links connecting a series of routers need to be scheduled. On the other hand, you can always let packet sources send as much data as they want, and then recover from congestion should it occur. This is the easier approach, but it can be disruptive because it is likely that many packets will be discarded by the network before congestion can be controlled. There are also solutions in the middle, whereby inexact allocation decisions are made, but congestion can still occur and hence some mechanism is still needed to recover from it. Whether you call such a mixed solution congestion control or resource allocation does not really matter. In some sense, it is both.

For our purposes, we discuss the problem in terms of congestion control, which has two points of implementation.

The hand that hath made you fair hath made you good.

—Shakespeare

At each router, it defines a queuing discipline. This queuing discipline specifies the order in which packets get transmitted, and as a consequence, affects which packets get dropped when congestion occurs. The queuing discipline also has the potential to segregate traffic, that is, to keep one user's packets from unduly affecting another user's packets. At the end hosts, the congestion-control mechanism paces how fast sources are allowed to send packets. This is done in an effort to keep congestion from occurring in the first place, and should it occur, to help eliminate the congestion.

This chapter starts by giving a general overview of congestion control. The second section then discusses different queuing disciplines that can be implemented on the routers inside the network, and the third section describes how TCP implements congestion control on the hosts at the edges of the network. The next section then explores various techniques that shift the burden of congestion control between the routers and the end hosts in an effort to avoid congestion before it becomes a problem. The chapter concludes with a discussion of a more active approach to congestion control called virtual clock, in which resources are reserved on behalf of an end-to-end flow of data.

8

Congestion Control

8.1 Issues in Congestion Control

Congestion control is a complex issue, and one that has been a subject of much study ever since the first network was designed. It is still an active area of research. One of the factors that makes congestion control complex is that it is not isolated to one single level of a protocol hierarchy. It is partially implemented in the routers or switches inside the network and partially in the transport protocol running on the end hosts. One of the main goals of this chapter is to define a framework in which these mechanisms can be understood, as well as to give the relevant details about a representative sample of mechanisms.

8.1.1 Network Model

We begin by defining three salient features of the network architecture. For the most part, this is a summary of material presented in the previous seven chapters that is relevant to the problem of congestion control.

Packet-Switched Network

We consider congestion control in a packet-switched network (or internet) consisting of multiple links and switches (or routers). Since most of the congestion-control mechanisms described in this chapter were designed for use on the Internet, and therefore were originally defined in terms of "routers" rather than "switches," we use the term router throughout our discussion. The problem is exactly the same, whether on a network or an internetwork.

In such an environment, a given source may have more than enough capacity on the immediate outgoing link to send a packet, but somewhere in the middle of a network, its packets encounter a link that is being used by many different traffic sources. Figure 8.1 illustrates this situation—two high-speed links are feeding a low-speed link. This is in contrast to shared-access networks like Ethernet and FDDI, where the source can directly observe the traffic on the network and decide accordingly whether or not to send a packet. We have already seen the algorithms used to allocate bandwidth on shared-access networks (Chapter 3). These access-control algorithms are, in some sense, analogous to congestion-control algorithms in a switched network.

Note that congestion control is not the same as routing. While it is true that a congested link can be assigned a large edge weight by the route-propagation protocol, and as a consequence, routers will route around it, "routing around" a congested link does not solve the congestion problem. To see this, we need look no further than the simple network depicted in Figure 8.1, where all traffic has to flow through the same router to reach the destination. Although this is an extreme example, it is common to have a certain router that it is not possible to route around.[1] This router can become congested, and there is nothing the routing mechanism can do about it. This congested router is sometimes called the *bottleneck* router.

---

[1] It is also worth noting that the complexity of routing in the Internet is such that simply obtaining a reasonably direct, loop-free route is about the best you can hope for—routing around congestion would be considered icing on the cake.

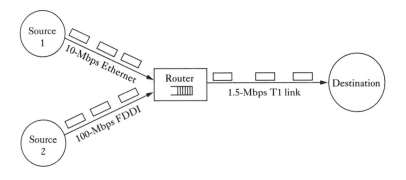

Figure 8.1 Congestion in a packet-switched network.

Connectionless Flows

We assume that the network is essentially connectionless, with any connection-oriented service implemented in the transport protocol that is running on the end hosts. (We explain the qualification "essentially" in a moment.) This is precisely the model of the Internet, where IP provides a connectionless datagram delivery service and TCP implements an end-to-end virtual circuit abstraction. Note that this assumption excludes early networks like X.25, in which a virtual circuit abstraction is maintained across a set of routers. (See Section 4.1.2.) In such networks, a connection setup message traverses the network when a circuit is established. This setup message reserves a set of buffers for the connection at each router, thereby providing a form of congestion control—a connection is established only if enough buffers can be allocated to it at each router. The major shortcoming of this approach is that it leads to an underutilization of resources—buffers reserved for a particular circuit are not available for use by other traffic even if they were not currently being used by that circuit. In effect, networks like X.25 address congestion control by doing hop-by-hop flow control. This chapter does not consider this approach any further.

We qualify the term *connectionless* because our classification of networks as being either connectionless or connection-oriented is a bit too restrictive; there is a gray area in between. In particular, the implication of a connectionless network that all datagrams are completely independent is too strong. The datagrams are certainly switched independently, but it is usually the case that a stream of datagrams between a particular pair of hosts flow through a particular set of routers. This idea of a *flow*—a sequence of packets sent between a source/destination host pair and following the same route through the network—is an important abstraction in the context of congestion control; it is one that we will use in this chapter. Note that a flow is essentially the same as a channel, as we have been using that term throughout this book. The reason we introduce a new term is that a flow is visible to the routers inside the network, whereas a channel is an end-to-end abstraction. Figure 8.2 illustrates several flows passing through a series of routers.

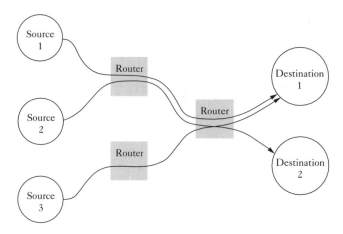

Figure 8.2 Multiple flows passing through a set of routers.

Because multiple related packets flow through each router, it sometimes makes sense to maintain some state information for each flow, information that can be used to make congestion-control decisions about the packets that belong to the flow. This state is sometimes called *soft state* because the correct operation of the network does not depend on it (each packet is still routed correctly without regard to this state), but when a packet happens to belong to a flow for which the router is currently maintaining soft state, then the router is better able to handle the packet. Note that this soft state is in contrast to a purely connectionless network that maintains *no* state at the routers and a purely connection-oriented network that maintains *hard state* at the routers.

Note that a flow can be either implicitly defined or explicitly established. In the former case, each router watches for packets that happen to be traveling between the same source/destination pair—the router does this by inspecting the addresses in the header—and treats these packets as belonging to the same flow for the purpose of congestion control. In the latter case, the source sends a flow setup message across the network, declaring that a flow of packets is about to start. While explicit flows are arguably no different than a connection across a connection-oriented network, we call attention to this case because even when explicitly established, a flow does not imply any end-to-end semantics, and in particular, it does not imply the reliable and ordered delivery of a virtual circuit. It simply exists for the purpose of resource allocation. Most of the mechanisms describe in this chapter are based on implicit flows.

Service Model

All but one of the congestion-control strategies presented in this chapter assume the best-effort service model of the Internet; the virtual clock algorithm presented in Section 8.5 is the exception. With best-effort service, each packet is treated in exactly the same way, with end hosts given no opportunity to ask the network that one of their flows be given certain guarantees. Defining a service model that supports some kind of guarantee—e.g., guaranteeing the bandwidth needed for a video stream—is currently an active subject of research. Such a service model is said to provide multiple *qualities of service* (QoS). The virtual clock mechanism is an example of a congestion-control mechanism that moves us toward a QoS-based service model. The next chapter describes an alternative service model that has been proposed, a model in which mechanisms like the virtual clock algorithm might be appropriate.

8.1.2 Taxonomy

There are countless ways in which congestion-control mechanisms differ, making a thorough taxonomy a difficult proposition. For now, we describe three dimensions along which congestion-control mechanisms can be characterized; more subtle distinctions will be called out during the course of this chapter. This taxonomy is primarily due to Lixia Zhang.

Router-Centric versus Host-Centric

Congestion-control mechanisms can be classified into two broad groups: those that address congestion from inside the network (i.e., at the routers or switches), and those that address congestion from the edges of the network (i.e., in the hosts, perhaps inside the transport protocol). Since it is the case that both the routers inside the network and the hosts at the edges of the network participate in congestion control, the real issue is where the majority of the burden falls.

 In a router-centric design, each router takes responsibility for deciding which packets get serviced and which are dropped, as well as for informing the hosts that are generating the network traffic how many packets they are allowed to send. In a host-centric design, the end hosts observe how many packets they are successfully getting through the network and adjust their transmission rates accordingly. Note that these two groups are not mutually exclusive. A network that places the primary burden for managing congestion on routers still expects the end hosts to adhere to any advisory messages the routers send, while the routers in networks that use end-to-end congestion control still have some policy, no matter how simple, for deciding which packets to drop when their queues do overflow.

Reservation-Based versus Feedback-Based

A second way that congestion-control mechanisms are sometimes classified is according to whether they use *reservations* or *feedback*. In a reservation-based system, the end host asks the network for a certain amount of capacity at the time a flow is established. Each router then allocates enough resources (buffers and/or percentage of the link's bandwidth) to satisfy this request. If the request cannot be satisfied at some router, because doing so would overcommit its resources, then the router rejects the flow. This is analogous to getting a busy signal when trying to make a phone call. In a feedback-based approach, the end hosts begin sending data without first reserving any capacity and then adjust their sending rate according to the feedback they receive. This feedback can either be *explicit* (i.e., a congested router sends a "please slow down" message to the host) or it can be *implicit* (i.e., the end host adjusts its sending rate according to the externally observable behavior of the network, such as packet losses).

Note that a reservation-based system always implies a router-centric congestion-control mechanism. This is because each router is responsible for keeping track of how much of its capacity is currently reserved and for making sure each host lives within the reservation it made. If a host sends data faster than it claimed it would when it made the reservation, then that host's packets are good candidates for discarding, should the router become congested. On the other hand, a feedback-based system can imply either a router- or host-centric mechanism. Typically, if the feedback is explicit, then the router is involved, to at least some degree, in the congestion-control scheme. If the feedback is implicit, then almost all of the burden falls to the end host; the routers silently drop packets when they become congested.

Window-Based versus Rate-Based

A third way to characterize congestion-control mechanisms is according to whether they are *window based* or *rate based*. The same distinction can be made for flow control, so this is a good time to clarify the difference between flow control and congestion control.

Both flow control and congestion control involve throttling the speed with which the source transmits packets. Flow control does this to keep the sender from overrunning the receiver, while congestion control does this to keep the sender from overloading the network. Both flow- and congestion-control mechanisms need to be able to express, to the sender, how much data it is allowed to transmit. There are two general ways of doing this: with a *window* or with a *rate*. We have already seen window-based transport protocols, such as TCP, in which the receiver advertises a window to the sender. This window corresponds to how much buffer space the receiver has, and it limits how much data the sender can transmit; that is, it supports flow control. This same window information can be used within the network to reserve buffer space, that is, to support congestion control. This is essentially what is done in X.25.

It is also possible to express flow and congestion control in terms of rate, that is, how many bits per second the receiver or network is able to absorb. While we have not studied any rate-based transport protocols in this book because this is still an open area of research, we can imagine such a protocol used to support video—the receiver says it can process video frames at a rate of 1 Mbps, and the sender adheres to this rate. As we will see later in this chapter, rate-based congestion control is a logical choice in a reservation-based system that supports different qualities of service—the sender makes a reservation for so many bits per second, and each router along the path determines if it can support that rate, given the other flows it has made commitments to.

Summary of Congestion Control Taxonomy

Classifying congestion-control mechanisms at two different points along each of three dimensions, as we have just done, would seem to suggest up to eight unique strategies. While eight different approaches to congestion control are certainly possible, we note that in practice two general strategies seem to be most prevalent; these two strategies are tied to the underlying service model of the network.

On the one hand, a best-effort service model usually implies that feedback is being used, since such a model does not allow users to reserve network capacity. This, in turn, means that most of the responsibility for congestion control falls to the end hosts, perhaps with some assistance from the routers. In practice, such networks use window-based information. This is the general strategy adopted in the Internet and the focus of most of this chapter.

On the other hand, a QoS-based service model probably implies reservations, which in turn depend on heavy router involvement. Moreover, it is natural to express such reservations in terms of rate, since windows are only indirectly related to how much bandwidth a user needs from the network. Because QoS-based service models are only now evolving, we limit our discussion of this general strategy to one mechanism—virtual clocks. Chapter 9 revisits this strategy in the context of a new service model.

8.1.3 Evaluation Criteria

The final issue is one of knowing whether a congestion-control mechanism is good or not. Recall that in the problem statement at the start of this chapter we posed the question of how a network *effectively* and *fairly* allocates its resources. This suggests at least two broad measures by which a congestion-control scheme can be evaluated. We consider each, in turn.

Effective Resource Allocation

A good starting point for evaluating the effectiveness of a resource allocation scheme is the two principal metrics of networking: throughput and delay. Clearly, we want as much throughput and as little delay as possible. While on the surface it might appear as though increasing throughput also means reducing delay, this is not the case. One sure way for a congestion-control algorithm to increase throughput is to allow as many packets into the network as possible, so as to drive the utilization of all the links up to 100%. We would do this to avoid the possibility of a link becoming idle, because an idle link necessarily hurts throughput. The problem with this strategy is that increasing the number of packets in the network also increases the length of the queues at each router. Longer queues, in turn, mean packets are delayed longer in the network.

To describe this relationship, some network designers have proposed using the ratio of throughput to delay as a metric for evaluating the effectiveness of a congestion-control scheme. This ratio is sometimes referred to as the *power* of the network:[2]

$$\text{Power} = \text{Throughput}/\text{Delay}$$

Note that it is not obvious that power is the right metric for judging congestion-control mechanisms. For one thing, the theory behind power is based on an M/M/1 queuing network that

---

[2]The actual definition is Power $= \text{Throughput}^\alpha/\text{Delay}$, where $0 < \alpha < 1$; $\alpha = 1$ results in power being maximized at the knee of the delay curve.

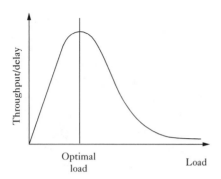

Throughput/delay (vertical axis)

Optimal load

Load

Figure 8.3   Ratio of throughput to delay as a function of load.

assumes infinite queues; real networks have finite buffers and sometimes have to drop packets. For another, power is typically defined relative to a single connection (flow); it is not clear how it extends to multiple, competing connections. Despite these rather severe limitations, however, no alternatives have gained wide acceptance, and so power continues to be used.

The objective is to maximize this ratio, which is a function of how much load you place on the network. The load, in turn, is set by the congestion-control mechanism. Figure 8.3 gives a representative power curve, where, ideally, the congestion-control mechanism would operate at the peak of this curve. To the left of the peak, the mechanism is being too conservative, that is, it is not allowing enough packets to be sent to keep the links busy. To the right of the peak, so many packets are being allowed into the network that increases in delay due to queuing are starting to dominate any small gains in throughput.

Interestingly, this power curve looks very much like the system throughput curve in a multiprogrammed computer system. System throughput improves as more jobs are admitted into the system, until it reaches a point when there are so many jobs running that the system begins to thrash (spends all of its time swapping memory pages) and the throughput begins to drop.

As we will see in later sections of this chapter, many congestion-control schemes are able to control load in only very crude ways. That is, it is simply not possible to turn the "knob" a little and allow only a small number of additional packets into the network. As a consequence, network designers need to be concerned about what happens even when the system is operating under extremely heavy load, i.e., at the rightmost end of the curve in Figure 8.3. Ideally, we would like to avoid the situation in which the system throughput goes to zero because the system is thrashing. In networking terminology, we want a system that is *stable*—where packets continue to get through the network even when the network is operating under heavy load. If a mechanism is not stable, the network may experience *congestion collapse*.

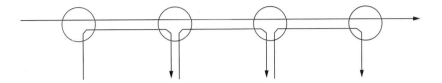

Figure 8.4 One four-hop flow competing with three one-hop flows.

Fair Resource Allocation

The effective utilization of network resources is not the only criterion for judging a congestion-control mechanism. We must also consider the issue of fairness. If more than one flow is sharing a particular link, then we would like for each flow to receive an equal share of the bandwidth. Of course, this definition presumes that a *fair* share of bandwidth means an *equal* share of bandwidth. An equally valid definition would be that each flow should be allocated some percentage of the available bandwidth, according to some allocation policy. To further complicate matters, we should also consider the length of the paths being compared. For example, as illustrated in Figure 8.4, what is fair when one four-hop flow is competing with three one-hop paths?

Assuming that fair implies equal and that all paths are of equal length, Raj Jain has proposed a metric that can be used to quantify the fairness of a congestion-control mechanism. Jain's fairness index is defined as follows. Given a set of flow throughputs $(x_1, x_2, \ldots, x_n)$, the following function assigns a fairness index to the flows:

$$f(x_1, x_2, \ldots, x_n) = \frac{\left(\sum_{i=1}^{n} x_i\right)^2}{n \sum_{i=1}^{n} x_i^2}$$

The fairness index always results in a number between 0 and 1. If all throughputs are the same, the fairness index is 1. If only k of the n flows receive equal throughput, and the remaining $n - k$ users receive zero throughput, then the fairness index is k/n.

8.2 Queuing Disciplines

Regardless of how simple or how sophisticated the rest of the congestion-control mechanism is, each router must implement some queuing discipline that governs how packets are buffered while waiting to be transmitted. The queuing algorithm can be thought of as allocating both bandwidth (which packets get transmitted) and buffer space (which packets get discarded). This section introduces two common queuing algorithms—FIFO and Fair Queuing—and identifies several variations that have been proposed.

8.2.1 FIFO

The idea of FIFO (first-in-first-out) queuing, also called first-come-first-served (FCFS) queuing, is simple: The first packet that arrives at a router is the first packet to be transmitted.

Given that the amount of buffer space at each router is finite, if a packet arrives and the queue (buffer space) is full, then the router discards that packet. This is done without regard to which flow the packet belongs to or how important the packet is.

FIFO queuing pushes all responsibility for congestion control out to the edges of the network. This is what is currently done in the Internet: IP routers implement FIFO queues and TCP takes responsibility for detecting and responding to congestion. (To be strictly accurate, not all IP routers use simple FIFO queues; some, for example, use the TOS, or type of service, bits in the IP header to classify packets into different priorities.)

If you think of a queuing discipline as deciding both which packets to transmit and which packets to discard, then FIFO intertwines these two functions in a single mechanism. It is possible, however, to use FIFO queuing to decide the order in which packets are transmitted, but to use some other algorithm to decide which packets to discard. For example, when a packet arrives and finds the queue full, rather than dropping that newly arriving packet, the router could select a packet at random from the queue to discard. A variation of this idea is discussed in Section 8.4.

Another variation on simple FIFO queuing is to implement priority queues. The idea is to have the sources mark each packet with a priority. The routers then implement multiple FIFO queues, one for each priority class. The router always transmits packets out of the highest-priority queue before moving on to the next priority queue. Within each priority, packets are still managed in a FIFO manner. This idea is a small departure from the best-effort delivery model, but it does not go so far as to make guarantees to any particular priority class. It just allows high-priority packets to cut to the front of the line.

The problem with priority queuing, of course, is how to keep all the sources from marking their packets as being high priority. Ultimately, there must be some form of "pushback" on users. One obvious way to do this is to use economics—the network could charge more to deliver high-priority packets than low-priority packets. How to implement such a scheme in a decentralized environment such as the Internet is far from clear.

8.2.2 Fair Queuing

The main problem with FIFO queuing is that it does not discriminate between different traffic sources, or in the language introduced in the previous section, it does not separate packets according to the flow to which they belong. This is a problem at two different levels. At one level, it is not clear that any algorithm implemented entirely at the source will be able to adequately control congestion with so little help from the routers. We will suspend judgment on this point until the next section when we discuss TCP congestion control. At another level, because the entire congestion-control mechanism is implemented at the sources and FIFO queuing does not provide a means to police how well the sources adhere to this mechanism, it is possible for an ill-behaved source (flow) to capture an arbitrarily large fraction of the network capacity. Considering the Internet again, it is certainly possible for a given application not to use TCP, and as a consequence, to bypass its end-to-end congestion-control mecha-

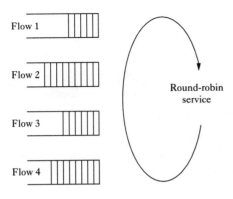

Figure 8.5   Fair queuing at a router.

nism. Such an application is able to flood the Internet's routers with its own packets, thereby causing other applications' packets to be discarded.

Fair queuing (FQ) is an algorithm that has been proposed to address this problem. The idea of FQ is to maintain a separate queue for each flow currently being handled by the router. The router then services these queues in a round-robin manner, as illustrated in Figure 8.5. When a flow sends packets too quickly, then its queue fills up. When a queue reaches a particular length, additional packets belonging to that flow's queue are discarded. In this way, a given source cannot arbitrarily increase its share of the network's capacity at the expense of other flows.

Note that FQ does not involve the router telling the traffic sources anything about the state of the router or in any way limiting how quickly a given source sends packets. In other words, FQ is still designed to be used in conjunction with an end-to-end congestion-control mechanism. It simply segregates traffic so that ill-behaved traffic sources do not interfere with those that are faithfully implementing the end-to-end algorithm. FQ also enforces fairness among a collection of flows managed by a well-behaved congestion-control algorithm.

As simple as the basic idea is, there are still a modest number of details that you have to get right. The main complication is that the packets being processed at a router are not necessarily the same length. To truly allocate the bandwidth of the outgoing link in a fair manner, it is necessary to take packet length into consideration. For example, if a router is managing two flows, one with 1000-byte packets and the other with 500-byte packets (perhaps because of fragmentation upstream from this router), then a simple round-robin servicing of packets from each flow's queue will give the first flow two-thirds of the link's bandwidth and the second flow only one-third of its bandwidth.

What we really want is bit-by-bit round robin, that is, the router transmits a bit from flow 1, then a bit from flow 2, and so on. Clearly, it is not feasible to interleave the bits from different packets. The FQ mechanism therefore simulates this behavior by first determining

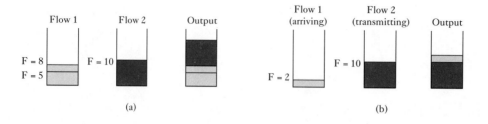

Figure 8.6 Example of fair queuing in action. (a) Shorter packets are sent first; (b) sending of longer packet, already in progress, is completed first.

when a given packet would finish being transmitted if it were being sent using bit-by-bit round robin, and then using this finishing time to sequence the packets for transmission.

To understand the algorithm for approximating bit-by-bit round robin, consider the behavior of a single flow and imagine a clock that ticks once each time a bit is transmitted from this flow. For this flow, let P_i denote the length of packet i, let S_i denote the time when the router starts to transmit packet i, and let F_i denote the time when the router finishes transmitting packet i. If P_i is expressed in terms of how many clock ticks it takes to transmit packet i (keeping in mind that time advances 1 tick each time this flow gets 1 bit's worth of service), then it is easy to see that $F_i = S_i + P_i$.

When do we start transmitting packet i? The answer to this question depends on whether packet i arrived before or after the router finished transmitting packet $i-1$ from this flow. If it was before, then logically the first bit of packet i is transmitted immediately after the last bit of packet $i - 1$. On the other hand, it is possible that the router finished transmitting packet $i - 1$ long before i arrived, meaning that there was a period of time during which the queue for this flow was empty, so the round-robin mechanism could not transmit any packets from this flow. If we let A_i denote the time that packet i arrives at the router, then $S_i = MAX(F_{i-1}, A_i)$. Thus, we can compute

$$F_i = MAX(F_{i-1}, A_i) + P_i$$

Now we move on to the situation in which there is more than one flow. For every flow, we calculate F_i for each packet that arrives. We then treat all the F_is as timestamps, and the next packet to transmit is always the packet that has the lowest timestamp—the packet that, based on the above reasoning, should finish transmission before all others.

Note that this means that a packet can arrive on a flow, and because it is shorter than a packet from some other flow that is already in the queue waiting to be transmitted, it can be inserted into the queue in front of that longer packet. However, this does not mean that a newly arriving packet can preempt a packet that is currently being transmitted. It is this lack of preemption that keeps the implementation of FQ just described from exactly simulating the bit-by-bit round-robin scheme that we are attempting to approximate.

To better see how this implementation of fair queuing works, consider the example given in Figure 8.6. Part (a) shows the queues for two flows; the algorithm selects both packets from flow 1 to be transmitted before the packet in the flow 2 queue. In part (b), the router has already begun to send a packet from flow 2 when the packet from flow 1 arrives. Though the packet arriving on flow 1 would have finished before flow 2 if we had been using perfect bit-by-bit fair queuing, the implementation does not preempt the flow 2 packet.

There are two things to notice about fair queuing. First, the link is never left idle as long as there is at least one packet in the queue. Any queuing scheme with this characteristic is said to be *work-conserving*. We discuss both work-conserving and non-work-conserving schemes in Section 8.5.4. One effect of being work-conserving is that if I am sharing a link with a lot of flows that are not sending any data, I can use the full link capacity for my flow. As soon as the other flows start sending, however, they will start to use their share and the capacity available to my flow will drop.

The second thing to notice is that if the link is fully loaded and there are n flows sending data, I cannot use more than $1/n$th of the link bandwidth. If I try to send more than that, my packets will be assigned increasingly large timestamps, causing them to sit in the queue longer awaiting transmission. Eventually the queue will overflow—although whether it is my packets or someone else's that are dropped is a decision that is not determined by the fact that we are using fair queuing.

It is possible to implement a variation of FQ, called *weighted fair queuing* (WFQ), that allows a weight to be assigned to each flow (queue). This weight logically specifies how many bits to transmit each time the router services that queue, which effectively controls the percentage of the link's bandwidth that that flow will get. Simple FQ gives each queue a weight of 1, which means that logically only 1 bit is transmitted from each queue each time around. This results in each flow getting $1/n$th of the bandwidth when there are n flows. With WFQ, however, one queue might have a weight of 2, a second queue might have a weight of 1, and a third queue might have a weight of 3. Assuming that each queue always contains a packet waiting to be transmitted, the first flow will get one-third of the available bandwidth, the second will get one-sixth of the available bandwidth, and the third will get one-half of the available bandwidth.

Note that a WFQ router must learn what weights to assign to each queue from the traffic sources, which suggests that WFQ depends on having these sources somehow communicate this information to the routers. This is a kind of reservation, although a rather weak one because these weights are only indirectly related to the bandwidth the flow receives. (The bandwidth available to a flow also depends, for example, on how many other flows are sharing the link.) We will see a proposal in Chapter 9 for using WFQ as a component of a more sophisticated resource allocation mechanism.

▶ Finally, we observe that this whole discussion of queue management illustrates an important system design principle known as *separating policy and mechanism*. The idea is to view each mechanism as a black box that provides a multifaceted service that can be controlled by a set of knobs. A policy specifies a particular setting of those knobs, but does not know (or care) about how the black box is implemented. In this case, the mechanism in question is the queuing discipline, and the policy is a particular setting of which flow gets what level of service (e.g., priority or weight). We discuss some policies that can be used with the WFQ mechanism in Chapter 9.

8.3   TCP Congestion Control

This section describes the predominant example of end-to-end congestion control in use today, that implemented by TCP. The essential strategy of TCP is to send packets into the network without a reservation and then to react to observable events that occur. TCP assumes only FIFO queuing in the network's routers, but also works with fair queuing.

TCP congestion control was introduced into the Internet in the late 1980s by Van Jacobson, roughly eight years after the TCP/IP protocol stack had become operational. Immediately preceding this time, the Internet was suffering from congestion collapse—hosts would send their packets into the Internet as fast as the advertised window would allow, congestion would occur at some router (causing packets to be dropped), and the hosts would timeout and retransmit their packets, resulting in even more congestion.

Broadly speaking, the idea of TCP congestion control is for each source to determine how much capacity is available in the network, so that it knows how many packets it can safely have in transit. Once a given source has this many packets in transit, it uses the arrival of an ACK as a signal that one of its packets has left the network, and that it is therefore safe to insert a new packet into the network without adding to the level of congestion. By using ACKs to pace the transmission of packets, TCP is said to be *self-clocking*. Of course, determining the available capacity in the first place is no easy task. To make matters worse, because other connections come and go, the available bandwidth changes over time, meaning that any given source must be able to adjust the number of packets it has in transit. This section describes the algorithms used by TCP to address these, and other, problems.

Note that although we describe these mechanisms one at a time, thereby giving the impression that we are talking about three independent mechanisms, it is only when they are taken as a whole that we have TCP congestion control.

8.3.1   Additive Increase/Multiplicative Decrease

TCP maintains a new state variable for each connection, called CongestionWindow, which is used by the source to limit how much data it is allowed to have in transit at a given time. The congestion window is congestion control's counterpart to flow control's advertised window. TCP is modified to have no more than the minimum of the congestion window and the advertised window number of bytes of unacknowledged data. Thus, using the variables defined in Section 6.2.4, TCP's effective window is revised as follows:

MaxWindow = MIN(CongestionWindow, AdvertisedWindow)
EffectiveWindow = MaxWindow − (LastByteSent − LastByteAcked).

That is, MaxWindow replaces AdvertisedWindow in the calculation of EffectiveWindow. Thus, a TCP source is allowed to send no faster than the slowest component—the network or the destination host—can accommodate.

The problem, of course, is how TCP comes to learn an appropriate value for CongestionWindow. Unlike the AdvertisedWindow, which is sent by the receiving side of the connection, there is no one to send a suitable CongestionWindow to the sending side of TCP. The answer is that the TCP source sets the CongestionWindow based on the level of congestion it perceives to exist in the network. This involves decreasing the congestion window when the level of congestion goes up and increasing the congestion window when the level of congestion goes down. Taken together, the mechanism is commonly called *additive increase/multiplicative decrease*.

The key question, then, is how does the source determine that the network is congested and that it should decrease the congestion window? The answer is based on the observation that the main reason packets are not delivered, and a timeout results, is that a packet was dropped due to congestion. It is rare that a packet is dropped because of an error during transmission. Therefore, TCP interprets timeouts as a sign of congestion and reduces the rate at which it is transmitting. Specifically, each time a timeout occurs, the source sets CongestionWindow to half of its previous value. This halving of the CongestionWindow for each timeout corresponds to the "multiplicative decrease" part of the mechanism.

Although CongestionWindow is defined in terms of bytes, it is easiest to understand multiplicative decrease if we think in terms of whole packets. For example, suppose the CongestionWindow is currently set to 16 packets. If a loss is detected, CongestionWindow is set to 8. (Normally, a loss is detected when a timeout occurs, but as we see below, TCP has another mechanism to detect dropped packets.) Additional losses cause CongestionWindow to be reduced to 4, then 2, and finally to 1 packet. CongestionWindow is not allowed to fall below the size of a single packet, or in TCP terminology, the *maximum segment size* (MSS).

A congestion-control strategy that only decreases the window size is obviously too conservative. We also need to be able to increase the congestion window to take advantage of newly available capacity in the network. This is the "additive increase" part of the mechanism, and it works as follows. Every time the source successfully sends a CongestionWindow's worth of packets—that is, each packet sent out during the last RTT has been ACKed—it adds the equivalent of 1 packet to CongestionWindow. This linear increase is illustrated in Figure 8.7. Note that in practice, TCP does not wait for an entire window's worth of ACKs to add 1 packet's worth to the congestion window, but instead increments CongestionWindow by a little for each ACK that arrives. Specifically, the congestion window is incremented as follows each time an ACK arrives:

Increment = (MSS × MSS)/CongestionWindow
CongestionWindow += Increment

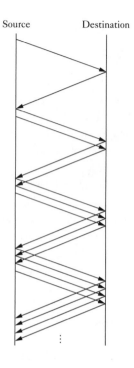

Source   Destination

Figure 8.7   Packets in transit during additive increase, with one packet being added each RTT.

That is, rather than incrementing CongestionWindow by an entire MSS each RTT, we increment it by a fraction of MSS every time an ACK is received. Assuming that each ACK acknowledges the receipt of MSS bytes, then that fraction is MSS/CongestionWindow.

This pattern of continually increasing and decreasing the congestion window continues throughout the lifetime of the connection. In fact, if you plot the current value of CongestionWindow as a function of time, you get a sawtooth pattern, as illustrated in Figure 8.8. The important thing to understand about additive increase/multiplicative decrease is that the source is willing to reduce its congestion window at a much faster rate than it is willing to increase its congestion window. This is in contrast to an additive increase/additive decrease strategy in which the window would be increased by 1 packet when an ACK arrives and decreased by 1 when a timeout occurs. It has been shown that additive increase/multiplicative decrease is a necessary condition for a congestion-control mechanism to be stable.

Finally, since a timeout is an indication of congestion that triggers multiplicative decrease, TCP needs the most accurate timeout mechanism it can afford. We already covered TCP's timeout mechanism in Section 6.2.5, so we do not repeat it here. The two main things to remember about that mechanism are that (1) timeouts are set as a function of both the average RTT and the standard deviation in that average, and (2) due to the cost of measuring

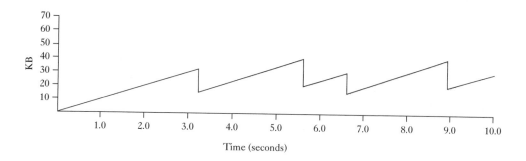

Figure 8.8   Typical TCP sawtooth pattern.

each transmission with an accurate clock, TCP only samples the round-trip time once per RTT (rather than once per packet) using a coarse-grained (500-ms) clock.

8.3.2   Slow Start

The additive increase mechanism just described is the right approach to use when the source is operating close to the available capacity of the network, but it takes too long to ramp up a connection when it is starting from scratch. TCP therefore provides a second mechanism, ironically called *slow start*, that is used to increase the congestion window rapidly from a cold start. Slow start effectively increases the congestion window exponentially, rather than linearly.

Specifically, the source starts out by setting CongestionWindow to 1 packet. When the ACK for this packet arrives, TCP adds 1 to CongestionWindow and then sends two packets. Upon receiving the corresponding two ACKs, TCP increments CongestionWindow by 2—one for each ACK—and next sends four packets. The end result is that TCP effectively doubles the number of packets it has in transit every RTT. Figure 8.9 shows the growth in the number of packets in transit during slow start. Compare this to the linear growth of additive increase illustrated in Figure 8.7.

Why any exponential mechanism would be called "slow" is puzzling at first, but it can be explained if put in the proper historical context. We need to compare slow start not against the linear mechanism of the previous subsection, but against the original behavior of TCP. Consider what happens when a connection is established and the source first starts to send packets, i.e., when it currently has no packets in transit. If the source sends as many packets as the advertised window allows—which is exactly what TCP did before slow start was developed—then even if there is a fairly large amount of bandwidth available in the network, the routers may not be able to consume this burst of packets. It all depends on how much buffer space is available at the routers. Slow start was therefore designed to space packets out so that this burst does not occur. In other words, even though its exponential growth is faster than linear growth, slow start is much "slower" than sending an entire advertised window's worth of data all at once.

Source   Destination

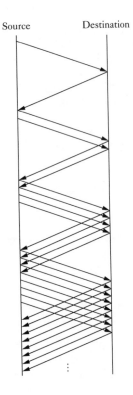

Figure 8.9   Packets in transit during slow start.

There are actually two different situations in which slow start runs. The first is at the very beginning of a connection, at which time the source has no idea how many packets it is going to be able to have in transit at a given time. (Keep in mind that TCP runs over everything from 9600-bps links to 2.4-Gbps links, so there is no way for the source to know the network's capacity.) In this situation, slow start continues to double CongestionWindow each RTT until there is a loss, at which time a timeout causes multiplicative decrease to divide CongestionWindow by 2.

The second situation in which slow start is used is a bit more subtle; it occurs when the connection goes dead while waiting for a timeout to occur. Recall how TCP's sliding window algorithm works—when a packet is lost, the source eventually reaches a point where it has sent as much data as the advertised window allows, and so it blocks while waiting for an ACK that will not arrive. Eventually, a timeout happens, but by this time there are no packets in transit, meaning that the source will receive no ACKs to "clock" the transmission of new packets. The source will instead receive one big cumulative ACK that reopens the entire advertised window, but as explained above, the source then uses slow start to restart the flow of data rather than dumping a whole window's worth of data on the network all at once.

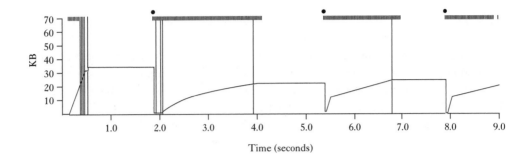

Figure 8.10 Behavior of TCP congestion control. Colored line = value of CongestionWindow over time; solid bullets at top of graph = timeouts; hash marks at top of graph = time when each packet is transmitted; vertical bars = time when a packet that was eventually retransmitted was first transmitted.

Although the source is using slow start again, it now knows more information than it did at the beginning of a connection. Specifically, the source has the current value of CongestionWindow, which, because of the timeout, has already been divided by 2. Slow start is used to rapidly increase the sending rate up to this value, and then additive increase is used beyond this point. Notice that we have a small bookkeeping problem to take care of, in that we want to remember the "target" congestion window resulting from multiplicative decrease as well as the "actual" congestion window being used by slow start. To address this problem, TCP introduces a temporary variable, typically called CongestionThreshold, that is set equal to the CongestionWindow value that results from multiplicative decrease. The variable CongestionWindow is then reset to 1 packet, and it is incremented by 1 packet for every ACK that is received until it reaches CongestionThreshold, at which point it is incremented by 1 packet per RTT.

In other words, TCP increases the congestion window as defined by the following code fragment:

```
{
    u_int    cw = state->CongestionWindow;
    u_int    incr = state->maxseg;

    if (cw > state->CongestionThreshold)
        incr = incr * incr / cw;
    state->CongestionWindow = MIN(cw + incr, TCP_MAXWIN);
}
```

where state represents the state of a particular TCP connection and TCP_MAXWIN defines an upper bound on how large the congestion window is allowed to grow.

Figure 8.10 traces how TCP's CongestionWindow increases and decreases over time and serves to illustrate the interplay of slow start and additive increase/multiplicative decrease.

This trace was taken from an actual TCP connection and shows the current value of CongestionWindow—the thick gray line—over time.

There are several things to notice about this trace. The first is the rapid increase in the congestion window at the beginning of the connection. This corresponds to the initial slow start phase. The slow start phase continues until several packets are lost at about 0.4 seconds into the connection, at which time CongestionWindow flattens out at about 34 KB. (Why so many packets are lost during slow start is discussed below.) The reason the congestion window flattens is that there are no ACKs arriving, due to the fact that several packets were lost. In fact, no new packets are sent during this time, as denoted by the lack of hash marks at the top of the graph. A timeout eventually happens at approximately 2 seconds, at which time the congestion window is divided by 2 (i.e., cut from approximately 34 KB to around 17 KB) and CongestionThreshold is set to this value. Slow start then causes CongestionWindow to be reset to 1 packet and to start ramping up from there.

There is not enough detail in the trace to see exactly what happens when a couple of packets are lost just after 2 seconds, so we jump ahead to the linear increase in the congestion window that occurs between 2 and 4 seconds. This corresponds to additive increase. At about 4 seconds, CongestionWindow flattens out, again due to a lost packet. Now, at about 5.5 seconds,

1 a timeout happens, causing the congestion window to be divided by 2, dropping it from approximately 22 KB to 11 KB, and CongestionThreshold is set to this amount;

2 CongestionWindow is reset to 1 packet, as the sender enters slow start;

3 slow start causes CongestionWindow to grow exponentially until it reaches CongestionThreshold;

4 CongestionWindow then grows linearly.

The same pattern is repeated at around 8 seconds when another timeout occurs.

We now return to the question of why so many packets are lost during the initial slow start period. What TCP is attempting to do here is to learn how much bandwidth is available on the network. This is a very difficult task. If the source is not aggressive at this stage, for example, if it only increases the congestion window linearly, then it takes a long time for it to discover how much bandwidth is available. This can have a dramatic impact on the throughput achieved for this connection. On the other hand, if the source is aggressive at this stage, as TCP is during exponential growth, then the source runs the risk of having half a window's worth of packets dropped by the network.

To see what can happen during exponential growth, consider the situation in which the source was just able to successfully send 16 packets through the network, causing it to double its congestion window to 32. Suppose, however, that the network happens to have just enough capacity to support 16 packets from this source. The likely result is that 16 of the 32 packets sent under the new congestion window will be dropped by the network; actually, this is the worst-case outcome, since some of the packets will be buffered in some router. This problem will become increasing severe as the delay×bandwidth product of networks increases. For example, a delay×bandwidth product of 500 KB means that each connection has the potential to lose up to 500 KB of data at the beginning of each connection. Of course, this assumes that both the source and the destination implement the "big windows" extension.

Some network designers have proposed alternatives to slow start, whereby the source tries to estimate the available bandwidth by means of more clever means of sending out groups of packets and seeing how many make it through. A technique called *packet-pair* is representative of this general strategy. In simple terms, the idea is to send a pair of packets with no spacing between them. Then, the source sees how far apart the ACKs for those two packets are. The gap between the ACKs is taken as a measure of how much congestion there is in the network, and therefore of how much increase in the congestion window is possible. The jury is still out on the effectiveness of approaches such as this, although the results seem promising.

8.3.3 Fast Retransmit and Fast Recovery

The mechanisms described so far were part of the original proposal to add congestion control to TCP. It was soon discovered, however, that the coarse-grained implementation of TCP timeouts led to long periods of time during which the connection went dead while waiting for a timer to expire. Because of this, a new mechanism called *fast retransmit* was added to TCP. Fast retransmit is a heuristic that sometimes triggers the retransmission of a dropped packet sooner than the regular timeout mechanism. The fast retransmit mechanism does not replace regular timeouts; it just enhances that facility.

The idea of fast retransmit is straightforward. Every time a data packet arrives at the receiving side, the receiver responds with an acknowledgment, even if this sequence number has already been acknowledged. Thus, when a packet arrives out of order—that is, TCP cannot yet acknowledge the data the packet contains because earlier data has not yet arrived—TCP resends the same acknowledgment it sent the last time. This second transmission of the same acknowledgment is called a *duplicate ACK*. When the sending side sees a duplicate ACK, it knows that the other side must have received a packet out of order, which suggests that an earlier packet might have been lost. Since it is also possible that the earlier packet has only been delayed rather than lost, the sender waits until it sees some number of duplicate ACKs and then retransmits the missing packet. In practice, TCP waits until it has seen three duplicate ACKs before retransmitting the packet.

Figure 8.11 illustrates how duplicate ACKs lead to a fast retransmit. In this example, the destination receives packets 1 and 2, but packet 3 is lost in the network. Thus, the destination will send a duplicate ACK for packet 2 when packet 4 arrives, again when packet 5 arrives, and so on. (To simplify this example, we think in terms of packets 1, 2, 3, and so on, rather than worrying about the sequence numbers for each byte.) When the sender sees the third duplicate ACK for packet 2—the one sent because the receiver had gotten packet 6—it retransmits packet 3. Note that when the retransmitted copy of packet 3 arrives at the destination, the receiver then sends a cumulative ACK for everything up to and including packet 6 back to the source.

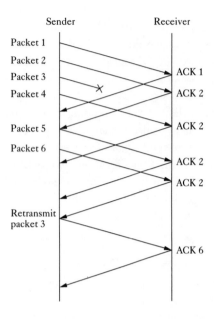

Figure 8.11   Fast retransmit based on duplicate ACKs.

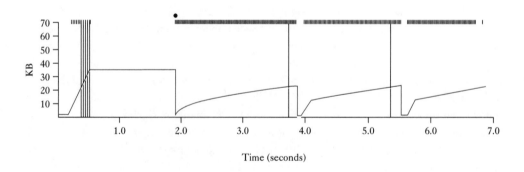

Figure 8.12   Trace of TCP with fast retransmit. Colored line = CongestionWindow; solid bullet = timeout; hash marks = time when each packet is transmitted; vertical bars = time when a packet that was eventually retransmitted was first transmitted.

Figure 8.12 illustrates the behavior of a version of TCP with the fast retransmit mechanism. It is interesting to compare this trace with that given in Figure 8.10, where fast retransmit was not implemented—the long periods during which the congestion window stays flat and no packets are sent has been eliminated. In general, this technique is able to eliminate about half of the coarse-grained timeouts on a typical TCP connection, resulting in roughly a

20% improvement in the throughput over what could otherwise have been achieved. Notice, however, that the fast retransmit strategy does not eliminate all coarse-grained timeouts. This is because for a small window size, there will not be enough packets in transit to cause enough duplicate ACKs to be delivered. Given enough lost packets—for example, as happens during the initial slow start phase—the sliding window algorithm eventually blocks the sender until a timeout occurs. Given the current 64-KB maximum advertised window size, TCP's fast retransmit mechanism is able to detect up to three dropped packets per window in practice.

Finally, there is one last improvement we can make. When the fast retransmit mechanism signals congestion, rather than drop the congestion window all the way back to 1 packet and run slow start, it is possible to use the ACKs that are still in the pipe to clock the sending of packets. This mechanism, which is called *fast recovery*, effectively removes the slow start phase that happens between when fast retransmit detects a lost packet and additive increase begins. For example, fast recovery avoids the slow start period between 3.8 and 4 seconds in Figure 8.12 and instead simply cuts the congestion window in half (from 22 KB to 11 KB) and resumes additive increase. In other words, slow start is only used at the beginning of a connection and whenever a coarse-grained timeout occurs. At all other times, the congestion window is following a pure additive increase/multiplicative decrease pattern.

8.4 Congestion-Avoidance Mechanisms

It is important to understand that TCP's strategy is to control congestion once it happens, as opposed to trying to avoid congestion in the first place. In fact, TCP repeatedly increases the load it imposes on the network in an effort to find the point at which congestion occurs, and then it backs off from this point. Said another way, TCP *needs* to create losses to find the available bandwidth of the connection. An appealing alternative, but one that has not yet been widely adopted, is to predict when congestion is about to happen and then to reduce the rate at which hosts send data just before packets start being discarded. We call such a strategy *congestion avoidance*, to distinguish it from *congestion control*.

This section describes three different congestion-avoidance mechanisms. The first two take a similar approach: They put a small amount of additional functionality into the router to assist the end node in the anticipation of congestion. The third mechanism is very different from the first two: It attempts to avoid congestion purely from the end nodes.

8.4.1 DECbit

The first mechanism was developed for use on the Digital Network Architecture (DNA), a connectionless network with a connection-oriented transport protocol. This mechanism could, therefore, also be applied to TCP and IP. As noted above, the idea here is to more evenly split the responsibility for congestion control between the routers and the end nodes. Each router monitors the load it is experiencing and explicitly notifies the end nodes when congestion is about to occur. This notification is implemented by setting a binary congestion bit in the packets that flow through the router; hence the name DECbit. The destination

Queue length

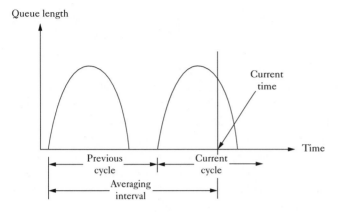

Figure 8.13   Computing average queue length at a router.

host then copies this congestion bit into the ACK it sends back to the source. Finally, the source adjusts its sending rate so as to avoid congestion. The following discussion describes the algorithm in more detail, starting with what happens in the router.

A single congestion bit is added to the packet header. A router sets this bit in a packet if its average queue length is greater than or equal to 1 at the time the packet arrives. This average queue length is measured over a time interval that spans the last busy + idle cycle, plus the current busy cycle. (The router is *busy* when it is transmitting and *idle* when it is not.) Figure 8.13 shows the queue length at a router as a function of time. Essentially, the router calculates the area under the curve and divides this value by the time interval to compute the average queue length. Using a queue length of 1 as the trigger for setting the congestion bit is a tradeoff between significant queuing (and hence higher throughput) and increased idle time (and hence lower delay). In other words, a queue length of 1 seems to optimize the power function.

Now turning our attention to the host half of the mechanism, the source records how many of its packets resulted in some router setting the congestion bit. In particular, the source maintains a congestion window, just as in TCP, and watches to see what fraction of the last window's worth of packets resulted in the bit being set. If less than 50% of the packets had the bit set, then the source increases its congestion window by 1 packet. If 50% or more of the last window's worth of packets had the congestion bit set, then the source decreases its congestion window to 0.875 times the previous value. The value 50% was chosen as the threshold based on analysis that showed it to correspond to the peak of the power curve. The "increase by 1, decrease by 0.875" rule was selected because additive increase/multiplicative decrease makes the mechanism stable.

8.4.2 RED Gateways

A second mechanism, called *Random Early Detection* (RED) gateways,[3] is similar to the DECbit scheme in that each gateway is programmed to monitor its own queue length, and when it detects that congestion is imminent, to notify the source to adjust its congestion window. RED gateways differ from the DECbit scheme in two major ways.

The first is that rather than explicitly sending a congestion notification message to the source, a RED gateway *implicitly* notifies the source of congestion by dropping one of its packets. The source is, therefore, effectively notified by the subsequent timeout. In case you haven't already guessed, RED gateways were designed to be used in conjunction with TCP, which currently detects congestion by means of timeouts (or some other means of detecting packet loss such as duplicate ACKs). As the "early" part of the RED acronym suggests, the gateway drops the packet earlier than it would have to, so as to notify the source that it should decrease its congestion window sooner than it would normally have. In other words, the gateway drops a few packets earlier than it would have to so as to cause the source to slow down, with the hope that this will mean it does not have to drop lots of packets later on. Note that RED gateways could easily be adapted to work with an explicit feedback scheme simply by *marking* a packet instead of *dropping* it.

The second difference is in the details of how a RED gateway decides when to drop a packet and what packet it decides to drop. To understand the basic idea, consider a simple FIFO queue. Rather than wait for the queue to become completely full and then be forced to drop each arriving packet, we could decide to drop each arriving packet with some *drop probability* whenever the queue length exceeds some *drop level*. This idea is called *early random drop*. All that RED adds to early random drop is the details of how to monitor the queue length and when to drop a packet.

First, RED computes an average queue length using a weighted running average similar to the one used in the original TCP timeout computation. That is, AvgLen is computed as

$$AvgLen = (1 - Weight) \times AvgLen + Weight \times SampleLen$$

where $0 <$ Weight < 1 and SampleLen is the length of the queue when a sample measurement is made. In practice, Weight is set equal to 0.002, and the queue length is measured every time a new packet arrives at the gateway.

Second, RED has two queue length thresholds that trigger certain activity: MinThreshold and MaxThreshold. When a packet arrives at the gateway, RED compares the current AvgLen with these two thresholds, according to the following rules:

    if AvgLen ≤ MinThreshold
    ⟶ queue the packet

---

[3]To be consistent with the terminology used throughout this book, we should probably call this a RED *router*. However, the name "RED gateway" is widely used in the literature, and so using the term "router" instead of "gateway" in this setting would be more confusing than helpful.

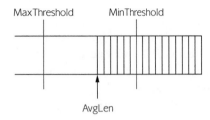

Figure 8.14   RED thresholds on a FIFO queue.

> if MinThreshold < AvgLen < MaxThreshold
> ⟶ calculate probability P
> ⟶ drop the arriving packet with probability P
>
> if MaxThreshold ≤ AvgLen
> ⟶ drop the arriving packet

That is, if the average queue length is smaller than the lower threshold, no action is taken, and if the average queue length is larger than the upper threshold, then the packet is always dropped. If the average queue length is between the two thresholds, then the newly arriving packet is dropped with some probability P. This situation is depicted in Figure 8.14. Note that the probability that a RED gateway chooses to drop a particular flow's packet(s) is roughly proportional to the share of the bandwidth that that flow is currently getting at that gateway—the more packets sent by a flow, the higher the chance that its packets will be selected for dropping.

The probability P of dropping a given packet is not a fixed value. Instead, it is a function of both AvgLen and how long it has been since the last packet was dropped. Specifically, it is computed as follows:

> TempP = MaxP × (AvgLen − MinThreshold) / (MaxThreshold − MinThreshold)
> P = TempP/(1 − count × TempP)

where count keeps track of how many newly arriving packets have been queued (not dropped) while AvgLen has been between the two thresholds. P increases slowly as count increases, thereby making sure that the gateway does not wait too long before dropping a packet. MaxP is typically set to 0.02, meaning that when the average queue size is halfway between the two thresholds, the gateway drops roughly 1 out of 50 packets.

Note that a fair amount of analysis has gone into setting the various RED parameters—e.g., MaxThreshold, MinThreshold, MaxP, and Weight—all in the name of optimizing the power function (throughput-to-delay ratio). The performance of these parameters has also been confirmed through simulation. It is important to keep in mind, however, that all of this analysis and simulation hinges on a particular characterization of the network workload. The real contribution of RED is a mechanism by which the gateway can more accurately manage its queue length. Defining precisely what constitutes an optimal queue length depends on the traffic mix and is a subject of further research.

For example, if the traffic is fairly bursty, then MinThreshold should be sufficiently large to allow the link utilization to be maintained at an acceptably high level. Also, the difference between the two thresholds should be larger than the typical increase in the calculated average queue length in one RTT. Setting MaxThreshold to twice MinThreshold seems to be a reasonable rule of thumb given the traffic mix on today's Internet.

We conclude our discussion of RED gateways by considering the more general question of when it is a good idea to drop packets before you are forced to by a full buffer queue. Consider an ATM network, for example. If you are sending AAL5 packets through a congested ATM switch, and the switch is forced to drop one of the cells from that packet, then the other cells will be useless to the end host; it will have to request that the entire AAL5 packet be retransmitted. Dropping these other cells, even though the switch has enough buffer space to hold them, makes a lot of sense. This technique has in fact been proposed and is called *partial packet discard* (PPD). A switch can be made even more aggressive by combining the idea of RED with the idea of PPD. That is, when an ATM switch is nearing congestion and the first cell of a new AAL5 packet arrives, the switch drops that cell and all the others cells that belong to that AAL5 packet.

8.4.3 Source-Based Congestion Avoidance

Unlike the two previous congestion-avoidance schemes, which depended on new mechanisms in the routers, we now describe a strategy for detecting the incipient stages of congestion—before losses occur—from the end hosts. We first give a brief overview of a collection of related mechanisms that use different information to detect the early stages of congestion, and then we describe a specific mechanism in some detail.

The general idea of these techniques is to watch for some sign from the network that some router's queue is building up and that congestion will happen soon if nothing is done about it. For example, the source might notice that as packet queues build up in the network's routers, there is a measurable increase in the RTT for each successive packet it sends. One particular algorithm exploits this observation as follows: The congestion window normally increases as in TCP, but every two round-trip delays the algorithm checks to see if the current RTT is greater than the average of the minimum and maximum RTTs seen so far. If it is, then the algorithm decreases the congestion window by one-eighth.

A second algorithm does something similar. The decision as to whether or not to change the current window size is based on changes to both the RTT and the window size. The window is adjusted once every two round-trip delays based on the product:

$$(\text{CurrentWindow} - \text{OldWindow}) \times (\text{CurrentRTT} - \text{OldRTT})$$

If the result is positive, the source decreases the window size by one-eighth; if the result is negative or 0, the source increases the window by one maximum packet size. Note that the window changes during every adjustment, that is, it oscillates around its optimal point.

Another change seen as the network approaches congestion is the flattening of the sending rate. A third scheme takes advantage of this fact. Every RTT, it increases the window size by one packet and compares the throughput achieved to the throughput when the window was one packet smaller. If the difference is less than one-half the throughput achieved when only one packet was in transit—as was the case at the beginning of the connection—the algorithm decreases the window by one packet. This scheme calculates the throughput by dividing the number of bytes outstanding in the network by the RTT.

A fourth mechanism, the one we are going to describe in more detail, is similar to this last algorithm in that it looks at changes in the throughput rate, or more specifically, changes in the sending rate. However, it differs from the third algorithm in that it calculates throughputs differently, and instead of looking for a change in the throughput slope, it compares the measured throughput rate with an expected throughput rate.

The intuition behind the algorithm, which is called TCP Vegas, can be seen in the trace of standard TCP given in Figure 8.15. (See the sidebar for an explanation of the name TCP Vegas.)   The top graph shown in Figure 8.15 traces the connection's congestion window; it shows the same information as the traces given earlier in this section. The middle and bottom graphs depict new information: The middle graph shows the average sending rate as measured at the source, and the bottom graph shows the average queue length as measured at the bottleneck router. All three graphs are synchronized in time. In the period between 4.5 and 6.0 seconds (shaded region), the congestion window increases (top graph). We expect the observed throughput to also increase,

Tahoe, Reno, and Vegas

The name "TCP Vegas" is a takeoff on earlier implementations of TCP that were distributed in releases of 4.3 BSD Unix. These releases were known as Tahoe and Reno (which, like Las Vegas, are towns in Nevada), and the versions of TCP became known by the names of the BSD release. TCP Tahoe, which is also known as BSD Network Release 1.0 (BNR1), corresponds to the original implementation of Jacobson's congestion-control mechanism and includes all of the mechanisms described in Section 8.3 except fast recovery.   TCP Reno, which is also known as BSD Network Release 2.0 (BNR2), adds the fast recovery mechanism, along with an optimization known as *header prediction*—optimizing for the common case that segments arrive in order.   TCP Reno also supports *delayed ACKs*—acknowledging every other segment rather than every segment—although this is a selectable option that is sometimes turned off. A more recent version of

but instead it stays flat (middle graph). This is because the throughput cannot increase beyond the available bandwidth. Beyond this point, any increase in the window size only results in packets taking up buffer space at the bottleneck router (bottom graph).

A useful metaphor that describes the phenomenon illustrated in Figure 8.15 is driving on ice. The speedometer (congestion window) may say that you are going 30 miles an hour, but by looking out the car window and seeing people pass you on foot (measured sending rate), you know that you are going no more than 5 miles an hour. The extra energy is being absorbed by the car's tires (router buffers).

TCP distributed in 4.4 BSD Unix adds the "big windows" extensions described in Section 6.2.

One thing you should take away from this discussion of TCP's lineage is that TCP has been a rather fluid protocol over the last several years, especially in its congestion-control mechanism. In fact, you would not even find univeral agreement about which technique was introduced in which release, due to the availability of intermediate versions of the code and the fact that patch has been layered on top of patch.

All that can be said with any certainty is that any two implementations of TCP that follow the original specification, while they should interoperate, will not necessarily perform well. Recognizing the performance implications of having TCP Tahoe interoperate with TCP Reno is a tricky business. In other words, you could argue that TCP is no longer defined by a specification, but rather by an implementation—the BSD implementation. The only question is, which BSD implementation?

TCP Vegas uses this idea to measure and control the amount of *extra* data this connection has in transit, where by extra data we mean data that the source would not have transmitted had it been trying to match exactly the available bandwidth of the network. The goal of TCP Vegas is to maintain the "right" amount of extra data in the network. Obviously, if a source is sending too much extra data, it will cause long delays and possibly lead to congestion. Less obviously, if a connection is sending too little extra data, it cannot respond rapidly enough to transient increases in the available network bandwidth. TCP Vegas's congestion-avoidance actions are based on changes in the estimated amount of extra data in the network, not only on dropped packets. We now describe the algorithm in detail.

First, define a given flow's **BaseRTT** to be the RTT of a packet when the flow is not congested. In practice, TCP Vegas sets **BaseRTT** to the minimum of all measured round-trip times; it is commonly the RTT of the first packet sent by the connection, before the router queues increase due to traffic generated by this flow. If we assume that we are not overflowing the connection, then the expected throughput is given by

$$\text{ExpectedRate} = \text{CongestionWindow} / \text{BaseRTT}$$

where **CongestionWindow** is the TCP congestion window, which we assume (for the purpose of this discussion) to be equal to the number of bytes in transit.

Second, TCP Vegas calculates the current sending rate, **ActualRate**. This is done by recording the sending time for a distinguished packet, recording how many bytes are trans-

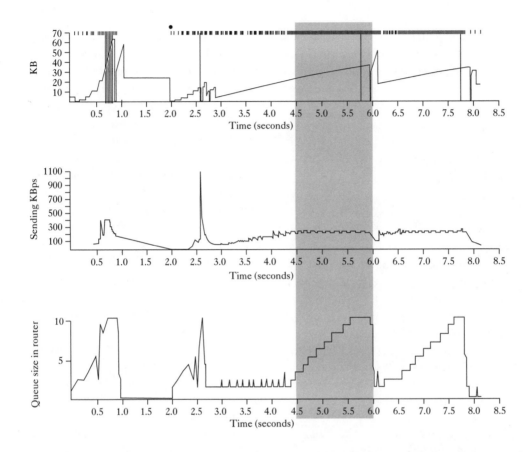

Figure 8.15 Congestion window versus observed throughput rate (the three graphs are synchronized). Top, congestion window; middle, observed throughput; bottom, buffer space taken up at the router. Colored line = CongestionWindow; solid bullet = timeout; hash marks = time when each packet is transmitted; vertical bars = time when a packet that was eventually retransmitted was first transmitted.

mitted between the time that packet is sent and when its acknowledgment is received, computing the sample RTT for the distinguished packet when its acknowledgment arrives, and dividing the number of bytes transmitted by the sample RTT. This calculation is done once per round-trip time.

Third, TCP Vegas compares ActualRate to ExpectedRate and adjusts the window accordingly. We let Diff = ExpectedRate − ActualRate. Note that Diff is positive or 0 by definition, since ActualRate > ExpectedRate implies that we need to change BaseRTT to the latest sampled RTT. We also define two thresholds, $\alpha < \beta$, roughly corresponding to having too little and too much extra data in the network, respectively. When Diff $< \alpha$, TCP Vegas increases the congestion window linearly during the next RTT, and when Diff $> \beta$, TCP

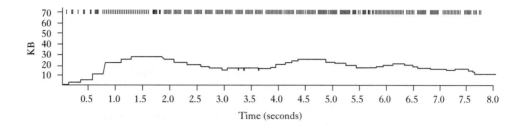

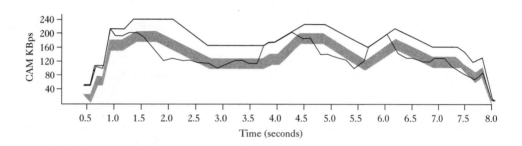

Figure 8.16   Trace of TCP Vegas congestion-avoidance mechanism. Top, congestion window; bottom, expected (colored line) and actual (black line) throughput. The shaded area is the region between the α and β thresholds.

Vegas decreases the congestion window linearly during the next RTT. TCP Vegas leaves the congestion window unchanged when $\alpha < \mathsf{Diff} < \beta$.

Intuitively, we can see that the farther away the actual throughput gets from the expected throughput, the more congestion there is in the network, which implies that the sending rate should be reduced. The β threshold triggers this decrease. On the other hand, when the actual throughput rate gets too close to the expected throughput, the connection is in danger of not utilizing the available bandwidth. The α threshold triggers this increase. The overall goal is to keep between α and β extra bytes in the network.

Figure 8.16 traces the TCP Vegas congestion-avoidance algorithm. The top graph traces the congestion window, showing the same information as the other traces given throughout this chapter. The bottom graph traces the expected and actual throughput rates that govern how the congestion window is set. It is this bottom graph that best illustrates how the algorithm works. The colored line tracks the ExpectedRate, while the black line tracks the ActualRate. The wide shaded strip gives the region between the α and β thresholds; the top of the shaded strip is α KBps away from ExpectedRate, and the bottom of the shaded strip is β KBps away from ExpectedRate. The goal is to keep the ActualRate between these two thresholds, that is, within the shaded region. Whenever ActualRate falls below the shaded region (i.e., gets too far from ExpectedRate), TCP Vegas decreases the congestion window because it fears that too many packets are being buffered in the network. Likewise, whenever ActualRate goes above the shaded region (i.e., gets too close to the ExpectedRate), TCP Vegas increases the congestion window because it fears that it is underutilizing the network.

Because the algorithm, as just presented, compares the difference between the actual and expected throughput rates to the α and β thresholds, these two thresholds are defined in terms of KBps. However, it is perhaps more accurate to think in terms of how many extra *buffers* the connection is occupying in the network. For example, on a connection with a BaseRTT of 100 ms and a packet size of 1 KB, if $\alpha = 30$ KBps and $\beta = 60$ KBps, then we can think of α as specifying that the connection needs to be occupying at least 3 extra buffers in the network and β as specifying that the connection should occupy no more than 6 extra buffers in the network. In practice, a setting of α to 1 buffer and β to 3 buffers works well.

Finally, you will notice that TCP Vegas decreases the congestion window linearly, seemingly in conflict with the rule that multiplicative decrease is needed to ensure stability. The explanation is that TCP Vegas does use multiplicative decrease when a timeout occurs; the linear decrease just described is an *early* decrease in the congestion window that, hopefully, happens before congestion occurs and packets start being dropped.

8.5 Virtual Clock

We conclude our discussion of congestion control by considering a mechanism—*virtual clock*—that is very different from those described in the previous sections. Instead of using feedback and being window-based, the virtual clock algorithm allows the source to make a reservation using a rate-based description of its needs. This approach takes us beyond the best-effort delivery model of the current Internet by allowing the source to ask the routers of the network to guarantee it a certain amount of bandwidth. Note that we are using the virtual clock algorithm as a representative

Evaluating a New Congestion-Control Mechanism

Suppose you develop a new congestion-control mechanism and want to evaluate its performance. For example, you might want to compare it to the current mechanism running on the Internet. How do you go about measuring and evaluating your mechanism? Although at one time the Internet's primary purpose in life was to support networking research, today it is a large, production network and therefore completely inappropriate for running a controlled experiment.

If your approach is purely end to end—that is, if it assumes only FIFO routers within the Internet—then it is possible to run your congestion-control mechanism on a small set of hosts and to measure the throughput your connections are able to achieve. We need to add a word of caution here, however. It is surprisingly easy to invent a congestion-control mechanism that achieves five times the throughput of TCP across the Internet. You simply blast packets into the Internet at a high rate, thereby

example of rate/reservation-based systems that are currently being designed and evaluated. Section 8.5.4 discusses related efforts in this area.

The idea of the virtual clock algorithm is quite elegant. It is modeled after time-division multiplexing (TDM), in which each flow is given a slice of time during which it can transmit on a shared link. The advantage of TDM is that each flow is guaranteed its share of the link's bandwidth, and flows are not allowed to interfere with each other. The disadvantage, however, is that TDM is not able to give one flow's unused bandwidth to another flow that has data to send. Since many applications do not transmit data at a constant bit rate, but instead have bursty transmissions, this is overly conservative. The virtual clock algorithm mimics the TDM behavior, but does so for a statistically multiplexed network by using a virtual definition of time to pace the transmission of data, rather than the real clock used by TDM.

8.5.1 Defining Rate

The virtual clock mechanism includes an explicit flow setup phase during which the source indicates its needs to the network. Similar to the establishment of a connection through a connection-based network, this involves a flow setup message that traverses a set of routers. Each router inspects the flow parameters and grants or denies the request based on its current load.

A flow's resource needs are expressed using two parameters: *average rate* (AR) and *average interval* (AI). For example, a flow might specify an AR of 100 packets per second and an AI of 100 ms. By specifying a particular AI/AR pair, the source is saying that over each time interval AI, dividing the total number of bytes it sends by AI will result in AR. The relevance of AR is obvious—it corresponds to the source's bandwidth needs. The importance of AI is that it puts a limit on the burstiness of the source, that is, how smoothly the bytes are spread out over time.

causing congestion. All the other hosts running TCP detect this congestion and reduce the rate at which they are sending packets. Your mechanism then happily consumes all the bandwidth. This strategy is fast but hardly fair.

Experimenting directly on the Internet, even when done carefully, will not work when your congestion-control mechanism involves changes to the routers. It is simply not practical to change the software running on thousands of routers for the sake of evaluating a new congestion-control algorithm. In this case, network designers are forced to test their systems on simulated networks or private testbed networks. For example, the TCP traces presented in this chapter were generated by an implementation of TCP that was running on an x-kernel-based network simulator. The challenge in either a simulation or a testbed is coming up with a topology and a traffic workload that are representative of the real Internet.

How a source selects a suitable AI is a good question, since it can take on a range of values:

$$1/AR \leq AI \leq \text{total flow duration}$$

If AI were set to its lower bound, then the source would be transmitting at a constant rate, much as in a circuit-switched network. On the other hand, if AI were as large as the total duration of the flow, then the source would be allowed to transmit data in an arbitrary manner, just as in a purely connectionless network. In general, each source selects an AI so that the average rate measured over each AI is relatively constant. This method of characterizing rate is similar (but not identical) to the *token bucket* method, described in Section 9.3.

There is one potentially troubling aspect of an explicit flow setup scheme such as the one just described—what about datagram and RPC-based traffic that cannot afford to set up a flow just for the sake of sending one or two packets? This problem is addressed by establishing a single permanent flow—call it flow 0—that is granted some fraction of the network's capacity. Datagram and RPC traffic can then be sent by means of flow 0. This would guarantee such traffic some percentage of the available capacity, while giving applications that are able to sustain a flow the opportunity to reserve bandwidth from the network.

8.5.2 Virtual Clock as a Queuing Discipline

To a first approximation, the virtual clock mechanism uses AR to set up the parameters for a queuing discipline that behaves much like weighted fair queuing. The router maintains a variable $VirtualClock_i$ for each flow i. It also computes a clock tick for flow i, denoted $VirtualTick_i$, that controls how fast the virtual clock for flow i advances. Assuming that all packets on flow i are the same size, then

$$VirtualTick_i = 1/AR_i$$

For example, if flow i has an AR of 200 packets per second, then $VirtualTick_i$ is set to 5 ms. Note that if packets are not all the same size, then $VirtualTick_i$ needs to be recalculated on a per-packet basis. To simplify the following discussion, we assume fixed-sized packets.

Upon receiving the first data packet in a flow, the router sets $VirtualClock_i$ to the current real time, as read from the system clock. Then, upon receiving each packet on flow i, the router advances the flow's virtual clock as follows:

$$VirtualClock_i = VirtualClock_i + VirtualTick_i$$

The router then stamps each packet with this setting of $VirtualClock_i$, and packets are queued and serviced in the order of increasing timestamps. When the router's buffer space is full, the packet with the largest timestamp is dropped. The end result is that packets from different flows are maximally interleaved in a round-robin manner.

To see better how the virtual clock algorithm works, consider the example pair of flows given in Figure 8.17, where real time is marked across the top and the order in which the packets are output is depicted on the bottom. In this example, flow 1 has an AR of 1000 packets

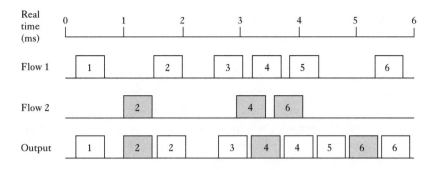

Figure 8.17 Example flows using virtual clock algorithm.

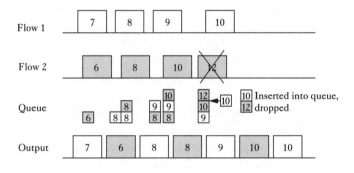

Figure 8.18 Example of discarding a packet using the virtual clock algorithm.

per second (thus, VirtualTick$_1$ = 1 ms), while flow 2 has an AR of 500 packets per second (thus, VirtualTick$_2$ = 2 ms). Notice how the packets are interleaved at a ratio of approximately 2-to-1, depending on exactly when each packet arrives at the router.

Continuing with this example, Figure 8.18 shows how the virtual clock algorithm drops packets when the router's queue overflows. For this example, suppose that the queue can hold only 3 packets. When the packet with timestamp 10 arrives on flow 1, the queue is already full (it contains packet 9 from flow 1 and packets 10 and 12 from flow 2), and so the packet with the largest timestamp (packet 12 from flow 2) has to be discarded.

Notice that like the FQ/WFQ algorithms, the virtual clock algorithm segregates flows and ensures that each flow receives the resources it has reserved. Although an aggressive or ill-behaved source is able to consume otherwise idle resources, it cannot disturb the service provided to other flows. It is also the case that datagram traffic that is using flow 0 can soak up any excess bandwidth.

8.5.3 Virtual Clock as a Flow Meter

As described so far, the virtual clock algorithm does not use the AI parameter, which was introduced to help quantify the burstiness of a flow. Thus, a particular source could choose to not send any packets for a long while—therefore its virtual clock would not advance—and then all of a sudden it could start sending a large burst of data. This would cause that flow's packets to be inserted early into the router's queue, potentially bumping packets that belong to other flows. In other words, the queuing discipline outlined above allows a flow to save up credits and then to use them in the future. To restrict a flow's ability to do this, the virtual clock mechanism also includes a flow monitoring component.

The idea is as follows. When flow i is set up, the router computes a control variable:

$$AIR_i = AR_i \times AI_i$$

Then, upon receiving AIR_i bytes worth of data on flow i, the router checks the flow in the following way. If $VirtualClock_i$ minus the real time is greater than some specified threshold, then the source is sending faster than it said it would (virtual time is advancing faster than real time) and the router sends an advisory message to the source. If, however, $VirtualClock_i$ is less than the real time, then the source is not sending data as fast as it said it would (virtual time is advancing more slowly than real time), and the router resets $VirtualClock_i$ to the real time. That is, virtual time is resynchronized with real time, meaning that the source is not allowed to accumulate "unused time" during one AI period in order to save it for use in the future.

Note that there is still a potential problem with a flow accumulating credit *within* an AI period of time; i.e., a burst could arrive late in a flow's AI period. The problem here is that we are using one variable (VirtualClock) to control both the queuing order and the flow monitoring. We can do better by introducing an auxiliary copy of the VirtualClock variable, called AuxVirtualClock, keeping this variable synchronized with the real time for every packet that arrives (rather than just once every time AIR bytes of data arrive) and using AuxVirtualClock for timestamps. Thus, upon receiving each packet on flow i, the router does the following:

$$AuxVirtualClock_i = MAX(real\ time, AuxVirtualClock_i)$$
$$VirtualClock_i = VirtualClock_i + VirtualTick_i$$
$$AuxVirtualClock_i = AuxVirtualClock_i + VirtualTick_i$$
$$Stamp\ packet\ with\ current\ value\ of\ AuxVirtualClock_i$$

In other words, $VirtualClock_i$ is resynchronized with the real time once for every AIR_i bytes of data on flow i, while $AuxVirtualClock_i$ is resynchronized with the real time once for every packet on flow i. This means that AuxVirtualClock is used to implement the queuing discipline, while VirtualClock meters the flow.

8.5.4 Other Rate-Based Mechanisms (ABR)

The virtual clock algorithm is just one of many rate-based service mechanisms that are being defined right now. In addition to guaranteeing a requested bandwidth to an end-to-end flow, these mechanisms also address the issues of bounding the delay and jitter (delay variation) experienced by those flows.

Broadly speaking, these various mechanisms can be classified as either *work-conserving* or *non-work-conserving*. The virtual clock algorithm is work-conserving because the router is never idle when there is a packet to send. In contrast, a non-work-conserving algorithm potentially can become idle even when it has packets buffered for transmission. What happens is that the router assigns each packet an *eligibility time*, which defines the earliest time the router will send that packet. Even when the server is idle, if no packets are eligible, none will be transmitted. The motivation for non-work-conserving algorithms is that they more carefully pace the transmission of packets, thereby improving the end-to-end jitter of each flow.

Of all the rate-based algorithms that have been proposed, the one we want to call attention to (in addition to virtual clock) is the *available bit rate* (ABR) mechanism that is being developed for use on ATM networks. Having been designed by a standards body, it is rather complex, so this section covers only a few of the high points.

We can think of an ATM virtual circuit as having two ends, the virtual source (VS) and the virtual destination (VD). They are "virtual" in the sense that they may be routers that connect the ATM network to another network, i.e., they may not be the true end-points of communication. ABR works only over an ATM network and is therefore not generally end to end. The VS or VD may even be an entity at the administrative boundary between, say, a private ATM network and a public network.

The ABR mechanism operates over an existing virtual circuit using a special ATM cell called a Resource Manager (RM) cell. The VS sends the cell to the VD and includes in it the rate at which it would like to send data cells. Switches along the path look at the requested rate and decide if sufficient resources are available to handle that rate, based on the amount of traffic being carried on other circuits. If enough resources are available, the RM cell is passed on unmodified; otherwise, the requested rate is decreased before the cell is passed along. At the VD, the RM cell is turned around and sent back to the VS, which thereby learns what rate it can send at.

The intention of ABR is to allow a source to increase or decrease its allotted rate as conditions dictate. As a consequence, RM cells are sent periodically and may contain either higher or lower requested rates. Also, the rate at which a source is allowed to send decays with time if not used. This is intended to discourage a source from requesting capacity "just in case."

There are a lot of difficult issues that must be resolved before this basic mechanism will work well. For example, it is desirable that a VS be able to start sending at some rate without having to wait the entire RTT before the RM cell returns. This is particularly important when you consider that the VS might be a router that just received a big burst of IP packets without prior warning, and if it doesn't send them out over the ATM network soon, its buffers may overflow. The idea in ABR is to allow a VS to start sending at some initial rate without waiting for the RM cell to return. If this rate is too low, however, it may be inadequate to deal with the traffic arriving at the VS, and if it is too high, then a number of virtual sources might be able to overwhelm a switch with a burst of data.

Another uncertain aspect of ABR is how it interacts with TCP's congestion-avoidance mechanisms. These mechanisms are finely tuned based on experience, and they work on the premise that there is nothing fancy going on in the network—if you send too fast, packets get dropped. With ABR, you can imagine that the VS might have to drop packets while it waits for an RM cell to return, even though there is in fact no real congestion in the network.

In any case, ABR products are likely to be deployed quite soon, at which point we will learn whether the mechanism it provides improves performance and what details still need to be worked out.

8.6 Summary

As we have just seen, the issue of congestion control is not only central to computer networking, it is also a very hard problem. Unlike flow control, which is concerned with the source not overrunning the receiver, congestion control is about keeping the source from overloading the network. In this context, most of our focus has been on mechanisms targeted at the best-effort service model of today's Internet, where the primary responsibility for congestion control falls on the end nodes of the network. Typically, the source uses feedback—either implicitly learned from the network or explicitly sent by a router—to adjust the load it places on the network; this is precisely what TCP's congestion-control mechanism does.

Independent of exactly what the end nodes are doing, the routers implement a queuing discipline that governs which packets get transmitted and which packets get dropped. Sometimes this queuing algorithm is sophisticated enough to segregate traffic (e.g., FQ), and in other cases, the router attempts to monitor its queue length and then signals the source host when congestion is about to occur (e.g., RED gateways and DECbit).

As suggested throughout this chapter, it is also possible to design a rate-based congestion-control mechanism in which source hosts reserve a desired quality of service from the network. The virtual clock mechanism is an example of a congestion-control mechanism designed in this mold, but it is not appropriate for a best-effort service model. We will continue this discussion in Chapter 9, where we introduce a new service model that supports multiple qualities of service, including the ability to reserve network bandwidth.

OPEN ISSUE

Inside versus Outside the Network

Perhaps the larger question we should be asking is how much can we expect from the network and how much responsibility will ultimately fall to the end hosts. The emerging reservation-based strategies certainly have the advantage of providing for more varied qualities of service than today's feedback-based schemes; being able to support different qualities of service is a strong reason to put more functionality into the network's routers. Does this mean that the days of TCP-like end-to-end congestion control are numbered? The answer is not so obvious. It is actually a fairly unlikely scenario that all the routers in a worldwide, heterogeneous network like the Internet will implement precisely the same resource-reservation algorithm. Ultimately, is seems that the endpoints are going to have to look out for themselves, at least to some extent. After all, we should not forget the sound design principle underlying the Internet—do the simplest possible thing in the routers and put all the smarts at the edges where you can control it. How this all plays out in the next few years will be very interesting indeed.

Beyond this basic question, there is another thorny issue lurking. While in the first section of this chapter we claimed that congestion control in a network and in an internet are the same problem—and they are—the issue becomes messy when the problem is being solved at *both* the network level and the internet level. Consider the case of running IP over ATM. If we try to program our IP routers to do something clever regarding resource allocation, then we could be in trouble if one of the underlying links is really implemented by an ATM virtual path and the ATM network is sharing that path with other traffic. This is because it is impossible for IP to promise some share of a link's bandwidth to a flow if the total bandwidth available on the link is variable. In a sense, there is a tug of war between ATM and IP over who owns the resource-allocation problem.

FURTHER READING

The recommended reading list for this chapter is long, reflecting the breadth of interesting work being done in congestion control. It includes the original papers introducing the various mechanisms discussed in this chapter. In addition to a more detailed description of these mechanisms, including thorough analysis of their effectiveness and fairness, these papers are must reading because of the insights they give into the interplay of the various issues related to congestion control. In addition, the first paper gives a nice overview of some of the early work on this topic (i.e., it summarizes the past), and the last paper surveys several emerging rate-based mechanisms (i.e., it gives a possible view of the future).

- Gerla, M., and L. Kleinrock. Flow control: A comparative survey. *IEEE Transactions on Communications*, COM-28(4):553–573, April 1980.

- Demers, A., S. Keshav, and S. Shenker. Analysis and simulation of a fair queuing algorithm. *Proceedings of the SIGCOMM '89 Symposium*, pages 1–12, September 1989.

- Jacobson, V. Congestion avoidance and control. *Proceedings of the SIGCOMM '88 Symposium*, pages 314–329, August 1988.

■ Ramakrishnan, K., and R. Jain. A binary feedback scheme for congestion avoidance in computer networks with a connectionless network layer. *ACM Transactions on Computer Systems* 8(2):158–181, May 1990.

■ Floyd, S., and V. Jacobson. Random early detection gateways for congestion avoidance. *IEEE/ACM Transactions on Networking* 1(4):397–413, August 1993.

■ Brakmo, L., and L. Peterson. TCP Vegas: End-to-end congestion avoidance on a global internet. *IEEE Journal of Selected Areas in Communication (JSAC)* 13(8):1465–1480, October 1995.

■ Zhang, L. Virtual clock: A new traffic control algorithm for packet switching networks. *ACM Transactions on Computer Systems* 9(2):101–124, May 1991.

■ Zhang, H., and S. Keshav. Comparison of rate-based service disciplines. *Proceedings of the SIGCOMM '91 Symposium*, pages 113–121, September 1991.

Beyond these recommended papers, there is a wealth of other valuable material on congestion control. For starters, two early papers by Kleinrock [Kle79] and Jaffe [Jaf81] set the foundation for using power as a measure of congestion-control effectiveness. Also, Jain [Jai91] gives a thorough discussion of various issues related to performance evaluation, including a description of Jain's fairness index.

More details on the various congestion-avoidance techniques introduced in Section 8.4 can be found in Wang and Crowcroft [WC92, WC91] and Jain [Jai89], with the first paper giving an especially nice overview of congestion avoidance based on a common understanding of how the network changes as it approaches congestion. Also, the packet-pair technique briefly discussed in Section 8.3.2 is more carefully described in Keshav [Kes91], and the partial packet discard technique suggested in Section 8.4.2 is described by Romanow and Floyd [RF94].

EXERCISES

1 Should flows be defined on a host-to-host basis or on a process-to-process basis? Discuss the implications of each approach to application programs. How would each scheme be implemented in the routers?

2 Suppose a congestion-control scheme results in a collection of competing flows that achieve the following throughput rates: 100 KBps, 60 KBps, 110 KBps, 95 KBps, and 150 KBps. Calculate the fairness index for this scheme.

3 Sketch the implementation of the weighted fair queuing algorithm. In particular, give the formula for F_i of packet i, assuming that W is the weight assigned to the flow.

4 Give an example of how non-preemption in the implementation of fair queuing violates the strict definition of bit-by-bit round-robin service.

5 Consider a simple congestion-control algorithm that uses linear increase/multiplicative decrease but not slow start, that works in units of packets rather than bytes, and that starts each connection with a congestion window equal to 1 packet. Give a detailed sketch of this algorithm. Plot the congestion window as a function of round-trip times for the situation in which the following packets are lost: 9, 25, 30, 38, and 50. For simplicity, assume a perfect timeout mechanism that detects a lost packet exactly 1 RTT after it is transmitted.

6 For the situation given in the previous problem, compute the effective throughput achieved by this connection. Assume that each packet holds 1 KB of data and that the RTT = 100 ms.

7 During linear increase, TCP computes an increment to the congestion window as

Increment = (MSS × MSS)/CongestionWindow

Explain why computing this increment each time an ACK arrives may not result in the correct increment. Give a more precise definition for this increment. (Hint: A given ACK can acknowledge more or less than one MSS's worth of data.)

8 Explain why coarse-grained timeouts are still possible in TCP even when the fast retransmit mechanism is being used.

9 Use the x-kernel simulator and trace tools to measure the effect of changing TCP's additive increase/multiplicative decrease mechanism. For example, you might try changing the rate at which the congestion window is increased or decreased.

10 Use the x-kernel simulator and trace tools to measure the effectiveness of TCP congestion control when the routers implement queuing disciplines other than FIFO, e.g., fair queuing and RED.

11 Use the x-kernel simulator and trace tools to measure the effectiveness of standard TCP versus TCP Vegas.

12 Discuss the relative advantages and disadvantages of marking a packet (as in the DECbit mechanism) versus dropping a packet (as in RED gateways).

13 For RED gateways, show that the router drops 1 in 50 packets when the average queue length is halfway between the two thresholds and the MaxP is 0.02.

14 Explain the intuition behind setting MaxThreshold = 2 × MinThreshold in RED gateways.

15 In RED gateways, explain why MaxThreshold is actually less than the actual size of the available buffer pool.

16 Sketch how an ATM switch would implement partial packet discard.

17 Explain the fundamental conflict between tolerating burstiness and controlling network congestion.

18 Discuss the ramifications of a large and a small AI in the virtual clock algorithm.

19 Consider a router that is managing three flows, on which packets arrive at the following times:

> flow A: 1, 2, 4, 6, 7, 9, 10
> flow B: 2, 6, 8, 11, 12, 15
> flow C: 1, 2, 3, 5, 6, 7, 8

(a) Suppose the router implements fair queuing. Plot the sequence of packets output by the router as a function of time. Assume that an infinite amount of buffering is available on the router.

(b) Suppose the router implements weighted fair queuing, where flows A and B are given an equal share of the capacity, and flow C is given twice the capacity of flow A. Plot the sequence of packets output by the router as a function of time. Assume that an infinite amount of buffering is available on the router.

(c) For (a) and (b) above, determine the minimum number of buffers that will be needed at the router to ensure that no packets are dropped. Assume that two packets can be transmitted during each time unit.

(d) Suppose the router implements the virtual clock algorithm, where flow A and flow B have specified an AR of 0.5 packets per time unit and flow C has specified an AR of 1 packet per time unit. Assume that the AI for all three flows is so large as to not influence this short trace, that the router can buffer only three packets, and that two packets can be transmitted during each time unit. Plot the sequence of packets output by the router as a function of time. Be sure to show what packets, if any, are dropped due to insufficient buffer space.

20 Give an argument why the congestion-control problem is better managed at the internet level than the ATM level.

P erformance has been an important aspect of nearly every topic covered in this book, for good reason, since it is often improvements in network performance that enable new classes of applications. With this continual push toward higher- and higher-speed networks, we have to wonder if the abstractions, mechanisms, architectures, and protocols we have been designing for the past 20 years will continue to work, or if instead some part of our fundamental infrastructure will break when we go faster.

First, we need to define what we mean by "faster." While it is likely that multi-terabit networks will one day be a reality, we aim our sights a bit lower by focusing on the gigabit networks that are now on the horizon. When you consider that most of us are still using 10-Mbps Ethernets and 1.5-Mbps long-haul T1 links, 1 Gbps easily qualifies as "high speed." At three orders of magnitude faster than a T1 link, 1 Gbps is enough bandwidth to force us to start thinking in terms of what happens in the limit, that is, what happens when an infinite amount of bandwidth is available.

So, what does happen at gigabit speeds? For one thing, the tradeoff between bandwidth and latency changes. While it is tempting to think of "high speed" as meaning that latency improves at the same rate as bandwidth, we cannot forget about the limitation imposed by the speed of light—the round-trip time for a 1-Gbps link is exactly the same as the round-trip time for a 1-Mbps link. Instead of being bandwidth poor, a situation that sometimes causes us to ignore the effects of round-trip times on the application, we are bandwidth rich and each RTT becomes more precious. The first section of this chapter discusses the resulting shift in focus from preserving bandwidth to tolerating and hiding latency.

A second thing that happens is that the bandwidth available on the network starts to rival the bandwidth available *inside* the computers that are connected to the network. What we mean by this is that the network bandwidth is within an order of magnitude of the memory and bus bandwidth of the host. If we are not careful in how we design the end hosts—

Now this is not the end. It is not even the beginning of the end. But it is, perhaps, the end of the beginning.

—Churchill

including both the host's architecture and the software running on that host—then we are not going to be able to deliver the gigabit bandwidth that the network provides all the way to the end applications that want to use it. The second section discusses this situation in more detail and introduces various techniques that have been proposed to deal with this problem.

A final thing that happens as the network becomes faster is that new applications, some never before imagined, start to emerge. While this is good news, quite often these applications need services from the network beyond just the ability to deliver bits at high rates. For example, high-speed networks are making video applications possible, but video needs performance guarantees, not just raw performance. New demands such as these often stress the network's underlying service model, a model that was developed for applications that ran at lower speeds. The third section of this chapter describes a new service model that is just now evolving and that may one day replace the current best-effort service model.

High-Speed Networking

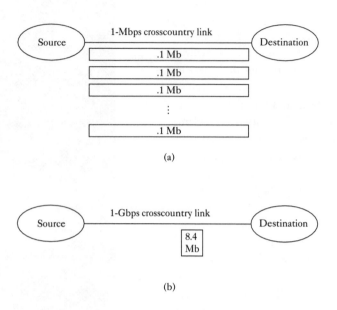

Figure 9.1   Relationship between bandwidth and latency. With an 8.4 Mb file, the 1-Mbps link has 84 pipes full of data (a); the 1-Gbps link has 1/12 of one pipe full of data (b).

9.1   Latency Issues

Although gigabit networks bring a dramatic change in the bandwidth available to applications—as much as 1000 times the bandwidth available on today's networks—in many respects their impact on how we think about networking comes in what does *not* change as bandwidth increases: the speed of light. That is, "high speed" does not mean that latency improves at the same rate as bandwidth; the crosscountry RTT of a 1-Gbps link is the same 100 ms as it is for a 1-Mbps link. This section considers the ramifications of this law of nature.

9.1.1   Latency/Throughput Tradeoff

To appreciate the significance of ever-increasing bandwidth in the face of fixed latency, consider what is required to transmit a 1-MB file over a 1-Mbps network versus over a 1-Gbps network, both of which have an RTT of 100 ms. In the case of the 1-Mbps network, it takes 100 round-trip times to transmit the file; during each RTT, 1% of the file is sent. In contrast, the same 1-MB file doesn't even come close to filling 1 RTT's worth of the 1-Gbps link, which has a delay × bandwidth product of 12.5 MB.

Figure 9.1 illustrates the difference between the two networks. In effect, the 1-MB file looks like a stream of data that needs to be transmitted across a 1-Mbps network, while it looks like a single datagram on a 1-Gbps network. To help drive this point home, consider that a 1-MB file is to a 1-Gbps network what a 1-KB *packet* is to a 1-Mbps network.

▶   Another way to think about the situation is that more data can be transmitted during each RTT on a high-speed network, so much so that a single RTT becomes a significant amount of time. Thus, while you wouldn't think twice about the difference between a file transfer taking 101 RTTs rather than 100 RTTs (a relative difference of only 1%), suddenly the difference between 1 RTT and 2 RTTs is significant—a 100% increase. In other words, latency, rather than throughput, starts to dominate our thinking about network design.

Perhaps the best way to understand the relationship between throughput and latency is to return to basics. The effective end-to-end throughput that can be achieved over a network is given by the simple relationship:

Throughput = TransferSize / TransferTime

For example, if it takes 10 ms to transfer 1 MB, then the effective throughput is 1 MB/10 ms = 100 MBps = 800 Mbps. (We assume that all uses of "Mega" in this discussion are equal.) What is interesting in the case we are now considering is that the transfer time in this formula depends not only on the bandwidth of the underlying network, but also on the latency of that network. In other words, we can define the transfer time as

TransferTime = Latency + 1/Bandwidth × TransferSize

where the 1/Bandwidth term reflects how long it takes to transmit a single byte at the given network bandwidth. For example, even if the underlying network bandwidth is 1 Gbps (meaning that it will take 1/1 Gbps × 1 MB = 0.8 ms to transmit 1 MB), an end-to-end transfer that requires 1 RTT of, say, 100 ms will have a total transfer time of 100.8 ms. This means that the effective throughput will be 1 MB/100.8 ms = 79.4 Mbps, not 1 Gbps. Clearly, transferring a larger amount of data will help improve the effective throughput, where in the limit, an infinitely large transfer size will cause the effective throughput to approach the network bandwidth. On the other hand, having to endure more than 1 RTT will hurt the effective throughput for any transfer of finite size and will be most noticeable for small transfers.

9.1.2 Implications

System designers have a common saying: bandwidth problems are solved with hardware, latency problems with software. Thanks to network hardware designers, we are entering a period in which we are bandwidth rich and latency poor, meaning that it is time to start building some good software. We now consider the implications of the emerging relationship between latency and throughput.

Congestion Control

In Chapter 8 we saw several congestion-control schemes, including the one used by TCP, that depend on the end hosts reacting to feedback from the network. On a high-speed network, however, a 10-MB file can be transmitted in a single RTT, meaning that the source has no opportunity to react to feedback if TCP's window size is greater than 10 MB; by the time any feedback would arrive, the host is done sending the data. Of course, this 10 MB of data might arrive at a router at the same time as 10 MB of data from another source, which could lead to congestion and massive packet losses.

In general, the problem is that even though we can calculate the potential delay × bandwidth product to be 10 MB, we have to remember that other flows might be using some fraction of this bandwidth. Finding the available bandwidth on the network is one of the things that TCP slow start is designed to do. The problem, however, is that slow start will require multiple RTTs instead of just one. For example, using a packet size of 1 KB, it will take slow start's exponential growth 14 RTTs to transmit a 10-MB file, assuming, of course, that the amount of data sent during each RTT can be successfully delivered. Clearly, we would want to work in units larger than 1 KB, but even a 128-KB packet would result in 7 RTTs to send a 10-MB file. To make matters worse, should doubling the congestion window cause this flow to exceed the available bandwidth during some round trip, as much as half of the data sent during that RTT might be dropped. On a 100 ms × 1-Gbps network, we are talking about losses on the order of 5 MB.

One alternative is to reserve the bandwidth before sending any data, which is clearly the right thing to do for a continuous stream of data generated by a video application. For a bulk transfer, however, this means one RTT to reserve the bandwidth (or to learn how much bandwidth is available), a second RTT to send the data (assuming that it all fit in one RTT, given the available bandwidth), and possibly a third RTT to tear down the reservation. In general, any protocol that requires a connection setup phase has the potential to turn a one round-trip job into a two round-trip job, effectively halving the throughput seen by the application.

Retransmissions

A second problem that is exacerbated by the relative importance of each RTT is the need to retransmit lost data. Suppose, for example, that a single ATM cell is dropped while transferring a 10-MB file across a 100 ms × 1-Gbps network. This will require a second RTT to retransmit the lost data, again halving the effective bandwidth realized by the application.[1] There is another consequence of having to retransmit this lost cell that should not be forgotten—the sender has to buffer the entire 10 MB in case some piece of it needs to be retransmitted, and the receiver has to buffer any data that arrives after some missing piece if it wants to deliver the data to the application in order.

One possible way to avoid retransmission delays and the associated buffering is to use *forward error correction* (FEC). The idea behind FEC is much like standard error detection, such as CRC, except that enough redundant information is encoded in each packet that the receiver can not only detect any errors, but also recover from them. Of course, single bit errors are not the only problem. A more likely scenario is that entire packets (or cells) of data are

---

[1]While this discussion focuses on applications that need reliable delivery and that are concerned about reducing the number of round trips needed to achieve it, keep in mind that some applications—e.g., interactive video and audio—cannot afford to wait even one RTT for a retransmission.

lost due to congestion. However, an FEC code can be calculated across a set of packets, so that it is possible to recover from the loss of one or more complete packets (cells).

Although specific FEC algorithms are beyond the scope of this book (see the references at the end of this chapter for example algorithms), it is interesting to note that FEC is, in some sense, the opposite of compression—FEC adds redundancy to the data, while compression removes redundancy. In fact, for data that is highly compressible, such as video and digital images, it is possible to use the natural redundancy in the data (rather than to compress it away) in lieu of FEC. Not compressing data (or adding redundancy to data) so as to facilitate FEC and to avoid retransmission delay is an example of trading bandwidth for latency.

Trading Bandwidth for Latency

The strategy of trading bandwidth for latency is well understood in computer systems and is likely to be a common approach in designing systems that run on high-speed networks. The idea is easy to understand if you consider accessing data objects in a remote storage server. The remote server might be an elaborate digital library, but it is sufficient to think in terms of a simple Unix file server. Suppose the client enters (does a cd to) a directory in the remote file system. Instead of running the risk of having to wait an entire RTT when later accessing a file in that directory, the client could retrieve the entire subtree that is rooted at that directory when the directory is first accessed. In effect, the client would be *prefetching* the files in that directory and then *caching* them for future use. In other words, the client would be spending bandwidth to retrieve files that it may never access, in return for not having to pay the latency to retrieve the files that it does access. Simply caching files you have already accessed is also a good idea, but it does not really involve trading any bandwidth.

In general, the prefetching strategy only works if you understand something about how users access the data objects. In the preceding example, we assumed that a client who visits a directory will also access some of the files in that directory. For a digital library—or to make the example more concrete, the WWW—you might gather statistics showing that when one object (page) is visited, then there is a good chance that the user will next choose to follow a particular link to some other object. This second object would be a good candidate for prefetching.

9.2 Throughput Issues

Being able to deliver data at 622 Mbps or 1.2 Gbps across the links and switches of a high-speed network is not anything to brag about if that data comes trickling into the application program on the destination host at Ethernet speeds. Why might this happen? There are several things that can go wrong between the time network data hits the back of a host and an application program running on that host is able to read and process that data.

While it may seem that computers are getting faster as rapidly as networks are getting faster, and therefore that delivering data to the application should not be a problem, it is important to remember that it is the computer's processor that is getting faster, not its memory.

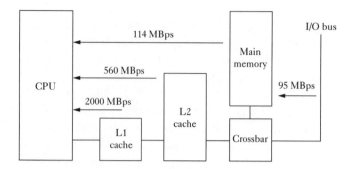

Figure 9.2   Memory bandwidth on a 175-MHz DEC Alpha workstation.

In fact, all of the problems in turning good network throughput into equally good application-to-application throughput can be traced to the host's memory bandwidth—the rate at which data can be moved between the host's memory and its CPU registers. This section first explains the memory bandwidth problem in more detail and then introduces several techniques that have been proposed to help mitigate the effects of limited memory bandwidth. In many respects, the issues discussed in this section lie at the intersection of computer architecture, operating systems, and computer networks.

9.2.1 Memory Bottleneck

To understand the effect a host's memory architecture can have on end-to-end network throughput, consider the block diagram given in Figure 9.2. This diagram shows the bandwidth available between various components of a 175-MHz DEC Alpha workstation. While this is certainly only one architecture, it is representative of the state of the art in workstation-class machines.

There are several things to notice about this diagram. The first is the bandwidth available on the I/O bus. Clearly, the I/O bus must be able to accept data at the rate it is transmitted over the network. In the case of this particular architecture, the 95-MBps (800-Mbps) bandwidth of the I/O bus appears sufficient to receive data off an STS-12 (622-Mbps) network, but not from an STS-24 (1.2-Gbps) network.[2] We say "appears sufficient" because it is not necessarily the case that the network adaptor can write into (read from) memory at this peak bandwidth. The real limitation is the size of the data block that is being transferred across the I/O bus, since there is a certain amount of overhead involved in each bus transfer. We will discuss this point more in the next subsection.

The second thing to notice about Figure 9.2 is the memory/CPU bandwidth, which is 114 MBps (956 Mbps). This is only slightly more than the bandwidth of the I/O bus, but fortunately this is a measured number rather than an advertised peak bandwidth. That is, this

---

[2]All MB in this discussion define mega to be 2^{20} and all Mb in this discussion define mega to be 10^6.

number reflects the fact that data is always transferred between main memory and the higher levels of the memory hierarchy in cache lines, e.g., 64 bytes on this machine. The principal ramification of this memory/CPU number is that it is of the same order of magnitude as the range of network bandwidths we are talking about. Thus, while it is possible to deliver packets across the I/O bus and into memory and then to load the data from memory into the CPU's registers at network bandwidths, it is impractical for the OS and application to go to memory multiple times for each word of data in a network packet, possibly because it needs to copy the data from one buffer to another. In particular, if the memory/CPU path is crossed n times— in either direction, read or write—then the best throughput you can hope for is $114\,\mathrm{MBps}/n$. The next subsection discusses techniques for keeping n as small as possible.

The third thing to notice is that not all the news is bad—memory caches are able to deliver high bandwidth to the CPU. The important question, however, is how effective the cache is in keeping the CPU from having to go to main memory to find network data. One problem is that first-level (L1) caches are usually small, able to hold on the order of only a packet or two. Second-level (L2) caches are typically bigger, on the order of 1 MB, but they have higher latencies than the on-chip cache. Beyond size, however, there are several other factors that impact the effectiveness of caches in accessing network data. The most important of these factors is that CPU scheduling may cause the execution of other programs to be interleaved with the processing of a network packet. By the time processing resumes, cached portions of the packet might have been replaced. There are a number of situations in which scheduling occurs during the processing of a packet: at the user/kernel boundary, in certain protocols (e.g., those that do reassembly), and between the device driver's interrupt handler and the rest of the protocol stack.

▶ As a final note on this discussion about memory bandwidth, it is important to recognize that there are many parallels between moving a message to and from memory and moving a message across a network. In particular, the effective throughput of the memory system is defined by the same two formulas given in Section 9.1.1. In the case of the memory system, however, the transfer size corresponds to how big a unit of data we can move across the bus in one transfer (i.e., cache line versus ATM cell versus large message), and the memory latency corresponds to "how far away" the memory is (i.e., on-chip cache versus off-chip cache versus main memory). Just as in the case of the network, the larger the transfer size and the smaller the latency, the better the effective throughput. Also similar to a network, the effective memory throughput does not necessarily equal the peak memory bandwidth (i.e., the bandwidth that can be achieved with an infinitely large transfer).

9.2.2 Techniques for Avoiding Data Transfers

The key to preserving the bandwidth that is delivered by high-speed networks through the end host—from the network device, through the OS and application program, and possibly to an output device (e.g., display)—is to avoid multiple transfers of the data between the CPU and main memory. This section identifies several potential data transfers and briefly describes techniques for efficiently handling or avoiding the transfer. Note that the following discussion does not include one of the most important techniques—a copy-free buffer manager. This is because we have already described such a mechanism—the x-kernel message abstraction—and we assume that such a mechanism is already used on low- and medium-speed networks.

Device/Memory Transfers

Before the application program can have any hope of accessing network data, the data must be moved between the network adaptor and main memory. As we saw in Chapter 3, the techniques most commonly used are direct memory access (DMA) and programmed input/output (PIO). With DMA, the network adaptor transfers data directly from/to main memory, without involving the CPU. PIO requires the processor to transfer every word between main memory and the adaptor in a programmed loop. While either technique can be used effectively for a 10-Mbps Ethernet, the ramifications of DMA and PIO are far reaching for a high-speed network.

With DMA, it is generally possible to transfer large blocks of data in a single bus transaction, thereby achieving transfer rates close to the limits of main memory and the I/O bus. DMA also has the advantage of being able to perform data transfers concurrently with activity by the processor(s), although contention for main memory access may decrease the efficiency of the processor during periods of heavy DMA traffic.

Although DMA typically supports large block transfers, it is not necessarily the case that the network adaptor can take advantage of this feature. Consider an ATM adaptor designed for the example architecture illustrated in Figure 9.2. For this particular I/O bus, it takes 8 clock cycles to acquire the bus for the purpose

> ## Network Device as a First-Class Citizen
>
> In many respects, the problem of turning good network bandwidth into equally good application-to-application bandwidth is an artifact of processors historically being so much faster than I/O devices. Little effort has been put into engineering the computer system for the sake of I/O. Thus we find gigabit-per-second network adaptors being attached to the same I/O bus as 38-Kbps serial lines are attached to.
>
> One question that computer designers are now beginning to explore is how we might move the network adaptor closer to the CPU. For example, instead of attaching it to the I/O bus, some have proposed connecting it directly to memory or even to the cache. In doing so, data could

of transferring data from the adaptor to host memory. This overhead is independent of the number of data bytes transferred. Thus, if you want to transfer the 48-byte payload of an ATM cell across the I/O bus, then the whole transfer takes 20 cycles: 8 cycles to acquire the bus and 12 cycles to transfer the data. (The bus is 32 bits wide, which means that it can transfer a 4-byte word during each clock cycle; 48 bytes divided by 4 bytes per cycle equals 12 cycles.) This means that the maximum bandwidth you can achieve is $12/(8+12) \times 800 = 480$ Mbps, not the peak 800 Mbps.

One way to improve on this situation would be to have the adaptor buffer one ATM cell, so that it could transfer a pair of cells (96 bytes) at a time across the bus. This would result in $24/(8 + 24) \times 800 = 600$ Mbps, which would be enough to keep up with the payload of a 622-Mbps STS-12 link. More generally, one could move complete AAL5 packets across the I/O bus, but this would imply that AAL5 segmentation and reassembly is implemented on the adaptor rather than on the host.

With PIO, not only is the CPU occupied during transfers from/to the device, but only a fraction of the peak I/O bandwidth is usually achieved. This is because the I/O bus transfers occur in either word or cache-line sizes. Nevertheless, there are situations in which PIO can be preferable to DMA. For example, computations on the data that occur in the kernel, such as checksum calculations, can sometimes be integrated with the PIO data movement, saving one trip to main memory. That is, the CPU computes the checksum for each word as it loads it from the device.

In addition, with carefully designed OS software, data can be read from the adaptor and written directly to the application's buffer in main memory, leaving the data in the cache. If the application reads the data soon after the PIO transfer, the data may still be in the cache. However, the PIO transfer from adaptor to application buffer must be delayed until the application is scheduled for execution in order to ensure sufficient proximity of data accesses for the data to remain cached. Loading data into the cache too early is not only ineffective but can actually decrease overall system performance by evicting live data from the cache. Unfortunately, delaying the transfer of data from adaptor to main memory until the receiving application is scheduled for execution requires a sub-

be written to and read from the network adaptor at memory or cache latencies. Still others have proposed treating the network adaptor as a co-processor, thereby making it accessible by means of register-to-register moves.

While proposals of this nature are quite dramatic, it is instructive to look at how computer architectures have changed in the last few years to support graphical displays. In essence, the demand for high-performance graphics led to a similar movement of the display device from the I/O bus onto the system board, making it possible to write into the frame buffer at memory speeds. The same could be done for networking, possibly resulting in a computer called a *gigabit workstation*.

stantial amount of buffer space in the adaptor. With DMA, instead of using dedicated memory resources on the adaptor, incoming data can be buffered in main memory. Using main memory to buffer network data has the advantage that a single pool of memory resources is dynamically shared among applications, the operating system, and the network subsystem.

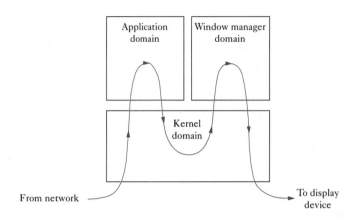

Figure 9.3   A packet traversing multiple protection domains.

Cross-Domain Transfers

Most operating systems support multiple protection domains (address spaces) so that one
faulty application cannot crash the whole system. Having protection domains means that
network packets must potentially cross one or more domain boundaries, since data accessible from one domain is typically not accessible from other domains. In the simplest case, a
data stream is handled by a single application process running on top of a conventional kernel
like Unix. In this case, each packet must cross the user/kernel boundary. In general, other
user processes, such as window managers and multimedia servers, introduce additional domain boundaries into the network data path. To make matters worse, the trend in operating
system design is toward microkernels, which push more and more OS functionality into user-
level servers, meaning that network data potentially crosses several domain boundaries. Figure 9.3 illustrates the path through the kernel and multiple user domains that a given packet
might need to traverse.

       As we have seen, software data copying as a means of transferring data across domain
boundaries exacerbates the memory bottleneck problem. As a result, there are a number of
techniques that rely on the virtual memory system to provide copy-free cross-domain data
transfer.

       One well-known technique, called *page remapping*, unmaps the pages containing net-
work packets from the sending domain and maps them into the receiving domain. Page remapping is illustrated in Figure 9.4. Page remapping has *move* rather than *copy* semantics, which
limits its utility to situations in which the sender needs no further access to the transferred
data. A variation on page remapping, sometimes called *copy-on-write*, shares the transferred
pages among the sending and receiving domains and delays copying until one of the sharing
domains attempts to write the shared data. Copy-on-write has *copy* semantics, but it can only
avoid physical copying when the data is not written by either the sender or the receiver after

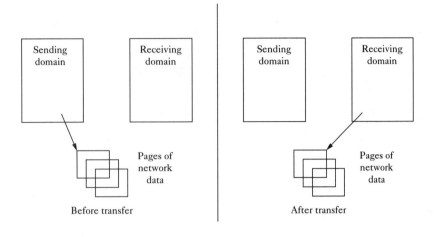

Figure 9.4 Page remapping.

the transfer. Both simple page remapping and copy-on-write require careful implementation to achieve good performance. The time it takes to switch to supervisor mode, acquire the necessary locks to kernel data structures, change virtual memory mappings for each page, and perform consistency actions on the host's memory-map hardware pose a limit to the achievable performance.

An alternative to page remapping, called *shared memory*, involves the use of buffers that are statically shared among two or more domains to avoid data transfers. As illustrated in Figure 9.5, shared memory avoids data transfer and its associated costs altogether. However, its use may compromise protection and security between the sharing protection domains, especially when extended to more than two domains. Since sharing is static—a particular page is always accessible in the same set of domains—prior knowledge of all the recipients of a data unit is required.

There is a hybrid technique, called *dynamic page sharing*, that combines page remapping with shared memory. We can view this technique in one of two ways. From one perspective, it is fundamentally a shared memory approach, with page remapping used to dynamically change the set of pages shared among a set of domains. From another perspective, it is fundamentally a page remapping approach, with pages that have been mapped into a set of domains cached for use by future transfers.

Data Manipulations

As we saw in Chapter 7, data manipulations—e.g., encryption, presentation formatting, compression, computing checksums—are one of the costliest aspects of data transfer. This is because reading, and possibly writing, each byte of data in a message involves memory loads

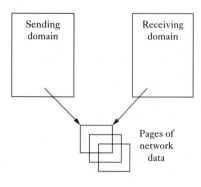

Figure 9.5   Shared memory.

or stores, which are relatively slow operations on modern reduced instruction set computer (RISC) architectures.

Integrated layer processing (ILP) has been suggested as a technique for addressing this problem. The aim of integration is to improve throughput by reducing the number of loads and stores of message data performed by protocols. Normally, network data is passed from one protocol to the next in the form of a complete message, buffered in a system data structure. Any protocol that manipulates the data in the message must load and possibly store each byte of the message. Integration combines data manipulations from a series of protocols into a pipeline that shares accesses to the message data structure, thereby reducing the number of memory accesses. Another way to say this is that the integrated implementation *streams* message data between protocols using registers.

Figure 9.6 illustrates the idea of ILP. The two for-loops in Figure 9.6(a) model a strictly layered implementation of two trivial (and artificial) data manipulations; the first adds one to every word of a message and the second takes the complement of every word in a message. These two loops would correspond to two separate protocol layers, each one processing every word of a message. In contrast, the single for-loop in Figure 9.6(b) models an integrated implementation of the same two data manipulations.

When the C code in the examples is compiled to run on a RISC architecture, the data manipulation steps result in the machine instructions noted in the comments. In the strictly layered loops, each time a word of data is manipulated, it is loaded and stored. In contrast, each word is loaded and stored only once in the integrated loop, even though it is manipulated twice. This is possible because the data word remains in a register between the two data manipulations. Hence, integrating the for-loops results in the elimination of one load and one store per word of data.

Because ILP serves to eliminate the redundant loads and stores associated with each data manipulation, it pays only when the amount of computation required by each manipulation is relatively small. If thousands of instructions are required for each word of data that

```
for( i = 0; i < 10000; i++ )
    msgData[i]++;                    /* LOAD, ADD, STORE */

for( i = 0; i < 10000; i++ )
    msgData[i] = ~msgData[i];        /* LOAD, COMPLEMENT, STORE */
```

(a)

```
for( i = 0; i < 10000; i++ ){
    temp = msgData[i];               /* LOAD */
    temp++;                          /* ADD */
    temp = ~temp;                    /* COMPLEMENT */
    msgData[i] = temp;               /* STORE */
}
```

(b)

Figure 9.6   For-loops modeling data manipulations. (a) Two original separate for-loops; (b) integrated version of the two for-loops.

is loaded into a register, then simply eliminating the load instruction and possibly a store instruction will have little impact. Thus, ILP is better suited for checksum and byte-swap computations than, say, DES or MPEG. Of course, as the processor/memory performance gap widens, more and more data manipulations will become good candidates for ILP.

One of the difficulties in realizing ILP is how to combine data manipulation loops from separate protocols without seriously compromising the modularity of the network software. One promising approach is to make ILP part of a protocol compiler, that is, a compiler that understands how to translate and optimize protocol code.

API Design

As we saw in Chapter 6, the application programming interface (API) defines the semantics for data transfer to and from the application program. The semantics defined by this interface can be a significant factor in the efficiency of the implementation. Consider, for example, the API defined by the Unix read and write system calls. Application programs are allowed to choose a contiguous data buffer in their address space with an arbitrary address, size, and alignment, and they have unconstrained access to that buffer. This low-level representation of data buffers makes it difficult for the system to avoid copying data.

One reason for this is that all virtual-memory-based techniques for cross-domain data transfer operate at the granularity of a page. If the user buffer's first and last address are not page aligned, the system must copy portions of the first and last page overlapped by the buffer.

Depending on the length of the user buffer, this can eliminate most of the benefits of using a copy-avoiding technique. A second reason that the API affects the efficiency of the network subsystem is that the semantics of the **write** system call permit the user process to modify (reuse) the user buffer immediately after the call returns. If this happens, the system must either copy the affected page or block the user process until the system is done with the previous data. The first approach re-introduces a copy, and the second approach may degrade the user's effective network bandwidth.

An API that lends itself to efficient data transfer methods should use an abstract data type, such as the x-kernel message, to represent data buffers. Application programs access the buffer type indirectly through its operations. They ask the system to create an instance when they need a buffer, pass/receive instances as arguments/results in system calls, and ask the system to deallocate the instance when the associated buffer is no longer needed. This gives the system complete control over buffer management, including address, alignment, method of transfer, and so on.

9.3 Integrated Services

One of the things that has happened as networks have become faster is that people have started to build applications that make use of the newly acquired speed, not just to do the same old things faster, but to do completely new things. In particular, increased bandwidths have enabled applications that send voice and video information. Video is a particularly high consumer of network bandwidth, while voice or audio information can be tolerably transmitted over 64-Kbps channels—not high speed by today's standards, but faster than early wide area network links. Also, both video and audio have increasing bandwidth requirements as the quality goes up, so that CD-quality audio might require closer to a megabit per second, while one can imagine using tens to hundreds of megabits per second to transmit very high-quality video.

There is more to transmitting audio and video over a network than just providing sufficient bandwidth, however. Participants in a telephone conversation, for example, expect to be able to converse in such a way that one person can respond to something said by the other and be heard almost immediately. Thus, the timeliness of delivery can be very important. We refer to applications that are sensitive to the timeliness of data as *real-time applications*. Voice and video applications tend to be the canonical examples, but there are others such as industrial control—you would like a command sent to a robot arm to reach it before the arm crashes into something.

The most important thing about real-time applications is that they need some sort of assurance *from the network* that data is likely to arrive on time (for some definition of "on time"). Whereas a non-real-time application can use an end-to-end retransmission strategy to make sure that data arrives *correctly*, such a strategy cannot provide timeliness: Retransmission only adds to total latency if data arrives late. Timely arrival must be provided by the network itself (the routers), not just at the network edges (the hosts). We therefore conclude that the best-

Figure 9.7   An audio application.

effort model, in which the network tries to deliver your data but makes no promises and leaves the cleanup operation to the edges, is not sufficient for real-time applications. What we need is a new service model, in which applications that need higher assurances can ask the network for them. The network may then respond by providing an assurance that it will do better or perhaps by saying that it cannot promise anything better at the moment. Note that such a service model is a superset of the current model: Applications that are happy with best-effort service should be able to use the new service model; their requirements are just less stringent. This implies that the network will treat some packets differently from others, something that is not done in the best-effort model.

9.3.1   New Service Model

At the time of this writing, the IETF is working toward standardization of a set of extensions to the best-effort service model of today's Internet. The idea behind standardizing a new service model is to enable networking equipment manufacturers to implement the new model and application writers to build new applications that use the new model, where everyone can have a common set of expectations about what the network provides. The rest of this section motivates and develops the new model, while Section 9.3.2 looks at the mechanisms that will be required to implement the model.

The first part of the model is that we now have two different types of applications: real-time and non-real-time. The latter are sometimes called "traditional data" applications, since they have traditionally been the major applications found on data networks. These include most popular applications like Telnet, FTP, email, Web browsing, and so on. All of these applications can work without guarantees of timely delivery of data. Another term for this non-real-time class of applications is *elastic*, since they are able to stretch gracefully in the face of increased delay. Note that these applications can benefit from shorter-length delays but that they do not become unusable as delays increase. Also note that their delay requirements vary from the interactive applications like Telnet to more asynchronous ones like email, with interactive bulk transfers like FTP in the middle.

Let's look more closely at the real-time applications. As a concrete example, we consider an audio application, as illustrated in Figure 9.7. Data is generated by collecting samples from a microphone and digitizing them using an analog-to-digital (A→D) converter. The digital samples are placed in packets, which are transmitted across the network and received at the other end. At the receiving host, the data must be *played back* at some appropriate rate. For example, if the voice samples were collected at a rate of one per 125 μs, they should be played back at the same rate. Thus, we can think of each sample as having a particular *playback time*: the point in time at which it is needed in the receiving host. In the voice example, each sample has a playback time that is 125 μs later than the preceding sample. If data arrives after its appropriate playback time, either because it was delayed in the network or because it was dropped and subsequently retransmitted, it is essentially useless. It is the complete worthlessness of late data that characterizes real-time applications. In elastic applications, it might be nice if data turns up on time, but we can still use it when it does not.

One way to make our voice application work would be to make sure that all samples take exactly the same amount of time to traverse the network. Then, since samples are injected at a rate of one per 125 μs, they will appear at the receiver at the same rate, ready to be played back. However, it is generally difficult to guarantee that all data traversing a packet-switched network will experience exactly the same delay. Packets encounter queues in switches or routers and the lengths of these queues vary with time, meaning that the delays tend to vary with time, and as a consequence, are potentially different for each packet in the audio stream. The way to deal with this at the receiver end is to buffer up some amount of data in reserve, thereby always providing a store of packets waiting to be played back at the right time. If a packet is delayed a short time, it goes in the buffer until its playback time arrives. If it gets delayed a long time, then it will not need to be stored for very long in the receiver's buffer before being played back. Thus, we have effectively added a constant offset to the playback time of all packets as a form of insurance. We call this offset the *playback point*. The only time we run into trouble is if packets get delayed in the network for such a long time that they arrive after their playback time, causing the playback buffer to be drained.

The operation of a playback buffer is illustrated in Figure 9.8. The left-hand diagonal line shows packets being generated at a steady rate. The wavy line shows when the packets arrive, some variable amount of time after they were sent, depending on what they encountered in the network. The right-hand diagonal line shows the packets being played back at a steady rate, after sitting in the playback buffer for some period of time. As long as the playback line is far enough to the right in time, the variation in network delay is never noticed by the application. However, if we move the playback line a little to the left, then some packets will begin to arrive too late to be useful.

For our audio application, there are limits to how far we can delay playing back data. It is hard to carry on a conversation if the time between when you speak and when your listener hears you is more than 300 ms. Thus, what we want from the network in this case is a guarantee that all our data will arrive within 300 ms. If data arrives early we buffer it until its correct playback time. If it arrives late, we have no use for it and must discard it.

To get a better appreciation of how variable network delay can be, Figure 9.9 shows the measured one-way delay across the Internet on one particular day in 1995. As denoted by the cumulative percentages given across the top of the graph, 97% of the packets have a latency

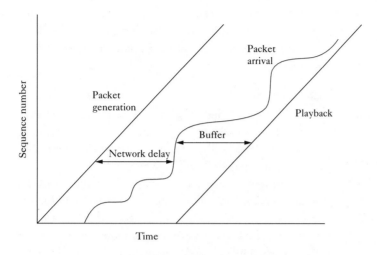

Figure 9.8   A playback buffer.

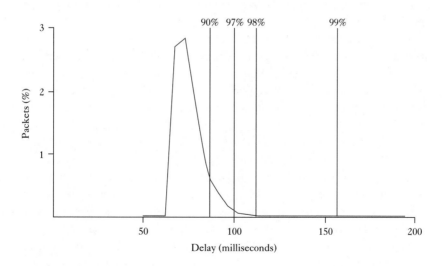

Figure 9.9   Example distribution of delays for an Internet connection.

of 100 ms or less. This means that if our example audio application were to set the playback point at 100 ms, then on average, 3 out of every 100 packets would arrive too late to be of any use. One important thing to notice about this graph is that the tail of the curve—how far it extends to the right—is very long. One would have to set the playback point at over 200 ms to ensure that all packets arrived in time.

Taxonomy of Real-Time Applications

Now that we have a concrete idea of how real-time applications work, we can look at some different classes of applications, which serve to motivate our service model. The following taxonomy owes much to the work of Clark, Braden, Shenker, and Zhang, whose papers on this subject can be found in the further reading section for this chapter.

The first characteristic by which we can categorize applications is their tolerance of loss of data, where "loss" might occur because a packet arrived too late to be played back. On the one hand, one lost audio sample can be interpolated from the surrounding samples with relatively little effect on the perceived audio quality. It is only as more and more samples are lost that quality declines to the point that the speech becomes incomprehensible. On the other hand, a robot control program is likely to be an example of a real-time application that cannot tolerate loss—losing the packet that contains the command instructing the robot arm to stop is unacceptable. Thus, we can categorize real-time applications as *tolerant* or *intolerant* depending on whether they can tolerate occasional loss. (As an aside, note that many real-time applications are more tolerant of occasional loss than non-real-time applications. For example, compare our audio application to FTP, where the uncorrected loss of one bit might render a file completely useless.)

A second way to characterize real-time applications is by their adaptability. For example, an audio application might be able to adapt to the amount of delay that packets experience as they traverse the network. If we notice that packets are almost always arriving within 300 ms of being sent, then we can set our playback point accordingly, buffering any packets that arrive in less than 300 ms. Suppose that we subsequently observe that all packets are arriving within 100 ms of being sent. If we moved up our playback point to 100 ms, then the users of the application would probably perceive an improvement. The process of shifting the playback point would actually require us to play out samples at an increased rate for some period of time. With a voice application, this can be done in a way that is barely perceptible, simply by shortening the silences between words. Thus, playback point adjustment is fairly easy in this case, and it has been effectively implemented for several voice applications such as the audio teleconferencing program known as VAT. Note that playback point adjustment can happen in either direction, but that doing so actually involves distorting the played back signal during the period of adjustment, and that the effects of this distortion will very much depend on how the end user uses the data. Intolerant applications will not in general be able to tolerate this distortion any more than they can tolerate loss.

Observe that if we set our playback point on the assumption that all packets will arrive within 100 ms and then find that some packets are arriving slightly late, we will have to drop

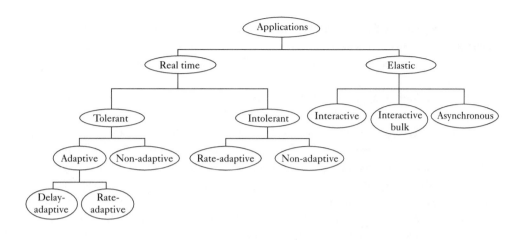

Figure 9.10   Taxonomy of applications.

them, whereas we would not have had to drop them if we had left the playback point at 300 ms. Thus, we should advance the playback point only when it provides a perceptible advantage and only when we have some evidence that the number of late packets will be acceptably small. We may do this because of observed recent history or because of some assurance from the network.

We call applications that can adjust their playback point *delay-adaptive* applications. Another class of adaptive applications are *rate adaptive*. For example, many video coding algorithms can trade off bit rate versus quality. Thus, if we find that the network can support a certain bandwidth, we can set our coding parameters accordingly. If more bandwidth becomes available later, we can change parameters to increase the quality. While intolerant applications will not tolerate the distortion of delay adaptivity, they may be able to take advantage of rate adaptivity.

To summarize, we have the following taxonomy of applications, as illustrated in Figure 9.10. First, we have the elastic and the real time, with a range of target delays for elastic applications. Within real time, we have the intolerant, which cannot accept loss or lateness of data, and the tolerant. We also find adaptive and non-adaptive real-time applications, which may in turn be rate adaptive or delay adaptive. What the Internet and most other networks provide today is a service model that is adequate only for elastic applications. What we need is a richer service model that meets the needs of any application in this taxonomy. This leads us to a service model with not just one class (best effort), but with several classes, each available to meet the needs of some set of applications.

Service Classes

For starters, consider a service class to support intolerant applications. These applications require that a packet never turn up late. The network should guarantee that the maximum delay that any packet will experience has some specified value; the application can then set its playback point so that no packet will ever arrive after its playback time. We assume that early arrival of packets can always be handled by buffering. This service is generally referred to as a *guaranteed* service.

Now consider an application that is tolerant of occasional lateness or loss, but is not adaptive. This application may be willing to take a statistical gamble that some fraction of its packets arrive late, since it knows that it can still deliver acceptable performance. Nevertheless, it needs some information about the likely delay that packets will experience in the network. Unlike the guaranteed service, what it needs is an "honest estimate" of maximum delay, which may occasionally be exceeded. It is not a hard upper bound. The intention of such a service is that it might allow more efficient use of network resources if an occasional late packet is allowed. This service class is often called *predictive*, since the maximum delay is predicted (perhaps wrongly on occasions) rather than guaranteed.

Delay-adaptive applications can also use predictive service. They might initially set their playback point based on an estimate of maximum delay provided by the network and then adapt to the observed behavior as time goes by. We can imagine that by adapting in this way, the application might perform better by moving to lower delays when the specified bound is too conservative, but backing off to longer delays when it is necessary.

We can also imagine another service class for delay-adaptive applications. Since they can adapt to observed delay, we can use a service that offers no quantitative specification of delay but simply attempts to control it in such a way that a delay-adaptive service will function reasonably well. The main criterion for such a service is that delay is controlled in such a way that the tail of the delay distribution is not too long; that is, we would like the vast majority of our packets to turn up within a bound that is useful to the application. At the time of this writing, the IETF is standardizing such a *controlled-delay* service which will offer three levels of delay service; the goal is to provide a choice of delay distributions where the maximum delay for each class is about an order of magnitude different from the neighboring class(es).

Finally, we need a service class for rate-adaptive applications. This is an area of ongoing research.

9.3.2 Mechanisms (RSVP)

Now that we have augmented our best-effort service model with several new service classes, the next question is how we implement a network that provides these services to applications. This section outlines the key mechanisms. Keep in mind while reading this section that the mechanisms being described are still in rough form; they are still being hammered out by the Internet design community. The main thing to take away from the discussion is a general understanding of the pieces involved in supporting the service model outlined above.

First, whereas with a best-effort service we can just tell the network where we want our packets to go and leave it at that, a real-time service involves telling the network something more about the type of service we require. We may give it qualitative information such as "use a controlled-delay service" or quantitative information such as "I need a maximum delay of 100 ms." In addition to describing what we want, we need to tell the network something about what we are going to inject into it, since a low-bandwidth application is going to require fewer network resources than a high-bandwidth application. The set of information that we provide to the network is referred to as a *flowspec*. This name comes from the idea that a set of packets associated with a single application and that share common requirements is called a flow, consistent with our use of the term "flow" in Chapter 8.

Second, when we ask the network to provide us with a particular service, the network needs to decide if it can in fact provide that service. For example, if 10 users ask for a service in which each will consistently use 2 Mbps of link capacity, and they all share a link with 10 Mbps capacity, the network will have to say no to some of them. The process of deciding when to say no is called *admission control*.

Third, we need a mechanism by which the users of the network and the components of the network itself exchange information such as requests for service, flowspecs, and admission control decisions. This is called *signalling* in the ATM world, but since this word has several meanings, we refer to this process as *resource reservation*, and it is achieved using a resource reservation protocol.

Finally, when flows and their requirements have been described, and admission control decisions have been made, the network switches and routers need to meet the requirements of the flows. A key part of meeting these requirements is managing the way packets are queued and scheduled for transmission in the switches and routers. This last mechanism is *packet scheduling*.

Flowspecs

There are two separable parts to the flowspec: the part that describes the flow's traffic characteristics (called the *Tspec*) and the part that describes the service requested from the network (the *Rspec*). The Rspec is very service specific and relatively easy to describe. For example, with a controlled-delay service, the Rspec might just be a number describing the level of delay required (1, 2, or 3). With a guaranteed or predictive service, you could specify a delay target or bound. (In the IETF's current guaranteed service specification, you specify not a delay but another quantity from which delay can be calculated.)

The Tspec is a little more complicated. As our example above showed, we need to give the network enough information about the bandwidth used by the flow to allow intelligent admission control decisions to be made. For most applications, however, the bandwidth is not a single number; it is something that varies constantly. A video application, for example, will generally generate more bits per second when the scene is changing rapidly than when it is still. Just knowing the long-term average bandwidth is not enough, as the following example illustrates. Suppose that we have 10 flows that arrive at a switch on separate input ports and that all leave on the same 10-Mbps link. Assume that over some suitably long interval each flow can be expected to send no more that 1 Mbps. You might think that this presents no problem. However, if these are variable bit-rate applications, such as compressed video, then they will occasionally send more than their average rates. If enough sources send at above

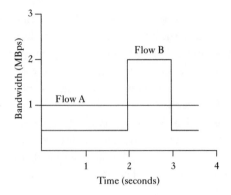

Figure 9.11   Two flows with equal average rates but different token bucket descriptions.

their average rates, then the total rate at which data arrives at the switch will be greater than 10 Mbps. This excess data will be queued before it can be sent on the link. The longer this condition persists, the longer the queue will get. At the very least, while data is sitting in a queue, it is not getting closer to its destination, so it is being delayed. If packets are delayed long enough, the service that was requested will not be provided. In addition, as the queue length grows, at some point we run out of buffer space and packets must be dropped.

Exactly how we manage our queues to control delay and avoid dropping packets is something we discuss below. However, note here that we need to know something about how the bandwidth of our sources varies with time. One way to describe the bandwidth characteristics of sources is called a *token bucket* filter. Such a filter is described by two parameters: a token rate r, and a bucket depth B. It works as follows. To be able to send a byte, I must have a token. To send a packet of length n, I need n tokens. I start with no tokens and I accumulate them at a rate of r per second. I can accumulate no more than B tokens. What this means is that I can send a burst of as many as B bytes into the network as fast as I want, but over a sufficiently long interval, I can't send more than r bytes per second. It turns out that this information is very helpful to the admission control algorithm when it tries to figure out whether it can accommodate a new request for service.

Figure 9.11 illustrates how a token bucket can be used to characterize a flow's bandwidth requirements. For simplicity, assume that each flow can send data as individual bytes, rather than as packets. Flow A generates data at a steady rate of 1 MBps, so it can be described by a token bucket filter with a rate $r = 1$ MBps and a bucket depth of 1 byte. This means that it receives tokens at a rate of 1 MBps but that it cannot store more than 1 token—it spends them immediately. Flow B also sends at a rate that averages out to 1 MBps over the long term, but does so by sending at 0.5 MBps for 2 seconds and then at 2 MBps for 1 second. Since the token bucket rate r is, in a sense, a long-term average rate, flow B can be described by a token bucket with a rate of 1 MBps. Unlike flow A, however, flow B needs a bucket depth B of at least 1 MB, so that it can store up tokens while it sends at less than 1 MBps to be used when it sends at 2 MBps. For the first 2 seconds in this example, it receives tokens at a rate of 1 MBps but spends them at only 0.5 MBps, so it can save up $2 \times 0.5 = 1MB$ of tokens, which it then spends in the third second (along with the new tokens that continue to accrue in that second) to send data at 2 MBps. At the end of the third second, having spent the excess tokens, it starts to save them up again by sending at 0.5 MBps again.

It is interesting to note that a single flow can be described by many different token buckets. As a trivial example, flow A could be described by the same token bucket as flow B, with a rate of 1 MBps and a bucket depth of 1 MB. The fact that it never actually needs to accumulate tokens does not make that an inaccurate description, but it does mean that we have failed to convey some useful information to the network—the fact that flow A is actually very consistent in its bandwidth needs.

Admission Control

The idea behind admission control is simple: When some new flow wants to receive a particular level of service, admission control looks at the Tspec and Rspec of the flow and tries to decide if the desired service can be provided to that amount of traffic, given the currently available resources, without causing any previously admitted flow to receive worse service than it had requested. If it can provide the service, the flow is admitted; if not, then it is denied. The hard part is figuring out when to say yes and when to say no.

Admission control is very dependent on the type of requested service and on the queuing discipline employed in the routers; we discuss the latter topic later in this section. For a guaranteed service, you need to have a good algorithm to make a definitive yes/no decision. The decision is fairly straightforward if weighted fair queuing (WFQ), as discussed in Section 8.2, is used at each router. For a predictive or controlled-delay service, the decision may be based on heuristics, such as "the last time I allowed a flow with this Tspec into this class, the delays for the class exceeded the acceptable bound, so I'd better say no" or "my current delays are so far inside the bounds that I should be able to admit another flow without difficulty."

Admission control should not be confused with *policing*. The former is a per-flow decision to admit a new flow or not. The latter is a function applied on a per-packet basis to make sure that a flow conforms to the Tspec that was used to make the reservation. If a flow does not conform to its Tspec—for example, because it is sending twice as many bytes per second as it said it would—then it is likely to interfere with the service provided to other flows, and some corrective action must be taken. There are several options, the obvious one being to drop offending packets. However, another option would be to check if the packets really are interfering with the service of other flows. If they are not interfering, the packets could be sent on after being marked with a tag that says, in effect, "this is a nonconforming packet—drop me first if you need to drop any packets."

Reservation Protocol

While connection-oriented networks have always needed some sort of setup protocol to establish the necessary virtual circuit state in the switches, connectionless networks like the Internet have had no such protocols. As this section has indicated, however, we need to provide a lot more information to our network when we want a real-time service from it. While there have been a number of setup protocols proposed for the Internet, the one on which most current attention is focused is called Resource Reservation Protocol (RSVP). It is particularly interesting because it differs so substantially from conventional signalling protocols for connection-oriented networks.

One of the key assumptions underlying RSVP is that it should not detract from the robustness that we find in today's connectionless networks. Because connectionless networks rely on little or no state being stored in the network itself, it is possible for routers to crash and reboot and for links to go up and down while end-to-end connectivity is still maintained. RSVP tries to maintain this robustness by using the idea of *soft state* in the routers. Soft state—in contrast to the hard state found in connection-oriented networks—does not need to be explicitly deleted when it is no longer needed. Instead, it times out after some fairly short period (say, a minute) if it is not periodically refreshed. We will see later how this helps robustness.

RSVP and ATM

Now that we've seen some highlights of RSVP, it is interesting to compare it with a more "conventional" signalling protocol from a connection-oriented network. Note that, at a high level, the goals of a connection-oriented signalling protocol and RSVP are the same: to install some state information in the network nodes that forward packets so that packets get handled correctly. However, there are not many similarities beyond that high-level goal.

Table 9.1 compares RSVP with the ATM Forum's current signalling protocol, which is derived from the ITU-T protocol Q.2931. (Recall

Another important characteristic of RSVP is that it treats multicast as a first-class citizen. This is not surprising, since the multicast applications found on the MBone, such as VAT and NV are obvious early candidates to benefit from real-time services. One of the insights of RSVP's designers is that most multicast applications have many more receivers than senders, as typified by the large audience and one speaker for a lecture carried on the MBone. Also, receivers may have different requirements. For example, one receiver might want to receive data from only one sender, while others might wish to receive data from all senders. Rather than having the senders keep track of a potentially large number of receivers, it makes more sense to let the receivers keep track of their own needs. This suggests the *receiver-oriented* approach adopted by RSVP. In contrast, connection-oriented networks usually leave resource reservation to the sender, just as it is normally the originator of a phone call who causes resources to be allocated in the phone network.

The soft state and receiver-oriented nature of RSVP give it a number of nice properties. One nice property is that it is very straightforward to increase or decrease the level of resource allocation provided to a receiver. Since each receiver periodically sends refresh messages to keep the soft state in place, it is easy to send a new reservation that asks for a new level of resources. In the event of a host crash, resources allocated by that host to a flow will naturally time out and be released. To see what happens in the event of a router or link failure, we need to look a little more closely at the mechanics of making a reservation.

from Section 4.3 that Q.2931 defines how a virtual circuit is routed across the network, as well as how resources are reserved for that circuit.) The differences stem largely from the fact that RSVP starts with a connectionless model and tries to add functionality without going all the way to traditional connections, whereas ATM starts out from a connection-oriented model. RSVP's goal of treating multicast traffic as a first-class citizen is also apparent in the receiver-driven approach, which aims to provide scalability for multicast groups with large numbers of receivers.

Initially, consider the case of one sender and one receiver trying to get a reservation for traffic flowing between them. There are two things that need to happen before a receiver can make the reservation. First, the receiver needs to know what traffic the sender is likely to send so that it can make an appropriate reservation. That is, it needs to know the sender's Tspec. Second, it needs to know what path the packets will follow from sender to receiver, so that it can establish a resource reservation at each router on the path. Both of these requirements can be met by sending a message from the sender to the receiver that contains the Tspec. Obviously, this gets the Tspec to the receiver. The other thing that happens is that each router looks at this message (called a PATH message), as it goes past, and it figures out the *reverse path* that will be used to send reservations from the receiver back to the sender in an effort to get the reservation to each router on the path. Building the multicast tree in the first place is done by mechanisms such as those described in Section 5.5.

Having received a PATH message, the receiver sends a reservation back "up" the multicast tree in a RESV message. This message contains the sender's Tspec and an Rspec describing the requirements of this receiver. Each router on the path looks at the reservation request and tries to allocate the necessary resources to satisfy it. If the reservation can be made, the RESV request is passed on to the next router. If not, an error message is returned to the receiver who made the request. (Actually, a range of options involving forwarding messages that failed at one or more routers are being considered by the IETF at present.) If all goes well, the correct reservation is installed at every router between the sender and the receiver. As long as the receiver wants to retain the reservation, it sends the same RESV message about once every 30 seconds.

RSVP	ATM
Receiver generates reservation	Sender generates connection request
Soft state (refresh/timeout)	Hard state (explicit delete)
Separate from route establishment	Concurrent with route establishment
QoS can change dynamically	QoS is static for life of connection
Receiver heterogeneity	Uniform QoS to all receivers

Table 9.1　Comparison of RSVP and ATM signalling.

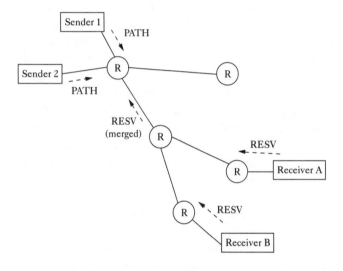

Figure 9.12　Making reservations on a multicast tree.

Now we can see what happens when a router or link fails. Routing protocols will adapt to the failure and create a new path from sender to receiver. PATH messages are sent about every 30 seconds, so the first one after the new route stabilizes will reach the receiver over the new path. The receiver's next RESV message will follow the new path and (hopefully) establish a new reservation on the new path. Meanwhile, the routers that are no longer on the path will stop getting RESV messages, and these reservations will time out and be released.

The next thing we need to consider is how to cope with multicast, where there may be multiple senders to a group and multiple receivers. This situation is illustrated in Figure 9.12. First, let's deal with multiple receivers for a single sender. As a RESV message travels up the multicast tree, it is likely to hit a piece of the tree where some other receiver's reservation has already been established. It may be the case that the resources reserved upstream of this point are adequate to serve both receivers. For example, if receiver A has already made a reservation that provides for a guaranteed delay of less than 100 ms, and the new request from receiver B is for a delay of less than 200 ms, then no new reservation is required. On the other hand, if the new request were for a delay of less than 50 ms, then the router would first need to see if it could accept the request, and if so, it would send the request on upstream. The next time receiver A asked for a mimimum of 100 ms delay, the router would not need to pass this request on. In general, reservations can be merged in this way to meet the needs of all receivers downstream of the merge point. The only catch is that the rules for merging can be complicated.

If there are also multiple senders to the tree, receivers need to collect the Tspecs from all senders and make a reservation that is large enough to accommodate the traffic from all senders. However, this may not mean that the Tspecs need to be added up. For example, in an audio conference with 10 speakers, there is not much point in allocating enough resources to carry 10 audio streams, since the result of 10 people speaking at once would be incomprehensible. Thus, we could imagine a reservation that is large enough to accommodate two speakers and no more. Calculating the correct overall Tspec from all the sender Tspecs is clearly application specific. Also, we may only be interested in hearing from a subset of all possible speakers; RSVP has different reservation "styles" to deal with such options as "reserve resources for all speakers," "reserve resources for any n speakers," and "reserve resources for speakers A and B only."

Packet Classifying and Scheduling

Once we have described our traffic and our desired network service and have installed a suitable reservation at all the routers on the path, the only thing that remains is for the routers to actually deliver the requested service to the data packets. There are two things that need to be done:

- associate each packet with the appropriate reservation so that it can be handled correctly, a process known as *classifying* packets;

- manage the packets in the queues so that they receive the service that has been requested, a process known as packet *scheduling*.

The first part is done by examining up to four fields in the packet: the source address, destination address, source port, and destination port. (In IPv6, it is possible that the FlowLabel field in the header could be used to enable the lookup to be done based on a single, shorter key.) Based on this information, the packet can be placed in the appropriate class. For example, it may be classified into one of three controlled-delay classes or it may be part of a guaranteed-delay flow that needs to be handled separately from all other guaranteed flows. In short, there is a mapping from the flow-specific information in the packet header to a single class identifier that determines how the packet is handled in the queue. For guaranteed flows, this might be a one-to-one mapping, while for other services, it might be many to one. The details of classification are closely related to the details of queue management.

It should be clear that something as simple as a FIFO queue in a router will be inadequate to provide many different services and to provide different levels of delay within each service. Several more sophisticated queue management disciplines were discussed in Section 8.2, and some combination of these is likely to be used in a router.

The details of packet scheduling ideally should not be specified in the service model. Instead, this is an area where implementers can try to do creative things to realize the service model efficiently. In the case of guaranteed service, it has been established that a weighted fair queuing discipline, in which each flow gets its own individual queue with a certain share of the link, will provide a guaranteed end-to-end delay bound that can readily be calculated. For controlled- and predictive-delay services, other schemes are being tested. One possibility includes a simple priority scheme in which all flows in a class are placed in one queue, there is one priority level per class, and the lowest delay class has the highest priority. The problem is made harder when you consider that in a single router, many different services are likely to be provided concurrently, and that each of these services may require a different scheduling algorithm. Thus, some overall queue management algorithm is needed to manage the resources between the different services.

9.4 Summary

At the beginning of this chapter, we asked the question, what breaks when we go faster? The answer is that three things break, but they can all be fixed. The first is that latency, rather than bandwidth, becomes our primary focus of concern. This is because while network bandwidth is improving at an astounding rate, the speed of light has remained constant. Fortunately, we can adjust for this by trading bandwidth for latency.

A second thing that breaks is our conception that computers are fast and I/O is slow. Gigabit networks make it necessary to design computer architectures and operating system software with the network foremost in our minds, rather than treating the network as a fast serial line. This is because network speeds are improving to the point that they are within the same order of magnitude as memory speeds. This situation is sometimes referred to as the memory bottleneck, and we examined several techniques to help mitigate its effects.

A third thing that breaks is the current best-effort service model. As networks have become faster, new applications such as real-time video have become possible. Often, however, these new applications need more than just raw speed. They also need a richer service model, one that provides for different qualities of service. This is perhaps the most drastic change that is required. In this context, we looked at the early stages of an effort to extend the Internet to support multiple qualities of service.

Although it is not explicitly stated in this chapter, there is much about the network architectures that have evolved over the past 20 years that does not break when networks move into the gigabit regime. Connectivity is still achieved through a hierarchical inter-

OPEN ISSUE
Realizing the Future

connection of machines, routers and switches still forward packets from one link to another, and end-to-end protocols still provide high-level communication abstractions to application programs.

What is apparent, however, is that computer networks will continue to evolve. Higher-speed technologies will be developed at the bottom of the network architecture, new applications will be introduced at the top of the network architecture, and the protocol layers in the middle will adapt to connect these new applications to the underlying technologies. Perhaps even more predictably, network designers will continue to argue about what functionality belongs at what layer. If nothing else, we hope that this book has imparted the message that computer networking is an active and exciting topic of study, and that it is a sound grasp of system design principles that will allow us to tackle each new challenge.

FURTHER READING

Our recommended reading list for this chapter is long, once again reflecting how active an area of research high-speed networking has become. The first paper gives an excellent discussion of how drastically high-speed networks have changed the latency/bandwidth tradeoff. The next five papers then discuss the issue of turning good host-to-host throughput into equally good application-to-application throughput. The first of these five (Druschel et al.) gives an overview of the general problem, the next two discuss the host/network interface, and the last two focus on OS techniques to avoid data copying. Finally, the last paper discusses various aspects of the new service model being designed for the Internet.

- Kleinrock, L. The latency/bandwidth tradeoff in gigabit networks. *IEEE Communications* 30(4):36–40, April 1992.

- Druschel, P., M. Abbot, M. Pagels, and L. L. Peterson. Network subsystem design. *IEEE Network (Special Issue on End-System Support for High Speed Networks)* 7(4):8–17, July 1993.

- Druschel, P., L. L. Peterson, and B. S. Davie. Experience with a high-speed network adaptor: A software perspective. *Proceedings of the SIGCOMM '94 Symposium*, pages 2–13, August 1994.

■ Edwards, A., G. Watson, J. Lumley, D. Banks, C. Calamvokis, and C. Dalton. User-space protocols deliver high-bandwidth performance to applications on a low-cost Gbps LAN. *Proceedings of the SIGCOMM '94 Symposium*, pages 14–23, August 1994.

■ Druschel, P., and L. L. Peterson. Fbufs: A high-bandwidth cross-domain transfer facility. *Proceedings of the Fourteenth ACM Symposium on Operating Systems Principles*, pages 189–202, December 1993.

■ Abbott, M., and L. L. Peterson. Increasing network throughput by integrating pro-tocol layers. *IEEE/ACM Transactions on Networking* 1(5):600–610, October 1993.

■ Braden, R., D. Clark, and S. Shenker. Integrated services in the Internet architec-ture: An overview. *Request for Comments* 1633, July 1994.

In addition to these papers, Partridge [Par94] gives an overview of the field of high-speed networking, covering many of the same topics discussed in this (and earlier) chapters.

There are several papers that examine OS issues related to efficiently implementing net-work software on end hosts. Three examples in addition to those enumerated above include Maeda and Bershad [MB93], Thekkath et al. [TNML93], and Pasquale et al. [PAM94]. There is also an assortment of papers that examine the network interface and how it interacts with the end host; examples include Drushel et al. [DPD94], Davie [Dav91], Traw and Smith [TS93], Ramakrishnan [Ram93], Edwards et al. [EWL+94], Metcalf [Met93], Kanakia and Cheriton [KC88], Cohen et al. [CFFD93], and Steenkiste [Ste94a].

To learn more about the new service model, see Clark et al. [CSZ92]. For more in-formation on alternative models for handling real-time traffic, see Ferrari [Fer90] and Ferrari and Verma [FV90, FV93]. To learn more about forward error correction, see Ohta and Ki-tami [OK91] and Biersack [Bie92].

Finally, we recommend the following live reference:

■ http://netlab.itd.nrl.navy.mil/onr.html: list of network-related research projects, many of which focus on high-speed networks.

E X E R C I S E S

1 Recall the proposed TCP extension described in Chapter 6 that allows window sizes much larger than 64 KB. Suppose that you are using this extended TCP over a 1-Gbps link with a latency of 100 ms to transfer a 10-MB file, and the TCP receive window is 1 MB. If TCP sends 1-KB packets (assuming no congestion and no lost packets):

(a) How many RTTs does it take until the send window reaches 1 MB? (Recall that the send window is initialized to the size of a single packet.)

(b) How many RTTs does it take to send the file?

(c) If the time to send the file is given by the number of required RTTs multiplied by the link latency, what is the effective throughput for the transfer? What percentage of the link bandwidth is utilized?

2 Compute the effective payload bandwidth for ATM over an STS-12 SONET link.

3 As pointed out in this chapter, latency gains importance as networks get faster. Compare the latency/bandwidth tradeoffs in high-speed networks with the overhead incurred by moving data items across an I/O bus. In which setting (high-speed network or I/O bus) is the situation more severe?

4 Suppose a workstation has a 32-bit-wide, 800-Mbps bus, which takes 8 cycles to acquire. Compute the effective bandwidth for one-word transfers, as can happen with PIO.

5 Suppose the workstation described in the previous problem is connected to an ATM adaptor that uses DMA, and that it takes 14 cycles to transfer the 48-byte payload of an ATM cell to memory. What is the effective payload bandwidth if the adaptor transfers each cell separately? What if it transfers two cells at a time?

6 Consider an ATM adaptor that can take advantage of DMA and that performs both demultiplexing and segmentation/reassembly on board. Suppose this adaptor is fitted into the workstation described in the previous two problems, such that the adaptor uses DMA to transfer entire AAL5 PDUs to memory. What is the effective bandwidth, assuming 4-KB PDUs?

7 In the description of DMA given in Section 9.2.2, only the 48-byte payloads of each ATM packet were transferred from the adaptor. This is possible if the demultiplexing function is performed on the adaptor and the payload is delivered into a VCI-specific buffer. Compare this method to that of transferring the entire ATM packet to memory, in terms of both bus utilization and effective payload bandwidth.

8 Consider a network adaptor that computes the TCP checksum for each packet, where the checksum is computed as the packet is transferred between host memory and adaptor memory and is then made available in some register. Identify the difficulties that arise on the sending side of a TCP/IP protocol stack that tries to take advantage of this adaptor. What might a system do to work around these difficulties?

9 For the network adaptor postulated in the previous problem, there are two options for when an incoming packet can be transferred from the adaptor to host memory: (1) in the device driver, and (2) not until TCP is invoked. Discuss the ramifications of each approach.

10 Consider the potential performance benefit of integrating N data manipulation layers, where we assume that both the loop overhead and the computation performed by each layer is negligible. If we also assume that the number of CPU cycles it takes to read a word of data from memory is the same as the number of cycles it takes to write a word of data to memory, then derive the cost, in terms of number of CPU cycles, for a serial implementation of N layers and an integrated implementation of N layers. Keep in mind that while all layers must read each word in a message, not all layers write each word back to memory.

11 Using the two formulae derived in the previous problem, next derive an expression for the relative increase in throughput due to integration. Use this expression to plot the relative improvement that results from integrating a checksum manipulation and a byte-swap manipulation.

12 Are the MPEG and DES data manipulations good candidates for integrated layer processing? Explain your answer.

13 Give an example of how the standard write system call can lead to an extra copy of the data being transmitted.

14 For some system to which you have access, measure the time it takes to zero-fill a page. Assuming it takes no time to perform a page remap, what is the best throughput a system will achieve if it has to zero-fill one-half of each page it maps? Why is it necessary to zero-fill a page before mapping it from one domain to another?

15 Consider the flow whose bandwidth requirements are illustrated in Figure 9.13. Assume that the pattern of the first 3 seconds repeats indefinitely. What are the rate and bucket depth parameters for the token bucket with the lowest rate that describes this flow?

16 Suppose, in the previous problem, that we instead wanted to use a token bucket depth of 1 byte. What would be the lowest rate we could use?

17 Consider the receiving side of a video stream that has a long-term average rate of 100 Mbps.

(a) What is the average interpacket gap if each packet is 1 KB size? (The interpacket gap should be measured from the first bit of one packet to the first bit of the next packet.)

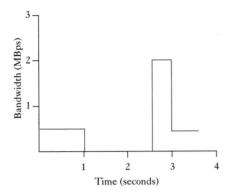

Figure 9.13 Bandwidth flow for exercise 15.

(b) Suppose the largest possible interpacket gap is 500 ms. Where should the playback point be set to ensure that all packets (frames) arrive in time?

(c) How much buffering is required to support this playback point?

18 Learn about the quality of service mechanisms that are being designed for ATM. Discuss the ramifications of running IP, with its new service model, on an Internet that includes ATM networks.

Network Management

A network is a complex system, both in terms of the number of nodes that are involved and in terms of the suite of protocols that can be running on any one node. Even if you restrict yourself to worrying about the nodes within a single administrative domain, such as a campus, there might be dozens of routers and hundreds—or even thousands—of hosts to keep track of. If you think about all the state that is maintained and manipulated on any one of those nodes—e.g., address translation tables, routing tables, TCP connection state, and so on—then it is easy to become depressed about the prospect of having to manage all of this information.

It is easy to imagine wanting to know about the state of various protocols on different nodes. For example, you might want to monitor the number of IP datagram reassemblies that have been aborted, so as to determine if the timeout that garbage collects partially assembled datagrams needs to be adjusted. As another example, you might want to keep track of the load on various nodes (i.e., the number of packets sent or received) so as to determine if new routers or links need to be added to the network. Of course, you also have to be on the watch for evidence of faulty hardware and mis-behaving software.

What we have just described is the problem of network management, an issue that pervades the entire network architecture. This appendix gives a brief overview of the tools that are available to system administrators to manage their networks.

A.1 SNMP Overview

Since the nodes we want to keep track of are distributed, our only real option is to use the network to manage the network. This means we need a protocol that allows us to read, and possibly write, various pieces of state information on different network nodes. The most widely used protocol for this purpose is the Simple Network Management Protocol (SNMP). SNMP is essentially a specialized request/reply protocol that supports two kinds of request messages: *get* and *put*. The former is used to retrieve a piece of state from some node, and the latter is used to store a new piece of state in some node. (SNMP also supports a third operation—*get-next*—which we explain below.) The following discussion focuses on the *get* operation, since it is the one most frequently used.

SNMP is used in the obvious way. A system administrator interacts with a client program that displays information about the network. This client program usually has a graphical interface. Whenever the administrator selects a certain piece of information that he or she wants to see, the client program uses SNMP to request that information from the node in question. (SNMP runs on top of UDP.) An SNMP server running on that node receives the request, locates the appropriate piece of information, and returns it to the client program, which then displays it to the user.

There is only one complication to this otherwise simple scenario: exactly how does the client indicate which piece of information it wants to retrieve, and likewise, how does the server know which variable in memory to read to satisfy the request? The answer is that SNMP depends on a companion specification called the Management Information Base (MIB). (This explains why SNMP's first name is "simple"—it doesn't tell the whole story.)

The MIB defines the specific pieces of information—the MIB *variables*—that you can retrieve from a network node. The next section describes a subset of the MIB variables.

Network management is a sufficiently large and important field that the IETF devotes an entire area to it. (The 50 or so IETF working groups are organized into nine areas.) There are well over 100 RFCs describing various aspects of SNMP and MIBs. The two key references, however, are Case et al. [CMRW93], which defines version 2 of SNMP (SNMPv2), and McCloghrie and Rose [MR91], which defines the second version of the mandatory MIB variables (MIB-II). Many of the other SNMP/MIB-related RFCs define extensions to the core set of MIB variables, for example, variables that are specific to a particular network technology or to a particular vendor's product. For a discussion of SNMP that provides more tutorial information than the RFCs, we recommend Rose's *The Simple Book: An Introduction to Internet Management* [Ros94].

A.2 MIB Variables

As mentioned in the previous section, a MIB defines the relevant variables for each component of a network node. This section gives the MIB variables for six different components; each component is called a MIB *group*. You will recognize that most of the groups correspond to one of the protocols described in this book, and nearly all of the variables defined for each group should look familiar. (Seeing if you recognize the MIB variables is a good way to test how much you remember from this book.)

Returning to the issue of the client stating exactly what information it wants to retrieve from a node, having a list of MIB variables is only half the battle. Two problems remain. First, we need a precise syntax for the client to use to state which of the MIB variables it wants to fetch. Second, we need a precise representation for the values returned by the server. Both problems are addressed using ASN.1.

Consider the second problem first. As we already saw in Chapter 7, ASN.1/BER defines a representation for different data types, such as integers. The MIB defines the type of each variable, and then it uses ASN.1/BER to encode the value contained in this variable as it is transmitted over the network. As far as the first problem is concerned, ASN.1 also defines an object identification scheme; this identification system is not described in Chapter 7. The MIB uses this identification system to assign a globally unique identifier to each MIB variable. These identifiers are given in a "dot" notation, not unlike domain names. For example, 1.3.6.1.2.1.4.3 is the unique ASN.1 identifier for the IP-related MIB variable ipInReceives; this variable counts the number of IP datagrams that have been received by this node. In this example, the 1.3.6.1.2.1 prefix identifies the MIB database (remember, ASN.1 object IDs are for all possible objects in the world), the 4 corresponds to the IP group, and the final 3 denotes the third variable in this group.

Thus, network management works as follows. The SNMP client puts the ASN.1 identifier for the MIB variable it wants to get into the request message, and it sends this message to the server. The server then maps this identifier into a local variable (i.e., into a memory location where the value for this variable is stored), retrieves the current value held in this variable, and uses ASN.1/BER to encode the value it sends back to the client.

A.2.1   System Group

These variables correspond to general parameters of the system (node) as a whole. For example, these variables record information about where the node is located, how long it has been up, the system's name, and so on. Notice that any variable of type **OBJECT IDENTIFIER** corresponds to a unique ASN.1 identifier, as described above. Most of the other types are self-explanatory.

```
Variable:
    sysDescr
Type:
    DisplayString (SIZE (0..255))
Description:
    A textual description of the entity. This value should
    include the full name and version identification of the
    system's hardware type, software operating system, and
    networking software. It is mandatory that this only
    contain printable ASCII characters.

Variable:
    sysObjectID
Type:
    OBJECT IDENTIFIER
Description:
    The vendor's authoritative identification of the network
    management subsystem contained in the entity. This value
    provides an easy and unambiguous means for determining
    "what kind of box" is being managed.

Variable:
    sysUpTime
Type:
    TimeTicks
Description:
    The time (in hundredths of a second) since the network
    management portion of the system was last re-initialized.

Variable:
    sysContact
Type:
    DisplayString (SIZE (0..255))
Description:
    The textual identification of the contact person for this
    managed node, together with information on how to contact
    this person.
```

Variable:
    sysName
Type:
    DisplayString (SIZE (0..255))
Description:
    An administratively assigned name for this managed node.
    By convention, this is the node's fully qualified domain
    name.

Variable:
    sysLocation
Type:
    DisplayString (SIZE (0..255))
Description:
    The physical location of this node (e.g., "telephone
    closet, 3rd floor").

Variable:
    sysServices
Type:
    INTEGER (0..127)
Description:
    A value that indicates the set of services that this
    entity potentially offers. The value is a sum. This
    sum initially takes the value zero. Then, for each layer
    L, in the range 1 through 7, that this node performs
    transactions for, 2 raised to (L - 1) is added to the
    sum. For example, a node that performs only routing
    functions would have a value of 4 ($2^{(3-1)}$). In
    contrast, a node that is a host offering application
    services would have a value of 72 ($2^{(4-1)} + 2^{(7-1)}$).
    Note that in the context of the Internet suite of
    protocols, values should be calculated accordingly:

    layer functionality
    1   physical (e.g., repeaters)
    2   datalink/subnetwork (e.g., bridges)
    3   internet (e.g., supports the IP)
    4   end-to-end (e.g., supports the TCP)
    7   applications (e.g., supports the SMTP)

    For systems including OSI protocols, layers 5 and 6 may
    also be counted.

A.2.2   Interfaces Group

The interfaces group of variables contains information about all the network interfaces (adaptors) attached to this node. This includes information about the physical address of each interface, as well as how many packets have been sent and received on each interface.

This group includes an example of two compound MIB variables: a table (**ifTable**) and a structure (**ifEntry**). Such compound variables explain the reason for the SNMP *get-next* operation. This operation, when applied to a particular variable ID, returns the value of that variable plus the ID of the next variable, e.g., the next item in the table or the next field in the structure. This aids the client in "walking through" the elements of a table or structure.

```
Variable:
    ifNumber
Type:
    INTEGER
Description:
    The number of network interfaces (regardless of their
    current state) present on this system.

Variable:
    ifTable
Type:
    SEQUENCE OF IfEntry
Description:
    A list of interface entries.  The number of entries is
    given by the value of ifNumber.

    Variable:
        ifEntry
    Type:
        IfEntry ::= SEQUENCE {
            ifIndex
                INTEGER,
            ifDescr
                DisplayString,
            ifType
                INTEGER,
            ifMtu
                INTEGER,
            ifSpeed
                Gauge,
            ifPhysAddress
                OCTET STRING,
            ifAdminStatus
                INTEGER,
            ifOperStatus
                INTEGER,
            ifLastChange
```

```
                              TimeTicks,
                       ifInOctets
                           Counter,
                       ifInUcastPkts
                           Counter,
                       ifInNUcastPkts
                           Counter,
                       ifInDiscards
                           Counter,
                       ifInErrors
                           Counter,
                       ifInUnknownProtos
                           Counter,
                       ifOutOctets
                           Counter,
                       ifOutUcastPkts
                           Counter,
                       ifOutNUcastPkts
                           Counter,
                       ifOutDiscards
                           Counter,
                       ifOutErrors
                           Counter,
                       ifOutQLen
                           Gauge,
                       ifSpecific
                           OBJECT IDENTIFIER
                  }
Description:
         An interface entry containing objects at the subnetwork
         layer and below for a particular interface.
```

A.2.3   Address Translation Group

The address translation group maintains information about the Address Resolution Protocol (ARP), and in particular, the contents of its address translation table.

```
Variable:
     atTable
Type:
     SEQUENCE OF AtEntry
Description:
     The Address Translation tables contain the NetworkAddress
     to "physical" address equivalences.  Some interfaces do
     not use translation tables for determining address
     equivalences (e.g., DDN-X.25 has an algorithmic method);
     if all interfaces are of this type, then the Address
     Translation table is empty, i.e., has zero entries.
```

```
Variable:
     atEntry
Type:
     AtEntry ::= SEQUENCE {
        atIfIndex
              INTEGER,
        atPhysAddress
              OCTET STRING,
        atNetAddress
              NetworkAddress
     }
Description:
     Each entry contains one NetworkAddress to "physical"
     address equivalence.
```

A.2.4 IP Group

This group defines variables related to IP, including its routing table, how many datagrams it has successfully forwarded, and statistics about datagram reassembly. Notice that many of the variables count how many times IP is forced to drop a datagram for one reason or another.

```
Variable:
     ipForwarding
Type:
     INTEGER {
        forwarding(1),      -- i.e., acting as a gateway
        not-forwarding(2) -- i.e., NOT acting as a gateway
     }
Description:
     The indication of whether this entity is acting as an IP
     gateway in respect to the forwarding of datagrams
     received by, but not addressed to, this entity.  IP
     gateways forward datagrams.  IP hosts do not (except
     those source-routed via the host).

Variable:
     ipDefaultTTL
Type:
     INTEGER
Description:
     The default value inserted into the Time-To-Live field of
     the IP header of datagrams originated at this entity,
     whenever a TTL value is not supplied by the transport
     layer protocol.

Variable:
     ipInReceives
Type:
     Counter
```

Description:
    The total number of input datagrams received from
    interfaces, including those received in error.

Variable:
    ipInHdrErrors
Type:
    Counter
Description:
    The number of input datagrams discarded due to errors in
    their IP headers, including bad checksums, version number
    mismatch, other format errors, time-to-live exceeded,
    errors discovered in processing their IP options, etc.

Variable:
    ipInAddrErrors
Type:
    Counter
Description:
    The number of input datagrams discarded because the IP
    address in their IP header's destination field was not a
    valid address to be received at this entity. This count
    includes invalid addresses (e.g., 0.0.0.0) and addresses
    of unsupported classes (e.g., Class E). For entities
    that are not IP gateways and therefore do not forward
    datagrams, this counter includes datagrams discarded
    because the destination address was not a local address.

Variable:
    ipForwDatagrams
Type:
    Counter
Description:
    The number of input datagrams for which this entity was
    not their final IP destination, as a result of which an
    attempt was made to find a route to forward them to that
    final destination. In entities that do not act as IP
    gateways, this counter will include only those packets
    that were Source-Routed via this entity, and the
    Source-Route option processing was successful.

Variable:
    ipInUnknownProtos
Type:
    Counter
Description:
    The number of locally addressed datagrams received
    successfully but discarded because of an unknown or

unsupported protocol.

Variable:
     ipInDiscards
Type:
     Counter
Description:
     The number of input IP datagrams for which no problems
     were encountered to prevent their continued processing,
     but which were discarded (e.g., for lack of buffer
     space). Note that this counter does not include any
     datagrams discarded while awaiting re-assembly.

Variable:
     ipInDelivers
Type:
     Counter
Description:
     The total number of input datagrams successfully
     delivered to IP user-protocols (including ICMP).

Variable:
     ipOutRequests
Type:
     Counter
Description:
     The total number of IP datagrams that local IP user-
     protocols (including ICMP) supplied to IP in requests for
     transmission. Note that this counter does not include
     any datagrams counted in ipForwDatagrams.

Variable:
     ipOutDiscards
Type:
     Counter
Description:
     The number of output IP datagrams for which no problem
     was encountered to prevent their transmission to their
     destination, but which were discarded (e.g., for lack of
     buffer space). Note that this counter would include
     datagrams counted in ipForwDatagrams if any such packets
     met this (discretionary) discard criterion.

Variable:
     ipOutNoRoutes
Type:
     Counter
Description:

The number of IP datagrams discarded because no route
could be found to transmit them to their destination.
Note that this counter includes any packets counted in
ipForwDatagrams that meet this "no-route" criterion.
Note that this includes any datagrams that a host cannot
route because all of its default gateways are down.

Variable:
      ipReasmTimeout
Type:
      INTEGER
Description:
      The maximum number of seconds that received fragments
      are held while they are awaiting reassembly at this
      entity.

Variable:
      ipReasmReqds
Type:
      Counter
Description:
      The number of IP fragments received that needed to be
      reassembled at this entity.

Variable:
      ipReasmOKs
Type:
      Counter
Description:
      The number of IP datagrams successfully re-assembled.

Variable:
      ipReasmFails
Type:
      Counter
Description:
      The number of failures detected by the IP re-assembly
      algorithm (for whatever reason: timed out, errors, etc).
      Note that this is not necessarily a count of discarded IP
      fragments since some algorithms (notably the algorithm in
      RFC 815) can lose track of the number of fragments by
      combining them as they are received.

Variable:
      ipFragOKs
Type:
      Counter
Description:

The number of IP datagrams that have been successfully
fragmented at this entity.

Variable:
    ipFragFails
Type:
    Counter
Description:
    The number of IP datagrams that have been discarded
    because they needed to be fragmented at this entity but
    could not be, e.g., because their "Don't Fragment" flag
    was set.

Variable:
    ipFragCreates
Type:
    Counter
Description:
    The number of IP datagram fragments that have been
    generated as a result of fragmentation at this entity.

Variable:
    ipAddrTable
Type:
    SEQUENCE OF IpAddrEntry
Description:
    The table of addressing information relevant to this
    entity's IP addresses.

    Variable:
        ipAddrEntry
    Type:
        IpAddrEntry ::= SEQUENCE {
            ipAdEntAddr
                IpAddress,
            ipAdEntIfIndex
                INTEGER,
            ipAdEntNetMask
                IpAddress,
            ipAdEntBcastAddr
                INTEGER,
            ipAdEntReasmMaxSize
                INTEGER (0..65535)
        }
    Description:
        The addressing information for one of this entity's IP
        addresses.

```
Variable:
    ipRoutingTable
Type:
    SEQUENCE OF IpRouteEntry
Description:
    This entity's IP Routing table.

    Variable:
        ipRouteEntry
    Type:
        IpRouteEntry ::= SEQUENCE {
            ipRouteDest
                IpAddress,
            ipRouteIfIndex
                INTEGER,
            ipRouteMetric1
                INTEGER,
            ipRouteMetric2
                INTEGER,
            ipRouteMetric3
                INTEGER,
            ipRouteMetric4
                INTEGER,
            ipRouteNextHop
                IpAddress,
            ipRouteType
                INTEGER,
            ipRouteProto
                INTEGER,
            ipRouteAge
                INTEGER,
            ipRouteMask
                IpAddress
            ipRouteMetric5
                INTEGER,
            ipRouteInfo
                OBJECT IDENTIFIER,
        }
    Description:
        A route to a particular destination.

Variable:
    ipNetToMediaTable
Type:
    SEQUENCE OF IpNetToMediaEntry
Description:
    The IP Address Translation table used for mapping from IP
    addresses to physical addresses.
```

```
Variable:
      IpNetToMediaEntry
Type:
      IpNetToMediaEntry ::= SEQUENCE {
            ipNetToMediaIfIndex
                  INTEGER,
            ipNetToMediaPhysAddress
                  OCTET STRING,
            ipNetToMediaNetAddress
                  IpAddress,
            ipNetToMediaType
                  INTEGER
      }
Description:
      Each entry contains one IpAddress to "physical" address
      equivalence.
```

```
Variable:
      ipRoutingDiscards
Type:
      Counter
Description:
      The number of routing entries that were chosen
      to be discarded even though they are valid.  One
      possible reason for discarding such an entry could
      be to free up buffer space for other routing entries.
```

A.2.5 TCP Group

The TCP group, as you might expect, maintains information about TCP connections involving this node. Variables that represent information about a particular TCP connection are transient; they persist only as long as the connection exists.

```
Variable:
      tcpRtoAlgorithm
Type:
      INTEGER {
            other(1),     -- none of the following
            constant(2), -- a constant rto
            rsre(3),      -- MIL-STD-1778, Appendix B
            vanj(4)       -- Van Jacobson's algorithm
      }
Description:
      The algorithm used to determine the timeout value used
      for retransmitting unacknowledged octets.
```

```
Variable:
      tcpRtoMin
```

Type:
     INTEGER
Description:
     The minimum value permitted by a TCP implementation for
     the retransmission timeout, measured in milliseconds.
     More refined semantics for objects of this type depend
     upon the algorithm used to determine the retransmission
     timeout. In particular, when the timeout algorithm is
     rsre(3), an object of this type has the semantics of the
     LBOUND quantity described in RFC 793.

Variable:
     tcpRtoMax
Type:
     INTEGER
Description:
     The maximum value permitted by a TCP implementation for
     the retransmission timeout, measured in milliseconds.
     More refined semantics for objects of this type depend
     upon the algorithm used to determine the retransmission
     timeout. In particular, when the timeout algorithm is
     rsre(3), an object of this type has the semantics of the
     UBOUND quantity described in RFC 793.

Variable:
     tcpMaxConn
Type:
     INTEGER
Description:
     The limit on the total number of TCP connections the
     entity can support. In entities where the maximum number
     of connections is dynamic, this object should contain the
     value "-1".

Variable:
     tcpActiveOpens
Type:
     Counter
Description:
     The number of times TCP connections have made a direct
     transition to the SYN-SENT state from the CLOSED state.

Variable:
     tcpPassiveOpens
Type:
     Counter
Description:
     The number of times TCP connections have made a direct

transition to the SYN-RCVD state from the LISTEN state.

Variable:
    tcpAttemptFails
Type:
    Counter
Description:
    The number of times TCP connections have made a direct
    transition to the CLOSED state from either the SYN-SENT
    state or the SYN-RCVD state, plus the number of times TCP
    connections have made a direct transition to the LISTEN
    state from the SYN-RCVD state.

Variable:
    tcpEstabResets
Type:
    Counter
Description:
    The number of times TCP connections have made a direct
    transition to the CLOSED state from either the
    ESTABLISHED state or the CLOSE-WAIT state.

Variable:
    tcpCurrEstab
Type:
    Gauge
Description:
    The number of TCP connections for which the current state
    is either ESTABLISHED or CLOSE-WAIT.

Variable:
    tcpInSegs
Type:
    Counter
Description:
    The total number of segments received, including those
    received in error. This count includes segments received
    on currently established connections.

Variable:
    tcpOutSegs
Type:
    Counter
Description:
    The total number of segments sent, including those on
    current connections but excluding those containing only
    retransmitted octets.

Variable:
     tcpRetransSegs
Type:
     Counter
Description:
     The total number of segments retransmitted - that is, the
     number of TCP segments transmitted that contain one or more
     previously transmitted octets.

Variable:
     tcpConnTable
Type:
     SEQUENCE OF TcpConnEntry
Description:
     A table containing TCP connection-specific information.

     Variable:
          tcpConnEntry
     Type:
          TcpConnEntry ::= SEQUENCE {
               tcpConnState
                    INTEGER,
               tcpConnLocalAddress
                    IpAddress,
               tcpConnLocalPort
                    INTEGER (0..65535),
               tcpConnRemAddress
                    IpAddress,
               tcpConnRemPort
                    INTEGER (0..65535)
          }
     Description:
          Information about a particular current TCP connection.
          An object of this type is transient, in that it ceases to
          exist when (or soon after) the connection makes the
          transition to the CLOSED state.

Variable:
     tcpInErrs
Type:
     Counter
Description:
     The total number of segments received in error (e.g., bad
     TCP checksums).

Variable:
     tcpOutRsts

```
Type:
    Counter
Description:
    The number of TCP segments sent that contain the RST flag.
```

A.2.6   UDP Group

Finally, we give the MIB variables that have been defined for UDP. Notice that these variables count, among other things, the total number of UDP datagrams that have been sent and received.

```
Variable:
    udpInDatagrams
Type:
    Counter
Description:
    The total number of UDP datagrams delivered to UDP users.


Variable:
    udpNoPorts
Type:
    Counter
Description:
    The total number of received UDP datagrams for which
    there was no application at the destination port.


Variable:
    udpInErrors
Type:
    Counter
Description:
    The number of received UDP datagrams that could not be
    delivered for reasons other than the lack of an
    application at the destination port.


Variable:
    udpOutDatagrams
Type:
    Counter
Description:
    The total number of UDP datagrams sent from this entity.


Variable:
    udpTable
Type:
    SEQUENCE OF UdpEntry
Description:
    A table containing UDP listener information.
```

```
Variable:
    udpEntry
Type:
    UdpEntry ::= SEQUENCE {
        udpLocalAddress
            IpAddress,
        udpLocalPort
            INTEGER (0..65535)
    }
Description:
    Information about a particular current UDP listener.
```

GLOSSARY

4B/5B: A type of bit encoding scheme used in FDDI, in which every 4 bits of data are transmitted as a 5-bit sequence.

AAL: ATM Adaptation Layer. A protocol layer, configured over ATM. Two AALs are defined for data communications, AAL3/4 and AAL5. Each protocol layer provides a mechanism to segment large packets into cells at the sender and to reassemble the cells back together at the receiver.

ABR: Available bit rate. A rate-based congestion-control scheme being developed for use on ATM networks. ABR is intended to allow a source to increase or decrease its allotted rate, based on feedback from switches within the network. Contrast with CBR, UBR, and VBR.

ACK: An abbreviation for *acknowledgment*. An acknowledgment is sent by a receiver of data to indicate to the sender that the data transmission was successful.

additive increase/multiplicative decrease: Congestion window strategy used by TCP. TCP opens the congestion window at a linear rate, but halves it when losses are experienced due to congestion. It has been shown that additive increase/multiplicative decrease is a necessary condition for a congestion-control mechanism to be stable.

ANSI: American National Standards Institute. Private U.S. standardization body that commonly participates in the ISO standardization process. Responsible for SONET.

API: Application programming interface. Interface that application programs use to access the network subsystem (usually the transport protocol). Usually OS-specific. The socket API from Berkeley Unix is a widely used example.

ARP: Address Resolution Protocol. Protocol of the Internet architecture, used to translate high-level protocol addresses into physical hardware addresses. Commonly used on the Internet to map IP addresses into Ethernet addresses.

ARPA: Advanced Research Projects Agency. One of the research and development organizations within the Department of Defense. Responsible for funding the ARPANET as well as the research that led to the development of the TCP/IP Internet. Known for a while as DARPA, the D standing for Defense.

ARPANET: An experimental wide-area packet-switched network funded by ARPA and begun in the late 1960s, which became the backbone of the developing Internet.

ARQ: Automatic repeat request. General strategy for reliably sending packets over an unreliable link. If the sender does not receive an ACK for a packet after a certain time period, it assumes that the packet did not arrive (or was delivered with bit errors) and retransmits it. Stop-and-wait and sliding window are two example ARQ protocols. Contrast with FEC.

ASN.1: Abstract Syntax Notation One. In conjunction with BER, a presentation-formatting standard devised by the ISO as part of the OSI architecture.

ATM: Asynchronous transfer mode. A connection-oriented network technology that uses small, fixed-size packets (called *cells*) to carry data.

ATM Forum: A key ATM standards-setting body.

authentication: Security protocol by which two suspicious parties prove to each other that they are who they claim to be.

autonomous system (AS): A group of networks and routers, subject to a common authority and using the same intradomain routing protocol.

bandwidth: A measure of the capacity of a link or connection, usually given in units of bits per second.

BER: Basic Encoding Rules. Rules for encoding data types defined by ASN.1.

best-effort delivery: The service model of the current Internet architecture. Delivery of a message is attempted but is not guaranteed.

BGP: Border Gateway Protocol. An interdomain routing protocol by which autonomous systems exchange reachability information. The most recent version is BGP-4.

BISYNC: Binary Synchronous Communication. A byte-oriented link-level protocol developed in the late 1960s by IBM.

bit stuffing: A technique used to distinguish control sequences and data on the bit level. Used by the HDLC protocol.

BLAST: An *x*-kernel protocol that performs fragmentation and reassembly of large messages.

block: An OS term used to describe a situation in which a process suspends execution while awaiting some event, such as a change in the state of a *semaphore*.

bridge: A device that forwards link-level frames from one physical network to another. Contrast with *repeater* and *router*.

broadcast: A method of delivering a packet to every host on a particular network or internet. May be implemented in hardware (e.g., Ethernet) or software (e.g., IP broadcast).

CBR: Constant Bit Rate. A class of service in ATM that guarantees transmission of data at a constant bit rate, thus emulating a dedicated transmission link. Contrast with ABR, UBR, and VBR.

CCITT: The now defunct *Comité Consultif International de Telegraphique et Telephonique*, a unit of the International Telecommunications Union (ITU) of the United Nations. Now replaced by ITU-T.

cell: A 53-byte ATM packet, capable of carrying up to 48 bytes of data.

CHAN: An *x*-kernel protocol that implements request/reply channels.

channel: A generic communication term used in this book to denote a logical process-to-process connection.

checksum: Typically a ones-complement sum over some or all of the bytes of a packet, computed and appended to the packet by the sender. The receiver recomputes the checksum and compares it to the one carried in the message. Checksums are used to detect errors in a packet and may also be used to verify that the packet has been delivered to the correct host. The term *checksum* is also sometimes (imprecisely) used to refer generically to error-detecting codes.

CIDR: Classless interdomain routing. A method of aggregating routes that treats a block of contiguous Class C IP addresses as a single network.

circuit switching: A general strategy for switching data through a network. It involves establishing a dedicated path (circuit) between the source and destination. Contrast with *packet switching*.

client: The requester of a service in a distributed system.

CLNP: Connectionless Network Protocol. The ISO counterpart to the Internet's IP.

clock recovery: The process of deriving a valid clock from a serially transmitted digital signal.

concurrent logical channels: Multiplexing several stop-and-wait logical channels onto a single point-to-point link. No delivery order is enforced. This mechanism was used by the IMP-IMP protocol of the ARPANET.

congestion: A state resulting from too many packets contending for limited resources, e.g., link bandwidth and buffer space on routers or switches, which may force the router (switch) to discard packets.

congestion control: Any network resource management strategy that has, as its goal, the alleviation or avoidance of congestion. A congestion-control mechanism may be implemented on the routers (switches) inside the network, by the hosts at the edges of the network, or by a combination of both.

connection: In general, a channel that must be established prior to use, e.g., by the transmission of some setup information. For example, TCP provides a connection abstraction that offers reliable, ordered delivery of a byte stream. Connection-oriented networks, such as ATM, are often said to provide a *virtual circuit* abstraction.

connectionless protocol: A protocol in which data may be sent without any advance setup. IP is an example of such a protocol.

context switch: An operation in which an operating system suspends the execution of one process and begins the execution of another. A context switch involves saving the state of the former process (e.g., the contents of all registers) and loading the state of the latter process.

CRC: Cyclic redundancy check. An error-detecting code computed over the bytes composing a packet and then appended to the packet by the network hardware (e.g., Ethernet adaptor). CRC provides stronger error detection than a simple checksum.

crossbar switch: A simple switch design in which every input is directly connected to every output and the output port is responsible for resolving contention.

CSMA/CD: Carrier Sense Multiple Access with Collision Detect. CSMA/CD is a functionality of network hardware. "Carrier sense multiple access" means that multiple stations can listen to the link and detect when it is in use or idle; "collision detect" indicates that, if two or more stations are transmitting on the link simultaneously, they will detect the collision of their signals. Ethernet is the best-known technology that uses CSMA/CD.

cut-through: A form of switching or forwarding in which a packet starts to be transferred to an output before it has been completely received by the switching node, thus reducing latency through the node.

DAN: Desk area network. A network that spans a desktop and interconnects devices typically enclosed within a computer; e.g., display, camera, disk. Contrast with LAN, MAN, and WAN.

datagram: The basic transmission unit in the Internet architecture. A datagram contains all of the information needed to deliver it to its destination, analagous to a letter in the U.S. postal system. Datagram networks are connectionless.

DCE: Distributed Computing Environment. An RPC-based suite of protocols and standards that support distributed computing. Defined by OSF.

DDCMP: Digital Data Communication Message Protocol. A byte-oriented link-level protocol used in Digital Equipment Corporation's DECNET.

decryption: The act of reversing an *encryption* process to recover the data from an encrypted message.

demultiplexing: Using information contained in a packet header to direct it upward through a protocol stack. For example, IP uses the ProtNum field in the IP header to decide which higher protocol (i.e., TCP, UDP) a packet belongs to, and TCP uses the port number to demultiplex a TCP packet to the correct application process. Contrast *multiplexing*.

demultiplexing key: A field in a packet header that enables demultiplexing to take place, e.g., the ProtNum field of IP.

DECbit: A congestion-control scheme in which routers notify the endpoints of imminent congestion by setting a bit in the header of routed packets. The endpoints decrease their sending rates when a certain percentage of received packets have the bit set.

DES: Data Encryption Standard. An algorithm for data encryption based on a 64-bit secret key.

distance vector: A lowest-cost-path algorithm used in routing. Each node advertises reachability information and associated costs to its immediate neighbors, and uses the updates it receives to construct its forwarding table. The routing protocol RIP uses a distance-vector algorithm. Contrast with link state.

DMA: Direct Memory Access. An approach to connecting hosts to I/O devices, in which the device directly reads data from and writes data to the host's memory. Also see *PIO*.

DNA/DECNET: Digital Network Architecture. An OSI-based architecture that supports a connectionless network model and a connection-oriented transport protocol.

DNS: Domain name system. The distributed naming system of the Internet, used to resolve host names (e.g., baskerville.cs.arizona.edu) into IP addresses (e.g., 192.12.69.35). The DNS is implemented by a hierarchy of name servers.

domain: Can refer either to a context in the hierarchical DNS name space (e.g., the "edu" domain), or to a region of the Internet that is treated as a single entity for the purpose of hierarchical routing. The latter is equivalent to *autonomous system*.

DS3: A 44.7-Mbps transmission link service offered by the phone company.

duplicate ACK: A retransmission of a TCP acknowledgment. The duplicate ACK does not acknowledge any new data. The receipt of multiple duplicate ACKs triggers the TCP *fast retransmit* mechanism.

EGP: Exterior Gateway Protocol. An early interdomain routing protocol of the Internet, which was used by exterior gateways (routers) of autonomous systems to exchange routing information with other ASs. Replaced by BGP.

encapsulation: The operation, performed by a lower-level protocol, of attaching a protocol-specific header and/or trailer to a message passed down by a higher-level protocol. As a message travels down the protocol stack, it gathers a sequence of headers, of which the outermost corresponds to the protocol at the bottom of the stack.

encryption: The act of applying a transforming function to data, with the intention that only the receiver of the data will be able to read it (after applying the inverse function, *decryption*). Encryption generally depends on either a secret shared by the sender and receiver or on a public/private key pair.

Ethernet: A popular local area network technology that uses CSMA/CD and has a bandwidth of 10 Mbps. An Ethernet itself is just a passive wire; all aspects of Ethernet transmission are completely implemented by the host adaptors.

exponential backoff: A retransmission strategy that doubles the timeout value each time a packet is retransmitted.

extended LAN: A collection of LANs connected by bridges.

fabric: The part of a switch that actually does the switching, that is, moves packets from input to output. Contrast with *port*.

fair queuing (FQ): A round-robin-based queuing algorithm that prevents a badly behaved process from capturing an arbitrarily large portion of the network capacity.

fast retransmit: A strategy used by TCP that attempts to avoid timeouts in the presence of lost packets. TCP retransmits a segment after receiving three consecutive duplicate ACKs, acknowledging the data up to (but not including) that segment.

FDDI: Fiber Distributed Data Interface. A high-speed token ring networking technology designed to run over optical fiber.

FEC: Forward error correction. A general strategy for recovering from bit errors introduced into data packets without having to retransmit the packet. Redundant information is included with each packet that can be used by the receiver to determine which bits in a packet are incorrect. Contrast with ARQ.

Fiber Channel: A bidirectional link protocol commonly used to connect computers (usually supercomputers) to peripherals. Fiber Channel has a bandwidth of 100 MBps and can span up to 30 meters. Used in the same way as HIPPI.

flow control: A mechanism by which the receiver of data throttles the transmission rate of the sender, so that data will not arrive too quickly to be processed. Contrast with *congestion control*.

forwarding: The operation performed by a router on every packet: receiving it on an input, deciding what output to send it to, and sending it there.

forwarding table: The table maintained in a router that lets it make decisions on how to forward packets. The process of building up the forwarding table is called routing, and thus the forwarding table is sometimes called a *routing table*.

fragmentation/reassembly: A method for transmission of messages larger than the network's MTU. Messages are fragmented into small pieces by the sender and reassembled by the receiver.

frame: Another name for a packet, typically used in reference to packets sent over a single link rather than a whole network. An important problem is how the receiver detects the beginning and ending of a frame, a problem known as framing.

Frame Relay: A connection-oriented public packet-switched service offered by the phone company. It is provided in ISDN as an alternative to X.25.

FTP: File Transfer Protocol. The standard protocol of the Internet architecture for transferring files between hosts. Built on top of TCP.

gopher: An Internet information service.

handle: In programming, an indentifier or pointer that is used to access an object.

hardware address: The link-level address used to identify the host adaptor on the local network.

HDLC: High-Level Data Link Control Protocol. An ISO-standard link-level protocol. It uses bit stuffing to solve the framing problem.

hierarchical routing: A multilevel routing scheme that uses the hierarchical structure of the address space as the basis for making forwarding decisions. For example, packets might first be routed to a destination network and then to a specific host on that network.

HIPPI: High Performance Parallel Interface. An ANSI-standard network technology capable of Gbps transmission rates, typically used to connect supercomputers to peripheral devices. Used in same way as *Fiber Channel*.

host: A computer attached to one or more networks that supports users and runs application programs.

HTML: HyperText Markup Language. A language used to construct World Wide Web pages.

HTTP: HyperText Transport Protocol. An application-level protocol based on a request/reply paradigm and used in the World Wide Web. HTTP uses TCP connections to transfer data.

IAB: Internet Activities Board. The main body that oversees the development and standardization of protocols of the Internet architecture. The IRTF and IETF are task forces of the IAB.

ICMP: Internet Control Message Protocol. This protocol is an integral part of IP. It allows a router or destination host to communicate with the source, typically to report an error in IP datagram processing.

IEEE: Institute for Electrical and Electronics Engineers. A professional society for engineers that also defines network standards, including the 802 series of LAN standards.

IETF: Internet Engineering Task Force. A task force of the IAB, responsible for providing short-term engineering solutions for the Internet.

IMP-IMP: A byte-oriented link-level protocol used in the original ARPANET.

integrated services: Usually taken to mean a packet-switched network that can effectively support both conventional computer data and real-time audio and video. Also, a name given to a proposed Internet service model that is being designed to replace the current best-effort service model.

integrity: In the context of network security, a service that ensures that a received message is the same one that was sent.

interdomain routing: The process of exchanging routing among different routing domains. BGP is an example of an interdomain protocol.

internet: A collection of (possibly heterogeneous) packet-switching networks interconnected by routers. Also called an internetwork.

Internet: The global internet based on the Internet (TCP/IP) architecture, connecting millions of hosts worldwide.

interoperability: The ability of heterogeneous hardware and multivendor software to communicate by correctly exchanging messages.

interrupt: An event (typically generated by a hardware device) that tells the operating system to stop its current activity and take some action. For example, an interrupt is used to notify the OS that a packet has arrived from the network.

intradomain routing: The exchange of routing information within a single domain or autonomous system. RIP and OSPF are example intradomain protocols.

IP: Internet Protocol (also known as IPv4). A protocol that provides a connectionless, best-effort delivery service of datagrams across the Internet.

IPng: Internet Protocol—Next Generation (also known as IPv6). Proposed version of IP that provides a larger, more hierarchical address space and other new features.

IRTF: Internet Research Task Force. A task force of the IAB, responsible for charting direction in research and development for the Internet.

ISDN: Integrated Services Digital Network. A digital communication service offered by telephone carriers and standardized by ITU-T. ISDN combines voice connection and digital data services in a single physical medium.

ISO: International Standards Organization. The international body that drafted the seven-layer OSI architecture, and a suite of protocols that has not enjoyed commercial success.

ITU-T: A subcommittee of the International Telecommunications Union, a global body that drafts technical standards for all areas of international analog and digital communication. ITU-T deals with standards for telecommunications, notably ATM.

JPEG: Joint Photographic Experts Group. Typically used to refer to a widely used algorithm for compressing still images that was developed by the JPEG.

Kerberos: A TCP/IP-based authentication system developed at MIT, in which two hosts use a trusted third party to authenticate each other.

LAN: Local area network. A network based on any physical network technology that is designed to span distances of up to a few thousand meters (e.g., Ethernet or FDDI). Contrast with DAN, MAN, and WAN.

latency: A measure of how long it takes a single bit to propagate from one end of a link or channel to the other. Latency is measured strictly in terms of time.

link: A physical connection between two nodes of a network. It may be implemented over copper or fiberoptic cable or it may be a wireless link, e.g., a satellite.

link-level protocol: A protocol that is responsible for delivering frames over a directly connected network (e.g., an Ethernet, token ring, or point-to-point link). (Also called link-layer protocol.)

link state: A lowest-cost-path algorithm used in routing. Information on directly connected neighbors and current link costs are flooded to all routers; each router uses this information to build a view of the network on which to base forwarding decisions. The OSPF routing protocol uses a link-state algorithm. Contrast with *distance vector*.

MAC: Media access control. Algorithms used to control access to shared media networks like Ethernet and FDDI.

MAN: Metropolitan area network. A network based on any of several new network technologies that operate at high speeds (up to several Gbps) and across distances wide enough to span a metropolitan area. Contrast with DAN, LAN, and WAN.

Manchester: A bit encoding scheme that transmits the exclusive-OR of the clock and the NRZ-encoded data. Used on the Ethernet.

MBone: Multicast Backbone. A logical network imposed over the top of the Internet, in which multicast-enhanced routers use tunneling to forward multicast datagrams across the Internet.

MD5: Message Digest version 5. An efficient cryptographic checksum algorithm commonly used to verify that the contents of a message are unaltered.

MIB: Management Information Base. Defines the set of network-related variables that may be read or written on a network node. The MIB is used in conjunction with SNMP.

MIME: Multipurpose Internet Mail Extensions. Specifications for converting binary data (such as image files) to ASCII text, which allows it to be sent via email.

Mosaic: A popular and free graphical World Wide Web browser developed at the National Center for Supercomputing Applications at the University of Illinois.

MPEG: Moving Pictures Expert Group. Typically used to refer to an algorithm for compressing video streams developed by the MPEG.

MTU: Maximum transmission unit. The size of the largest packet that can be sent over a physical network.

multicast: A special form of broadcast in which packets are delivered to a specified subgroup of network hosts.

multiplexing: Combining distinct channels into a single, lower-level channel. For example, separate TCP and UDP channels are multiplexed into a single host-to-host IP channel. The inverse operation, *demultiplexing*, takes place on the receiving host.

name resolution: The action of resolving host names (which are easy for humans to read) into their corresponding addresses (which machines can read). See DNS.

NDR: Network Data Representation. The data-encoding standard used in the Distributed Computing Environment (DCE), as defined by the Open Software Foundation. NDR uses a receiver-makes-right strategy and inserts an architecture tag at the front of each message.

Netscape: A popular graphical WWW browser.

network-level protocol: A protocol that runs over switched networks, directly above the link level.

NFS: Network File System. A popular distributed file system developed by Sun Microsystems. NFS is based on SunRPC, an RPC protocol developed by Sun.

NIST: National Institute for Standards and Technology. The official U.S. standardization body.

node: A generic term used for individual computers that make up a network. Nodes include general-purpose computers, switches, and routers.

NRZ: Non-Return to Zero. A bit encoding scheme that encodes a 1 as the high signal and a 0 as the low signal.

NRZI: Non-Return to Zero Inverted. A bit encoding scheme that makes a transition from the current signal to encode a 1 and stays at the current signal to encode a 0.

NSF: National Science Foundation. An agency of the U.S. government that funds scientific research in the United States, including research on networks and on the Internet infrastructure.

NV: Network Video. A videoconferencing application that runs over the MBone.

OC: Optical Carrier. The prefix for various rates of SONET optical transmission. For example, OC-1 refers to the SONET standard for 51.84-Mbps transmission over fiber. An OC-n signal differs from an STS-n signal only in that the OC-n signal is scrambled for optical transmission.

ONC: Open Network Computing. A version of SunRPC that is being standardized for the Internet.

OSF: Open Software Foundation. A consortium of computer vendors that have defined standards for distributed computing, including the NDR presentation format.

OSI: Open Systems Interconnection. The seven-layer network reference model developed by the ISO. Guides the design of ISO and ITU-T protocol standards.

OSPF: Open Shortest Path First. A routing protocol developed by the IETF for the Internet architecture. OSPF is based on a *link-state* algorithm, in which every node constructs a topography of the Internet and uses it to make forwarding decisions.

packet: A data unit sent over a packet-switched network. Also see *frame* and *segment*.

packet switching: A general strategy for switching data through a network. Packet switching uses store-and-forward switching of discrete data units called packets, and implies *statistical multiplexing*.

participants: A generic term used to denote the processes, protocols, or hosts that are sending messages to each other.

peer: A counterpart on another machine that a protocol module interoperates with to implement some communication service.

PGP: Pretty Good Privacy. A collection of public domain software that provides privacy and authentication capabilities using RSA and that uses a mesh of trust for public key distribution.

physical-level protocol: The lowest layer of the OSI protocol stack. Its main function is to encode bits onto the signals that are propagated across the physical transmission media.

Ping: A Unix utility used to test the RTT to various hosts over the Internet. Ping sends an ICMP ECHO_REQUEST message, and the remote host sends an ECHO_RESPONSE message back.

PIO: Programmed Input/Ouput. An approach to connecting hosts to I/O devices, in which the CPU reads data from and writes data to the I/O device. Also see *DMA*.

poison reverse: Used in conjunction with *split horizon*. A heuristic technique to avoid routing loops in distance-vector routing protocols.

port: A generic term usually used to mean the point at which a network user attaches to the network. On a switch, a port denotes the input or output on which packets are received and sent.

POTS: Plain old telephone service. Used to specify the existing phone service, in contrast to ISDN, ATM, or other technologies that the telephone companies offer now or may offer in the future.

process: An abstraction provided by an operating system to enable different operations to take place concurrently. For example, each user application usually runs inside its own process, while various operating system functions take place in other processes.

promiscuous mode: A mode of operation for a network adaptor in which it receives all frames transmitted on the network, not just those addressed to it.

protocol: A specification of an interface between modules running on different machines, as well as the communication service that those modules implement. The term is also used to refer to an implementation of the module that meets this specification. To distinguish between these two uses, the interface is often called a *protocol specification*.

pseudoheader: A subset of fields from the IP header that are passed up to transport protocols TCP and UDP for use in their checksum calculation. The pseudoheader contains source and destination IP addresses and IP datagram length, thus enabling detection of corruption of these fields or delivery of a packet to an incorrect address.

public key encryption: Any of several encryption algorithms (e.g., RSA), in which each participant has a private key (shared with no one else) and a public key (available to everyone). A secure message is sent to a user by encrypting the data with that user's public key; possession of the private key is required to decrypt the message, and so only the receiver can read it.

QoS: Quality of service. Packet delivery guarantees provided by a network architecture. Usually related to performance guarantees, such as bandwidth and delay. The Internet offers a best-effort delivery service, meaning that every effort is made to deliver a packet but delivery is not guaranteed.

RED: Random Early Detection. A queuing discipline for routers in which, when congestion is anticipated, packets are randomly dropped to alert the senders to slow down.

repeater: A device that propagates electrical signals from one Ethernet cable to another. There can be a maximum of two repeaters between any two hosts in an Ethernet. Repeaters forward signals, whereas *bridges* forward *frames*, and *routers* and *switches* forward *packets*.

reverse-path broadcast (RPB): A technique used to eliminate duplicate broadcast packets.

RFC: Request for Comments. Internet reports that contain, among other things, specifications for protocols like TCP and IP.

RIP: Routing Information Protocol. An intradomain routing protocol supplied with Berkeley Unix. Each router running RIP dynamically builds its forwarding table based on a *distance-vector* algorithm.

router: A network node connected to two or more networks that forwards packets from one network to another. Contrast with *bridge*, *repeater*, and *switch*.

routing: The process by which nodes exchange topological information to build correct forwarding tables. See *forwarding*, *link-state*, and *distance-vector*.

routing table: See *forwarding table*.

RPC: Remote Procedure Call. Synchronous request/reply transport protocol used in many client/server interactions.

RSA: A public key encryption algorithm named after its inventors: Rivest, Shamir, and Adleman.

RSVP: Resource Reservation Protocol. A protocol for reserving resources in the network. RSVP uses the concept of *soft state* in routers and puts responsibility for making reservations on receivers instead of on senders.

RTT: Round-trip time. The time it takes for a bit of information to propagate from one end of a link or channel to the other and back again; in other words, double the latency of the channel.

scrambling: The process of XORing a signal with a pseudorandom bit stream before transmission to cause enough signal transitions to allow clock recovery. Scrambling is used in SONET.

segment: A TCP packet. A segment contains a portion of the byte stream that is being sent by means of TCP.

SELECT: A synchronous demultiplexing protocol of the *x*-kernel.

semaphore: A variable used to support synchronization between processes. Typically a process *blocks* on a semaphore while it waits for some other process to signal the semaphore.

server: The provider of a service in a client/server distributed system.

session: An *x*-kernel object that implements the endpoint of a channel.

signalling: At the physical level, denotes the transmission of a signal over some physical medium. In ATM, signalling refers to the process of establishing a virtual circuit.

silly window syndrome: A condition that occurs in TCP that may arise if, each time the receiver opens its receive window a small amount, the sender sends a small segment to fill the window. The result is many small segments and an inefficient use of bandwidth.

sliding window: An algorithm that allows the sender to transmit multiple packets (up to the size of the window) before receiving an acknowledgment. As acknowledgments are returned for those packets in the window that were sent first, the window "slides" and more packets may be sent. The sliding window algorithm combines reliable delivery with a high throughput. See ARQ.

slow start: A congestion-avoidance algorithm for TCP that attempts to pace outgoing segments. For each ACK that is returned, two additional packets are sent, resulting in an exponential increase in the number of outstanding segments.

SMDS: Switched Multimegabit Data Service. A service supporting LAN-to-WAN connectivity, to be offered by U.S. telephone companies. SMDS will be used to bridge related technologies like ATM or *Frame Relay*.

SMTP: Simple Mail Transfer Protocol. The electronic mail protocol of the Internet.

SNA: System Network Architecture. The proprietary network architecture of IBM.

SNMP: Simple Network Management Protocol. An Internet protocol that allows the monitoring of hosts, networks, and routers.

socket: The abstraction provided by UNIX that provides the application programming interface (API) to TCP/IP.

soft state: Connection-related information contained in a router that is cached for a limited period of time rather than being explicitly established (and requiring explicit teardown) through a connection setup.

SONET: Synchronous Optical Network. A clock-based framing standard for digital transmission over optical fiber. It defines how telephone companies transmit data over optical networks.

source routing: Routing decisions performed at the source before the packet is sent. The route consists of the list of nodes that the packet should traverse on the way to the destination.

split horizon: A method of breaking routing loops in a distance-vector routing algorithm. When a node sends a routing update to its neighbors, it does not send those routes it learned from each neighbor back to that neighbor. Split horizon is used with *poison reverse*.

statistical multiplexing: Demand-based multiplexing of multiple data sources over a shared link or channel.

stop-and-wait: A reliable transmission algorithm in which the sender transmits a packet and waits for an acknowledgment before sending the next packet. Compare with *sliding window* and *concurrent logical channels*. See also ARQ.

STS: Synchronous Transport Signal. The prefix for various rates of SONET transmission. For example, STS-1 refers to the SONET standard for 51.84-Mbps transmission.

subnetting: The use of a single IP network address to denote multiple physical networks. Routers within the subnetwork use a subnet mask to discover the physical network to which a packet should be forwarded. Subnetting effectively introduces a third level to the two-level hierarchical IP address.

SunRPC: Remote procedure call protocol developed by Sun Microsystems. SunRPC is used to support NFS. See also ONC.

switch: A network node that forwards packets from inputs to outputs based on header information in each packet. Differs from a *router* mainly in that it typically does not interconnect networks of different types.

switching fabric: The component of a switch that directs packets from their inputs to the correct outputs.

T1: A standard telephone carrier service equal to 24 ISDN circuits, or 1.544 Mbps.

TCP: Transmission Control Protocol. Connection-oriented transport protocol of the Internet architecture. TCP provides a reliable, byte-stream delivery service.

Telnet: Remote terminal protocol of the Internet architecture. Telnet allows you to interact with a remote system as if your terminal is directly connected to that machine.

throughput: The observed rate at which data is sent through a channel. The term is often used interchangeably with *bandwidth*.

token bucket: An admission control algorithm. Conceptually, processes accumulate tokens over time, and they must spend a token to transmit a byte of data and then must stop sending when they have no tokens left. Thus, overall bandwidth is limited, with the accommodation of some burstiness.

token ring: A physical network technology in which hosts are connected in a ring. A token (bit pattern) circulates around the ring. A given node must possess the token before it is allowed to transmit. FDDI is an example of a popular token ring network.

TP4: OSI Transport Protocol Class 4. The most powerful OSI transport protocol. TP4 is the ISO equivalent of TCP.

transport protocol: An end-to-end protocol that enables processes on different hosts to communicate. TCP is the canonical example.

tunneling: Encapsulating a packet using a protocol that operates at the same layer as the packet. For example, multicast IP packets are encapsulated inside unicast IP packets to tunnel across the Internet to implement the MBone. Tunneling will also be used during the transition from IPv4 to IPv6.

two-dimensional parity: A parity scheme in which bytes are conceptually stacked as a matrix, and parity is calculated for both rows and columns.

Tymnet: An early network in which a *virtual circuit* abstraction was maintained across a set of routers.

UBR: Unspecified Bit Rate. The "no frills" service class in ATM, offering best-effort cell delivery. Contrast with ABR, CBR, and VBR.

UDP: User Datagram Protocol. Transport protocol of the Internet architecture that provides a connectionless datagram service to application-level processes.

unicast: Sending a packet to a single destination host. Contrast with *broadcast* and *multicast*.

URL: Uniform resource locator. A text string used to identify the location of Internet resources. A typical URL looks like http://www.bellcore.com. In this URL, http is the protocol to use to access the resource located on host www.bellcore.com.

VBR: Variable Bit Rate. One of the classes of service in ATM, intended for applications with bandwidth requirements that vary with time, such as compressed video. Contrast with ABR, CBR, and UBR.

VCI: Virtual circuit identifier. An identifier in the header of a packet that is used for virtual circuit switching. In the case of ATM, the VPI and VCI together identify the end-to-end connection.

virtual circuit: The abstraction provided by connection-oriented networks such as ATM. Messages must usually be exchanged between participants to establish a virtual circuit (and perhaps to allocate resources to the circuit) before data can be sent. Contrast with *datagram*.

virtual clock: A service model that allows the source to reserve resources on routers using a rate-based description of its needs. Virtual clock goes beyond the best-effort delivery service of the current Internet.

VPI: Virtual Path Identifier. An 8-bit or 12-bit field in the ATM header. VPI can be used to hide multiple virtual connections across a network inside a single virtual "path," thus decreasing the amount of connection state that the switches must maintain. See also *VCI*.

WAN: Wide area network. Any physical network technology that is capable of spanning long distances (i.e., crosscountry). Compare with DAN, LAN, and WAN.

weighted fair queuing (WFQ): A variation of *fair queuing* in which each flow can be given a different proportion of the network capacity.

well-known port: A port number that is, by convention, dedicated for use by a particular server. For instance, the Domain Name Server receives messages at well-known UDP and TCP port 53 on every host.

WWW: World Wide Web. A hypermedia information service on the Internet.

X.25: The ITU packet-switching protocol standard.

X.400: The ITU electronic mail standard. The counterpart to SMTP in the Internet architecture.

X.500: The ITU directory services standard, which defines an attribute-based naming service.

XDR: External Data Representation. Sun Microsystems's standard for machine-independent data structures. Contrast with ASN.1 and NDR.

x-kernel: An object-oriented framework for implementing network protocols developed at the University of Arizona.

zone: A partition of the domain name hierarchy, corresponding to an administrative authority that is responsible for that portion of the hierarchy. Each zone must have at least two name servers to field DNS requests for the zone.

REFERENCES

[Bar95]   Barlow, J. P. Electronic frontier: Death from above. *Communications of the ACM* 38(5):17–20, May 1995.

[Bat68]   Batcher, K. E. Sorting networks and their applications. *Proc. 1968 Spring AFIPS Joint Computer Conference* 32:307–314, 1968.

[BCDB95]   Borden, M., E. Crawley, B. Davie, and S. Batsell. Integration of real-time services in an IP-ATM network architecture. *Request for Comments* 1821, August 1995.

[BDMS94]   Bowman, C. M., P. B. Danzig, U. Manber, and M. F. Schwartz. Scalable internet resource discovery: Research problems and approaches. *Communications of the ACM* 37(8):98–107, August 1994.

[BG92]   Bertsekas, D., and R. Gallager. *Data Networks*. Prentice Hall, Englewood Cliffs, NJ, second edition, 1992.

[BG93]   Bjorkman, M., and P. Gunningberg. Locking effects in multiprocessor implementations of protocols. *Proceedings of the SIGCOMM '93 Symposium*, pages 74–83, September 1993.

[Bie92]   Biersack, E. Performance evaluation of forward error correction in ATM networks. *Proceedings of the SIGCOMM '92 Symposium*, pages 248–257, August 1992.

[Bla87]   Blahut, R. E. *Principles and Practice of Information Theory*. Addison-Wesley, Reading, MA, 1987.

[BLNS82]   Birrell, A., R. Levin, R. Needham, and M. Schroeder. Grapevine: An exercise in distributed computing. *Communications of the ACM* 25:250–273, April 1982.

[BM95]   Bradner, S., and A. Mankin, editors. *IPng: Internet Protocol Next Generation*. Addison-Wesley, Reading, MA, 1995.

[Boo95]   Boorsook, P. How anarchy works. *Wired* 3(10):110–118, October 1995.

[BPY90]   Bowman, M., L. L. Peterson, and A. Yeatts. Univers: An attribute-based name server. *Software—Practice and Experience* 20(4):403–424, April 1990.

[BS88]   Bic, L., and A. C. Shaw. *The Logical Design of Operating Systems*. Prentice Hall, Englewood Cliffs, NJ, 1988.

[Buf94]   Buford, J. F. K. *Multimedia Systems*. ACM Press/Addison-Wesley, Reading, MA, 1994.

[CFFD93]   Cohen, D., G. Finn, R. Felderman, and A. DeSchon. ATOMIC: A low-cost, very-high-speed, local communications architecture. *Proceedings of the 1993 Conference on Parallel Processing*, August 1993.

[Cha93]   Chapin, A. L. The billion node internet. In D. C. Lynch and M. T. Rose, editors, *Internet System Handbook*, chapter 17, pages 707–716. Addison-Wesley, Reading, MA, 1993.

[CJRS89]   Clark, D. D., V. Jacobson, J. Romkey, and H. Salwen. An analysis of TCP processing overhead. *IEEE Communications* 27(6):23–29, June 1989.

[Cla82]   Clark, D. D. Modularity and efficiency in protocol implementation. *Request for Comments* 817, July 1982.

[Cla85]   Clark, D. D. The structuring of systems using upcalls. *Proceedings of the Tenth ACM Symposium on Operating Systems Principles*, pages 171–180, December 1985.

[CLNZ89]   Chen, S. K., E. D. Lazowska, D. Notkin, and J. Zahorjan. Performance implications of design alternatives for remote procedure call stubs. *Proceedings of the Ninth International Conference on Distributed Computing Systems*, pages 36–41, June 1989.

[CMRW93]   Case, J., K. McCloghrie, M. Rose, and S. Waldbusser. Structure of management information for version 2 of the simple network management protocol (SNMPV2). *Request for Comments* 1442, April 1993.

[Com95]   Comer, D. E. *Internetworking with TCP/IP. Volume I: Principles, Protocols, and Architecture*. Prentice Hall, Englewood Cliffs, NJ, third edition, 1995.

[CP89]   Comer, D. E., and L. L. Peterson. Understanding naming in distributed systems. *Distributed Computing* 3(2):51–60, May 1989.

[CS93]   Comer, D. E., and D. L. Stevens. *Internetworking with TCP/IP. Volume III: Client-Server Programming and Applications, BSD Socket Version*. Prentice Hall, Englewood Cliffs, NJ, 1993.

[CS94]   Comer, D. E., and D. L. Stevens. *Internetworking with TCP/IP. Volume III: Client-Server Programming and Applications, AT&T TLI Version*. Prentice Hall, Englewood Cliffs, NJ, 1994.

[CSZ92]   Clark, D., S. Shenker, and L. Zhang. Supporting real-time applications in an integrated services packet network: Architecture and mechanism. *Proceedings of the SIGCOMM '92 Symposium*, pages 14–26, August 1992.

[CZ85]   Cheriton, D. R., and W. Zwaenepoel. Distributed process groups in the V kernel. *ACM Transactions on Computer Systems* 3(2):77–107, May 1985.

[Dav91]   Davie, B. S. A host-network interface architecture for ATM. *Proceedings of the SIGCOMM '91 Symposium*, pages 307–316, September 1991.

[DP93]   Druschel, P., and L. L. Peterson. Fbufs: A high-bandwidth cross-domain transfer facility. *Proceedings of the Fourteenth ACM Symposium on Operating Systems Principles*, pages 189–202, December 1993.

[DPD94]   Druschel, P., L. L. Peterson, and B. S. Davie. Experience with a high-speed network adaptor: A software perspective. *Proceedings of the SIGCOMM '94 Symposium*, pages 2–13, August 1994.

[dTeT92a] de Telegraphique et Telephonique, C. C. I. Open systems interconnection: Specification of abstract syntax notation one (asn.1). CCIT Recommendation X.208, 1992.

[dTeT92b] de Telegraphique et Telephonique, C. C. I. Open systems interconnection: Specification of basic encoding rules for abstract syntax notation one (asn.1). CCIT Recommendation X.209, 1992.

[DY75]   Drysdale, R. L., and F. H. Young. Improved divide/sort/merge sorting networks. *SIAM Journal on Computing* 4(3):264–270, September 1975.

[EWL+94] Edwards, A., G. Watson, J. Lumley, D. Banks, C. Calamvokis, and C. Dalton. User-space protocols deliver high performance to applications on a low-cost Gb/s LAN. *Proceedings of the SIGCOMM '94 Symposium*, pages 14–23, August 1994.

[Fer90]   Ferrari, D. Client requirements for real-time communications services. *IEEE Communications* 28(11), November 1990.

[Fin88]   Finkel, R. A. *An Operating Systems Vade Mecum*. Prentice Hall, Englewood Cliffs, NJ, 1988.

[FLYV93] Fuller, V., T. Li, J. Yu, and K. Varadhan. Classless interdomain routing (CIDR): An address assignment and aggregation strategy. *Request for Comments* 1519, September 1993.

[FV90]   Ferrari, D., and D. Verma. A scheme for real-time channel establishment in wide-area networks. *IEEE Journal of Selected Areas in Communication (JSAC)* 8(3):368–379, April 1990.

[FV93]   Ferrari, D., and D. Verma. Distributed delay jitter control in packet-switching internetworks. *Journal of Internetworking: Research and Experience* 4:1–20, 1993.

[GG94]   Gopal, I., and R. Guerin. Network transparency: The plaNET approach. *IEEE/ACM Transactions on Networking* 2(3):226–239, June 1994.

[Gia94]   Giagioni, E. A structured tcp in standard ml. *Proceedings of the SIGCOMM '94 Symposium*, pages 36–45, August 1994.

[Hed88]   Hedrick, C. Routing information protocol. *Request for Comments* 1058, June 1988.

[Hei93]   Heinanen, J. Multiprotocol encapsulation over ATM Adaptation Layer 5. *Request for Comments* 1483, July 1993.

[HMPT89]   Hutchinson, N., S. Mishra, L. Peterson, and V. Thomas. Tools for implementing network protocols. *Software—Practice and Experience* 19(9):895–916, September 1989.

[Hol91]   Holzmann, G. J. *Design and Validation of Computer Protocols*. Prentice Hall, Englewood Cliffs, NJ, 1991.

[HP96]   Hennessy, J. L., and D. A. Patterson. *Computer Architecture: A Quantitative Approach*. Morgan Kaufmann, San Francisco, CA, second edition, 1990.

[HP95]   Holzmann, G. J., and B. Pehrson. *The Early History of Data Networks*. IEEE Computer Society Press, Los Alamitos, CA, 1995.

[Huf52]   Huffman, D. A. A method for the construction of minimal-redundancy codes. *Proceedings of the IRE* 40(9):1098–1101, September 1952.

[Jac88]   Jacobson, V. Congestion avoidance and control. *Proceedings of the SIGCOMM '88 Symposium*, pages 314–329, August 1988.

[Jaf81]   Jaffe, J. M. Flow control power is nondecentralizable. *IEEE Transaction on Communications* COM-29(9):1301–1306, September 1981.

[Jai89]   Jain, R. A delay-based approach for congestion avoidance in interconnected heterogeneous computer networks. *ACM Computer Communication Review* 19(5):56–71, October 1989.

[Jai91]   Jain, R. *The Art of Computer Systems Performance Analysis: Techniques for ExperimentalDesign, Measurement, Simulation, and Modeling*. John Wiley & Sons, New York, 1991.

[Jai94]   Jain, R. *FDDI Handbook: High-Speed Networking Using Fiber and Other Media*. Addison-Wesley, Reading, MA, 1994.

[JBB92]   Jacobson, V., R. Braden, and D. Borman. TCP extensions for high perfor-
           mance. *Request for Comments* 1323, May 1992.

[KC88]   Kanakia, H., and D. R. Cheriton. The VMP network adaptor board (NAB):
           High-performance network communication for multiprocessors. *Proceedings of
           the SIGCOMM '88 Symposium*, pages 175–187, August 1988.

[Kes91]   Keshav, S. A control-theoretic approach to flow control. *Proceedings of the SIG-
           COMM '91 Symposium*, pages 3–15, September 1991.

[Kle75]   Kleinrock, L. *Queuing Systems. Volume 1: Theory.* John Wiley & Sons, New
           York, 1975.

[Kle79]   Kleinrock, L. Power and deterministic rules of thumb for probabilistic prob-
           lems in computer communications. *Proceedings of the International Conference
           on Communications*, June 1979.

[KP91]   Karn, P., and C. Partridge. Improving round-trip time estimates in reliable
           transport protocols. *ACM Transactions on Computer Systems* 9(4):364–373,
           November 1991.

[KPS95]   Kaufman, C., R. Perlman, and M. Speciner. *Network Security: Private Com-
           munication in a Public World.* Prentice Hall, Englewood Cliffs, NJ, 1995.

[Lau94]   Laubach, M. Classical IP and ARP over ATM. *Request for Comments* 1577,
           January 1994.

[Lei94]   Leiner, B., guest editor. Issue on internet technology. *Communications of the
           ACM* 37(8), August 1994.

[Lin93]   Lin, H.-A. P. Estimation of the optimal performance of ASN.1/BER transfer
           syntax. *Computer Communications Review* 23(3):45–58, July 1993.

[LMKQ89]   Leffler, S. J., M. K. McKusick, M. J. Karels, and J. S. Quarterman. *The Design
           and Implementation of the 4.3BSD UNIX Operating System.* Addison-Wesley,
           Reading, MA, 1989.

[LTWW94]   Leland, W., M. Taqqu, W. Willinger, and D. Wilson. On the self-similar na-
           ture of ethernet traffic. *IEEE/ACM Transactions on Networking* 2:1–15, Febru-
           ary 1994.

[Mal93]   Malkin, G. Rip version 2 carrying additional information. *Request for Comments*
           1388, January 1993.

[MB93]   Maeda, C., and B. Bershad. Protocol service decomposition for high-
           performance networking. *Proceedings of the Fourteenth ACM Symposium on Op-
           erating Systems Principles*, pages 244–255, December 1993.

[MD93]   McKenney, P. E., and K. F. Dove. Efficient demultiplexing of incoming TCP packets. *Proceedings of the SIGCOMM '92 Symposium*, pages 269–280, August 1993.

[Met93]   Metcalf, R. Computer/network interface design lessons from arpanet and ethernet. *IEEE Journal of Selected Areas in Communication (JSAC)* 11(2):173–180, February 1993.

[Min93]   Minoli, D. *Enterprise Networking: Fractional T1 to SONET, Frame Relay to BISDN*. Artech House, Norwood, MA, 1993.

[Moy94]   Moy, J. Ospf version 2. *Request for Comments* 1583, March 1994.

[MP85]   Mogul, J., and J. Postel. Internet standard subnetting procedure. *Request for Comments* 950, August 1985.

[MR91]   McCloghrie, K., and M. Rose. Management information base for network management of tcp/ip-based internets: Mib-ii. *Request for Comments* 1213, March 1991.

[Mul90]   Mullender, S. Amoeba: A distributed operating system for the 1990s. *IEEE Computer* 23(5):44–53, May 1990.

[Nat94]   National Research Council, Computer Science, and Telecommunications Board. *Realizing the Information Future: The Internet and Beyond*. National Academy Press, Washington, DC, 1994.

[Nel92]   Nelson, M. *The Data Compression Book*. M&T Books, San Mateo, CA, 1992.

[NYKT94]   Nahum, E. M., D. J. Yates, J. F. Kurose, and D. Towsley. Performance issues in parallelized network protocols. *Proceedings of the First USENIX Symposium on Operating System Design and Implementation (OSDI)*, pages 125–137, November 1994.

[OCD+88]   Ousterhout, J. K., A. R. Cherenson, F. Douglis, M. N. Nelson, and B. B. Welch. The Sprite network operating system. *IEEE Computer* 21(2):23–36, February 1988.

[OK91]   Ohta, H., and T. Kitami. A cell loss recovery method using FEC in ATM networks. *IEEE Journal of Selected Areas in Communication (JSAC)* 9(9):1471–1483, December 1991.

[OP91]   O'Malley, S., and L. Peterson. Tcp extensions considered harmful. *Request for Comments* 1263, October 1991.

[Ope94]   Open Software Foundation. *OSF DCE Application Environment Specification*. Prentice Hall, Englewood Cliffs, NJ, 1994.

[OPM94]   O'Malley, S. W., T. A. Proebsting, and A. B. Montz. Universal stub compiler. *Proceedings of the SIGCOMM '94 Symposium*, pages 295–306, August 1994.

[Pad85]   Padlipsky, M. A. *The Elements of Networking Style and Other Essays and Animadversions on the Art of Intercomputer Networking*. Prentice Hall, Englewood Cliffs, NJ, 1985.

[PAM94]   Pasquale, J., E. Anderson, and P. K. Muller. Container shipping: Operating system support for I/O-intensive applications. *IEEE Computer* 27(3):84–93, March 1994.

[Par94]   Partridge, C. *Gigabit Networking*. Addison-Wesley, Reading, MA, 1994.

[PB61]   Peterson, W. W., and D. T. Brown. Cyclic codes for error detection. *Proceedings of the IRE* 49:228–235, January 1961.

[Per92]   Perlman, R. *Interconnections: Bridges and Routers*. Addison-Wesley, Reading, MA, 1992.

[Per93]   Perlman, R. Routing protocols. In D. C. Lynch and M. T. Rose, editors, *Internet System Handbook*, chapter 5, pages 157–182. Addison-Wesley, Reading, MA, 1993.

[Pet88]   Peterson, L. L. The Profile naming service. *ACM Transactions on Computer Systems* 6(4):341–364, November 1988.

[PF94]   Paxson, V., and S. Floyd. Wide-area traffic: The failure of poisson modeling. *sigcomm94*, pages 257–268, London, UK, August 1994.

[Pry91]   De Prycker, M. *Asynchronous Transfer Mode: Solution for Broadband ISDN*. Ellis Horwood, Chichester, England, 1991.

[Ram93]   Ramakrishnan, K. K. Performance considerations in designing network interfaces. *IEEE Journal of Selected Areas in Communication (JSAC)* 11(2):203–219, February 1993.

[RF89]   Rao, T. R. N., and E. Fujiwara. *Error-Control Coding for Computer Systems*. Prentice Hall, Englewood Cliffs, NJ, 1989.

[RF94]   Romanow, A., and S. Floyd. Dynamics of TCP traffic over ATM networks. *Proceedings of the SIGCOMM '94 Symposium*, pages 79–88, October 1994.

[RL95]   Rekhter, Y., and T. Li. A border gateway protocol 4 (bgp-4). *Request for Comments* 1771, March 1995.

[Rob93]   Robertazzi, T. G., editor. *Performance Evaluation of High-Speed Switching Fabrics and Networks: ATM, Broadband ISDN, and MAN Technology*. IEEE Press, Piscataway, NJ, 1993.

[Ros86]   Ross, F. E. FDDI—a tutorial. *IEEE Communications* 24(5):10–17, May 1986.

[Ros94]   Rose, M. *The Simple Book: An Introduction to Internet Management.* Prentice Hall, second edition, 1994.

[Sal78]   Saltzer, J. Naming and binding of objects. *Lecture Notes on Computer Science* 60:99–208, 1978.

[SB89]   Schroeder, M. D., and M. Burrows. Performance of Firefly RPC. *Proceedings of the Twelfth ACM Symposium on Operating Systems Principles*, pages 83–90, December 1989.

[Sch94]   Schneier, B. *Applied Cryptography: Protocols, Algorithms, and Source Code in C.* John Wiley & Sons, New York, 1994.

[Sha48]   Shannon, C. A mathematical theory of communication. *Bell Systems Technical Journal* 27:379–423, 623–656, 1948.

[Sho78]   Shoch, J. Inter-network naming, addressing, and routing. *Seventeenth IEEE Computer Society International Conference (COMPCON)*, pages 72–79, September 1978.

[SHP91]   Spragins, J., J. Hammond, and K. Pawlikowski. *Telecommunications: Protocols and Design.* Addison-Wesley, Reading, MA, 1991.

[Sit92]   Sites, R. L. *Alpha Architecture Reference Manual.* Digital Press, Maynard, MA, 1992.

[Sri95a]   Srinivasan, R. RPC: Remote procedure call protocol specification version 2. *Request for Comments* 1831, August 1995.

[Sri95b]   Srinivasan, R. XDR: External data representation standard. *Request for Comments* 1832, August 1995.

[Sta90]   Stallings, W. *Local Networks.* Macmillan, New York, third edition, 1990.

[Sta91]   Stallings, W. *Data and Computer Communications.* Macmillan, New York, third edition, 1991.

[Ste94a]   Steenkiste, P. A. A systematic approach to host interface design for high speed networks. *IEEE Computer* 27(3):47–57, March 1994.

[Ste94b]   Stevens, W. R. *TCP/IP Illustrated. Volume 1: The Protocols.* Addison-Wesley, Reading, MA, 1994.

[SW95]   Stevens, W. R., and G. R. Wright. *TCP/IP Illustrated. Volume 2: The Implementation.* Addison-Wesley, Reading, MA, 1995.

[Swe95]   Swerdlow, J. L. Information revolution. *National Geographic* 188(4):5–37, October 1995.

[Tan88]   Tanenbaum, A. S. *Computer Networks*. Prentice Hall, Englewood Cliffs, NJ, second edition, 1988.

[Tan92]   Tanenbaum, A. S. *Modern Operating Systems*. Prentice Hall, Englewood Cliffs, NJ, 1992.

[Ter86]   Terry, D. Structure-free name management for evolving distributed environments. *Sixth International Conference on Distributed Computing Systems*, pages 502–508, May 1986.

[TL93]   Thekkath, C. A., and H. M. Levy. Limits to low-latency communication on high-speed networks. *ACM Transactions on Computer Systems* 11(2):179–203, May 1993.

[TNML93]   Thekkath, C. A., T. D. Nguyen, E. Moy, and E. D. Lazowska. Implementing network protocols at user level. *IEEE/ACM Transactions on Networking* 1(5):554–565, October 1993.

[TS93]   Traw, C. B. S., and J. M. Smith. Hardware/software organization of a high-performance ATM host interface. *IEEE Journal of Selected Areas in Communications (JSAC)* 11(2):240–253, February 1993.

[UI81]   USC-ISI. Transmission Control Protocol. *Request for Comments* 793, September 1981.

[VL87]   Varghese, G., and T. Lauck. Hashed and hierarchical timing wheels: Data structures for the efficient implementation of a timer facility. *Proceedings of the Eleventh ACM Symposium on Operating Systems Principles*, pages 25–38, November 1987.

[Wat81]   Watson, R. Identifiers (naming) in distributed systems. In B. Lampson, M. Paul, and H. Siegert, editors, *Distributed System—Architecture and Implementation*, pages 191–210. Springer-Verlag, New York, 1981.

[WC91]   Wang, Z., and J. Crowcroft. A new congestion control scheme: Slow start and search (Tri-S). *ACM Computer Communication Review* 21(1):32–43, January 1991.

[WC92]   Wang, Z., and J. Crowcroft. Eliminating periodic packet losses in 4.3-Tahoe BSD TCP congestion control algorithm. *ACM Computer Communication Review* 22(2):9–16, April 1992.

[Wel84]   Welch, T. A technique for high-performance data compression. *IEEE Computer* 17(6):8–19, June 1984.

[WM87]   Watson, R. W., and S. A. Mamrak. Gaining efficiency in transport services by appropriate design and implementation choices. *ACM Transactions on Computer Systems* 5(2):97–120, May 1987.

[WMB94]   Witten, I. H., A. Moffat, and T. C. Bell. *Managing Gigabytes.* Van Nostrand Reinhold, New York, 1994.

[YHA87]   Yeh, Y.-S., M. B. Hluchyj, and A. S. Acampora. The knockout switch: A simple, modular architecture for high-performance packet switching. *IEEE Journal of Selected Areas in Communication (JSAC)* 5(8):1274–1283, October 1987.

[ZL77]   Ziv, J., and A. Lempel. A universal algorithm for sequential data compression. *IEEE Transactions on Information Theory* 23(3):337–343, May 1977.

[ZL78]   Ziv, J., and A. Lempel. Compression of individual sequences via variable-rate coding. *IEEE Transactions on Information Theory* 24(5):530–536, September 1978.

INDEX